Administrative Law Governance in Asia
Comparative perspectives

This book examines administrative law in Asia, exploring the profound changes in the legal regimes of many Asian states that have taken place in recent years. Political democratization in some countries, economic change more broadly and the forces of globalization have put pressure on the developmental state model, wherein bureaucrats governed in a kind of managed capitalism and public-private partnerships were central. A more market-oriented regulatory state model seems to be emerging in many jurisdictions, with emphases on transparency, publicity and constrained discretion. The book analyzes the causes and consequences of this shift from a socio-legal perspective, showing clearly how decisions about the scope of administrative law and judicial review have an important effect on the shape and style of government regulation. Taking a comparative approach, individual chapters trace the key developments in the legal regimes of major jurisdictions across Asia, including China, Japan, Korea, Malaysia, Taiwan, Hong Kong, Indonesia, Singapore, the Philippines, Thailand, and Vietnam. They demonstrate that, in many cases, Asian states have shifted away from traditional systems in which judges were limited in terms of their influence over social and economic policy, toward regulatory models of the state involving a greater role for judges and law-like processes. The book also considers whether judiciaries are capable of performing the tasks they are being given, and assesses the profound consequences the judicialization of governance is starting to have on state policy-making in Asia.

Tom Ginsburg is Professor of Law at the University of Chicago. His research interests focus on comparative public law, international law, law and development and East Asia. His publications include *Institutions and Public Law* (2005, co-editor), *International Commercial Arbitration in Asia* (2002, 2nd edition 2005, co-editor), *Legal Reform in Korea* (2004, editor) and *Judicial Review in New Democracies* (2003).

Albert H. Y. Chen is Chan Professor in Constitutional Law, Faculty of Law, University of Hong Kong. His research interests include constitutional law, comparative law and legal and political philosophy. His publications include *The Basic Law and Hong Kong's Future* (1988, co-editor), *An Introduction to the Legal System of the People's Republic of China* (3rd edn 2004) and *Human Rights in Asia* (Routledge 2006, co-editor).

Routledge law in Asia
Series editor Randall Peerenboom

Asian Discourses of Rule of Law
Theories and implementation of rule of law in twelve Asian countries, France and the U.S.
Edited by *Randall Peerenboom*

Human Rights in Asia
A comparative legal study of twelve Asian jurisdictions, France, and the USA
Edited by *Randall Peerenboom, Carole J. Petersen, and Albert H.Y. Chen*

Support for Victims of Crime in Asia
Edited by *Wing-Cheong Chan*

Administrative Law and Governance in Asia
Comparative perspectives
Edited by *Tom Ginsburg and Albert H.Y. Chen*

Administrative Law and Governance in Asia

Comparative perspectives

Edited by
Tom Ginsburg and Albert H. Y. Chen

LONDON AND NEW YORK

First published 2009
by Routledge
2 Park Square, Milton Park, Abingdon, Oxon OX14 4RN

Simultaneously published in the USA and Canada
by Routledge
270 Madison Avenue, New York, NY 10016

*Routledge is an imprint of the Taylor & Francis Group,
an informa business*

© 2009 Editorial selection and matter, Tom Ginsburg and
Albert H.Y. Chen; individual chapters, the contributors

Typeset in Times New Roman by Keyword Group Ltd
Printed and bound in Great Britain by CPI Antony Rowe, Chippenham Wiltshire

All rights reserved. No part of this book may be reprinted or reproduced or utilized in any form or by any electronic, mechanical, or other means, now known or hereafter invented, including photocopying and recording, or in any information storage and retrieval system, without permission in writing from the publishers.

British Library Cataloguing in Publication Data
A catalogue record for this book is available from the British Library

Library of Congress Cataloging in Publication Data
Administrative Law and Governance in Asia: Comparative perspectives/
 edited by Tom Ginsburg and Albert H.Y. Chen
  p. cm. – (Routledge law in Asia series ; 4)
Simultaneously published in the USA and Canada.
Includes bibliographical references and index.
 1. Administrative law–Asia, 2. Administrative agencies–Asia.
 3. Rule of law–Asia. 4. Human rights–Asia. 5. Rule of law.
 6. Human rights. I.Ginsburg, Tom. II. Chen, Hongyi, 1957-

KNC620.A93 2008
342.5′06–dc22   2008018504

ISBN 10: 0-415-77683-X (hbk)
ISBN 10: 0-415-77731-3 (pbk)

ISBN 13: 978-0-415-77683-7 (hbk)
ISBN 13: 978-0-415-77731-5 (pbk)

Contents

List of Contributors	vii
Preface	ix
ALBERT H.Y. CHEN AND TOM GINSBURG	

1 The judicialization of administrative governance: causes, consequences and limits   1
TOM GINSBURG

PART I
General perspectives   21

2 On the regulatory dynamics of judicialization: the promise and perils of exploring "judicialization" in East and Southeast Asia   23
MICHAEL W. DOWDLE

3 Agencification, regulation and judicialization: American exceptionalism and other ways of life   38
COLIN SCOTT

4 Riding the accountability wave? Accountability communities and new modes of governance   59
KANISHKA JAYASURIYA

PART II
Northeast Asia and Greater China   79

5 Administrative law and judicialized governance in Japan   81
HITOSHI USHIJIMA

6 Government reform, judicialization, and the development of public law in the Republic of Korea   101
JONGCHEOL KIM

7	Democracy-driven transformation to regulatory state: the case of Taiwan JIUNN-RONG YEH	127
8	Administrative law, politics and governance: the Hong Kong experience JOHANNES CHAN	143
9	More law, less courts: legalized governance, judicialization, and *dejudicialization* in China RANDALL PEERENBOOM	175

PART III
Southeast Asia 203

10	The juridification of administrative complaints and review in Vietnam JOHN GILLESPIE	205
11	The emergence of administrative justice in Thailand under the 1997 Constitution PETER LEYLAND	230
12	Administrative law and judicialized governance in Malaysia: the Indian connection GAN CHING CHUAN	257
13	The judicialization of governance: the case of Singapore JOLENE LIN	287
14	"Government by judiciary" in the Philippines: ideological and doctrinal framework RAUL C. PANGALANGAN	313
15	Administrative law and judicial review in Indonesia: the search for accountability STEWART FENWICK	329
16	Conclusion: reflections on administrative law and judicialized governance in East and Southeast Asia ALBERT H.Y. CHEN	359
	Index	381

Contributors

Johannes Chan, S.C., is Professor and Dean, Faculty of Law, the University of Hong Kong.

Albert H.Y. Chen is Professor in Constitutional Law at the University of Hong Kong.

Michael W. Dowdle is Chaired Professor of Governance and Globalization, *Institut d'Études Politiques de Paris* (Sciences Po), Paris, France.

Stewart Fenwick is a development consultant and was Team Leader, Indonesia-Australia Legal Development Facility, Jakarta, 2004–2008.

Gan Ching Chuan is Associate Professor, Faculty of Law, University of Malaya, Kuala Lumpur, Malaysia.

John Gillespie is Professor of Law and Director of the Asia-Pacific Business Regulation Group, Monash University, Melbourne, Australia.

Tom Ginsburg is Professor of Law at the University of Chicago.

Kanishka Jayasuriya is Senior Principal Research Fellow, Asia Research Centre, Murdoch University, Perth, Australia.

Jongcheol Kim is Associate Professor of Law at the College of Law, Yonsei University, Seoul, Korea.

Peter Leyland is Professor of Public Law, London Metropolitan University.

Jolene Lin is Assistant Professor, Faculty of Law, The University of Hong Kong.

Raul C. Pangalangan is Professor of Law at the University of the Philippines.

Randall Peerenboom is Professor of Law, La Trobe University; Associate Fellow, Centre for Socio-Legal Studies, Oxford University; and Director of the China Rule of Law Program, Oxford Foundation for Law, Justice and Society.

Colin Scott is Vice Principal for Research and Innovation, University College Dublin College of Business and Law and Professor of EU Regulation and Governance, University College Dublin School of Law.

Hitoshi Ushijima is Professor of Law at Chuo University in Tokyo, Japan.

Jiunn-rong Yeh is Professor of Law, National Taiwan University, Taipei.

Preface

Albert H.Y. Chen and Tom Ginsburg

The phenomenon of judicialization is attracting increasing attention in socio-legal studies. In a wide variety of countries and settings, courts and court-like processes are playing an increasingly important role in politics and society. The causes of this trend are complex, and not completely understood. Nor, we are quick to point out, is the trend a universal one. Nevertheless, we believe the growing role of courts is significant enough to warrant further examination.

We take as our target of inquiry administrative law, governance and regulation, and focus on a particular region of the world, East and Southeast Asia. Although a number of studies have examined judicialization in other regions of the world, few have examined the phenomenon in Asia. Yet, as the most dynamic region of the world economy, Asia offers an excellent environment to test general theories about law and governance.

Administrative law is a particularly important arena in which to examine the role of courts. East Asia has long been considered the homeland of developmental capitalist regimes that rely on state direction rather than unrestrained market forces to shape national economies. Whether or not this image is correct is a controversial question, and we take no position on it here. Regardless of the truth of the image, it was largely reflected in traditional structures of administrative law that kept the courts out of policymaking and left fairly wide zones of discretion for government bureaucrats. Yet in recent years, we have seen significant reforms to the administrative law regimes in most jurisdictions in the region. It is thus an ideal time to examine the changing roles of administrative law in the regulatory sphere, both to understand governance in individual Asian countries as well as to test broader comparative hypotheses. We believe the studies in this volume expand our knowledge of law and governance in Asia as well as our general understanding of judicialization and administrative law.

The papers in this volume were originally presented at the conference on *Administrative Law and Judicialized Governance in Asia*, held at the university of Hong Kong on June 29–30, 2007. The editors are greatful to Dean Johannes Chan of the Faculty of Law, HKU, Professor Donald Lewis, Director, East Asia Economic Law Program, HKU, and Dean Heidi Hurd and the Asian Law, Politics and Society Program at University of Illinois College of Law, for financial support of the conference. Special thanks to Ms. Flora Leung of the Centre for Comparative and Public Law, HKU, for her excellent administrative support. In addition, we offer our sincere thanks to Sara Lisagor and Vysali Soundararajan for research assistance in preparing the manuscript and to the Reverend Samuel R. Vandegrift for his superb editorial assistance.

1 The judicialization of administrative governance

Causes, consequences and limits

Tom Ginsburg

In recent years, there has been increasing attention to the phenomenon of judicialization, the expansion of the range of activities over which judges exercise significant authority. Judges around the world now routinely make important policy decisions that only a few years ago would have been seen as properly the purview of bureaucrats, politicians, and private actors.[1] Beyond the direct involvement of judges in decision-making, judicialization can also refer to the expanding use of trial-like procedures for making governmental decisions and the extension of law-like processes into new social spheres.

Whereas recent studies have examined judicialization in a variety of regional contexts,[2] the overwhelming emphasis is on judicialization in Europe and the United States.[3] But of course there is far more to the world than the North Atlantic. One of the motivations for this volume is to ask whether and to what extent judicialization has occurred in East and Southeast Asia. It analyzes this issue in a particularly crucial context: the sphere of administrative law and regulation. Though much more attention in the nascent judicialization literature is devoted to constitutional issues,[4] most citizens are far more likely to encounter the state in the routine matters that are the stuff of administrative law rather than in the rarified sphere of constitutional law.

Administrative law is a mode of "regulating regulation,"[5] a particular way of ensuring that government observes certain rules in its interaction with society. I characterize administrative law as operating at two levels: retail and wholesale. The retail level concerns administrative interaction with private parties, what is called administrative justice in the UK. The wholesale level, which is less uniformly conceived as part of the domain of judicial control, concerns the formation of sub-legislative rules. Despite continuing doctrinal divergences and quite different institutional structures, there has been substantial convergence in the core elements of administrative law systems, with a right to present one's case before agencies, to receive reasons for adverse decisions, and the right to challenge administrative decisions before third party decision-makers. Particularly when judges have the power to review decisions of regulators, administrative law provides a crucial locus of state–society interaction, a channel for determining how and if participation can occur and rights can be protected. Judicial review of administrative action and enforcement of constitutional guarantees of fair procedures have been important constraints on regulatory decision-making.

East and Southeast Asia provides an important regional context for examining administrative law and regulation. For many years, the dominant trope in discussions of the Asian state was the developmental state,[6] an image of state-led economic growth in which bureaucratic supermen used vast grants of discretion to pick economic winners and losers. A large debate concerns the extent to which this imagery matched reality, but the very existence of the debate suggests that there was the appearance of substantial state discretion, in contrast with conventional economic theory. However, in the mid-1990s, as a result of several forces, this image began to lose power and East Asian states began to transform toward a more liberal regulatory model. This model included privatization, establishment of administrative procedures acts and the emergence of greater constitutional constraint on regulatory actors.

This shift has significant consequences for law and courts. Although law was not a major concern for first-generation analysts of the Asian state, the developmental state model contained an implicit model of law in general and administrative law in particular. Administrative law in the region tended to be formalistic and to govern a relatively small range of transactions. A paradigmatic practice, known in Japan as "administrative guidance" and by other euphemisms elsewhere, consisted of government suggesting a course of action by private parties that would be followed even if government lacked the formal legal power to force the course of action it was suggesting. Contrary to some imagery, such behavior is hardly the exclusive competence of Asian bureaucrats, but is found in virtually every regulatory system to one degree or another. Nevertheless, the notion that Asian bureaucracies during the high-growth period exercised a lot of discretion remains powerful. The statutory frameworks governing bureaucratic action were not extensive. The powerful Northeast Asian economies of Japan, Korea and Taiwan did not even pass their first general administrative procedures acts until the 1990s.

Beyond this, judicial authorities would tolerate fairly vague legislative pronouncements that empowered bureaucratic authorities. Particularly when compared with vigorous systems of administrative review by courts that operated under the American, French and German constitutional traditions, Asian courts seemed to be reticent to become involved in regulatory governance. Administrative courts did exist in some countries but the combination of judicial deference and powerful bureaucracies meant that their scope was not extensive at all.

This structural feature had consequences for firm strategy. With relatively underdeveloped formal legal guarantees, firms had to invest in specific relationships with regulatory authorities. Firms were dependent on state authorities for information, access to markets, and even capital during the high-growth period. Their investment in such relationships meant there was a corresponding disincentive to push for change. There was thus no winning domestic coalition supporting more transparent and open styles of regulation. So long as bureaucratic–business relationships were stable, the legal equilibrium was sustainable as well.

A number of factors, explored in great detail in the case studies in this volume, combined to put pressure on this situation. This chapter first describes the concept of judicialization, with special attention to the context of administrative governance. It next describes the various theories of why the shift is occurring, focusing on three categories of explanation: politics, economics and general features of the global environment. The chapter then considers some of the consequences of the shift and speculates briefly on the limits of judicialization. The discussion is generic in the sense that it does not purport to explain any single country experience, but rather to provide some considerations that may operate to a greater or lesser extent in various contexts.

The concept of judicialization of governance

The judicialization of politics is now an established concept, with an expanding literature tracing the myriad spheres in which courts are now making and influencing policy decisions that previously had not been within their purview.[7] By judicialization of governance, we have in mind a broad conception of the expansion of judicial involvement in the formation and regulation of public policy. Expanded judicial power may come at the expense of bureaucratic power, as in the establishment of vigorous systems of judicial review of administrative action and judicially policed processes of sub-legislative rule formation. It may come at the expense of politicians, so that political decision-making is shaped and constrained by higher order principles articulated by judges. And it may come at the expense of private actors, who find their own freedom to create and organize rules is constrained by judicially created or enforced public policies.

Judicialization involves more than simply the direct articulation and application of rules by judges; it also involves decisions by other political actors made in the shadow of judicial processes. An agency that refrains from certain conduct, or provides extensive legal justification for actions that it does take, or introduces trial-like processes to defend itself from claims of arbitrariness, may be acting to avoid being brought before courts. In this sense the sphere of judicialized governance is broader than it might initially appear and it may also be difficult to trace its precise boundaries.

A related concept is that of juridification: the spread of legal discourse and procedures into social and political spheres where it was previously excluded or was minimal.[8] Hirschl notes that this has long been a concern of social theory, as rationalized processes. A particularly interesting contribution is exemplified by Morgan[9] who identifies the spread of cost–benefit analysis in the economic sphere as a kind of quasi-judicialization, in which technocratic discourse is employed to evaluate individual cases against "higher" criteria of rationality. We focus instead on judicialization, not because juridification is unimportant, but because judicialization is one window on the broader and more amorphous process of juridification.

The most elaborate elucidation of the judicialization concept is by Stone Sweet, who roots the concept of judicialization in dyadic social relationships and a shift to third parties.[10] Dyadic social relations are sustained by reciprocity. Reciprocity can be stable for a very long time, but sometimes it can break down, as parties disagree over rights and obligations. Once conflict occurs, one party might be able to force its view on the other, but if not, the dyad is likely to turn to a third party to help resolve the dispute.[11] When a third party enters the picture to resolve disputes and help the dyad partners coordinate their expectations, governance begins.

The triadic structure of dispute resolution involves, inherently, the articulation of rules and the generation of a normative structure that helps guide future behavior. This also engenders a discourse about the application of rules that itself becomes embedded into the reasoning and strategic calculus of the governed. Future dyadic interaction occurs in light of this normative structure, and a feedback cycle develops whereby new conflicts that emerge are again sent to the triadic dispute resolver, with the questions becoming ever more refined over time. This is the process of judicialization.

In the Asian context, one can view relational, reciprocity-based networks of exchange as being essentially dyadic in character. Firms contract with each other, and enforce the contracts through reciprocity-based sanctions. Firms also interact with government in essentially dyadic ways, with each firm seeking to establish relationships and norms of cooperation with government actors. Judicialization involves the partial displacement of relational governance with more arms-lengths transactions, both among firms and with the state. Arms-lengths transactions require triadic dispute resolution—a third party to help the dyadic parties coordinate their actions and understandings. This role can, and increasingly is, played by courts.

Two issues, however, are not fully specified in Stone Sweet's theory. The first concerns the *timing* of judicialization. Why does judicialization emerge when it does? This issue is raised in Hirschl's account of constitutionalization, in which he argues that departing hegemonic elites are likely to turn over power to independent courts as a way of governing in the future.[12] When one thinks one will be out of power, governing by independent courts becomes a way of ensuring that one's policies are not overturned. Does the same logic apply in the administrative sphere?

A second issue not fully clear from Stone Sweet's work is whether or not judicialization is a one-way process. That is, once a political system has allowed courts into various spheres of governance, is there a way to put the proverbial humpty-dumpty of state discretion back together again? Stone Sweet's theory is not teleological, but does suggest a kind of developmental trajectory in which judicialization, if unchecked, is a continuously expanding process. On the other hand, a large institutionalist literature on courts has established that courts are embedded in broader systems of governance.[13] Judicial decisions constrain other political actors, but are also constrained by them in important ways. Other actors have in their power myriad tools to constrain the operation of courts and to shape the sphere of judicialized governance.[14] Can they ever reverse the process? A complete account of judicialization in spheres of governance would include not only a discussion of its establishment but also of its endurance.

To really understand the issues of timing and whether judicialization is reversible, one needs an understanding of its origins and consequences. It is to these issues that we now turn.

Causes of judicialization

One can trace three separate categories of explanation for the expanded role of courts in governance generally. We focus on economic, political and international factors.

Economic factors

Economic globalization is an important force in the judicialization of national regulatory processes. The rapidly intensified scope and scale of global transactions, combined with liberalization of trade and capital flows, has allowed new entrants to appear in many domestic markets. These actors had less extensive relationships with the local bureaucracies, and indeed suffered comparative disadvantage vis-à-vis favored local actors who were embedded in networks of reciprocity. The new players may have been less willing to trust the word of a local bureaucrat potentially connected to the firm's competitors. This meant that administrative informalism and reciprocity-based political economy had less efficacy for these "outside" actors. Instead, new entrants were likely to view their relationships with bureaucracy in formal terms. They were more likely to rely on legally defined rights and duties, to demand transparency in rule formation and application and to challenge "guidance" that did not benefit them.

We have few studies of how the entry of new firms from outside changes *local* firms' regulatory strategies, but one can imagine that the dynamic is epidemiological in character. Conceiving of pre-judicialized governance as a stable equilibrium of reciprocity-based contracting arrangements, one can suppose that new entrants might disrupt the equilibrium. Demands for transparency, initiated from outside, decrease bureaucratic leverage over local firms as well as foreign firms, and may shift power toward business in general. A bureaucracy that cannot manipulate information is one that is weaker. Thus strategic moves that originate with foreign or outside firms (e.g., aggressively collecting on bad loans in mid-1990s Japan) can become rational for local actors as well. If new strategic equilibria emerge, and these rely on courts to a greater extent, judicialization may resemble a process of infection (though I don't intend the pejorative normative implications of that term).

An underappreciated factor in globalization discourse is that it is a two-way street. Capital not only flows into economies from outside, but "inside" capital can also flow out. This shifts the balance of power in business–government relations. Regulatory demands are constrained by the ability of firms to exit when demands are unreasonable, empowering business vis-à-vis the government. Arguably, the great shift in Japan in the 1990s to switch from "ex ante planning" forms of regulation to "ex post correction" reflected this dynamic of shifting incentives.[15]

The former model requires firms to invest in specific relationships with bureaucrats to gain information, while the latter more legalistic model allows firms to plan rationally on the basis of objective language, and gives access to courts for ex post correction of arbitrary policies.

Liberalization also means that vital services—telecommunications, electricity, health care, working-class housing, transportation systems, financial services—are increasingly provided by privately owned companies rather than government monopolies. Where government has less involvement in direct service provision, it has less leverage over private parties to informally contain conflict among businesses, punish misbehavior or forestall insolvency. This in turn places new demands on the courts, and reduces the relative power of agencies to resist challenge.

Economic complexity is another structural factor that was no doubt at work in recent years. When Asian economies were primarily engaged in primary production or simple industrial manufacturing, regulatory decisions were relatively simple in character. As an information- and service-based economy came into effect, the old models of regulation proved inapposite. No regulatory agency, even one staffed with bureaucratic supermen, is able to anticipate all the changes in a complex, global economy. Information about regulatory needs is thus scarcer, creating pressure for new more flexible forms of regulation and the delegation of more decisions about implementation to private parties. On the other hand, complex economic circumstances require ever more expert technocratic solutions to unanticipated problems. Furthermore, ordinary citizens have a more difficult time evaluating the effects of regulation.

One way to resolve this tension is to allow for new and flexible forms of regulation, but to set up a second actor to monitor the performance of the primary regulators. A guardian institution becomes almost necessary in a situation which both demands highly technical solutions to complex problems, but is pervaded by distrust of the authorities to always implement the solutions on their own.[16] As in standard principal-agent theory, a simple solution is to hire a second agent to watch the first, to provide a second look at the decisions of the regulators.

We thus see powerful economic forces at work that encourage the development of judicial review of administrative action. The dynamic I have described is one of secular increases in economic complexity, combined with the entry of new firms, putting pressure on old systems of relational governance.[17] As demands for regulatory transparency, initially championed by outsiders, take root, local actors may change their strategies and become less willing to abide by the implicit terms of relational regulation. A dynamic of judicialization ensues.

Political factors

The above account can explain forces pushing for change, but does not explain the particular timing of changes in particular countries. Here a number of specific political factors may be necessary to provide local impetus for the shift. In Japan, a combination of bureaucratic scandal and incompetence, as well as the failure of the vaunted Ministry of Finance to cope with the popping of the financial bubble in the early 1990s, put pressure on the systems of relational governance. The brief loss of power of the long-ruling Liberal Democratic Party further ruptured the link between politics and bureaucracy, and provided the impetus for the passing of more transparent governance framework. This in turn changed the strategies of private actors, who no longer had to rely on government for crucial regulatory information.

The Asian Financial Crisis of 1997, which began in Thailand and spread most profoundly to Korea and Indonesia, provided further impetus for breaking old networks of business–government collaboration.[18] Many of these relationships had been sustained by implicit promises of government assistance and favorable action in return for overall deference by firms. As the crisis erupted, implicit and explicit promises were broken, providing an impetus for major political reform in some countries, such as Thailand (where the 1997 "People's Constitution" was passed) and Indonesia (where Suharto's 30-year dictatorship began to rapidly erode, ultimately falling two years later).

These stories highlight the importance of the political dimension of economic regulation. Politics, both in the narrow interest sense and a broader structural sense, have a profound impact. A good amount of research has tied the expansion of judicial power to fragmentation of political power.[19] As it becomes more difficult to produce legislation, courts have more policy space in which to insert themselves into policymaking without fear of legislative correction or discipline by other political actors.

The chief factor fragmenting political power in Asia in recent years has been the wave of democratic consolidation. It is seldom appreciated that East and Southeast Asia is the main region of the world in which third-wave democracies have in fact become consolidated.[20] Since the mid-1980s, the Philippines, South Korea, Taiwan, Indonesia, and Thailand have all become democracies, and only Thailand has suffered any significant backsliding (though it remains to be seen what the long-term implications of that backsliding will be).

Democracy, by definition, implies political competition and is typically associated with the structural fragmentation of political power. Compared to autocratic regimes, this means that courts have more room in which to work. Furthermore, there is more demand for judicial monitoring of bureaucrats in democracies than there is in dictatorships, because the time horizons of rulers are typically shorter. A bureaucrat who does not like the instructions coming from her political superiors need only wait until the next election, when the superior may be out of power and a new boss in place in her stead. Principal-agent problems are thus exacerbated by democracy and competition for political power.

Democracy, however, cannot explain the expansion of judicial power in one-party states such as Vietnam, China and Singapore, to the extent it has occurred. In these countries, political and economic factors suggest a different logic. All-powerful parties face difficulties making credible commitments to economic actors that they will not expropriate wealth.[21] Even if the central sovereign is committed to market-oriented policies, lower-level bureaucrats may seek to abscond with wealth. The regime thus faces principal-agent problems, and these are exacerbated in an era of economic complexity, as described earlier. Setting up an independent court system with the power to publicly constrain lower-level state actors may in fact enhance economic growth by providing credible commitments to economic actors. This "hand-tying" aspect of judicial power is well known among scholars of administrative law, and is exemplified by the adoption of administrative law systems in authoritarian countries such as China and Indonesia under Suharto.[22]

This political story seems to differentiate the functions of judicial oversight of administrative governance in dictatorship and democracy. Whereas in democracies, courts are needed because of extensive principal-agent problems associated with the competition for political power, in dictatorships they are needed precisely *because* political power is so concentrated. Since it will govern for a very long time, the Chinese Communist Party cannot credibly promise not to interfere with local property rights; an independent public review of alleged bureaucratic wrongs helps to make the Party's promises more believable, and enhances the central regime's ability to implement uniform policy throughout a large and diverse country.

In short, specific political coalitions may be necessary to trigger a shift toward judicialized governance. Once in place in the regulatory realm, however, judges provide important services for sovereigns. Judicialization is remarkably adaptable, thriving in a wide range of political environments.

It is perhaps telling that the rule of law discourse has become so ubiquitous that, like markets, no one questions its relevance. Not only was the rule of law a crucial component of the Washington Consensus, but it also seems to be a component of the so-called "Beijing Consensus."[23] While the Washington Consensus featured democracy, law and markets as the three interlinked components, the Beijing Consensus substitutes autocracy for democracy, under the guise of "stability." The consensus among consensuses is that judges are important actors in the structure of governance.

But what kind of judges? There are obviously vastly different conceptions of the proper role of the judge in different systems. Legal traditions may provide ideational structure that constrains and facilitates judicialization, though it is my own view that legal traditions and legal origin provide much less of a constraint than typically imagined. We have seen the emergence of vigorous constitutional and administrative courts in civil law jurisdictions and these have had profound impact on the administrative state.[24] Still, ideas about the proper role of judging matter, and can be viewed as ideological structures within which judges must operate.

Perhaps more important than broad traditions are local interest-group structures. Epp[25] focusing on what he calls the Rights Revolution, emphasizes that judges cannot insert themselves into new policy domains without demand from the public, and without the crucial intervening variable of "support structures." By this, he means a relatively independent bar and interest groups that are willing to utilize

The judicialization of administrative governance 9

the courts to advance their own strategic goals. Clearly the passive structure of judicial decision-making relies on others to bring cases to courts, and so courts must form alliances with interest groups and the bar in order to be in a position to influence policies. These "support structures" are mutually constitutive of judicialization: judges need the support structures, but the availability of litigation-based possibilities for social change will in turn encourage extra-judicial actors to bring cases to court.

No doubt the internal politics of the legal system itself, or what Halliday *et al*[26] call the notion of the "legal complex," provide resources and constraints in this regard. For example, the creation of *new* administrative and constitutional courts may provide a conducive environment for judicialization, as judges seek to articulate a role for themselves and cannot rely on old patterns of deference or ducking the tough cases. The emergence of new constitutional courts is particularly important. Direct examination of administrative action for constitutionality is part of the general trend toward judicialization. If a court can set aside legislation passed by a democratically elected parliament because of its non-conformity with the constitution, surely a court can also set aside actions of unelected bureaucrats for the same reason. The same logic leads toward expanded judicial supervision of administrative actions under delegated statutory authority. If judges can examine administrative action for conformity with the constitution, it is hardly objectionable that other judges examine the same action for conformity with the statutory dictates of the legislature itself. Now the courts are not attacking the legislature but serving it. So the expansion of constitutional review, by increasing the prestige of courts and their reputation as guardians of rights, may naturally lead toward greater supervision of administrative action.

International factors

We would be remiss not to discuss certain international factors at play in the governance shift. These have two components: institutional and ideational.

The chief institutional force for greater judicialization is the emergence of supranational regulatory regimes that constrain domestic policymaking. Trade and investment regimes typically involve supranational adjudication and review of local governmental practices.[27] As explicitly discriminatory practices shrink in scope, these regimes have increasingly confronted regulatory decisions previously thought to be "domestic" in character. This process has developed further outside Asia, which still lacks equivalent regional regimes to the North American Free Trade Agreement and the European Union. The GATT/WTO regime, however, has had a profound impact on Asian political economies. The shift from the GATT to the WTO had significant consequences for domestic regulatory organization. Article X of the GATT 1994 requires that "Laws, regulations, judicial decisions and administrative rulings of general application [...] shall be published promptly..." and administered "in a uniform, impartial and reasonable manner," notably by independent administrative tribunals or procedures.[28] Similar requirements for independent and transparent regulation are found in the newer agreements on services and intellectual property. It is thus clear that international commitments expand the scope of judicial oversight at a national level.

While the WTO agreements do not explicitly require institutional change in non–trade-related sectors, in some countries, notably China, they seemed to trigger broader institutional reforms. China agreed to impartial and uniform implementation of its commitments and of trade-related laws; to substantial transparency and notice and comment procedures of those laws, regulations and measures; and most dramatically, to set up and maintain impartial judicial review of all administrative action. The WTO became, in essence, an amendment to the Chinese constitution. Internal forces wished to "lock in" commitments before they could be whittled away at the local level, and third-party monitoring, locked in by international agreements, provided the mechanism.

The Chinese accession illustrates also that the international commitment device can help provide transparency *within* a country, enhancing predictability for domestic actors by constraining government. Thus WTO requirements of publication of laws and regulations; notice of new measures and provision for comment and independent adjudication and sites of appeal will have substantial effects on administrative law systems. The WTO secretariat itself claims that transparency is especially important with respect to domestic regulations aimed at legitimate public policy objectives that might have an effect on international competition, such as public health or protection of the environment.[29] By extending the right to comment on new regulatory measures to those outside national borders, the WTO expands judicial or at least adjudicative evaluation of rule-making.

Beyond the institutional impact of the international environment on local regulatory systems, there is an ideational element to the spread of judicialized governance. The salience of the legal solution increases as it becomes adopted in more and more countries. This represents a process of policy diffusion, in which the probability of a country adopting a policy or institution increases with the number of similar countries that adopt the solution.

A simple explanation of the diffusion process is that it represents a kind of trend, in which countries copy institutions that appear to have worked in other countries. Sociologists might attribute this to the emergence of a world society, in which certain norms and institutions become standard scripts and signs of modernity.[30]

A more optimistic take is that diffusion follows from a process of learning. When confronted with similar problems of economic complexity, transnational regulation and political diffusion, it makes sense to adopt the judicial "solution" of monitoring bureaucratic performance. The fact that other countries have delegated decisions to judges, and the particular solutions adopted by judges have not produced unmitigated disaster, provides information to the later adopter. In some cases, the adoption of an institutional solution in one country can also increase the costs and benefits for other countries considering reforms. An intriguing possibility is that law, globally, represents a kind of network good, in which legalization or judicialization in one country makes it more desirable for neighbors or similar countries to adopt the same solution. As one country adopts judicialized governance, it gains access to the global "conversation" of judges that have analyzed similar problems.

Regardless of whether the network conjecture is correct, there is little doubt that international factors do affect the conception of the proper role of the judge in domestic legal systems. Both the "legalization" of world politics and increased transnational exchange among judges help shape views of the judicial role.

Conclusion

Reviewing these various causes suggests that no single theory can explain variation in the timing and extent of judicialization. What I have suggested instead is that it is the interaction of local political conditions (including politics within the legal system) with structural constraints in the economy that lay the basis for judicialization. Many of the pressures for transferring power to judges are global in nature, driven by international regimes and economic forces. At the same time there are numerous contingencies that constrain and dictate the process, including the patterns and performance of business–government relations,[31] local political coalitions, and the structure, role conception and preferences of the judiciary itself.

Consequences of judicialization

A separate concern of many of the papers in this volume is to understand the consequences of the shift to judicialized governance. This raises tricky methodological issues. It is difficult to measure the impact of judicialization in any given policy area, because the consequences extend beyond the cases decided by judges. Changes in regulatory behavior that occur in the shadow of judicial decision-making, that is in response to *potential* decisions by judges, have an equally profound effect and ought to be considered in any complete account of judicial impact. More loosely, one might include the process of juridification, the expansion of "legal" modes of policy justification and discourse within the regulatory sphere.[32] Juridification focuses not on the mere achievement of judicial policy preferences but rather on a shift in the way policies are articulated and constructed.

The normative debate over judicialization is perhaps best developed in the context of the American administrative state, the national context in which judges have played the most visible and sustained role in supervising the administrative state. Some suggest that the judicial "solution" to problems of administrative governance will engender as many problems as it resolves. Others are more optimistic, seeing judges as crucial defenders of rights whose role in governance is on the whole positive. This section begins by describing the American experience and then moves on to look at broader concerns.

An American interlude

It is perhaps worthwhile to consider the American experience briefly to better articulate the critiques. The American administrative state arises somewhat later than its continental counterparts, in part because of the constitutional jurisprudence of the Supreme Court which viewed regulation as an interference with the twin values of property and freedom of contract. It took a massive and sustained political coalition in the wake of the Great Depression to overcome this resistance, after which the Supreme Court acquiesced to administrative regulation.[33] The New Deal then granted large amounts of administrative discretion to expert agencies on the basis of broadly worded statutes and minimal judicial review. Opponents of the regulatory state were able to push for the adoption of an Administrative Procedures Act (APA) in 1946, which represented a compromise set of constraints on regulation.

Toward the late 1950s and early 1960s, there was a shift in the underlying politics of administration in the United States. President Eisenhower's address at the close of his administration warned Americans of the takeover of government by an "industrial-military complex."[34] An academic book, *Silent Spring*,[35] detailed how industrialization was creating incredible environmental problems. And the "cultural revolution" of the counter-culture and free speech movements created great distrust in traditional institutions. In short, there was fear that the expert administrators who were running the government were not doing such a good job. Furthermore there was a fear that they were regulating not in the interest of the general public, but in the interest of the various parties they were supposed to regulate. Policymaking was a closed circle in which the general public lost out.[36] Distrust set in.

Interestingly, the courts seemed to respond to this shift by increasing the rigor of judicial review. The first steps were to demand more record-keeping by agencies. In a case involving highway traffic safety regulation, *Automotive Parts and Accessories Assn. v. Boyd,* the court dealt with an argument from a private party that the agency had not clearly responded to comments given in the "notice-and-comment" process. The court warned the agency that its statement of policy that accompanied the final rule must allow courts to see "major issues of policy" and why the agency reacted to them as they did. In another case, *United States v. Nova Scotia*, the court demanded that the agency also make a record of the underlying science on which it based its own regulations—even though the APA had imposed no such requirement.[37] The rationale for these shifts was that the courts had a statutory requirement to engage in the process of judicial review on the basis of the whole record. If an agency did not keep a record (as the Food and Drug Administration did not in the *Nova Scotia* case) then the court would be unable to properly evaluate the agency action and thus would not be able to accomplish its own duty. Thus the courts began by demanding greater records from agencies—without any clear statutory basis.

The next step was to scrutinize the records with more rigor. And here too the courts began to act more aggressively. Led by the United States Court of Appeals for the DC Circuit (which is in fact the final court of appeal for much administrative action because of the Supreme Court's discretion not to take cases), the courts began to find an increasing range of administrative actions to be "arbitrary and capricious."[38] They did so, nominally, as a procedural matter, by saying that the agencies needed to take a "hard look" at the evidence before them. In practice, this also meant that the courts too would take a "hard look" at the agency's actions. The Supreme Court redefined arbitrary and capricious review to include a requirement that courts undertake a "substantial inquiry" and conduct a "searching evaluation" of the evidence.[39] This included an inquiry into whether the agency has acted in the scope of its authority, and whether on the facts, the decision is reasonably within the range of discretion. It would be arbitrary and capricious if an agency has not considered relevant factors or made a clear error of judgment. All these moves tended to blur the line between the supposedly deferential "arbitrary and capricious" test and the more intrusive "substantial evidence" test.[40] Those who opposed particular regulations were happy to have courts intervene to ensure their participation and to ensure that agencies evaluated evidence properly.

Ultimately, of course, administrative decision-making involves policy choices among many competing alternatives. Deciding what level of public safety merited what level of requirements on manufacturers involves complex tradeoffs of risk, price and technical feasibility. No matter what decision is made, someone will be unhappy and will utilize the availability of judicial review to challenge that decision. Thus the shift toward activist judicial review inevitably involved the courts deeply in policy. And this, of course, led to the question asked since the time of the Romans, namely, who guards the guardians of legality?[41]

Gradually, the United States Supreme Court, which became dominated by conservatives beginning in the 1980s, began to cut back on the "activist" approach of courts. First, they told the lower courts to stop imposing new procedural requirements beyond the scope of the APA onto regulated parties.[42] Then, in one of the most important administrative law decisions known as *Chevron*,[43] the Supreme Court announced that, when agencies were involved in interpreting the laws they were supposed to apply, courts should defer to agency interpretations of law. This decision obviously shifted the balance of power back to the agencies, away from the lower courts. It reflected a judicial philosophy on the Supreme Court that wanted to let the administrators be administrators, and keep judges from the fundamental policy choices. It also kept judicial review focused on the one thing judges could do with confidence: evaluating whether the statute was unclear. Henceforth, courts that wanted to limit agencies would have to focus on questions other than the substantive interpretation of agency statutes; instead they would have to look at issues like the agency findings of fact, the procedures to be used and the reasons given for governmental action.[44]

And yet, despite recalibration by the Supreme Court, the judiciary remains deeply involved in regulatory governance. It is a case of one step back after four steps forward. It is thus not surprising that the United States has been the locus of massive debates about the proper role of judges. Many asked why it was that that courts ought to be able to substitute their own vision of policy for those of "expert" administrators. The logic of having a second body review the decisions of a primary regulatory depends on the second body *sometimes* over-ruling the first. If courts do not do this, then their utility as a mechanism of accountability is lost. But, being non-expert, judges are always subject to critiques when they do intervene. One might see the judicialization of administrative governance as inherently unstable—it responds to felt needs, but generates its own challenges.

Costs and benefits

What are the consequences of judicialization? Critics familiar with the American experience described above have identified several. First of all there are the decision costs associated with overly involved procedures.[45] Comparative studies of regulation repeatedly find that, across advanced industrial democracies, the substantive outcomes of regulation are frequently the same, but that the costs and manner of obtaining these outcomes differ dramatically across regulatory systems.[46] The American system is particularly costly, contentious and wasteful in achieving regulatory goals, with conflict pervading the process from rule formation to enforcement. This entails potentially serious delays and expense, with repeated re-consideration of issues in different fora.

Besides the decision costs, Kagan's magisterial critique of American "adversarial legalism" suggests that over-judicialization entails costs in terms of legal uncertainty. The possibility of judicial over-turning of decisions made at the bureaucratic and political levels mean that there is inherent uncertainty in the regulatory process. Legal norms in such circumstances may be particularly malleable and indeterminate, ultimately undermining the utility of law for social and economic ordering. Rather than serve to constrain bureaucratic discretion, legal uncertainty may perversely empower bureaucrats by discouraging parties from undertaking costly and unpredictable challenges.

Finally, Kagan critiques what might be called cultural consequences of over-judicialization, helping to perpetuate a legal culture of "adversarial legalism." As private actors respond to institutional structure, they entrench adversarial patterns of behavior that promote defensive regulation and over-proceduralization. Instead of seeking cooperative and mediate solutions, parties will use the availability of courts to make unbending rights-based demands. These patterns then become the norms expected for future regulatory iterations.

To these challenges and critiques, a number of sophisticated defenses of judicial involvement have emerged. The most common one, though difficult to evaluate empirically, is that judicial involvement as a monitor of regulatory processes and a guarantor of transparency leads to better quality and more legitimate regulation. Decisions that agencies know will be reviewed and written in such a way as to justify their outcomes and reasoning, perhaps more so than decisions taken solely by a primary actor without review. This may result in better justified, more legitimate governmental processes.

A sophisticated institutional proposal, associated with Dorf[47] emphasizes the potential role of courts in participating in broader processes of democratic experimentalism. Institutions are sites for deliberation, experimentation and transformation, and courts have certain unique qualities that render them skilled in this regard. One should not, then, throw out the baby with the bathwater—some of the benefits from judicialization, including more reasoned and better justified policies, and presumably also procedural fairness, ought to be sustained and indeed extended.

Another line of defense is to note that the purported excesses of judicial involvement in policymaking are overstated. Positive political theorists have provided the most recent elaboration of an old institutionalist argument that observes that courts are always embedded in larger political contexts. Preferences of bureaucrats and politicians matter. Political authorities in particular have myriad tools to discipline courts and to shape the realm of judicial involvement in terms of which issues courts can hear and at what stage. Because other actors can constrain and correct courts, judicial involvement should not be such a great concern, for it is always shaped by the preferences of other actors. In the administrative sphere, this argument typically emphasizes that judges are ultimately subject to control by politicians[48] and so are less likely to undertake truly unpopular policies.

This raises the question of whether judicialization is a one-way street, or whether it is in fact reversible in some fundamental sense. Once one moves to a system of governing with judges, can one ever return? What are the limits of judicialization? These questions are particularly important for understanding how regulatory systems may evolve in the future.

Limits

To understand the limits of judicialized governance, one must consider which of the various driving forces described above are truly primary. If one believes that the main causes of judicialization are global and economic in character, one might expect little scope for reversal or change. Indeed, one might predict convergence across countries in the trend of judicialization, for most countries are embedded in both global regulatory regimes and the global economy. On the other hand, if one believes that local politics is the key factors, one might anticipate more possibility for variation. For example, dominant political actors (e.g., the Chinese Communist Party) may be able to expand the scope of bureaucratic informalism, (re-) constructing tight links between regulators and regulated parties and relying on such tools as administrative guidance. They may do so to capture the benefits of flexible, even responsive, regulation in circumstances of dynamic change. Furthermore, dominant parties have the ability to use the party apparatus itself to monitor and punish bureaucratic errors and malfeasance. This means there is less need to use third-party monitoring in the first place.

Still, administrative law frameworks, like primary regulatory rules, have the quality of establishing their own communities around them once in place. The much criticized Administrative Procedures Act in the United States has never been changed despite numerous proposals to do so. Interest groups develop around the legal opportunities that are made available to them, and may resist efforts to restrict their access (or expand access for their opponents). Nor is it likely that specialized administrative courts can be disbanded without a major constitutional revolution. While we have seen the establishment of *new* administrative courts and specialized benches (e.g., in Korea, Indonesia and Thailand, with similar proposals circulating in Japan), it is rare to see an administrative court merged into the ordinary court system. In short, then, inertia can make switching costs of change prohibitive and the disbanding of institutions difficult. When judicial control becomes an effective solution to the problem of regulatory power, it itself becomes resistant to easy change.

The key variable, then, may be the political communities that grow up around judicial structures. If a strong independent bar develops, for example, it may find that there is good business to be done using administrative law tools to obtain benefits for private parties. Interest groups may develop litigation-based strategies for shaping regulatory outcomes. And, to the extent that judicialization delivers better and more legitimate policies, as the proponents of extensive judicial involvement have argued, the public may play an important role as a bulwark against interference with judicial involvement. All these actors can help defend courts against overt political interference.[49]

Stone Sweet models judicialization as a feedback cycle, of continuous articulation and refinement of governance. His stylized model does not purport to examine the endurance of judicialization, but suggests that the continued viability of judicial involvement in regulatory governance depends on the specific political configurations in place. Judicialization is sustained by concrete actors who rely on it in strategic encounters. If these actors are or become powerful enough, the feedback cycle can indeed become embedded and resist change. On the other hand, the scope of judicial power in the regulatory arena is subject to ultimate control by strong political actors. A dominant political coalition can limit and shape the scope of judicial involvement in governance. Whether it wishes to do so, though, may depend on the deeper processes of juridification. If judicial articulation of normative structure becomes taken for granted and part of the culture, dominant parties may accept it as part of the landscape, an unquestioned constraint. When this happens, judicialization is indeed irreversible.

Conclusion

Many of the writings on judicial involvement in regulatory governance concern the European Union and the United States, large federalisms with multiple levels of regulators in non-hierarchical relationships. The chapters in this volume will consider the extent to which similar phenomena have occurred in the context of nation-states in Asia, where regional architecture is still in a nascent phase. The chapters describe administrative law frameworks, many of which are in flux, that have for the most part seen greater involvement by judges in constraining regulated parties.

This chapter has considered, at a broad level, some of the causes and consequences of judicialization of administrative governance. It has speculated that judicialization is a process with multiple causes whose interaction dictates the scope of judicial involvement. Though international factors and economic change play an important role in pressuring systems to move toward judicialization, local political circumstances play a crucial role in dictating the timing and scope of judicialized governance. More importantly, local factors may dictate the sustainability of the judicial solution to problems of bureaucratic oversight.

As for the normative question about whether all this is a good thing, much depends on where one stands. As a positive matter, we can say that judges who insert themselves into the regulatory process are likely to be seen as performing a crucial role in governance, and if they are doing their jobs properly, will occasionally be criticized for over-stepping their "natural" boundaries. Criticism comes with the territory, and is a sign that judges in the region are becoming more like their counterparts elsewhere.

Notes

1 N. Tate and T. Vallinder, *The Global Expansion of Judicial Power*, New York: New York University Press, 1995.
2 See especially: R. Sieder et al., eds., *The Judicialization of Politics in Latin America*, Basingstoke: Palgrave Macmillan, 2005; Also: R. Gargarella et al., eds., *Courts and Social Transformation in New Democracies: An Institutional Voice for the Poor?*, Aldershot: Ashgate Publishing, 2006.
3 J. Ferejohn, "Judicializing Politics, Politicizing Law", *Law & Contemporary Problems*, 65, 2002, pp.41–68; A. Stone Sweet, *The Birth of Judicial Politics in France*, New York: Oxford University Press, 1992.
4 R. Hirschl, *Towards Juristocracy: The Origins and Consequences of the New Constitutionalism*, Cambridge: Harvard University, 2004; T. Ginsburg, *Judicial Review in New Democracies: Constitutional Courts in Asian Cases*, New York: Cambridge University Press, 2003.
5 T. Ginsburg and R. Kagan, eds., *Institutions and Public Law: Comparative Approaches*, New York: Peter Lang, 2005.
6 C. Johnson, *MITI and the Japanese Miracle*, Stanford: Stanford University Press, 1982; K. Jayasuriya, ed., *Law, Capitalism and Power in Asia*, London: Routledge, 1999.
7 A. Stone Sweet, *Governing with Judges: Constitutional Politics in Europe*, New York: Oxford University Press, 2000; J. Ferejohn, and P. Pasquino, "Rule of Democracy and Rule of Law", in J. M. Maravall and A. Przeworski, eds., *Democracy and The Rule of Law*, New York: Cambridge University Press, 2002; N. Tate and T. Vallinder, *The Global Expansion of Judicial Power*, New York: New York University Press, 1995; Hirschl, op. cit.; M. Shapiro and A. Stone Sweet, *On Law, Politics, and Judicialization*, New York: Oxford 2002; J. Ferejohn, "Judicializing Politics, Politicizing Law", *Law & Contemporary Problems*, 65, 2002, pp.41–68; R. H. Pildes, "The Supreme Court, 2003 Term: Foreword: The Constitutionalization of Democratic Politics", *Harvard Law Review*, 118, 2004, pp.29–154.
8 R. Hirschl, "The New Constitutionalism and the Judicialization of Pure Politics Worldwide", *Fordham Law Review*, 75, 2006, pp.723.
9 Morgan, "The Internationalisation of Economic Review of Legislation: Non-Judicial Legalisation", in T. Ginsburg and R. Kagan, eds., *Institutions and Public Law: Comparative Approaches*, New York: Peter Lang, 2005.
10 Stone Sweet and Shapiro, op. cit.
11 M. Shapiro, *Courts: A Comparative and Political Analysis*, Chicago: University of Chicago Press, 1981.

12 R. Hirschl, op. cit.
13 Ginsburg and Kagan, eds., op. cit.
14 Thus one should not speak of juristocracy (cf. Hirschl 2004) so much as judicial participation in broader patterns of governance.
15 Recommendations of the Justice System Reform Council: For a Justice System to Support Japan in the 21st Century (June 12, 2001).
16 M. Shapiro, *Who Guards the Guardians? Judicial Control of Administration*: Athens: University of Georgia Press, 1988.
17 C. Milhaupt, "A Relational Theory of Japanese Corporate Governance: Contract, Culture, and the Rule of Law", *Harvard International Law Journal*, 37, 1996, pp.3–64.
18 A. MacIntyre, *The Power of Institutions: Political Architecture and Governance*, Ithaca: Cornell University Press, 2003.
19 R. Kagan, *Adversarial Legalism: The American Way of Government*, Cambridge: Harvard University Press, 2002; J. M. Ramseyer, "The Puzzling (In)Dependence of Courts", *Journal of Legal Studies*, 23, 1994, pp.721–747; Ginsburg, op. cit.
20 A brief consideration of the democratic status in other regions of the world confirms this. Russia and the former Soviet Republics have settled into a pattern of renewed authoritarianism, albeit with the trappings of democracy; Latin America is undergoing a wave of populism and strongman rule; Africa has seen democratic stagnation; and democracy has been stillborn in much of the Arab world. Only in Central Europe and the Southern Cone of Latin America (with Brazil) has democracy been consolidated on any kind of large scale during the "Third Wave".
21 D. C. North and B. R. Weingast, "Constitutions and Commitment: The Evolution of Institutions Governing Public Choice in Seventeenth-Century England", *Journal of Economic History*, 49, 1989, pp.803–832; T. Ginsburg and T. Moustafa, eds., *The Politics of Courts in Authoritarian Regimes*, New York: Cambridge University Press, 2008.
22 Ibid.; Jayasuriya, ed., op. cit., p.17.
23 J. Cooper Ramo, *The Beijing Consensus*, London: Foreign Policy Centre, 2004; R. Peerenboom, *China Modernizes: Threat to the West or Model for the Rest?*, New York: Cambridge University Press, 2007.
24 B. David, "Magic Memos, Collusion, and Judges with Attitude: Notes on the Politics of Law in Contemporary Indonesia" in K. Jayasuriya, ed., *Law, Capitalism and Power in Asia*, London: Routledge, 1999, pp.233–52; P. Leyland, "Droit Administratif Thai Style: A Comparative Analysis of the Administrative Courts in Thailand", *Australian Journal of Asian Law*, vol.8, no.2, 2005, pp.121–154; Ginsburg, op. cit.
25 C. Epp, *The Rights Revolution*, Chicago: University of Chicago Press, 1998.
26 T. Halliday et al., *Fighting for Political Freedom: Comparative Studies of the Legal Complex and Political Liberalism*, Oxford: Hart Publishing, 2007.
27 J. Goldstein et al., "Introduction: Legalization and World Politics", *International Organization*, 54, 2000, p.385.
28 General Agreement on Tariffs and Trade 1994, 15 April 1994; Marrakech Agreement Establishing the World Trade Organization, Annex 1A, art X, 1867 UNTS 187, 33 ILM 1153 (1994). Note that Article X.3(c) qualifies the obligation so as not to "require the elimination or substitution of procedures in force in the territory of a contracting party on the date of this Agreement which in fact provide for an objective and impartial review of administrative action even though such procedures are not fully or formally independent of the agencies entrusted with administrative enforcement. Any contracting party employing such procedures shall, upon request, furnish the Contracting Parties with full information thereon in order that they may determine whether such procedures conform to the requirements of this subparagraph".
29 WTO 1999, The Fundamental WTO Principles of National Treatment, Most-Favored Nation and Transparency.

30 J. Meyer, "The World Polity and the Authority of the Nation-State" in A. Bergesen, ed., *Studies of the Modern World-System*, New York: Academic Press, 1980, pp.109–37.
31 A. MacIntyre, *Business and Government in Industrializing Asia*, Ithaca: Cornell University Press, 1997.
32 G. Majone, *Evidence, Argument, and Persuasion in the Policy Process*, New Haven: Yale University Press, 1989.
33 B. Ackerman, *We the People Vol 1.*, Cambridge: Harvard University Press, 1992; but also for an account that emphasizes earlier developments see: S. Skowrenek, *Building a New American State: The Expansion of National Administrative Capacities, 1877–1920*, New York, Cambridge University Press, 1982.
34 Dwight David Eisenhower, Farewell Address, January 17, 1961 ("In the councils of government, we must guard against the acquisition of unwarranted influence, whether sought or unsought, by the military-industrial complex. The potential for the disastrous rise of misplaced power exists and will persist".)
35 R. Carson, *Silent Spring*, New York: Houghton Mifflin, 1962.
36 The economic theory of collective action, developed by Olsen 1971, provided intellectual underpinnings for this idea: since small groups with a lot at stake are likely to care more about policies than large groups like consumers or taxpayers, the interests of industry are likely to win out over the general interest.
37 568 F. 2d 240 (2d Cir. 1977).
38 E.g. *Motor Vehicle Manufacturing Assn v. State Farm*, 463 U.S. 29 (1983).
39 *Citizens to Preserve Overton Park v. Volpe*, 401 U.S. 402 (1971).
40 *Association of Data Processing Service Organizations v. Federal Reserve Board*, 745 F 2d 677 (D.C. Cir. 1984).
41 M. Shapiro, *Courts: A Comparative and Political Analysis*, Chicago: University of Chicago Press, 1981.
42 *Vermont Yankee Nuclear Power Corp. v. NRDC*, 435 U.S. 519 (1978).
43 *Chevron USA v. NRDC*, 467 U.S. 837 (1984). The issue concerned an environmental law that required the Environmental Protection Agency (EPA) to regulate emissions from each "stationary source of pollution" and said that new sources had to have the best available technology to minimize pollution. Previously, the EPA had interpreted "source" to mean each smokestack in a polluting factory. After the election of the pro-business President Reagan, the EPA passed a rule stating that manufacturers could treat each factory as a single source, so that new technology need not be used for every smokestack, but only where required if total pollution from the whole factory increased. In dealing with this question, the court announced a famous two-step test for considering agency interpretations of law. First, courts were to ask if the statutory language being interpreted was unclear. If the answer was yes, then the court was to defer to reasonable agency interpretations of the law. In other words, the agency was seen to have as much or more expertise in interpreting statutes than the court.
44 Chevron was thrown into some confusion by a later case, *United States v. Mead Corp.*, 120 S. Ct. 2164 (2001), and many scholars believe this will be subject to clarification by the Supreme Court in coming years.
45 A. Samaha, "Undue Process", *Stanford Law Review*, 59, 2006, pp.601–72.
46 R. Kagan, op. cit. 2002; J. Wilson, *Bureaucracy*, New York: Basic Books, 1989; R. Kagan and L. Axelrad, *Regulatory Encounters: Multinational Corporations and American Adversarial Legalism*, Berkeley: University of California Press, 2000.
47 M. Dorf, "Legal Indeterminacy and Institutional Design", *New York University Law Review*, 78, 2003, pp.875–981; M. Dorf and C. F. Sabel, "A Constitution of Democratic Experimentalism", *Columbia Law Review*, 98, 1998, pp.267–473.
48 J. M. Ramseyer and E. Rasmusen, *Measuring Judicial Independence: The Political Economy of Judging in Japan*, Chicago: University of Chicago Press, 2003.
49 Epp, op. cit.

Part I
General perspectives

2 On the regulatory dynamics of judicialization

The promise and perils of exploring "judicialization" in East and Southeast Asia

Michael W. Dowdle

Introduction

The notion of judicialization could be a very potent concept. As I hope to show in this chapter, judicialization offers a powerful tool to identify and understand particular kinds of regulatory and constitutional change. However, in order to do so, we need to treat that notion with a lot more care than is commonly the case. In particular, the idea of "judicialization" tends to conflate into a single category a wide diversity of regulatory dynamics that have a similarly wide diversity of developmental implications. An exploration of judicialization in East and Southeast Asia may give us our most detailed mapping to-date of what our emerging, "post-industrial" regulatory world might look like. In order to do this, we must first understand and correct the potential analytic problems described above that are too often latent in the concept of judicialization.

A history of judicialization

In order to better comprehend these potential problems, we must understand the "history" of judicialization – i.e., the history of the courts' role in public policy decisionmaking. Contemporary analyses invariably treat "judicialization" as a very recent phenomenon. But in fact, as we shall see, it has a long history. Courts have a long history as active agents of public policy[1]. It was only toward the end of the nineteenth century that the constitutional role of the courts was re-defined in its present, more policy-neutral terms. Thus, the phenomenon of judicialization does not necessarily represent a new development: it could represent a return to an older way of doing things.

Judicialization and the original function of the courts

The modern notion of judicialization is used to describe the modern evolutionary process through which courts are assuming increasingly central roles in national and supranational policy formation. However, it is often forgotten that prior to the twentieth century, the Anglo-American court system—the system that serves as the principal template for the idea of a "constitutionalized" judiciary—initially emerged, first and foremost, as policy devices. In fact, English constitutional thought had long held that judges were members of the executive branch. (Montesquieu, by contrast, regarded them as a part of the legislature.)

In both England and the early United States, sitting justices would sometimes hold concurrent positions in the executive cabinet. Indeed, prior to the end of the nineteenth century, in both the United Kingdom and the United States, the judiciary was probably the *principal* constitutional device used to construct national policy relating to localized governance.[2] The Anglo-American judicial system developed and implemented national policy through the precedential development of the "common law." We in the Anglo-American system don't often think of the development of "the common law" as a form of national policy. But we might recall that in both France and later Germany, one of their very first policy decisions in the process of creating and unifying their modern nation-states was to draft and enact national legislation that standardized and codified precisely those areas of "private law" that the Anglo-American constitutional systems left to the courts to regulate. In a similar vein, up until the end of the nineteenth century, the common law was such an important centralizing policy device in the United Kingdom and the United States that both jurisdictions instructed judges to interpret potentially competing policy initiatives of both local and national governments so as to preserve the existing common law policies in the domain of private law.

What gave the common law courts this distinctive capacity to develop and promote central policy *vis-à-vis* the other branches of government during this era? In pre-modern societies, like that of both England and America prior to the late nineteenth century, executives and legislatures operated at a significant remove from local governance. Both were relatively small and operated largely out of a single place. Their capacity to govern a widely flung and widely diverse collection of localities was abstract at best. By contrast, the courts operated locally by co-opting some aspects of the functionality of local governance. This allowed them to directly and proactively regulate local behavior in a way that other centralized regulators could not. This unique power of local regulation, combined with their power of precedent, gave them a unique capacity to develop national policy in the regulation of local affairs. Indeed, the centrality of the courts to central policy formation during the first century of American constitutionalism was such that the historian Steven Skowronek refers to this period of American administrative history as the period of "courts and parties," referring to what he saw as the two principal vehicles for national public policy formation in nineteenth century America.[3]

In doing this, four distinctive aspects facilitated the courts' institutional authority. The first we might call the power of concurrent jurisdiction. Courts are not precluded from issuing policy decisions simply by virtue of the fact that some other governmental entity has authority over that area of policy. In fact, much of court-initiated policy is issued in (hopefully harmonious) concurrence with and in response to pre-existing national or local policy initiatives on the same subject. A second aspect would later be termed the "convening power," the power to compel both local citizenry and local administrators to appear before it to discuss local affairs. A third aspect is the power of application, the courts' unique power to directly apply their "law" to real world situations. These two latter powers allowed courts to proactively make and implement local policy decisions independently of local government. By contrast, the more remote executive and legislative branches were limited to passively reviewing local policy implementation (or frolic) after these actions had already at least partially occurred. Finally, and related to the power of application, the courts also enjoy the power of finality. In areas of concurrent authority, the court's decision was generally final, not only with regard to the local government, but also in many important aspects with regard to the other two branches of the national government.

Modernism and the retreat of the courts' policymaking capacities

The courts' role as policy devices changed radically with the advent of administrative bureaucratization, however. Bureaucratization allowed administrative organs to expand in size and competence so as to begin more directly and proactively overseeing and shaping local governance. With such capacities, there was no longer need for the kind of parallel localized governance structures that the courts provided. In a word, administrative bureaucratization rendered the courts, at least in their original constitutional role, somewhat "redundant."

The result was a significant retreat in the courts' formal contribution to public policy formation. This development is most clearly seen in nineteenth century England, as paradoxically attested to in Dicey's hagiography to England's older tradition of judge-centric constitutionalism, his vision of "rule of law" constitutionalism.[4] Dicey's vision of rule-of-law constitutionalism was motivated by a desire to restore the English judiciary to its earlier role in public policy formation—a role that Dicey saw as dangerously threatened by the rapid growth of the English administrative state.

On the other side of the Atlantic, the story is a bit more complicated, partly because the development of administrative bureaucracy, at least at the federal level, was more fitful in the United States than it was in the United Kingdom. After a continuous period of executive challenge, particularly from the Theodore Roosevelt and Woodrow Wilson administrations, the American courts first acquiesced to their new, subordinate role by the early 1910s.[5] But the Republican administrations of the 1920s arrested the federal administration's bureaucratization, and this worked to temporarily invigorate at least some aspects of the courts' traditional policymaking capacities. The courts and the administration then engaged in a second round of competition over policymaking and control in the 1930s, with the administration winning decisively in *NLRB v. Jones & Laughlin Steel* in 1937.[6]

Subsequent attempts to restore the courts to policymaking oversight capacity, most notably the Dicey-inspired Administrative Procedure Act of 1946[7] and the open government acts of the 1960s, were of only marginal effectiveness.

As documented by Jerry Mashaw in the late 1970s and more recently by Elena Kagen, the courts' role in national public policymaking and enactment remains minor—although the court-centric focus of Anglo-American legal education has tended to magnify that role in Anglo-American legal consciousness.[8]

As the courts' policymaking function receded, their perceived constitutional role of the courts also began to change. Instead of being affirmative instruments of a national centralization, courts were increasingly seen in more politically neutral and policy-neutral terms—as simple "resolvers of disputes." Their expertise morphed from one that focused on divining the organic policy wisdoms of a metaphysical "law" to one focused on more mechanistic interpretation of statutes and other forms of positive norms (like the Restatements in many areas of the private law).[9] In America, this change in constitutional role is evinced by the emergence in the late nineteenth century of the conceptual conundrum that would later be known as the "counter-majoritarian difficulty"—that question of why non-elected courts should, in a democracy, enjoy a constitutional trump over elected legislatures and executives at both the national and the local levels. So long as courts are perceived as enjoying independent and distinctive *policymaking* authority, their capacity to override the policymaking authority of these other regulators within their areas of competence did not raise serious issues. It was only when the courts were reconceptualized as distinctively "apolitical"—i.e., as distinctively removed from policy formation—that their long-standing regulatory overlap with other governmental entities became problematic.

This is the vision of courts that continues to inform our constitutional understanding to this day. It is the vision that informs our understanding of the "rule of law." But it is also a vision that describes a political arrangement that is much more contingent and fragile than is normally recognized.

Modernism and industrialization

Underlying the emergence of this more "modernist" vision of the distinctively apolitical role of courts in constitutional governance that we associate with "rule of law" was the concurrent emergence of industrialization and managerial capitalism. We noted above how one of the principal attributes that recommended courts as opposed to administrations as the principal motor for localizing centralized governments was their distinctively localized character. This localized character gave court-developed policy a unique flexibility in application. Although less predictable a priori than rule-based governance, such flexibility was necessary in an environment in which local conditions were unknowable to more remote administrative policymakers.

Industrialization changed all this by increasingly harmonizing and standardizing the economic and social space of the nation. A harmonized and standardized regulatory space is much more responsive to rule-based regulation. In such an environment, bureaucracies become more efficient regulatory implementers than courts, because local variance and local opacity—the two factors that courts are most adapt at confronting—are no longer significant issues.

There is good reason, however, to suspect that the industrialized world, and the kind of harmonized and standardized regulatory environments that it tends to generate, is in decline. National economies are fragmenting and are simultaneously being swallowed by transnational economic forces. There is evidence that economies of scale may be tapping out, and that industrial survival increasingly depends on flexibility rather than on simple cost-per-unit. As a result, regulatory environments are becoming more complex, more opaque, and therefore less susceptible to bureaucratic, rule-based regulation. The phenomenon of judicialization may reflect this trend.

In other words, "judicialization" may represent the emergence of a growing antithesis to "rule of law." This, I think, could make it a very powerful analytic tool. Contemporary efforts to comprehend "law and development" have invariably treated "rule of law" as the natural mode of regulation. Deviations from this mode have been treated as aberrational. For this reason, promotion of regulatory effectiveness has been invariably regarded as simply a process of removing unnatural—or "political"—impediments to this natural state of regulatory functioning.

But rule of law, as we have seen, is really the product of and dependent up the distinctive form of social and economic stability and rationalization produced by industrialization and managerial capitalism. And it depends on the "improbable [regulatory and economic] stability"[10] for its effectiveness. Therefore, it is really "rule of law," and not its absence, which is exceptional. Even at its height, both modern industrialism and its attendant rule-of-law only really colonized the core regulatory environments of the world economy. Efforts to export them to the more peripheral regions of that economy have invariably failed. It has traditionally been presumed that this failure is due either to some flaw in the method of exportation (see the critiques of law and development) or some flaw in the recipient polity (see the literature on "good governance"). Our exploration of the nature of this regulatory model suggests something else—that it is the presence of rule-of-law rather than its absence that is innately aberrational. If this is the case, then law and development may need to begin developing regulatory models that do not depend on the rule-of-law metrics. Investigations into the phenomenon of "judicialization" could be used to help rectify this oversight.

Kinds of judicialization

To develop such new regulatory models we must be much more precise in defining "judicialization." To date, analyses of the phenomenon of judicialization have tended to conflate into one rubric what are in fact a number of very different kinds of regulatory phenomena, each with distinct developmental implications. Before any investigation into judicialization can be analytically useful then, we must distinguish between its different forms of manifestation.

Before taking a detailed inventory as to what judicialization might be, it is helpful first to clarify what it is not. Consider the following. Historically, the question of when and where one might smoke was determined largely by private and social norms or "soft law." Beginning around the 1980s, however, many local governments in the United States began passing legislation regulating where people could smoke. Naturally, the courts were often called upon to interpret and fill in the gaps of this new legislation, and this in turn invariably involved them in a new area of policymaking.

Nevertheless, it would be a mistake to count this as an example of "judicialization." The increase in judicial policymaking described above is simply concomitant to increased regulation generally. Courts are a foundational part of government regulation, and the more government regulation, the more areas of social and political life the courts help regulate. Judicialization, by contrast, seems to describe a phenomenon that is different from mere regulatory expansion. It seems to describe an expansion in judicial role relative to other governmental actors. Borrowing from the terminology of Joseph Schumpeter, we might say that juridicalization involves a "dynamic" as oppose to "static" expansion of the judicial role of public policymaking—an expansion that implicates changes in the internal dynamics of regulatory governance *per se*.

What might be the nature of this distinctively *dynamic* expansion? The answer to this question is not so simple, because as discussed below, courts actually have multiple constitutional roles. And each of these particular roles provides a distinctive pathway for judicialization with its own developmental dynamics and implications.

A return to the historical analysis of the courts' traditional regulatory role helps to illustrate this point. As we saw, courts originally emerged as devices for developing and implementing centralizing policymaking in a pre-modern regulatory environment. Of course, they still retain this capacity, so one potential dimension for judicialization is this traditional one of centralization.

A good present-day example of this kind of judicialization can be found in Zhu Suli's analysis of China's recent judicial and legal development. According to Zhu, a Professor of Law at Beijing University, a dominant political motive behind China's recent turn to "rule of law" is the same one that catalyzed the development of "rule of law" in England some 700 years ago—i.e., a desire to get local governments to conform to central policy initiatives.[11] And along these lines, in those regulatory areas in which we do find significant and sustained interest in developing centralized policy, such as those relating to social stability and promoting private economic activity, we find evidence of an enhanced policy role for the courts, a distinctly dynamic enhancement because it comes at the expense of the regulatory powers of local administrative government. Thus, we find high levels of court involvement in matters relating to economic relations, corporate governance, business organization, in matters relating to the WTO, and ordinary crime control. Conversely, in policy areas in which significantly developed centralized policy is yet to appear, such as corruption or regulation of marriage and family relationships, the courts' policy voice has often been (but not always—see next) much more distinctively absent.[12]

When most scholars talk about "judicialization," especially in a comparative context, they are most likely talking about this particular centralizing form of judicialization.[13] This is also the form of judicialization that resonates consonantly with the developmentalist notion of "rule of law." Rule of law sees the role of the courts as one of resolving disputes in ways that are most consistent with an abstract law—i.e., laws that are uniformly applied throughout the realm. This requirement of uniformity gives this law and the decisionmaking it generates an innately centralizing character. The distinctly centralizing role of courts in this vision is evinced by the observation that when polities have trouble with localities that ignore central legal mandates, one of the typical "rule of law" responses is that of "court reform."[14] In this way, it sees a properly functioning court to be an important step toward the development of a more centralized and uniform legal system in the face of local resistance.

In thinking about this aspect of judicialization, however, we have to be careful not to conflate "centralization" with "state power." Some forms of centralization work against state power. For example, the judicialization of Europe described by Shapiro would appear to be an example of a centralization form of judicialization, but it is centralizing at a transnational level rather than a state level. In this way, it works to weaken rather than strengthen national power. Indeed, much of the developmentalist interest in judicialization would seem to be of this sort: many developmentalist applications of judicialization—such as in the context of WTO or intellectual property or human rights—use it as a device for weakening a state's capacity to resist larger international norms. For them, "centralizing" role of the judicialization is a super-national rather than a national phenomenon.

But as we have also seen, with the advent of the modern administrative state, the state had much less need for this particular function of the courts. This did not, however, render courts obsolete. As explained above, the courts acquired a number of specialized powers in their pre-modern stages. With the retreat of the logic of centralization, these special powers have been increasingly adapted to serve other needs and interests, implying its own unique dimension for judicialization.

Take, for example, the convening power. As noted above, one of the ways in which the courts were able to take over local governance is by compelling others to participate, face-to-face, in judicial decision-making processes. Combined with the fact that courts operate locally, this gives the courts a unique capacity to gather and make use of local knowledge. Courts can use their convening power to compel the input and decisional participation of a much wider diversity of actors, including local actors, than can other centralized governmental entities. Many believe that this, in turn, allows them to craft more nuanced regulatory responses to complex social problems.

Michael Dorf and Charles Sabel have recently referred to this particular use of courts as a form of "experimentalism." Using innovative American "drug courts" as their principal example, they show how courts can use the distinctive advantage in gathering local knowledge to catalyze useful experimentation in the regulation of many recalcitrant social problems. In this way, the courts' convening power, combined with the courts' case-by-case decisionmaking, gives the courts a capacity to generate policy that is more flexible and adaptable than modernist, Weberian regulation.

This is another possible trajectory for judicialization, one that works to promote regulatory flexibility and local adaptability rather than centralized uniformity. Indeed, this trajectory actually tends to *decentralize* regulation, and for this reason has been strongly associated with post-modern—or post-industrial, or post-Fordist—regulatory environments, which many see as particularly dynamic and ever-changing and thus more demanding of institutional flexibility and adaptability than of institutional uniformity. The use of the courts in this manner is not new. Indeed, the original role of the jury was precisely to facilitate the court's capacity to gather and make use of the community's local knowledge in rendering its decisions.

Citizens, too, frequently make use of the courts' localized convening power, but they do so often for reasons that are not meaningfully termed experimentalist. Because of their convening function, courts provide a unique forum in which ordinary citizens can engage with the state. For most citizens, a court represents the one forum in which the state must respond, directly and publicly, to a complaint. This gives the court a unique, expressive functionality. This too can be a distinctive trajectory of judicialization.

This particular usage of courts is most obviously articulated in the idea of "civil disobedience." Civil disobedience is not concerned with using the courts to compel government to adopt a particular policy response. Under the classic doctrine of civil disobedience, the dissenting citizen fully expects to go to jail. She then seeks to use the court to demonstrate the state's inability to provide a rational or moral justification for the particular policy over which she dissents.

This expressive trajectory of judicialization is also readily apparent in Asia, and particularly in China. It was at the heart of Zhang Yimou's internationally acclaimed movie, *Jiu Qu's Story*, which chronicled the efforts of a rural peasant in China to use the newly reformed administrative litigation process in order to get a village cadre to "explain his way of reasoning to me." More recently, it is also seen in the emergence of a small community of lawyers in China who are using trials of political dissidents as vehicles to articulate opposition to China's political regime. In doing so, they have no expectation of actually winning these cases. Indeed, they have been criticized for sometimes seeming to sacrifice the interests of their clients in pursuing this more expressive agenda.

Another possible trajectory that judicialization can take is that of simple resistance. This is the trajectory that makes us aware of the innate finality of judicial decisions. The fact that a court's decisions are often significantly difficult to overturn makes the courts an attractive venue for promoting policy initiatives that cannot be otherwise advanced through the political environment. In the context of American constitutional law, this particular functionality for the courts was famously acknowledged by Justice Stone in the third paragraph of his famous fourth footnote to *Caroline Products Co. v. U.S.* in which he acknowledged the court's special role in advancing the necessary interests of those "discrete and insular minorities" whose abilities to protect themselves politically would otherwise be swallowed-up in more majoritarian forms of political policy formation. A similar concern led Albert Venn Dicey to advance his distinctively court-centric vision of British constitutionalism in the late nineteenth century, as discussed above.[15]

In many ways, this trajectory of resistance resembles the judicialized trajectory that Martin Shapiro famously captured in his work on triadic dispute resolution, and that Tom Ginsburg later expanded upon in his insurance theory for judicial review.[16] All of these metaphors—triadicism, insurance, resistance—emphasize the distinctly third-party nature of the judicial entity in its dispute-resolving role. However, the first two emphasize the purportedly "neutral" and disinterested character of the judicial *decisionmaker*. By contrast, the metaphor of "resistance" emphasizes the innately *coercive* nature of the judicial *decision*. Because judicial resolutions occupy the final stage of the regulatory process, they represent an intrinsically and distinctly coercive form of dispute resolution. As the product of a third-party decisionmaker that for the most part is non-negotiable after it is issued, a judicial decision is, or has the innate capacity to be, imposed upon the parties irrespective of their consent.

This gives judicial forms of dispute resolution an intrinsically anti-cooperative character. This character is often recognized in the context of discussions of "Asian" legal culture, but it has been well documented in the context of the West as well. In Stewart Macauley's famous study of the contract dispute practices of local businesses in the Wisconsin dairy industry, for example, he found that these businesses would often prefer to forgo litigation even when they were certain they would win the case.[17] The metaphor of "resistance" is meant to highlight a corollary implication of Macauley's observation, one that suggests that parties will tend to resort more to judicial dispute resolution in situations in which they are (1) politically or socially subordinated within the relevant regulatory environment, and (2) no longer interested in pursuing more cooperative solutions to their disputes with stronger parties.

Of course, to say that a particular trajectory of judicialization is driven by "resistance" says nothing about what is being resisted. We must be careful to avoid conflating "resistance" with the struggles of the little against the big or the local against the global. Thus, just as advocates of local empowerment can use the courts to resist centralization or globalization, so too can advocates of centralized or globalized regulation use courts to resist local regionalism within the context of that local environment. Indeed, as discussed above, this was one of the original intents behind the development of the English court system. The key element of this trajectory lies in its distinctly anti-cooperative nature. Sometimes, in other words, judicialization can be the product of a breakdown in other, more socialized, means of social coordination.

For convenience, we might label these different forms of judicialization "centralizing," "experimental," "expressive," and "resistive" respectively. As we shall see ahead, what is important about this classification is that each of these trajectories has its own, distinctive developmental implications. But before we examine these implications, we might first note that many real-world incidents of judicialization will involve more than one of these trajectories. For example, beginning in the middle 1990s, China experienced a form of judicialization in which rural activists began a conscious campaign of using the courts to challenge the expropriation of property by local governments. In doing so, this campaign was actually composed of each of the four kinds of judicialization described earlier. Key to the activists' claims was a belief that the challenged local expropriations violated central law and norms, and in this way the activists could be seen as seeking to promote greater centralized control over local and aberrant political actors. As a general matter, the activists did not expect to win their cases—it is a universally known fact that local courts are often controlled by the very local actors that the activists seek to challenge. Their litigation was intended more to attract publicity as well as central-level attention and sympathy to their plight. In this way, their efforts to judicialize a policy problem also evinced a strong expressive element, and of course, they were using the courts to resist and challenge the actions of local power structures. The litigation was a distinctly confrontational strategy brought about by a feeling that the expropriating local governments would not deal with them in good faith, and that the most effective resolution to this issue would therefore have to be at least in part coercive rather than cooperative. Finally, litigatory activists discussed the results of their various litigation strategies in order to develop more robust understandings of the kinds of claims, publicity and pressures that were more effective in provoking either positive centralized intervention or significant local acquiescence. In this way, their judicialization evinced a distinctive experimentalist element to it as well.

The reason why this action provoked such diversity of judicialization trajectories is that it operated within and through a diversity of regulatory environments. The different trajectories represent the different dynamics of these regulatory environments. So, for example, in evoking national law and political norms, these litigation efforts significantly impacted the national efforts to regulate land expropriation. From the perspective of this regulatory environment, the judicialization trajectory this litigation represented appears centralizing. On the other hand, the kind of regulatory response that these activists sought to provoke was more political—administrative and civil societal—than juridical. Within these national administrative and parliamentary regulatory orbits, such as those of the Ministry of Civil Affairs or the Party's Propaganda Department for example (which was responsible for regulating the press's reporting of these litigations), the judicialization trajectory would be primarily expressive. And finally, the social networks these activists formed among themselves can also be regarded as a particular regulatory environment, in that it did serve to coordinate and promote these litigations, and it was from the perspective of this environment that this "judicialization" was experimentalist.

Developmental implications

As mentioned above, each of these trajectories has its own distinct developmental implications. Obviously, a centralizing judicialization would suggest the development of a more centralized, and hence stronger, state-level regulatory environment. But it would also suggest that that environment is not rationalized (or modernized) in a way that would allow for more modern administrative forms of centralization. By contrast, resistive judicialization would seem to imply a general retreat in regulatory efficacy (within that particular regulatory environment, of course), since it would suggest a breakdown in the common interests and goals that make coherent regulation possible.[18] Expressive judicialization could seem to portend an evolution of more pluralist regulatory frameworks—frameworks in which a growing number and diversity of social voices are seeking to affect regulatory decisionmaking. And finally experimentalist judicialization could signal the emergence of more dynamic, post-industrial or post-Fordist regulatory environments, environments in which regulatory adaptability is becoming more critical to regulatory success than regulatory predictability.

The symbiosis between judicialization trajectories and developmental trajectories is very apparent in the rural activism example discussed immediately above. That activism took place at a time when China's central government was beginning to try to crack down on local corruption and autonomy. Furthermore, China's local rural administrative environments are still largely pre-industrialized, and thus they are not amenable to more modernist, administrative forms of centralization.

At the same time, however, local political society in China was also experiencing the rapid emergence of civil–society-like regulatory structures. But these structures were of very ambiguous legality in China's political environment, and were often subject to sporadic local crackdowns. As a result, they developed loose-linked organizational networks that were particularly adept at exploiting local political opportunities and adapting to sudden political threats. This is precisely the kind of regulatory development that Dorf and Sabel associate with judicial "experimentalism."

Beyond this, China's larger, national-level political society was correspondingly experiencing the emergence of an increasing diversity of political voices all demanding inclusion into various forms of regulatory decisionmaking. It was in this regulatory realm, that of national-level politics and policy formation, that this judicialization took on its more expressive manifestation. And finally, the overall effect of all this was to reduce the autonomy of local rural government—from above through centralization, and from below by the advent of a meaningful civil society. And it was in this regulatory realm that this judicialization was experienced as resistive.

So, what does all this tell us? As noted above, the standard model of judicialization invariably presumes a single functionality for the courts: that of neutrally resolving disputes (i.e., what Shapiro captures with the term "triadic logic"). In the realm of constitutional law, this perspective equates "judicialization" with effective judicial review—in which courts set new constitutional policy norms (solely) through the process of independently resolving disputes over constitutional norms between other constitutional actors.

Viewed from this perspective, the "judicialization" in China that we just explored would seem to hold little developmental significance. In these cases, the Chinese courts have not been particularly neutral or "triadic" in their decisionmaking, nor have they been notably effective in "resolving" the disputes before them. When they decide for the government, as they generally do, the petitioners will invariably "appeal" that decision to higher-level political processes, in effect moving the dispute elsewhere. Even if they decide for the petitioners, the local governments will frequently ignore the judgment, and thus again perpetuate the dispute.

Indeed, some might legitimately question whether the framework discussed above actually even constitutes "judicialization." As we described in the introduction, the notion of judicialization refers to increased judicial participation in policymaking at the expense of some other governmental entity. In the story told here, we have increased litigation, but we have not testified to any apparent increase in judicial contribution to policymaking. This is consistent with much literature on Chinese law that portrays Chinese courts as making no significant contribution to regulatory development in China, precisely because they lack independence, neutrality, and effective powers of judicial review.

But the regulatory mapping that this more involved understanding of judicialization provides us with a much more robust understanding of the possible trajectories of China's regulatory development. What this more nuanced mapping of judicialization allows us to see is how at least some aspects of constitutional development in China can be the product of the interaction of a number of different regulatory systems. The Chinese case involves four distinct regulatory systems, each with its own distinct set of concerns. There is a national administrative regulatory system that is seeking to concentrate policy and regulatory control; localized regulatory systems that are seeking to resist threats to their political autonomy; emerging private advocacy groups at the national level seeking to find support for the various policy initiatives they are advocating; and local emergent civil-society groups seeking ways to affect local decisionmaking.

The interaction of these different regulatory systems appears to have generated some degree of constitutional development in China. Centralized administrative agencies are trying to exert greater centralized control over local government. Local civil-society organizations are trying to adapt this control to their own particular needs, and local governments are in turn trying to resist this adapted control. This competition is replicated at the national-level, as different national-level interests seek to adapt different elements of this conflict to their own ends. This, in turn, results in a new, pluralist form of national political competition, which requires new kinds of political norms to regulate. Many see the regulation of national political pluralism to be a *sine qua non* of constitutionalism, and so the emergence of these new norms would represent an important contribution to China's constitutional development.

In this case, judicialization appears to be a product of the fact that the courts are the one, principal constitutional organ to play a significant role in each of these four regulatory environments. The judiciary is the only constitutional body to have both national and local institutional manifestations. It is the constitutional entity whose decisionmaking is most accessible to the everyday citizenry, and hence to still embryonic civil-society structures such as those local resistance organizations that drove this process of judicialization. The courts were thus uniquely situated to provide the conduits through which the particular changes in one of these regulatory systems were transmitted and translated to changes in the others.

Moreover, and critically, the conduits the courts provide among these different regulatory systems were not symmetrical. The courts played different roles in these different regulatory systems, and these different roles affect the kind of information and institutional pressures the courts were transmitting. The asymmetrical nature of the courts' transmission function resulted from the development of a positive rather than a negative feedback loop among these regulatory systems. Positive asymmetric feedback is particularly conducive to systemic change. It is the positive rather than the negative character of the courts' inter-systemic feedback that resulted in this inter-systemic interaction's dynamic, transformative effect on the larger constitutional system.

Indeed, my suspicion is that a similar story may underlie many other incidents of judicialization. The courts' particular character as creatures of a remote and central-level government that nevertheless operate very much "locally" makes them especially sensitive to the structural symbiosis between central and local regulatory systems. When one of these two systems is perturbed in such a way as to affect this regulatory symbiosis, it is the courts that are best placed to transmit this disturbance so as to allow for complementary adjustments of the other relevant regulatory systems. This would explain, for example, why one of the paradigmatic examples of modern day judicialization is found in the European Union, an entity in which the relationships between central and local regulatory systems is still very much in flux.

Conclusion

In dissecting judicialization in this manner, however, we need to be aware of three additional and complicating factors. The first of these is the possibility of we might call "judicial surrogates." We need to remember that a "court" is a wholly artificial designation. Nothing stops a polity from choosing to name something a "court" even where it fails to fulfill any of the constitutional functions of a court in the constitutional sense of the term. Even more importantly, nothing stops a polity from creating court-like structures that are not formally labeled as courts—what we might call "judicial surrogates." Perhaps the most well-known example of such a surrogate is the French *Conseil d'Etat*. Although often referred to as an "administrative court," the *Conseil d'Etat* is, as a formal matter, not a court at all. It is an administrative agency. This formal distinction seems irrelevant to us now, but we should not forget that a century ago this same formality of labeling caused A. V. Dicey to completely mischaracterize the nature and character of French administrative law. As a general matter, the more alien the constitutional system, the greater the likelihood that problems of formal (mis)naming and judicial surrogates will skew efforts to analyze judicialization.

A second factor that needs to be considered is the possible emergence of new judicial functionalities such as experimentalism. If the courts' constitutional roles are themselves changing, then does this count as a kind of judicialization? David Dolinko, for example, has recently argued that in the context of the criminal law, a particular form of judicial experimentalism known as 'restorative justice' actually represents a retreat of court criminal functionality, because it effectively dejudicializes findings of criminality.[19]

This last fact brings me to a final concern about the notion of "judicialization." This is that the whole idea of judicialization could threaten to essentialize and universalize the modern common law's (pre-modern) fetishization of courts and judges. At least some of the examples of judicialization that I have seen cited in the literature seem to reflect more of a growth in the role that a distinctly remote, political and increasingly international "regulation" plays in everyday lives, rather than a growth in the courts' powers per se vis-à-vis other regulatory entities. For this reason, it may be best overall to talk simply in terms of *changes* in the courts' constitutional functionalities rather than in terms of *increases* (or decreases) of one particular aspect of the courts' constitutional functionality.

Nevertheless, despite these concerns, I hope I have shown that the notion of judicialization can represent a very powerful tool for analyzing the dynamics of regulation and regulatory change. However, in order for it to do so, the concept of judicialization must be treated with particular care.

Notes

1 In examining the constitutional history of the courts, we will look overwhelmingly at Western European history, and in large part to Anglo-American history. This is simply because our now increasingly global vision of "constitutionalism" today derives primarily from these particular histories. Therefore, these are also the histories that (often tacitly) inform our received understanding of "judicialization."
2 See also S. Skowronek, *Building a New American State: The Expansion of National Administrative Capacities, 1877–1920*, New York: Cambridge University Press, 1982.
3 Ibid.
4 D. Schneiderman, "A. V. Dicey, Lord Watson, and the Law of the Canadian Constitution in the Late Nineteenth Century," *Law and History Review*, 16, 1998, pp.495–526.
5 See generally Skowronek, op. cit.; see also L. Hand, "The Search of Justice," *Harvard Law Review*, 29, 1915, p.617.
6 301 U.S. 1 (1937).
7 On Dicey's influence, see M. Horowitz, *The Transformation of American Law, 1870–1960: The Crisis of Legal Orthodoxy*, Oxford and New York: Oxford University Press, 1992, pp. 225–28.
8 See, e.g., E. Kagan, "Presidential Administration," *Harvard Law Review*, 114, 2001.
9 See Hand, op. cit.
10 B. Jessop, "Regulationist and Autopoieticist Reflections on Polanyi's Account of Market Economies and the Market Society," *New Political Economy*, 6, 2001, p.213.
11 See Z. Suli, *Song fa Xiaxiang: Zhonguo Jiceng Sifa Zhidu Yanjiu* [Sending Law to the Countryside: Research on China's Basic Level Judicial System], Beijing: The Chinese University of Law and Politics Press, 2000; See also F. K. Upham, "Who Will Find the Defendant if He Stays with His Sheep? Justice in Rural China," *Yale Law Journal*, 114,

2005, p.1675; Compare with discussion of English legal development in J. Baker, *An Introduction to English Legal History*, London: Oxford University Press, 1971.

12 Compare S. Whiting, "Law and Its Substitutes: Contracting and Dispute Resolution among Chinese Firms," in T. Leng and Y. Chu, eds., *China's Grassroots Democracy and Local Governance* (under revision); with M. Woo and Y. Wang, "Civil Justice in China: An Empirical Study of Courts in Three Provinces," *American Journal of Comparative Law* (forthcoming); Cf. R. P. Peerenboom, "Seek Truth from Facts: An Empirical Study of the Enforcement of Arbitral Awards in the People's Republic of China," *Empirical Research on International Commercial Arbitration*, London: Kluwer Law International, 2004.

13 A. Stone Sweet, *Governing with Judges: Constitutional Politics in Europe*, Oxford: Oxford University Press, 2000.

14 See, e.g., S. Lubman, *Bird in a Cage*, Stanford: Stanford University Press, 2000.

15 Dicey, see note [7].

16 M. Shapiro, *Courts*, Chicago: University of Chicago Press, 1981; T. Ginsburg, *Judicial Review in New Democracies*, New York: Cambridge University Press, 2003.

17 S. Macaulay, "Non-contractual Relations in Business: A Preliminary Study," *American Sociological Review*, 28(1), pp.55–67.

18 See M. Olson, *The Logic of Collective Action: Public Goods and the Theory of Groups*, Cambridge, Harvard University Press, 1971.

19 See, e.g., David Dolinko's critique of restorative justice, which can be seen as a form of judicial experimentalism, in D. Dolinko, "Restorative Justice and the Justification of Punishment," *Utah Law Review*, 319(1), 2003.

3 Agencification, regulation and judicialization
American exceptionalism and other ways of life

Colin Scott

Introduction

Much of the contemporary debate about the rise of regulation (or the regulatory state) in Europe, Asia and elsewhere, focuses on processes of agencification – the establishment of independent or semi-independent agencies and allocation to them of regulatory tasks, many of which were previously the responsibility of ministers or, in some cases, business undertakings. In some instances agencies are created to undertake new roles not previously regarded as part of the tasks of government. This focus on agencies is a product both of the dominance of the American model of government in public policy thinking about regulation, and a reflection of the priority given to the establishment of independent agencies by international organizations such as the WTO and the OECD.[1] In many countries regulation-by-agency has taken on the status of a solution in search of public policy problems.

Agencies, however, are not the only show in town. Whereas there are examples of the creation of regulatory agencies in all the EU member states and in most of the member states of the OECD, there are important regulatory functions which remain within the remit of government ministries (even where there are regulatory agencies in the sector), and also regulatory functions exercised by non-state actors. The regulatory state shift is characterized not only by the creation of agencies, but also by a separation of policy making and operational functions (sometimes within single ministries), and a tendency towards greater use of formal rules as the basis for standard setting and enforcement.[2] Proliferation of agencies is only part of the picture. Indeed, the fragmentation in governance capacity associated with non-state and supranational regulation, when combined with alternatives to legal rules as the basis for control, take us further from an agency-focused regulatory state model and, as I have argued elsewhere, towards a post-regulatory model of governance.[3]

This chapter suggests that a regime's approach, which analyzes the variety of state and non-state actors participating within any given regulatory space, might provide a better framework within which to understand the nature and contribution of agencies to regulatory activity. The regimes approach has important implications for understanding the nature and problems of judicialization, since our emphasis is on judicialization as it affects all of the actors in the regime, and not just agencies (where they exist). More generally this approach offers a different perspective on the critical question of state capacity for regulatory governance.

The chapter starts with an analysis of the peculiar hold which the regulatory agency form has in discussions of the rise of regulation and proceeds to elaborate on the alternative regimes approach. The main part of the chapter seeks to re-conceptualize judicialization as it affects regulatory regimes, examining the different contexts within which judicialization might arise, and concluding with an assessment of both functional and normative implications.

Agencification: Pressures and processes

Ideas of regulation, and in particular of the rise of regulation and the regulatory state are closely linked to an ideal typical conception of regulatory agencies, which appears to derive largely from institutional structures in the United States. Though these structures are replicated (and perhaps even originated) at state level, it has been the Federal Independent Regulatory Agency (FIRA) model which has captured the imagination of policy makers in both domestic and supranational governmental organizations.

The FIRA model appears to have originated in the tribunal structure adopted for the Interstate Commerce Commission, established in 1888, which was in turn copied either from the British Railways and Canals Commission established in 1873[4] or from a number of state commission structures established in the 1860s and 1870s.[5] The innovation in the ICC structure was that in addition to the tribunal-type powers to receive and issue determinations in respect of complaints relating to provisions relating to such matters as pricing and provision of common carriage on the railways,[6] the Commission was also given authority and indeed a duty to keep itself informed of matters relating to the operation of the railroad industry, of its own initiative, and with related investigatory powers and without the requirement of a complaint (s. 12). This duty was subsequently enlarged so as to permit *enforcement* of the Act on the initiative of the Commission, and not only in response to complaints.[7] The Commissioners had judicial-type appointments and, notwithstanding the innovation of the own-initiative investigatory powers, were substantially restricted to enforcement action triggered by complaints. Subsequently the ICC sought to take on a greater own-initiative jurisdiction. Critically the ICC's attempts to set rules concerning rates were struck down by the Supreme Court in 1897.[8] Accordingly, it was only with express provision for rule making, introduced by legislation 1906[9] that the ICC was able to fully take on the combination of rule making, investigatory and enforcement powers which typify the FIRA model of the twentieth century. Subsequently the ICC was assigned powers to regulate telecommunications, and these were transferred to the new Federal Communications Commission in 1934.

The origins of the ICC in the tribunal structure are critical to understanding the constitution and powers of FIRAs. First, the fact of the ICC being a tribunal supported judicial-type appointment and independence of the Commissioners.

Second, the origins in the tribunal model have sustained a focus on both complaints and adversarial procedures as the basis both for action and for processes within the FIRAs. The capacity for independent rule making was an add-on to the investigatory and complaint-handling power, and fell to be processed in the same legalistic fashion. A third, and related, point is that the combination of independence and legal process associated with the agencies underpinned the acceptability of extensive delegation of rule-making powers to agencies.

The timing and location of the evolution of the US FIRAs is also significant. The ICC emerged in a period of small government, and in which the courts, and by extension tribunals, were important in resolving disputes often conceived of as being concerned with private rights over property.[10] The gradual extension of the capacity of the FIRA from tribunal to full regulator occurred at a time when institutional alternatives were not available for resolving disputes that required not only adjudication but also sectoral rules. The New Deal period is widely seen as one of increasing power for independent agencies, and further steps were taken to structure the use of these powers juridically by the passage of the Administrative Procedure Act 1946. It is claimed that the distrust of government and its constraint by law and the courts is a distinctive feature of contemporary American government which distinguishes it from government in other jurisdictions.[11]

Skipping forward to the 1980s and debates about the 'rise of the regulatory state in Europe'[12] and elsewhere,[13] the governmental and institutional context is very different. The rise of regulation, precisely converse to the nineteenth-century US history, is largely, though not exclusively, a response to the problem of big government. In this dimension, governments struggling with unmanageable public enterprises were seeking mechanisms to shrink the state.[14] Taking a lead in these reforms the UK government progressively transformed state-owned enterprises (SOEs) into privately owned companies, and, at the same time established regulatory agencies.[15] There is no sense in which the emergent agencies evolved from a court or tribunal structure. They were initially conceived of as mechanisms for controlling the worst effects of private monopoly, notably exerting controls over prices, 'holding the fort' until competition arrived under planned policies of liberalization.[16] The functions assigned to these agencies derived partly from a separation of operational and policy functions exercised by the former SOEs, and partly from the oversight functions held by government ministries. These agencies, while originating with a focus on price control, acted as a magnet for a variety of other issues, including quality of service and related problems, and subsequently the array of functions linked to promoting competition in the various sectors.[17]

These new UK agencies then, in contrast with the US experience, grew out of functions transferred from SOEs and ministries, and in a context within which the undertaking and the ministry were both to remain of central importance to the governance of the sectors concerned. It is unsurprising that the new agencies were not to have the degree of independence associated with the US agencies. Ministers retained key powers, including over-rule making. The limited capacity of the agencies to change the ground rules was, in most cases, subject to the consent of the regulated firm involved, or requiring of a report from an independent competition authority.[18] Such limited rule changes as might be made were subject to being called in by the minister at any time. Thus ministries remained deeply involved in day-to-day regulatory affairs, and maintained contacts not only with the agencies, but also directly with the former SOEs.[19] The tendency of this institutional history to support limited powers and independence for agencies was further supported by traditions within the Westminster governmental systems generally under which powers to make rules are jealously guarded by legislatures and governments.[20]

Although the privatization context was significant to processes of agencification in the United Kingdom, it was not the only context. A further dimension to the big government problem was identified in the heart of the government machine itself, and many operational tasks such as payment of social security and the operation of prisons were transferred to agencies which remained legally part of the parent department, but with a degree of autonomy and their own chief executive, often appointed from outside the public service.[21]

The history of financial services regulation was also quite distinctive, in the sense that the often implicit regulatory functions were, prior to 1986, largely being exercised through processes of self-regulation subject to light oversight from the Bank of England and the UK Treasury.[22] Without fully addressing the policy of liberalization adopted for the financial services sector, it is sufficient to say that regulation within the domain has seen a progressive move from informal self-regulation to a more hybrid regime involving statutory self-regulators and a new agency, the Securities and Investment Board, established in 1986, to a more centralized regulatory regime now very largely the responsibility of a statutory agency, the Financial Services Authority, established in 2000.[23] Thus the financial services story does represent a significant advance of government regulatory capacity into an area it had previously left to industry self-regulation. It was accompanied by reforms in other sectors where self-regulation in both contractual and statutory forms remains important, the former being illustrated by advertising self-regulation and some areas of consumer protection more generally, the latter by self-regulation of professions in areas such as law and medicine. Moran describes this process as a shift away from 'club government' towards regulatory governance.[24] This history is significant because it is so markedly different from American experience, but, in some ways closer to patterns of government in other countries which depend to a greater degree on implicit regulation and informal steering capacity in respect of non-state actors in order to govern.

The 'rise of the regulatory state' in the United Kingdom then was, perhaps, seeking to capitalize on some of the advantages of the US FIRA model, but under conditions where many of the features of the model were unavailable or unthinkable. What were the arguments in favour of the regulatory agency model? The main justifications put forward are related to the desirability of independence and expertise in the regulatory function.[25]

Independence is significant in at least two ways. Most obviously, and contrary to the experience of the SOE period, regulation is to be independent from the firms providing services so that no one firm has advantages in its capacity to set or enforce rules. Independence also relates to the relationship to government. To the extent that government has financial interests in former SOEs (notably through retention of shares) and/or strategic interests (e.g., in the protection of national champions) then it is desirable that the regulatory functions are exercised independently of those interests. A key reason for privatizing network industries was to remove the capacity of government to prioritize macro-economic policies over the efficient running and pricing of the utility sectors.[26] A somewhat wider point underlines the tendency within Westminster systems for pendulum-swing politics under which, for example, policies of privatization and regulation under one government, might be reversed under a succeeding government. The charging of agencies with regulatory functions, and more particularly the entrenching of regulatory rules within a form of contractual licence, reduces the scope for the exercise of governmental discretion and thus enhances the credibility of the regime among investors who are being asked to put private capital into former SOEs and new entrant competitors, in part as compensation for historic public under-investment.[27]

The expertise argument in favour of agencies also takes a number of forms. First there is the suggestion that where regulatory functions are exercised within divisions of larger ministries there is a lack of focus and a tendency to movement of staff in and out of different parts of the organization, where in many cases those staff have limited expertise and limited time to acquire it. Agencies may be in a position to recruit their own staff, rather than draw on generalist public servants. Related to this, where an agency can establish autonomy in terms of pay and conditions, it may develop greater flexibility in terms both of pay and terms of engagement so as to be able to attract a wider range of expertise to the organization. A distinct but related element to the argument concerns the single-function nature of agencies, as compared to all-purpose ministerial departments. The pursuit of the agency's functions may benefit both from the sustained focus of the organization to its task, and to the public profile of agency heads which would rarely be accorded the head of a division within a ministry.

Somewhat distinct from both the independence and autonomy arguments, a key attraction of agencification for governments lies in the potential to transfer functions in difficult policy areas such that blame can be attached to others when things go wrong.[28] Within the Westminster systems, the potential for blame-shifting is not as great as might first appear because it is difficult for ministers to insulate agencies to the extent that they can claim they were powerless to intervene when it was apparent that things were going wrong.

The early history of agencification in the UK in the 1980s and 1990s significantly undermines the claims both to independence and expertise in the new agencies. Although the new agencies possessed independent capacity for judgement, we have noted already that they were constrained by the rights and powers both of firms and ministries in terms of their capacity for independence of action.[29] Independence was further constrained by procedural requirements linked to enforcement, which, as is typical within Westminster systems, required application to a court prior to any formal sanctions being applied to regulatees. Furthermore the new UK agencies had limited capacity to capitalize on the potential for greater expertise as they were initially tied to employing ministry staff on ministry terms and conditions.

Over a period these limits on expertise and independence have eased somewhat as agencies have taken on rights to recruit their own staff, set their own pay and conditions and, in respect of some matters issue rules autonomously, and apply sanctions without application to a court. In two fields in particular, competition policy and financial services regulation, the agency form has evolved to permit direct application of sanctions, and in the case of financial services also to issue rules.[30] These gradual changes only slightly qualify the overall picture in which the making of rules largely remains with ministers and legislature, the formal enforcement of rules requires application to a court (which may or may not understand the objectives of the regime) leaving agencies with autonomous capacity largely only in respect of their monitoring functions. Agencies have been able to work within these limits to claim a larger amount of the policy space than their limited formal capacities might suggest, but it has not been through the exercise of legal capacity, and thus deviates significantly from the US model. The significance of self-regulation within the UK system is also at variance with the US system. Paradoxically, self-regulatory bodies frequently do possess the full range of regulatory functions – to make rules, monitor for compliance and apply sanctions – without the necessity of recourse to others.

The US and UK history with agencies provide two starting points to thinking about agencification. Canada followed the US model quite closely for a period in the middle of the twentieth century, leading one Canadian commentator to coin the phrase 'governments in miniature' to capture the idea of the executive body with all the rule making, monitoring and enforcement powers of government in a single agency.[31] But Canada has subsequently pulled back from that experience, pushing rule-making powers back towards legislative institutions.[32] Australia followed a model of agencies not dissimilar to that of the United Kingdom, though it favoured Commission structures over the single Director General model initially used in the United Kingdom. New Zealand initially rejected the creation of new agencies in favour of a combination of implicit ministerial regulation and the application of ordinary competition rules.[33] Difficulties with policies of liberalization have subsequently led New Zealand towards the agency model for the network industries, while a need to institutionalize regulatory cooperation with Australia in such areas as food safety has led to some joint agencies being established.

Evaluating the broader European experience with the establishment of regulatory agencies, Fabrizio Gilardi has tested the hypothesis that the chief reason for establishing agencies is to maximize the credible commitment of governments to stable and predictable regulatory regimes by minimizing their own capacity to intervene in the sectors concerned. Were such a hypothesis correct, Gilardi suggests, we would expect to find that agencies had a high degree of independence. Having developed an independence index, the patterns Gilardi found were quite mixed, both by sector and country. He found some evidence for the proposition that credibility, and thus independence, were more significant in the establishment of agencies in sectors where the market was being liberalized. But there were significant exceptions, for example in the decision of the German government to retain electricity regulation within government. Belgian and German governments gave to regulatory agencies in telecommunications only limited independence. In other sectors, such as food safety and pharmaceuticals evaluation, agencies tend to be less independent or functions retained within government. Financial markets regulators tend to fall somewhere in between network industries and the food/pharmaceutical sectors in terms of independence.[34]

At the level of the European Union many new agencies have been created since the 1970s. But it is telling that these agencies typically only have limited powers and limited autonomy from the main executive organ of the Union, the European Commission. The European Environment Agency, for example, is chiefly a gatherer of information, while the Food Safety Agency, established in the wake of the BSE crisis of the 1990s, is chiefly an expert adviser to the European Commission.[35]

The pattern in Asia is diverse. During key phases of development many Asian states were characterized by highly centralized discretionary governmental power, with rather weak capacity for shaping the conduct of others. Modest transitions from development to regulatory state mode in some countries represents an attempt at developing more legally constrained and less direct forms of governance.[36] It has been argued that the establishment of successful regulatory agencies requires a high degree of state capacity and consequently is more challenging to some of the weaker Asian state structures.[37] Malaysia created regulatory agencies across a number of key industry sectors linked to privatization, including energy and communications. Hong Kong and Singapore have also adopted agency models in some sectors, though in the Singaporean case, the agency for telecommunications regulation combined this sector with the broader industrial development function.[38] The decision of the Singapore government to accelerate the process of liberalization in the telecommunications sector, in order to comply with commitments to the WTO, tested the credibility of its commitment to the monopoly licence issued to Singtel. US$1.2 billion in compensation was paid for the early ending of the monopoly in 2000.[39]

In Japan, with the exception of the historically weak Fair Trade Commission (FTC) in the area of competition policy, the preference has been to retain regulatory functions within super-ministries and also local authorities, while simultaneously deploying extra-legal means of persuasion to steer social and economic behaviour.[40] As Ginsburg[41] notes in his chapter, Japanese government has historically been highly dependent on administrative guidance which would be referred to elsewhere as 'soft law'.[42] We might hypothesize that differing models generate very different relationships affecting behaviour within the regulatory space.

There is no doubting that most countries are subject to pressures to create agencies. Such pressures come from the spread of ideas that agencies provide the most effective means of steering social and economic behaviour, at one remove from the political priorities of government, and, in particular from the take-up of these ideas by major international institutions capable of linking provision of loans and grants to reforms along these lines. The WTO has also sought to emphasize the importance of regulatory capacity having some independence from government, for example in telecommunications, so as to better ensure a level-playing field for new entrants from other countries. However, we must also observe that the pattern of changes is highly diverse. I have noted already that cultural factors within the political-administrative structures of many European states make the adoption of agencies with the powers of US FIRAs almost unthinkable. Within the Asian states Japan shows a strong cultural resistance to administrative structures which shift power away from central ministries. Within the Asian context generally, a culture of centralization within government is balanced by highly diverse state capacity. Thus in Singapore the proliferation of agencies, discussed in Chapter 13 by Jolene Lin, are indicative both of a centralized and strong state capacity, in a very small state, which, in these ways is rather exceptional. Many states exhibit much weaker state capacity, making the establishment of credible state agencies more challenging.

Regulatory regimes

The dispersed nature of governance is key theme of contemporary studies of regulation. The institutional separation of capacity for making norms, monitoring compliance and enforcement, observable within many regimes, supports an analysis which emphasizes the operation of regimes rather than discrete actors.[43] The concept of regulatory space alerts us to the many actors present within regulatory regimes: ministries, firms, consumers and consumer groups, NGOs, supranational governmental non-governmental bodies and so on.[44]

Understanding a regime requires an analysis of the often changing capacities and roles played by these actors, and some understanding of both their worldview and interests shape the way they act. This pattern of fragmentation is accentuated if we recognize that formal legal capacities are only part of regulatory regimes. Even such formal legal capacities are often widely dispersed. Thus though legislatures and ministers may have exclusive right to make primary and secondary legislation, legally binding rules can also be set by contracts, as with self-regulatory regimes, within supply contracts. Provision for monitoring (e.g., by third parties) and application of sanctions can also be provided for in contracts. The classic analysis of Christopher Hood supplements the legal authority to act with other tools of government based on 'treasure', 'nodality' and 'organization'.[45] The capacity to encourage behaviour through expenditure of money, through the position at the centre of information networks and through the direct use of organizational capacity is, very obviously, not restricted to governmental actors.

The analysis is important not only for an understanding of what is going on within regulatory regimes, but also for understanding what may be possible in terms of governance capacity. Thus within states with weak capacity for legal provision and enforcement, alternative instruments may be developed which place greater emphasis on expenditure (if the 'treasure' is available) or on the capacity of government to shape social and economic behaviour through education, information, advice and the deployment of informal authority to shape views and thus actions in respect of appropriate and inappropriate conduct.

Observations of the significance, capacity and effects of a wide range of actors within regulatory regimes underpin discussion of 'decentred regulation'[46] and 'nodal governance'[47] which rather directly challenge the focus on regulatory agencies. The arguments in favour of this re-conceptualization have been put extensively elsewhere. The main focus of this chapter is to examine the implication of the shift away from conceiving of agencies as the key actors within regulatory regimes for discussion of judicialization.

The focus on capacities and interests of actors in their interactions does not exhaust the insights offered by a broadly institutionalist approach. One of the key puzzles associated with judicialization in the EU members states lies in the variety of experiences.[48] As member states have liberalized key network industries it is notable that in some an explosion of litigation has resulted. Germany is a key example. Whereas in many others, relations between ministries, regulators and an increasing number of firms continue to be governed in more bureaucratic fashion. This experience suggests that other institutional variations are at play, but these are difficult to specify with precision.

Judicialization within regulatory regimes

The concept of judicialization has been much discussed, particularly in the political science literature. There is a tendency to use the term to refer to the encroachment of judicial decision making on moral and political spheres where decision making would previously have been non-judicial.[49] By extension, judicialization within regulatory regimes might be taken to refer to a process of displacement of technical, bureaucratic or political decision making about regulation with judicial decision making through courts and tribunals. Whereas the emphasis, in Alec Stone Sweet's work in particular, has been in a transformation from dyadic to triadic decision making, that is from bilateral and reciprocal relations, to one where bilateral disputes are adjudicated by a third party (a court or tribunal),[50] it has long been apparent that, with the possible exception of the United States, regulatory governance is typified as much by multilateral engagements in respect of decisions which could be characterized as polycentric.[51] If this claim is correct then judicialization represents a narrowing of the basis of decision and framing it as involving an adversarial and bilateral dispute, where in practice, many parties and competing interests may be involved.

The focus on the incursion of courts and tribunals into decision making within the judicialization literature, although widely followed, neglects the possibility that the character of decision making within public and private bureaucracies might change, even though there is little evidence of greater involvement of courts and tribunals. Thus an agency might regard itself as being more constrained in its decision making, and involve its legal team from an earlier stage, or with greater intensity in reaching conclusions, and might find that the legal teams of firms are more regularly involved in meetings in regulatory matters than hitherto, even though no tendency towards greater litigation is evident. Even if this transformation is not strictly within the concept of judicialization it does arguably come within the German concept of 'juridification', within which the governance of social and economic spheres comes progressively to be shaped by juridical norms and processes to a greater extent.[52]

Litigation is, of course, more visible than these more nebulous indicators of juridification, the latter being only discoverable in any systematic way through fairly micro-level empirical research. Thus, obvious evidence of judicialization may ground hypotheses about its effects on a wider trend to juridification. However, the converse is not true. An absence of litigation does not provide evidence either way in respect of juridification.

A position on the nature and relative significance of agencies within the regulatory regimes of a jurisdiction is significant in shaping perspectives on the nature and effects of judicialization. Within the unique context of the United States, we can see that the agency model which retains a central position within regulatory governance emerged from the judicial form of the tribunal, and though it was extended to incorporate more proactive investigatory and enforcement capacity, it nevertheless remained essentially judicial in its organization and processes. Within this context the oft-criticized judicialization of regulation is readily explicable. It is not that the model was once non-judicialized and became infected. Rather, the model adopted is a key part of the underpinnings of 'adversarial legalism' in the United States, and this is reflected in the centrality of regulatory processes in the both study and research in administrative law.[53]

The pre-history of regulatory agencies in many European countries was not courts, but rather ministries and SOEs. Processes of privatization, liberalization and re-regulation in many sectors of the economy from the 1980s, some driven by domestic priorities, and others by European Community legislation, disrupted the essentially bureaucratic and non-judicial organization of these economic and social activities, though they did not challenge the polycentric character of decision making over the sectors involved. Competitive pressures unleashed by liberalization, and the arrival of new entrant firms from other member states, might have been expected to put pressure on the somewhat informal ways of governing, even within new and more arms-length regulatory regimes. The case of British Telecom was instructive. On the one hand, they tried to maintain a senior position as dominant incumbent within a pattern of largely informal relationships with regulator and ministry within the regime established in 1984.[54] On the other hand, they took up opportunities aggressively to assert their rights to compete as new entrants in other jurisdictions, including the use of litigation as a key strategic instrument. While the UK regulator OFTEL (until 2003, subsequently OFCOM) has been the subject of relatively little litigation, the German telecoms regulator RegTP has been deluged.[55] But within both these regimes, the picture with agencies involves only a small part of the story. In the next section, I examine the range of potentially judicialized relationships, and the conditions which may lead to judicialization.

In some instances regimes have been re-programmed to significantly enhance the juridical element, often as the quid pro quo for the introduction of more stringent powers associated with agencies, for example by setting up specialist tribunals or appeals mechanisms within which regulated firms can challenge regulatory decisions. In the United Kingdom, for example, the ratcheting of agency powers over firms in competition policy generally, combined with the devolution of Commission enforcement powers, has been accompanied by the allocation of responsibility to a specialist Competition Appeal Tribunal (CAT), established in 2003, to hear appeals from decisions of agencies (and in some cases ministers) in respect of regulatory matters, and to hear actions for damages under competition law.[56] The CAT is a judicial body but, in common with tribunals in England and Wales more generally, comprises a legally qualified chair accompanied by two experts, typically with expertise in economics. Similarly, the establishment of the Financial Services Authority in the United Kingdom in 2000 was accompanied by the creation of the Financial Service and Markets Tribunal to which appeals against FSA decisions could be brought.[57] Intriguingly, while these two tribunals are kept very busy, a similar Irish tribunal for the communications sector – the Electronic Communications Appeal Panel (ECAP) – though busy with three of four appeals against the Communications Regulator for its first two years, 2004 and 2005, has recently been abolished, having heard no appeals since 2005.

Although the ECAP case is an intriguing exception, it appears to be almost inevitable that the establishment of specialist tribunals to hear regulatory appeals will tend to increase judicialization of regulatory decision making, taking affected regimes somewhat closer to the tribunal origins and adversarial style of the American agencies. Many of the US federal agencies retain a division of administrative law judges *within the agency*, whereas the UK model has the tribunal wholly external to the agency. Within the European context, the independent hearings officers within the European Commission Competition Directorate General perhaps come closest to the internal but independent judicial function.[58]

The analysis which follows is suggestive of the various relationships which *have the potential to* give rise to processes of judicialization. None of these scenarios should be viewed in isolation, since the takeoff of judicialization affecting one set of relationships is liable to spill over to other relationships within the regulatory space, though not in a predictable fashion. The effects of the various pressures for judicialization are liable to be mediated through both national politic-administrative cultures and the more specific cultures both of particular sectors and the legal system. Thus, notwithstanding the existence of similar external pressures generally, a regime within which there is a cultural hostility to judicialization might be expected to experience different responses to one where judicial involvement in decision making is more generally accepted.

Agency-regulated firm

In respect of the classic agency-regulated firm relationship we have two contrasting scenarios. Within the first, the agency is unhappy with the compliance of the firm

Agencification, regulation and judicialization 49

with rules set variously by legislation, ministers or the agency itself. Research over many domains suggests that though they may possess formal powers many enforcement agencies use education and advice to steer firms towards compliance and frequently save legal enforcement as a device 'of last resort'.[59] This is less likely to be true where the infraction is regarded as so serious that no alternative to prosecution is possible, as with breach of health and safety rules resulting in serious injury or death, or failures in safety critical plant such as nuclear installations. In some instances agencies may use formal enforcement symbolically, to demonstrate the presence by making an example of one firm encouraging the others.[60] Such strategies carry risks, and are liable to backfire where enforcement actions are unsuccessful in the courts. The unpredictability of responses of courts to what in many instances are rather unfamiliar processes of regulatory enforcement may encourage agencies to be cautious about litigation.

On the other side of the relationship, regulated firms may use litigation to challenge regulatory decisions. Challenges may be on the basis of decisions made or sometimes decisions not made by an agency. Key decisions made by agencies might include allocation of licences or the making of rules. Where, as is common, these powers are retained within ministries, the scope for legal challenge may be restricted to enforcement actions by agencies. Again firms are likely to be very cautious about litigating, aware that they too face reputational, and perhaps financial risks, from adverse decisions. On the other hand, in concentrated sectors firms may have deeper pockets than regulators, and may use threats of litigation as part of a strategy of steering agencies towards their view of particular regulatory issues.[61] Under conditions of liberalization new entrant firms, which have less stake in the relationship with an agency, may be thought more likely to litigate than is true of dominant incumbents. An added factor here is that where new entrants come from other countries they may lack the kind of social embeddedness within social networks which tend to inhibit litigation. Network sectors provide a particular case where the interests of firms are diffuse and the competing strategies of differently placed firms may counterbalance each other in dealings with an agency (or, for that matter a ministry).

In those regimes which make extensive use of licensing, the decisions of licensing authorities are liable to have a particularly significant impact. Within the common law world, greater intensity in the application of principles of procedural fairness is applied where an authority proposes to remove a licence from a firm than where a licence is not to be renewed and, attracting list protection, where a licence is not to be granted.[62] Licences have been compared to property rights for this reason.[63]

Thinking about regulatory regimes more generally, it is hypothesized within sociological research on law enforcement that where regulatees and enforcers have relatively low relational distance (because staff share history or training and/or there is frequent interaction) they are less likely to resort to litigation.[64] Research on relations between enforcement agencies and regulated businesses,[65] and between oversight agencies and public bodies has provided support for the hypothesis.[66] The hypothesis may be of particular significance in regulatory spaces occupied simultaneously by sectoral and competition agencies. All other things being equal, competition agencies are likely to have a higher relational distances to firms (less in common, less contact, etc.) and accordingly more prone to escalating to formal sanctions processes. Something of this thinking lies behind the decision of the Australian government to abolish the sectoral regulator for telecommunications, AUSTEL, after only eight years, in 1997 and transfer its telecommunications competition regulation powers to the general competition authority, the Australian Competition and Consumer Commission.[67] The relational distance hypothesis is developed chiefly to address enforcement behaviour of agencies, but may be equally valid in considering ways in which firms seek to 'enforce' against agencies.

Where the courts recognize that the power to make decisions on important social and economic matters within regulatory regimes has been allocated by legislation to agencies, common law courts may tend towards a non-interventionist approach, seeking to channel decisions within the regulatory framework. On the other hand, where a rights-based and adversarial conception of regulation takes hold, as in the United States, the courts may tend towards a more interventionist role.

Agency – Third party (consumer, interest group)

In contrast to the very direct and often concentrated stake that regulated firms have in regulatory decision making, although consumers (whether industrial or residential) may, in aggregate be strongly affected, the effects they feel in isolation are likely to be much less central to their well-being than would be true for regulated firms. Accordingly, we would expect such consumers to engage in less litigation. Litigation is, perhaps, most likely where consumers are relatively large and/or organized. It is often observed that large consumers of energy and telecoms services (i.e. large multinational firms) were a key driving force behind European Community policies on network liberalization, but that involvement largely fell short of litigation.[68] As to organized groups of consumers their effects in judicialization are likely to be sporadic rather than systematic.

Agency – Ministry

I have noted that in many countries it is difficult for ministries to give away autonomy to agencies. Within regimes where this proposition is true it is unlikely that ministers with other less drastic means to rein in agencies would need to litigate. Evidence of litigation would tend to suggest that an agency had become more independent than the ministry was comfortable with. There are a number of instances in the United Kingdom of third parties, rather than agencies themselves, challenging ministerial orders to agencies on grounds that they were *ultra vires*.[69]

Agency – Self-regulatory body

In some jurisdictions self-regulatory bodies have significant roles within regimes which also involve agencies. Thus in the communications sector in Australia,

Agencification, regulation and judicialization 51

there is both an industry ombudsman scheme and an industry standards body both operating within a statutory context alongside the regulator, the ACCC. The Telecommunications Industry Ombudsman scheme is explicitly concerned to maintain a conciliatory and non-juridical approach to dispute resolution.[70] In the United Kingdom, similarly, there is a self-regulatory ombudsman scheme, created under pressure from the agency in 2003, and to transfer low-level complaint handling away from the agency. Additionally, the UK regulator, OFCOM, is dependent on a self-regulatory body, ICSTIS (now re-named Phonepay Plus), for the regulation of terms and conditions and complaint handling relating to premium rate telephone services, and a separate self-regulatory body, the Advertising Standards Authority, for the regulation of broadcast advertising content. Litigation here is relatively unlikely since an agency is likely to have sufficient suasion with government that if it is not satisfied with the way a self-regulatory regime, nested within a statutory regime is operating, it may seek to displace self-regulation with statutory regulation.

A key exception to the general absence of juridical relations affecting agency links to self-regulation is where a meta-regulatory agency is established to oversee self-regulation, as has happened with medical and legal self-regulation in a number of jurisdictions including Australia and the United Kingdom. The UK Council for the Regulation of Health Care Professionals was established with specific powers to refer to the High Court unduly lenient disciplinary proceedings against healthcare professionals.[71] Here the choice of judicialization was made by government in the way the regime was restructured.

Ministry-regulated firm

Where ministries retain enforcement capacities a central issue of regulatory style is defined by the extent to which formal enforcement is resorted to, as opposed to informal methods of suasion, where infractions are detected. In many jurisdictions ministries may prefer informal routes and reserve any formal sanctions to the most egregious of cases. Alternatively, ministries may prefer to address long-standing problems with legislation rather than litigation. Where agencies are established to carry out enforcement the issue is not likely to arise. On the other side, firms may use litigation processes to challenge the ways in which ministries develop regulatory regimes. The opportunity for such litigation is dependent on the institutional factors which characterize both constitutional and administrative law regimes in a particular jurisdiction. Thus, some jurisdictions, and notably the United States, permit challenge to primary legislation on constitutional grounds (interference with property rights being a classic reason).[72] In other instances, notably the United Kingdom, opportunities are restricted to challenge of secondary legislation on relatively narrow administrative law grounds. Challenges by third parties may be possible, though in many systems of administrative law such third parties may lack standing where they are not directly affected. In the United Kingdom, key challenges to ministers over rule making have concerned government implementation of EC legislation for the telecommunications sector.[73]

Ministry – European Commission

Within the European Union a key source of judicialization in recent years has arisen from obligations associated with membership. Where administrative infringement proceedings by the European Commission fail to elicit compliance there is a judicial stage which may ultimately lead to fines.[74] Sluggishness in implementing liberalization measures in such areas as energy, telecommunications and postal services has, in practice, been a key cause of such litigation. Similar litigation risks are faced by ministries in respect of trade obligations, such as those arising from membership of the WTO.

European Commission – Regulated firms

There are few supranational regulators with direct enforcement capacity against firms. One of the few examples is the European Commission, but only in its competition policy role. Whereas the Commission has engaged in much administrative enforcement, and this has frequently given rise to legal proceedings at the suit of the undertaking targeted, recent reforms have transferred much of the enforcement responsibility to National Competition Authorities (NCAs) (albeit in parallel with the Commission's responsibilities). Accordingly, a decline in such litigation is likely (though it may be displaced to the national level). The Commission is not removed from the scene, but rather operates less directly, seeking to steer the enforcement conduct of NCAs through network activities.[75]

Firm – Firm

Some regulatory regimes are substantially built on the capacity of firms to enforce against each other. The US anti-trust regime famously uses the incentive of triple damages for successful complainants both to encourage private actions and to punish violators.[76] Another key example was provided by the regime established to accompany privatization of telecommunications in New Zealand. In the highly contentious area of interconnection terms, essential for new entrants to gain access to the dominant incumbent infrastructure to provide competing services, the New Zealand government opted to let the firms litigate using general competition rules relating to abuse of dominant position as the normative basis, rather than the detailed sectoral rules developed and implemented by agencies in most jurisdictions.[77] The result was a high degree of judicialization but a concern that the result was unworkable in terms of delivering competition, such that the government had to use 'implicit' regulatory powers to persuade the firms to find workable agreements.[78] In more competitive sectors litigation by competitors may be more viable, and is a key plank of the US anti-trust regimes which penalizes infractions with treble damages as an incentive to the damaged competitor to enforce the rules.

Where contracts are used as the basis for regulation by one firm of another then judicialization may be possible where things go wrong. However, we should note the general tendency, observed in socio-legal research, for reluctance among business people to resort even to strict contractual terms, let alone litigation.[79] Such contractual regulation may, of course, form part of a larger statutory or self-regulatory regime. For example, a regulated or self-regulated firm may impose conditions in contracts in order to ensure its own compliance, and its position may be imperilled by breaches by the other party. An example is provided by the case of a retailer who requires accreditation of products as fairly traded, organic or compliant with the rules of the Forest Stewardship Council, who would risk reputational damage and possibly prosecution for misleading practices, if products acquired as being compliant were, in fact, not so. Thus damages may be sought where losses result.

Third party – Regulated firm

In general we might not expect third parties such as consumer and environmental groups to enforce rules directly against firms. However, in some instances the legal regime is adapted directly to encourage this. Consumer group enforcement of consumer protection laws has become a key principle of European Community consumer law, extending now beyond enforcement of rules on unfair terms in consumer contracts[80] to a range of other issues. The theory underlying this is that such third-party enforcement may compensate for a complacent regulator. However, it creates the risk that the overzealous third-party enforcer may disrupt effective but more consensual regulatory relations with litigation.[81]

Self-regulatory body – Regulated firm

Self-regulation is frequently not simply a voluntary engagement for a firm, but a necessity if it is to trade effectively in its sector. Thus, the first point is that even though joining a self-regulatory regime may be formally voluntary it maybe a de facto pre-condition to market participation. I should also observe at this point that compliance within self-regulatory regimes is not a voluntary matter. Any self-regulatory regime worth the name will have enforcement capacity against members. Where a self-regulator has the powerful position which derives from the necessity for businesses to join if they are to participate in the market then it is tantamount to a licensing authority, as well as frequently combining rule-making and enforcement powers. Self-regulators often combine all the regulatory powers, but paradoxically the courts may give less intense scrutiny to decision making because any action contrary to the rules can be rectified by modification of the rules, an option not open to many government agencies.[82] In many jurisdictions self-regulatory bodies are considered to fall outside the scope of judicial review, leaving dissatisfied members to pursue contractual actions when dissatisfied with the conduct of the organization.

Conclusion

The rise of the regulatory state, where this has been seen, frequently involves delegation of tasks to agencies on a greater scale than has been seen before. But this does not imply that the agencies which are created are regulatory agencies in the American style. The US history is one in which greater powers have been given to agencies than elsewhere, and the accompanying legal constraints are a key part of the unique style of adversarial legalism associated with American government.

We should not assume that agencies are the be-all and end-all of regulation, nor that the diffuse patterns of delegation to agencies, where these are created, are likely to lead to judicialization in the American style. Rather there seem to be some other, general factors at play creating pressures for judicialization, but also inhibitors, many of which appear to be peculiar to particular national systems.[83] Within the European Union, a key source of judicialization in the member states, the development of the 'new governance' provides evidence of a move beyond legalistic ways of thinking about governing, towards mechanisms which give greater play to processes both of competition and, in particular the kind of community governance which develops within networks.[84] Similar ideas are expressed in different terms in discussion of a shift from authority, as the modality of governance, to other modalities based on incentives and learning.[85] These developments, it is claimed, form part of a wider pattern of democratic experimentalism.[86] Thus, to tackle Ginsburg's question[87] – does judicialization represent a one-way street or is there a way back? – there is some evidence that the EU governance structures are on the way back, in limited ways, in some sectors.

There is no judicialization index which can be deployed to compare the extent of judicialization in different jurisdictions. For the reasons of institutional history, already noted, it would be surprising if any country emerges which could challenge the pre-eminent position of the United States as the most highly judicialized in its regulation, and public administration more generally. Processes of market liberalization might, all other things being equal, tend to push particular regimes towards greater judicial involvement, as they put pressure on long-standing less formal governance relationships. Alongside this, the award of more stringent or complete regulatory powers to agencies has tended to be accompanied by more extensive rights of appeal, and in some cases institutionalization of these rights in new tribunals. This institutional choice is likely also to push regimes towards greater judicial involvement. A third factor, linked to liberalization, is the growth of regional and global trade regimes which create pressures both for dominant firms and also for governments which result in disputes being articulated in juridical terms. Although the more developed example is the European Union, we have seen substantial litigation in the WTO appellate panel also. But these factors do not overwhelm the institutional cultures found within particular jurisdictions, so the responses to these pressures is mediated through peculiar national factors, which should lead us to expect apparently similar policy changes yielding markedly different instances of judicialization.

Are the effects of judicialization negative or positive? This is likely to depend on your point of view. For some, judicialization is a side effect of the breaking down of cosy relationships between governments and suppliers of utilities services, and financial and professional services. It is but part of a wider process in which the expectations placed on service providers are better articulated and more amenable to challenge, not only by government and by agencies but also by consumers and interest groups. Thus judicialization is part of process by which service providers and regulators are better and more transparently held to account for what they do. For others the spectre of judicialization is that it will create a world of more defensive and cautious service provision and regulation, in which litigation risks are recognized and minimized, at the expense of vitality and innovation within the sectors affected. Key social values may be displaced by juridical values, and service providers will find themselves less able to focus on what they are supposed to do. The basis for decisions over polycentric issues is liable to be narrowed to a bilateral contest over rights in the particular case. At the outside the weight of expectation placed on the legal system, in terms of holding to account and ensuring proper delivery by service providers, may cause it to collapse or have its legitimacy challenged.[88]

Finally, there is the possibility that judicialization may imply different things in diverse jurisdictions. Thus for some jurisdictions it might represent simply a tendency towards formalization in the way that relationships are governed, whereas in others it might be perceived as a complete recasting of relationships from familiar to novel forms. Thus there may be reasons to perceive any judicialization trend differently in different spaces and different times.

Notes

1 OECD, *Regulatory Reform*, Paris: OECD 1997.
2 M. Loughlin and C. Scott, 'The Regulatory State', in P. Dunleavy et al., eds, *Developments in British Politics 5*, Basingstoke: Macmillan, 1997.
3 C. Scott, 'Regulation in Age of Governance: The Rise of the Post-Regulatory State', in J Jordana and D Levi-Faur, eds, *The Politics of Regulation*, Cheltenham: Edward Elgar, 2004, pp.145–74.
4 Railways and Canals Act 1873; M. Dimock, *British Public Utilities and National Development*, London: Allen & Unwin, 1933.
5 C. Aitchison, 'The Evolution of the Interstate Commerce Act 1887–1937', *George Washington Law Review*, 5, 1927.
6 Interstate Commerce Act 1887, Section 13.
7 Atchison, op. cit., pp.317–19.
8 *ICC v. Cincinatti N. O. and T.P Railway Company* 167 US 479.
9 Atchison, op. cit., pp.327–8.
10 R. Epstein, *Takings: Private Property and the Power of Eminent Domain*, Cambridge: Harvard University Press, 1985.
11 R. Kagan. 'Globalization and Legal Change: The "Americanization" of European Law?', *Regulation & Governance,* vol.1. no.2, 2007, pp.99–120.
12 G. Majone, 'The Rise of the Regulatory State in Europe', *West European Politics*, 17, 1994, pp.77–101.

13 D. Levi-Faur, 'The Global Diffusion of Regulatory Capitalism', *The Annals of the American Academy of Political and Social Science*, 598, 2005, pp.12–32.
14 H. Feigenbaum et al., *Shrinking the State: The Political Underpinnings of Privatization*, Cambridge: Cambridge University Press, 1999.
15 T. Prosser, *Law and the Regulators*, Oxford: Oxford University Press, 1997.
16 S. Littlechild, *Regulation of British Telecommunications' Profitability*, London: Department of Trade and Industry, 1983.
17 C. Hall et al., *Telecommunications Regulation: Culture, Chaos and Interdependence Inside the Regulatory Process*, London: Routledge, 2000.
18 Prosser, op. cit.
19 Hall et al., op. cit.
20 M. Loughlin and C. Scott, 'The Regulatory State', in P. Dunleavy et al., eds, *Developments in British Politics 5*, Basingstoke: Macmillan, 1997.
21 O. James, *The Executive Agency Revolution in Whitehall*, Basingstoke: Palgrave-Macmillan, 2003.
22 J. Black, *Rules and Regulators*, Oxford: Oxford University Press, 1997.
23 M. Moran, *The British Regulatory State: High Modernism and Hyper-Innovation*, Oxford: Oxford University Press, 2003.
24 Ibid.
25 M. Thatcher and A. Stone Sweet, 'Theory and Practice of Delegation to Non-Majoritarain Institutions', *West European Politics*, 25, 2002, pp.1–22.
26 T. Prosser, *Nationalised Industries and Public Control: Legal, Constitutional and Political Issues*, Oxford: Blackwell, 1986.
27 B. Levy and P. Spiller, eds, *Regulation, Institutions and Commitment*, Cambridge: Cambridge University Press, 1996.
28 C. Hood and H. Rothstein, 'Risk Regulation Under Pressure: Problem Solving or Blame-Shifting?', *Administration & Society*, 33, 2001.
29 Hall et al., op. cit.
30 R. Baldwin, 'The New Punitive Regulation', *Modern Law Review*, 67, 2004, pp.351–83.
31 J. Willis, 'Administrative Decision and the Law: The Views of a Lawyer', *Canadian Journal of Economics and Politics*, 24, 1958, pp.502–11.
32 B. Doern, 'A Political-Institutional Framework for the Analysis of Competition Policy Institutions', *Governance*, 8, 1995, 195–217.
33 C. Flood, Colleen, 'Regulation of Telecommunications in New Zealand: Faith in Competition Law and the Kiwi Share', *Competition and Consumer Law Journal*, 3, 1992, pp.119–221.
34 F. Gilardi, 'Policy Credibility and Delegation to Independent Regulatory Agencies: A Comparative Empirical Analysis', *Journal of European Public Policy*, 9, 2000, pp.873–93.
35 C. Scott, 'Agencies for European Governance: A Regimes Approach', in D. Geradin et al., eds, *Regulation Through Agencies: A New Paradigm for EC Governance*, Northampton: Edward Elgar, 2005.
36 T. Ginsburg, Chapter 1, in this volume, 2008.
37 M. Painter and S. Wong, 'The Telecommunciations Regulatory Regimes in Hong Kong and Singapore: When Direct State Intervention Meets Indirect State Policy Instruments', *Pacific Review*, 20, 2007, pp.173–95.
38 Ibid.
39 Ibid., p.184.
40 R. Kagan, 'Introduction: Comparing National Styles of Regulation in Japan and the United States', *Law and Policy*, 22, 200, pp.225–44; U. Schaede, *Cooperative Capitalism: Self-Regulation, Trade Associations and the Antimonopoly Law in Japan*, Oxford: Oxford University Press, 2000.

41 Ginsburg, op. cit.
42 F. Snyder, 'The Effectiveness of European Community Law: Institutions, Processes, Tools and Techniques', *Modern Law Review*, 56, 1993, pp.19–54.
43 M. Eisner, *Regulatory Politics in Transition*, Baltimore: Johns Hopkins University Press, 2000.
44 L. Hancher and M. Moran, eds, *Capitalism, Culture and Regulation*, Oxford: Oxford University Press, 1989; C. Scott, 'Analysing Regulatory Space: Fragmented Resources and Institutional Design', *Public Law, 2001*, pp.329–53.
45 C. Hood, *The Tools of Government*, London: Macmillan, 1984.
46 J. Black, 'Decentring Regulation: The Role of Regulation and Self-Regulation in a "Post-Regulatory" World', *Current Legal Problems*, pp.103–46, 2001.
47 S. Burris et al., 'Nodal Governance', *Australian Journal of Legal Philosophy*, 30, 2005.
48 M. Thatcher, 'Delegation to Independent Regulatory Agencies: Pressures, Functions and Contextual Mediation', *West European Politics*, 25, 2002, pp.125–47.
49 M. Shapiro and A. Stone Sweet, *On Law, Politics, and Judicialization*, Oxford: Oxford University Press, 2002.
50 Ibid.
51 L. Fuller, 'The Forms and Limits of Adjudication', *Harvard Law Review*, 92, 1978, pp.353–409.
52 G. Teubner, 'Juridification: Concepts, Aspects, Limits, Solutions', in R. Baldwin et al., eds, *Socio-Legal Reader on Regulation*, Oxford: Oxford University Press, 1998 (orig. pub. 1987).
53 R. Kagan, *Adversarial Legalism: The American Way of Law*, Cambridge: Harvard University Press, 2003.
54 C. Hall et al., op. cit.
55 Thatcher, op. cit.
56 Enterprise Act 2002, section 12, Sched 2.
57 Financial Services and Markets Act 2000, Section 132.
58 Doern, op. cit.
59 P. Grabosk and J. Braithwaite, *Of Manners Gentle: Enforcement Strategies of Australian Business Regulatory Agencies*, Melbourne: Oxford University Press, 1986.
60 K. Hawkins, *Law as Last Resort: Prosecution Decision Making in a Regulatory Agency*, Oxford: Oxford University Press, 2002.
61 C. Hall et al., op. cit.
62 *McInnes v. Onslow-Fane* [1978] 1 W.L.R. 1520.
63 C. Reich, 'The New Property', *Yale Law Journal*, 73, 1964, pp.733–87.
64 D. Black, *The Behavior of Law*, New York: Academic Press, 1976.
65 Grabosky and Braithwaite, op. cit.
66 C. Hood, Christopher et al., *Regulation Inside Government: Waste-Watchers, Quality Police, and Sleaze-Busters*, Oxford: Oxford University Press, 1999.
67 M. Kerf and D. Geradin, *Controlling Market Power in Telecommunications: Antitrust v. Sector-Specific Regulation*, Oxford: Oxford University Press, 2003.
68 W. Sandholtz, 'The Emergence of a Supranational Telecommunications Regime', in W. Sandholtz and A. Stone Sweet, eds, *European Integration and Supranational Governance*, Oxford: Oxford University Press, 1998.
69 C. Scott, 'The Juridification of Regulatory Relations in the UK Utilities Sectors', in J. Black et al., eds, *Commercial Regulation and Judicial Review*, Oxford: Hart, 1998, pp.36–8.
70 A. Stuhmke, 'The Rise of the Australian Telecommunications Industry Ombudsman', *Telecommunications Policy*, 26, 2002, pp.69–85.
71 NHS Reform and Health Care Professions Act 2002.
72 R. Epstein, *Takings: Private Property and the Power of Eminent Domain*, Cambridge: Harvard University Press, 1985.

73 C. Scott, 'The Juridification of Regulatory Relations in the UK Utilities Sectors', in J. Black et al., eds, *Commercial Regulation and Judicial Review*, Oxford: Hart, 1998, pp.35–36.
74 M. Mendrinou, 'Non-Compliance and the Commission's Role in Integration', *Journal of European Public Policy*, 3, 1996, pp.1–22.
75 I. Maher, 'Competition Law in the International Domain: Networks as a New Form of Governance', *Journal of Law and Society*, 29, 2002, pp.111–37.
76 R. Bork, 'The Goals of Antitrust Policy', *The American Economic Review*, 57, 1967, pp.242–53.
77 Flood, op. cit.
78 C. Scott, 'The Proceduralization of Telecommunications Law', *Telecommunications Policy*, 22, 1998, pp.243–55.
79 S. Macaulay, 'Non-Contractual Relations in Business: A Preliminary Study', *American Sociological Review*, 28, 1963, pp.55–83.
80 Unfair Terms in Consumer Contracts Directive 93/13/EEC Art 7(2).
81 I. Ayres and J. Braithwaite, *Responsive Regulation: Transcending the Deregulation Debate*, Oxford: Oxford University Press, 1992.
82 C. Scott, 'The Juridification of Regulatory Relations in the UK Utilities Sectors', in J. Black et al., eds, *Commercial Regulation and Judicial Review*, Oxford: Hart, 1998, pp.38–41.
83 Thatcher, op. cit., p.134–36.
84 J. Scott and D. Trubek, 'Mind the Gap: Law and New Approaches to Governance in the European Union', *European Law Journal*, 8, 2002, pp.1–18.
85 Painter and Wong, op. cit., p.178.
86 O. Gerstenberg, 'Law's Polyarchy: A Comment on Cohen and Sabel', *European Law Journal*, 3, 1997, pp.343–58.
87 Ginsburg, op. cit.
88 Teubner, op. cit.

4 Riding the accountability wave?
Accountability communities and new modes of governance

Kanishka Jayasuriya

Introduction

The old certainties of administrative law – its location, nature, and purpose – are dissolving; administrative law is now much more varied, diverse, and diffused. As Sedley[1] argues, this 'systematic dispersal of the sites of power beyond the confines of what we had learned to recognize as the state, old certainties of public law are no longer there'.[2] While some might take exception to this extension of the boundaries of administrative law, there is little doubt that one of the striking transformations in the industrialized and newly industrialized world is that the exercise of public power is now taking place in sites outside the formal structures of governmental power – a process which decentres and fragments the state.

The decentring of public governance is a structural process occurring in countries with established systems of administrative law as well as in those with less secure or non-existent foundations of administrative law. Nevertheless, these issues are more pressing in newly industrializing countries, where the evolution of administrative law differs sharply from that which occurs in developed democracies. In established democracies these new mechanisms are layered on older instruments of administrative law, while in developing and newly industrialized countries, such as China, these decentred sites are a primary component of the emerging new regulatory state.[3] And again, in countries such as post-authoritarian Indonesia, it may simply encompass constituting rather than reconstituting the public domain.

Decentring, in this context, means that governance is located in multiple sites, engages a number of non-state actors in governance, and deploys a range of techniques of governance that move beyond the traditional structures of public law.[4] These new modes of governance – such as private-public partnerships and the growing importance of transnational non-governmental standard-setting organizations – challenge our conception of the state as a coherent and unified entity; this in turn suggests that conventional mechanisms of accountability to regulate the exercise public power are being challenged and transformed.[5] For instance, the thrust of a substantial literature on regulatory governance at the global or the national level is towards a search for substitute mechanisms of accountability and monitoring operating outside formal governmental institutions.[6] All of this invariably raises fundamental questions about the application of what amounts to a new administrative law in these novel modes of governance.

The development of these new modes of governance is the outcome of a complex set of structural forces that come under the generic label of neo-liberalism. Although it is not within the scope of this paper to examine the nature of these new forces, it is possible to identify four crucial determining factors or drivers: first, the growing trend towards privatization and deregulation of key areas of economic and social governance leading to new public-private governance arrangements that sit uneasily with traditional conceptions of administrative law; second, the influence of non-governmental – often transnational – agents in the management and regulation of domains considered as public governance; third, the growth of independent administrative agencies such as central banks and financial supervisory bodies often connected to transnational policy networks; and fourth, the development of transnational regulation, administrative rules, and adjudication such as the World Trade Organization (WTO) or bilateral investment treaties, producing hybrid forms of national and transnational governance. Of course, these determining factors cannot simply be reduced to neo-liberalism as each of these has its own independent effects on the shape and form of governance. But what is clear is that the thrust of this process is towards a decentring of governance and administrative regimes.[7]

Such deep-seated changes in modes of governance are of course laden with complex questions about the nature and role of public law principles in these new decentred sites. However, this is not simply a question of extending public law principles to these new sites of public power, but rather one of constituting and defining the 'public' in these new sites of governance. For this reason accountability, it seems, is everywhere and is invested with virtuous qualities. Here, we develop the concept of 'accountability communities' which give expression to the 'public' within the various modes of governance, and make those who exercise public power accountable.[8] This facilitates the application of public law principles – if not public law itself – within new modes of governance. At the same time these new mechanisms of 'accountable governance' are about establishing systems of political rule through which new political relationships are constituted within these new modes of governance.[9] And one of the defining characteristics of this extension of public law norms and principles to the new modes of governance is that accountability remains anchored to specific technical or instrumental goals of the transnational policy regimes, especially to those such as the WTO seeking to promote a specific conception of economic order.

The essay advances three key propositions:

- administrative law in these decentred sites of governance operates through the explicit constitution of a public domain in various specialized functional policy and private orders;
- systems of accountability are vital dimensions through which the public domain is reconstituted, that is, they serve to organize and constitute a system of political rule;

- an implication of this reconstitution of the public domain is that it leads to growing instrumentalization of law. This may prove attractive to political leaders in East Asia particularly in the case of China because it reinforces and facilitates a technocratic form of politics which may well influence the future trajectories of post authoritarian political regimes in the Asian region.

Global administrative law and the exercise of public power

It is useful to examine this process of state decentring through the prism of global administrative law.[10] Global administrative law locates – partially and imperfectly as the case may be – notions of *review, monitoring,* and *participation* in the administrative acts of international public agencies and through the actions of international non-governmental organizations such as standard-setting organizations. In fact, a striking development over the past two decades in Asia is the intersection between international law, regulation, and national governance. In this regard, what is of special interest to us is that the new forms of transnational regulation are not easily identifiable hard law of international treaties; rather, they are more likely to appear in the shape of regulatory standards and even privately organized or monitored public standards.[11] One example of this transnational regulation is the entry of China into the WTO and the concomitant legal changes in the national system of administrative law. Other examples are the emergence of new dimensions of transnational regulatory governance that range from networks of central bankers (e.g. the East Asian Central Bankers network)[12] public-private partnerships (e.g. the Global Fund for Malaria eradication)[13] to private standard-setting organizations around issues such as promotion of various codes of labour standards.[14] Standard-setting organizations, in particular, have gained in significance as a means of governing production networks that cross national jurisdictions. These organizations are especially relevant for understanding the governance of emerging transnational production processes in China.[15]

These are diverse forms of rule making but Kingsbury, Krisch, and Stewart[16] have argued that these processes can be subsumed under the rubric of global administrative law in that they go beyond traditional conceptions of international administrative law. Global administrative law focuses on 'administrative procedure, on principles of reasoned decision making, and on mechanisms of review'[17] within diverse sites of transnational governance. A primary dynamic of this expansion of administrative law is that the 'members of different national communities are increasingly subject to the effects of measures adopted by the authorities of different national communities'.[18] Implicit in this definition of global administrative law is the fact that the reach of administrative law or other rule-making bodies go beyond national boundaries and may be the effects of diverse actors, including other national governments, supranational authorities, and private organizations.

Proponents of global administrative law have clearly identified a discernible trend in global governance towards the use of instruments of administrative law rather than the more conventional hard law tools of international treaty. It is a development that reflects an emerging administrative and regulatory system that transcends the traditional dualisms of municipal and international law where transnational relationships take place, and regulatory spaces created through the utilization of administrative agreements while at the same time enrolling private actors to undertake regulatory functions. Boundaries are crossed and spanned in these decentred sites of governance such that at any given level 'a boundary can be defined, separating governmental and non-governmental institutions or public employees from private individuals, but the significance of the boundary will depend on the micro-analysis of the interactions that occur across it, and on either side'.[19] It is this boundary crossing and spanning nature of global administrative law, creating network-like forms that compels us to rethink the way we conceptualize emerging forms of post-Westphalian statehood. It remains the case that the identification of such boundary spanning features of the new modes of governance is not unique to the global administrative law perspective, and has much in common with other perspectives such as transnational regulatory governance or legal pluralism that have identified a similar emergence of new forms of transnational regulatory or policy fields that cut across all domains of governance.[20] This much is now familiar.

However, in the context of this discussion, what is relevant here is that global administrative law not only makes possible the creation of regulatory networks but may also establish systems of accountable governance. It is this system of accountable governance that helps to constitute a public domain within these regulatory networks. Therefore, the distinctive feature of the concept of global administrative law is that it brings to this debate a focus on public law principles and values in the context of the decentred sites of global regulatory governance. Consequently, for our discussion, the decisive point is that public power is constituted in these networks which span the conventional national and governmental boundaries of public law and compels us to focus more squarely on forms of public power and authority in these new sites of governance.

Here, emergent mechanisms of accountable governance remain at the heart of making various forms of global public power accountable in diverse forms of global rule making and administrative law ranging from the WTO dispute resolution mechanisms to various private standard-setting organizations such as labour or international accounting standards. Accountability is the glue – albeit not the only one – that holds together the various elements within a transnational regulatory sphere. For this reason some have argued that we are in the midst of a new accountability revolution, or what Goetz and Jenkins[21] call a 'new accountability agenda'.

This new accountability agenda is increasingly the focus of many developmental programmes within the World Bank and the IMF,[22] new institutional forms such as citizen report cards introduced in Ho Chi Minh City,[23] and the emergence of specialized global accountability networks such as the ombudsman network.[24] It is entirely unexceptional to say that administrative law is about accountability, what lies at the core of any notion of administrative law is the idea that public officials and agencies be held accountable to those affected by their administrative decisions. However, accountability is not simply about the identification and enumeration of a set of good governance elements, but a system of political rule and authority, making this highly significant as a form of global public law established and enforced within the nation state.

In so far as accountability practices create spaces of transnational public authority, it becomes a distinctive dimension of global administrative law. The notion that these forms of administration and regulation are about political authority and rule is a dimension that is obscured in the literature. Yet the question is: how do we go about defining the nature of this political relationship, and, more importantly, what is to represent the 'public' in the extension of accountability to various decentred modes of governance? Here, what counts in the various forms of transnational regulation or administration is not so much the identifiable elements of administrative law – such as review and monitoring – but the way these elements combine to constitute a set of public relationships that lie between the national and international, and between the public and private sphere. This foreshadows a more distinct political conception of public law as an 'assemblage of rules, principles, canons, maxims, customs, usage, and manners that condition and sustain the activity of governing'.[25]

The political dimension of administrative law as a practice of political governance or rule is rarely acknowledged in the technocratic vocabulary used in the academic literature and policy practice. It is a striking omission, especially in the context of countries such as China where we find that notions of administrative law – global or otherwise – are no longer anchored in a recognizable conception of democratic determination or the rule of law. This is not merely a theoretical lacuna in the literature. The deeper political fact is that these new forms of accountable governance enable principles such as fairness and participation to be readily divorced from more substantive and thicker versions of the rule of law. These developments may indeed reinforce what Peerenboom has called a thin version of the rule of law.[26]

One such important public law value that has assumed some significance in the implementation of global regulatory programmes is the principle of participation – that is, the notion that clients or recipients of programmes need to be involved in the process of formulating and implementing governance programmes. Take, for example, the case of the Poverty Reduction Strategy Papers (PRSP) of the World Bank and the IMF. The PRSP is a nationally formulated policy document that provides mechanisms for consultation and deliberation, including those with non-governmental organizations, and deliberates on policy strategies for poverty reduction. These strategies serve to implement the social standards and objectives of international financial institutions such as the IMF/World Bank.[27] The PRSP is not only a policy strategy, but also a road map of the participatory and audit process required to qualify for World Bank/IMF approval. Furthermore, PRSP is linked to the so-called Comprehensive Development Framework (CDF), and is viewed as a method of giving concrete shape to some of the key objectives of the CDF.[28]

Participation itself becomes an important objective in various international programmes such as the implementation of social funds or the promotion of localized participation such as the initiative on grass-roots democracy in Vietnam.[29] Another prominent example of the importance of participation in World Bank programmes is the one billion dollar Kecamatan Development Program (KDP) that was implemented across villages all over Indonesia. KDP sought to promote 'community empowerment' through the development of participatory mechanisms. A major justification for KDP was that targeting the 'community' in this way would lead to a happy marriage between participation and technocratic policy making because policy would be less prone to be captured by corrupt bureaucracies or patronage networks.[30]

These World Bank programmes demonstrate that the notion of participation becomes a means through which public law principles are given expression within the systems of global regulatory governance. But these public law values are articulated within the domain of specific policy regimes. Hence, the purpose of participation and deliberation in these regulatory systems is concerned with problem solving or the effective management of policy rather than the achievement of a legitimate political consensus.[31] Hence, for example, IMF and OECD programmes have been developed to promote and enforce greater transparency in the financial and commercial practices of developing and newly industrial countries.[32] However, as Rodan[33] has argued, these notions of transparency remain confined to a restricted notion of economic, rather than political transparency.

These examples underscore the fact that this participation takes place outside the 'political society', and the boundaries of the 'public' are defined in terms of the pursuit of a particular configuration of macro-economic objectives. In other words, participation is not seen as an end in itself, but rather, as an instrumental fashion of pursuing technocratic aims of the policy regime. Hence, accountable governance within global regulatory regimes can be said to constitute a system of political authority that defines the 'public' in functional or policy terms and implicitly ties this 'public' accountability to technocratic rationales.

Accountability communities and the reconstitution of the public domain

Global administrative law is a special kind of beast because accountability becomes a method not just of allowing redress for those affected by administrative decisions but also a way of determining the nature and role of the 'accountability community' to which 'account' must be given. However, the more substantive question at stake here is the process through which the 'public' is defined in these global regulatory regimes. The public domain itself is now the focus of concerted political action through which new boundaries and definitions of 'publicness' are asserted, contested and regulated.[34] This therefore helps us to constitute the 'public' to which this accounting must be given.

Global administrative law reconstitutes the public domain by creating various forms of 'publicness' and it does this through creating accountability communities within various policy or issues-specific sites of governance. Accountability communities are composed of public and/or private organizations which perform watchdog and monitoring activities in relation to the specific functionally based regulatory regimes – private or public or a combination of both – within and beyond national boundaries. These communities are distinguished by a specific control over accountability language and practices – in other words, over epistemic resources. Control over these epistemic resources are particularly valuable in regulatory settings in which there are interdependent public and private actors acting in complex issue areas or sectors that overlap national boundaries. In undertaking these regulatory activities these communities help to create various forms of publicness within such regulatory regimes. In this sense they exercise public power within the context of these functionally based regulatory regimes but also constitute the public domain within these regulatory regimes.

However, there is a fundamental paradox in the emergence of these new accountability communities: the incorporation of some public law principles into the regulatory regime at the same time subordinates these principles to various specific broader policy objectives in policy regimes such as those pertaining to the environment, trade, or public health. Consequently the emergence of functionally differentiated accountability communities transforms political conflict into issues of technocratic management such that there are 'no parties with projects to rule, no division of powers, and no aspiration of self-government beyond the aspiration of statehood aspirations identified precisely as what we should escape from'.[35]

Evidence of this technocratic politics can be found in the developmental programmes committed to the pursuit of good governance; but this is only to the extent that it ensures the successful achievement of developmental objectives. In fact, even when administrative grievance procedures are enshrined within these programmes they become incorporated in such a way that subordinates conventional rule of law objectives to broader governance objectives. For example, the PRSP is a nationally 'owned' governance programme which provides an administrative framework for the formulation and deliberation of policy strategies on poverty reduction. As we have seen, the PRSP is a vehicle through which international financial institutions such as the IMF and the World Bank sets broad social standards and objectives which are then localized and implemented by governmental agencies in conjunction with the participation of non-governmental groups. In this sense the PRSP establishes a particular accountability community as it explicitly calls for dialogue and participation with a range of government and non-governmental stakeholders. In fact, the World Bank constantly reaffirms that the PRSP is not simply about producing a public document, but is itself a means of furthering a dialogue or deliberation on poverty related issues.[36] 'Ownership', figures high on the recent policy lexicon of international development agencies.

In terms of our argument, the PRSP serves to establish an accountability community through which public law principles such as fairness, participation, and review, find expression within a legally mandated accountability community composed of private actors, transnational organizations, and national governments. Yet these accountability communities are subordinate to the pursuit of the broad policy objectives of regimes that are also themselves beyond political contestation. Similarly, while public law principles become important in the operation of accountability communities, these principles are applied within a domain that is outside the formal governmental structures. As Harrington and Turem[37] argue in a related context, we need to 'locate "accountability" in concrete sites and contexts, and allows us to see the relationship between distinct accountability discourses and broader social, political, economic, and legal relations they are part of'.[38] Framing the issue in these terms has the distinct virtue of identifying and analyzing developing forms of accountability and public law in terms of 'how it is understood, shaped, and ultimately mobilized as a powerful political symbol to legitimate a certain type of regulatory regime'.[39] Accountability communities mobilize different understandings of accountability and this has implications for our understanding of the nature of state transformation.[40]

This conceptualization of accountability communities recalls Rubin's metaphor of a network in which accountability actors form an important node of regulatory authority within a transnational network. In this way it can include private standard-setting bodies, adjudicating tribunals such as the WTO dispute resolution mechanisms, or the international criminal tribunal for the former Yugoslavia (ICTY). In short, these are 'accountability communities' that establish nodes of public authority within organizations or networks that span boundaries between the national and transnational or the public and private, thereby creating functionally differentiated sites of governance. Accountability communities constitute a public domain which shapes the organization of political authority within functionally regulatory regimes.

Accountability communities and private rule making

Accountability communities also form around standards established by private organizations such as accounting standard bodies or labour standard monitoring organizations. This private standard setting involves 'what might be called "soft enforcement", that is, reputation and transparency to leverage public pressure to ensure the commitments made by the firm are upheld'.[41] In this way it constitutes a 'public domain' within private production and commercial regimes. Labour standards in particular represent an interesting example of the development of transnational accountability communities around international NGOs and monitoring organizations.[42] Such standard-setting organizations need to be seen as a way of incorporating public law principles through accountability communities within complex transnational production chains. One such way is the development of various forms of corporate conduct that have evolved in the aftermath 'of several well-publicized scandals involving child labour, hazardous working conditions, excessive working hours, and poor wages in factories supplying the major global brands, multinational corporations have developed their own "codes of conduct"'.[43]

Reinforcing these codes of conduct has been a vital shift within the ILO from labour rights to the protection of labour standards, towards an emphasis on substance rather than process, and greater attention to decentralized systems of enforcement.[44] As Alston argues this 'trajectory has involved a gradual hardening of initially soft standards, an incremental strengthening of supervisory processes and the adoption, with the acquiescence of governments and other actors, of innovative promotional and other measures'.[45]

Decentralized systems, such as the use of instruments of code of conduct, serve to constitute an accountability community but one limited to a 'public domain' located within private economic orders. In effect this means that, as Alston indicates, this shift towards core labour standards is detached from a conception of political rights and empowerment and increasingly becomes a flexible notion to be incorporated in various policy regimes such as bilateral trade agreements. Examples are the US-Cambodia agreement on access for garments, or private economic orders such as through corporate and NGO codes of conduct.

The Cambodia-US bilateral textile trade agreement, which included labour standards, is especially revealing on this score,[46] because it required substantial compliance with international core labour standards. As a result of this agreement, the Cambodian government, together with the ILO[47] and the Ministry of Commerce, requires registration with the inspection regime of the ILO's Better Factories Program in order to export. The establishment of such an inspection regime is innovative, and has led to more effective compliance with core labour standards. Yet the focus on 'better factories' has been at the expense of the expansion of representative politics in the political domain which of course would be central to a notion of labour rights.

In the Cambodian case, the approach of the Better Factories Program, as Hughes[48] has cogently argued, has led to a separation of issues of standards and wider power relationships between labour and employers. These effects are similar to other standard-setting programmes such as the OECD Guidelines for Multinational Enterprises. The OECD guidelines are voluntary codes of conduct accompanied by what are called National Contact Points (NCPs) that police these guidelines.[49] The NCP system allows non-governmental organizations to have a monitoring role in private economies. However, such an incorporation of public law principles is located within the private economic order, thus subordinating these principles to the economic functions.

The enforcement of international standards requires the creation of accountability communities and these communities exercise a form of public power within private spheres of economic order. For example, it has been argued that accountability is merely a question of subjecting those exercising public power to monitoring and greater scrutiny. From this there develops a line of reasoning suggesting that not only administrative but also political accountability can be found when accountability practices perform 'the democratic function of enabling democratic "stakeholders" to exercise some degree of political control over the "public" decision-making processes that impact upon their lives'.[50] Hence, various forms of non-electoral accountability mechanisms are developed, which have been central to emerging notions of reflexive global regulation, although such a reflexive regulation is itself a form of political rule creating relationship between rulers and the ruled.

It is readily apparent that the Macdonald and Macdonald[51] argument recognizes that what is novel here is the exercise of public power within private domains or outside formal governmental structures. But what arguments about non-electoral accountability obscure is – as Hughes[52] clearly illustrates with respect to the Cambodian case – the impact of the reconstitution of the public domain on the form of representation as well as the nature[53] of contestation allowed within these new sites of public governance. For this reason, an emphasis on principles and procedures rather than on rights reconstitutes representation outside political structures and subordinates it to the functions or goals formulated within various public or private policy regimes.

Clearly, the emergence of private standard-setting organizations such as labour standards and monitoring mechanisms or new codes of corporate governance reflects the development of new forms of public power. In much of the literature on diffused or dispersed governance and transnational regulation there is an assumption that public law principles are now secured through different systems of accountability.[54] Therefore, for some like Dorf and Sabel[55] the new global accountability cascade represents the triumph of the politics of pragmatism; experimentalism as politics becomes significantly focused on learning and puzzling about policy problems rather than power. But this preoccupation with technical analysis of regulation tends to neglect the more important political questions: how is the public domain reconstituted and how are new forms of political rule organized? Hence we need to be more circumspect about the growing interest in notions such as responsive regulation or other ways of describing decentred regulatory activities all of which in one way or another highlight the importance of accountability as an expression of public law principles, but only at the expense of occluding the wider political relationships that underpin these practices of accountability.

However, this does not mean, as we have argued, that there is no conception of the 'public' in these transnational regulatory domains, but as Keohane and Grant[56] argue, these various practices of accountability substitute for democratic politics. Their analysis, however, is persuasive only on the assumption that they regard both democracy and accountability as concepts more akin to responsiveness than to the contestation and conflict of representative democracy. Yet this analysis, like much of the literature on new governance, tends to obscure the fact that accountability is a method of ordering political relationships that involve the allocation of material stakes, the mobilization of ideological principles, and the exercising of political authority. The broader point to be made here is that the development of new transnational administrative standards has created a public domain within private economic orders at the expense, or in place of, the representative sphere of political society. In this sense the process described above is analogous to what some have described as the judicialization of politics,[57] though this essay would suggest that it is better described as a process of juridification that takes place in sites outside the formal governmental apparatus as well. At a more normative level, it is clear that

Legal instrumentalism and technocratic politics

From the foregoing, it is clear that the diffusion and fragmentation of public law create new methods and forms of public monitoring, review, and even grievance mechanisms, that lie outside the formal governmental process. The burgeoning academic literature on law and new governance has produced a veritable proliferation of terms such as 'responsive regulation', 'reflexive regulation'[58] or 'democratic experimentalism', 'transnational regulation' to identify these mechanisms. Yet this literature has failed to provide a more comprehensive examination of the ramifications of these new modes of governance for the normative project of the rule of law, especially in developing countries.

In the case of global administrative law, the normative understanding of the rule of law is challenged on at least three fronts. First, new forms of global regulation have multiple sources, are increasingly fragmented, and challenge the rule of law assumption about the notion of legal supremacy and a single source of sovereignty. Second, new types of global law often depend on new forms of representing a 'public' – defined in functional or policy terms – and challenge the rule of law as somehow linked to, or connected with, notions of political representation. Third, transnational legal regulation works through increasingly flexible, soft forms of standard setting which challenges the notion of rule of law as consisting of legal predictability and certainty.

But what really is a striking departure from various conceptions of the rule of law embodied within these new modes of governance is its explicit legal instrumentalism. Not only is legal instrumentalism important, but the argument here is that it may well constitute a neo-liberal version of the rule of law that resonates with the possible direction of East Asia's post-authoritarian political transformation. To get to the heart of this argument we must examine the nature of administrative law. Administrative law – decentralized or otherwise – presents difficulties for the normative theory of law because 'modern governments generally employ 'tactics' rather than laws, and thus has a tendency to use the law tactically or as 'instruments of managerial policy'. This in turn has meant that positive law often forms part only – and not necessarily the constitutive part – of an administrative scheme, and this presents obvious problems of legal interpretation'.[59] In a liberal democratic society this suggests that administrative law reflects a combination of two kinds of association – what Oakeshott[60] called a 'purposive and enterprise organisation' directed at achieving policy goals and objectives, and a 'civic association as a non-purposive civic association'. This has always been a balancing act but the shift towards decentred sites of public law has tilted the balance towards an 'enterprise' mode of association.

In policy regimes such as the WTO, administrative law is subordinate to the policy and managerial goals of the regime.[61] As we have shown, even rights

70 *Kanishka Jayasuriya*

issues such as labour standards are now incorporated and subordinated within the broader frame of a policy regime such as a bilateral trade agreement. Similarly, the development of forms of transnational juridification of governance through such organs as the WTO dispute settlement mechanism, or the Court of Arbitration for Sport set up to determine dispute in sports are highly specialized policy-specific forms of judicialized governance. Nothing is more illustrative of this instrumentalism than the fact that in those cases where international agencies promote the 'rule of law'[62] it is often in the service of broader policy objectives such as secure property rights.[63] Taken together with the development of specific accountability communities administrative law takes on an instrumental and functional role that has tilted sharply towards making the law subordinate to technocratic objectives.

In a recent provocative statement Tamanaha – writing mostly in the context of the United States – has noted that legal instrumentalism has become such a pervasive feature that 'individuals and groups within society will endeavour to seize the law, and fill in, interpret, and apply the law, to serve their own ends'.[64] In essence the argument is that law is pushed towards what Damaska[65] illuminatingly calls 'a policy impending mode of law'.[66] Legal instrumentalism leads to the advance of private good at the cost of its 'manifestation as *public* power that is to be wielded in furtherance of the *public good*. The legitimacy of the law, its claim to obedience, is based upon this claim'.[67] Consequently the problem for Tamanaha is that this growing instrumentalization of law is at the expense of the diminution of the public good which saps the legitimacy of the rule of law. There is much to offer in this account of contemporary trends. Yet, Tamanaha's account of legal instrumentalism remains a story of the triumph of instrumental theories of jurisprudence that have limited relevance for our understanding of the relationship between global administrative rules and legal instrumentalism in the newly industrializing countries of Asia.

However, Tamanaha's account is useful to frame the discussion of legal instrumentalism presented here. In this context there are two problems with his argument and both relate to the fact that what counts is not legal instrumentalism *per se* but the tilting of the balance between instrumentalist and non-instrumentalist versions of law so that the new administrative law is subordinate to the kind of policy regimes analyzed above. One problem is that instrumentalism needs to be located within the historical context of neo-liberalism. A distinctive aspect of legal instrumentalism in a neo-liberal context is the explicit subordination of law to the policy or technocratic objectives of policy regimes, especially those relating to economic governance. Hence, the legal form of global administrative law reflects the operation of social political forces which have created a more explicit form of legal instrumentalism. Consequently the emergence of instrumentalism reflects a basic reorientation of political authority rather than a shift away from a conception of the public good.

But how does this play in terms of the wider debates over the historical evolution of the rule of law particularly in the 'hard case' of China? Well, for one, it alerts us to the fact that the rule of law itself needs to be contextualized by embedding it within a broader set of social and political forces. Intriguingly in the case of China we see that what we have identified as a tendency towards legal instrumentalism may well provide the foundations for the growing importance of legalism in the institutions of new governance, particularly those linked to, or operating within, a transnational context. However, this requires that if 'we are to understand the likely path of development of China's system, and the reasons for differences in its institutions, rules, practices, and outcomes, we need to rethink rule of law'.[68] In this exercise, legal instrumentalism is part of a wider understanding of legalism as an exercise in state building. It is a nice twist to the Weberian model of legal rationality[69] where instead of legal rationality being the outcome of a process of historical evolution, it becomes a set of routines and practices used to create particular instrumental forms of governance.

The other and potentially more serious problem with Tamanaha's argument is that it depends on a vague notion of the public good and assumes that most forms of instrumentalism provide avenues for the promotion of private agendas as against the public good. But the focus on the public good deflects our attention away from the fact that it is the nature of public power that is at issue rather than the pursuit of private interests at the expense of the public good. Rather, the question that needs to be asked is this: what is the nature of the structural relationship between rulers and ruled within these new modes of governance? In fact, as we have seen, accountability communities emergent within new sites of public governance embody forms of political rule that depend on the mobilization of certain conceptions of the public good conceived in terms of the ends of a particular regulatory regime.

The nub of the argument here is that 'accountability communities' – whose functions are aligned to the objectives and goals of specialized policy and legal regimes – lead to a form of politics that is essentially technocratic. In fact to label this as 'legal instrumentalism' runs the risk of overlooking the more important point that it is instrumentalism of a *particular* kind, especially in relation to the 'accountability cascades' of transnational regulation, that facilitates technocratic forms of political rule. Take for example, the case of labour and social standards that depend on an 'accountability community' extending public law norms to the private economic domains. Certainly this falls within the ambit of what Morgan[70] calls 'technocratic accountability', that is, 'the delegation of the communicative processes of revelation, explanation and justification to an arms length, neutral and independent institution'.[71] However, delegation may not be the crucial issue; rather, as we have suggested in the case of labour, it is the way 'publicness' itself is constructed so as to embody notions of representation that favour certain ways of managing and organizing conflict in preference to others. Hence it is an understanding of technocratic problem solving within the policy making process rather than the robust contestation of interests within the formal political arena.

Nevertheless, these technocratic 'accountability cascades' may well serve to further important norms of participation and responsiveness within various policy regimes. In the case of China we find that complex birth control policies and programmes are usually associated with coercive command and control regulatory techniques. However, as Greenhalgh and Winckler[72] point out, the birth rules were designed in terms of meeting international standards of quality care and choice. They state that 'most remarkably this included an emphasis in the program itself on human rights, partly to mobilize the public against program abuses, partly to provide birth workers with concrete standards of conduct'.[73] Similarly Hughes[74] points out that in Cambodia, the Better Factories Program is quite consistent with, and perhaps even reinforce, various neo-patrimonial tendencies within the Cambodian state in the period after the UN intervention. In a similar fashion Rodan[75] has pointed out how the Singaporean government has selectively used various practices of transparency to reinforce its own authoritarian rule. His work points out the malleable character of the concept of transparency once it is removed from a conception of political empowerment and becomes the transparency of commercial relationships.

In the instances of both Cambodia and Singapore, legal instrumentalism furthered the extension of public law norms but only to the extent that these norms were confined within the technocratic objectives of the programme. Such forms of technocratic accountability narrows political contestation to specific issues of administrative participation and efficiency. It is, however, beyond the confines of this essay to explore the politics of 'accountability cascades', but it may suggest – particularly in the case of China – a political strategy to contain the permissible extent and nature of conflict and means for addressing it. More speculatively, it might, in the Asian context, present a possible post-authoritarian regime trajectory that focuses on a configuration between neo-liberalism, technocratic accountability, and new forms of legalism.

Conclusion: Governance and state transformation

Accountability, 'involves social interaction and exchange, in that one side, that calling for the account, seeks answers and rectification, while the other side, that being held accountable, responds and accepts sanctions'.[76] In this sense, what we could term 'accountability cascades'[77] – some of which are driven by global regulation and rules – take place within varied and diffused sites of power in and outside the state. Therefore, these forms of accountability seek to extend the norms of public law to new sites of governance. In this process an important role is played by accountability communities which are a crucial component of new regulatory regimes that span the hard territorial boundaries of the national state. Accountability communities are constituted within discrete policy regimes that may be either private or public, or a combination of the two. Instead of the 'hard' territorial boundaries of the 'Westphalian state' the boundaries of the accountability communities are defined by the softer and more flexible boundaries of the policy or regulatory regime.

One implication of these accountability communities is that they reconstitute the public domain within these new regulatory regimes. Accountability communities embody public law principles, participation, review, and reasoned decision making, but these principles function within and are subordinate to the broader objectives of the regulatory regime. It takes place outside the formal governmental or political society, and as such, marginalizes political contestation. Consequently the new systems of accountable governance may well be intimately linked to the relocation of politics independent of formal political systems. For this reason it is as much about the process of state 'construction as it is about destruction'.[78] After all, what is distinctive about the perspective of accountability as a mode of political regulation is the transformation of the relationship between citizen and state, or in effect what Nettl[79] termed 'stateness'.[80]

It follows that an understanding of state transformation should be at the forefront of the analysis of emerging transnational regulatory regimes and accountability communities. Global administrative law is part of a broader process of state transformation that involves new technocratic institutions pertinent to the refinement of political rule. Accountability communities establish new forms of stateness that suggest different ways of defining relationships between the individual and the state. Administrative law of the old or the new variety is as much about expanding state power as it is about limiting and constraining executive power. Therefore, understanding this 'statecraft' is an important issue for any future research agenda. This takes on particular relevance in the context of the growing importance of private standard-setting organizations such as labour standard monitoring agencies.

Finally, the development of new accountability communities has ramifications for our understanding of the rule of law. It may well reinforce a form of legal instrumentalism that lends support to what Peerenboom calls a 'thin theory of the rule of law'. He argues that 'a thin theory stresses the formal or instrumental aspects of rule of law – those features that any legal system allegedly must possess to function effectively as a system of laws, regardless of whether the legal system is part of a democratic or non-democratic society, liberal or theocratic'.[81] It is important to locate these developments in the context of the operation of the fragmented policy and legal regime produced not just by global rules but also as an outcome of the broader process of neo-liberal restructuring. In fact, within these policy regimes it may be possible, as Greenhalgh and Winckler[82] argue with respect to Chinese birth control programme, that various forms of participation and notions of choice will be allowed to operate but within the constraints of the instrumental or technocratic management of the policy regime. For this reason accountability communities and the broader process of global administrative law may be crucial to the remaking of state structures in the Asia Pacific.

Notes

1. S. Sedley, 'Foreword', in M. Taggart, ed., *The Province of Administrative Law*, Oxford: Hart, 1997.
2. Ibid.; For an overview of some of these changes in the nature of administrative law, also see: A. Aman, 'Administrative Law for a New Century', in M. Taggart, ed., *The Province of Administrative Law*, Oxford: Hart, 1997.

3 In fact, because of the absence of an older layer of administrative law in many parts of Asia, it may well be that new modes of administrative law become adopted more quickly than in established liberal democracies.
4 K. Jayasuriya, 'Globalization and the Changing Architecture of the State: Regulatory State and the Politics of Negative Coordination', *Journal of European Public Policy*, vol.8, no.1, 2001a, pp.101–23; C. Offe, *Modernity and the State: East, West*, Cambridge: MIT Press, 1996.
5 For example, one of the main thrusts of the New Public Management (NPM) movement is to move towards giving greater autonomy and flexibility to a range of public sector agencies. It is clear that the NPM is having a substantial impact on the restructuring of the public sector in developed as well as developing countries, and, indeed, its core themes have been embraced by the World Bank.
6 For a broader analysis of changes in global governance see: K. Jayasuriya, *Reconstituting the Global Liberal Order: Legitimacy and Regulation*, Oxford: Routledge, 2005.
7 For a discussion of this in the context of the multi level governance, see: L. Hooge and G. Marks, 'Unraveling the Central State, But How? Types of Multi-level Governance', *American Political Science Review*, vol.97, no.2, 2003, pp.233–43. They identify the importance of specialized functional agencies and organizations as emerging respatialization of governance.
8 An excellent overview of different notions and practices of accountability can be found in M. Dowdle, 'Public Accountability: Conceptual, Historical and Epistemic Mapping', in M. Dowdle, ed., *Public Accountability: Design, Dilemmas and Experiences*, New York: Cambridge University Press, 2006.
9 David Kennedy expresses this in an alternative way in his book on humanitarian intervention as a form of rulership. See D. Kennedy, *The Dark Side of Virtue: Reassessing International Humanitarianism*, Princeton: Princeton University Press, 2004.
10 B. Kingsbury, et al., 'The Emergence of Global Administrative Law', *Law and Contemporary Problems*, vol.68, no.3–4, 2005, pp.15–61.
11 Jayasuriya, op. cit., 2005; K. Jayasuriya, 'Globalization, Law, and the Transformation of Sovereignty: The Emergence of Global Regulatory Governance', *Indiana Journal of Global Legal Studies*, vol.6, no.2, 1999, pp.425–55; R. Hall and T. Biersteker, eds, *The Emergence of Private Authority in Global Governance*, Cambridge: Cambridge University Press, 2002; A. Slaughter, 'The Real New World Order', *Foreign Affairs*, vol.76, no.5, 1997, pp.183–97; D. Zaring, 'International Law by Other Means: The Twilight Existence of International Financial Regulatory Organisation', *Texas International Law Journal*, vol.33, no.2, 1998, pp.281–330; V. Haufler, *A Public Role for the Private Sector. Industry Self-Regulation in a Global Economy*, Washington DC: Carnegie Endowment for International Peace, 2001.
12 On East Asian financial networks and cooperation see: J. Amyx, 'A Regional Bond Market for East Asia? The Evolving Political Dynamics of Regional Financial Cooperation', *Pacific Economic Papers*, No. 342, 2004.
13 For more information see <http://www.theglobalfund.org/en/about/malaria/default.asp>. Accessed 23 May 2005.
14 For an overview of corporate codes of conduct, see: R. Jenkins, et al., eds, *Corporate Responsibility and Ethical Trade: Codes of Conduct in the Global Economy*, London: Earthscan, 2002.
15 In particular, emerging systems of regulating labour standards have gained importance and visibility especially in the context of the booming Chinese economy.
16 Kingsbury, et al., op. cit.
17 Kingsbury, et al., op. cit., p.28.
18 S. Battini, 'The Globalisation of Public Law', 2007. Available at SSRN: <http://ssrn.com/abstract=895263>. Accessed 27 May 2007.

19 E. Rubin, *Beyond Camelot: Rethinking Politics and Law for the Modern State*, Princeton: Princeton University Press, 2005, p.50.
20 K, Jayasuriya, 'Globalization, Sovereignty, and the Rule of Law: From Political to Economic Constitutionalism?', *Constellations* vol.8, no.4, 2001b, pp.442–60; F. Snyder, 'Economic Globalisation and the Law in the 21st Century', in S. Austin, ed., *The Blackwell Companion to Law and Society*. Oxford: Blackwell Publishing, 2004; G. Teubner, ' "Global Bukownia": Legal Pluralism in a World Society', in G. Teubner, ed., *Global Law without a State*, Dartmouth: Aldershot, 1997.
21 A. Goetz and R. Jenkins, *Reinventing Accountability: Making Democracy Work for Human Development*, London: Palgrave Macmillan, 2004.
22 K. Jayasuriya, *Statecraft, Welfare and the Politics of Inclusion*, London: Palgrave Macmillan, 2006.
23 See: Vietnam Development Report, *Governance*, Joint Donor Report to the Vietnam Consultative Meeting, Hanoi, 2005. For more details on participatory programmes see: UNDP, *Deepening Democracy and Increasing Popular Participation in Vietnam*, UNDP Vietnam Policy Dialogue Paper, Hanoi, 2006. Interestingly the UNDP argues that: 'Citizens should be active in deciding local planning priorities and participating in decision-making forums for government and public services. Furthermore, the aim of participatory democracy is not just to get everyone around the table, but also to improve the quality of deliberation and participation in these new public arenas' (UNDP 2006: 5). Here participation is the capacity of citizens – through empowered citizenship – to air grievances and monitor the activities of administrative agencies. For more on reform policies within the state, see: M. Painter, 'The Politics of State Sector Reform in Vietnam: Contested Agendas and Uncertain Trajectories', *Journal of Development Studies*, vol.41, no.2, 2005, pp.261–83.
24 C. Harlow and R. Rawlings, 'Promoting Accountability in Multi-Level Governance', *European Governance Papers*, no.C-06–02, 2006. Available at: <http://www.connexnetwork.org/eurogov/pdf/egp-connex-C-06–02.pdf>
25 Martin Loughlin, *The Idea of Public Law*, Oxford : Oxford University Press, 2003, p.30.
26 R. Peerenboom, *China's Long March Toward Rule of Law*, New York: Cambridge University Press, 2002.
27 H. Weber, 'Reconstituting the Third World? Poverty Reduction and Territoriality in the Global Politics of Development', *Third World Quarterly*, vol.25, no.1, 2004, pp.187–206.
28 P. Cammack, 'The Mother of All Governments: The World Bank's Matrix for Global Governance', in R. Wilkinson and S. Hughes, eds, *Global Governance: Critical Perspectives*, Routledge, 2002, pp.36–53.
29 UNDP, op. cit.
30 T. Carroll, 'Power, Poverty Reduction and Attempting Socio-Institutional Neoliberal Transformation: The World Bank's Kecamatan Development Program (KDP)'. Paper presented at the second workshop on North-South Development Issues and the Global Regulatory Framework, The Hague: Institute of Social Studies, November 2006.
31 As Steele notes, a fundamental distinction between deliberative models of democratic legitimacy and problem solving lies in the fact that in the latter 'the subject matter of deliberation is more likely to be an individual decision for action, rather than the adoption of a formal legal standard or other law. This means that participation of this type is likely to be a requirement of law (if law is involved at all), instead of being a part of the process of legislation. See: J. Steele, 'Participation and Deliberation in Environmental Law: Exploring a Problem-Solving Approach', *Oxford Journal of Legal Studies*, vol.21, no.3, 2001, pp.415–42.
32 S. Soederberg, 'Grafting Stability onto Globalization? Deconstructing the IMF's Recent Bid for Transparency', *Third World Quarterly*, vol.22, no.5, 2001, pp.849–67; G. Rodan,

33 Rodan, op. cit.
34 J. Newman, 'Restating a Politics of the Public', *Soundings*, 32, Spring 2006, pp.162–76.
35 M. Koskeniemmi, 'The Fate of Public International Law: Between Technique and Politics', *Modern Law Review*, vol.70, no.1, 2007, pp.1–30.
36 For the World Bank's view on Participation see: World Bank, *World Development Report 1996: From Plan to Market*, Oxford: Oxford University Press, 1996.
37 C. Harrington and Z. Turem, 'Accounting for Accountability in Neoliberal Regulatory Regimes', in M. Dowdle, ed., *Public Accountability: Designs, Dilemma and Experiences*, New York: Cambridge University Press, 2006.
38 Ibid., p.201.
39 Ibid., p.201.
40 It should also be clear that these new global accountability regimes differ, and cannot be easily subsumed under the heading of horizontal and vertical accountability in the way proposed by O'Donnell in his approach to democratic transitions. Vertical accountability refers to the relationship between citizen and the state established through regular competitive elections; horizontal accountability refers to the checks and balances on executive power within the state. G. O'Donnell, 'Delegative Democracy', *Journal of Democracy*, vol.5, no.1, 1994, pp.55–69.
41 V. Haufler, *A Public Role for the Private Sector. Industry Self-Regulation in a Global Economy*, Washington DC: Carnegie Endowment for International Peace, 2001, p.3.
42 H. Arthurs, 'Private Ordering and Workers' Rights in the Global Economy: Corporate Conduct as a Regime of Labour Market Regulation', in J. Conaghan, et al., eds, *Labour Law in an Era of Globalization: Transformative Practices and Possibilities*, Oxford: Oxford University Press, 2001.
43 R. Locke, et al., 'Does Monitoring Improve Labour Standards? Lesson from Nike', *Sloan School Working Papers*, no.4612–06, 2006.
44 P. Alston, '"Core Labour Standards" and the Transformation of the International Labour Rights Regime', *European Journal of International Law*, vol.15, no.2, 2004, pp.457–521; For a response to Alston's arguments on labour rights, see: B. Langille, 'Core Labour Rights – The True Story', *European Journal of International Law*, vol.16, no.3, 2005, pp.437–61. But his argument fails to tackle the real normative differences between locating public authority within private orders and the enhancing claims to labour rights through political empowerment. The broader context here is the collapse of class politics in both developed and developing societies.
45 Alston, op. cit., p.461.
46 S. Polaski, 'Cambodia Blazes a New Path to Economic Growth and Job Creation', *Carnegie Papers*, no.51, 2004.
47 The programme is built around a series of random inspections and uses both ILO standards and Cambodian labour law to provide a checklist of more than 500 items. For an overview of the Better Factories Program see <http://www.betterfactories.org/ILO/default.aspx?z=1&c=1>. Accessed 26 May 2007. The best analysis of this is in C. Hughes, 'Transnational Networks, International Organization and Political Participation in Cambodia: Human Rights, Labour Rights and Common Rights', *Democratization*, Vol.14, no.5, 2007, pp.834–52.
48 Ibid.
49 Any interested party such as a NGO who believes that violation of the guidelines has occurred can take the issue up with NCP of the country where the alleged violation took place or the NCP of the country where the company has its headquarters. For the Guidelines see <http://www.oecd.org/document/28/0,2340,en_2649_34889_2397532_1111,00.html>. Accessed 26 May 2007.

50 T. Macdonald and K. Macdonald, 'Non-Electoral Accountability in Global Politics: Strengthening Democratic Control in the Global Garment Industry', *European Journal of International Law*, vol.17, no.1, 2006, pp.89–119.
51 Ibid.
52 Hughes, op. cit.
53 Macdonald and Macdonald (2006) make much of non-electoral accountability but less attention is paid to the more crucial issue of representation though their work is notable for its close analysis of how standard monitoring organizations fare in relation to various notions of democracy. For this reason, this is a much more sophisticated work than those with democratic deliberation and experimentalism in various forms of labour standard monitoring. In this context see the work of A. Fung, et al., *Can We Put an End to Sweatshops? A New Democracy Form on Raising Global Labour Standards*, Boston: Beacon Press, 2001.
54 J. Freeman, 'Extending Public Accountability through Privatization: From Public Law to Publicization', in M. Dowdle, ed., *Public Accountability: Design, Dilemmas and Experiences*, New York: Cambridge University Press, 2006; R. Grant and R.O. Keohane, 'Accountability and Abuses of Power in World Politics', *American Political Science Review*, vol.99, no.1, 2005, pp.29–44; Macdonald and Macdonald, op. cit. For example, Freeman argues that: 'Rethinking what accountability requires is necessary because public law tends to define accountability as formal and hierarchical, whereas public-private arrangements function as horizontal networks' (Freeman 2006: 109–10). See also: J. Freeman, 'Extending Public Law Norms through Privatization', *Harvard Law Review*, 116, 2003, pp.1285–352. But, what is the relevant 'public' in this context and what forms of contestation are allowed and what is disallowed?
55 M. Dorf and C. Sabel, 'A Constitution of Democratic Experimentalism', *Columbia Law Review*, 98, 1998, pp.267–473.
56 Keohane and Grant, op. cit.
57 R. Hirschl, 'The New Constitutionalism and the Judicialisation of Pure Politics Worldwide', *Fordham Law Review*, 75, 2006, pp.721–53; See: T. Ginsburg, *Judicial Review in New Democracies: Constitutional Courts in Asian Cases,* New York: Cambridge University Press, 2003, for an analysis of the process of judicialization in East Asia.
58 For reflexive regulation, see: G. Teubner, 'Substantive and Reflexive Elements in Modern Law', *Law and Society Review*, vol.17, no.2, 1983, pp.239–86, for probably one of the most sophisticated statements on self-regulatory regimes.
59 M. Loughlin, *The Idea of Public Law*, Oxford : Oxford University Press, 2003, p.27.
60 M. Oakeshott, *On Human Conduct*, Oxford: Clarendon Press, 1975.
61 R. Howse, 'From Politics to Technocracy – and Back Again: The Fate of the Multilateral Trading Regime', *American Journal of International Law* vol.96, no.1, 2002, pp.94–117.
62 We need to recognize the influential role of law and economics jurisprudence in these forms of legal instrumentalism.
63 D. Trubek and A. Santos, eds, *The New Law and Economic Development: A Critical Appraisal*, New York: Cambridge University Press, 2006.
64 B. Tamanaha, 'The Perils of Pervasive Legal Instrumentalism', *Montesquieu Lecture Series, Tilburg University*, Vol. 1, 2005, Available at SSRN: http://ssrn.com/abstract=725582
65 M. Damaska, *The Faces of Justice: A Comparative Approach to Legal Process*, New Haven and London: Yale University Press, 1986.
66 Though he did not use this to refer to the common law regimes and for this reason it is intriguing to see how much of what he described as a 'policy implementing mode' can now be applied to all kinds of different legal jurisdictions.
67 Tamanaha, op. cit., p.65.

68 R. Peerenboom, *China's Long March Toward Rule of Law*, Cambridge: Cambridge University Press, 2002, p.5.
69 M. Weber (Translation from Max Weber), *Wirtschaft und Gesellschaft* (second edn) [*Max Weber on Law in Economy and Society*], New York: Simon and Schuster, 1925.
70 B. Morgan, 'Technocratic v. Convivial Accountability', in M. Dowdle, ed., *Public Accountability: Design, Dilemmas and Experiences*, New York: Cambridge University Press, 2006.
71 Ibid., p.246.
72 S. Greenhalgh and E. Winckler, *Governing China's Population: From Leninst to Neoliberal Biopolitics*, Stanford: Stanford University Press, 2005.
73 Ibid., p.149.
74 Hughes, op. cit.
75 Rodan, op. cit.
76 R. Mulgan, *Holding Power to Account: Accountability in Modern Democracies*, London: Palgrave Macmillan, 2003, p.555.
77 I use the term 'accountability cascade' because it has a connection to what Lutz and Sikkink call 'justice cascades' in global governance. See: E. Lutz and K. Sikkink, 'The Justice Cascade: The Evolution and Impact of Foreign Human Rights Trials in Latin America', *Chicago Journal of International Law*, vol.2, no.1, 2001, pp.1–34.
78 Harrington and Turem, op. cit., p.205.
79 J.P. Nettl, 'The State as a Conceptual Variable', *World Politics*, vol.20, no.4, 1968, pp.559–92.
80 The benefit of this formulation is that it allows us to focus on the process of state transformation and state building and the processes through which new notions of stateness are created. Instead of locating the impact of neo-liberalism on some quantum of state power this approach allows us to explore how globalization changes the internal architecture of the state.
81 Peerenboom, op. cit., p.3.
82 Greenhalgh and Winckler, op. cit.

Part II
Northeast Asia and Greater China

5 Administrative law and judicialized governance in Japan

Hitoshi Ushijima

Introduction

Japanese administrative law is in transition. Since 1868 when the new Meiji government replaced the feudal *Edo-bakufu* government, Japan has had a tradition of a powerful administrative branch with relatively modest legislative and judicial branches, a configuration deemed necessary in order to develop and effectively manage the country. Administrative law has played a supporting role in this framework. However, in recent years a set of new statutes has begun to establish procedural controls over governmental actions and expanded opportunities to obtain extensive judicial review.[1] This can be considered a form of judicialization, expanded dispute resolution or policy-making by judicial or quasi-judicial procedure[2] in the judicial or administrative branch, which some see as a global trend (as described by Ginsburg (Chapter 1) and Peerenboom (Chapter 9) in this volume.

Since the "Bubble Economy" burst in the early 1990s, Japan has been trying to carry out a wide range of social reforms, including those related to administrative law and the judicial system, while it has been struggling with depression and deflation. These reforms do not only derive from depression itself, but are the fruit of social change in Japan and globalization as well.

This chapter will first present an overview of Japan's administrative law regime, and then provide a brief description of Japan's reforms of administrative law and judicial system from a legal perspective. These reforms are intertwined with each other and have a distinctively Japanese character. This chapter will also consider the future of "administrative law and judicialized governance," especially the short-term consequences of reforms and their future. It focuses especially on two aspects: (1) administrative procedures and legal control of "administrative guidance" (*Gyosei-shido*), and (2) judicial review of administrative action.

The thesis of this chapter is two-fold. First, in the current social condition, two major reforms of administrative law and the judicial system are expected to enhance judicialized governance in administrative law, which appears to be rooted in the Constitution of Japan. How these reforms will work in practice will depend on how individuals or parties in society take advantage of the opportunities they present.

82 *Hitoshi Ushijima*

Second, Japan is also cautious about over-judicialization in society, as exemplified in overly adversarial administrative processes or high rates of litigation. Judicial governance or judicialization of administrative governance in Japan will result from the balance of these two factors: greater opportunities for judicialization, along with concern about over-judicialization.[3]

The administrative state

The constitutional and statutory framework of administrative law and judicial review: A brief history

Japan's modern administrative law was born when it opened the country in the middle of the nineteenth century. Initially, Japanese reformers referred to German and French law to replace the traditional Japanese administrative law that had been influenced by imperial Chinese law. Since then, Japanese administrative law that has been heavily influenced by ideas of European Continental legal system, especially the German legal system, though it also has had its own unique development.

The 1946 Constitution, adopted after World War II under American influence, incorporated fundamental legal ideas such as "rule of law" and "due process of law" into the Constitution. Yet Japan's pre-war administrative law theory survived, even as the legal system embraced constitutional value such as civil rights protection, democracy, and respect for international harmony. A substantial number of Japanese administrative law scholars and practicing lawyers continue to refer to German and French law to resolve administrative law issues. For example, the German notion of "administrative disposition" (*Gyosei-koi*) has had great influence on Japan's administrative law theory.

The Constitution of Japan provided for two major changes on judicial power from the perspective of administrative law: first, it provided the judiciary with the power to determine the constitutionality of governmental actions, and second, it prohibited the establishment of extraordinary tribunals such as a Constitutional Court or Administrative Court, thus following the American model of a judicial system.[4]

Without an Administrative Court, Japan was forced to develop administrative law and judicial review of administrative action using civil procedure in ordinary courts. However, during the occupation, the GHQ (General Headquarters of Allied Forces) itself realized that the Anglo-American judicial model did not fit the Japanese system when a judicial injunction was issued against a governmental activity directed by the GHQ (*Hirano* case).[5] This marked the return to the traditional system influenced by German or French ideas, since this was the reference point for the majority of Japanese academics and practicing lawyers at the time. In 1962, Japan finally passed the Administrative Litigation Law (ALL), after some transitional statutes, while it maintained the system without a distinct administrative court.[6] The ALL provided for some types of public-law based administrative litigation, including *Torikeshi-sosho*, a type of challenge to final administrative decisions (*Gyosei-shobun*). Civil procedure was to be applicable to administrative litigation so long as it does not conflict with the character of administrative litigation.[7]

A small judiciary practicing extreme forms of judicial self-restraint would be a distinctive feature of Japan's administrative law and judicial review in practice, at least at times (though not entirely during the 1960s and early 1970s in lower courts). This would partly derive from a dual system in which judges and practicing lawyers have little career overlap. Judges serve as a member of judicial bureaucracy, allegedly under administrative or political control.[8]

It should be noted that in-house government lawyers working at the Ministry of Justice include judges who are seconded during the rotation and promotion process and come back to the judiciary after serving a fixed term in a professional capacity. Judges reviewing administrative actions may have experience as legal counsel for the national government (though they do not decide cases they had dealt with as counsel). Some believe this practice may influence judicial review of administrative action.

The legislative process

There are two distinct characteristics of the Japanese legislative process: first, substantial involvement of the bureaucracy in designing legislation; and second, approval of the ruling Liberal Democratic Party (LDP, *Jiyu-Minshu-To*) before introducing bills.[9]

Substantial bureaucratic involvement in designing bills is critical because most major bills are introduced by the Cabinet. The merit-based civil service system, under which a small number of senior officials are appointed by the Cabinet, has become a systematic barrier such that even the LDP, which has ruled almost continuously since 1955, cannot easily design bills to control the bureaucracy which might infringe their interests.

Second, a wide variety of interests are considered and compromised within the LDP before bills are introduced. Traditionally the Cabinet cannot introduce any bill without the approval of the LDP.[10] Some LDP legislators are supported by particular industries ("*Zoku-gi'in*"), and substantially work with bureaucrats at the relevant ministry to produce bills protecting industry interests.[11] Since lawmaking involves compromise among competing interests, the process produces simple and vague regulatory laws with minimal public participation, making judicial review of administrative action difficult. Courts have generally not been able to exercise extensive judicial review over the loose regulatory statutes, though there are some exceptions.

Administrative process

A preference for informality is also a distinguishing characteristic of the Japanese administrative law and process. Informality has, in this chapter, two meaning: (1) avoidance of legalized decision-making; and (2) avoidance of trial-type procedures.[12]

Administrative Guidance (AG) is a famous example of this preference for informality. A typical example of AG is performed to achieve administrative goals when an administrative agency does not have explicit statutory powers, but instead provides industry with guidance as to what course of action to take without any legal sanctions.[13] An agency sometimes performs AG for internal reasons. The operation and legal control of AG have been extensively studied by both Japanese and foreign lawyers. For foreign lawyers, AG is treated as a kind of magic tool to implement Japan's industrial policy. For Japanese lawyers, AG is treated as evidence of a gap between Japanese law in action and the theoretical requirements of the rule of law or the *Rechtsstaat*, which calls out for explanation.[14]

Traditionally AG has been considered to have the potential to conflict with the rule of law because it is sometimes unreviewable. AG is generally not subject to the *Torikeshi-sosho* procedure provided by the ALL, because it is not *Gyoseishobun*, that is, a final administrative action with legal effect. With regard to damages suits, another form of legal constraint, it is sometimes difficult to file claims against an act of AG because the private party typically follows the guidance "voluntarily," even if in the shadow of implicit threats to sanction the party. Some legal constraints have been provided at the outer boundaries of AG, and courts have declared some types of AG to be unlawful when they conflict with the principle of voluntariness, but the courts have never prohibited AG outright because of a recognition of its practical benefits.

Regulatory reform

Under the banner of Administrative Reform (*Gyosei-Kaikaku*), the Japanese government has been engaged in regulatory reform and deregulation since the late 1980s. The general principles of regulatory reform or deregulation have been that economic regulation should be abolished unless reasons for regulation are still supported; social regulation, such as environmental or safety regulation, should be minimal; and when regulation is needed, *ex post* regulation through administrative supervision or judicial review is preferred to *ex ante* regulation through AG or licensing.[15] A law providing for the experimental deregulation, which allows local exceptions to national regulation, was also enacted in 2002.

The Japanese business establishment, including such groups as *Keidanren*, have been acting as pressure groups pushing regulatory reform and deregulation. Another source of pressure is from foreign countries, particularly the U.S., which has argued that Administrative Guidance functions as non-tariff barriers and that deregulation is required to protect equal opportunities for foreign business. Japanese consumers, on the other hand, sometimes insist on stricter regulations in some areas such as safety, environmental, or consumer policy.

Another factor is the amendment of the Cabinet Law (*Naikaku Ho*), carried out with other reforms of the national government organization (*Chuo Shocho Kaikaku*) in 2001. The Cabinet office has been a major advocate of regulatory reform, challenging objections by the bureaucracy. The amended Cabinet Law provides more Cabinet power, spurring reforms.

Reform of administrative law

New statutes

Since the Administrative Procedures Law (APL) was first enacted in 1993, several major statutes in administrative law were enacted or amended: (1) the Information Disclosure Law (IDL), which provides the right to disclosure of information held by the national government,[16] enacted in 1999; (2) the Privacy Law was largely amended,[17] and related new laws were enacted in 2003; (3) the Administrative Litigation Law (ALL), which provides for legal challenge to governmental activities, was largely amended in 2004; and (4) the APL was amended to include a rulemaking procedure in 2005. In addition, the Local Government Law (LGL) and related laws were largely amended in 1999 and the Whistleblower Protection Law was enacted in 2004.

These statutory reforms mark a major historical change in Japanese administrative law. Under the APL, whose objective was to protect individual rights and interests by promoting fairness and transparency, governmental agencies are bound to provide more opportunities for notice-and-hearing, to create standard and transparent application or disposition procedures, and to perform Administrative Guidance in accordance with legal boundaries. The IDL was an important statute for enhancing government accountability. The Privacy Law and related statutes partly aim for harmonization with privacy rules in the EU and the U.S. as well as for the securing of constitutional value of privacy protection. The recently amended ALL was designed to overcome narrow case law in some areas such as standing. The amended APL adds a notice-and-comment rulemaking procedure, incorporating the experience of "public comment procedure on regulation setting or amendment," that had operated under a cabinet resolution for a short period.[18] The recently amended LGL redistributes the roles of national and local governments and provides more power to local government through decentralization.

The purposes of these reforms are infiltration of the "rule of law" to society,[19] for example through fair procedures and transparency (APL); accountability of open government (IDL); more protection of individual rights through administrative litigations (ALL); and decentralization by transferring authority from the national to local government (LGL). These ideas are not Japanese traditional ones (except decentralization, because Japan was transformed into centralized governmental system only after 1868) and we should examine why Japan carried out such major administrative law reforms.

Cause: Why administrative law reform?

There are several factors contributing to administrative law reform from political economy and law-and-society perspectives.

First, the Japanese society itself has been changing. As a highly industrialized and mature society, Japanese industries are ready to accommodate a more market-oriented economy and policy than before. The relationship between the government and business is not the same as during the 1960s and 1970s, which was characterized by the paternalistic industrial policy of MITI (the Ministry of International Trade and Industry) and submissive corporate behavior, sometimes known under the rubric of "Japan, Inc." Business is a bit more independent than before, as is government. The APL changed the relationship between business and government by providing for illegal Administrative Guidance and the new ALL facilitates citizen or business challenges to governmental actions. In other words, the great shift from "*ex ante* planning" and employing administrative guidance to "*ex post* correction" by administrative disposition and judicial review was intended to obtain more transparency and fair procedure. Informal tools such as administrative guidance are not prohibited but delineated in an APL statutory scheme, described below.

Citizens' groups or NGOs are becoming more willing to use the judiciary. There are a large number of public-documents-disclosure suits and Local Citizen's Suits (*Jumin-sosho*), challenging local governments' public expenditures. Cases in these two areas appear to be more acceptable to courts than do general administrative law cases.[20]

Second, Japan has been trying to establish a legal system whose rules are harmonized with those of other OECD or WTO member countries to share common values to promote free and fair trade. The Privacy Law is a good example. The other new statutes described above also promote fairness and transparency of governmental activities as well. These reforms will accommodate Japan to globalization and promote free trade in which international or foreign firms enter Japanese markets with fewer non-tariff barriers and gaps of administrative or judicial regulations than in other countries. The Justice System Reform Council (JSRC), in its final report in 2001, described the goal of judicial reform as establishing in Japan a rule of law or legal order embracing liberty and fairness, which would be the basis of Japan's contribution to the development of international society.[21] These reforms have been adopted by the major ruling party, the LDP, which seeks to maintain its political power by pursuing support of the people and business. Similarly, further reforms of the civil-servant system and quasi-governmental entities established by law (*Tokushu-hojin* or *Dokuritsu-Gyosei-hojin*) are currently on the political agendas under the topic of administrative reform.

Administrative remedies

Distinct from judicial remedies, private parties have the right to seek *post-hoc* administrative remedies *after* final administrative decision (*Gyosei-shobun*) as well as a hearing *before* administrative decisions. The Administrative Appeal Law (AAL) providing this *post-hoc* procedure was enacted in 1962 in place of the old Administrative Appeal Law (*Sogan Ho*) in 1890. The Japanese government is currently planning to amend the AAL substantially to give more procedural protection in the administrative process in accordance with procedural development of the APL and ALL. In July 2007, the Review Committee on the Administrative Appeal System (*Gyosei-Fufuku-Shinsa-Seido-Kentoukai*) under the Ministry of Internal Affairs and Communications submitted a final report, which proposes a wide variety of amendments to the AAL and APL, including an independent council procedure (AAL amendment proposal) and remedies against illegal AG (APL amendment proposal). Three bills, the new AAL, amendment of APL, and a related law were introduced to the National Diet on April 11, 2008, but failed to be passed due to relatively low priority and time pressures in the Diet. They are expected to be reintroduced to the next session of the National Diet in Fall 2008.

Japanese lawyers are very cautious about over-judicialization in administrative process, though they recognize that some judicialized structure is needed to produce better administrative decisions and private rights protection, as seen in APL and AAL frameworks as well as the final report by the above Commission. The APL provides for a pre-termination oral hearing only in the case of severe adverse actions such as a license revocation, and the AAL provides written *post-hoc* hearing unless a party requests an oral hearing. Neither APL nor AAL hearings are trial-type hearings, though they are evidentiary hearings to some extent. The report proposed two major amendments to the fundamental structure of the AAL: (1) the introduction of a hearing examiner (*Shinsa-in*) who will preside over a more adversary process than is currently the case, and (2) an independent council procedure, which produces opinions that are not legally binding but generally binding in practice. The independent council procedures are currently seen in some Japanese administrative law schemes such as that on Information disclosure, and the report seems to draw on these successful experiences.

Evidence of Japan's preference for modest or balanced procedural protection in the administrative process is found in an area which already has trial-type procedures. In economic regulation, the Anti-monopoly Law was amended, effective in 2006, to provide for hearing *after* Japan's Fair Trade Commission's (JFTC) final decision to issue, for example, a cease-and-desist order or an imposition of civil penalties. The hearing was transformed from a hearing *before* a JFTC decision having legal effect.[22]

Judicial system reform

Overview

Since 1999, the Japanese government has been carrying out large-scale reforms of the judicial system. The JSRC was established within the Cabinet to propose a basic policy of judicial reform in 1999 and its final report was submitted to the Cabinet in 2001. Based on this report, the Japanese government started to engage in the judicial system reform establishing the Plan of Judicial System Reform (*Shiho-seido Suishin Keikaku*) during 2001–2004 and Headquarters of Judicial System Reform (*Shiho-seido Suishin Kaikaku Honbu*), which supervises this plan.

This reform covers extensive areas: the civil justice system, the criminal justice system, including the introduction of lay participation (*Saiban'in*) in criminal procedure, establishment of special court of intellectual property, new forms of legal aid, promotion of more judicial intervention in administrative actions, and a new system of legal education. From a historical viewpoint, this reform is the third major one in modern Japanese history, building on the post-World War II reforms and the effort to establish a modern judicial system in the latter half of the nineteenth century. It should be noted that this judicial reform was largely designed by the Cabinet with the support of the ruling parties, the Ministry of Justice, the Supreme Court, and the Federation of the Japanese Bar Associations (Nichiberen), incorporating a wide variety of interests. The legislative body supported the reform process through passage of the necessary statutes. Amendment of the ALL is a part of the judicial reform as noted above and will be discussed further below.

Legal education

Legal education is one major arena of judicial system reform as noted above. There are two major changes in legal education related to administrative law and judicialized governance. First, a new legal educational system was established to change legal education and to produce more lawyers.[23] Seventy-four new graduate schools of law nationwide were established to provide a more process-oriented legal education, incorporating the case method and clinical programs. Students will study at a new graduate school of law for two or three years, depending on their previous experience of legal studies. Law schools are required to admit substantial numbers of students with some work experiences or without undergraduate legal studies. Undergraduate legal education still continues to exist but it is not prerequisite to entering a law school.

Second, administrative law has become a mandatory subject area for study and is one of the new subjects on the bar examination.[24] This change will produce administrative law-conscious lawyers. Some have argued that the low rate of administrative litigation, both in suits filed and in win rates, comes from both judges[25] and practicing lawyers unfamiliar with administrative law theory.

It is not clear why these two major changes were accomplished without any strong pressure group; indeed the only interest group activity seemed to be resistance to the reforms from some practicing lawyers who fear losing their markets.[26] However, we can speculate on two major reasons for the reforms: (1) a major ruling party, the LDP, partly supported by the opposition JDP, has been trying to challenge the traditionally strong bureaucracy through administrative, regulatory, and judicial reforms, and producing administrative law-conscious lawyers,[27] (2) business and consumer groups support this policy.[28]

Administrative law and judicialized governance: Current status of major areas[30]

Administrative procedures and legal control of Administrative Guidance provided by the APL

As described above, the APL provides a new statutory framework for fair procedure and transparency, introducing both more legalization and judicialization into the administrative process. Administrative Guidance is subject to greater judicial control and the national and local governments are required to provide private parties with notice-and-hearing in more cases in administrative process. The IDL and new ALL will assist in this regard. Altogether, it seems as if Japan is heading toward more judicialized governance in administrative law, though there is always discussion of how far we should go in this direction. It will take a long time for public officials (especially at the local level) and judges to fully understand ideas of fair procedure. This means that legal education is particularly important to sow the seeds of long-term reform.

Purpose and scope

The legislative purpose of the APL is to protect citizens' interests through fair procedure and transparency.[31] The original APL of 1993 had largely three parts: (1) application procedure (Shinsei ni Taisuru Shobun); (2) procedure of adverse action (Furieki-Shobun); (3) principles and procedural control of Administrative Guidance (AG).[32]

License or permission application procedure

In practice, AG traditionally played an important role in the economy, and formal applications were sometimes held up during AG. For example, a high-rise condominium building permit might not be given within the statutory time limit when the developer was complying with AG by voluntarily changing the plan to accommodate neighborhood request. In these instances withholding the permit was part of a process of negotiation between a local government agency and a private party. AG used to be the only administrative tool local government could use when the scope of local government ordinance was arguably limited by national statutes before 1999, when the Local Government Law was greatly amended to expand the regulatory scope of local ordinances. However, as a matter of protection of private rights that is within statutory framework, the APL made basic rules of application procedures.

There are four major rules: (1) a requirement to establishing and publicly announcing internal rules (Shinsa-Kijun) to govern the review process for applications (art.5); (2) a requirement (though not legally binding) to establish a standard time period for review (art.6); (3) the initial decision must either be to begin reviewing the application, request correction of the application, or to deny the application when there is a severe defect in the application (art. 7); and (4) disclosure of reasons in cases of denial.

Rules (1) and (4) are provided to promote transparency and to bring more opportunities for judicial review. Indeed, they were developed with reference to Supreme Court cases. This can be regarded as a dialogue between legislation and judicial lawmaking, and can be seen as some evidence of judicial governance in administrative law.

Rules (2) and (3) are provided to regulate certain type of AG such as when an agency holds an application until a private party changes an application or submits extra-statutory documents requested by AG. These rules function as regulation of AG in this regard.

Procedure of adverse actions

The APL provides three major rules on procedure of adverse actions: (1) a requirement (though not legal binding) of setting internal rules for adverse action decision-making (*Shobun-kijun*); (2) disclosure of reasons for adverse actions; and (3) the right to be heard. Rules (1) and (2) are supposed to perform the same function as the equivalent provisions of application procedure. As to Rule (3), the APL provides two kinds of hearing prior to adverse actions: (1) notice and oral hearing (*Chomon*); and (2) notice and written hearing (*Benmei no Kikai no Fuyo*) (art. 13). Oral hearings have more procedural protection prior to severe adverse actions such as license revocation than do written ones, which are utilized prior to less severe adverse actions such as license suspension. It should be noted that oral hearing is not a trial-type hearing but a quasi-triadic structure, in which the hearing examiner presides to produce a record and summary report by which an agency makes a decision based on fact-finding at hearing.

Principles and procedural control of administrative guidance

The court has declared that some types of AG are unlawful, especially when a request to a private party transmitted through AG was in fact enforced notwithstanding the lack of legal power to do so. This section considers several examples related to city planning and building construction.

In the first example, a construction company made a donation to a city government in the shadow of AG and a threat that the government would not provide drinking water to the company's newly built condominium.[33] The company requested reimbursement of the donation thereafter insisting that it was forced to make it. The court held that the request for a donation was unlawful because it went beyond the scope of AG that a private party would follow voluntarily.

In the second example, a city government actually failed to provide drinking water to a newly built condominium due to non-compliance with AG.[34] The city mayor, responsible for ensuring the water supply, was prosecuted for a violation of the Drinking Water Law, which requires compulsory water supply. The issue was whether non-compliance with AG is a sufficient reason to fail to supply water. The court answered in the negative.

Finally, in the third example, a city government asked a company informally to change the building plan of a condominium, and the company sought administrative relief. The government continued to perform AG and[35] the private party requested damages due to the delay of obtaining building permit. The court declared that AG is lawful so long as voluntariness of the private party is evident but that, once a party expresses serious and clear unwillingness to comply, AG will generally be unlawful.

The APL provides three substantive rules and two procedural rules, incorporating these Courts' decisions. First, administrative agencies can engage in AG only within the relevant statutory scope and must recognize that compliance with AG must be voluntary. As a corollary, administrative agencies should not produce adverse decisions simply because of non-compliance with AG (art. 32). This rule was drawn partly from the nature of AG and partly from caselaw. Second, when administrative agency staff use AG to encourage applicants to withdraw or modify their application, they cannot continue engaging in AG when the applicant expresses an intent not to comply with AG (art. 33). This rule also reflects case law.

Third, where an administrative agency cannot exercise authority or does not intend to do so, agency staff should not compel an applicant to comply with AG by threatening to exercise formal authority (art. 34).

Fourth, as a procedural matter agency staff are required to provide, upon request by private parties, a written statement stating the purpose and content of the AG, as well as the name of the responsible person (art. 35).

Fifth, as a procedural matter, when an administrative agency directs AG to a certain category of private parties to achieve a similar purpose, it should make the guidelines publicly available (art. 36). Guidelines of AG (*Shido-yoko*), which local governments typically set for AG in city planning, is one example of this category of acts.

These rules are intended to provide for fair procedure and transparency without hindering the flexibility and practicality of AG. Thus, the Court will examine AG in particular cases to articulate these statutory rules in further depth, elaborating issues such as the scope of prohibited (or admissible) adverse action against non-complying parties.[36]

A "No-action letter" system was introduced by national agencies in the form of the "agency reference on prospective law application" (*Gyosei-kikan ni yoru Horei-tekiyo Jizen-kakunin Tetuzuki*). This system does not have statutory basis but is based on a Cabinet resolution.[37] An agency's opinion expressed by a no-action letter is substantially trusted by business and constrains the agency from acting contrary to its expressed policy.[38]

Notice-and-comment rulemaking procedure (Iken-Kobo-Tetsuzuki)

The APL was amended in 2005 to incorporate a notice-and-comment rulemaking procedure, with which national agencies had some experience under a Cabinet resolution adopted a few years earlier. Japan's rulemaking procedure is also required when an agency is setting (1) internal standards for reviewing applications and for making adverse decisions, and (2) internal guidelines for issuing AG as required by the APL (articles 5, 12, 36), as well as making rules under statutory delegation. The procedure is roughly similar to American notice-and-comment informal rulemaking procedure, but it is not clear how an interested party could challenge a rule.

The procedure requires a rulemaking agency to post the proposed rule in the government register and on a website and to allow any person to submit written comments on that rule. An agency will decide on the final rule after examining all opinions submitted and post the final rule in the government register and on the web, along with a summary of opinions, and a statement as to why the agency took or did not take these comments into account. There is no provision for a second rulemaking procedure when an agency substantially changes the initial rule, but as a matter of interpretation of the APL, agencies are statutorily required to follow the same procedures for a second round in such an event.

Judicial review of administrative action: New provisions of amended ALL

Background and purpose

The ALL was amended and is expected to facilitate enhanced opportunities for private parties to obtain judicial review and to control governmental actions. Recent data show two distinguishing characteristics of Japan's use of courts: (1) a relatively small number of suits filed challenging government comparing with other highly developed countries; and (2) a low rate of cases in which the plaintiff prevails in challenging government.[39]

As to the small (though gradually increasing) number of cases (see Table 5.1), this partly results from the low rate of plaintiff successes (a bit more than 10 per cent, see Table 5.1). Many important cases challenging governmental actions have been said to have been lost in courts due to threshold questions such as lack of standing. On the other hand, the Constitution provides for the right of access to the courts (art. 32). If governmental actions were not subject to judicial review, it would conflict with the concept of rule of law by placing some governmental actions beyond the law. This was one reason that the ALL was amended to enhance judicial intervention. Even if a case gets over jurisdictional hurdles, parties may lose when the administrative discretion in question is not easily subject to judicial scrutiny.

Courts were originally expected to develop vigorous caselaw under the old ALL, adopted some 40 years earlier. However, with some exceptions, courts did not play an active role, in part because neither judges nor lawyers were very familiar with administrative law. Most of the amended ALL is not new but rather simply expands the possibility of judicial development of the law.

Table 5.1 Number of administrative litigations in recent years

	New cases	Final resolution at first instance	Plaintiff-prevailing rate at first instance (%)	New appeals to the Supreme Court
2002	1,662	2,208	17.8	613
2003	1,858	2,503	15.1	709
2004	1,859	2,708	13.8	710
2005	1,882	2,454	9.8	764
2006	2,093	2,565	11.0	735

Source: General Secretariat of the Supreme Court, Hoso-jiho, vol. 59, no. 9, 2007, pp. 149, 152–153, 159.

Since the passage of the new ALL, the Supreme Court has, as expected, stepped forward to develop the law more vigorously. New judges who have studied administrative law as a mandatory subject will be in a better position to review administrative law cases than judges under the old system.

The bill amending the ALL was drafted by the Cabinet based on a final report of the Study Group of Administrative Litigation (*Gyosei-sosho Kentokai*), which consisted of judges, Ministry of Justice officials, practicing lawyers from the Japanese Federation of the Bar Associations (*nichibenren*), and law professors. This is a typical example of the Japanese style of legislation, in which a council of mixed membership makes a proposal to the Ministry or the Cabinet, and we saw the same process in setting the agenda of judicial reform or in the legislative proposal of the APL.[40]

Some important parts of the new ALL include: (1) standing (*Genkoku-tekikaku*); (2) declaratory judgment (*Kohojo-no-tojisya-sosho*); (3) mandamus (*Gimuzuke-sosho*); and injunction (*Sashitome-soho*).[41]

Standing

Article 9 of the ALL provides for standing to file a "Torikeshi-sosho" when a plaintiff has an interest protected by law and needs a remedy. The amended article 9 added section 2 which deals with third-party (party who is not a receiver of a disposition) standing. When a third party files a suit, courts should consider: (1) the intent and purpose of the law as well as its provisions; and (2) the substance and nature of the third party's interests should an administrative decision in question be made. Section 2 of amended article 9 also requires courts to refer to the intent and purpose of any related laws that share a purpose with the law at issue, and to take into account the substance and nature of the interests infringed, along with the manner and extent of infringement if an illegal administrative decision in question is made.

The case law of standing, especially in cases filed by a third party, has been generally regarded to be too narrow, but it appears to be moving gradually toward a wider direction. The court declared two criteria in deciding standing: (1) the third party should have an interest, protected by the law at issue, that is or will be infringed; and (2) this interest should be an individual interest protected by the law, *not* a purely collective interest. Thus, the court typically denied standing of parties whose only interest was as a consumer or a cultural interest. On the other hand, the court has allowed standing in cases involving business competition, disturbance by airplanes, and safety regulation. The new section 2 of article 9 of the amended ALL incorporates the court's interpretive policy in two major cases, *Niigata Airport* and *Monju*. In the *Niigata Airport* case, neighbors challenged an airline's license to stop disturbance by airplanes, and the court declared that standing depended not simply on the intent and purpose of the law at issue but also of related laws that share a purpose as well (substantially equivalent to the new section 2 of article 9 of the ALL). In the *Monju* case, neighbors challenged the safety of a nuclear power plant, and the court declared an interpretive policy of standing that takes into account the substance and nature of the interests infringed, as well as the manner and extent of infringement in the event of an illegal administrative decision (substantially equivalent to the new section 2 of article 9 of the ALL).

Since *Monju*, the court has allowed standing in cases in which neighbors challenge safety regulations, such as those related to landslide prevention, and has shown some sympathy to other kinds of interests such as the right to sunlight. In the *Odakyu Railway* case after amendment of ALL, the court went further to allow standing of neighbors, with no real property interests, who lived within the designated area of environmental assessment by the Tokyo Metropolitan government and who challenged city plans including a railway reconstruction permit, alleging environmental interests that would be infringed by construction.

From the description of judicially created law on standing above, we see Japan's two styles of judicial governance in administrative law. First, there is an attitude of judicial modesty: the court shows a tendency to interpret laws in a narrow, positivistic manner. Indeed, the ALL was amended because courts did not fully exercise their powers to develop the law in the judicial process. The law did *not* restrict judicial power or over-rule judicial lawmaking as sometimes occurs in the Anglo-American system, but rather promoted the development of judicial law. The modest approach of Japanese courts on standing is rooted in the difficulties of finding distinction of legally protected and unprotected interests. Some argue that the requirement of legally protected individual interests should be removed. However, the court has maintained the same basic framework, while applying it more flexibly.

Second, there is the modest legislative attitude: the amended ALL confirms the developments of the court's recent judicial law. Some argue that the amendment of the ALL falls short of the position needed and the ALL should have provided for standing based on an "injury in fact" criteria instead of legally protected interests. However, the final report of the Study Group did not take this legislative policy, nor did Parliament.

Declaratory judgment

The German-style *Torikeshi-sosho* procedure is inadequate for parties to challenge certain agency decisions. Some statutes have threshold requirements of finality or ripeness, legal effect, or unilateral character of decisions (*Shobunsei*) before challenges can be made. The ALL provides that *Torikeshi-sosho* is a suit challenging a final administrative decision (*Gyosei-shobun*) or its equivalent. However, many argue that the court's interpretation of this provision is too narrow. A private party should be able to file a suit, under the Constitutional right of access to courts, to confirm legality of its actions beforehand, when changing internal interpretive agency rules invoke prosecutorial authority in party's violation of regulation. There was a discussion, at the Research Committee, as to whether this threshold requirement would be deregulated or not, but the Study Group concluded that a declaratory judgment invoking article 4 would be suitable for this issue in which the *Torikeshi-sosho* procedure was inadequate. Article 4, which provides a form of civil procedure in public law, was amended to allow a party to use this form of litigation in such cases.

Mandamus and injunction

The original ALL did not prohibit mandamus and injunction but provided no provision for them. Only a few court decisions were passed in this area under the ALL. Thus, the amended ALL also added provisions of mandamus and injunction, though the threshold requirements are very strict.

Conclusion: The future of judicialized governance in administrative law

This chapter concludes with some speculations on the future. First, the two major reforms of administrative law and the judicialized system will enhance judicial governance in administrative law, which appears to be rooted in the Constitution of Japan, so as to accommodate changes in Japanese society. However, the level of judicialization will ultimately depend on how individuals or parties in society take advantage of these reforms and continue to develop them. Second, Japan is also cautious about over-judicialization of governance and the regulatory process. The judicialization of administrative governance in Japan will reflect a balance between these two forces.

Two other issues are relevant here. First, it is important to design and enhance mechanisms for public participation into statutory schemes. Relatively few provisions for public participation are found in Japan's national laws, though such participation provisions are increasing.[42] Instead, some local governments have been trying to incorporate public participation into ordinances.[43] The relative lack of public participation provisions leads to judicial restraint, both because of difficulties in finding illegality as well as the lack of reviewability.

Second, new forms of public-private partnership[44] will be one of the challenging issues for governance and accountability. Public service by private business is an example. Some new or amended statutes are now provided for an extensive role for private parties, with government and civil society existing in partnership. For example, under the current system, building permits are partly provided by some private corporations certified by the national government and under local government supervision.[45] Under this system, it becomes important to know how the government controls private entities activities. Another example is found in the contracts between private care-service-providers and consumers under the Public Insurance for Nursing Law,[46] which changed the basic policy of public service provided by public agency, promoting quality of service by competition. This regulatory change is not unique in Japan and is an example of global trends of privatization of public service.

Table of statutes cited

Administrative Appeal Law (*Gyosei-fufuku-shinsa Ho*) (AAL), Law No. of 1962.

Administrative Litigation Law (ALL) (*Gyosei-jiken Sosyo Ho*), Law No. of 1962.

Administrative Procedures Law (APL) (*Gyosei tetsuzuki Ho*), Law No. 88 of 1993.

Anti-monopoly Law (*Shiteki-dokusen no Kinshi oyobi Kousei-torihiki no Kakuho ni kansuru Horitsu*), Law No. 54 of 1947.

Basic Law Concerning National Civil Servant System Reform (*Kokka-Koumu in Seido Kaikaku Kihon Ho*), Law No. 68 of 2008.

Building Standards Law *(Kenchiku-kijun Ho)*, Law No.25 of 1950.

Cabinet Law (*Naikaku Ho*), Law No. 5 of 1947.

Drinking Water Law (*Suido Ho*), Law No. 177 of 1957.

Information Disclosure Law (IDL) (*Gyosei-kikan no Hoyusuru Joho no Kokai ni Kansuru Horitsu*), Law No. of 1999.

Local Government Law (LGL) (*Chiho-jichi Ho*), Law No. 67 of 1947.

Privacy Protection Law (*Kojin-joho no Hogo ni Kansuru Horitsu*), Law No. 57 of 2003.

Privacy Protection Law on Administrative Agency Holding Information (*Gyosei-kikan no Hoyusuru Kojin-joho no Hogo ni Kansuru Horitsu*), Law No. 58 of 2003.

Public Insurance for Nursing Law (*Kaigo Hoken Ho*), Law No. 123 of 1997.

Solid Waste Disposal Law (*Haikibutsu no Shori oyobi Seiso ni Kansuru Horitsu*), Law No.137 of 1970.

Whistleblower Protection Law (*Koheki Tsuho-sya Hogo Ho*), Law No. 122 of 2004.

Notes

1 This is also applicable to South Korea and Taiwan, as described in Chapters 6 and 7 of this volume. Japanese scholars have recently begun to refer to these active judiciaries with regard to constitutional and administrative litigation, particularly through meetings of the East Asian Administrative Law Association and the Japan Public Law Association.
2 Judicialization involves legalism, adversariness, and independent decision-making, whether in the judicial process or administrative process. The particular configuration of judicialization depends on the particular society in which it is found. See Robert Kagan, *Adversarial Legalism*, Cambridge, MA: Harvard University Press, 2002.
3 The concept of "government-governance" in Japan usually refers to the political or administrative branch or process and does not usually indicate the judicial branch and its process. However, the role distribution among the three branches of government are always important topics in Japanese constitutional and administrative law. Thus, "judicialized governance" is a useful new perspective in Japan to understand governance by the judicial branch or quasi-judicial procedure in the administrative process.
4 Constitution of Japan, Art. 76. Before World War II, Japan had an Administrative Court located only in Tokyo, which was the first and final instance independent from the old Supreme Court *(Taishin'in)*, drawn from the European continental legal system. A type of litigation challenging adverse governmental actions was statutorily based and

strictly restrained in its governmental system. This system was based on the European continental judicial system, that is dichotomy of public and private law, which has been much criticized but is still partly alive in the Supreme Court cases. See, for example, Case of *Osaka International Airport*, in which the court declared no standing to file a civil procedure injunction against airplane traffic at a government-run airport, Minshu vol. 35, p.1369 (Sup. Ct., Dec. 16, 1981); Case of *Takarazuka City Ordinance*, in which the court held that local government cannot file a civil procedure injunction without an explicit statutory basis because the case does not involve case or controversy, Minshu vol. 56, p.1134 (Sup. Ct., July 9, 2002).
5 Mr. Hirano, a representative of parliament, requested and obtained an injunction at the Tokyo district court on a governmental decision to purge him due to his undemocratic character.
6 Although the Constitution prohibits the establishment of extraordinary tribunals exercising final judicial power, it allows the judicial system to have special tribunals under the authority and supervision of the Supreme Court (art. 76).
7 Art. 7 of ALL.
8 John O. Haley, Judicial Independence in Japan Revisited, *Law in Japan*, no.25, pp.1–18, 1995. Setsuo Miyazawa, Administrative Control of Japanese Judges, in Philip S. C. Lewis, ed., *Law and Technology in the Pacific Community*, Boulder, CO: Westview Press, 1991. Some judges seem to prefer conciliation *(Wakai)* at court over deciding cases against government.
9 It should be noted that this may be subject to change. First, the current government consists of a coalition between the LDP and *Komei* party (*Komei-To*), and coalition government may introduce some changes in the system. Second, the Japan Democratic Party (JDP, *Minshu-To*) increased its power since the last House of Councillors (*Sangi'in*) election in 2007, and we have observed greater JDP influence on legislation.
10 This custom functions through floor votes in which party discipline is high. However, ex-Prime Minister Koizumi broke with this custom when the Cabinet introduced bills to privatize the Japanese Postal Service.
11 Mathew D. McCubbins and Gregory W. Noble, The Appearance of Power: Legislators Bureaucrats and the Budget Process in the United States and Japan, in Peter Cowhey and Mathew D. McCubbins, *Structure and Policy in Japan and the United States: An Institutionalist Approach,* Cambridge: Cambridge University Press, 1995. This phenomenon is sometimes known as the iron triangle of politics, bureaucracy, and industry, in which senior officials are recruited by regulated industries after retirement ("*Amakudari*," whose literal meaning is "coming down to real world from heaven"). While the society benefits from the talents of senior officials, there is a concern that senior officials at a Ministry might distort regulatory policy in favor of certain interests, expecting a future career. The Japanese government has been trying to change this traditional *Amakudari* system but is finding it very difficult to break. However, reform of the civil-servant system should have an impact. The Basic Law Concerning National Public Service System Reform enacted on June 23, 2008, will further regulate Amakudari and related issues.
12 See below. This means Japanese style of regulation would be opposite to American one. See Kagan, op. cit.
13 AG is performed by both national and local governments as a regulatory technique. At the national level, AG is well-known as a tool for industrial policy, while local governments use AG to fill gaps between national statutes and local needs in areas such as city planning. With respect to national AG, see generally Michael Young, Judicial Review of Administrative Guidance: Governmentally Encouraged Consensual Dispute Resolution in Japan, *Columbia Law Review*, 1984(923–8). With respect to local AG, see generally Ramseyer and Nakazato, *Japanese Law: An Economic Approach* 1999, pp.205–11; Takehisa Nakagawa, Administrative Informality in Japan: Governmental

Activities Outside Statutory Authorization, *Administrative Law Review*, vol.52, no.1, Winter 2000. AG is also performed when an administrative agency *does* have an explicit statutory power to exercise. An agency issues guidance as a procedure prior to Disposition (*Gyosei-shobun*), the legalized decision on statutory basis.

14 Both an agency and a private party will often prefer informal AG to formal legalized Disposition based on statutory power because it is relatively cost-effective and preserves ongoing relationships. Thus, there is a question of transparency, especially when a private party might wish to avoid disclosure of negative information.

15 Three Year Plan of Promotion of Deregulation (Cabinet resolution, March 31, 1998).

16 Local information disclosure ordinances were enacted beginning in the 1980s. When the national government enacted its law, it incorporated local governments' experience and case law on these laws.

17 This Privacy Law provides a regulatory framework concerning documents held by non-governmental bodies as well as common basic rules applicable to both public and private institutions. As to documents and data held by the national government, the new Privacy Protection Law on Administrative Agency Holding Information was enacted in the same year as the Privacy Law.

18 Cabinet resolution (March 23, 1999).

19 See Final report of the Justice System Reform Council, 2001.

20 Note removed.

21 This is a unique phenomenon of the current state of administrative litigation. It results from national courts' willingness to render decisions against local governments, and reflects both the statutory framework and case law developed in the *Torikeshi-sosho*. Most local ordinances (*Jorei*) which provides for public documents disclosure do not limit standing, adopting an "any-person rule." Local Citizen's Suits (*Jumin-sosho*), provided for in the LGL and influenced by the American idea of taxpayer's suit, may be filed without any particular standing limit so long as the plaintiff is a local citizen and has exhausted administrative remedies. Thus, standing in these two types of suits are clearly wider than standing under the *Torikeshi-sosho*, provided in ALL, to challenge final governmental decisions. Furthermore, as a matter of interpretation, courts have arguably been limiting standing under the *Torikeshi-sosho*, and Local Citizen's Suit have been employed in part to avoid these standing limitations to challenge governmental activities. The National IDL involves the same statutory framework, even though there is no citizen's suit challenging national public money spending.

22 It is arguable that the "rule of law" concept is shared in global arena. It sometimes refers to legalism or juridification and there is discussion in the area of "law and development" topics. However, the JSRC refers to the rule of law as a basis for the Japanese Constitution. From this point, the JSRC appears to regard judicial control of governmental (legislative and administrative) actions, pursuing justice, as a core element of "rule of law."

23 The Report by the Advisory Panel on Basic Issues Regarding the Anti-Monopoly Act to the Secretary of the Cabinet Office, submitted on June 26, 2007, pp.33–46 (English Version) suggests that ex-ante hearings should be readopted. On the other hand, the JFTC is reported to be planning to take out *post-hoc* administrative procedure to provide full scope of judicial review of JFTC's actions with no *prior* administrative procedure based on request by Keidanren and Ministry of Economy, Trade, and Industry. See *Asahi-Shinbun* January 25, 2008.

24 One of the differences between the Japanese and American systems of legal education is that Japan has maintained undergraduate legal education. While the Japanese system produces more law-conscious graduates for society, those who focus on legal studies through both undergraduate and graduate schools would need to make an effort to broaden their perspective beyond the legal arena.

25 Administrative law is a subject of public law, just as is constitutional law.
26 As described above, courts dealing with civil cases review administrative actions. Only the Tokyo and Osaka district courts have special benches (*Senmonbu*) to deal with administrative litigation, while some districts courts specify particular benches (*Shuchubu*) dealing with administrative litigation though not exclusively.
27 There is always a pro-and-con discussion within the bar and government about increasing the number of lawyers. However, on July 18, 2008, the Japan Federation of Bar Associations (*Nichiberen*) issued a new proposal which partly suggest governmental policy of increasing number of lawyers be changed toward slow and steady manner.
28 More lawyers should be required as well as "judicial system" reform to achieve recent regulatory policy that *ex post* correction should be preferred to *ex ante* planning.
29 Recommendation by the JSRC pointed out the necessity of expansion of lawyers population to meet social demand, that is, (1) more access to courts and lawyers, especially rural areas, (2) expedited civil and criminal procedure, (3) expansion of the scope of lawyers' activities.
30 Standards of judicial review, judicial control of rulemaking or standard setting, open government (information disclosure) and judicial review, and governmental liability are other major areas this chapter does not cover.
31 Article 1 of APL.
32 A procedural provision of the notification to an agency (*Todokede*) constitutes a separate chapter and provision. The idea of this provision, legal obligation of notification to an agency, is fulfilled when a notification in accordance with legal requirement arrives at an agency office (art. 37), can be understood in the same way as application procedure which provides agency's obligation of starting review application upon receipt. This provision prohibits agency's refusal to receive a notification by private parties in the case of non-compliance with extra-statutory requirement of AG, which is sometimes seen in administrative practice, as is the case with no start to review application in the case of non-compliance with AG.
33 Minshu Vol. 47, p. 574 (Sup.Ct. Feb. 18, 1993).
34 Hanrei-jiho No. 1328, p. 16 (Sup.Ct. Nov. 18, 1989).
35 Minshu Vol. 39, p. 989 (Sup.Ct. July 16, 1985).
36 Publicity of AG non-compliance would be a good topic whether it would be within scope of admissible action. It is not legal sanction but brings certain disadvantages of private parties depending on situations.
37 Cabinet resolution March 27, 2001.
38 There is no statute or judicial law on this issue, but issues of estoppel would be raised.
39 Table 5.1 does not include governmental liability cases, which are also an important tool to control government, but does include tax and intellectual property cases.
40 The records of discussion at the council or study group are made public through websites.
41 Mandamus or injunction is a translation of Japanese concepts similar to the Anglo-American counterpart, though the Japanese legal system does not follow all of the relevant rules found in common law or equity. Other than parts designated, amendment of the ALL includes: (1) providing that the defendant will be a government entity in which an individual agency exercised authority (Art. 11); (2) more jurisdiction over administrative litigation, concentrated in major district courts (Art. 12); (3) a longer period (3 months to 6 months) to challenge administrative action (Art. 14); (4) a notice requirement, at the time of administrative dispositions, about the possibility of administrative litigation (Art. 46); (5) providing for court power to order submission of agency records or documents that explain further reasons of a decision (Art. 23); and (6) deregulating the requirement of tentative judicial orders (Art. 25), and providing temporary mandamus and temporary injunction (Art. 37–5).
42 E.g. Art. 15 of Solid Waste Disposal Law, as amended in 1997, which provides for an opportunity for notice-and-comment hearings on environmental issues involving local

people and municipalities prior to prefectural government's approval for establishment of a solid waste disposal facility. This participation provision was supposed to abolish a common practice of AG issued by prefectural government, with no statutory basis, requesting submission of documents showing local people's agreement with the establishment of the facility. This custom might be a barrier to establishing new facilities as the Law intended, and would involve financial transfers between industry and a limited number of local people.

43 Some city governments have recently enacted public participation ordinances by which local people have the right to participate in some kind of hearing important issues before final decisions are made.

44 Privatization, standard-setting by private parties, or self-regulation are also good examples, as well as regulation or public service by private entities provision. See generally Jody Freeman, Private Parties, Public Functions and New Administrative Law, *Administrative Law Review*, vol.52, no.3, 2000, pp.813–58.

45 Art. 6–2 of Building Standards Law.

46 This law applies to the elderly and handicapped who need care.

6 Government reform, judicialization, and the development of public law in the Republic of Korea

Jongcheol Kim

Introduction

This essay reports recent changes in public law with special reference to government reform and the attendant changing role of the judiciary in South Korea. We begin with a description of the two topics and their relationship. Next, we trace the government reforms in both the Kim Dae Jung (1997–2002) and Roh Moo Hyun (2002–2007) administrations, focusing on the establishment of mechanisms to enhance transparency and public participation. We then discuss the role of the courts and the phenomenon of judicialization.

Government reform in Korea

In this section, we argue that government reform in Korea has three primary causes: democratization, globalization, and informatization.[1] We treat each in turn.

Democratization

First, democratization has led to pressures to enhance participation. The year 2007 marked the twentieth anniversary of the Constitution which resulted from the "People's Uprising of June, 1987." Koreans are justifiably proud of the emergence of constitutional democracy during this period. However, democratization is neither a simple nor a short process in which everything follows mechanically from one successful ignition. The restoration of the citizen's power to choose their representatives and chief executive, though one of the main achievements of the 1987 Uprising, is not the end of the story, but rather the beginning of a process, providing a mechanism for further developments. Ongoing reforms of both state and society are inevitable to eradicate the legacy of longstanding authoritarianism. Those citizens wounded by political, economic, social, and cultural hardship associated with the dictatorship and its discriminatory social and economic policies adopted in the name of industrialization need to be healed. At the same time, the resources accumulated during that painful period must be sublimated rather than discarded away with the dark side of the old legacy.

This double project can be accomplished by, on the one hand, compensating victims and rehabilitating their damaged reputations and, on the other hand, restructuring state and societal arrangements tainted by the authoritarian patterns of thought and behavior. For the latter in particular, government reforms at institutional, organizational, and operational levels to enhance popular sovereignty, the rule of law, and the separation of powers are inevitable.

Globalization

The need for comprehensive political and social reforms is also strengthened by the rapid change in international circumstances, namely globalization. Globalization refers to the rapidly increased flow of capital and commodities across national borders, blurring state boundaries, especially in terms of the economy. Globalization demands transparency, efficiency, and effectiveness, challenging the basis of the developmental state which dominated Korea before 1987. The developmental state model had centered on a dominant role for the bureaucracy in national economic and social planning, acting as a self-appointed guardian for selected Korean private firms, at the expense of foreign and non-favored domestic firms. But this role may not be appropriate for a global era.

The demands of efficiency and effectiveness in government functioning forces the state to change its function and institutional structures. Diverse public policy ideas such as New Public Management, governance, privatization, "co-opetition" (the juxtaposition of cooperation and competition in public service), and policy networks are being advanced as models for government reform.[2]

Informatization

The development of what is sometimes called the information society, or knowledge-based society, is another background for comprehensive reform. Informatization or the transition from industrial society to knowledge-based society, transforms not only our values and visions but also communicative modes and skills in both private and public sectors. For example, computerization has led most democracies to develop programs of E-Government, in which a great deal of public service is performed and delivered online. Public access to government information and public participation in policy-making through online government system is also enhanced.[3] Easier communication across the state-society boundary changes values, and requires transformation of the government system itself.

Judicialization in Korea

The second main topic is judicialization. The Roh Moo Hyun Presidency, the fourth since the establishment of the 1987 Constitution, can be identified above all as the "period of judicialization." During Roh's tenure in office, we witnessed the growing influence of the ordinary and constitutional courts on matters which were once considered purely political. Evidence of this new constitutional trend includes the first impeachment trial against the President in the history of Korean constitutional democracy, which resulted in the curtailment of presidential power by the Constitutional Court while rejecting the impeachment charge; the decision holding unconstitutional the Special Act for the Construction of the New Administrative Capital, which had been the most ambitious agendum of the Roh Administration; and the temporary suspension of the Saemangeum Reclamation Project, considered to be one of the biggest development projects in Korean modern history. In addition, virtually every political conflict between pro-Roh political forces and anti-Roh forces ended up in the docket of the Constitutional Court at some point.[4]

Apart from the peculiar politico-legal circumstances of the Roh Government, judicialization has two major sources in Korea. First, there is strong public demand for judicial control over the government activities as a means of advancing democratization. The authoritarian period had featured an imperial presidency together with bureaucracy-led industrialization. Legislative and judicial control over the administration remained only a formality, provided in constitutional and statutory texts but never realized in practice. Even after 1987, the legacy of the imperial presidency remains through the effective curtailment of control and through the de facto presumption of executive supremacy by the use of various law enforcement offices, such as the police, prosecutors' office, and tax office to intelligence office. This presumption has diminished with the passage of time, and was greatly reduced by the inauguration of the Roh Moo Hyun Administration in 2003.

Second, government reform initiatives in Korea tend to strengthen judicialization. Not only do judges tend toward a greater consideration of policy matters, but a juristic interpretation of the law has become an important criterion for the evaluation of government policies and actions, in both formulation and implementation. Some features of government reform, such as decentralization or privatization, require new mechanisms for enhanced accountability of public actors. Vertical administrative control mechanisms of old, based upon a centralized and well-rationalized bureaucratic hierarchy, cannot cope with decentralized, government activities as effectively as judicialization in association with professional and public accountability mechanisms.

Government reforms in Kim Dae Jung and Roh Moo Hyun administrations

Outline of the government reform process since 1998

In 1997, Kim Dae Jung won the presidential election by defeating the candidate of the Grand National Party, the successor of the longstanding ruling parties that had been in power since 1948. This was arguably the first transfer of power through election since 1948, as the earlier election of Kim Young Sam in 1992 had in large part been acted with the military and the Roh Tae Woo Administration.

To eradicate the old legacy of authoritarian rule and the immediate economic crisis, the the Kim Government proclaimed its ambition for a "second nation-building," with government reform as a key element. Strongly influenced by the New Public Management Model, the Kim Government pursued "a small but efficient and better-serving government," implemented through privatization of public services and reinvention of government organization.

The Roh Moo Hyun Administration, launched in 2003 under the motto of "participation government," shifted the Kim Government's reform agenda toward more decentralization and public participation. This did not involve the total abandonment of the market-oriented, performance-based approach to government renovation, but rather a reorientation of government reform initiatives. For example, the downsizing of government apart from public enterprises was no longer pursued, on the ground that compared to the Western countries with well-established welfare states, the size of government in Korea was relatively small.[5]

Roh designated the Presidential Committee on Government Innovation and Decentralization (PCGID) to produce the agenda for reform, and this Committee suggested ten key national goals. Five of these were related to government reform: "removing corruption in society and creating a service-oriented administration"; "realizing political reform"; "building a science- and technology-centered society"; and "decentralization and balanced regional development." To implement these goals, PCGID announced a program of participatory "transparent and effective government" with five objectives: (1) to create an efficient, streamlined, and strongly competitive government oriented towards streamlined government with strong competitiveness; (2) to craft a service-oriented government that provides quality service to the people; (3) to encourage maximum transparency; (4) to promote decentralization and shared authority and responsibility in government; and (5) to build a participatory government equally open to all. According to the road-map, 23 national agendas consisting of 150 specific tasks were divided into five categories: (1) administrative reform; (2) personnel reform; (3) financial reform; (4) decentralization; and (5) E-government.[6]

Administrative law change pertaining to government reform

Changes in government have been accompanied by changes in administrative law as the primary locus of state-society interchange. This section briefly describes these reforms in terms of the objectives and goals of administrative reform.

Efficiency

Evaluation system reform

After evaluating the government reforms of previous administrations, PCGID came to the conclusion that the evaluation system itself should be renovated in order to enhance the efficiency, effectiveness, and accountability of government functions and secure public confidence in government. It pointed out four causes of the inefficient evaluation system: (1) duplication of similar evaluation of policy and performance of each administrative office; (2) lack of long-term vision and strategy; (3) inefficient self-evaluation of each administrative office; and (4) ineffective use of evaluation result due to the lack of a consolidated performance-based management.[7] In response to these findings PCGID proposed the establishment of a consolidated evaluation system by enacting the "Basic Law for Evaluation of Government Activities" (BLEGA). BLEGA established the Government Performance Evaluation Committee (GPEC) which is co-chaired by the Prime Minister and in which a non-governmental member of the Committee is designated to conduct final deliberations and resolve outstanding issues in government performance evaluation (Art. 9 of BLEGA).

In contrast to the renovated government performance evaluation system, an internal-control mechanism, the Board of Audit and Inspection (BAI) functions as outside evaluators of government performance. The BAI carry out performance audits under the authority of the Evaluation Research Institute, newly established under the BAI Act. A new initiative, the Bill for the Audit of Public Institutions, currently pending in the National Assembly, is an attempt to make the BAI more efficient and effective in its audit process as part and parcel of the consolidated evaluation system. The thrust of this Bill lies in the separation of the legal audit from the performance audit. As per the Bill, the BAI as the supreme audit institution, changes its main task from legal audits to performance audit and evaluations while legal audits are delegated to internal inspectors.

Policy coordination reform

PCGID saw the increasing complexity of policy issues in the modern state, with its concomitant disharmony between the concerned departments and agencies, as another cause of government inefficiency and declining public confidence. In response, the Prime Ministerial Decree, "An Order for the Coordination of Administration Tasks," was enacted. According to this Order, every department intending to make a policy overlapping with other departments' mandates and references should inform and consult with the other departments. When there are conflicts between relevant departments and they fail to reach a harmonious resolution, the Prime Minister, the Minister of the designated department for relevant government matters, or the Minister of the Office for Government Policy Coordination can each, depending on the nature and severity of the difficulties, help resolve the issues. From 2003 to 2005, the policy coordination system dealt with approximately 197 cases, of which 176 cases were completely resolved.[8]

Reform for decentralized organizational design

As a result of its analysis of administrative functioning and circumstances, PCGID has adopted a view favoring decentralized organizational design as the most effective mechanism to respond to rapid changes in the administrative environment, with particular emphasis on the enhancement of the autonomy of each administrative office and flexible operation of public services. To meet these goals, the Government Organization Act was revised. In addition to reshuffling the agencies, the revision is notable for its personnel system reforms.[9] First, the Senior Public Officials Group (SPOG) system consolidated the senior public officials of each administrative office into one personnel pool. This allowed the appropriate person to be placed in any particular position, based on performance and career development, effectively abolishing the departmental personnel barrier and enhancing exchange among senior officials. SPOG is composed of "director-general or above level positions in the central government covering approximately 1,500 positions."[10] Additionally, this flexible personnel program is accompanied by an open competition system like the Open Position System,[11] the job posting system,[12] and agency flexible management. Second, each central administrative department and agency is given discretion to determine the titles for mid-level personnel. Unlike the earlier system which determined position titles based on a hierarchical grade system across the government, this new system allows the department or agency to assign officials regardless of grades, giving greater flexibility in personnel allocation. It also allows departments to organize themselves based on a total budget for personnel, rather than a specified number of staff. Third, while the Ministry of Planning and Budget controls the total budget allocated for personnel expenses under the total personnel expenditure system, each administrative office enjoys wide discretion in determining the composition of personnel as long as it falls within the total budget allocated.

Another reform aimed at increasing the autonomy of agencies can be found in the consecutive revision of the Executive Operating Agency Act (EOAA)[13] first enacted in 1999 under the Kim Dae Jung Administration. The Executive Operating Agency (EOA) is an agency that is given wider discretion in performing designated administrative functions, while the policy-making function remains within the central agency. This system facilitates the separation of policy-making and administrative functions, the introduction of an entrepreneurial culture and competition, increased discretion on the part of the executive officer, greater accountability for performance, and contractual relations as an accountability mechanism between the executive officer and department on the one hand and the executive officer and agency staff on the other.[14] The revised EOAA, modified upon the recommendation of PCGID, extends the scope[15] and autonomy of the EOA in several ways. First, there are now two categories of EOA, administrative and entrepreneurial, of which the latter has greater autonomy. Second, the executive officer is given the discretion to spend within the assigned budget. Third, the personnel quotas under certain grades are consolidated so as to increase autonomy and flexibility in organizational formation. Fourth, high-level administrative offices like *Cheongs*(Administrations at the Vice Ministerial level)[16] may be designated as EOAs.

Transparency

Information disclosure system reform

The Roh Moo Hyun Administration identifies itself as the "Participation Government." Participation requires the sharing of information necessary to form a political opinion, and as such, freedom of information is protected as one of the basic rights in democracy. As early as 1988, the Korean Constitutional Court recognized the right to know as a constitutional right based upon several articles in the Korean Constitution, including Article 21 which guarantees freedom of expression in conjunction with Article 1 which guarantees popular sovereignty, Article 10 which deals with human dignity and values, Article 34(1) which deals with the entitlement of all people to a life worthy of human beings (Art. 34(1)).[17]

However, without any implementing legislation, the right to know would have no substantive implications for the real world. On December 31, 1996, the National Assembly passed the Official Information Disclosure Act which came into effect on January 1, 1998. Between 1998 and 2003, applications for information disclosure exploded nearly seven times, from 26,086 to 192,295 requests. Although the application acceptance rate (i.e., information disclosure rate) reached almost 90 percent, people were dissatisfied with the degree and quality of information disclosure.[18] The reasons for dissatisfaction included the continuing need for secrecy to protect essential and sensitive information, the lack of specific standards for the refusal of disclosure requests, and the difficulties on the part of people in accessing the sources of information, on which to formulate requests.

PCGID recommendations for active disclosure of information by public authorities were enacted in the 2004 revision of the Official Information Disclosure Act. The main features of the 2004 revision of the Act can be summarized as follows. First, instead of the passive disclosure system of old in which information was disclosed based on an application for disclosure, the new system required (in principle) that public authorities[19] disclose certain categories of information[20] on a regular basis without request, that is, a positive disclosure system with advanced disclosure. Public authorities have a statutory obligation to prescribe the scope, method, and frequency of disclosure "in advance" (Art. 7). Second, the revision introduced a list system in which the types of information and where public authorities collect and maintain such information is accessible to the public. Third, the revision made non-disclosure available in only a narrow set of circumstances. It became both more difficult to fall under the non-disclosure category and this categorization was more strictly enforced. For example, identifiable personal information is subject to non-disclosure only if there is fear for the infringement of state secrets or of the individual's right to privacy. Information that is so classified must be prescribed in the form of statute, delegated order, and rules[21] as per Article 9(1). Fourth, the deliberation period for disclosure was reduced from fifteen to ten days (Art. 11(1)). In the event of non-disclosure, authorities must make prompt notification of the relevant applications of the fact that delineates specifically and explicitly the grounds for non-disclosure and the procedure in which to appeal the decision (Art. 13(4)). Fifth, professional participation in the decision-making process for information disclosure was strengthened so as to increase public confidence over non-disclosure decisions. The Act mandates the establishment of an Information Disclosure Council. This body deliberates on whether or not to disclose information. The Council's composition includes half that must be drawn from outside experts with an in-depth knowledge of the working of public authorities or of the work of disclosing information (Art. 12). As an attendant mechanism for increasing public confidence in non-disclosure decisions, the Minister of Government Administration and Home Affairs makes an annual report on the operation of information disclosure during the preceding year to the National Assembly before the ordinary session of the National Assembly opens (Art. 26). Sixth, the Act establishes the Presidential Information Disclosure Committee, responsible for the coordination and deliberation on matters concerning the formulation of an information disclosure policy and the improvement of the current information disclosure system, the setting of information disclosure standards, and the evaluation of the actual operational state of information disclosure by public authorities (Art. 22).

Administrative procedure law reform

Transparency in administrative procedure increases public participation while increasing public confidence in the administrative process. As early as 1996, the Administrative Procedures Law was enacted and revised substantively two times in the course of government reform. The Act provides as a general administrative procedure such standard tools as a requirement of issuing a disposition upon proper application, selective formal hearing, public hearing, pre-announcement of administrative legislation, and pre-announcement of administration.[22] In 2002, apart from some technical changes, the law was revised to strengthen the effect of such administrative processes as hearing and public hearing (Art. 35–2 and Art. 39–2). The 2007 revision contemplates a notice that concerned parties may apply for both administrative adjudication and administrative litigation (Art. 26) and stipulates procedures for public hearing (Arts. 38, 38–3, 39, 39–2).[23] It also requires public agencies to notify relevant agencies and local government and other public authorities (Art. 42(3)).

Transparency of discretion

Administrative discretion operating without legal constraint may result in bureaucratic arbitrariness contrary to the rule of law. However, wide discretion might have merit as a catalyst for industrialization: this was the claim of the developmental state model that was prevalent until the 1990s. However, as democratization and globalization has proceeded, the merits of discretion have become outweighed by its negative side-effects, including a lack of predictability of government activities and the unfairness which capricious discretion might sometimes produce.

PCGID offered two recommendations to combat the potential negative consequences of wide discretion. First, legislation and subordinate legislation should be rephrased so as to be as clear and as systematically arranged as possible. Toward that end, each Ministry is to make a master plan for consolidation and systematization of legislation under its purview. Second, with regard to new legislation, each Ministry is recommended to submit its proposed bills or regulations for review by the Ministry of Legislation.[24]

Participation

Public participation in administration

Public participation in administration takes three forms: (1) participation in the decision-making process; (2) participation in the post-decision-making process; and (3) participation in the political process affecting administration. The first category is concerned with consultation, public hearing, public access to public information, citizens' initiative, and referendum. The second category covers grievance redress, citizens' request for audit and inspection, administrative adjudication, and litigation. The third includes recall, participation in personnel committee, and civil society activity. As some reforms have been addressed here under various sections, I will focus here on reforms to foster positive public participation, such as citizens' request for audit and inspection, citizens' initiative, referendum, and recall.

Citizens' request for audit and inspection[25]

The Anti-corruption Act of 2001 introduced public participation in anti-corruption movement in the form of citizens' request for audit and inspection. Any citizen aged 20 or over may request an inspection from the Board of Audit and Inspection (BAI)[26] by presenting a petition signed by not fewer than a certain number of citizens as prescribed by the Presidential Decree when they see public organizations seriously harm public interest or their involvement in an act of corruption.[27] Whether to conduct such inspection is determined by the National Audit and Inspection Request Deliberation Commission prescribed by the Regulations of the BAI.

As far as local administration is concerned, the Local Government Act endows any citizen aged 19 or over residing within its jurisdiction with the right to request an audit and inspection from the relevant Minister in case of local government at the upper level like City and Do or from City Mayor/Do Governor in case of local government at the lower level like Si/Gun/autonomous Gu (Art. 16).

Citizens' lawsuits

Generally speaking, status as a citizen or resident does not confer a right to challenge a law or administrative action in Korea. However, in 2005, the amendment of the Local Government Act introduced a kind of citizen lawsuit similar to taxpayer lawsuits permitted in many states, though not in federal level, in the U.S.A.[28] According to the Act, the residents, having made a request for inspecting certain matters, are entitled to raise a lawsuit under certain conditions prescribed by the Act against the unlawful acts or the fact of neglect related to the matters requested for inspection against the head of relevant local government. The object of lawsuits include those matters concerning: (1) the payment of public money; (2) the acquisition, management, and disposition of property; (3) the conclusion and execution of contract for trade, lease, undertaking, and others with the partner of competent local government; and (4) the neglect of imposition and collection of public money, such as local tax, fees for use, service charge, and fine for default. The conditions contemplated by the Act are the delay of inspection requested, residents' dissatisfaction with the result of inspection requested or with the implement of the request for measures, the failure on the part of the relevant head of local government of execution of the request for measures made by the relevant upper authorities.[29]

Resident lawsuits take four forms: (1) lawsuits demanding a suspension of the whole or part of the relevant acts; (2) lawsuits demanding a cancelation or alteration of the relevant acts; (3) lawsuits demanding a confirmation of unlawfulness of particular actions or omissions; and (4) lawsuits demanding compensation for damages or making a request for a return of unlawful gains by local government actors or other related parties.

One notable criticism is that the request for audit and inspection as a preliminary condition for a resident lawsuit is too narrow a requirement.

Citizens' participation in budget-making process

In the Korean Constitution, the power to make a budget plan is exclusively given to the executive (Art. 54(2)), though the power of final decision on the budget is given to the National Assembly. If public participation in budget-making process were to be permitted, transparency and efficiency of budget may be enhanced. To this end, the Local Government Finance Act of 2005 introduced a system of residents' participation in the budget-making process by permitting the head of local government to allow for residents' participation in the budget-making process as prescribed by Presidential Decree. The Enabling Order of the Local Government Finance Act contemplates public hearing, informal talk, on-line or off-line questionnaires, public subscription for project, and so on.

It is a sign of progress that there is a legal basis for citizens' input into budget-making. However, this mechanism is not sufficient because its success depends entirely on introduction by the head of local government.

Citizens' initiatives

Citizens' initiatives are an important method for fostering popular participation in government, especially as a complement to representative democracy. Although no citizens' initiatives have yet been introduced in central administration and politics, the Local Government Act of 1999 provides for citizens' ability to request enactment and revision/abolition of municipal ordinances (Art. 15). Although it has a statutory basis, such requests can only be introduced if each local assembly enacts enabling municipal legislation. The request itself is legally binding only if the citizen garners the signatures of between 1/50 and 1/20 of all the residents 19 years of age or older. In addition, certain subjects are excluded from the object of citizens' request. They include those matters involving violating Acts and subordinate statutes; related to the imposition/collection or reduction/exemption of local taxes, user fees, commission, charges; and relating to the establishment/alteration of administrative structure or matters in opposition to establishment of public facilities.

Referendum

Referendum has become increasingly popular in modern democracy as the deficiencies of representative democracy come under attack. The Korean Constitution introduces referendum in only two cases: on the one hand, in the stage of final confirmation of constitutional revision and, on the other hand, when the President proposes referendum on policies concerning foreign affairs, reunification, and so on.

In 2004, however, the Local Government Act prescribes residents' voting on the proposal of the heads of local governments regarding major matters which have caused an excessive burden, or have a significant effects on residents (Art. 13–2(1)). The Residents' Voting Act of 2004 is a special Act designated by the Local Government Act to provide the object, requirements for proposal, and procedure, and so on. of the residents' voting. The object of the Act is divided into two categories: matters related to local government's functions and national policies concerning establishment/alteration of local government or establishment of public facilities. The latter is different from the former in two ways. The latter, first, has merely a consultative character with no binding force and, second, only the relevant Minister of central government is entitled to make an initiative. As far as the former is concerned, three kinds of initiatives are provided: by the heads of local governments; by the local assemblies with a strict majority rule, with the attendance of more than one half of the total members, and with a concurrent vote of two-thirds or more of the members present; and by residents with the joint signature of the majority of residents not less than 19 years of age as determined by the Presidential Decree, within the scope between no less than 1/20 and no more than 1/5 of the total residents of the area. Generally, two criticisms have been raised: first, the objective of residents' voting is too limited to facilitate public participation in administration and politics; second, the requirement of joint signature for a motion of residents' voting is too restrictive.[30]

Recall

Recall is a sort of direct democratic procedure by which citizens can oust their representatives from office.[31] It is different from referendum or citizen initiatives in that it presupposes indirect democracy, that is, representative democracy. At the constitutional level, Korea does not have a recall system. However, there has been a strong demand from civil society for the introduction of recall because the cartelized professional politicians tend to ignore their constituents and to easily become corrupt. As a matter of fact, the Special Act for Decentralization based upon PCGID's recommendation provides that "the State and Local Governments shall make efforts to strengthen residents' direct participation system such as the residents' recall system" (Art. 14).

Responding to this increasing social and political demand, the National Assembly passed the Residents' Recall Act in 2006, which came into effect in May 2007. According to the Act, residents with the joint signature of more than 10 percent (in the case of City Mayor or Do Governor), 15 percent (in the case of the lowest local government), or 20 percent (in the case of members of local assemblies) of local residents may give rise to petitions for the recall of the heads of local government or members of local assemblies[32] (Art. 7). If the votes for recall become a majority based upon a quorum of one-third or more, the heads or representatives can be removed from their offices (Art. 22). In the course of the recall process, the powers of the relevant local leaders are to be suspended (Art. 21). However, petitions for recall are not allowed when less than one year has passed since the beginning of the term or the previous recall election, or less than one year remains in the term (Art. 8).

As soon as the law came into effect, the first case was brought up in August 2007. The Mayor of Hanam City, a southern satellite city of Seoul, became the first target of recall under the new system. The recall activists challenged the Mayor's plan to introduce a public crematorium. However, on September 13, 2007, a week before the voting date, recall voting was suspended by the court. The court invalidated the recall petition on the grounds that it failed to meet the required number of joint signatures as some signatures failed to include a written reason for the petition as required by law. The court stated that having unlimited ability to recall without stating reasons would make local democracy unstable instead of upgrading it.

Ombudsman

Ombudsman refers to a state official or agency that controls administrative activity in the interests of the citizen by providing a safeguard against maladministration. The Korean Ombudsman system has two major functions: inspection and redress of grievances. A clear-cut differentiation between the two is impossible especially as the two functions sometimes overlap with each other. The function of inspection is mainly undertaken by the Board of Audit and Inspection (BAI)[33] while the function of grievance redress is by the Ombudsman of Korea. BAI's mandate covers not only inspection but also audit, and the inspections tend to focus on improper administration in general rather than direct protection of the people. Thus, the Ombudsman's office was set up as a distinct office, initialy in 1994 to cope with public grievances, based upon the Basic Law Governing Administrative Regulations and Civil Petition Affairs.

However, its institutional independence was in doubt and public participation in processing their complaints was very restricted. PCGID recommended the expansion of Ombudsman to enhance transparency and fairness of administration by strengthening public participation in the grievance redress system. In response to this recommendation, the Ombudsman of Korea Establishment and Operation Act 2005 was enacted.

According to this Act, the Ombudsman system became a dual system, with a National Ombudsman administration serving as the statutory agency responsible for redressing public grievances and improving the administrative process, while Citizen Ombudsman agencies were set up in each local government, to check local administration with the support of the National Ombudsman. The National Ombudsman Agency was shifted from a Prime Ministerial agency to a Presidential one, and its independence in terms of personnel management and function was improved. To facilitate public complaints, the Act endows the Ombudsman with power to make recommendation for improving improper administration to the National Assembly and the President and relevant administrative offices, to report on special matters within its mandate to the President and the National Assembly, and to refer complaints to the BAI for thorough audit and inspection (Arts. 37 to 40).

What is notable in the new Ombudsman system apart from institutional changes is the strengthened participation-reinforcing system. First, mediation between those grieved and the concerned administrative office is introduced when there are a plurality of parties involved or there are high social consequences expected. Second, the public's access to the Ombudsman is improved by providing an on-line portal specialized for government grievances and extending the Ombudsman's mandate to cover the role of collection and distribution of information regarding grievance redress overall for administrative offices.

E-Government

E-Government involves every aspect of government reform thus far described: efficiency, transparency, and participation together with accountability—which in turn will be touched upon later in the course of discussing judicialization.

As a matter of fact, E-Government has become one of main points on the agenda for public sector reform across the whole globe in the 1990s[34] in the wake of the information revolution pre-1980.[35] Korea was not an exception. The computer revolution pushed Korean government to undertake automation of material tasks in the 1970s and build up five national networks—administration, finance, education and research, defense, and security—in the 1980s.

This information infrastructure led to the foundation of the Information Super-Highway and the establishment of the Ministry of Information and Communications as a key driving force for E-Government within governmental structure in 1990s. In 1995, the Framework on Informatization Promotion Act was enacted, which paved the way for the launch of official government homepages and Internet-based public service such as real estate registration in 1998. Finally, in 2001, the National Assembly driven by the Kim Dae Jung Administration's active plan for E-Government passed the first comprehensive legislation on E-Government, the Promotion of Digitalization of Administrative Works for E-Government Realization Act. The basic contents of this Act included computerization of administrative management, computerization of civil service facing citizens, and reduction of documentation service.

This first E-Government legislation was successfully implemented and was succeeded by the Roh Government's vision of developing "the World's Most Open E-Government." The Roh Government's E-Government policy became much more concretized to 31 tasks which in turn contemplated 45 subtasks.[36] In 2007, the National Assembly amended the long title of the Promotion of Digitalization of Administrative Works for E-Government Realization Act to the simple title, the E-Government Act, and in so doing, several amendments were added.[37] The amendments were made to enhance information security, to enhance the protection of personal information, and to evaluate performance in relation to informatization, and to promote informatization projects by administrative offices, international relations on E-Government and the cooperation of information officers of all public authorities.

Summary

Government reform in Korea during the last decade has changed not only the ideals and practices of public administration but also the legal regime governing administration. Values underlying government reform range from efficiency, transparency, participation to accountability. To put these values into effect in public administration, wide dimensions of institutional, organizational, procedural, operational transformations at national and local levels have taken place. Accompanying these changes, a legal regime that featured a developmental state was replaced by that of a regulatory state, which in turn is evolving into a new governance model.[38]

A legal regime based upon a governance model represents a dynamic, reflexive and flexible paradigm where the relationship between the governed and the governors becomes interdependent rather than oppressive. It features empowerment of individuals and social groups, cooperative competition of administrative actors, public participation in the decision-making process, organizational and personnel flexibility of administrative agencies, diversity of administrative actions, open and good administration, decentralization and autonomy or self-regulation of subordinate actors, and performance orientation of administrative actions.

Judicialization and government reform in Korea

The transformation of the legal regime accompanying government reform reflects not only the change of organization and function of public administration but also the change of dispute resolution paradigms in public law. The role of the judiciary in relation to public administration expands, as well as new trends toward extra-judicial dispute resolution. This change is a reflection of another important attribute of good governance, governmental accountability.

Accountability and judicialization

Accountability, as Professor Dawn Oliver puts it,

> "has been said to entail being liable to be required to give an account or explanation of actions and, where appropriate, to suffer the consequences, take the blame or undertake to put matters right if it should appear that errors have been made."[39]

In modern constitutional states, democracy and the protection of human rights require administrative offices to give effect to such values and principles. One tool to accomplish this requirement is accountability of administrative actors. Accountability, in Professor Oliver's terms, can be divided into four categories depending upon four classes of body; accountees such as politicians, the public, the courts, and a range of auditors: political, public, legal, and administrative accountabilities.[40]

The structure or operation of traditional government, featuring centralized, control-oriented, secrecy-driven bureaucratic hierarchy, matches up little accountability on the part of bureaucrats partly because traditional public law system tends to provide simple, limited accountability mechanism. The traditional public law system heavily depends upon political accountability which itself tends to focus on very limited, big social issues which can easily attract wide public attention rather than ordinary matters of civil services. Legal accountability is also limited, though definitely not meaningless, because judges tend to restrain themselves from policy matters and as a result public authorities tend to enjoy wide discretion. Administrative accountability, the essence of which lies in audit and inspection, tends to lack independence in its function, on the one hand, and on the other, to narrow down the scope of accountability to the matters of financial accounts. Public accountability does not have much room in the traditional accountability systems because, generally speaking, it is public authorities that are responsible for administrative activities, and because the public is supposed to have no standing in the administrative process unless they are personally affected in legal terms, the public has little say.

Government reform, accompanied with a regulatory or governance model in which government observes and promotes such values as transparency, efficiency, effectiveness, and participation forces a transformation in the old regime of accountability. Our focus here is legal or quasi-legal accountability, that is, judicialization.

Basic ideas and political backgrounds of judicialization in Korea

The rule of law, an essential element of constitutionalism, is a principle under which administrative bodies must be subject to the law. According to the Korean Constitution, in particular Article 37(2), any actions of the state power should have a statutory basis, and abide by the principle of proportionality.[41] To implement this, the Korean Constitution provides not only for administrative adjudication and litigation but also constitutional adjudication through the mechanism of constitutional complaints.

This normative ideal and institution of the rule of law makes judges supreme controllers of all government powers. For example, they may be able to decide whether or not legislation or delegated legislation should be struck down because it is contrary to constitutional law or human rights, whether or not the actions of a public body may be cancelled on the ground that they are in contradiction with constitutional law or statute, whether the President and other high-level administrative and judicial officials should be removed from their offices because their activities encroach upon constitutional law or statutory law.

However, the dictates of reality make this ideal merely a daydream because judges constrain themselves or give in to coercive political pressures. On the one hand, judges might think that it is inappropriate for them to decide policy matters in legal terms because they lack professional knowledge and experience of policy matters. On the other, authoritarian rule or despotism associated with the developmental state has hindered judges from becoming involved in social or economic policy issues.[42]

The latter phenomenon has been consistently eroded in the course of democratization, and judges have expanded their purview. What is of importance to see is that as the pendulum swings the other way, another problem emerges. A legalistic approach begins to become favored so that matters once dealt with through administrative or political processes are increasingly brought before the courts. The judiciary in the broadest sense, including the Constitutional Court, has taken an activist position in a number of controversial cases where delicate political interests are involved.

One of the factors providing space for legalist judicial activism in recent years is the public's attitude toward or confidence in various public actors, that is, legislative, administrative, and judicial branches. In the course of democratization, the Korean public demonstrated relatively low levels of confidence in all state branches compared to actors in private sector. Among the three branches, however, the judiciary has enjoyed a relatively higher evaluation, though the judiciary has been one of the main targets of reform, an important agenda in Korean society since 1987. The public prefers the seemingly neutral decisions of the courts over the politicians and bureaucrats who led the developmental state and are now viewed as corrupt. Another factor may be what some perceive to be Koreans' peculiar tendency to prefer a clear-cut result by exhausting every possible ways, political or legal, to achieve their goals rather than take a middle way to compromise differences.

Judicialization in context

This section identifies illustrative cases, as well as providing statistics and accounts of institutional reforms to document the extent of judicialization of administrative governance in Korea.

Cases

Saemangeum Reclamation Project case

In May 16, 2006, the Supreme Court ended a five-year lawsuit in favor of the government in a controversial administrative case.[43] Thanks to the court's decision, the government resumed construction work on what is called the Saemangeum Reclamation Project, originally planned to transform 40,100 hectares of mudflats in coastal areas in *Cheonbuk* (North Cholla) Province into farmland and a freshwater reservoir. This 15-year national project, budgeted to cost 2.5 trillion won ($2.2 billion), had to endure on-and-off construction because of different decisions between the Seoul Administrative Court and the Appellate Court. In 2001, more than 3,500 residents and environmental activists challenged the project on environmental grounds before the Seoul Administrative Court, which first suspended the Project in 2003. In an appeal by the defendant, the Ministry of Agriculture and Forestry and the Prime Minister, the Seoul Appellate Court defied the lower court's decision and the construction work was resumed in 2004. However, it was suspended once again by the Seoul Administrative Court in a retrial in 2005 when about 85 percent of the budget had already been spent and 92 percent of the construction work had been completed, with only 2.7 kilometers of the total 33-kilometer-long seawall left to complete. In December 2005, the Appellate Court once again reversed the lower court's decision of suspension and finally the case was referred to the Supreme Court.

The main issues at stake in the Supreme Court were two: first, whether or not procedural defects in the decision-making process can render the whole project void; and second, whether or not the reclamation project would cause an environmental disaster without countervailing economic merits. On both counts, 11 Justices out of 13 including the Chief Justice answered in the negative.

Two implications of this case deserve to be mentioned here. First, the courts did not restrain themselves from becoming involved in policy matters. They took an active role in determining whether a major national project with a huge budget was discordant with the law or legal principles. Second, the courts made it clear that there would be a certain limit on discretion on the part of administrative offices, and established standards of judicial review.

The "Salamander" case

In 2003, environmental activists filed a lawsuit demanding an injunction to block construction of a roughly 13-kilometer-long tunnel through Mt. Cheonseong, south of Daegu in South-East Korea, on the high-speed railroad. This case became prominent for two reasons. First, salamanders that inhabit, Mt. Cheonseong's highland swamps would be affected and were joined by "their friends" as parties to the case against the Korea Railway Facilities Corp in 2004. Both the Ulsan District Court in the first instance and the Busan Appellate Court found that salamanders were not entitled to standing, because they are merely "natural things" entitled to no legal personality. The plaintiffs appealed to the Supreme Court which confirmed the lower court's decisions in 2006. Second, a two-month hunger strike by an environmentalist Buddhist nun called Jiyul drew media attention and even the Prime Minister intervened to help arbitrate between environmentalist groups and the Corporation.

Ultimately, the Supreme Court dismissed the plaintiff's argument that the right to environment protected by Article 35 of the Constitution provides a direct cause of action for injunctive relief, and that the plaintiff's environmental interests were infringed by the construction work. Although this case is a civil law injunction case and because the defendant was a private entity in the Korean legal system, the issue at stake is, like the Saemangeum Reclamation Project case, how to weigh environmental interests against development interests in administrative decision-making. Both cases show how the courts have begin to play a much more active role in the decision-making process in Korea.

Statistics

As Table 6.1 shows, the amount of administrative litigation in the first instance increased by around four times between 1998 and 2005. Although the exact reasons for the increase of administrative litigation need to be examined in detail, it would be safe to say from these statistics that more and more administration is checked by the courts in terms of legal accountability. Furthermore, as we see in the salamanders case, there are likely many more cases which are not categorized as administrative litigation because a private entity is the object of the litigation, although the nature of the case is in reality no different from administrative cases.

Institutions

Another factor indicating judicialization is institutional change. Our focus here is two-fold: increasing quasi-judicial committees involved public law matters, on the one hand, and on the other, administrative litigation law reform to expand jurisdiction.

Table 6.1 Administrative litigations in the first instance in Korea: 1998–2005

Years	Total	For plaintiff	For agency	For both in part	Withdrawal	Others	Increase
1998	3,198	653	1,201	91	990	263	N/A
1999	8,174	1,855	3,268	298	2,174	579	4,976
2000	8,309	1,579	3,344	291	2,512	583	135
2001	10,635	1,736	4,014	337	3,880	668	2,326
2002	11,482	1,698	4,326	426	4,523	509	847
2003	10,799	1,631	4,259	386	4,110	413	−683
2004	11,997	1,789	4,887	478	4,217	626	1,198
2005	13,360	1,673	5,709	517	4,500	961	1,363

Source: Supreme Court Judicial Statistics.[44]

Increasing quasi-judicial committees

Traditionally, Koreans have preferred social dispute resolution mechanisms rather than resorting to judicial processes because of the strong influences of tradition, custom and group morality. Even in the 1960s and 1970s, surveys found that Koreans' modern legal consciousness was not high.[45] However, a survey in 1994 painted a different picture. A litigation explosion was underway, and Koreans were deemed litigious. The 1994 survey presumed that the increase in legal consciousness was a result of the increased "rights consciousness" associated with democratization and decreased confidence in legislative and administrative authority (Park, G. J., 1998: 95).[46]

However, the increase of litigation has given rise to delay of judicial process and unsatisfactory judicial service so that there has been a strong demand for Alternative Dispute Resolution (ADR) not only in private law but also in public law areas. ADR in Korean public law in general includes administrative adjudication, mediation, and arbitration.

Article 107(3) of the Korean Constitution guarantees administrative adjudication as a preliminary dispute resolution mechanism, though it is not compulsory for the individual affected by administrative actions or inactions to exhaust it before raising administrative litigation. Most administrative offices establish administrative adjudication committees within their hierarchical organization as an appeal process challenging administrative actions. As far as central government offices and local governments are concerned, the Administrative Adjudication Committee instituted under the Prime Minister is in charge of that function. This Committee deals with around 20,000 applications every year, which has been increased five times since 1998 as shown in Table 6.2. Thanks to the E-Government project, individuals can submit adjudication requests online and track cases to see where they are in the process. There is also the Administrative Adjudication Act that defines the process and basic principles regarding administrative adjudication, delegated to the National Assembly as per Article 107(3) of the Constitution. The same provision also sets up one constitutional guideline for the legislature to follow in making the Act: the administrative adjudication process should be in conformity with the principles of judicial procedures.

Many public laws have now introduced mediation as a mechanism for resolving disputes.[47] Table 6.3 shows the situation.

Arbitration has been introduced in the areas of press law and labor relations. For example, the Press Arbitration Commission has been set up under the Government Information Agency and an Arbitration Committee affiliated to the Labor Relations Commission under the Ministry of Labor. As a matter of fact, most arbitration and mediation established under public law are designed to resolve private interest disputes, except pure public law disputes such as local government disputes or environmental disputes. For this reason, some argue that ADR under public law involving private disputes does too much harm to party autonomy, and the increasing use of ADR would harm the original judicial function.[48] However, it should be borne in mind that ADR in public law enhances participation of the

Table 6.2 Administrative adjudication in the ACC Korea: 1998–2006

Year	Application	Deliberation/judgment				Rate of acceptance (%)	Withdrawal/ transfer
		Subtotal	For the plaintiff	For the agency	Dismissal		
1996	3,991	3,346	1,455	1,770	121	43.5	100
1997	8,131	7,231	2,779	4,102	350	38.4	85
1998	6,855	7,336	2,423	4,657	256	33.0	118
1999	8,028	8,055	2,066	5,589	400	25.6	76
2000	9,226	8,844	1,900	6,266	678	21.5	128
2001	12,692	12,252	2,891	8,624	737	23.6	106
2002	11,725	10,678	2,175	7,858	645	20.4	576
2003	13,831	13,165	2,501	10,028	636	18.9	281
2004	20,082	19,114	3,372	14,945	797	17.6	526
2005	22,292	21,131	3,102	17,157	872	14.6	884
2006	19,540	18,590	2,958	15,037	595	15.9	480

Source: The Administrative Adjudication Committee homepage in Korean.
(www.simpan.go.kr/index.jsp)

Table 6.3 Mediation institution in Korea

Commission	Affiliated ministry
Local government dispute resolution commission	The ministry of government administration & home affairs
Medical examination and mediation commission	The ministry of health & welfare
Employment equality commission	The ministry of labor
Construction dispute resolution commission	The ministry of construction & transportation
Patent rights deliberation and mediation commission	The ministry of culture & tourism
Program deliberation and mediation commission	The ministry of information & technology
Environmental dispute resolution commission	The ministry of environment
Labor relations commission	The ministry of labor
Electronic commerce dispute resolution commission	The ministry of commerce, industry, & energy
Mediation committee of the national human rights commission, mutual aid dispute resolution commission	The ministry of construction
Consumer dispute mediation commission	The Korea consumer agency
Personal information protection dispute mediation commission	The Korea information security agency

Source: Reorganized by the author but basically based on Kim E. (2006: 194–195).

public in administration and dispute resolution and it is the very parties that can and should decide what are their best interests in dispute resolution.[49]

Administrative litigation law reform

In recent years, administrative litigation law reform is taken on board in academia and practice. The Administrative Litigation Act (ALA) was enacted first in 1951 and permitted very limited appeals challenging administrative actions. As the society developed, ALA was considerably revised in 1984 to extend the scope of administrative litigation and rationalization of the process. What is notable is the introduction of litigation for affirmation of nullity (litigation instituted to seek the affirmation of effectiveness or ineffectiveness and the existence or non-existence of a disposition or other act by an administrative agency) and litigation for affirmation of illegality of an omission (litigation instituted to affirm the illegality of an omission despite the legal obligation to act on the part of an administrative agency). In addition, citizens' lawsuits and agency litigation have a clear and separate legal basis according to ALA 1984. In 1994, another revision of ALA took place in that administrative adjudication is transformed from a compulsory preliminary procedure to optional procedure before administrative litigation and a special court for administrative litigation in the first instance may be established.

However, there has been increasing vocal calls to expand the scope of administrative litigation to enhance legal accountability and protection of citizens' rights, and to resolve procedural difficulties associated with administrative as opposed to civil litigation. To respond to this demand, in 2002 the Supreme Court set up a Committee for ALA Revision and gave to it the special terms of reference to analyze problems of ALA and to propose solutions. The Committee produced a number of recommendations in 2004. These recommendations include the introduction of litigation for mandamus, preventive injunction, provisional injunction, the power to request for administrative materials, the permission to change the form of action between administrative and civil litigation, the expansion of the scope of appeals to cover delegated legislation, and the expansion of the standing of appeals litigation from those with directly concerned legal interests to those with legal interests regardless of direct administrative relationships. However, the recommendation of a Supreme Court Committee failed to get through the National Assembly.

In the meantime, the Ministry of Justice (MOJ) also recognized the need for ALA reform and set up a Special Sectional Committee for ALA Revision in 2006 and recommended a number of proposals in May 2007.[50] These recommendations will be examined via public hearings[51] and debates and then the final revision bill will be submitted to the National Assembly in September 2007. The focus of the MOJ's recommendation is basically similar to that of the Supreme Court's proposals in that litigation for mandamus, preventive injunction, provisional injunction, the power to request for administrative materials, and the permission of the change of the form of action between administrative and civil litigations are introduced. However, MOJ's proposal rejects – above all – the expansion of appeals litigation which has caused an informal conflict between the Supreme Court and the Constitutional Court. At the present constitutional adjudication system, the Constitutional Court has competence to review the constitutionality of delegated legislation in the form of constitutional complaints. However, if the Supreme Court's proposal to expand appeals litigation to delegated legislation is put into practice, the Constitutional Court loses such a power owing to the exhaustion rule[52] plus the statutory prohibition of constitutional complaints challenging judicial decisions according to Article 68(1) of the Constitutional Court Act. Let alone the informal objection of the Constitutional Court, the expansion of appeals litigation has worried some commentators and public officials because it would allow judges too much power to control administrative actions.

Conclusion

I have tried to describe what is taking place in Korea with regard to government reform, public law, and judicialization, along with their legal and political implications. The Korean case demonstrates that a program of government reform requires a new mechanism for enhancing accountability of public actors and thus legal accountability is implicated. These dynamics are not peculiar to Korea but universal in most contemporary democracies. Although these topics are not unique, the causes stem from peculiarities embedded in constitutional arrangements, socio-political and legal cultures particular to Korea. For example, the increasing importance of legal accountability or judicialized governance may be a universal trend, but both their institutional and cultural backgrounds and results could not be the same or similar, despite the commonalities.

As far as Korea is concerned, it should be stressed that apart from universal causes of judicialization such as the rationalization of administrative process, the lack of popular confidence in administration and political parties, or politicians and administrators' avoidance of their responsibilities, political motivation and special interests have played an important role in the acceleration of reform. Democratization produces political diversity. Political diversity increases political instability, which is a threat to the vested politics that has dominated the past 60 years of Korea's modern political history. A political confederation between the old political elites, bureaucrats, and privileged businesses is on the brink of deconstruction, or at least significant readjustment. The mantra of the rule of law might be the last but best resort for the vested interests, especially in the business sector or politics, to defy democratic reforms. What makes this more attractive for the vested in business sector is that the Korean judiciary is arguably one of the most elitist and economically conservative organizations around. Judges are those who passed the notoriously hard state judicial/bar exam, which has produced only 1,000 qualified candidates since 2001. Their personal ambition tends to center on promotion to higher level posts in the judicial career system. The career system is a centralized judicial administration system at the top of which lies the Judicial Administration Office belonging to the Supreme Court.

Furthermore, the Korean Constitution institutionalizes constitutional review of legislation and subordinate legislation. It means that even legislation itself can be void according to judicial interpretation of the Constitution or statutes. In this constitutional arrangement, without preliminary or parallel reform of the judiciary toward decentralization and democratization, democracy itself can be in danger. Judicialization is an ambivalent phenomenon. On the one hand, it can control the abuse of political and administrative powers in the direction of protecting human rights and other constitutional values, thereby enhancing constitutionalism. On the other hand, judicialization can distort democratic visions enshrined in the Constitution by replacing constitutional values with the preferences of a small group of unaccountable judges in the bench. The ambivalence of judicialization persuades us to take a middle route. The judicial powers are entitled to review political and administrative decisions but only on certain conditions and in a self-contained manner. Such conditions include democratic constitution of the judicial powers, prudential exercise of judicial powers based upon persuasive reasoning and rationales, and the reservation of the critical public sphere for the judicial powers. To reiterate once again, the judges are not in a good position to determine which policy is better in a micro decision-making process, and they are better in determining what the Constitution and law prohibits or permits, that is, the boundary setting within which the autonomous actors in political and administrative sphere can decide the best policy and interests. To avoid charges of juristocracy, judicialized governance should envisage a transition from a developmental state toward a regulatory state or new governance stage, in the context of Koreans' quest for more perfect constitutional democracy.

Notes

1 Song, Hee Joon, *Building E-Government through Reform*, Seoul: Ewha Womans University Press, 2004, ch.1.
2 J. Kim, "From the Bureaucratic State to the Contracting State?: Evaluating Kim Dae Jung Administration's Government Reinvention Policy", *Korean Journal of Law and Society*, no.20, 2001, pp.67–95; J. S. Kang, *Understandings on Government Innovation: The Participatory Government's Innovation Strategy and Logic of Practice*, Seoul: Korea Institute of Public Administration, 2005.
3 National Computerization Agency, *National Informatization Whitepaper*, 2005.
4 A recent example of this trend of judicialization is President Roh Moo Hyun's decision to file a constitutional complaint to the Constitutional Court in June 2007. He challenged the National Election Commission's finding that a series of speeches breached the neutrality obligation of public servants required by the Election Law.
5 J. H. Eun, A Study on the Korean Participatory Government's Strategy of Reinventing Government, Seoul: Korea Institute of Public Administration, 2005.
6 PIGID White Paper, *Administrative Reform of the Participatory Government*, Seoul: PCGID, 2005.
7 Ibid., pp.31–2.
8 Ibid., p.168.
9 See, for example, the creation of the Defense Acquisition Program Administration belonging to the Minister of Defense, the upgrading of the Korea Meteorological Administration and Korea National Statistical Office to a vice ministerial agency, the

10 Namkoong, Keun, "Civil Service Reform in the Participatory Government: Civil Service System in Transition", at PCGID homepage.
11 This system, introduced in 1999 and legally enforceable, is one in which the government is encouraged to recruit a certain percentage of professionals from the private sector human resource pool.
12 This system, introduced during the Kim Dae Jung Administration, is an intra-competitive recruitment program in which an administrative office voluntarily designates job posting positions for which only career civil servants can apply.
13 The revision has taken place a total of five times, three of which were during the Roh Government in 2004, 2005, and 2006.
14 Korean EOA models *executive agency* of the U.K., *crown entity* of New Zealand, *special operating agency* of Canada, *business unit* of Department of Administrative Services of Australia, *performance-based organization* of the U.S.A, all of which were popular in the name of government reform in late twentieth century. See: Y. Choi, *A Study on Governance System in a Transition era*, Seoul: Korea Institute of Public Administration, 2005, p.79. However, it should be borne in mind that the status and scope of function of these agencies vary partly due to different administrative law and history.
15 The number of EOA was increased from 10 in 2000 to 44 as of June 2007 in Korea.
16 According to the Government Organization Act, central administrative departments and agencies in principle divided into three categories: *Bus* (Ministries), *Cheos* (Ministries at the Agencies-Ministerial level), and *Cheongs* (Administrations at the Vice Ministerial level). There are 18 *Bus*, 4 *Cheos*, 18 *Cheongs* as of June 2007. The first EOA at *Cheong* level is the Intellectual Property Office, under the Ministry of Commerce, Industry and Energy, which became EOA in 2006.
17 KCC, 88Hun-Ma22, Sep. 4, 1989.
18 PCGID, op. cit., p.242.
19 According to the Act, public authorities include state agency, local government, government-invested institutions provided for in Article 2 of the Framework Act on the Management of Government-Invested Institutions and other institutions prescribed as such by the Presidential Decree (Art. 2 (3)).
20 At present, information falls under this category when it is information pertaining to any policy that has a substantial impact on the life of the people; information pertaining to any work or any project, and so on. which is undertaken under a state policy and requires the spending of a significant amount of money; information that is needed to perform the administrative overseeing of detailed budget spending and project evaluation outcome; and other information that is prescribed by the heads of public authorities (Art. 7(1)).
21 Delegated orders and rules are limited by the Act to the rules of the National Assembly, the rules of the Supreme Court, the rules of the Constitutional Court, the rules of the National Election Commission, the Presidential Decree and municipal or local ordinances (Art. 9(1)).
22 Apart from this general administrative procedure law, a number of special laws provide public participation in decision-making, such as opinion-gathering, public hearing, consultation, influence evaluation, and so on. For example, the Basic Law for Environmental Policy provides influence evaluation, opinion-gathering, public hearing, and the National Land Planning and Use Act contemplates public hearing, opinion-gathering, public notice.
23 What is outstanding in this procedural change is the introduction of electronic public hearing with condition of parallel off-line public hearing (Art. 38–2).
24 PCGID, op. cit., pp.259–64.
25 The National Assembly as the representative of people is also entitled to request to the BAI audit and inspection pursuant to the National Assembly Act Art. 127–2.

26 To safeguard the required independence, request for audit and inspection with regard to the administrative affairs executed by the National Assembly, courts, the Constitutional Court, Election Commissions, or the Board of Audit and Inspection should be made to the heads of the concerned institutions.
27 There are statutory exceptions from citizens' request for audit and inspection, which include matters pertaining to (1) national security and confidential information, (2) the appropriateness of an investigation, trial, and execution of penalty, and (3) private right relationship or individual privacy.
28 Hall, Daniel, *Administrative Law – Bureaucracy in a Democracy*, Upper Saddle River, NJ: Pearson Prentice-Hall, 2006.
29 See generally: I. Ham, "A Study on the Object of the Residents' Lawsuit", *Public Law*, vol.34, no.4–1, 2006, pp.27–53.
30 E. J. Kim, *A Study of Administrative Law and Participatory Governance*, Seoul: Ewha Womans University Ph.D. dissertation, 2006, pp.179–80.
31 J. Kil, "A Legal Study on Residents' Recall", *Public Law*, vol.34, no.1, 2006, pp.55–92.
32 Members of local assemblies elected by a proportional election system are excluded from the recall system (Art. 7).
33 The Korea Independent Commission Against Corruption (KICAC) is a presidential agency established in 2002 pursuant to the Anti-Corruption Act of 2001 that is functionally independent and serves to improve laws and institutions so as to prevent as well as weed-out corruption through the formulation and implementation of anti-corruption policies and specialized inspection. This corruption policy and inspection system provides both protection and rewards for whistleblowers, the first in Korean legal history.
34 It was known that the term "Electronic Government" first appeared in the Clinton Administration's report for government reform, titled "Creating a Government that Works Better and Costs Less: From Red Tapes to Results". MOGAHA, *The 2005 Annual Report for E-Government*, Seoul: MOGAHA, 2006, p.12.
35 Song, op. cit.
36 Specific indicators of success of this vision include: an 85 percent increase in online public services; top ten global ranking for business support competiveness; reduction in civil service applicants to three per year; an increase in utilization of E-Government programs to 60 percent. E-Government. MOGAHA, op. cit., p.13.
37 K. Cheon, "Legal Problems on the Establishment of the E-Government", *Study on the American Constitution*, vol.18, no.1, 2007, pp.81–117; J. K. Kim, "A Study on the Administrative Law Issues of the E-Government", *Public Law*, vol.35, no.1, 2006, pp.145–83.
38 For various models, see: Ginsburg, Tom, "Judicialization of Administrative Governance: Causes, Consequences and Limits", paper presented in International Conference on "Administrative Law and Judicialized Governance in Asia: Comparative Perspectives" organized by Center for Comparative and Public Law, University of Hong Kong, 2007.
39 Oliver, Dawn, *Constitutional Reform in the UK*, Oxford: Oxford University, 2003, p.48.
40 Ibid., ch.3.
41 KCC, 89Hun-Ga95, Sep. 3, 1990.
42 J. Kim, "Tasks and Perspectives of the Korean Presidential System: With focus on Roh Moo Hyun Administration(1)", *Horits Jiho*, vol.77, no.8, 2005b, pp.99–105.
43 Supreme Court, 2006Du330, May 16, 2006.
44 Statistics from 2002 can be traced in Korean at the Supreme Court Homepage (http://www.scourt.go.kr/justicesta/JusticestaListAction.work?gubun=10).
45 J. Kim, op. cit., 2005b.
46 G. J. Park, 1988. "Dispute Resolution System in Korean Legal Culture", *Yonsei Law Review*, 8:79–112.

47 It is also noticeable that de facto mediation is used more and more recently even without a legal basis in administrative adjudication and litigation process. In addition, to rationalize the administrative process and to enhance "cooperative administration" by institutionalizing conflict influence evaluation, conflict mediation meetings and/or councils, a Basic Bill for Conflict Management of Public Authorities was submitted to the National Assembly in 2005 but failed to be enacted. See generally N. Kim, "Mediation in Public Law as a Means of Conflict Management", *Public Law*, vol.31, no.4–2, 2006, pp.209–34.
48 Another critique is that the mediation is lacking independence and professionalism because of strong influence from the relevant agencies. See: N. Kim, op. cit., p.226.
49 N. Kim, op. cit.
50 See generally: B. Bae, "On Administrative Litigation Act", in MOJ, *Materials for a Public Hearing on Administrative Litigation Act Revision*, 2007, pp.3–15.
51 The first hearing took place on May 23, 2007.
52 Article 68(1) of the Constitutional Court Act requires the applicants for constitutional complaint to exhaust all possible legal processes for redress.

7 Democracy-driven transformation to regulatory state
The case of Taiwan

Jiunn-rong Yeh

Introduction

In the 1960s and 1970s, the developed world, led by the United States, sought to modernize the developing world by promoting industrialization and rule of law. Many Asian states, including Taiwan, received extensive U.S. aid and modernized many of their institutions. These developmental states were phenomenally successful, and produced the Asian economic miracle.

While contributing to economic success in Taiwan, modernization efforts did not successfully substantiate the rule of law as envisaged. Indeed, the phenomenal economic development was achieved under an authoritarian regime that extended strong control over society. Law and legal institutions became instrumental, serving the development-driven authoritarian regime but not constraining it. In this context, modernization efforts contributed to the formation of a developmental favored economic growth over the rule of law, and social stability over open democracy.

In the last decade or so, many Asian countries began to depart from the developmental state model, exhibiting a transformation from unfettered regulatory discretion to more legal and procedural constraints. Among them, Taiwan is iconic in its illustrative development path from a "milk cow" base for launching national recovery in the 1950s, through the *in situ* economic development in the 1970s and 1980s, followed by democratic transition since the mid-1980s.[1] Major legislation directed to procedural rationality and greater regulatory controls has begun shaping a regulatory environment that leans toward being more transparent, participatory, and even deliberative. Legal institutions, lawyers and due process have become much more noticeable in policy making. Nowadays, national leadership positions are occupied by such renowned lawyers as President Ma Ying-jeou, former President Chen Shui-bian, former Vice-President Annette Lu, and former Premier Chun-Shun Chang. This impressive concentration of lawyers is unusual even for advanced democracies.

What has driven this transformation, however, is not yet clear and in need of sound explanation. One possible answer is that Asian states, including Taiwan, have simply become less development-driven and shifted their focus somehow. But this rather simplistic answer fails to account for when and why this change occurred. An alternative explanation, by contrast, would look into the dynamics of these developments and identify—even compare—forces of change contributing to this transformation. Democratization, for example, may trigger institutional changes that provide substantive and procedural controls over regulatory authorities while at the same time empowering civil society. To an important degree, progress made in the process of democratization may entail a transition from a developmental state model to a regulatory state. But are these two the same or different? In what ways and to what extent are these two transitions—one political, the other regulatory—the same transition or two different transitions?

In this paper, I present two models of governance, the developmental state and regulatory state, and compare their institutional and operational aspects. This comparison is followed by an analysis into the driving forces behind the transition, with special attention to the democratization process beginning in the late 1980s. It concludes with the process-centric character of the transformation, providing strong impetus for democratic consolidation in the modern regulatory state.

From the developmental state to the regulatory state

In the past five decades or so, Taiwan has gone through the developmental state phase, and, with the vigor of a more open and democratic society, moved toward a regulatory state model. This section of the paper depicts these two distinct pictures of Taiwan: one as a developmental state before 1987; the other as a fledgling regulatory state after 1987. These institutional and operational aspects are often reflected in various legal or policy instruments by the legislative, judicial, or administrative branches. Beyond state powers, whether and to what extent civil society establishes any relationship—formal or informal—with state apparatus is equally important for observation.

Picturing the developmental state before 1987: Technocracy, modernization, and development

The record of rapid economic growth, Taiwan made during the 1980s, is commonly referred to as miraculous. Development-oriented policies, government enterprises, close—or even tightly controlled—relationships between government and corporations were the primary attributes.

A developmental state operates at two levels: institutional and operational. Institutionally, it favors technocrats for public governance and finds the legal regime and its main players—lawyers—hostile or at least unfriendly. Courts, bar associations, and law schools are not at the center of policy making or management in a developmental state. At the operational level, a developmental state focuses on economic development as the primary goal of state policy, emphasizing public construction and moving up the technological ladder over goals of social welfare and equal distribution. Hardware expenditure is disproportionately higher than its software counterpart.

Legislation

Up until 1987, Taiwan was under Martial Law[2] and the constitutionally authorized period of "Mobilization for Suppression of the Communist Rebellion."[3] During this period, legislation mostly served as an instrument of political control for the party state. Most importantly, several pieces of legislation provided for strict economic controls in the name of mobilization.[4] Major utilities and government enterprises were granted either monopolies or certain privileged status via legislative enactments and official endorsements. This established the official way by which government resources poured into those sectors that were either owned by government or closely affiliated with it. The developmental state during this period was directly engaged in economic development with the strong hand of the government. In this sense, the developmental state in Taiwan was a state-undertaking development, rather than a state-facilitating development.

Other than legislative instruments that entrenched government entities into particular economic sectors, formal legislative authorization was minimal. Development policies were mainly incarnated in policy statements and administrative regulations without any need for prior legislative authorization. Legislative enactments were used mainly to establish government or quasi-government entities and to grant them official status. In this way, legislative functions in a developmental state were rather limited but mainly provide tax incentives, funding and human resources.[5]

Judicial adjudication

Legal institutions did not play a prominent role in the developmental state. In Taiwan, the Constitutional Court (the Council of Grand Justices) was created in the late 1940s and continued to function throughout the authoritarian period. But the court hardly exercised meaningful constitutional supervision before the 1980s, in part due to the three-fourths vote threshold to render constitutional interpretations, as well as the larger political environment.[6]

Similarly, the Administrative Court was established very early in the authoritarian period and the Administrative Litigation Act had been effective for a long time. These institutions, however, provided only limited checks on the bureaucracy before 1987. Despite permitting individual litigation against administrative agencies, administrative litigation was limited to challenges against concrete administrative acts, so many issues were nonjusticiable. The Administrative Court had limited capacity, with only one instance. The Court was not very aggressive in nullifying or suspending administrative acts; the exceptional cases in which the Court did so primarily concerned tax exemptions or regulatory fees with minor policy significance.

In 1980, the State Compensation Act was enacted to provide compensation for government wrongdoings. The Act represented, to a certain extent, a response to the emergence of rights consciousness in the middle classes after two decades of rapid economic growth. Certain grievances, particularly concerning consumer and environmental protections, were addressed. But the Act had rigid conditions and required a cumbersome process, so it functioned as neither an effective nor sufficient check with government powers.[7]

In sum, before 1987, legal institutions were in place but their functions were highly constrained. Judges, despite their quality and professional training, were largely seen as part of the bureaucracy. In a developmental state, the bureaucracy including the judiciary was conceived of as serving developmental purposes, and judicial independence in its institutional sense was minimal, if not a myth.

Executive control

In a developmental state, policy making is inevitably dominated by the technocracy. Before 1987, Taiwan was both a party state and a developmental state. The decision-making center was, not surprisingly, the Kuomintang party apparatus and in the Executive Yuan, both of which were mainly occupied by the same group of technocrats. In the 1970s and 1980s, premiers (Presidents of the Executive Yuan in Taiwan's constitutional system) were either of military background or well-trained agricultural or industrial engineers, or economists, a clear sign of a developmental state.[8]

In the internal operations of the Executive, the budget was allocated strongly in favor of visible hardware construction at the expense of social security and distributive justice. The authorities also put a strong hand in steering the focus of industrial development by identifying major critical industries, providing incentives and necessary assistance through policy announcement or programs. The widespread installation of industrial parks or import-export free zones are typical examples of this pro-development industrial policy.

Civil society

Authoritarian regimes rarely support, and usually suppress, civil society. To the extent that civil society includes business organizations and labor unions, a developmental state must manipulate its relationship with these organizations, treating them as instrumental to state-centered development. Taiwan before 1987 was often described as a corporatist state, in which the party state extended and entrenched its influence over civic and business organizations, professional associations and academic institutions. Not until the mid-1980s did voluntary social organizations begin burgeoning. Even the National Bar Association was controlled by lawyers who had served as military judges. This was the legacy of the notorious "back door" policy for admitting lawyers: the national bar exam admitted less than 1 percent of the applicants who graduated from the law schools, while creating a "back door" channel for far larger numbers of retired military judges or senior bureaucrats to enter the bar each year.

Picturing the regulatory state after 1987: Democratization, rule of law, and the regulatory state

The year 1987 was a watershed in the history of Taiwan. It was the year when the Martial Law Decree was lifted, political liberalization began, and cross-straits contacts were reopened. Parallel to these profound changes in the political sphere, Taiwan also underwent a transition from the developmental state to a more open—even if somewhat disoriented—regulatory state.

In a regulatory state, it is the private sector that takes the lead in development while the government's role is to maintain a free and fair market with legal enforcement. A regulatory state is not, or at least not necessarily, a capitalist state. It may be a welfare state, where government regulations serve not only to police a free market but also, more importantly, to render equitable redistribution.

A regulatory state also operates in two ways: institutional and operational. Institutionally, legally trained bureaucrats are more favored in the public sector. Because administrative decisions are always subject to review by courts, lawyers play a relatively more important role in the agencies. At the operational level, government policies focus on policing fair competition of the market on the one hand and enhancing public welfare on the other. With economic development already having been achieved to a certain scale, equitable redistribution becomes a more acute issue. Economic growth and hardware expenditure no longer necessarily prevail as the dominant policies. As in the developmental state model, these institutional and operational managements may be analyzed through legal or policy instruments by the legislative, judicial, or administrative branches, as well as a particular relationship between civil society and state apparatus.

Legislation

With the lifting of the Martial Law Decree, past repressive measures were suspended and replaced with more liberal rules. A series of new pieces of legislation were passed, such as the revised Publication Act, the Assembly and Parade Act, the Maintenance of Public Order Act, and the Media Broadcasting Act. The liberal tendency of new legislative enactments continued and was further strengthened with the ending of the period of "Mobilization for Suppression of the Communist Rebellion" in May 1991. This liberalizing and democratizing moment created an unprecedented institutional opportunity for the strong exercise of legislative powers.

Around this time, the Legislative Yuan, whose seats were finally opened for competitive elections in 1992, began to seek greater influence over policy making and ramped up its controls over executive powers. As mentioned earlier, the primary functions of a regulatory state are twofold: maintaining a fair market and facilitating public welfare. It was no surprise that legislative efforts since 1992 included both aspects. Regarding the maintenance of free and competitive market, a series of laws were passed, most importantly the Fair Trade Act of 1991 and

Consumer Protection Act of 1994. Regarding the facilitation of public welfare, the Environmental Impact Assessment Act of 1994 and the National Health Insurance Act of 1996 were key junctures.

Besides regulatory reforms rendered by the legislative branch, stricter controls over executive powers were also made rather explicit. Some of these legislative enactments were responses to the growing demands of the citizenry in a rapidly democratizing society. As Table 7.1 indicates, significant legislation included the Act on Property Declaration by Public Servants of 1993, Data Protection Act

Table 7.1 Major legislation

Years	Major incidents	Legislation
1912–1948 (1945–1948)	1945 end of Japanese colonization	Administrative Petition Act (1930) Administrative Litigation Act (1932) Administrative Enforcement Act (1932)
1949–1986	1949 Nationalist relocated to Taiwan	State Compensation Act (1980)
1987–1991	1987 Lifting the martial law decree 1988 Lifting the ban on political parties 1991 Terminating the mobilization period	Maintenance of Public Order Act (1991) Fair Trade Act (1991)
1992–1999	1992 First open reelection for national representatives	Assembly and Parade Act (1992) Act on Property-Declaration by Public Servants (1993) Environmental Impact Assessment Act (1994) Consumer Protection Act (1994) Data Protection Act (1995) National Health Insurance Act (1996) Major Revisions to Administrative Appeal Act (1998) Major Revisions to Administrative Litigation Act (1998) Major Revisions to Administrative Enforcement Act (1998) Government Procurement Act (1998)
2000–2007	2000 Regime change	Administrative Procedure Act (2000) Police Power Exercise Law (2003) Public Referendum Act (2003) Campaign Finance Act (2004) Administrative Penalty Act (2005) Major Revisions to Administrative Enforcement Act (2005) Government Information Disclosure Act (2005)

Source: Compiled by author.

of 1995, major revisions to Administrative Appeals Act of 1998, major revisions to Administrative Litigation Act of 1998, major revisions to Administrative Enforcement Act of 1998, Government Procurement Act of 1998, and the Administrative Procedure Act (APA) of 2000.[9]

Despite aggressive legislative efforts illustrated above, however, certain developmentalist policies and powers were maintained by government agencies. This was particularly true for industrial policies concerning high-tech and cutting-edge technologies, in areas such as nanotechnology and biotech. Yet, facing an increasingly assertive legislature, developmental policies were progressively subject to formal authorization and written into law.

Judicial adjudication

Administrative laws were clearly on the rise beginning in the 1990s as a mode of legislative control over the executive. In 1998, major revisions to the Administrative Litigation Act added new instances for administrative litigation, expanded standing to sue, increased litigation types and, most importantly, for the first time allowed public-interest litigation.[10] These changes inevitably led to a significant increase in judicial control over administrative powers and policy making. A certain amount of judicial activism was observed, particularly in the early years of the Supreme Administrative Court invalidating administrative rules.[11] The Administrative Courts began to function more aggressively in reviewing agency actions. As Table 7.2 indicates, lumping data from three Administrative Courts in Taipei, Taichung and Kaohsiung, the rate at which courts grant relief to the individual citizens averaged around 18–20 percent, a sharp increase from previous years.

In 1993, the procedure of Constitutional Court was significantly revised. Most important was the lowering of the threshold for issuing constitutional interpretations: from three-quarters to two-thirds. A more open, adversarial process was introduced for the Constitutional Court, allowing resolutions of constitutional

Table 7.2 Taiwan administrative court rulings: 2000–2007

Years	Total	For plaintiff (A)	For agency (B)	For both in (A)+(B)=(C)	(A)+(C)	(A)+(C) %
2000	1,247	934	307	6	940	75.4
2001	3,646	504	2,992	150	654	17.9
2002	5,274	730	4,261	283	1,013	19.2
2003	6,344	918	5,050	376	1,294	20.4
2004	6,090	648	5,056	386	1,034	16.9
2005	6,384	543	5,518	323	866	13.6
2006	6,326	651	5,419	256	907	14.3
2007(Jan–Apr)	1,954	252	1,619	83	335	17.1

Source: By author, based on the Judicial Yuan Statistics, available at www.judicial.gov.tw/juds/report/sg-2.htm (last visit June 6, 2007).

controversial issues to be more publicly scrutinized. Beginning in the 1990s, the ratio of unconstitutional rulings rises rather significantly. Judges, lawyers, and legally trained professionals became more actively involved in many areas, extending beyond litigation.

Executive control

Due to the focus on the maintenance of a free and fair market and its legal enforcement, legally trained experts and lawyers have a much more pronounced position in a regulatory state. This was also observed in Taiwan after 1987. Today, major offices of policy making at the highest level are all held by lawyers, including the President, Vice-President, Premier, and Ministers. It was not true, however, that legal expertise has penetrated into the entire bureaucracy. Rather, lawyers are on the surface, like a layer of chocolate frosting, with technocrats still serving as the main body of the cake.

In terms of budget allocation, while economic and industrial sectors still prevail, there has been a growing expenditure on public welfare, cultural diversity, and social justice. This tendency was exemplified by the introduction of the national health insurance program after the enactment of the National Health Insurance Act, substantially shifting the focus of the regulatory state.

Civil society

Since 1987, liberalization has led to a vibrant civil society in Taiwan. With the abrogation of outdated laws that restricted civil organization, citizen activism began to increase. The media have enjoyed freedom of press in the most profound way, in contrast to the severely controlled situation before the transition. More and more civic organizations, many of which are organized by lawyers or other professionals, enjoy full-scale freedom and organizational autonomy. The corporatist state has began to erode. While the old pattern of tight relationships between certain corporate organizations and the government continues, relational influence upon policy formulation has been on the decline. It should also be noted that the rise of civil society in Taiwan has gone hand in hand with globalization and the increasing density of international networks. An increasing number of civil organizations have international partners and expressed their activism beyond borders. What effect this will have on the emerging regulatory state in Taiwan is yet to be seen.

Analyzing the transition

The two illustrations drawn above highlight Taiwan's transition from a developmental state to a regulatory state subject to an unprecedented level of judicial scrutiny and procedural rationality in the performance of regulatory functions. It is not yet clear, however, what caused a transformation of such magnitude and orientation and how we are to evaluate the features of this transformation.

Driving forces of the transition: Democracy driven

What caused the transformation from a developmental state to a regulatory state in Taiwan? There are three possible explanations.

Development factor

One view is that the driving force behind Taiwan's transition from a developmental state to a regulatory state was the realization that rapid growth came at the expense of the environment, social justice, and, in some cases, minority rights. Once these deficiencies were realized, social forces demanded a shift toward more balanced approaches was made. Since the beginning of the 1990s, a number of social groups became outspoken in demanding a new focus on environmental and social policy. The Democratic Progressive Party (DPP) made social policy their top campaign issue for the legislative election in 1995, with significant success.

While this explanation has some power, it is incomplete. Although the current DPP government has leaned more toward social policy since it took office in 2000, the differences are relatively minor. The current government may be less development-driven than its predecessors but demands for economic performance and growth have remained strong. To be sure, there is a difference among the major political parties in their orientations toward development or social, but it remains rather minor. Major political parties in Taiwan remain development-driven. Even after 2000, this still holds true, with only a slightly different orientation leaning toward social policy.

International factor

Another explanation for the transformation focuses on international factors. Like other Asian economies, Taiwan is very dependent on international trade; even more than other economies, it strives to gain international recognition because of its distinct history. Taiwan's accession to WTO required it to make significant commitments with regard to transparency and rationality. In the process of debate over domestic legislation such as the APA and the Government Information Disclosure Act, advocates made a strong argument that Taiwan should "run with the herd" and follow global trends toward institutional reform.

This international element, however, should not be overemphasized, particularly with regard to Taiwan. It is true that many states in the region are susceptible to international pressure because of their needs for international loans and aid. But, except for a period of U.S. aid in the 1960s, Taiwan did not follow this path. It is true that the accession to the WTO—or the desire to accede—facilitated the improvement of the rule of law and administrative transparency in Taiwan.[12] But international pressure focused only on some policy areas, mainly involving trade-related sectors. The driving forces for the broad transformation must lie somewhere else.

Democracy factor

The dominant factor underlying Taiwan's transformation from a developmental state to a regulatory state was democratization. While Taiwan remains focused on development as a central policy goal even after the regime change in 2000, the process of democratization has institutionally transformed the nature of the regulatory regime in the direction of transparency, participation, deliberation, and partnership.[13]

Major legislative initiatives pushing toward transparency, participation, and accountability are rooted in the period of democratization beginning in the mid-1980s. From the beginning of that period, the DPP as the main opposition force adopted an institutionalist approach by participating in elections and seeking broader representation in the Legislature, though it also used demonstrations and street protests at particular times when public mobilization was helpful. This *"reform from within"* strategy pushed the KMT into a competition to enact quasi-constitutional legislative measures, such as the Administrative Procedural Act, Act for Property Declaration for Public Servants, and Government Procurement Act. This dynamic explains why there has been an avalanche of legislation leading to more transparent and accountable governance in the years of democratization. Regime change in 2000 intensified this development, but the momentum was compromised due to gridlock in the Legislature as a result of divided government.

In the general climate of democratization, courts displayed a significant change in style and activism. As the result of legislative empowerment, administrative courts, and the Constitutional Court adjudicated more cases with increasing neutrality and activism, sending signals to the political sectors to improve regulatory rationality. The general empowerment from a more liberal political environment and greater social diversity also contributed to this particular style of judicial activism. Democratic input into constitutional adjudication by the Council of Grand Justices is illustrative. Elsewhere, I analyze the steady but steep rise of constitutional adjudication pushing for rule of law, political liberalization, economic liberalization, and internationalization by the Council since the beginning of the democratization.[14]

The role of democracy in facilitating judicialization is illustrated by Taiwan's democratic transition. Three elements account for this claim.

Empowerment

First, legislative empowerment of the judiciary, directly or indirectly, through legislation in the process of democratization has helped expand the policy space for courts to adjudicate issues of regulatory relevance. The APA and enhanced systems for administrative litigation have vested courts with more power to examine the processes and substance of regulatory matters. The procedural enactments directed at transparency, participation, deliberation, and partnership have changed the operational dynamics among bureaucrats, industry, and society involved in regulation toward more engagement in courts. For example, thanks to legislative authorization of the expansion of administrative courts in 1998, cases regarding judicial scrutiny on administrative regulation have been substantially increased.[15]

Trust

Second, the liberalization of regulatory processes in the wake of democratization has placed courts in a monitoring position directed to identifying and correcting regulatory errors. The burgeoning of mass media in the democratic era has established a media-court link in monitoring the regulatory state. Any media report into a possible abnormality of regulatory matters would most probably end up with a court investigation in a contested political environment. For example, when the opposition legislators challenged Premier Shieh, former Kausiung Mayor, and the media-extended report on the alleged abnormality of the Kausiung Transit System in 2005, the courts were soon flooded with suits concerning criminal charges and legality of administrative actions.

Spillover

Third, many regulatory issues tend to spill over to the courts in a contested political environment because the contending political forces could only resort to the independent third parties. In the context of Taiwan's democratic transition, courts shoulder more functions in answering to the institutional spillover of the regulatory decision making. In recent years, for example, the courts were called upon to review the constitutionality of National Communication Commission, national fingerprint program and national health insurance cost allocation between local and central governments, issues that could have been resolved politically but failed due to political gridlock.

Analyzing the feature of the transition: Process-centric feature and impact

While there has been a growing trend toward judicial influence in the regulatory governance, the manner in which courts exercise their influence may have divergent impact on regulatory politics. Courts may exert their powers by strongly imposing values and opinions they hold. In doing so, the judicialization of regulatory governance would lead to an important shift in regulatory powers toward the court. Judges would not merely second-guess right answers to regulatory choices but, even more aggressively, substitute their own preferred policy for those of regulators. In other instances, however, courts may be more deferential, influencing policy in a more dialectic manner by providing only general policy directions or by focusing on procedural elements in regulatory process. This approach avoids the danger of courts becoming the primary regulator while still ensuring that the regulatory process becomes more transparent, law-abiding, democratic, and even deliberative. I shall call the former version as a *thick* concept of judicialization of regulatory governance, the latter one *thin*.

As much evidence indicates, the judicial function in Taiwan's current transition leans toward the thin model described earlier. In analyzing both legislative measures and judicial rulings issues during the process of democratization, I find that both the legislature and the judiciary have exercised their increasing mandates in a process-sensitive manner. Judicial decisions have leaned toward more dialectic approaches, encouraging dialogue between divergent actors rather than substituting judicially preferred policies for those of the regulatory authorities. This approach has prevented the regulatory state from becoming a judicialized state or a legislative state.

Process-centric transformation in a legislative dimension

Major procedural legislation enacted in the period of democratization has had a profound impact on the transformation to a regulatory state. Instead of superseding regulatory authorities, the legislature chose to establish general procedural frameworks of decision making. This was supported by a coalition of reform forces across political parties engaging in a political competition for reform. The Administrative Procedure Act, the Financial Disclosure Act, the Campaign Finance Act, the Government Procurement Act, the Environmental Impact Assessment Act, the Administrative Litigation Act, and the Government Information Disclosure Act all resulted from this procedural approach. This line of legislation, promulgated after the democratic transition, did not establish an immediate reallocation of resources. Instead, the statutes set up long-term institutional frameworks for regulatory transparency, participation, and rationality. These procedural requirements entailed constraints in the delivery of regulatory functions, but they also set up a decision-making framework that facilitated the discharge of regulatory functions. With these legislative enactments, regulatory policies were made and implemented in a more transparent, participatory, and deliberative fashion.

Process-centric transformation of judicial adjudication

In the development of judicialized governance, courts were called upon to deal with major disputes of profound policy importance in the areas of economic establishment and social security scheme. The following discussion of relevant judicial rulings illustrates how courts resorted to procedural solutions rather than second guessing policy decisions of the bureaucracy. The three cases—The Electronic Toll Collection, Nuclear Installation, and National Health Insurance cases—exemplify both judicialization and the process-centered approach.

The Electronic Toll Collection case

After the cabinet reshuffle in early 2006, Premier Su faced the so-called Electronic Toll Collection (ETC) controversy, a huge political case. The ETC project was funded by a BOT (build, operate and transfer) mechanism to provide a speedy toll system for highway users.[16] The government was subjected to media criticism, however, because of an insufficient number of users and controversial installation fees. Worse yet, the Supreme Administrative Court approved a lower court ruling indicating that the public selection process was flawed and voiding the decision by the selection committee commissioning Far Eastern Electronic Toll Collection Co. (FETC) to set up the system for Taiwan Freeway Bureau. The embattled government surely did not anticipate or welcome the decision. Still, by focusing on the procedural errors in the selection process, the decision allowed the government to correct its errors by reopening the decision-making procedure. The court did not pick among rival companies, as anticipated by media, but rather provided directions to the government, defusing the political crisis at the time.

The Nuclear Installation controversy

Soon after the regime change in 2000, the DPP government announced the termination of the Fourth Nuclear Power Plant installation after a six-month period of reevaluation by a special task force. This decision led to political turmoil. The legislature, still controlled by the former ruling party, the KMT, refused to receive the Premier and threatened to recall the President. Opponents also filed a suit before the Council of Grand Justices to determine whether the decision to cancel the installation was unconstitutional. In Interpretation No. 520, the Council laid out four possible resolutions of the issue and demanded the executive and the legislature fulfill their respective procedural duties. The court indicated that the executive bore a duty to report to the legislature explaining why it chose to cancel the installation,[17] but at the same time the legislature bore a duty to listen to the executive. This procedural resolution of the matter not only saved the court from political retaliation but also facilitated political dialogues among political branches. In the end, the matter was resolved by a joint declaration between the executive and the legislature, declaring a long-term goal of establishing a nuclear free homeland while continuing to build the Fourth Nuclear Plant. The resolution was eventually written into law.[18]

The National Heath Insurance divide

The establishment of the national health insurance program in 1996 was a great leap forward for social welfare policy in Taiwan. This ambitious compulsory program has in general been received positively, but the financial allocation issue has remained controversial since its introduction. One of the financial issues was the allocation of costs between central and local governments; Taipei and Kaohsiung municipal governments constantly complained about their financial burdens. Taipei municipal government refused to contribute to the contributions, as specified by the law, resulting in a series of administrative disputes and litigation. The tension became worse as the Mayor of Taipei and the national executive were major figures in opposing political parties, making judicial decision on the matter more politically sensitive.

In Interpretation No. 550, the Council of Grand Justices proclaimed that both the central and local governments bore constitutional duties of supporting a national health insurance program. The allocation of financial burdens to local governments such as Taipei City by the National Health Insurance Act was constitutional. The court did not clearly indicate, however, how much financial cost borne by local governments is constitutional. Instead of indicating any concrete amount, the court takes a pro-negotiation approach. The court indicated that since local governments were required to share financial costs, they must be given sufficient opportunities to participate in the course of policy formulation. Thus, the national government must discuss and consult with local governments when drafting such policies to avoid possibly unreasonable outcomes and must work out sound plans for allocation of costs. In addition, the court also demanded that the legislature, in revising relevant laws, allows representatives of local governments to be presented as observers during relevant sessions and to express their concerns. Again, this ruling showed a consistent tendency of the court that was unwilling to intervene in substantive policies but took a rather procedural approach.

The impact of the transition

The democracy-driven transformation from a developmental state to regulatory state may risk moving to the opposite extreme. On the one hand, the judiciary may overstep regulatory authorities by second-guessing regulatory choices, seizing the momentum of judicial empowerment in the climate of democratization. On the other hand, in contrast to the development-driven regulatory regime, the legislature may exercise pork-barrel politics to supersede the executive, taking advantage of the imposition of regulatory constraints. In the process of the transformation from developmental state to regulatory state, there is a risk of domination by either the judiciary or the legislature, and neither is particularly desirable. The process-centric feature of the transformation becomes thus more significant.

The judicialization of a regulatory state may render regulatory policies subject to second-guessing by the courts at the expense of political accountability. Over-politicization, on the other hand, would turn a developmental state into a bargaining game with politicized interventions in bureaucratic justice. And last but not least, the capture of regulatory governance may risk regulatory policies falling into the hands of the regulated, primarily industry. In the transitional move to a regulatory state, it is important to address demands for social reforms while at the same time preserving spaces for policy formation. As the experience of Taiwan has shown, a democracy-reinforcing, process-centric pattern may be a better model worthy of special attention.

Conclusion

In this paper, I analyze the driving forces for the transformation in Taiwan, after presenting the dynamics of the transition from a developmental state to a regulatory state. I argue that Taiwan has indeed transitioned from a developmental state to a regulatory state with increasing procedural rationality and substantive legal controls over the regulatory regime. This transition is, however, largely democracy-driven. Given (or because of) this democracy-driven transition, certain growth-driven tendencies have continued and in some cases become even more entrenched.

The transition took place in Taiwan not as a result of explicit government policies, but rather as an inevitable consequence of democratization. Major legislation facilitating the forming of a regulatory state was introduced in the backdrop of democratization in the 1990s in parallel with certain pressures from international network. Increasing judicial controls over regulatory matters were made possible on the one hand by legislative enactments and on the other hand by democratization. More importantly, when looking into the dynamics of the regulatory state in Taiwan, institutional constraints on the regulatory state bear a strong procedural nature as demonstrated by both major legislation and court rulings. This process-centric feature enjoys the potency of developing a dialectic regulatory environment that may possibly prevent the risk of judicialization while reinforcing more open, deliberative democratic governance.

Notes

1 J. Yeh, "Institutional Capacity-Building toward Sustainable Development: Taiwan's Environmental Protection in the Climate of Economic Development and Political Liberalization," *Duke Journal of Comparative & International Law*, vol.6, 1996a, p.229.
2 The Martial Decree declared in 1949 was lifted on July 15, 1987.
3 The period was formally terminated in May 1991 when the "Temporary Provisions Effective During the Period of Communist Rebellion" were abrogated and the Constitution was revised with the additional articles.
4 J. Yeh, "Constitutional Reform and Democratization in Taiwan: 1945–2000," in P. Chow ed., *Taiwan's Modernization in Global Perspective*, Westport: Praeger Publishers, 2002a, pp.47–77.
5 In order to attract foreign investment, for example, the Act to Facilitate Investment was promulgated to provide tax incentives and assistance in the form of land or financial support.
6 W. Chang, "The Role of Judicial Review in Consolidating Democracy: The Case of Taiwan," *Asia Law Review*, vol.2, no.2, 2005, pp.73–88; J. Yeh, "The Function of Constitutional Interpretations by Council of Grand Justice: 1949–1998," *National Taiwan University Law Review*, vol.28, no.2, 1999, pp.1–63. (in Chinese).
7 J. Yeh, "The Spillover of State Liability: A General Review on the State Compensation Act," *National Taiwan University Review*, vol.24, no.2, 1995, pp.123–47.
8 Premiers Yu Kou-Hwa and Sun Yun-Hsuan were the best examples of this feature.
9 Since 2000, another wave of new legislative enactments included the Police Power Exercise Law of 2003, Government Information Disclosure Act of 2005, Public Referendum Act of 2003, Administrative Penalty Act of 2005.
10 A parallel development happened in the environmental regulatory area in the form of citizen suits. Today, most environmental statutes authorize citizen suits, allowing environmental groups to file complaints to the courts for agency inaction in enforcing environmental regulation.
11 J. Yeh and W. Chang, 2002. "Transitional Court and the Rule of Law: On Judicial Activism of the Supreme Administrative Court in Reviewing Administrative

Rules," *Journal of Social Sciences and Philosophy*, vol.14, no.14, 2002, pp.515–559 (in Chinese).
12 With regard to the Administrative Procedural Act, at least some government agencies were convinced that the enactment would be helpful for international recognition.
13 J. Yeh, *Confronting Administrative Procedure Act: Taiwan's Procedural Capacity-building*, Taipei: Angle Publishing, 2002b (in Chinese); R. J. Daniels and M. Trebilcock, "The Political Economy of Rule of Law Reform in Developing Countries," *Michigan Journal of International Law*, no.26, 2004, pp.99–140.
14 Yeh, op. cit., 1999.
15 Yeh and Chang, op. cit.
16 Once operational, drivers will not need to stop and pay tolls, improving traffic flows, energy efficiency and air quality. In the future, drivers will not only enjoy the audio-visual equipment in the cars through the telematics system, but also improvement in car security and safety. Furthermore, many new services can be combined to offer convenience and efficiency: navigation, travel information, roadway information, mobile commerce, multimedia entertainments, and motorcade management.
17 The Council indicated that the Premier or related ministers of the Executive Yuan had to, within a reasonable time, submit a report to the Legislative Yuan and subject [themselves] to interpellation.
18 The nuclear free homeland joint declaration was written into the Basic Law of the Environment. Article 23 of the Law provides that relevant authorities of the government have to development feasible implementations plan for the realization of the nuclear free homeland in Taiwan. The Executive Yuan submitted a bill for the implementation of the nuclear-free homeland in 2003, but it has not yet been passed by the Legislature.

8 Administrative law, politics and governance
The Hong Kong experience

Johannes Chan

Judicial review of administrative actions was almost unheard of in Hong Kong before 1950. Even as late as 1988, there were only 29 applications for judicial review.[1] The number of applications then rose exponentially after 1990. In the last few years, the number remains at about 150 applications per year. An overwhelming number of these applications are directed at the Government (as opposed to other public bodies).[2] These applications cover virtually every aspect of governance including immigration policy, such as the establishment of an appeal tribunal over the exercise of discretion of the Director of Immigration,[3] levy on foreign domestic helpers;[4] housing policy, such as public housing rental policy[5] and privatization of commercial utilities in public housing estates;[6] telecommunication issues, such as interconnection charges between fixed and mobile telecommunication networks;[7] environmental policy issues, such as the scope of the power of the Director of Environmental Protection to approve an environmental assessment report submitted by the Airport Authority,[8] the appropriateness of the criteria on audibility adopted in a noise abatement notice,[9] and harbour reclamation;[10] public employment policy such as civil servants' pay cut,[11] localization policy,[12] and the validity of a scheme governing the minimum in-flight rest period for cabin staff on ultra long-range flights;[13] town planning,[14] political structure;[15] and education policy such as allocation of primary school locations,[16] criteria for operating primary first-year classes at government-aided schools,[17] and school-based management for government-aided religion-run schools.[18]

In many of these cases the court is brought to the forefront of the illusory boundary between law and policy. Many of these decisions have profound political, economic or social consequences. This chapter explores the reasons for this phenomenon, and argues that, among other factors, the rise in the application of judicial review is indeed a negative verdict on the democratic development, or more accurately, the lack of it, in Hong Kong.

A historical perspective

As a former colony, Hong Kong inherited the British administrative law system, a system based on the rule of law and the principle of separation of powers.

Under the classic view of administrative law, the role of the court was to ensure that the executive branch of the Government was kept within the confines of law.[19] Prior to the 1950s, few attempted to challenge the Government's exercise of powers.

Various reasons might explain this situation. First, the majority of the population in Hong Kong consisted of refugees from Mainland China. Most of them regarded Hong Kong as a place of temporary sojourn. It was a 'borrowed place at a borrowed time'. Hence, very few of them showed enthusiasm to become involved with the Government as long as the Government left them alone. This was reinforced by the traditional Chinese cultural inclination to avoid confrontation in courts as much as possible. Indeed, for a long period of time the main mode of contact between the Government and the people was criminal law. Second, the political system was relatively closed. Her Majesty appointed the Governor and vested wide powers in him. He was advised by an Executive Council, whose members were appointed by him. He was the President of the Legislative Council, which comprised only official and appointed members. Prominent businessmen and social leaders were appointed to either the Legislative Council or the Executive Council. Under such a system, those with the means to challenge the Government's action in courts also had access to the Government in other fora and would find it more effective to negotiate with the Government in those fora than in court. Third, the language of the law rendered the law quite inaccessible to the general public. It was only in the late 1980s that the Chinese language became an official language for law that enjoyed equal authenticity with the English language version.[20] The very nature of common law aggravated the problem of access, the principles of which were scattered in stacks of law reports. Fourth, there was a paucity of lawyers in Hong Kong.[21] Civic education and rights discourse were virtually non-existent. Indeed, civic education in formal curriculum was not introduced until the early 1980s.

Furthermore, a major fire in 1953 led to the introduction of massive low cost public housing. Together with the political changes in the Mainland and the improved economy in Hong Kong, the sojourn attitude was gradually replaced by increasing identification with the territory and a correspondingly increased interest in the governance, particularly among the generations born after World War II. The riot in 1967, a spillover of the Cultural Revolution across the border, led the Government to re-consider its policy and governance in Hong Kong. A number of draconian laws, including the Public Order Ordinance, the Societies Ordinance and the Emergency Regulations Ordinance, were passed during the riot. However, because China could easily control Hong Kong simply by turning off the water supply to Hong Kong, and Britain was 8,000 miles away, the Government considered that a repressive regime relying on the draconian powers it had would only lead to further confrontations and would not be the best way to maintain stability and prosperity in the territory. Instead, it adopted a benign policy and contained public dissatisfaction on issues of public concerns by improving the livelihoods of the ordinary members of the community. Hence, under the leadership of Governor MacLehose, the 1970s saw massive construction of public housing projects and the establishment of the powerful Independent Commission Against Corruption, with its determination to wipe out corruption.

Both measures had long-term impact on the development of Hong Kong. The Chinese language was formally recognized as an official language (except for law). The Government also established an extensive network of consultative bodies and appointed its critics to these bodies. This process, known as administrative absorption, successfully absorbed a lot of pressure from the Government. Hence, notwithstanding the rapid development of administrative law in Britain in the 1960s and the 1970s,[22] there was no corresponding increase in judicial review in Hong Kong. Indeed, as a result of its economic success, the major crisis faced by Hong Kong during this period was the large-scale influx of illegal immigrants and asylum seekers, particularly those from Mainland China and Vietnam. This posed a major problem for Hong Kong in the following two decades, and many judicial review applications were related to this problem.

This scene began to change again in the 1980s. China had emerged from the Cultural Revolution, and the new leadership under Deng Xiaoping was determined to rebuild the country. The conclusion of the Sino-British negotiation on the future of Hong Kong shattered any lingering hope that Hong Kong could remain under any form of British administration in the future. Indeed, China would resume sovereignty over Hong Kong in 1997, something that was received with mixed feeling. On the one hand, there was natural national pride that Hong Kong would eventually re-unite with the motherland. On the other hand, China did not have a proud record in terms of protection of human rights. Sadly, many people in Hong Kong were once victims of the communist regime in China. Never in the history of Hong Kong had human rights become so real and so imminent an issue. During the drafting process of the Basic Law between 1985 and 1990, the entire community was engaged in debates on constitutional issues such as central-local relationship, democratic development and human rights protection. The outcome was a much more rights conscious community, and to some extent, a more polarized community.

On July 1, 1997, Hong Kong became a Special Administrative Region of the People's Republic of China under the model of 'one country, two systems'. It is governed by the Basic Law, which is the constitution of the HKSAR as well as a piece of domestic legislation on the Mainland. Hong Kong was to enjoy a high degree of autonomy, with legislative, executive and independent judicial power, including the power of final adjudication. However, it later transpired that the final power of adjudication does not include a final power of interpretation of the Basic Law, which is vested in the Standing Committee of the National People's Congress; the promise of an ultimate goal of direct election of the Chief Executive and the Legislative Council does not carry a timetable or a roadmap.[23] Foreign affairs and defence fall within the jurisdiction of the Central People's Government, but Hong Kong, given its extensive international linkage, particularly in the area of trade, is given considerable freedom in entering into international relationships.

The Basic Law enshrines a separation of powers.[24] In 2007, the Chief Executive of the HKSAR Government was elected by an 800 member Election Committee and appointed by the Central People's Government. An Executive Council in policy making assists him, and he must consult the Executive Council before making important policy decisions.[25] A bill passed by the Legislative Council may take effect only after it is signed and promulgated by the Chief Executive.[26] The Chief Executive may refuse to sign a bill passed by the Legislative Council and return it to the Legislative Council for re-consideration if he considers it incompatible with the overall interest of the HKSAR.[27] However, if the Legislative Council passes the bill again by not less than a two-thirds majority of all members, the Chief Executive will either have to sign and promulgate the bill or dissolve the Legislative Council.[28] He can only dissolve the Legislative Council once in each of his terms.[29] In return, the Legislative Council may impeach the Chief Executive on the ground of a serious breach of law or dereliction of duty.[30] The Judiciary is independent of the other two branches of Government. It exercises judicial power independently and may continue to refer to and follow precedents of other common law jurisdictions.[31] The power of final adjudication is vested in the Court of Final Appeal, which may, and does invite overseas judges from other common law jurisdictions to sit on the Court of Final Appeal.[32] Thus, in short, the Basic Law prescribes a checks and balances system.

Currently, the Legislative Council comprises 30 members returned by geographical election by universal adult franchise, and 30 members returned by 28 functional constituencies. Article 68 of the Basic Law provides that the Legislative Council shall be constituted by election, and the ultimate aim is the election of all the members of the Legislative Council by universal suffrage. The Basic Law, through its Annex, further prescribes the formation of the first three terms of the Legislative Council and a procedure for further democratization of the Legislative Council after 2007 if there is a *need* to do so. Since 2003, there has been a strong voice in the community to democratize the Legislative Council. As the demand for direct election of the Chief Executive in 2007 and direct election of all the members of the Legislative Council in 2008 grew stronger, the Standing Committee of the National People's Congress (NPCSC), on its own motion, issued an interpretation of the relevant provisions of Annex I and II of the Basic Law, according to which the power to determine whether there was a need to change the method of formation of the Legislative Council rested with the Central Government and not the HKSAR.[33] It further decided that there was no need to do so for the election of the Legislative Council in 2008, and that any change in 2008 in the number of directly elected seats should be accompanied by a corresponding change in the number of functional constituency seats. While the NPCSC's interpretation successfully stifled any further demand for direct election in 2007/2008, it also has the effect of increasingly polarizing the community. The Government unsuccessfully introduced a modest reform package in 2005. Soon thereafter the pan-democratic parties tried to push for direct election of the Chief Executive and of all the members of the Legislative Council in 2012, as well as reform of corporate votes and re-grouping of functional constituencies in functional constituency election in 2008. The Government lamented over its defeat in the reform package in 2005 and refused to consider any further changes in 2008. In December 2007, the NPCSC decided that direct election for the Chief Executive could only take place in 2017, and direct election of all members of the Legislative Council could only take place afterwards, which would be in 2022 at the earliest. The decision has come as a major disappointment to many people in Hong Kong. Not only has direct election for the Chief Executive been pushed back for ten years, it remains to be seen what hurdles would be set up in the process, for example, a nomination process which may effectively serve as a screening process to screen out 'undesirable candidates'. Some Chinese senior government officials have also been reported to have said that functional constituency election was not inconsistent with the principle of direct election by universal suffrage.[34]

Mr. C. H. Tung was appointed as the first Chief Executive of the HKSAR. Not a member of a political party or a civil servant, he lacked political legitimacy and the experience required to run a huge, complex Government machinery. He has the trust of Beijing, but that is not enough to steer a highly sophisticated metropolis with widely diverse interests. He has some vision of how he wants to lead Hong Kong, but he was too ambitious and lacked the political skills to carry these ideas through. Worse still, shortly after he assumed the position of Chief Executive, Hong Kong was hit hard by the Asian financial crisis, followed by natural disasters such as SARS and bird flu. With dwindling economic performance and a high unemployment rate, dissatisfaction of his governance grew. Tung's response was to attempt to isolate or marginalize his critics, resulting in his being further estranged from the community. The abortive attempt to introduce national security legislation finally led to his downfall, after half a million people took to the streets to express their anger and frustration. He stepped down in 2005, merely half way through his second term of office.

During his term of office, the relationship between the Executive Government and the Legislative Council had gone from bad to worse. Neither party liked one another. To some extent this was also a systemic issue. Without a party system or the support of political parties, it is difficult for the Executive Government to secure the support of the Legislative Council on controversial issues. As a result, the Government tried to bypass the Legislative Council if possible. The Legislative Council, half of whose members are selected by direct election in geographical constituencies, expects to play a more central role in policy debates. Not being able to do so, some members became highly critical of the Government, sometimes going beyond the limits of rationality and thus reinforcing mistrust of one another. The Legislative Council is itself divided between those who support and those who oppose the Government. Votes are sometimes cast on the basis of personal rivalry rather than on the merits of the issues in question. The result is a crippled and defensive Government that is unable to carry out most of its policies and a fragmented Legislative Council that is unable to agree on anything. When the Government became increasingly distanced from the general public, closing its ear to critical views, and checks and balances between the Legislature and the Executive Government continued to be eroded, the court became the natural alternative choice to pursue social and political agendas.

The trend of judicialization

The term 'judicial review' embraces two inter-related types of review. There is the narrower British notion of review of administrative decisions under which the role of the court is to determine the legality but not to second-guess the wisdom or appropriateness of the administrative decisions. There is also a broader notion of constitutional review in which the court has to determine the compatibility of legislative provisions or administrative decisions with the constitutional requirements of the Bill of Rights and the Basic Law. Under the broad notion of constitutional review, it is inevitable that the courts will have to examine to some extent the merits of the legislative provisions and the administrative decisions of the Government. In Hong Kong, both types of judicial review applications are heard by the High Court. There is no centralized Constitutional Court or Administrative Law Court.

Four key factors have shaped the development of administrative law in Hong Kong from the 1990s onwards. First, Hong Kong continues to prosper economically. It has successfully transformed from a manufacturing economy in the 1960s, taking advantage of cheap labour costs in Hong Kong, to an international financial centre in the mid-1980s relying on its sophisticated infrastructure and legal system. The administration has grown increasingly sophisticated. This is accompanied by a trend of devolution of administrative powers of the Central Government to statutory bodies, notably in the areas of public health and housing[35] and the establishment of an extensive array of regulatory bodies, especially in the areas of finance, economy and professional matters.[36]

Second, in preparation for its withdrawal from Hong Kong, the British Government was eager to consolidate the social, economic and political system in Hong Kong and to nurture a group of social leaders who would be sympathetic to Western values. The Bar in particular had been very vocal in maintaining the rule of law and defending human rights, and many members of the Bar had subsequently emerged as influential political leaders. Despite its economic success, the political system in Hong Kong in the mid-1980s was still rather backward. Indeed, functional constituency election, a form of elitist election, was introduced in 1985. The first geographical election to the Legislative Council, albeit for 18 out of 60 seats, was not held until 1991, six years before the Chinese resumption of sovereignty over Hong Kong. The resumption of sovereignty elicited high public expectation of democratization of the political process, and the failure to meet this public expectation in the following two decades has had a profound impact on the development of constitutional and administrative law in Hong Kong.

Third, the enactment of the Hong Kong Bill of Rights Ordinance in 1991 hammered the last nail into the coffin of the old system, marking a new era of constitutional review. Unlike Britain's unwritten constitution, Hong Kong's was always a written constitution, namely the Letters Patent and the Royal Instructions before 1997, and the Basic Law after 1997. Before 1997, any legislation that was inconsistent with the Letters Patent would be null and void, and the power to declare on the consistency of local legislation with the Letters Patent was naturally vested

The Hong Kong experience 149

in the judiciary. The British conception of supremacy of Parliament was never practised in Hong Kong. The legislative power of the Hong Kong Legislature has always been circumscribed by the provisions of the Letters Patent, and it is for the courts in Hong Kong to construe those limits in the Letters Patent. In other words, the power of constitutional review always existed in Hong Kong. It had not resulted in any significant jurisprudence before the 1990s, but this was largely due to the content of the Letters Patent. It was an archaic form of constitution, setting out nothing but the barebones of governance – the appointment and powers of the executive, the legislature and the judiciary – without any human rights provisions. Hence it gave little room for challenging administrative decisions, and as a result, the provisions of the Letters Patent have been invoked on only a few occasions before the 1990s.[37] The enactment of the Bill of Rights in 1991 thus filled a major gap in the constitutional regime.[38] The courts were soon faced with all kinds of challenges against legislative provisions or executive excess that were not possible to bring before the court before the introduction of the Bill of Rights. With an enhanced scope to review legislation under the new constitutional set-up, the judiciary has had to re-examine its role and limits. This has posed a major challenge to the judiciary since 1991, and, the change of sovereignty and the coming into force of the Basic Law in 1997 merely continued the process under a new and more complicated political system.

Fourth, the Basic Law's coming into force in 1997 presented a new constitutional regime in Hong Kong. The Hong Kong Court of Final Appeal was established to replace the Privy Council as the highest appellate court. In order to maintain the high standard of respectability of the court, the Chief Justice invited a panel of very distinguished overseas judges to serve on the Court of Final Appeal, and introduced a permanent practice of having an overseas judge in every substantive hearing before the Court of Final Appeal. At the same time, it soon transpired that the power of final interpretation of the Basic Law was vested not in the Hong Kong courts, but in the Standing Committee of the National People's Congress, a political body that can exercise the power of interpretation at any time even without any judicial reference from Hong Kong under Article 158 of the Basic Law. This additional political constraint means that the judiciary has to tread carefully between asserting its independence and autonomy and its role as guardian of the rule of law and human rights on the one hand, and respecting the sovereign and not encroaching on the other side of an elusive boundary of autonomy on the other hand.[39]

Administrative system in Hong Kong

The administrative process is a complex process. Statutory powers are set out in primary legislation and elaborated in secondary legislation, which is supplemented by practices and procedures contained in internal circulars, guidelines, notices, memoranda and other forms of writings, not all of which are available outside the administrative agencies. There are different mechanisms to hold public bodies accountable. Legality of administrative actions is determined by the court. The Ombudsman checks against maladministration,[40] and the Commissioner of Audit ensures proper spending of public revenue.[41] There are over 400 statutory bodies with advisory and consultative bodies on virtually every aspect of government administration. The powers and functions of these bodies vary significantly, and they usually include a majority of public members who serve on a voluntary basis. There are also a large number of regulatory bodies, many of them related to professional conduct and disciplines.

Judicial review

Judicial review lies at the centre of administrative law. It is based on an inherent jurisdiction of the superior court to supervise inferior courts and tribunals. Its principles are scattered in the common law. There is no Administrative Procedural Law as such.[42] However, this has not prevented the court from superimposing the common law fundamental principles of fairness on the decision-making processes of public bodies.[43] In a system that subscribes to the doctrine of supremacy of Parliament, the efficacy of judicial review has been doubted, but the courts have proven to be resilient and innovative. They are able to resist even the most patent statutory encroachment of their jurisdiction.[44] Similar eagerness to assert its jurisdiction is found in *Solicitor v. Law Society of Hong Kong*, where the Court of Final Appeal held that a statutory provision proclaiming the judgement of the Court of Appeal as final did not preclude the aggrieved party from further appealing to the Court of Final Appeal.[45]

Broadly speaking, the doctrinal position of traditional judicial review is that it concerns the exercise of public powers. Judicial review is not about regulation of private relations. This public/private dichotomy has long proved to be problematic, if not unworkable.[46] It has proved to be particularly problematic in Hong Kong in the context of the management, use and development of land.

With the exception of St John's Cathedral, all land in Hong Kong is held by lease, and the title can always be traced back to the Crown or Government. This is reinforced by Article 7 of the Basic Law that provides that the management, use and development of land and the lease or grant to individuals or corporations for use or development shall be the responsibility of the Government. Given the scarcity of land supply in Hong Kong, land has been one of the most important resources of the Government. Indeed, a land lease is not just a grant of property right to the lessees. It is also used as a major planning instrument under which the Government could impose general and special conditions related to land use planning, and could take into account public interest considerations in determining whether to grant or extend a lease.[47] Land is sold in public auctions or by private grants. The premium in land sales constitutes a major source of revenue of the Government, and the Government has deliberately maintained a high land price policy by controlling the supply of land so that it could maintain a low tax system. It is thus artificial to argue that in granting or refusing to grant or extend a lease the Government is acting in its private capacity.

However, the court reached a different conclusion. In *Canadian Overseas Development Co Ltd v. Attorney General*,[48] the appellant (developer) intended to develop one of its sites in Fairview Park, New Territories. Under a special condition in the new grant, only buildings in accordance with a master layout plan approved by the Crown were permitted. The appellant submitted a master layout plan, which was rejected by the Crown. Leave to apply for judicial review was granted *ex parte* but was set aside subsequently on the grounds that in refusing to approve the master layout plan, the Crown was performing a private contractual obligation and exercising a contractual right governed by private law.

This reasoning is hardly convincing. On the facts of that case, the site was one of the largest residential developments in the New Territories. It was almost a small town of its own. That explained why the new grant envisaged the preparation of a master layout plan, which is part of the process of land use planning under the Town Planning Ordinance.[49] The plan covered details such as road construction, provision of amenities, specific land use and so on. It is difficult to see how the exercise of a power to approve or otherwise a master layout plan would be a matter of private law. Indeed, why should a landlord be concerned with the detailed planning and use of land when the land was leased for a considerable period, which, for all practical purposes, could be regarded as an outright sale? The restriction could only be justified by public interest. It is artificial to suggest that the Crown was acting as a private landlord in such circumstances. The Court of Appeal held that it was bound by *Hang Wah Chong v. Attorney General*,[50] where the Privy Council held that the Director of Public Works, in demanding a premium for modification of certain special conditions in the land lease to allow redevelopment, was acting in the private domain as a landlord.. However, *Hang Wah Chong* was decided on the basis of two specific conditions in the Crown lease, and the Privy Council expressly noted that some provisions in the Crown lease were obviously of a public nature.[51] There was no justification to expand the principle to cover every aspect of a Crown lease. Nor would such a categorical approach be consistent with subsequent development on the distinction between public law and private law. Unfortunately, *Hang Wah Chong* was subsequently affirmed by the highest court and was almost elevated unjustifiably to become a general principle of law. In *Director of Lands v. Yin Shuen Enterprises Ltd*, Lord Millet, delivering the judgement of the Court of Final Appeal, held:[52]

> Secondly, in deciding whether to grant or withhold its consent to a modification of the terms of a lease, the Government does not exercise a public law function but acts in its private capacity as landlord… It thus has an absolute right if it chooses to demand a premium, however large, for granting a modification of the terms of the lease, or to withhold its consent altogether, however unreasonably.

The same point was affirmed by the Court of Final Appeal in *Ying Ho Ltd v. Secretary for Justice*,[53] and more recently, by Hartmann J. in *Rank Profit Industries Ltd v. Director of Lands*.[54] By this stage, the benefit of the Government was treated to be the same as the benefit to the public. Hartmann J noted that 'in that context, it had been authoritatively decided in *Hang Wah Chong* that the Government acted in the capacity of a landlord and was entitled to exercise its powers for its own benefit – that is, for the benefit of the public.[55] This extension of *Hang Wah Chong* emasculates any distinction between private and public law. Ironically, *Hang Wah Chong* clearly drew a distinction between the Government acting as a landlord and as Government.[56]

The distinction between private and public law can be traced back to *O'Reilly v. Mackman*,[57] which first introduced the principle of procedural exclusivity for public law claims. It was once heralded as marking the long-awaited introduction of public law into English common law. Two decades since this decision, the wisdom of a rigid distinction between public law and private law is generally doubted if not discarded. Lord Woolf once observed extra-judicially that the procedural exclusivity rule led to wholly undesirable procedural wrangles and suggested that it be emasculated altogether.[58] Ironically, in Hong Kong, in the context of land use and development, the distinction has been emasculated but for a different reason. Given the complexity and the multi-dimensional nature of land use planning and policy, the court is reluctant to interfere unduly with these types of decisions. The obscure distinction between private and public law provides a convenient excuse not to entertain such challenges in the first place.

A major obstacle to bringing judicial review applications in Hong Kong lies in the prohibitive legal costs. This obstacle is partially removed by the readiness of the Legal Aid Department to grant legal aid in appropriate cases, the readiness of some members of the legal profession to act on a *pro bono* basis in litigation and the willingness of the court to make pre-emptive cost orders and indemnity cost orders. In *Chan Wai Yip Albert v. Secretary for Justice*,[59] the court confirmed that it has an inherent jurisdiction to make a 'pre-emptive costs order' directing that no order as to costs would be made against an applicant regardless of the outcome of the case if such course was in the interest of justice, taking into account the strength of the case and the public interest in litigating the matter. Such an order will remove a grave concern of an applicant of the risk of bearing the legal costs of the opposing party should the application fail. In *Society for the Protection of Harbour Ltd v. Town Planning Board (No. 2)*,[60] the Court of Final Appeal upheld an indemnity cost order on the grounds that the Society was a charitable organization; that it was reasonable for the Society to resort to litigation when other attempts had failed; that the issue was undoubtedly a matter of public importance and that the Society did not stand to make any personal gains from the litigation. These are encouraging developments and are of great significance in promoting public interest litigation.

Another important development that has made it easier to apply judicial review is the court's liberal stance on the requirement of *locus standi* and its readiness to grant declaratory relief.[61] While it is necessary for an applicant to show that he has an interest in a judicial review application, the court is prepared to adopt a rather liberal test of standing and prefers to resolve a dispute on its substantive merits rather than on pure technical procedural grounds. Thus, a civil service trade union with at least one of its members who would be affected by a localization policy introduced by the Government was held to have sufficient standing to bring the judicial review application,[62] and a member of the public who has no right to vote in any functional constituency has sufficient standing to challenge the functional constituency system.[63] Related to this issue of standing is that an applicant has to show that he has sufficient interest to obtain a declaratory relief, as it is not the function of the court to engage in academic or hypothetical debates. On the other hand, the court is prepared to entertain a question of law when there is a genuine dispute even when its resolution may not have direct or immediate impact on the factual dispute before the court. This is a discretionary power that the court will exercise with caution only when required by the public interest. Thus, in *Chit Fat Motors Company v. Commissioner for Transport*,[64] it was held that although

> the court will not give an advisory opinion on hypothetical facts ... Sometimes ... the question is said to be hypothetical or academic only because the real dispute that drove the parties to litigation (sometimes called the *lis*) happens no longer to be in the existence at the time of the hearing, even though the relevant facts giving rise to the dispute had actually taken place. In these types of situations, the court had discretion to determine the question before it even though there was no longer a *lis*.

This is of particular significance in public law, as 'the duties of public bodies fall to be exercised on a continuing basis not only in relation to the parties before the court but also perhaps to others in the future'.[65]

It is also interesting to note the identity of the applicants in judicial review cases. Apart from the aggrieved persons who are directly affected by a decision of a public authority, there are also trade unions and non-governmental organizations. In some of the judicial review applications, the applicants were carefully chosen so as to ensure that they would be eligible for legal aid.[66] In recent years there are also a number of judicial review applications that were brought by the civil servants against the Government. In *Association of Expatriate Civil Servants of Hong Kong v. Secretary for the Civil Service*,[67] the expatriate civil servants, who used to be a privileged group in the civil service during the colonial regime, challenged the localization policy which was introduced in the late 1980s to pave way for Chinese civil servants to reach the top positions of the civil service. In *Senior Non-Expatriate Officers' Association v. Secretary for the Civil Service*, a group of directorate grade officers challenged the Government's decision to prohibit all directorate officers to serve on the Selection Committee, a body set up by the PRC Government to select the first Chief Executive of the HKSAR.[68] This is a notable case because the directorate officers in the Hong Kong Civil Service are the 'cream' in the civil service. It is unprecedented for this group of civil servants to initiate legal action against the Government. Both of these cases reflect the degree of anxiety and uncertainty among senior civil servants before the change of sovereignty. Yet the trend did not stop after the handover. In *Association of Expatriate Civil Servants of Hong Kong v. Chief Executive of the HKSAR*,[69] the applicants challenged the Public Service (Administrative) Order 1997 and the Public Service (Disciplinary) Regulation on the ground that they provided for the appointment and removal of holders of public office contrary to the provisions of the Basic Law, as these orders/regulations were executive orders adopted without the sanction of the Legislative Council. In *Secretary for Justice v. Lau Kwok Fai Bernard*,[70] the issue was the legality of the Public Officers Pay Adjustment Ordinance,[71] which was introduced by the Government to reduce the pay level of civil servants in order to reduce government expenditure during the economic downturn.

These cases were met with varying degrees of success. However, the interesting point of these cases is that they show that the communication channel, even between senior civil servants and the Government, has broken down, and even senior civil servants have to resort to judicial action to resolve disputes with the Government. Civil servants form the backbone of the Government. Career stability has always been the prime concern of civil servants. There are also well-established mechanisms for resolution of disputes within the civil service. When senior civil servants are prepared to take the Government to court, it is always a dangerous sign on governance. Indeed, shortly after the decision of the Court of Final Appeal in the *Bernard Lau* case, the then Chief Executive was forced by mounting public discontent to step down from his office.[72]

Other administrative bodies and tribunals

Article 10 of the Bill of Rights provides for a right to fair hearing by an independent and impartial tribunal. Article 10 requires, in the administrative context, either a body whose decision-making process complies with the requirements of Article 10, or its decision is subject to review by a body which complies with the requirements of Article 10, in which case being a body which has full jurisdiction to review both law and merits.[73] Traditionally, most of the administrative decisions (particularly those made by licensing authorities) were made by the administrative bodies, and the only appeal was by petitioning the Governor in Council. It was considered that such a system would not be able to satisfy the requirements of Article 10. As a result, an Administrative Appeals Board and a Municipal Service Appeals Board were introduced. They are chaired by a member of the judiciary, who sits with two public members drawn from a panel. The Boards have jurisdiction to hear appeals from a large number of specified administrative bodies, and the appeal is by way of a rehearing. The hearing resembles a judicial hearing, albeit with much less formality. The extent of formality at the hearing depends on whether the parties are represented.

The Ombudsman is another statutory body charged with the jurisdiction to consider any complaints of maladministration by a wide range of Government and public bodies. Apart from acting on complaints, it can also initiate its own investigation. In general, it has received full co-operation of Government departments and its recommendations are generally well received. This may partly be due to a relatively low public profile adopted by successive Ombudsmen.[74]

Another important statutory body ensuring the accountability of the Government is the Director of Audit. This is an independent statutory office entrusted with the duty of monitoring the spending of Government departments and many statutory bodies. It conducts regular audits and publishes regular reports. It has been quite critical of any misuse of public funds by various Government departments and/or statutory bodies. In contrast to the Ombudsman, the Director of Audit adopts a relatively high public profile and its reports usually receive widespread public attention and are well received by the community. The reports are followed up by the Finance Committee of the Legislative Council.

Finally, the Chief Executive may appoint a Commission of Inquiry to investigate incidents of public concern.[75] A number of high profile Commissions have been appointed in recent years.[76] In most cases the Commission will include a senior judge. The hearing resembles a court hearing, and is conducted in public. The Commission is assisted by its own legal representation. In 2007, the Chief Executive appointed a two-member Commission to investigate allegations of interference with academic freedom by two senior Government officials. The Commission found the allegations against the former Permanent Secretary for Education partially substantiated, and its report led to her early retirement. While the Commission of Inquiry is an effective way to deal with factual disputes of public controversies, it is expensive and its credibility depends heavily on the persons appointed as Commissioners. There were a few occasions in the last ten years when the Legislative Council, and in one case, the Ombudsman as well, decided to set up their own investigation.[77] This kind of political gamesmanship is highly unsatisfactory and results in multiple proceedings, sometimes with completely different results that satisfy nobody.

Judicialization or de-judicialization of governance?

Since the 1990s, the rapid growth in the number of judicial review applications and the diversity of cases brought before the court has resulted in a much closer judicial scrutiny of a wide diversity of administrative actions. Administrative bodies are expected to achieve a minimum standard of fairness. Thus, it was held that there was a duty to hear the parents before their child was to be expelled from a school, even when the school had been acting at all times in good faith.[78] Where reasons were required or were provided for an administrative decision, they should be clear and adequate in the circumstances.[79] The courts were entitled to expect the reasons to be sufficiently clear without its having to resort to guesswork. Thus, the Obscene Articles Tribunal was required to set out its reasons and not merely adopt the statutory criteria for its classification of articles as obscene or indecent.[80] It was not sufficient as a proper consultation exercise for a public officer from the Education Department to inform the outgoing principal of a school of a decision to take the school out of the Primary One Admission School List, which decision might put the ability of the school to continue operations at grave risk.[81] It was unreasonable for the Commissioner for Television and Entertainment Licensing to impose his own standards of morality and decency outside the framework of the

Control of Obscene and Indecent Articles Ordinance in setting conditions of licence under the Amusement Game Centres Ordinance for games played in centre for those of 16 years of age or above.[82] A high standard of fairness should be adopted in deportation cases and it was not sufficient for the Director of Immigration to rely merely on the UNHCR's unexplained rejection of the applicant's refugee status in making a determination to deport the applicant to his country where he claimed he would be subject to torture.[83] Discovery was ordered of documents in relation to any general guidance in respect of persons on a watch-list or other categories into which the applicants fell in order to enable the court to decide fairly a complaint that the applicants were denied entry into Hong Kong on the ground of their religious beliefs and affiliation.[84]

The court is aware of the trend of increasing judicial intrusion into administration and has warned against unnecessary judicialization. Thus, in *Tse Lo Hong v. Attorney General*,[85] the late Jerome Chan J warned against excessive lawyering in approaching judicial review. In that case, the court had to determine whether a police disciplinary tribunal properly understood the technical meaning of 'corroborative evidence' when it characterized the evidence of two supporting witnesses as being corroborative of the complaint against the respondent police officer. Chan J held:

> It is the function of a court in a judicial review to supervise the exercise of quasi-judicial powers of the administration. However, in doing so, it is not the function of the court to subject a determination of a domestic tribunal to a lawyer's relentless knife in a judicial surgical dissection. That determination cannot be construed like a statute. Nor should it be subject to the punishment of fine surgical analysis in isolated compartments. A statement made in a determination should not be segregated and be put to a pathetically literal construction out of context.

Likewise, in holding that the Obscene Articles Tribunal was obliged to give reason for its determination on obscenity and indecency, the Court of Final Appeal adopted a realistic approach and held that the reasons could be brief.[86] The court looked to see if the Tribunal had properly addressed the substantial issues before it and why it had come to its decisions. In this regard, while the court held that public officers or statutory bodies are under a duty to act fairly, this duty does not always include a duty to give reasons for their decisions, and it is not for the court to second-guess the professional judgement of a disciplinary committee except where it could be seen that it had plainly misread the evidence and come to a plainly wrong decision.[87] Nor does fairness require legal representation in all circumstances; a restriction to written submission before the Disciplinary Committee of the Stock Exchange of Hong Kong was upheld.[88]

While judicialization under traditional judicial review is largely confined to procedural matters, the broader type of judicial review allows a much wider scope for judicial intervention in administrative actions. Ginsburg argues that there are three factors – economic, political and international – that account for an expanded role of the judiciary in governance.[89] Of the three factors, the political factors dominate the case of Hong Kong. The change in the political status of Hong Kong has led to an increasingly rights-conscious culture. This was reinforced by the introduction of the Bill of Rights in the early 1990s. The new constitutional era in 1997 and the replacement of the prestigious Privy Council by the court of Final Appeal in Hong Kong have precipitated a strong consciousness on the part of the court to establish its reputation, to assert its autonomy and to prove its independence, yet knowing fully well that there are limits that it could not go beyond.[90] Finally, the lack of progress in democratization and the public frustration with both the Legislative Council and the Executive Government have resulted in a preference for the court as a forum to push for social progress. The resort to courts for settling disputes, notably by the civil servants, is itself a reflection of the fragmentation of political powers. At the same time, judicialization of governance is received with mixed feelings by the judiciary and is checked by judicial self-restraint. The following subsections will describe how the judiciary responds to the judicialization process.

Getting ready: The device of substantive legitimate expectation and proportionality

Legitimate expectation

In the landmark decision of *Ng Siu Tung v. Director of Immigration*,[91] the Court of Final Appeal extended the doctrine of legitimate expectation to cover substantive protection. Indeed, the first landmark case on legitimate expectation also came from Hong Kong. In *Attorney General v. Ng Yuen Shiu*,[92] the Privy Council held that where a public authority charged with a duty of making a decision promised to follow certain procedures before reaching that decision, good administration required that it should act by implementing the promise if the implementation did not conflict with the authority's statutory duty. In that case, it was held that having promised to consider each case on its merits upon the discontinuance of the 'touch base' policy, the Director of Immigration could not retract from that promise by removing an illegal immigrant without affording him an opportunity to be heard. This is sometimes referred to as procedural legitimate expectation. The court has for some years been hesitant to hold that the promise made in such circumstances is enforceable, as it may unnecessarily hamper the Government's ability to change a policy. Thus, only a decade ago, the doctrine of substantive legitimate expectation was still labelled by the English Court of Appeal as 'wrong in principle' and 'heretical'.[93]

On the other hand, important as it may be, procedural legitimate expectation leaves an aggrieved person with little remedy if he has been properly heard. He relied on a promise made by the Government, and yet the promise could be withdrawn without any consequence. Thus, over the years, the court has held the Government to its promise on various occasions . In *Wong Pei Chun v. Hong Kong Housing Authority*,[94] the Commissioner for Resettlement assured in writing the residents at Rennie's Mill could reside in the area indefinitely; many of them were nationalist soldiers of Kuomintang Government who came to settle in Hong Kong after 1949. Confining the principle of legitimate expectation to procedural protection, the court held that it was an abuse of power for the Government to breach the promise some 35 years later when the Government decided to remove the residents in order to carry out urban redevelopment.

The principle of substantive legitimate expectation received renewed interest in England[95] and was finally and authoritatively established in *Ng Siu Tung*. Following the judgement of the Court of Final Appeal in *Ng Ka Ling v. Director of Immigration*,[96] the applicants in *Ng Siu Tung* would have been entitled to a right of abode in Hong Kong. As a matter of case management, these applicants were advised not to join in the litigation, but were assured that they would be treated in the same way as the applicants in *Ng Ka Ling*, which was intended to be a test case. Subsequently, *Ng Ka Ling* was reversed by an interpretation of the Standing Committee of the National People's Congress pursuant to Article 158 of the Basic Law, which provided that 'judgements previously rendered shall not be affected'. The applicants in *Ng Siu Tung* claimed that they were given the expectation that they would be treated in the same way as the applicants in *Ng Ka Ling* and be granted a right of abode in Hong Kong. In this sense they were claiming a substantive benefit. The Court of Final Appeal upheld their claim and held that, where the conduct of a public officer, whether by way of promise, representation, practice or policy, gave rise to a legitimate expectation of a substantive outcome or benefit, it would be an abuse of power to refuse to honour such a legitimate expectation in the absence of any overriding reason of law or policy. This decision was soon followed both locally and overseas, and it greatly enhanced the role of judicial scrutiny of administrative actions.[97]

From Wednesbury to proportionality

Gone are the days when judicial review was only concerned with the rules of natural justice or other procedural idiosyncrasies. Even before the advent of the Bill of Rights, the courts were presented with all sorts of issues that challenged the fundamental yet illusive distinction between law and politics and between procedural irregularities and substantive merits. One of the best examples is the increasing dissatisfaction of the traditional *Wednesbury* unreasonableness test as a means to monitor widespread discretionary powers that are conferred by Parliament on the Executive Government.[98]

Short of accepting proportionality as an independent ground for judicial review,[99] the court has come to accept that any restriction on fundamental human rights has to satisfy the proportionality test.[100] It is implicit in the proportionality test that the court must ask not only whether human rights considerations have been taken into account, but also *how* they have been taken into account. As Lord Steyn pointed out: 'The doctrine of proportionality may require the reviewing court to assess the balance which the decision maker has struck, not merely whether it is within the range of rational or reasonable decisions'.[101] It goes beyond the traditional grounds of review 'inasmuch as it may require attention to be directed to the relative weight accorded to interests and considerations'.[102]

Although the proportionality test is largely confined to human rights cases, there is no rational principle that it should not be applied to other types of judicial review cases. Parliament could always be presumed to be able to confer a power, the exercise of which should not exceed what is necessary for the attainment of the statutory objectives. The more important the statutory objectives are, the graver the restrictions on the exercise of discretionary power should be. Whether this is called a proportionality test or a sliding scale of reasonableness is irrelevant, but it does highlight the point that the court has to engage in the review of the merits of a decision, even though the intensity of that review may vary from case to case, depending on the importance and the nature of the subject matter.[103] This principle has been accepted in *Society for Protection of the Harbour Ltd v. Chief Executive in Council (No. 2)*, where the court held that a more rigorous standard than that of *Wednesbury* unreasonableness is called for in scrutinizing the justification for Harbour reclamation in light of the unique legal status of the Harbour.[104]

On the other hand, the court has repeatedly warned that it is not the function of the court to evaluate government policy. Perhaps the starkest warning against excessive judicialization is the reminder of the Privy Council in approaching the Bill of Rights. Commenting on an earlier observation that the Bill of Rights introduced a new era of constitutional review, Lord Woolf observed:[105]

> While the Hong Kong judiciary should be zealous in upholding an individual's rights under the Hong Kong Bill, it is also necessary to ensure that disputes as to the effect of the Bill are not allowed to get out of hand. The issues involving the Hong Kong Bill should be approached with realism and good sense, and kept in proportion. If this is not done the Bill will become a source of injustice rather than justice and it will be debased in the eyes of the public.

Thus, the court is hesitant to be involved in issues concerning political structure. In *Lee Miu Ling v. Attorney General*,[106] the applicant challenged the functional constituency system as a violation of the right to vote by universal and equal suffrage guaranteed by Article 21 of the Bill of Rights. Functional constituency is a unique feature in Hong Kong, under which a member of the functional constituency is entitled to vote for the return of a member to the Legislative Council. It creates an elitist group whose members enjoy a vote in addition to the vote in geographical constituency. The size of the electorate of the functional constituencies varies significantly; the smallest one might have only about 40 members.[107] This system has long been criticized for being discriminatory.[108]

The applicant argued that first, the conferral of an extra vote on members of functional constituencies on the ground of their property or functions violated the right to vote by universal and equal suffrage. Second, the great disparity in size of each functional constituency resulting in great disparity in the voting powers of different members of different functional constituencies further violated the right to vote by equal suffrage. Both arguments were rejected by the Court of Appeal. To address the first point, functional constituency elections were provided for by the Letters Patent, the contemporary constitution of Hong Kong that was immune from Bill of Rights challenge. On the second point, the court held that once functional constituency was found to be constitutional, a variation in size of different functional constituencies was an inevitable result, and the test was whether sensible and fair-minded people would condemn the degree of variation as irrational and disproportionate. The court answered the question in the negative. Moreover, the applicant, not being a member of a functional constituency, had no status to challenge the disparity in voting power.

It is not easy to follow the reasoning of the court in formulating its test. The proper test should be whether a sensible and fair-minded person would consider the degree of variation rational and proportionate. By asking a negative question, the court effectively reversed the burden of proof by asking the applicant who was asserting her right to prove the worth of her right, rather than asking the Government to justify the restriction of her right. The formulation of the test resembles the *Wednesbury* unreasonableness test, which has a very high threshold.

On other occasions the court is less subtle. In *Ng King Luen v. Rita Fan*, the court refused to grant leave to challenge the legality of the Provisional Legislative Council, which was appointed by the Chinese Government pending the election of the first Legislative Council of the HKSAR when it became impossible to constitute the First Legislative Council before 1997 as a result of the breakdown of the Sino-British negotiation on political reform. The Provisional Legislative Council began to operate across the border in Shenzhen in the first half of 1997 alongside the Legislative Council in Hong Kong. Keith J warned that the courts were not concerned with political matters and must stand back from this type of political conflict.[109] Likewise, in *Chan Shu Ying v. Chief Executive of the HKSAR*,[110] the applicant unsuccessfully challenged the Government's decision to abolish Regional Council and Urban Council as part of its political reform package.

In contrast, in *Secretary for Justice v. Chan Wah*,[111] the applicant successfully challenged the electoral arrangements for the election of village representatives, which was open only to indigenous villagers of the New Territories, that is, descendants by patrilineal descent of ancestors who in 1898 were residents of villages in the New Territories. It was held that 'public affairs' under Article 21 of the Bill of Rights would cover all aspects of public administration at all levels, including at the village level. It is an unreasonable restriction on the right to take part in public affairs to exclude non-indigenous villagers, who, like the applicant, have spent their whole life in the village, as candidates in the village election. It is also an unlawful discrimination on the grounds of sex under the Sex Discrimination Ordinance to have treated male and female non-indigenous villagers who have married an indigenous villager differently regarding their right to vote in the village election. Although Article 40 of the Basic Law protects the lawful traditional rights and interests of indigenous inhabitants of the New Territories, the court held that the deprivation of the political rights of the non-indigenous inhabitants was unnecessary for the protection of the lawful traditional rights and interests of the indigenous inhabitants.

The culmination of these cases is that while the courts have positively affirmed a wider power of review of administrative decisions by adopting the principle of proportionality, it has chosen to exercise this power cautiously. Yet this principle remains a powerful device for the courts to decide how far they wish to step into the issue of governance.

Engine for social reform

The advent of the Bill of Rights and then the Basic Law has dramatically shifted the focus of judicial review. The subject of inquiry has increasingly been shifted to a query of appropriateness of an administrative decision in the name of constitutionality. The court is perceived to be an effective engine for social/political reform, and the devices of substantive legitimate expectation and the doctrine of proportionality enable the court to perform this role if it wishes. The new role, or the perceived new role, is best illustrated by a number of cases involving harbour reclamation, mechanisms for reducing rents in public housing, privatization of retail and commercial facilities in public housing estates and regularization of interception of telecommunication.

Harbour reclamation

The Harbour Reclamation case is a good illustration of resorting to legal action to force a change in government policy.[112] For many years the Government has treated the Victoria Harbour as a convenient source of land supply. A huge amount of land has been reclaimed over the years. Around 1994, the Town Planning Board unveiled a massive plan of further reclamation. This led to the enactment of a private member's bill shortly before the handover to create a presumption against reclamation. Around 2002, the Town Planning Board submitted to the Chief Executive in Council a draft plan for constructing a bypass to ease traffic congestion at the central area. The plan required a substantial amount of reclamation. The applicant had lodged objections to the plan but failed to persuade the Board to reduce the amount of reclamation. As a result, the judicial process was launched. The Board argued that it had taken into account the statutory presumption against reclamation and considered that the presumption had been displaced by wider public interest. The proper weight to be attached to the competing factors was a matter for the Board, and the court should not intervene unless the decision of the Board was considered *Wednesbury* unreasonable. This was rejected by the Court of Final Appeal, which adopted an 'overriding and compelling present need' test. Given the statutory intention and the irreversible nature of reclamation, the presumption could only be displaced when cogent and persuasive evidence showed there was an overriding, present public need, that there was no other reasonable alternative to satisfy the public need and that the reclamation was kept to a minimum.

It remitted the plan to the Town Planning Board for re-consideration. Alongside the high profile litigation, the applicant launched a highly successful public campaign to protect the harbour, which effectively aroused public concern and sympathy for the cause of protecting the harbour from further unnecessary and unjustifiable reclamation. The litigation has not only resulted in a re-consideration of the reclamation plan and a substantial reduction of the scale of previously proposed reclamation, it has also led to structural changes through the establishment of a Harbour Enhancement Committee by the Government and to a more vigilant scrutiny by both the public and the Government of any further proposed reclamation.

Public housing

Two other highly controversial pieces of litigation concern the Hong Kong Housing Authority, a statutory body responsible for the provision of affordable rental public housing for about 30 per cent of the total population in Hong Kong. *Ho Choi Wan v. Hong Kong Housing Authority* turned on the proper interpretation of section 16(1A) of the Housing Ordinance, which provides that any 'determination of variation of rent' shall not exceed 10 per cent of the median rent to income ratio (MRIR).[113] As a result of economic recession, this ratio had exceeded 10 per cent since mid-2000. The response of the Housing Authority was to freeze the rent and defer any rent review, despite a long and consistent practice of over 20 years to conduct biannual rent review. There was strong public demand for a reduction in rent. The Housing Authority argued that it had a legal obligation to bring down the rent to a level that was within the statutory limit only when it decided to vary the rent. It had no such obligation when the rent remained unchanged. The tenants were not impressed by such an argument, which was said to run contrary to the legislative purpose of protecting the tenants from unaffordable rent. The contra-indicated effect of the Housing Authority's argument would be that in times of economic success, the MRIR would go up and leave room for rent increase, whereas in times of economic recession when reduction of rent would be most pressing, the Housing Authority could freeze and hence maintain a high rent. They further argued that in light of the consistent past practice, they had a legitimate expectation that the Housing Authority would conduct a rent review biannually and would not defer rent review for over four years, thereby maintaining a high level of rent.

The Court of Final Appeal rejected the argument of legitimate expectation on the basis that any such expectation would have been defeated by the introduction of a three-year-review cycle by the legislation. It further held that, as a matter of statutory construction, there was no duty to comply with the statutory ceiling if there was no variation of rent. This is a justifiable conclusion in light of the rather convoluted and poor drafting. However, this construction would mean that the Housing Authority could not reduce the rent if after the reduction, the MRIR remained at a level above 10 per cent. To get out of this difficulty, the court held that 'variation' could only mean 'upward adjustment', and therefore the phrase 'any determination of variation of rent' in section 16A of the Housing Ordinance did not extend to a decision to reduce rent. Thus, the Housing Authority was free to reduce rent, even if the reduction did not result in bringing the MRIR down to the statutory ceiling. This is a rather strained interpretation. At the heart of the matter, it was a question of housing policy involving allocation of scarce public resources. It was an important, and indeed rather emotional issue affecting over 2.4 million people living in public housing. The problem was compounded by a poorly drafted and ill-thought-out legislative scheme, and the court was forced to interpret the garbled scheme. Section 16A was eventually repealed and replaced by a more sensible rent adjustment mechanism in June 2007.

The second housing decision concerns a privatization attempt by the Housing Authority to divest the retail and parking facilities within its housing estates to Link REIT, a unit trust to be listed on the Hong Kong Stock Exchange. Link REIT would acquire these assets and facilities through a global offering, and on completion of the global offering, these assets would be managed by its subsidiaries that would adopt a market-oriented approach.[114] The applicant, a public housing tenant, challenged the decision on the ground that the Housing Authority had no authority to sell (and would hence be no longer in control of) its assets under section 4(1) of the Housing Ordinance, which requires the Housing Authority 'to secure the provision of housing and such amenities ancillary thereto'. The challenge was rejected on a simple ground that, as a matter of construction, the obligation of the Housing Authority under section 4(1) was merely to secure the provision of those facilities. Section 4(1) did not require the Housing Authority to be the direct provider. It would discharge its obligations so long as these facilities were available, albeit provided by Link REIT, a third party over whom the Authority had no control.

This case has attracted considerable criticism from all quarters. The tenants were worried that the rent would rise sharply once the management of the facilities was put into the hands of a corporation that would adopt a market-oriented approach, especially at a time of economic recession. This worry indeed proved to be real. The application was brought on the day before the deadline for applications for units in Link REIT, and successfully pushed back the listing of the company. Those who had applied for the units and expected to make a profitable speculation complained that the litigation was brought with ulterior motives. Others criticized the Housing Authority for planning a major privatization project in such a cavalier manner. In light of these circumstances, Bokhary PJ emphasized in his judgement that 'the question presented to the court in this appeal is a pure question of legal capacity to be decided as a matter of statutory interpretation'.

Interception of telecommunication

Leung Kwok Hung v. Chief Executive of the HKSAR provides another classical example.[115] Although the Telecommunications Ordinance authorizing interception of telecommunication has long been acknowledged to be incompatible with the Bill of Rights, the Government has refused to change the law. A private member's bill to amend the Ordinance was successfully passed by the Legislative Council in June 1997. The bill was to come into effect on a date to be appointed by the Government. For eight years after its enactment the Government still failed to appoint an operation date. When the legality of telephone interception was eventually and successfully challenged in a criminal trial,[116] the Government's response was to introduce an Executive Order. It was only after the decision of the Court of Final Appeal and with a deadline of six months imposed by the judiciary that the Government was prepared to rush through a piece of amending legislation. By then, the Government, through its intensive lobbying efforts, secured the passage of the new law by rejecting virtually every single amendment proposed by legislators from the pan-democratic camp in the Legislature irrespective of the merits of the proposed amendments. This is another illustration of frustration at the political level that is one of the direct contributing causes to the flooding of political cases before the courts.

This case is significant in another aspect. It shows the innovation of the judiciary in balancing individual rights and public interest. The Government argued strenuously that a power to intercept telecommunication was crucial to the operation of law enforcement agencies. If the court were to hold that there was no legal basis for such operation, and as it would take time for the Government to introduce the necessary legislation, there would be a lacuna in the law which would pose serious threat to the enforcement of law and order. The Court of Final Appeal affirmed that the court has an inherent jurisdiction to suspend the operation of a declaration in exceptional cases, just as it has an inherent jurisdiction to grant a declaration in the first place.[117] In that case, the court suspended the operation of the declaration of unconstitutionality for a period of six months so as to afford the Government time to introduce the necessary legislation.

These cases are nice illustrations of the ineffectiveness of the political process to address political disputes. In *Ng Siu Tung*, it was easy for the Government to grant the applicants an amnesty to stay in Hong Kong. After all, the number of applicants was finite by then. Its stubborn refusal led to further litigation in what was already a highly controversial political crisis. In *Leung Kwok Hung*, the Government refused to regularize its power on interception of telecommunication for more than ten years. The refusal to bring into operation a bill which has been passed by the Legislative Council for eight years would have precipitated a political crisis in many established democracies. The Government was forced to legalize the exercise of this draconian power only after judicial intervention, and the ensuing legislative process fully revealed the abrasive treatment of opposition. The Harbour case is another typical example of the Government's abrasiveness. There was a change in attitude only after protracted litigation and major public campaigns. In the Housing cases, the court was reluctantly drawn into difficult policy issues, and had to make sense out of an impossible rent control scheme. Likewise, in the *Link REIT* case, it was unthinkable in any democracy that a privatization project affecting 2.4 million people could be carried out without any proper consultation or debates at the Legislature. The Government simply circumvented the Legislative Council. The critics had to initiate legal proceedings to delay the listing, which itself had grave financial consequences, and the court was asked to pronounce, albeit indirectly, on the appropriateness of such a cavalier privatization scheme. These cases dragged the court to the forefront of governance and blurred the dividing line between law and policy. Reluctant as it may be, the court was forced to become the 'involuntary hero' in the political tug of war between the legislature and the executive.

Conclusion

The establishment of a new constitutional order is having a profound impact on the role of the judiciary. In line with the common law tradition, the court perceives itself as the guardian of the rule of law. A strong Court of Final Appeal was established upon the change of sovereignty, and it is natural for the court to assert its independence and to build up its reputation. By and large, it has laid down a reasonably liberal tradition in approaching constitutional review. The principles of legal certainty and proportionality are firmly established in the human rights context. This liberal approach in constitutional review naturally influences the judicial approach in traditional judicial review, especially when the jurisdiction of both types of review is exercised by the same court. For instance, it is believed that the principle of proportionality will soon become part of the general law of judicial review of administrative action. On the whole, judicial scrutiny has improved the quality of the Government's decision-making process and heightened awareness of fairness, rationality and equity in governance. Despite the political overtones of many cases before the court, the judiciary has maintained its independence and impartiality. The diversity and complexity of the cases that have been handled by the court and the sophistication it has adopted in approaching these issues are highly impressive. The court is willing, able and ready to adopt a more active role in governance.

At the same time, the new sense of identity of the court's constitutional role is coupled with a fragmentation of political power at the political level. The pan-democratic parties, who won their seats through direct geographical election, have a strong popular mandate, yet they are not given any significant role in governance. The huge gap in expectation and reality leads to a critical, if not sometimes hostile, attitude towards the administration. At the other end, the Executive Government has no vote or party alliance in the Legislature to ensure support of its policies and to secure the passage of necessary legislation. The Legislative Council, particularly with the hostile attitude of some of its members towards the Government, is regarded by the administration at best as a nuisance. Alliance with some political parties is transient and unreliable. Such alliance also leads to polarization of an already fragmented Legislative Council. The structural problems in the constitutional system and the tension and mutual distrust between the Legislative Council and the Executive Government result in frustration on both sides. While it is obvious that political reform is urgently required to break the deadlock of the strenuous relationship between the Legislature and the Executive, any further democratization of the political process by strengthening the political legitimacy of the Chief Executive and the Legislative Council is skeptically received. It is a concern, or at least a perceived concern, of Beijing, that democratization will lead to political instability. Discussion on political reform is plagued with the vague and emotional concept of sovereignty and nationalism, which can hardly lead to rational debates. This tension has spread to discussions of other social and political issues. Frustration and helplessness at the political forum shifted the focus to the judiciary as a forum for making the Government accountable and responsive. Litigation thus becomes an instrument for social progress.

The judiciary itself is aware of this political shift and has been treading the path carefully. Given its limited scope of inquiries and resources, the court is not the best forum to deal with policy matters that have far-reaching consequences. It, quite properly, confines itself to the resolution of legal issues, although on some occasions the distinction between law and politics is particularly fine.[118] It has developed self-restraint by adhering to traditional concepts such as amenability to judicial review, or resorting to a vague balancing process inherent in the concept of proportionality, or by introducing the new concept of deference to the Legislature or the Executive Government through the doctrine of margin of appreciation. Nonetheless, the Chief Justice has still found it necessary to remind the public on two successive Openings of the Legal Year on the proper role of the judiciary in judicial review:[119]

> ... the courts do not assume the role of the maker of the challenged decision. The courts are concerned and only concerned with the legality of the decision in question, adjudged in accordance with common law principles and the relevant statutory and constitutional provisions. It follows that the courts' judgement can only establish the limits of legality. The courts could not possibly provide an answer to, let alone a panacea for, any of the various political, social and economic problems which confront society in modern times.

Looking from another perspective, the resort to judicial challenges as a means for pushing legal or political reform is itself a result of a democracy deficit.[120] In a democratic system, the political process provides for reconciliation and compromise of different interests by a rational means. A democratic Legislature ensures the accountability of the Executive Government and guards against an over-zealous, over-paternalistic or over-conservative Government. It is difficult for the Legislative Council to discharge this role when half its members are chosen by functional constituencies representing narrow interests derived from different sects. At the same time, the Government tried to bypass the Legislature whenever possible and marginalized the democratically elected members of the Legislature, who make up the remaining half of the Legislative Council and have a strong popular mandate. When political dialogue is dominated by mistrust and suspicion, when the political process is no longer dictated by reasoning, when opposite views are treated with hostility, ridicule or even contempt, and when broadmindedness, tolerance and plurality which form the basis of a democratic society are conspicuously absent in the political process, those who are frustrated or disillusioned could only resort either to street politics or to the court.

The erosion of other brakes against arbitrary decisions aggravates this situation in the political system, which would not have happened had there been a democratic government. An independent Executive Council, an extensive array of statutory and consultative bodies and an impartial and professional civil service would be able to serve as some forms of braking forces against an excess of powers by providing independent and impartial advice to the Government. Since the resumption of sovereignty in 1997, appointments to various statutory and consultative bodies were increasingly made on the ground of political loyalty or expediency rather than on merits or expertise. As a result of the introduction of the so-called 'ministerial system', the independent members of the Executive Council were replaced by ministers chosen by the Chief Executive. Both measures have resulted in a Government that is increasingly distanced from the public views. The ministers, who are no more than an *ad hoc* group with no common vision or platform and little experience in public administration, have weakened the trust for the civil service and their role as a braking force against hastily made decisions. Contrary to the original design, senior civil servants rather than the ministers continue to shoulder political responsibilities and have from time to time taken the blame for bad policy decisions. In return, the civil servants respond by becoming more reluctant to offer their independent views. When all these devices break down and when the Legislature no longer provides an effective check or balance against the Executive Government, the court becomes the last resort to hold the Government accountable.

The emergence of a strong court determined to establish its independence and reputation accelerates the process of judicialization of administration. The court is perceived to be an effective instrument for engineering social or political changes and for ensuring public accountability of the Government. When these social/political issues are presented as legal issues and are so addressed, it ossifies judicialization of administrative decisions and emasculates the distinction between law and policies. This is to a large extent a negative verdict and a sign of frustration of the political process. If the political forum remains ineffective and if there is continued erosion of the checks and balances system, this trend of resorting to the judiciary to resolve political disputes will inevitably continue. If there is still little progress in the process of democratization, the courts are likely to continue to be dragged into policy debates and governance issues and will have to continue to straddle between the fine lines of law and governance. When the judiciary is unable to handle the frustration of this unmet yet unrealistic expectation, the rule of law will be undermined.

Notes

1 The figure is set out in the judgement of Barnett J in *Re Sum Tat-man* [1991] 2 HKLR 601 at 613. Out of the 29 applications, 26 were granted leave.

2 Applications against the Government have increased from fewer than 100 in 2004 to 130 in 2005 and 128 in 2006, representing an almost 25 per cent growth in the subsequent two years: Benedict Lai, 'Recent Trends and Developments of Judicial Review in Hong Kong', a paper presented in the 20th Biennial Lawasia Conference, 6–8 June 2007, Hong Kong (available at www.doj.gov.hk/eng/public/pdf/lo20070608e.pdf).
3 In *R v. Director of Immigration, ex parte Chan Heung Mui* [1993] 3 HKPLR 533 at 551, Godfrey J criticized the absence of any avenue for appeal against a decision of the Director of Immigration refusing to allow an illegal immigrant to remain in Hong Kong on humanitarian ground, as the Director was put in a difficult position in making such a decision when his duty is to keep illegal immigrants out. In *Mok Chi Hung v. Director of Immigration* [2001] 2 HKLRD 125, Cheung J (as he then was) expressed his discomfort with the decision of the Director of Immigration even though he held that the court should not interfere with the removal order.
4 *Julita F Raza v. Chief Executive in Council* [2005] 3 HKLRD 561.
5 *Ho Choi Wan v. Hong Kong Housing Authority* [2005] 8 HKCFAR 628.
6 *Lo Siu Lan v. Hong Kong Housing Authority* [2005] 8 HKCFAR 363.
7 *PCCW-HKT Telephone Ltd v. The Telecommunications Authority*, HKAL No. 112/2006 (13 Feb 2007).
8 *Shiu Wing Steel Ltd v. Director of Environmental Protection and Airport Authority of Hong Kong* [2006] 3 HKLRD 487.
9 *Noise Control Authority v. Step In Limited* [2005] 1 HKLRD 702.
10 *The Society for the Protection of Harbour v. Town Planning Board* [2004] 1 HKLRD 396; The *Society for the Protection of Harbour v. Chief Executive in Council (No. 2)* [2004] 2 HKLRD 902.
11 *Secretary for Justice v. Lau Kwok Fai Bernard* [2005] 8 HKCFAR 304.
12 *Association of Expatriate Civil Servants of Hong Kong v. Secretary for the Civil Service* [1996] 6 HKPLR 333.
13 *Cathay Pacific Airways Fight Attendants Union v. Director-General of Civil Aviation and Cathay Pacific Airways Ltd Interested Party* [2007] 2 HKC 393.
14 E.g., *Henderson Real Estate Agency Ltd v. Lo Chai Wan* [1997] 7 HKPLR 1 (on whether planning intention was misunderstood).
15 *Chan Shu Ying v. Chief Executive of the HKSAR* [2001] 1 HKLRD 641.
16 *Equal Opportunities Commission v. Secretary for Education, Health and Welfare* [2001] 2 HKLRD 690.
17 *Lam Yuet Mei v. Permanent Secretary for Education and Manpower* [2004] 3 HKLRD 524; *Cheng's Educational Fund Limited v. Secretary for Education and Manpower*, HCAL 61 of 2005 (2 Sept 2005).
18 *Catholic Diocese of Hong Kong v. Secretary for Justice* [2006] HKEC 2141.
19 This is sometimes known as the red light theory: see C. Harlow and R. Rawlings, *Law and Administration*, London: Weidenfeld and Nicolson, 1984.
20 Official Languages (Amendment) Ordinance 1987, which came into effect in 1989.
21 The first law school was established in the University of Hong Kong in 1969.
22 Some of the most important cases in administrative law, such as *Ridge v. Baldwin [1964] AC 40*, *Anisminic Ltd v. Foreign Compensation Commission* [1969] 2 AC 147, were decided during this period.
23 See Articles 45 and 68 of the Basic Law. For a discussion on the constitutional reform, see Chan J. and Harris L. eds, *Hong Kong's Constitutional Debates*, Hong Kong: Hong Kong Law Journal Ltd, 2005.
24 This is endorsed by a number of judgements: see *Leung Kwok Hung v. President of Legislative Council of the HKSAR* [2007] HKEC 788 (27 April 2007); *HKSAR v. Hung Chan Wa* [2006] 3 HKLRD 841; *Lau Cheong v. HKSAR* [2002] 2 HKLRD 612. However, the Beijing Government, and to a certain extent, the HKSAR Government, contends that the governance system should be executive-led.

25 Articles 54 and 56 of the Basic Law.
26 Article 76.
27 Article 49.
28 Articles 49 and 50.
29 Article 50.
30 Article 73(9).
31 Article 84.
32 Article 82.
33 Interpretation issued on 6 April 2004.
34 Li Fei, *Ming Pao*, Dec 2007.
35 For example, public hospitals are under the Hospital Authority and public housing is managed by the Hong Kong Housing Authority.
36 For example, the Securities and Futures Commission, Insider Dealing Board, Town Planning Board, Tax Appeal Board, Equal Opportunities Commission, Personal Data (Privacy) Commission.
37 See, for example, *Ho Po Sang v. Director of Public Works* [1959] HKLR 632; *Deacon Chiu v. Attorney General* [1992] 2 HKLR 84.
38 The Bill of Rights Ordinance provided that any pre-existing legislation shall be construed consistently with the Bill of Rights, and if they could not be so construed, they were repealed to the extent of inconsistency. Pre-existing legislation was defined to be legislation in existence on 8 June 1991, the date when the Bill of Rights Ordinance came into force. It further provided that any subsequent legislation should be construed consistently with the Bill of Rights without setting out the consequence if such legislation could not be so construed. However, the Letters Patent was amended at the same time that if any subsequent legislation was inconsistent with the International Covenant on Civil and Political Rights as applied to Hong Kong, they would be of no effect. The linkage was that the Bill of Rights Ordinance incorporated into domestic law the ICCPR as applied to Hong Kong. Therefore, any subsequent legislation that was inconsistent with the Bill of Rights would be inconsistent with the ICCPR as applied to Hong Kong and was struck down by the Letters Patent. The amendment of the Letters Patent followed closely the language of Article 39 of the Basic Law.
39 For more detailed discussion, see Yap Po Jen, 'Ten Years of the Basic Law: The Rise, Retreat and Resurgence of Judicial Power in Hong Kong', *Common Law World Review*, vol.36, no.2, 2007, pp.166–91.
40 Ombudsman Ordinance (Cap 397).
41 Audit Ordinance (Cap 122).
42 Nor is there any centralized Constitutional Court or Administrative Law Court.
43 *R. v. Secretary for Home Affairs, ex parte Doody* [1993] 3 WLR 154.
44 See, for example, *Anisminic Ltd v. Foreign Compensation Commission* [1969] 2 AC 147 and the line of authorities on ouster clause. See also *Thai Muoi v. Hong Kong Housing Authority* [2000] HKEC 596; *Kwan Shung King v. Housing Appeal Tribunal* [2000] 2 HKLRD 764.
45 [2004] 1 HKLRD 214.
46 The leading English case on this point is *R. v. Panel on Take-overs and Mergers, ex parte Datafin plc* [1987] 1 QB 815, under which it was held that there was no universal test to determine whether an action of a public body fell within the realm of public law. The court has to take into account a whole range of factors, including the sources of power and the nature of the functions to be performed. See also *Ngo Kee Construction Co Ltd v. Hong Kong Housing Authority* [2001] 1 HKC 493 at 507, per Cheung J (as he then was).
47 See *Hong Kong and China Gas Co Ltd v. Director of Lands* [1997] 3 HKC 520 at 526 where the Director of Lands refused to extend a land grant after taking into account

the interest of the community in the case of an emergency, the maintenance of gas depot in a residential community and the disadvantage of the site being unavailable to other potential lessees at a significant premium if the lease were extended. The court held that the Director was exercising a public function. Compare *Kam Lau Koon v. Secretary for Justice* [1998] 2 HKLRD 876 at 882, where the court found that the Director was not exercising a public function when he refused to renew the lease of land for the use as a Taoist temple for public worship. The two decisions are not easily reconcilable.

48 [1991] 1 HKC 288.
49 Cap 131, s 4(1).
50 [1981) 1 WLR 1141. This case was doubted in *R. v. Thurrock Borough Co, ex parte Blue Circle Industries plc* [1994] 2 PLR 1.
51 Ibid., at 1145–46, per Lord Edmund-Davies: 'The various Conditions of Sale well illustrate the wide range of roles played by the Director in exercising his discretion. As regards some of the conditions, the Director's role may, almost certainly, be that of protector of the public interest. The vital question is whether for the purposes of special conditions 6 and 7 he can properly be regarded as being entitled to act in his capacity of land agent for the Crown. It is not open to serious doubt that those conditions relate directly to the landlord's interests, economic and otherwise, and their Lordships conclude that the Director was entitled to act, and did act, in that role when granting his qualified approval to the applicants' plan in 1976'.
52 [2003] 6 HKCFAR 1 at 14E.
53 [2005] 1 HKLRD 135 at 171, where Riberio PJ noted that the Government did not act as a fiduciary *vis-à-vis* land developers in respect of any discretion reserved to itself under conditions of grant.
54 [2007] 2 HKC 168.
55 See Hartmann J, ibid., at 183.
56 This distinction was confirmed in *R. v. Thurrock Borough Co, ex parte Blue Circle Industries plc* [1994] 2 PLR 1.
57 [1983] 2 AC 237.
58 Lord Woolf, *Access to Justice* (1996), at p.250. See also Lord Slynn in *Mercury Communications Ltd v. Director General of Telecommunication* [1996] 1 WLR 48 at 57; Lord Lowry in *Roy v. Kensington and Chelsea Family Practitioners Council* [1992] 1 AC 624 at 635.
59 HCAL 36/2005 (19 May 2005). See also *HSBC International Trustee Ltd v. Tam Mei Kam* HCMP 16/2004, *Re Biddencare* [1994] 2 BCLC 160.
60 [2004] 2 HKLRD 95. See also *New Zealand Maori Council v. Attorney General of New Zealand* [1994] 1 AC 466 at 485, per Lord Woolf, and the warning by Hartmann J in *Leung Kwok Hung v. President of the Legislative Council*, HCAL 87/2006 (Ruling on Costs: 27 April 2007) and *Leung Kwok Hung v. Clerk to the Legislative Council*, HCAL 112/2004 (Ruling on Costs: 13 October 2004).
61 On the other hand, the Court of Final Appeal has raised the threshold for granting leave to apply for judicial review from a potentially arguable test to a reasonably arguable test: *Peter Po Fun Chan v. Winnie Cheung*, FACV No. 10/2007 (30 Nov 2007).
62 *Association of Expatriate Civil Servants of Hong Kong v. Secretary for the Civil Service* [1996] 6 HKPLR 333.
63 *Lee Miu Ling v. Attorney General* [1995] 5 HKPLR 585, but the court held that not being a member of any functional constituency, the applicant had no standing to challenge the disparity in voting power between different functional constituencies.
64 [2004] 1 HKC 465 at 472–3, per Ma CJHC. See also *Koo Sze Yiu v. Chief Executive of HKSAR* [2006] 3 HKLRD 455, below, on the inherent power of the court to suspend a declaration.
65 Ibid., at 472.

66 E.g. *Lee Miu Ling v. Attorney General* [1995] 5 HKPLR 585; *Ho Choi Wan v. Hong Kong Housing Authority* [2005] 8 HKCFAR 628; *Lo Siu Lan v. Hong Kong Housing Authority* [2005] 8 HKCFAR 363; *Leung Kwok Hung v. Chief Executive of the HKSAR* [2006] HKEC 816.
67 [1996] 6 HKPLR 333.
68 [1997] 7 HKPLR 91.
69 [2005] 3 HKLRD 164.
70 [2005] 8 HKCFAR 304.
71 Cap 580.
72 For details, see Petersen C., 'Hong Kong's Spring of Discontent: The Rise and Fall of the National Security Bill in 2003', in Fu Hualing, et al., eds, *National Security and Fundamental Freedoms: Hong Kong's Article 23 under Scrutiny*, Hong Kong: Hong Kong University Press, 2005, ch 1.
73 *Ma Wan Farming Ltd v. Chief Executive of the HKSAR* [1998–99] 8 HKPLR 386. See also *Commissioner of Inland Revenue v. Lee Lai Ping* [1993] 3 HKPLR 141; *R. v. Lift Contractors' Disciplinary Board, ex parte Otis Elevator Company (HK) Ltd* [1994] 4 HKPLR 168. It was reversed on appeal on the ground that an appeal against the Disciplinary Board lied at the Court of Appeal and was by way of rehearing. This would satisfy the requirements of Article 10.
74 Except during the term of Mr So Kwok Wing, who was accused of adopting too high a public profile against the Government. He has initiated various high profile investigations against the Government, such as the Airport Enquiry. Mr So was succeeded by the present Ombudsman, Ms Alice Tai, who was the Judicial Administrator before her appointment as Ombudsman.
75 Commissions of Inquiry Ordinance (Cap 86).
76 E.g. inquiry into the accident on New Year's Eve at Lan Kwai Fong (chaired by Bokhary J); inquiry into the riot at Pak Shek Detention Centre (chaired by Denis Chang SC), inquiry into the chaos in the first few days of operation of the new Airport (chaired by Woo JA), inquiry into the handling of SARS (chaired by Professor Rosie Young), inquiry into allegations of academic interference (chaired by Yeung JA).
77 The Legislative Council decided to set up its own inquiry into the SARS tragedy, under which about 300 persons were killed by the deadly disease, when it was not satisfied of the independence of the Committee of Inquiry set up by the Government. In 1997, the Legislative Council, the Ombudsman, and the Government each set up their own inquiry into the administrative chaos experienced during the opening of the new airport.
78 *R. v. English Schools Foundation* [2004] 10 HKPLR 1004; see also *Fok Lai Ying v. Governor in Council* [1997] 7 HKPLR 327 where the Privy Council held that there was a duty to hear a person before the Governor in Council decided on the resumption of her land. The land was part of an indigenous village, and the indigenous inhabitants were consulted of the proposed resumption. The applicant was not an indigenous inhabitant and was left out of the consultation process. The application eventually failed on factual grounds.
79 *Capital Rich Development Ltd v. Town Planning Board* [2007] 2 HKLRD 155, at paras 97 & 98; *Anderson Asphalt Ltd v. Town Planning Board* [2007] 3 HKLRD 18, para 53.
80 *Oriental Daily Publisher Ltd v. Commissioner for Television and Entertainment Licensing Authority* [1998] 4 HKC 505.
81 *Lam Yuet Mei v. Permanent Secretary for Education and Manpower* [2004] 3 HKLRD 524.
82 *Wong Kam Kuen v. Commissioner for Television and Entertainment Licensing* [2003] 10 HKPLR 739. See also *Commissioner of Police v. Municipal Services Appeals Board* [2005] 1 HKC 170.
83 *Secretary for Security v. Prabakar* [2005] 1 HKLRD 289.

84 *Chu Woan Chyi v. Director of Immigration* [2005] 4 HKC 303. The Applicants were residents of Taiwan and each of them was in possession of a multi-entry visa. They intended to come to Hong Kong to attend a conference on the teachings and practice of Falun Gong.
85 [1995] 5 HKPLR 112 at 116.
86 *Oriental Daily Publisher Ltd v. Commissioner for Television and Entertainment Authority* [1998] 4 HKC 505.
87 *Tong Pon Wah v. Hong Kong Society of Accountants* [1998–99] 8 HKPLR 585 at 597.
88 *Stock Exchange of Hong Kong Ltd v. New World Development Co Ltd* [2006] 2 HKLRD 518.
89 Ginsburg T., 'Judicialization of Administrative Governance: Causes, Consequences and Limits', above, in this volume. While Hong Kong is a member of WTO, the WTO Agreement had only limited effect on the administration in Hong Kong. In *Ngo Kee Construction Co Ltd v. Hong Kong Housing Authority* [2001] 1 HKC 493, it was held that the WTO Agreement on Government Procurement 1994 was an unincorporated international treaty and therefore its provisions could not serve as the underpin for the Government's tendering process.
90 For a more detailed discussion of the role of the court in constitutional matters during the first ten years of the HKSAR, see Albert Chen, 'Constitutional Adjudication in Post-1997 Hong Kong', *Pacific Rim Law and Policy Journal*, no.15, 2006, pp. 627–82; Yap Po Jen, 'Ten Years of the Basic Law: The Rise, Retreat and Resurgence of Judicial Power in Hong Kong', *Common Law World Review*, vol.36, no.2, 2007, pp.166–91; Chan J., 'Basic Law and Constitutional Review: The First Ten Years', *Hong Kong Law Journal*, no.37, 2007, pp.407–47.
91 [2002] 1 HKLRD 561.
92 [1983] 2 AC 629.
93 *R. v. Secretary of State for the Home Department, ex parte Hargreaves* [1997] 1 WLR 906 at 924–5.
94 [1996] 2 HKLRD 293.
95 See also *R. v. North and East Devon Health Authority, ex parte Coughlan* [2000] 2 WLR 262.
96 [1999] 2 HKCFAR 4.
97 See *R. v. Secretary of State for the Home Department, ex parte Zeqiri* [2002] UKHL 3. It has generated a large number of cases in Hong Kong, see, for example, *Cathay Pacific Airways Flight Attendants Union v. Director General of Civil Aviation* [2007] 2 HKC 393; *Ho Choi Wan v. Hong Kong Housing Authority* [2005] 8 HKCFAR 628. For further discussion of this doctrine, see Forsyth & Williams, 'Closing Chapter in the Immigration Children Saga: Substantive Legitimate Expectations and Administrative Justice in Hong Kong', *Asia Pacific Law Review*, 2002 29–47; Li & Leung, 'The Doctrine of Substantive Legitimate Expectation: The Significance of *Ng Siu Tung and Others v. Director of Immigration*', *Hong Kong Law Journal* no.32, 2000 471–96; Tai & Yam, 'The Advent of Substantive Legitimate Expectations in Hong Kong: Two Competing Visions', *Public Law*, 2002 688–702.
98 In *R. (Daly) v. Secretary of State for the Home Department*, Lord Cooke expressed his frustration and considered the *Wednesbury* test 'an unfortunate retrogressive decision in English administrative law: [2001] 2 AC 532 at 549.
99 An argument that proportionality constituted a fourth ground for judicial review alongside illegality, procedural irregularities and impropriety was rejected by the House of Lords in *R. v. Secretary of State for the Home Department, ex parte Brind* [1991] 1 AC 696.
100 *Leung Kwok Hung v. HKSAR* [2005] 3 HKLRD 64 at 183, per Li CJ. See also *R. v. Lord Saville of Newdigate, ex parte A* [2000] 1 WLR 1855 at 1867. For a more

detailed argument, see Chan J., 'A Sliding Scale of Reasonableness in Judicial Review', *Acta Juridica*, no.233, 2006.
101 *R(Daly) v. Secretary of State for the Home Department* [2001]2 AC 532 at 547.
102 Ibid.
103 See *Minister for Aboriginal Affairs v. Peko-Wallsend Ltd* [1985] 162 CLR 24 at 41–2, per Mason J; *R. v. Secretary of State for the Home Department, ex parte Launder* [1997] 1 WLR 839 at 867, per Lord Hope.
104 *Society for Protection of the Harbour Ltd v. Chief Executive in Council (No. 2)* [2004] 2 HKLRD 902 at 929–30. Despite the rhetoric, the manner the court applied this sliding scale test was not much different from the Wednesbury unreasonable test. It highlights the uneasiness of the court to interfere with the executive assessment of competing factors. For a more detailed discussion, see J. Chan, 'A Sliding Scale of Reasonableness in Judicial Review' [2006] *Acta Juridica* 233.
105 *Attorney General v. Lee Kwong-kut* [1993] 3 HKPLR 72 at 100.
106 [1995] 5 HKPLR 585.
107 Regional Council Functional Constituency, whereas the largest has 487,000 voters.
108 The Human Rights Committee has concluded in its Concluding Observations on the Fourth Periodic Report of the United Kingdom on Hong Kong that functional constituency elections were incompatible with Article 25 of the ICCPR: 'The Committee considers that the electoral system in Hong Kong does not meet the requirements of Article 25, as well as Articles 2, 3 and 26 of the Covenant. It underscores in particular that only 20 of 60 seats in the Legislative Council are subject to direct popular election and that the concept of functional constituencies, which gives undue weight to the views of the business community, discriminates among voters on the basis of property and functions. This clearly constitutes a violation of Article 2, paragraph 1, 25(b) and 26'. Reproduced in [1996] 5 HKPLR 641 at 644, para 19.
109 *Ng King Luen v. Rita Fan* [1997] 1 HKLRD 757.
110 [2001] 1 HKLRD 641. Mr Justice Hartmann held that the right to take part in the conduct of public affairs under Article 25 of the ICCPR included not only participation in situations which have legislative, executive or administrative powers but also participation in institutions which, while not possessed of those powers, do have the power by way of open debate, consultation and advice to have a real influence on public affairs. It is for each jurisdiction, through its constitution and its law, to decide the modalities best suited to meet the changing conditions of its own society which at the same time comply with Article 25. In Hong Kong, it has chosen to place executive and administrative powers in the hands of the Government, whereas legislative power is vested in the Legislative Council. It has further chosen to create a number of District Councils which are able to debate local needs and to influence the Government in its formulation and implementation of policies to meet those needs. Thus, through the establishment of both the Legislative Council and the District Council, the requirements of Art 25 were held to have been met.
111 [2000] 9 HKPLR 610.
112 *The Society for the Protection of Harbour v. Town Planning Board* [2003] 3 HKLRD 960 (CFI); [2004] 1 HKLRD 396 (CFA). There are two separate challenges to two separate outline zoning plans. The earlier discussion on proportionality refers to the challenges to the Central reclamation, whereas this part refers to the challenges to the Wanchai reclamation. For a more detailed discussion of these cases, see J. Chan, 'A Sliding Scale of Reasonableness in Judicial Review' [2006] *Acta Jurisdica* 223–56.
113 [2005] 8 HKCFAR 628.
114 *Lo Siu Lan v. Hong Kong Housing Authority* [2004] HKEC 1521 (CFI); [2004] HKEC 1541 (CA); [2005] 8 HKCFAR 363.
115 [2006] HKEC 239 (CFI); [2006] HKEC 816 (CA); sub nom *Koo Sze Yiu v. Chief Executive of the HKSAR* [2006] 3 HKLRD 455 (CFA).

116 *Secretary for Justice v. Shum Chiu* [2006] HKEC 2335. See also *HKSAR v. Chan Kau Tai* [2006] 1 HKLRD 400 and *HKSAR v. Mo Yuk Ping* [2005] HKEC 1318; *HKSAR v. Li Man Tak* [2005] HKEC 1309.
117 *Koo Sze Yiu v. Chief Executive of the HKSAR* [2006] 3 HKLRD 455.
118 The public housing rental case, the *Link Reit* case and the Harbour reclamation case described above are particularly apposite examples of the fine distinction between law and politics.
119 Speech of the Chief Justice at the Ceremonial Opening of the Legal Year 2006 (9 Jan 2006) (available at www.judiciary.gov.hk/en/other_info/speeches.htm).
120 In a typical democratic system, the role of the judiciary is to check against majority dictatorship or to balance against a vocal and well organized minority that is able to hijack political agendas: for a useful discussion, see Wheare K.C., *Modern Constitutions*, Oxford University Press, 2nd ed, 1966; Bruce Ackerman, 'Beyond Carolene Products', *Harv L Rev*, vol.no.98, no.713, 1985. In Hong Kong, the main problem of democracy deficit is the absence of checks and balance against the Executive Government so that the judiciary becomes a major venue for ensuring good governance and accountability of the Government.

9 More law, less courts
Legalized governance, judicialization, and *dejudicialization* in China

Randall Peerenboom

The global trend has been toward the judicialization of social, economic and political issues. Civil law countries, newly established democracies and even authoritarian regimes have now adopted various forms of constitutional review that greatly expand the policy-making capacity of judges.[1] In administrative law, there is a heavier emphasis on judicial review, and, in many countries, a transition from soft/procedural to hard/substantive review, which allows judges in effect to substitute their judgment for that of administrative agencies.[2]

As part of this judicial expansion, courts now regularly review both specific acts and abstract acts (generally applicable administrative rules). In so doing, they are aided by a series of increasingly onerous rules that require agencies to base their decisions on cost–benefit analysis, take notice and comment provisions seriously, establish a written record, give reasons for their decisions and even in some cases respond to specific comments from the public.

To be sure, not all states have followed the United States so far down the substantive review path.[3] Nor for that matter has "hard review" prevailed in the U.S. Since the Chevron case, judicial review has also arguably been softer, with courts required to show more deference to agency decisions. Furthermore, courts have always been considerably more political than suggested by the naive civic textbook account of judges as neutral arbiters who faithfully apply the law. Nevertheless, even accepting such qualifications, there has been a marked trend overall for courts to be more involved in policy making, acting more like political agents that can and do overrule the decisions of the legislature and administrative agencies.[4]

In China, there has been an undeniable shift toward *legalized*[5] governance, including a wide range of administrative reforms that seek to implement "administration according to law" (*yifa xingzheng*).[6] However, China offers mixed support for the *judicialization* of administrative law or governance more broadly. Although there has been an increased reliance on courts to handle an expanding range of cases, and administrative litigation has become an accepted feature of the PRC political-legal landscape, the courts continue to play a complementary role to political-administrative mechanisms in dispute resolution and an even more limited role in the making of key policies. Moreover, there are signs of retrenchment—a reversal of judicialization or *dejudicialization*—as it has become increasingly evident that courts are not the proper venue for resolving many of the socially, politically and economically contentious issues that typically arise in a developing country undergoing rapid and fundamental change, especially one as large, diverse and complex as China.

The first section provides a brief overview of the many efforts to legalize governance. The second section examines the role of the courts in dispute resolution in general, and in administrative litigation in particular. The third section applies the main explanations in the theoretical literature for the judicialization of administrative law and governance to China. These theories have been developed largely in light of the histories of economically advanced democracies in Euro-America or the experiences of newly established democracies. The fourth section goes beyond existing theories to explore other explanations for the relatively more limited role of courts in China. Some of the reasons are China-specific, or particular to non-democracies or democracies dominated by a single party, particularly with respect to *politically sensitive cases*. Others reflect the specific challenges that middle-income countries face and the difficulties courts have handling the *growing pains cases* that arise in developing countries. The fifth section discusses dejudicialization. The sixth section concludes with some thoughts about the likely direction of future developments in China; some observations about the limits of existing theory to explain developments in authoritarian regimes; and a reminder that, even assuming judicialization is desirable in developed democracies, expecting courts in developing countries to resolve economically, politically and socially contentious issues may be asking too much of a still evolving institution.

The "legalization" of administrative law and governance

The government's efforts to establish a socialist rule of law state have resulted in major changes affecting virtually all aspects of the legal-political system. Although beyond the scope of this chapter, reforms have led to significant changes in Party-state relations, state-society relations and major governing institutions including the people's congresses, the procuracy, police and the legal profession, as well as to the judiciary.[7] Judicial reforms fall into three broad categories: efforts to make the adjudicative process more efficient and just; reforms aimed at enhancing the quality and professionalism of judges and attempts to increase the authority and independence of the courts. Most recent judicial reforms fall into the first two categories, although the autonomy and independence of the courts have also been strengthened.[8]

The plethora of reforms aimed at establishing rule of law and improving governance have been effective. As of 2004, China's legal system ranked in the 41st percentile on the World Bank's rule of law index. As rule of law and other good governance indicators are highly correlated with wealth, China's performance is best judged relative to other countries in its income class.[9] China performs better than average in its lower-middle-income class on rule of law, as it does on most other core indicators of good governance,[10] and indeed on most indicators of human rights and well-being with the exception of civil and political rights.[11]

Administrative law has been one of the most active areas of reform. The wide-ranging reforms to the administrative law regime include: acceptance of a new conception of governance based on the principle of administration according to law (*yifa xingzheng*); strengthening of the administrative law regulatory framework; improvements in the quality of the civil service; the limited albeit not insignificant efforts at deregulation; recent measures to increase transparency and public participation and last but not least the attempts to strengthen the various mechanisms for reining in state actors.[12]

A new conception of governance: yifa xingzheng and limited government

In March 2004, the State Council issued the Implementation Outline for Promoting Administration by Law in a Comprehensive Way, and announced the goal of realizing a law-abiding government in ten years. The concept of a limited government is now increasingly accepted (although debates continue about how big the state should be, and its proper role in the economy and provision of social services). Also, whereas in the past the purpose of administrative law was considered to be how to facilitate efficient government and ensure that government officials and citizens alike obey central policies, administrative law is now understood to entail a balancing of government efficiency with the need to protect individual rights and interests.

Constructing the regulatory framework for an administrative law regime

The last 15 years have witnessed a flurry of national and local legislative activity. In terms of national laws alone, the Administrative Litigation Law was passed in 1989, providing a general basis for citizens to sue government officials. In 1990, the Administrative Supervision Regulations and the Administrative Reconsideration Regulations were passed. In 1994, the State Compensation Law was passed, followed by the Administrative Penalties Law in 1996. The Administrative Supervision Regulations and Administrative Reconsideration Regulations were amended and upgraded to laws in 1997 and 1999 respectively. The Administrative Licensing Law was promulgated in 2003, followed by the Administrative Compulsory Enforcement Law in 2005. The NPC is now considering a draft Administrative Procedure Law (APL). The law is not expected to be passed for several years, however, as numerous technical, conceptual and political problems have yet to be worked out. Nevertheless, the passage of an APL within the next decade would still be much earlier in the developmental arc than in other East Asian development states such as Japan, Taiwan and Korea, all of which only passed such laws in the 1990s.

Improving the civil service

The 1993 provisional regulations for civil servants were followed by the Law on Civil Servants in 2005. These acts changed the way government officials were selected and promoted and introduced a rotation system. Recruitment of officials for key government positions is now more competitive and transparent. Recruitment notices and qualification requirements are made public, the nomination process is more democratic and candidates must pass exams and then yearly appraisals.

In addition, the CPC Central Committee issued the Regulations on the Work of Selecting and Appointing Leading Party and Government Cadres in 2002, followed in 2004 by the Provisional Regulations on the Open Selection of Leading Cadres of the Party and Government and the Interim Provisions on the Work of Competition for Posts in the Party and Government. The regulations provide for open and competitive recruitment and cover all aspects of the process, including application, selection standards and procedures, examination and promotion procedures and supervision and discipline.

Limited deregulation and privatization

During the era of the centrally planned economy, administrative agencies were integrally involved in commercial activities. A ministry would be responsible for carrying out Party policies and regulating the industry; and, as the department in charge of a particular industry, it would be responsible for allocating resources, resolving disputes between companies under its charge and ensuring that such companies met their quotas. In many cases, companies affiliated with the ministries had a virtual monopoly. It became clear early in the reform period that the transition to a market economy required separating government from enterprises. Ministries were divided in two, with the ministry retaining responsibility for regulating but distancing itself from commercial activities. In the process, new companies were established or existing companies reorganized. State-owned enterprises (SOEs) were given greater autonomy in operating. Many small and medium-sized state-owned enterprises have been sold off. The government has also allowed investors to purchase shares, generally minority shares, in larger SOEs.

In recent years, the State Council has embarked on an ambitious program to overhaul the administrative review system for foreign and domestic companies alike in an effort to enhance efficiency and reduce corruption. The new approach confirms a change in policy toward greater deregulation and reliance on market forces. China's entry into the WTO, and the recently enacted Administrative Licensing Law, have provided further impetus, and legal guidelines, for a more streamlined approval and registration system. By the end of 2004, the number of projects that needed government review and approval was cut in half. Some local governments have attempted to establish "one-stop" approval processes for foreign investment projects. Nevertheless, most projects, including foreign investment projects, are still subject to numerous, often overlapping, approval and registration requirements.

The passage of the Law on Enterprise Bankruptcy and Anti-Monopoly Law in 2007 are also part of the drive to enhance market efficiency and competitiveness.

While the general trend toward increased marketization and competition is clear and remains unchanged, there are signs of retrenchment in industrial policy. In December 2006, the State Council announced that seven industries were to remain under "absolute" state control: armaments, electricity, oil, telecommunications, coal, civil aviation, and shipping. In addition, several others would remain under "relatively strong" state control, including manufacturing, automobiles, electronics, architecture, steel, metallurgy, chemicals, surveillance, science and technology. The goal is to cultivate 30 to 50 globally competitive enterprise groups. The government is also developing a system similar to that in the U.S. to investigate the impact of economic transactions on national security, and to investigate and retaliate against trade barriers in other countries.[13] Meanwhile, the bankruptcy law contained a temporary carve-out through 2008 for certain state-owned enterprises.[14] Further, the Anti-Monopoly Law does not adequately address administrative monopolies and sectors dominated by large SOEs, which have been the main areas of concern. In light of the above, skeptics have questioned the assumption that China's leaders are committed to increased market competition, arguing that the real rationale behind the law is the desire to maintain and extend economic control.[15]

More, albeit still limited, transparency and public participation

The government has sought to achieve greater accountability and efficiency by enhancing transparency and increasing the channels for public participation in the rule-making, implementation and supervision processes. As noted, the NPC is now drafting an Administrative Procedure Law. As is often the case, local governments have already passed their own procedural regulations. China's WTO accession agreement also requires that the public, including foreign companies, be given an opportunity to comment on commercial regulations before they become effective (but unfortunately not before they are promulgated). The NPC has also been soliciting public comment on major laws, in accordance with the Law on Legislation. In general, both the NPC and administrative agencies solicit opinions from academic experts during the law- and rule-making processes.

Recent years have seen attempts to expand the use of hearings both for NPC laws and administrative rules.[16] There are currently a number of projects and experiments on hearings that seek to address issues ranging from when hearings should be held, how the public is to be notified, who should be able to attend and speak at such hearings (especially if the number of people wishing to attend the hearing and speak is very large), how the hearings should be conducted and how the government should respond to inquiries or recommendations from the public.

In 2007, the State Council passed the Regulations on Open Government Information. Prior to that, numerous provincial and municipal governments had passed open government information regulations. Most government agencies now also have websites where regulations and other information are made available to the public. The amount of information available to the public, and the degree of user-friendliness, vary widely. Broad central and local state secret laws and regulations prohibit the dissemination and discussion of information of general public concern on a range of issues, from family planning policies to corruption and to the number of persons subject to the death penalty.

The State Council has acknowledged that considerably more needs to be done in making government more transparent and service-oriented. A 2005 report noted that some officials have not attached much importance to efforts to increase openness, that regulations are incomplete or not implemented, and that some departments have only made half-hearted, formalistic efforts at compliance.[17] It called on local governments to pass access to information acts and to make public through the media, websites, information centers and public hearings information on government budgets, procurements and tax revenues, land takings, major investment projects, bankruptcies and the distribution of assets and license and registration requirements. It also called for sanctions for government officials that falsify progress reports or fail to take action in carrying out the directive.

The government has also experimented with citizen committees to supervise and advise on government work.[18] At the central level, the Development and Reform Commission has established an Expert Consultation System. At the provincial level, Shanxi recently established the Government Decision-making Consultation Committee, and invited 60 experts to participate as consultants on key decisions made by the provincial government. Hunan established the Academics and Experts Consultation System, set up the Opinion Poll Center in the Provincial Statistics Bureau and established the Public Opinion Collection and Analysis Mechanism. Having created the Governor and Expert Symposia and Foreign Consultant Invitation System, Guangdong now holds a symposium every two years where the heads of the top 50 enterprises in the world are invited to advise the governor on economic development in Guangdong. Hainan established a system where regulations and official documents are sent out for review by outside legal counsel before being sent to the governor for signature. Hebei has also established legal expert consultation bodies in 11 city governments and more than half of the county governments.

Even the procuracy, one of the most conservative and least open institutions, has jumped on the bandwagon. Beginning in October 2003, the procuracy established citizen supervision committees in ten provinces. The system is now used by 86 percent of procuratorates nationwide. The committee is charged with conducting independent appraisals of cases the procuracy placed on file for investigation but later decided to withdraw or terminate prosecution. According to the Democracy White Paper: "They can also participate, upon invitation, in other law-enforcement examination activities organized by the people's procuratorates regarding crimes committed by civil servants, and make suggestions and comments on violations of law and discipline discovered. By the end of 2004, a total of 18,962 people's supervisors had been selected, who had supervised the conclusion of 3,341 cases."[19]

Improvement of mechanisms to check administrative power

The government has sought to strengthen the various mechanisms for checking administrative power and providing citizens with remedies against wayward state actors who exceed or abuse their powers. These mechanisms include legislative supervision;[20] the national audit system;[21] administrative reconsideration; administrative litigation; administrative supervision;[22] party discipline committees and *shuanggui* (non-judicial detention) procedures;[23] the letter and petition system;[24] supervision by consultative committees, NGOs, the media and other civil society actors[25] and local and inner party elections.[26] Nevertheless, further reforms are needed to fully realize the potential of these mechanisms.[27]

Provisional summary

China has developed many political-administrative mechanisms for governing and handling disputes, in addition to litigation in the courts. These mechanisms are codified in law, and thus reflect a long-term trend toward legalization and a law-based society.[28]

Some commentators have expressed concerns that administrative developments have been overly top-down, with a heavy emphasis on promulgation of new laws, harmonization of the increasingly dense legislative network, rationalization and centralization of the regulatory bureaucracy and efforts to change the attitudes of government officials and institutional norms and culture within government agencies.[29] This approach may, critics claim, ignore more recent trends in regulatory theory that call for more bottom-up, experimental approaches, or suggest that greater use be made of negotiated rule making (reg-neg), self-regulation (including restorative justice) and the contracting out of government services. These debates about the proper mix of regulatory tools are part of a larger debate about whether China must first establish a modern Weberian regulatory regime or whether it can leapfrog past that stage to a post-modern, post-industrial, post-Fordist phase.[30]

To be sure, legal reforms have been much more bottom-up than often portrayed. Moreover, China has already adopted some of these more fashionable contemporary regulatory techniques. China is well-known for its pragmatic approach to reforms that relies heavily on local experimentation to test various approaches before adopting national policies. It has also experimented with contracting out of government services, including such core government functions as policing, in part because as a lower-middle-income country the state simply lacks the resources and capacity to do everything.[31] Furthermore, the law-making and rule-making processes, at least at the national level, involve repeated rounds of solicitation of, and input from, a wide variety of actors, including academics, representatives of affected industries and companies, relevant ministries and increasingly private citizens. Thus, the process in China is consistent with current global trends toward transparency, civil society participation and reg-neg approaches involving the various stakeholders.

The government is constantly experimenting with a wide variety of regulatory techniques in an effort to rationalize governance, improve efficiency and enhance its legitimacy by better serving citizens and protecting their rights. As in other countries, however, there are dramatically divergent opinions about the relative effectiveness of various techniques and the proper mix.

Judicialization with and within limits

The courts are undeniably playing a much larger role in dispute resolution than in the past. The number of cases rose rapidly through the 1980s and 1990s to around eight million cases per year, while mediation has been decreasing, and arbitration remains insignificant.[32] Administrative litigation cases also rose sharply to 90,000–100,000 cases per year.

The global trend toward judicialization, with a politically more salient role for the judiciary, is evident not only in the increased volume of cases but also in the wide range of controversial economic, social and political disputes now being funneled into the courts.

- Courts have been given jurisdiction over minority shareholders suits against SOEs for disclosure violations, raising a number of complicated issues regarding how to prove damages and what happens if a state-owned enterprise loses the suit, and the liabilities force the company into bankruptcy, leading to massive layoffs and an increase in social instability.
- The courts are also being inundated with labor disputes from factory workers suing over unlawful termination and unsafe working conditions, and migrant workers seeking unpaid wages and protesting compulsory overtime in excess of the number of hours stipulated in the Labor Law.
- Retirees are suing their former employees or the local government for failure to pay pensions, raising important social policy issues in the absence of an effective welfare system.
- Courts are hearing an expanding range of discrimination claims brought with respect to the rights of migrant workers, education, the retirement age for female workers, diseases such as hepatitis and AIDS and the unequal treatment of urban and rural residents in wrongful death cases.
- Land disputes are rising dramatically both in urban and rural areas as governments in pursuit of economic growth requisition land for developers, again raising issues of corruption and collusion.
- Social activists have sought to bring suits against the local government for forced abortions and other violations of family planning policies and regulations.
- Citizens, often aided by newly formed (and sometimes not licensed) environmental groups, are seeking to close down polluting enterprises in their area.

- Courts are also handling cases that touch on sensitive national security issues or affect social stability, including cases involving very broadly defined state secrets regulations that are used against whistleblowers who reveal government corruption or malfeasance.
- A rising number of cases involve freedom of speech, assembly and religion, including the rights of citizens to form NGOs: in one much publicized case, Dong Jian brought an administrative litigation suit against the Ministry of Health after the Ministry failed to respond formally to Dong's application to establish an NGO to promote eye care.
- In addition, many cases raise the issue of social justice as those who have lost out in the course of economic reforms look to the courts for protection: what are people entitled to given the government's goal of establishing a harmonious society (*hexie shehui*) or at least a *xiaokang* society?[33]

Support structures[34] for judicialization are also growing fast. Social activists and special interest groups are using the courts to press their agendas. A number of lawyers and law firms now specialize in "impact litigation." They are often based in or closely associated with legal aid centers, or supported by and linked to universities or the national or local bar association. At the annual Impact Litigation Forum, experts discuss the ten most significant cases for that year, chosen by experts and the public via Internet voting.[35] In 2005, the event was widely covered in over two million press reports. In general, there is something of a "law craze" in China nowadays: controversial cases are widely debated in the print media and on the Internet; radio and television programs regularly discuss the ins and outs of new laws and legal developments and people flock to sensationalist trials (over 50 million people attended trials in 2005 alone).

Not surprisingly, courts are more powerful than ever before. This is evident in the high rate of administrative litigation cases where courts quash administrative agency decisions or a case is withdrawn after the agency changes its decision. Plaintiffs prevail in whole or in part in approximately 30 to 40 percent of administrative litigation cases in China, in comparison to 12 percent in the U.S. and just 8 to 12 percent in Japan and Taiwan. Another indicator is the low number of cases (less than 0.3 percent) supervised by the procuracy or people's congress that result in a changed verdict.[36] The enhanced stature of the court is also evident in the high acquittal rates for lawyers in cases where police and procuracy prosecute lawyers on trumped-up charges of falsifying evidence.[37] Further, whereas in the past, plaintiffs in labor suits often lost, with the court often upholding the decision of the labor arbitration committee, today the majority wins in court—with plaintiffs enjoying a higher success rate in courts than in arbitration.[38] In short, the courts, once described as no different than the post office,[39] are now able to stand up to the people's congress, procuracy, police and other state actors.

In a related yet rather unusual development given the civil law structure in China, the SPC plays a limited but important policy-making role by issuing a wide variety of interpretations of laws, even though the court's legal basis for doing so is far from solid. These interpretations are more detailed, and often longer, than the law itself, and generally reflect the experiences of the courts in dealing with issues that have arisen in the course of interpreting and implementing the laws.[40]

Limits on judicial review of specific acts

Despite the signs of judicial expansion, the role of the courts in dispute resolution and policy making remains limited, particularly with respect to certain types of cases or issues. The total number of disputes submitted to the courts has leveled off,[41] as has the number of administrative law suits.[42]

Doctrinal shortcomings explain to some extent the relatively small number of administrative cases. For instance, the Administrative Litigation Law (ALL) allows parties to bring suit when their "legitimate rights and interests" are infringed by a specific administrative act of an administrative organ or its personnel. This requirement has been construed narrowly to prevent those with only indirect or tangential interests in an act from bringing suit. The narrow interpretation prevents interest groups or individuals acting as "private attorney generals" from challenging the administration. Moreover, citizens may only challenge decisions that affect their personal or property rights. This excludes other important rights, most notably civil rights such as the rights to march and to demonstrate, freedom of association and assembly and rights of free speech and free publication.[43]

A difficult issue faced by all systems is what level of deference judges should show to administrative agencies. The ALL authorizes the court to annul or remand for reconsideration administrative decisions if the agency makes its decision without sufficient essential evidence, incorrectly applies laws or regulations, violates legal procedures or exceeds or abuses its authority. These standards, in the hands of an aggressive judiciary, could develop in a way that practically permits the courts to review acts for their appropriateness. For instance, both "exceeding authority" and "abuse of authority" have been interpreted in other countries to include principles of proper purpose, relevance, reasonableness, consistency with fundamental rights and proportionality. However, Chinese courts have not been aggressive in using these potentially broad standards to review agency acts.

Similarly, judges could use the insufficiency of evidence standard to take a "hard look" at the factual basis for decisions. They could force agencies to establish a record by setting a high standard for the type, quality and quantity of evidence required to justify an agency decision. There is some movement in that direction.[44] In accordance with local rules, some courts will refuse to accept agency statements about what happened at a hearing unless a record is kept. Courts have also refused to recognize administrative rules that have not been properly filed for review.

In general, however, the courts have been reluctant to hold agencies to procedural requirements. They do not require agencies to develop a detailed record, give reasons for their actions or respond to individual public comments—all of which support a more substantive review. This may in part be a reflection of a traditional emphasis on substantive rather than procedural justice. In addition, China has yet to pass an Administrative Procedure Law. Accordingly, procedural requirements are contained in piecemeal legislation and tend to lack detail. Many reformers hope, perhaps somewhat unrealistically, that the proposed Administrative Procedure Law will go a long way toward addressing the problem.

Although there is no theoretical reason why the courts could not develop broad standards of review, in practice their stature in the political hierarchy combined with their dependence on local government for funding and personnel decisions, has resulted in a less aggressive approach to judicial review. However, the SPC's Second Five-Year Agenda, in addition to revising the rules for administrative litigation, calls for structural reforms to prevent interference in administrative cases, including the centralization of funding. In some cases, a stronger and more aggressive judiciary would be desirable. However, it is debatable whether decision and policy making by government officials is being replaced with decision and policy making by judges as a general matter.

Judicial and constitutional review of laws and regulations

In China, courts do not have the power to review abstract acts (generally applicable administrative rules). They may only review specific acts, and then only for their legality rather than for their appropriateness. Nevertheless, courts in effect carry out a type of abstract review by basing their decisions on higher-level legislation while ignoring inconsistent local level legislation.

The courts' refusal to follow local regulations often leads agencies to change policies, though in some cases only after overcoming considerable local resistance. For instance, in one case, the Guangxi People's Congress passed regulations imposing a toll on non-residents, in violation of national laws. The regulation was challenged in court, with the High People's Court deciding in favor of the plaintiff. The High Court sought instruction from the SPC, and based its decision on the SPC's reply. Nevertheless, the Guangxi People's Congress threatened to remove the judge if he decided in favor of the plaintiffs. The People's Congress relented only after the SPC intervened on behalf of the judge and insisted that the court uphold the national law.

Because the courts cannot declare regulations invalid, the local government could continue to impose tolls on non-residents, who would then have to challenge the action again in court. This is highly inefficient, and leads to unequal and unfair treatment. While other administrative and legislative entities do have the authority to declare lower-level legislation invalid, the processes involved are cumbersome, and not all can be initiated by individual complainants. As a result, one intermediate court judge in the infamous "seed case" attempted to strike down a local regulation, declaring it invalid *ab initio* (*zi sheng wuxiao*). Her action caused an uproar and almost resulted in her termination for exceeding her authority. Neither the executive nor legislative branch appears ready to concede authority for even this limited form of review to the courts.

China has yet to establish a dedicated constitutional review body. The NPC Standing Committee is formally charged with constitutional interpretation and review, although it rarely performs these functions, and when it does, it does so primarily for the purpose of ensuring consistency between higher- and lower-level legislation rather than protecting individual rights.

There has been considerable debate about the need to establish a more effective constitutional review procedure,[45] with some advocating review by general courts as in the U.S. (although this seems ill-advised and in any event highly unlikely), some favoring review by the SPC and still others favoring a special constitutional court. There are also many differences of opinion about the powers of the review body and the nature, scope and details of review.

Explaining the limited judicialization: application of general theories

Theories to explain the global trend toward judicialization can be grouped into three categories: political, economic and normative.[46]

Political theories

Two closely related political theories center on the role of ruling parties. In the *political insurance theory*, members of ruling parties that face the risk of losing power in the near future cede power to the courts as a way of ensuring that their policies will be reviewed by a third party, rather than simply overturned by the incoming party, and also as a way of ensuring that they themselves will be treated fairly.[47] The *separation of powers/divided government* theory suggests that politicians cede power to the court to avoid deadlock in systems where one party may control the legislature while the other party wins the presidency and controls the executive branch.

Applied to China, these theories would predict limited judicialization given that China is effectively a single-party state. Party and state functions are formally separate, and in fact there is a much higher degree of separation than the stereotype of China as an authoritarian regime dominated by the Party suggests. Nevertheless, courts do not review Party decisions.

While these theories seem successful in predicting limited judicialization, they fail to explain why judicialization has occurred to the extent it has in China (or for that matter in other authoritarian regimes).

Another theory focuses on the need to police the boundaries between central and local governments in a *federal system*. China, however, is a unitary system. That said, the general principle behind the theory—the need for the central government as principal to police local governments as agents—is certainly applicable, and goes some way toward explaining judicialization in China. Economic reforms have resulted in significant decentralization, and led to an incentive structure that virtually ensures principal-agent problems because local officials are assessed and promoted to a large extent based on their ability to deliver economic growth and social stability. Thus, local governments often pass local regulations or make decisions at odds with central policies in their headlong rush to generate growth.

Giving judges the power to review administrative decisions is one way for the center to rein in wayward local officials.

Nevertheless, administrative litigation is only one of many means for reining in local officials. It is not even the most powerful. The nomenklatura system and the incentive structure for promotions, Party sanctions and ultimately criminal sanctions are more powerful tools. Moreover, the decision not to allow courts to review abstract acts and various doctrinal rules limits the power of courts to act as the Party's agent to control local officials. Thus, the need to police local agents provides at best only a partial explanation for the role of courts in China today.

Still another theory suggests that political actors may cede power to the courts as a way of *diffusing responsibility*. Both democratic and authoritarian regimes may find it advantageous to funnel divisive issues to the court as a way of maintaining elite level consensus, deflecting popular discontent away from the regime, and allowing disgruntled citizens a forum to blow off steam, thus maintaining legitimacy for the ruling party.

The Party's desire to diffuse responsibility by having the normal state organs (the legislature, courts, administrative agencies, etc.) assume responsibility for daily governance is one of the motivations for the move toward legalized governance and rule of law.[48] During the Mao era, the Party was responsible for virtually all decisions, big and small, including the disastrous Great Leap Forward and Cultural Revolution. The Party was also burdened by the Marxist dogma of scientific rationalism, and the belief in a single right answer to complex social, political and economic issues. With economic and social reforms leading to a more pluralistic society, it became impossible to maintain the myth of a single right answer.

While the diffusion theory has some explanatory power, it too should not be overstated. The Party continues to be responsible—and to be held accountable in the eyes of the citizenry—for all major policies. No one would expect the courts to be key decision-makers given their stature and the structural limits typically found in traditional civil law systems.

Economic theories

The most straightforward and powerful explanation for judicialization is economic reforms. Investors need a forum for resolving disputes fairly and efficiently. In a reasonably complex economy, relational contracting and informal mechanisms for resolving (horizontal) disputes between contracting parties are inadequate. In general, litigation increases as economies develop; and legal institutions are strengthened as countries become richer. As the more than four million civil cases a year in China demonstrates, there is more to the slogan "a market economy is a rule of law economy" than mere rhetoric.

A variant of this theme attributes the *degree* of judicialization to the *degree* of economic liberalization: freer markets require more legalistic modes of regulation because informal, hierarchical means of control are not adequate.

Ginsburg[49] suggests this explains the trend away from administrative discretion in other East Asian developmental states, while Gillespie[50] suggests that in Vietnam the Party's continued intervention in the market has enhanced administrative discretion and hindered the development of administrative litigation and the administrative law regime more generally.

In China, the transition from a centrally planned economy to today's more market-based economy has decentralized decision-making. The role of the former State Planning Commission and other regulating agencies has changed from one of comprehensive management over both general policy-making and daily operational decisions for state-owned enterprises to a focus on general macro-development and regulatory issues, as suggested by the renaming of the Commission to the State Development and Reform Commission.

However, given large sectors dominated by administrative monopolies and state-owned enterprises, one would expect the degree of judicialization, at least in economic cases involving these entities, to be limited. While some would argue that this is in fact the case, the overall trend is to treat state-owned enterprises like other entities. For instance, in January 2005, the State Council issued regulations emphasizing that SOEs owned by the central government are to handle independently—and to be liable for—major legal disputes.[51]

China's accession to the WTO also required judicial review of administrative actions and the consistent application of laws and regulation. However, rather than being seen as an external force compelling China to make unwanted changes and thus a radical departure from existing practices, WTO accession should be viewed as a continuation of China's internal reform process.

A somewhat narrower economic-based explanation for judicialization looks to the need for the political regime to demonstrate a credible commitment to investors, and in particular to demonstrate its commitment to avoid vertical takings. As Ginsburg[52] puts it: "Since it will govern for a very long time, the Chinese Communist Party cannot credibly promise not to interfere with local property rights; an independent public review of alleged bureaucratic wrongs helps to make the Party's promises more believable."

In China, the government has demonstrated its commitment to investors over the last 25 years, and it has been rewarded with annual FDI inflows that rival, and sometimes surpass, those of the U.S. However, it has not been because the courts have imposed real restraints on vertical takings. Rather, the state has been bound by the political need for economic growth, required to maintain legitimacy and retain power. Thus, a two-track system has developed. Central and local governments have been careful to avoid taking property from businesses for fear of poisoning the business environment. Yet they have frequently confiscated land from, and relocated, private citizens—and they have done so in the name of economic development (though in the process many officials have benefited from kick-backs and bribes). For a variety of reasons discussed shortly, the courts have not been effective in dealing with land takings involving private citizens. In fact, land takings have been the single biggest reason for the rapid rise in large-scale protests, which are increasingly turning violent.

Normative theories

The globalization of law, flying today under the banner of rule of law and good governance, has been inspired by, or in service to, an increasingly comprehensive and assertive international economic law regime, and an increasingly comprehensive and assertive international human rights regime. An independent and activist judiciary with wide powers of constitutional and administrative review is often seen as beneficial to both economic growth and the protection of human rights (though the biggest determinant of rights enjoyment in most cases is wealth).[53]

In China, the dominant theory of law in general, and administrative law in particular, now accepts the need to balance efficiency/the control function, with equity/the protection of human rights. However, the courts provide at best limited protection of civil and political rights when the exercise of such rights threatens sociopolitical stability. Moreover, as in most countries, economic rights are generally not justiciable. To the extent that rights-protection has fueled judicialization in China, it has mainly been the protection of property interests needed to ensure growth. This type of two-track system—restraints on civil and political rights and protection of property rights and the commercial interests of businesses—is a general feature of the East Asian model of development.[54]

A variant on this theme is that countries today need independent, rights-protecting courts to be considered legitimate in the eyes of the world public and their own citizens. Given the crackdown in Tiananmen in 1989 and the continued slow pace of political reform in China today, it is safe to say that the greater role for the courts has not been the result of Chinese leaders bowing to international pressure, at least from the human rights community. An increasingly confident China has come to realize the foreign pressure to take rights more seriously is inconsistent and marginalized within the overall foreign policy goal structure of most countries, including the U.S.[55] Within China, legitimacy has been performance-based. Indeed, poll after poll shows most Chinese citizens are reasonably satisfied with the government, happy with their lives and optimistic about the future.[56] Again, the main driving force comes from the transition to a market economy.

However, with citizens now more conscious of their rights, and the government having promised the rule of law, people have turned to the courts to obtain relief in all sorts of cases. As in other East Asian countries, sustaining the dual-track system has proven difficult.

Local explanations for limited judicialization

The standard view attributes the limited role of the courts in China to the nature of the political regime. There is no doubt that there is considerable truth to this explanation when it comes to civil and political rights that are perceived to threaten sociopolitical stability. However, the standard view cannot explain why courts are playing a significant role in China in many areas. Nor can it explain the more limited role of the courts in certain types of cases that do not involve the exercise of civil and political rights.

The main reason for limited judicialization in China is that courts are not the best forum for resolving the types of complex social, economic and political issues that arise in a lower-middle income country such as China. As in other developing countries at its level of wealth, the courts (and other institutions) are relatively weak. Moreover, many of the problems are not amenable to judicial solution—courts simply cannot come up with effective and enforceable remedies.

Many of the disputes are essentially economic in nature, including claims for retirement payments and other welfare benefits, labor suits, challenges to the taking of land and the amount of compensation offered, attempts to force domestic companies to comply with environmental standards typically found in developed states, suits to enforce judgments against state-owned enterprises that are in fact insolvent and so on. The courts cannot make good on the plaintiffs' legal entitlements in such cases: there is no effective remedy. If the state had adequate resources to satisfy these claims, it would have done so.

Further, many of these cases involve conflicting fundamental policy goals. Environmental protection cases, for instance, are difficult because people themselves are conflicted about how to balance the need for clean air and water with the need for economic growth. The court will meet resistance no matter how it decides such cases. Needless to say, enforcement is extremely difficult if not impossible.[57] Similarly, in addition to the conflict of interest between developers and homeowners, land taking cases highlight the tension between the desire to modernize and the desire to retain historical areas.

Land cases highlight another problem: the lack of clear rules, often the result of postponing difficult policy decisions usually made by the legislature.[58] Funneling compensation claims for the taking of rural or urban land into the courts forces judges to decide the controversial issue of who is entitled to the windfall from rising real estate prices. Urban residents, especially those that worked for the government or state-owned enterprises, are often living in housing originally allocated to them by the state for free, and then sold to them at heavily subsidized rates. When the land is requisitioned, the court must decide how much the homeowners should be compensated. Should the current residents be entitled to fair market value for their housing *and* the land use rights, even though the land use rights may be unclear, and they obtained the housing at subsidized prices? Those affected may argue that they worked hard for the state for years for low wages, and deserve the windfall. But they have already benefited relative to others who did not have the opportunity to purchase their housing at below-market prices. Similar issues arise in the countryside, although farmers may have a greater normative claim to the sales from land use rights given the discriminatory policies that transferred wealth from rural to urban areas through artificially low prices for agricultural products and the large wealth differential between rural and urban areas today.

Because rural land is owned collectively, rural taking cases also raise the difficult issues of who speaks for the collective, and whether a few holdouts who want to push for higher compensation can block the majority. Such cases also raise the specter of massive social instability should farmers, having sold the land and run through the money, end up without means to support themselves.

Disputes between newly created homeowner associations and developers and their affiliated management companies also present problems for the court. The regulatory system in this area is new and evolving. Many of the disputes occurred before there were any rules in place. Even now, there are differences between the relevant provisions of the 2007 Property Law and the more detailed administrative regulations that have governed up to now and remain effective. Further, these cases often involve allegations of corruption and collusion between the defendants and local government officials. They pit one powerful group, real estate developers, against increasingly powerful private citizens who are themselves often government officials or members of the nouveau riche with strong government connections.

The problems with the courts should not be overstated, as they often are. Courts are able to handle most cases reasonably well, and parties are relatively satisfied with their performance, at least in comparison to other countries.[59] However, courts are considerably less successful at handling certain types of cases, which can be broadly categorized as politically sensitive cases and cases that reflect the growing pains of developing countries.[60]

The courts' failure to provide an adequate remedy in these cases, especially the growing pains cases, is one of the reasons for the rapid rise in large-scale social protests, from 58,000 in 2003 to over 74,000 in 2004 alone. It also explains the massive upsurge in letters and petitions, even though writing letters to or visiting government officials rarely produces a satisfactory result. In the face of this upsurge, the State Council amended the Regulations on Letters and Visits in 2005. The amendments strengthened the rights of citizens in some respects. For instance, the Regulations call for greater procedural fairness, increased powers for the letter and visits offices to respond to citizen complaints and enhanced supervision of government officials involved in the process, including through the imposition of legal liability for those who do carry out their duties. However, the authorities appear to be increasingly worried that too many people are blocking government offices, interfering with officials trying to do their work and upsetting social stability. The Regulations limit the petitioner to three appeals to successively higher-level administrative agencies. The 2005 Public Security Administration Punishments Law suggests that the government will start to crack down on those who repeatedly petition government offices.

Retrenchment—dejudicializing disputes

Both judges and government officials appear to have realized the problems with funneling certain types of cases to the courts. One sign of the pushback on judicialization is the attempt to limit access to the courts in controversial cases, notwithstanding the general trend toward greater access through legal aid, the waiving of court fees, the simplification of filing procedures, etc.

- Courts will sometimes refuse to accept politically sensitive cases. In some cases, they will even recommend to the plaintiffs that they file a case in a higher-level court or another jurisdiction.
- As noted, the courts have interpreted standing requirements narrowly to prevent "private attorney general" lawsuits and to prevent parties from challenging agency decisions that limit their civil and political rights in administrative litigation suits.
- The courts are also resisting pressure from people's congresses and the procuracy to retry cases through the discretionary supervision procedure. In addition, the courts have issued rules to prevent parties from repeatedly petitioning the court to retry cases.[61] If parties are still unhappy with the results after exhausting the normal appeal process, they should look to other political or administrative channels for a remedy.
- Another technique is to require that parties first exhaust their administrative remedies. Labor advocates have long called for the abolition of the requirement that workers first go through arbitration before going to court. However, a Supreme Court interpretation in 2006 provided only limited relief, allowing workers to go directly to court in wage arrears cases where they have written proof of unpaid wages from the employer, and no other claims are raised.[62] In contrast, the 2007 Labor Dispute Mediation and Arbitration Law went the other way, providing for binding arbitration in certain cases including failure to pay wages or worker's compensation. The law also emphasized mediation and appears to create an additional administrative channel for workers to bring suit.[63]

The government has also sought to relieve pressure on courts by limiting the ability of citizens to challenge taking and compensations decisions. In 2001, the State Council issued the Urban Housing Demolition Administrative Regulation, which requires developers negotiate a demolition agreement with residents and provide details for calculating compensation. However, the Demolition Regulation also provides that the developer can apply for a "forced demolition" if the residents do not accept a developer's compensation proposal that has been approved by municipal authorities. And while the Demolition Regulation allows the residents to challenge a municipally approved compensation proposal in court, it also stipulates that the courts cannot stop or suspend a forced demolition that has been approved by the municipality. More generally, the government has enacted a series of measures to prevent land taking disputes from arising in the first place, including shifting the authority upward to provincial governments; re-emphasizing the need for local officials to hold hearings on taking decisions and compensation amounts; requiring that land sales be through a public bidding process; attempting to cool the red hot real estate sector; and amending the Land Management Law and passing the Property Law to clarify and better protect people's rights.[64]

A second sign of dejudicialization is the renewed emphasis on mediation. In response to the difficulties of deciding cases when laws and policies are unclear and the citizenry deeply divided about the proper outcome, the Supreme People's

Court has recently begun to re-emphasize mediation, even in administrative litigation cases. The SPC clearly hopes that mediation will allow the parties to reach a mutually acceptable solution, thus allowing the courts to avoid having to make hard decisions that are difficult to enforce. Nevertheless, the renewed emphasis on mediation is striking for two reasons. First it bucks the trend over the last 25 years for more litigation and less mediation. Second, the court's endorsement of mediation in administrative cases, reflected in the forthcoming amendments to the ALL, is a reversal of the previous policy that prevented mediation in such cases.[65] Previously, mediation was prohibited to avoid agencies putting pressure on parties to withdraw their suits. The reversal suggests that plaintiffs are now more confident in their rights, and thus less likely to bow to agency pressure to withdraw their suits out of fear of retaliation. It also suggests that agencies fear lawsuits less than in the past. This may be because administrative litigation is now an accepted practice, but it may also result from agency officials believing their actions are now in compliance with law.[66]

Still another sign is the attempt to address the problems created for the courts by the rapid rise in mass plaintiff cases. Many of the most contentious cases—environmental, labor, land takings, social security issues—involve multiple parties. The number of such cases has shot up in recent years: there were 538,941 multi-party suits in 2004, up 9.5 percent from 2003. The courts are frequently unable to provide an effective remedy in these cases, which often attract the attention of the media. The disgruntled plaintiffs then take to the streets in protest or besiege government officials with letters and visits. Courts have developed a number of techniques to reduce public pressure, including breaking the plaintiffs up into smaller groups, emphasizing conciliation and providing a spokesperson to meet with, and explain the legal aspects of the case to, the plaintiffs and the media in the hopes of encouraging settlement or even withdrawal of the suit.

In a related move, the authorities have sought to rein in activist litigation support groups. In 2006, the All China Lawyers Association issued guidelines that seek to reach a balance between social order and the protection of citizens and their lawyers in exercising their rights.[67] The guidelines remind lawyers to act in accordance with their professional responsibilities. Lawyers should encourage parties and witnesses to tell the whole truth and not conceal or distort facts; they should avoid falsifying evidence; they should refuse manifestly unreasonable demands from parties; they should not encourage parties to interfere with the work of government agencies; they should accurately represent the facts in discussions with the media and refrain from paying journalists to cover their side of the story and they should report to and accept the supervision of the bar association. On the other hand, bar associations shall promptly report instances of interference with lawyers lawfully carrying out their duties to the authorities, and press the authorities to take appropriate measures to uphold the rights of lawyers. Where necessary, local bar associations may enlist support from the national bar association.

More generally, the government has closed down or put pressure on some NGOs and law firms that have become too active in pressing for change. Some individual lawyers have been arrested, experienced intimidation or had their licenses revoked in the process of representing criminal defendants or citizens challenging government decisions to requisition their land for development purposes and the amount of compensation provided.[68] Meanwhile citizens seeking to protect their property rights, uphold environmental regulations or challenge government actions have been beaten by thugs and gangs, sometimes with links to the local government, or they have been detained for their efforts.[69]

Finally, as is generally true, globally, some of the newer administrative techniques that involve self-regulatory systems or shift policy and decision-making to private actors present different accountability issues from the traditional administrative agency-dominated process.[70] In many cases, judicial review is not possible or at least not the main mechanism for achieving accountability. Thus, the global and Chinese trends toward heightened judicial review of administrative policy and decision-making is offset to some extent by the trend toward greater reliance on these new techniques that decenter and fragment government power.

Conclusion

Courts are only one avenue to resolve disputes and to address social tensions, and they are generally something of a last resort in any country. Given the current level of development and the nature of the disputes, courts in China are unable to provide adequate redress in certain types of cases, most notably politically sensitive ones and the kind of cases that reflect the growing pains typical of developing countries. Pushing these disputes into the courts results in discontented parties venting their anger in the streets. It also undermines the authority of the judiciary at a time when the various state organs are jockeying for power in the new polity that is emerging as a result of the sustained reforms and institution-building of the last 25 years.

A certain amount of judicial retrenchment is therefore a judicious choice at this stage. There is a need to think through more carefully which institutions are best suited to handle which types of disputes, and to avoid overwhelming the courts with cases they are not capable of handling adequately. Dejudicialization, however, will, and should, be limited to certain areas. The general trend will continue to be toward greater judicialization, including administrative cases.

With amendments to the ALL expected soon, there will be an expansion of the courts' role in handling routine ALL cases, particularly those that deal with local officials, because this serves the state's interest in ensuring local officials follow central laws and regulations. Furthermore, the overriding emphasis on maintaining strong economic growth in order to maintain legitimacy suggests a more active role for the courts in protecting property rights and ensuring that agency decisions are efficient, rational and responsive to commercial demands. Courts will also take procedural issues more seriously in administrative litigation cases once the APL comes out, although it is unlikely that the courts will move very far down the path toward robust substantive review in the near future. In addition, courts will continue to take rights more seriously, in administrative cases and generally, at least when the exercise of such rights does not threaten sociopolitical stability, and it is within their power to offer a remedy.

The establishment of a constitutional court or some other viable mechanism for conducting constitutional review is possible, although it does not seem likely in the near future. Ackerman[71] recommends that constitutional courts in new democracies focus first on human rights cases, rather than cases that would involve courts overturning decisions by other state organs, which could result in a backlash. In contrast, Shapiro[72] argues that constitutional review is most likely to be successful when "(1) it is a solution to an acute commitment problem, (2) when a constitutional court is serving politically and economically powerful interests or (3) when it has served such interests in the past and uses the legitimacy accumulated earlier to move on to the service of the less powerful." Thus he concludes that a newly established constitutional court is more likely to be successful if it focuses on federalism issues rather than on human rights issues.

China is not a new democracy. The experiences of constitutional courts in other authoritarian regimes (or democracies dominated by a single party), including in Asia, suggest that one should not expect such a body to play an active role in the early years in protecting civil and political rights. A constitutional review body in China is much more likely to focus at first on principal-agent relations—that is, conflicts between central and local laws. Over time, it may also take on division of power issues among state organs. A significant role in rights-protection is most likely to come only later.[73]

It bears noting that this book project, and the larger projects of exporting a neoliberal market economy, liberal democracy and rule of law are based on certain ideological assumptions largely derived from the experiences of economically advanced Western countries, the U.S. in particular. The central tenets of this ideology are: judges should be important political actors; constitutional and judicial review are essential for the adequate protection of rights and for sustained economic growth; courts must be independent of the ruling party and other state actors to function properly (and indeed, the more independent, the better); privatization and liberalization are necessary for economic growth; good governance requires transparency, public participation and a court-driven rule of law; politically and normatively, the ultimate goal is democracy and a liberal interpretation of rights that prioritizes personal freedoms over collective goods.

Every project must start somewhere, and there is an obvious logic to starting with the experiences of successful states. However, there are two problems with this approach. First, it is not clear to what extent these common assumptions apply to developing countries.[74] Developing countries face special issues. Most obviously, the state lacks the resources to prevent many problems from arising in the first place. In general, institutions are weaker than in developed countries. Corruption, including judicial corruption, is usually more prevalent. As the experiences of many developing democracies show, independent but corrupt courts are surely no guarantor of justice.

Second, the study of the role of courts in authoritarian regimes is only beginning.[75] It has been generally assumed that courts are merely a façade for an oppressive regime that wants to "pull the wool over the eyes" of the international community and foreign investors. However, this view ignores many interesting legal developments in authoritarian regimes. To be sure, institutions may differ, and seemingly similar institutions may play different roles. China has developed a number of institutions including adjudicative committees, individual case supervision by people's congresses and the procuracy and political-legal committees that serve as an interface between the Party, government and courts. These institutions should not be dismissed simply because they are different, or would not be permitted in liberal democracies. Of course, they *may* be problematic, and in need of reform or abolishment, but that determination should be based on an understanding of the context in which they operate and empirical studies that verify the institutions' advantages and disadvantages.

China demonstrates that increasingly assertive and independent courts are possible within an authoritarian regime, albeit within certain limits. Authoritarian regimes, like other regimes, must maintain legitimacy. Given the lack of elections, their legitimacy is even more heavily dependent on sustaining economic growth. Moreover, if the government repeatedly and loudly promises rule of law, passes laws that provide people with a wide range of rights and carries out public education campaigns to raise people's consciousness of their rights, then people will seek to have their rights upheld in whatever forum they can, including the courts. Further, the state is continually extolling judges to become more professional, and requiring that they undergo continual training. External pressure from companies, citizens and international opinion motivate judicial improvement. In addition, and perhaps most significantly, internal pressure from within the judiciary itself is leading to greater professionalism and an enhancement of the stature and authority of the courts.

Painting the courts as agents for "the oppressive regime," with individual judges celebrated as rogues who sometimes thwart the best attempts of Big Brother to force them to be faithful servants of the "Party" line, distorts reality. The Party is not monolithic. There are many different factions within the Party—being a member of the Party tells us less about the political views of a judge than their being a Democrat or Republican in the U.S., or a socialist or centralist in France. Individual Party members hold widely divergent views—much like other members of society—regarding rule of law, judicial review, constitutional law, the rights of criminals, etc. For that very reason, there is no "Party line" on many particular issues. The Party provides a general policy direction: promote growth; maintain social stability. In most economic, administrative and criminal cases, the Party just wants the parties to feel the process was fair and the outcome just.

Thus, there is still considerable room for expansion of the role of the courts in every day cases. Moreover, the range of difficult cases, particularly growing-pains cases but also politically sensitive cases, will narrow over time as China becomes more prosperous and stable with more politically confident leaders.

Finally, the inability to overcome resistance from entrenched interests within the state itself is one of the main reasons developing countries frequently experience the "middle-income blues," where reforms stall and progress grinds to a halt.[76] Contrary to conventional wisdom that would prescribe no role for the Party in judicial affairs, only the Party has the authority to push through difficult institutional reforms, particularly those that affect the balance of power among the major state organs. Paradoxically, PRC courts cannot continue to enhance their authority and independence without Party support for legal reforms in general, and for the courts in particular, as they struggle to professionalize and carve out space in the still evolving political order; but such support comes at the cost of the courts being able to challenge core Party interests lest they bite the hand that feeds them. Courts are not born with independence and authority. In every country, courts must learn to cope with other, often more powerful, political actors. The future of rule of law in China will be determined in no small part by how this negotiated process between the courts, the Party and other state actors plays out.

Notes

1 A. Stone, *Governing with Judges: Constitutional Politics in Europe*, Oxford: Oxford University Press, 2000; T. Ginsburg, *Judicial Review in New Democracies*, New York: Cambridge University Press, 2003; R. Hirschl, *Towards Juristocracy*, Cambridge: Harvard University Press, 2004; P. Leyland and G. Anthony, *Textbook on Administrative Law 5th edition*, Oxford: Oxford University Press, 2005; T. Ginsburg and T. Moustafa, eds., *The Politics of Courts in Authoritarian Regimes*, forthcoming.
2 M. Shapiro, and A. Stone Sweet, *On Law, Politics and Judicialization*, Oxford: Oxford University Press, 2002.
3 Ibid.
4 T. Ginsburg, and R. Kagan, eds., *Institutions and Public Law*, New York: Peter Lang, 2005.
5 "Legalization" and "legalized governance" are awkward and convoluted ways of expressing the notion of a law-based order, much as "judicialization" and "juridicification" are, respectively, awkward and convoluted ways of expressing the notions of an expanded role for courts, and an expansion of legal discourse and modes of analysis into other spheres.
6 R. Peerenboom, *China's Long March Toward Rule of Law*, Cambridge: Cambridge University Press, 2002; R. Peerenboom, *China Modernizes: Threat to the West or Model for the Rest?* Oxford: Oxford University Press, 2007; Office of Legislative Affairs (OLA),*Undertaking Administration According to Law: Review and Prognosis*, report prepared for the Asian Development Bank, 2008; D. Yang, *Remaking the Chinese Leviathan: Market Transition and the Politics of Governance in China*, Stanford: Stanford University Press, 2004.
7 Peerenboom, op. cit., 2002; A. Chen, *An Introduction to the Legal System of the People's Republic of China*. 3rd ed., Hong Kong: LexisNexis/Butterworths, 2004; S. Lubman, *Bird in a Cage: legal reforms in China after Mao*, Stanford: Stanford University Press, 1999; D. Yang, *Remaking the Chinese Leviathan: Market Transition and the Politics of Governance in China*, Stanford: Stanford University Press, 2004; Supreme People's Court 2008; M. Dowdle, "Of Parliaments, Pragmatism, and the Dynamics of Constitutional Development: The Curious Case of China," *New York University Journal of International Law and Politics*, vol.35, no.1, 2002.
8 R. Peerenboom, "Judicial Independence in China," forthcoming 2008; B. Liebman, "China's Courts: Restricted Reforms," *China Quarterly*, forthcoming 2007a.
9 Peerenboom, op. cit., 2007a.

10 D. Kaufmann, et al., Governance Matters III: Governance Indicators for 1996–2004, available at http://info.worldbank.org/governance/kkz2004/sc_chart.asp; Peerenboom, op. cit., 2007.
11 Peerenboom, op. cit., 2007a.
12 OLA, op. cit.; Peerenboom, op. cit., 2002; Peerenboom, op. cit., 2007a; Yang, op. cit.
13 See Chapter VII of the 2004 Foreign Trade Law. The Law calls for investigations of the impact of foreign trade on the competitiveness of domestic industries as well as national security, and contemplates such remedies as anti-dumping measures, countervailing duties or safeguards. Each year, MOFCOM issues reports on trade and investment barriers in over 20 countries, including the E.U., U.S. and Japan. The reports are similar to the U.S. Trade Representative's annual National Trade Estimate Report on Foreign Trade Barriers. While largely political theater, the reports have been used to protest Japan's quantitative restrictions on imports of laver, resulting in Japan's opening of the laver market to Chinese producers.
14 T. Halliday, "The Making of China's Bankruptcy Law," Oxford: Oxford Foundation for Law, Justice and Society, 2007.
15 M. Williams, "Competition Policy and Law," Oxford: Oxford Foundation for Law, Justice and Society, 2007.
16 OLA, op. cit.
17 State Council Opinion on the Further Promoting Openness in Governmental Affairs, March 24, 2005.
18 OLA, op. cit.
19 State Council, White Paper: Building of Political Democracy in China, Oct. 19, 2005.
20 Dowdle, op. cit., 2002.
21 Yang, op. cit.
22 Peerenboom, op. cit., 2002.
23 F. Sapio, "*Shuanggui*: Extra-legal detention by Commissions for Discipline Inspection," *China Information*, vol.22, no.1, forthcoming, 2008.
24 C. Minzner, "Xinfang: An Alternative to the Formal Legal System," *Stanford Journal International Law*, 42, 2006.
25 OLA, op. cit.; Peerenboom, op. cit., 2008.
26 Yang, op. cit.
27 See generally Peerenboom 2002, 2008; OLA, op. cit.
28 The exception is *shuanggui* detention, although even there the Party has issued a number of directives to limit and regulate the procedure.
29 M. Dowdle, "Comments on 'Undertaking Administration in Accordance with Law: Review and Prospects" Asian Development Bank Report: Rule of Law in China: Review and Prospects, 2007.
30 Peerenboom, op. cit., 2002.
31 Mertha (A. Mertha, *The Politics of Piracy: Intellectual Property in Contemporary China*, Ithaca: Cornell University Press, 2005) has shown how companies have hired private investigation firms to collect evidence to document intellectual property violations and in some cases have even paid the public security a fee to raid the violating companies and confiscate counterfeit goods. Stephen Frost has also documented how the government is encouraging and relying on companies to ensure compliance with labor laws in their supply chains. H.L. Fu, and D.W. Choy, "Policing for Profit: Fiscal Crisis and Institutionalized Corruption of Chinese Police," in S. Einstein and M. Amir, eds., *Police Corruption: Paradigms, Models and Concepts: Challenges for Developing Countries*, Huntsville: Office of International Criminal Justice, 2003, Chapter 21, discuss contracting out of policing. Tanner (M. S. Tanner, "Campaign-Style Policing in China and Its Critics," in B. Bakken, ed., *Crime, Punishment and Policing in China*, Lanthan, MD: Rowman & Littlefield, 2005) argues that the reliance on strike hard campaigns, which draw heavily on citizen-involvement in reporting crime, is due in no

small measure to the low ratio of professional police to citizens. While acknowledging traditional aspects to the campaigns, Dutton (M. Dutton, "Toward a Government of the Contract: Policing in the Era of Reform," in B. Bakken, ed., *Crime, Punishment and Policing in China*, Lanthan, MD: Rowman & Littlefield, 2005) points out that they reflect a general trend from a political-based to a market/contract-based philosophy found in policing and society more generally during the reform era.

32 Zhu Jingwen, *Zhongguo falu fazhan baogao (1979–2004)* [*China Legal Development Report (1979–20045)*], Beijing, 2007.

33 Very roughly, *xiaokang* refers to a society in which the differences between the rich and poor are not so great as to undermine social stability. A harmonious society is a much higher standard, and would more like the minimal compromises and accommodations required to achieve a *xiaokang* society. A harmonious society would require in addition that individuals are given the opportunity to achieve a certain degree of self-fulfillment—a notion vaguely akin to the capabilities approach adopted by Sen and Nussbaum. An even loftier idea would be *datong*—literally "great unity." This state is a utopian ideal, capable of various interpretations ranging from the Marxist ideal of "to each according to their needs" to a Millian state in which all obtain self-realization and fulfillment to a state in which procedural and substantive notions of equality would merge. A. Sen, "Capability and Well-being," in M. Nussbaum and A. Sen, eds., *The Quality of Life*, New York: Oxford University Press, 1993; M. Nussbaum, "Capabilities and Human Rights," *Fordham Law Review*, vol. 66, 1997, p.273.

34 C. Epp, *The Rights Revolution*, Chicago: University of Chicago Press, 1998; T. Moustafa, *The Struggle for Constitutional Power: Law, Politics, and Economic Development in Egypt*, Cambridge: Cambridge University Press, 2007.

35 China's Impact Litigation Forum (*Zhongguo yingxiangxing susong luntan*), 2006, available at www.imlawyer.org.

36 R. Peerenboom, "Judicial Accountability and Judicial Independence: An Empirical Study of Individual Case Supervision in the People's Republic of China," *The China Journal*, 2006.

37 Fu Hualing, "When Lawyers are Prosecuted: The Struggle of a Profession in Transition," available at http://ssrn.com/abstract=956500, 2006.

38 E. Michelson, "The Practice of Law as an Obstacle to Justice: Chinese Lawyers at Work," *Law & Society Review*, vol. 1, 2006.

39 D. Clarke, "Power and Politics in the Chinese Court System: The Enforcement of Civil Judgments," *Columbia Journal of Asian Law*, vol. 1, 1996.

40 R. Peerenboom, "Courts as Legislators: SPC Interpretations and the Need for Procedural Reforms to Increase Transparency and Public Participation," Oxford: Oxford Foundation for Law, Justice and Society, 2007b.

41 X. He, "Recent Decline in Chinese Economic Caseload: Exploration of a Surprising Puzzle," *The China Quarterly,* vol.190, 2007.

42 Zhu, op. cit.

43 On the other hand, the courts have expanded their jurisdiction in some areas. For instance, courts have held that universities may be sued under the ALL, contrary to the widespread belief that they fell outside the scope of the ALL.

44 W. Gan, "Sifa shencha dui yifa xingzheng de zhongyao yingxiang" ["The Important Impact of Judicial Review on Administration According to Law"], Asian Development Bank Report: Rule of Law in China: Review and Prospects, 2007. On file with author.

45 Cai Dingjian, "Constitutional Supervision and Interpretation in the People's Republic of China," *Journal of Chinese Law*, vol. 219, 1995.

46 See generally Ginsburg and Kagan, op. cit., Ginsburg and Moustafa, op. cit.

47 J. M. Ramseyer, "The Puzzling (In)Dependence of Courts," *Journal of Legal Studies*, 23, 1994, pp.721–47; Ginsburg, op. cit., 2003.

48 Peerenboom, op. cit., 2002.

49 See Tom Ginsburg's chapter, "Judicialization of Administrative Governance: Causes, Consequences and Limits," in this book.
50 See John Gillespie's chapter, "The Juridification of Administrative Complaints and Review in Vietnam," in this book.
51 The State Council Asset Supervision and Administration Commission will provide assistance when there are no laws or policies, or the law and policies are unclear, or when there has been unfair competition. However, the Commission's support includes making sure that the company's legal rights are protected according to law and that the company carries out its legal responsibilities. The Commission's actions must be in accordance with law, fair and just. See Provisional Measures for the Management of Major Legal Disputes Involving Central Government State Owned Enterprises, effective March 1, 2005.
52 See Tom Ginsburg's chapter, "Judicialization of Administrative Governance: Causes, Consequences and Limits," in this book.
53 Peerenboom, op. cit., 2007.
54 Ibid., Peerenboom and Chen 2008; K. Jayasuriya, ed., *Law, Capitalism and Power in Asia*, London: Routledge, 1999.
55 W. Ming, "Democracy and Human Rights in Chinese Foreign Policy: Motivation and Behavior," in Y. Deng and F. Wang, eds., *China Rising*, Lanham: Rowman and Littlefield, 2006.
56 Peerenboom, op. cit., 2007.
57 B. van Rooij, *Land and Pollution Regulation in China: Law-Making, Compliance, Enforcement; Theory and Cases*, Leiden: Leiden University Press, 2006.
58 This may be one reason why courts are more successful in obtaining autonomy and independence in authoritarian regimes and developing more countries more generally when the legislature develops first (J. Couso, "Judicial Independence in Latin America: The Lessons of History in Search for an Always Elusive Ideal," in T. Ginsburg and R. Kagan, eds., *Institutions and Public Law*, New York: Peter Lang, 2005.; Dowdle, op. cit., 2002). To be sure, in China, people's congresses also impede judicial independence by engaging in individual case supervision. They formally also have the right to appoint and remove judges. That said, local governments and agencies are a much bigger threat to the courts in practice.
59 R. Peerenboom, "Assessing Implementation of Law in China: What's the Standard?" In *Making Law Work* (Marina Svensson ed.), forthcoming 2009; He Xin, "Economic Contract Enforcement in China: An Empirical Study from a Basic-level court in the Pearl River Delta," forthcoming.
60 The renewed emphasis on mediation, discussed below, is driven in part by problems handling politically sensitive and growing pains cases. In addition, however, it is driven by a third type of case: civil cases where people are not happy with results because of the perceived lack of competence of judges, actual or suspected corruption, the feeling that laws are at odds with local norms, difficulties in enforcing the judgment, or simply the plaintiff's lack of understanding or unrealistically high expectations of what a legal system can do. Such problems exist more in rural areas and in basic level courts. Thus, it is not surprising that rural courts have for years settled cases through mediation at a much faster rate than urban courts. H. L. Fu Hualing and R. Cullen, "From Mediatory to Adjudicatory Justice: The Limit of Judicial Formalism in China," forthcoming 2009. However, in the longer terms, the general trend will be toward judicialization of these types of cases once ongoing efforts to professionalize the judiciary address the problems in basic level and rural courts.
61 The number of cases reversed or remanded as a percentage of the cases actually reviewed has risen steadily since 1998 because the courts have been much more rigorous in screening cases. As a result, the number of cases supervised has decreased in recent years from a peak in 1999–2000. R. Peerenboom, "Judicial Accountability and Judicial

Independence: An Empirical Study of Individual Case Supervision in the People's Republic of China," *The China Journal*, 2006; Zhu, op. cit.

62 Several Issues Concerning the Applicable Law for the Trial of Labor Disputes Cases, August 14, 2006. Granted, one should not expect the SPC to forge new rights given their tenuous legal basis for issuing interpretations. Even the limited change in the SPC's interpretation would appear to be at odds with the Labor Law and thus technically invalid.

63 Whether the law will provide relief for the courts remains to be seen. The ranges of cases subject to "final" arbitration is limited. And, rather oddly, the law still allows workers and even employers to challenge the limited range of cases subject to "final" binding arbitration in the courts.

64 Congressional-Executive Committee on China (CECC), *Annual Report*, 2004. Available at www.cecc.gov/pages/annualRpt/annualRpt04/CECCannRpt2004.pdf

65 Shapiro (Shapiro and Sweet, op. cit.) suggests that the logic of resolution may lead courts to emphasize mediation or issue judgments that attempt to "split the loaf": courts come into existence as a way of providing parties in a dyadic relationship a neutral third-party mechanism for resolving disputes. Yet the courts' neutrality will be called into question whenever it issues a judgment in favor of one of the parties, and even more so if over time it appears the courts systematically favor certain parties over others. In one sense, this theory would seem to have even greater purchase in China, where losing parties frequently assume they lost because the other side biased the court against them through some form of inappropriate influence. In fact, however, the trend has been for courts to issue more "winner-take-all" decisions, rather than trying to split the loaf. D. Clarke, et al., "The Role of Law in China's Economic Development," 2006, available at http://ssrn.com/abstract=878672. Before the SPC's attempt to breathe new life into judicial mediation, the number of cases resolved through court-mediated settlements had dropped dramatically. Zhu, op. cit.

66 However, SPC judge Gan Wen (Gan Wen. "Sifa shencha dui yifa xingzheng de zhongyao yingxiang" ["The Important Impact of Judicial Review on Administration According to Law"], Asian Development Bank Report: Rule of Law in China: Review and Prospects, 2007. On file with author.) suggests that the fear of administrative litigation has led agencies to adopt softer, more citizen-friendly, approaches such as mediation; to rely less on fines and other coercive sanctions and to be more responsive to people's request for information.

67 Guidance Notice of the All-China Lawyers Association regarding Lawyers' Handling of Multi-party Cases, March 20, 2006.

68 Fu Hauling, op. cit.

69 CECC, op. cit.

70 Dowdle, op. cit. 2006.

71 Ackerman, *The Future of Liberal Revolution*, New Haven: Yale University Press, 1992.

72 Shapiro and Stone Sweet, op. cit.

73 In the 2001 *Qi Yuling* case, the SPC seemed to signal that rights set out in the constitution would be directly justiciable, that is, even if there are no implementing law and regulations. However, that case was extremely controversial, and this line of reasoning has not been developed in subsequent cases.

74 Peerenboom, op. cit., 2007 and 2008.

75 Tom Ginsburg and Tamir Moustafa, eds., *Rule by Law: The Politics of Courts in Authoritarian Regimes*, New York: Cambridge University Press, 2008.

76 Peerenboom, op. cit., 2007.

Part III
Southeast Asia

10 The juridification of administrative complaints and review in Vietnam

John Gillespie

Introduction

The juridification of administrative complaints and review in Vietnam is closely linked to the creation of a mixed-market economy. The term "juridification" describes a tendency toward governance through legal rules, legal professionals and judicial power. Foreign investment and membership of international trade agreements, especially the WTO, has generated pressure for juridification. Over time party leaders have come to believe that law-based regulation is necessary to stimulate economic development and check the powers of the executive government. This transformation involves shifting some regulatory power from the executive to enable courts to resolve disputes.

To some extent this reallocation of regulatory power mirrors judicialization in other East Asian countries discussed in this volume.[1] This chapter argues, however, that low domestic demand for law-based review coupled with a political reluctance to support judicial review over executive action is slowing judicialization in administrative courts.

A central concern in all administrative systems is finding ways to control the behavior of state officials. The *Hong Doc* Code of the Le Dynasty in fifteenth-century Vietnam, for example, promoted strict adherence to Neo-Confucian morality, backed by draconian punishments, to minimize regulatory abuses by the mandarins.[2] More recently during the high-socialist period (1954–1986), party leaders attempted to control malfeasance by politicizing the command economy. Contemporary leaders are now experimentally deregulating concessionary licensing to curb bureaucratic corruption in the mixed-market economy.

Changes in the political economy have undoubtedly contributed toward the diverse and protean administrative responses in Vietnam, but they are not the only contributing factors. This chapter draws on the concept of juridification to understand how ideas animate administrative change.[3] It is a slippery concept that stresses the role of discourse and epistemological assumptions in shaping legal preferences. It postulates that epistemological assumptions guide the way officials conceptualize political, economic and legal problems, define their strategic interests and devise regulatory responses to secure their interests.[4] It is posited in this chapter that epistemological assumptions determine the way the state and non-state actors in Vietnam respond to political power and to domestic and global pressure to juridify administrative complaints and review.

Juridification also suggests the need to decenter the analysis to understand regulatory change produced by the diffusion of legal ideas and practices that bypass or take place at the periphery of state agencies. For example, international legal education, business standards and trade agreements such as supply-chain agreements inculcate administrative ideas and practices with little reference to state-based political, legal and economic structures.

The changing role of legality in state administration is outlined in the first part of this chapter. The discussion then investigates social demand for the juridification of administrative processes. It next assesses the scope for juridification in administrative complaints and court review of administrative action. The chapter concludes that administrative complaint and review processes are highly contextual and negotiated, and judicialization is unlikely to progress without the active political support of the party.

The changing role of legality in state administration

Constructing the law-based state

Commencing in the 1960s, Vietnamese lawmakers imported Soviet administrative law with few concessions to local precepts and practices.[5] The central principles of socialist legality (*phap che xa hoi chu nghia*) provided the conceptual building blocks for administrative law. Although the theory has been modified over the intervening decades, basic concepts such as law is the "will of the ruling class" (*y chi cua giai cap thong tri*) and the party leads the state and society remains unchanged.[6] The state borrowed "state economic management" (*nha nuoc quan ly kinh te*) from the Soviet Union to regulate the command economy. It used administrative instruments such as party "policy regimes" and state socio-economic plans to manage economic production.[7]

Soviet legality proved far too abstract and legalistic for administrative regulation in Vietnam.[8] Instead the party conflated Soviet organizational principles such as democratic centralism (*tap trung dan chu*) and "state economic management" with neo-Confucian and traditional moral principles as a pragmatic way to bring authorities "in touch with the people" (*duong loi quan chung*).[9] Since the people responded more to personal interaction than to abstract plans and law, state officials were encouraged to develop personal relationships to micro-manage state businesses and cooperatives.[10] The substantive content of regulation was much less important than finding flexible and situationally relevant solutions to local problems.[11] This highly discretionary regulatory style became known as "reason and sentiment in carrying out the law" (*ly va tinh trong viec chap hanh phap luat*)—a practice that produced outcomes without technically and rigidly applying the law.

Inconsistencies between laws, plans, and "policy regimes" did not especially matter in the command economy, because regulators syncretically constructed solutions from a wide range of sources. But as the mixed-market economy gained momentum in the late 1980s, officials could no longer simply suppress market pathologies. Although the need for a new regulatory approach was obvious, the operation of the market did not provide conceptual insights about how to achieve this objective. Party leaders were compelled to search elsewhere for new ways to resolve market problems.

Regulatory debates during the period concerned the compatibility of "state economic management" with private commercial rights. Party leaders were attracted to the neo-liberal deregulatory arguments promoted by multi-lateral agencies.[12] According to this discourse the administrative system needed powers to correct market failures as well as clear legal demarcations between public and private spheres. It also needed institutions (especially courts) that allowed entrepreneurs to enlist state power to protect property rights and enforce contracts. But, after decades of socialist discretionary control, party leaders resisted the liberal notion that businesses can do anything that is not prohibited by law. They preferred the "asking-giving" administrative mechanism that forced businesses to seek official permission for each new venture.

The *nha nuoc phap quyen* (law-based state) doctrine adopted by the Seventh Party Congress in 1991 reflected this dualist thinking.[13] Modeled on constitutional principles formulated in Gorbachev's Soviet Union, it sought to implement state policy through authoritative and compulsory law; equality before the law; and the use of law to constrain and supervise state administration.[14] Party leaders in Vietnam refused, however, to abandon core socialist principles that privileged party "leadership" over the state and society.[15] As a consequence, the administrative system superimposed imported rights-based commercial legislation over Leninist organizational structures such as "state economic management," "democratic centralism" and "party leadership."

Further pressure for administrative reform arose in the late 1990s when "hot spots" erupted throughout rural Vietnam, which directly and occasionally violently challenged state officials and institutions. At the same time complaints from the private sector about opaque and constantly changing regulations, intrusive government inspection and official corruption became more difficult to ignore.[16] Press reports during this period depict an administrative system that is struggling to fairly and competently regulate commercial activity.[17]

After years of internal debate the party in 2005 promulgated legal and judicial reform strategies.[18] The Legal Sector Reform Strategy links public administrative reform to the broader law reform agenda. Considerable attention is devoted to making state bodies, especially the executive, more accountable to the public. A similar theme runs through the Judicial Reform Strategy. It also emphasizes public access to justice by putting lawyers on a more equal footing with judges and procurators. Yet both strategies subordinate administrative reforms to longstanding socialist principles that promote party leadership over the state and society.

The following discussion seeks to understand how the party and state will respond to pressure for administrative change. The next section examines the hypothesis raised by Ginsberg (Introduction in this volume) that as businesses outgrow networks and transact with strangers they will demand arms-length law-based relationships with state officials. Subsequent parts will deal with administrative complaint mechanisms and judicial review of administrative action. Particular attention is given to structural and epistemological constraints to judicialization. The final part of the next section deals with political limitations to the judicialization of administrative courts.

Demand for law-based interactions with state officials

Demand from domestic companies

As the economy grows in size and complexity, some theorists believe that domestic entrepreneurs will want to legalize their relationship with state regulators.[19] Theorists from this tradition maintain that personal relationships and negotiated outcomes are not up to the task of stabilizing large-scale economic regulation. Empirical research about business networks in Vietnam suggests, however, a more complex development trajectory.

Drawing on neo-liberal economic principles, the Enterprise Law 1999 deregulated market access for domestic business in Vietnam. Previously, local authorities used licensing gateways to proactively "manage" private investment according to local interpretations of state socioeconomic plans.[20] As anticipated, the deregulation of market entry unleashed a wave of incorporations and domestic investment.[21]

Many commentators have interpreted the surge of incorporations following the Enterprise Law as evidence for a broad-based shift by domestic businesses away from transacting through business networks toward legal formality and "rational" administration—a shift toward juridification.[22] Some studies about the implementation of the Enterprise Law seemed to support this view, because they show that domestic investors preferred deregulated market access to proactive "state economic management."[23] Other studies demonstrated that deregulation leaves firms vulnerable to claims by predatory state officials, because business licenses provided irrefutable evidence that business were operating unlawfully.[24]

Empirical studies that examined companies in five industry groups in Northern Vietnam reveal the importance of business networks in mediating state administration. They challenge the conventional view that firms rushed to incorporate after the enactment of the Enterprise Law to gain access to corporate rules and administrative certainty. In fact, firms incorporated to gain access to government benefits such as VAT invoices, infrastructure tenders, import/export permits and loans from state banks. Few were attracted to, or even aware of, the legal benefits of incorporation such as limited liability, internal management rules and the capacity to raise equity capital. A similar disinterest in commercial legislation was observed in the reaction of firms toward the raft of laws introduced to comply with international treaties commitments (especially the US-Vietnam Bilateral Trade Agreement (BTA) and WTO).

More importantly for this study, findings point out that most firms prefer personal rather than depersonalized law-based interactions with state regulators.[25] They expressed satisfaction with existing arrangements, even though personal relationships with state officials were invariably secured and maintained with bribes.

Empirical studies also intimate that as firms grow in size and search for new markets they did not, as Stone Sweet suggests,[26] gravitate toward arms-length, law-based relationships with state regulators. Instead, they sought membership of business networks benefiting from privileged access to state officials. For example, a large Ho Chi Minh–based computer retailer struggled to expand into the Hanoi market until it bought its way into an established retail network. Members of the network negotiated standard tax payments with local officials in the Dong Da District in Hanoi. Payment formulas were loosely based on business turnover and aimed to moderate excessive claims by officials and prevent socially disruptive preferential deals. They also gave traders leverage over new market entrants, who were expected to comply with local trading rules and distribution cartels in return for receiving the payment formula. Officials tacitly supported the network by negotiating payment relationships only with retailers familiar with the formula.

Some business networks considered in the study did not directly engage with state officials, but most used group numbers and pooled resources to leverage preferential treatment. Networks mainly cultivated local officials, who often feel more responsible to businesses in their locality than do higher-level authorities. Local officials are expected to personalize decisions to overcome rigidities in central laws, provide privileged information, enforce debts and selectively enforce administrative and criminal sanctions. They use "reason and sentiment in carrying out the law" to find contextually relevant solutions. In this syncretic decision-making process, exogenous normative sources such as central laws are not considered absolute, universal or immutable, but rather alternate sources of guidance.

Local officials are not hermetically sealed-off from global legal texts and discourse that promotes law-based outcomes, but the dominant modes of thought that shape their world-views differ from those circulating at elite levels. For local officials "state management" is not found in legal texts, but rather it is personally negotiated with businesses by applying "reason and sentiment in carrying out the law." This is an extension of the "asking-giving" mechanism that developed during the socialist period.

Local officials protect private property and profits that have been accumulated by network members in politically and socially responsible ways—a practice that gives state support for the network's trading standards. In short, state officials carry out many of the functions statutory rules and formal administrative processes fail to perform.

Even though the study found little current demand among domestic companies for laws to check state power, movement in this direction cannot be ruled out. To grow, some private companies will eventually need to access capital markets and secure state protection for their intellectual property rights. It is also possible that as the regulatory environment becomes more ordered by laws and legal processes, and especially if administrative courts gain enough discretionary power to effectively review administrative decisions (discussed below), law-based administration is likely to appear more credible to domestic businesses.

In another development, supply-chain agreements entered between international buyers, and Vietnamese manufacturers are changing attitudes about law-based regulation. In one representative case, US buyers such as Nike contractually bound Vietnamese footwear manufacture (Maxsport) to adopt labor standards that exceeded domestic requirements. Maxsport was also required to implement a logistics management regime that tracked every stage of manufacture to ensure that production reached quality standards and delivery schedules.

Maxsport acts like a node in a network. It imports the new organizational thinking through supply-chain agreements and then spreads this knowledge to sub-contractors and suppliers. The new organizational thinking bypasses state institutions and stimulates domestic firms to create novel ways of dealing with each other.

In summary, many private investors form hybrid state–private business networks that harness or at least moderate state power. Business networks have a regulatory effect that extends well beyond their members. For example, some business networks establish trading norms and modes of dealing with state officials that influence firms outside the network. In these regulatory communities firms "trade in the shadow" of the network. Administrative power is co-opted by business networks in ways that fragment the hierarchies envisaged by law-based administration.

Demand from state-owned enterprises

Most state-owned enterprises (SOEs) have even less to gain from legally circumscribing state power than private companies. This project may weaken their close political and personal relationships with state administrative agencies. Although the number of privatizations has increased over the last few years, state authorities generally retain a controlling interest of over 50 percent of issued shares.[27] This practice has ensured that privatized entities remain receptive to state policies.

Conflicts between SOEs and state regulators are generally resolved politically rather than through formal legal processes. Evidence suggests that directors of SOEs use their supervising agency, either a ministry or provincial people's committee, to negotiate settlements with other state regulators. Recently, however, SOEs have begun using business associations to lobby regulators. For example, Vietnam Steel Corporation and its privatized offshoots use the Vietnam Steel Association, which is led by a retired senior official from the Ministry of Industry, to negotiate with state authorities to protect the industry against import competition.[28] It is possible that as the interests and operational logics of government and privatized SOEs diverge, this sector will see more value in legal rules defining and constraining state regulatory power.

Global pressure for reform: International agencies and trade agreements

Following the East Asian Financial Crisis in 1997, international agencies such as the World Bank, Asian Development Bank and UNDP called for the government to "rationalize" state administration. This entailed defining state entities and their relationships and powers with clear and general rules.[29] The underlying assumption was that "rationalized governance" is a prerequisite for economic development. But little happened until Vietnam ratified a Bilateral Trade Agreement with the United States in 2001 and began the final round of negotiations to enter the WTO.

International agencies produced a standard list of reforms required to "rationalize governance" and showed little patience for the idea that optimal regulatory settings are specific to national economic, political and epistemological contexts. Reforms included enhancing transparency and accountability of administrative systems, curbing corruption and strengthening institutional oversight of administrative operations. The key thrust of this neo-liberal agenda was to de-couple state agencies from their embeddedness in local structures and traditions and open the administrative system to globalized legal texts and processes.[30] Reforms aimed to replace "reason and sentiment in carrying out the law" with a procedural "rule of law."

Rivaling and perhaps surpassing Soviet legal assistance during the high-socialist period, international agencies have funded hundreds of law reform projects in Vietnam. There are some differences in the approach taken by international agencies. For example, Japanese agencies are more willing to work around the government's economic planning than neo-liberal oriented agencies such as the World Bank, IFC and Asian Development Bank. But international agencies are united in their support for Public Administration Reform programs that aim to streamline administrative procedures, close licensing gateways, privatize SOEs and enhance accountability through citizen complaint procedures and administrative courts.[31] These initiatives were revised in 2001 to reflect Vietnam's commitments under the BTA and WTO to separate policy formulation from regulation and improve the public's right to claim compensation for administrative abuses.[32]

Although international agencies provided many (but certainly not all) of the ideas employed by PAR initiatives, the way these ideas are implemented by Vietnamese agencies reflects domestic political, economic and social concerns more than global visions of "rationalized governance."[33] For example, six months after the Enterprise Law deregulated market entry, local authorities had shifted their discretionary powers over companies to other licensing gateways that were more resistant to PAR reforms.

Foreign investor support for administrative reform

Western, and to a lesser extent Japanese and other multinational investors, support the global push for public administrative reforms. Their internal bureaucracies are staffed by lawyers and their accountants plan and organize business activities according to external policies and laws. They prefer an operational environment governed by legal transparency, codified legal standards and judicially defined boundaries between state and private interests. Foreign investors compensate for their exclusion from local business networks that give domestic firms influence over state officials by advocating a "rule of law" that levels the regulatory playing field.

Take, for example, the tax dispute concerning a Taiwanese construction company in Ho Chi Minh City.[34] After construction commenced on the Phu My Hung apartment project in 2003, the Ministry of Planning and Investment (MPI) increased the tax rate from 10 to 25 percent per annum, claiming that residential construction attracted a higher tax impost than civil construction. Lawyers acting for the company persuaded the Ministry of Justice to issue an Official Letter stating that "civil construction" projects include residential apartments and that article 121 of Decree No. 24 Implementing the Foreign Investment Law 2000 gave foreign investors legal protection against future tax increases.[35] When MPI refused to follow the Official Letter and reduce the tax, the Office of Government ordered the Ministry of Finance, MPI and the Ho Chi Minh City People's Committee to resolve the impasse.

For six months it seemed the investors were successful in persuading MPI to forgo tax revenue and base its decision-making on Decree No. 24. However, in August 2004, the prime minister intervened in the dispute by issuing a decision that forced the Phu My Hung Corporation to pay the 25 percent tax.[36] In this case politics intervened, but lawyers believe that more generally dialogical exchanges between foreign investors and elite-level officials generate common perspectives about the importance of using laws to circumscribe state power.

To summarize, domestic regulatory networks blur legal distinctions between public and private spheres and by implication challenge hierarchical concepts of administrative law. Particularly at the local level, many regulatory decisions are made outside legally defined administrative pathways. Typically, decision-making takes place in an ongoing series of decentered negotiations between state officials and business networks. In this fragmented regulatory environment, international donor agencies and foreign investors struggle to "rationalize" administrative decision-making.

For local officials to change their administrative style it seems likely they must also change their identity—from "economic managers" to economic regulators. Otherwise law-based administrative practices will become assimilated by an older regulatory system based on "reason and sentiment in carrying out the law."

It is interesting to consider briefly the factors that may stimulate demand for "rational" administration. Far from inducing demand, the surge of foreign investment generated by accession to the WTO is likely to push domestic firms toward defensive networks. Firms studied believed that business networks could co-opt nationalistic state officials to protect them against foreign competition.

Domestic demand for "rational administration" is more likely to occur when state officials are no longer capable of protecting business networks. This may happen if anti-corruption initiatives force local officials to follow central legal rules rather than negotiated agreements with business networks. But central authorities are unlikely to mobilize the political capital required to control local officials without an economic shock, such as the East Asian Economic Crisis[37] that generates a broad reform consensus.

The diffusion of international legal standards and practices is also slowly generating local demand for "rational" administration. As the rules become evermore complex, supply-chain agreements are infusing domestic firms with rule-based organization systems that require professional managers. Because the managers are accountable for legal compliance, they are likely to prefer arms-length, law-based interactions with state officials. Similar professional bureaucracies are forming in firms adopting ISO management standards and firms dealing frequently with international traders and lawyers. Although it is still embryonic, the diffusion of legal standards through non-state pathways is likely in the long term to generate significant demand for "rational" administration.

Administrative complaints mechanisms

In contrast to the tepid local support for the "rationalization" of administrative power, domestic forces enthusiastically use formal and informal administrative complaint mechanisms. The precise numbers of complaints are not publicly available, but officials estimate they number in the hundreds of thousands each year.[38] Approximately 60 percent concern the administration of land and housing, about 20 percent arise from the enforcement of court judgments and the remaining 20 percent relate to commercial matters such as company registration, permit conditions and administrative fines.

Complaints are communicated through many channels. Some are sent to village heads, party officials and the National Assembly. Others are conveyed through formal mechanisms established by the Law on Complaints and Denunciations 2004, Ordinance Guiding the Administrative Courts 1996 (as amended) and *Van Phong Tiep Dan Cua Trung Uong Dang va Nha Nuoc* (Office to Receive Citizen's Complaints of the Central Committee of the Party and the State).

Popular enthusiasm for administrative complaint mechanisms seems to contradict the previous observation that domestic firms are generally indifferent toward law-based "rational" dealings with state officials. One possible explanation, which is explored in the following discussion, is that most complaint mechanisms, with the exception of administrative courts, use non-legal techniques such as "reason and sentiment in carrying out the law" to resolve disputes.

The law on complaints and denunciations

There is a long history in Vietnam of using petitions to "complain and denounce" (*giai quyet khieu nai to cao*) administrative abuses.[39] What is comparatively recent is the notion that public officials are legally accountable to the public. Imperial Vietnam did not accept legal limits to the power of the ruler. During the high-socialist period, citizens were permitted to complain to state authorities, but as morally perfected beings, party cadres were assumed to know best and the people were expected to defer to their greater wisdom. Party pronouncements encouraged citizens to view their rights as collective entitlements and denounced personal complaints as bourgeois individualism.[40]

The complaints system came under pressure for reform during the early stages of *doi moi* reform. The number of complaints rapidly increased from 88,802 in 1991 to 131,920 in 1996. To make matters worse, the increasing complexity of complaints arising from the mixed-market economy created a backlog of unresolved cases. By this time, PAR initiatives and other donor reforms were beginning to change elite-level attitudes toward public complaints. Party pronouncements reflected this epistemological shift by emphasizing the people's "democratic" rights to challenge and review administrative action.

This new thinking appeared in the Law on the Settlement of Complaints and Denunciations 1998 (as amended), which exposed a wider range of official action to review. For example, the public were permitted to not only complain about executive action, but also about abuses by other arms of the state (judiciary, procuracy, National Assembly and state president) together with state-owned enterprises, political organizations (including the party) and individual cadres. In another change, the law placed more emphasis on the responsibilities of officials to resolve complaints. For example, officials were required to resolve complaints within fixed timelines and give reasons for their decisions; penalties were stipulated for non-compliance. Most significantly, the law gave complainants clear pathways to appeal decisions either to higher administrative authorities or to the administrative courts.

Vietnam's membership of international trading agreements has also animated reforms. Both the BTA and WTO require Vietnam to give investors access to transparent and independent review over administrative acts and/or omissions that adversely affect business activities.[41] During the WTO accession negotiations, Vietnam agreed to give businesses a right to refer any administrative decision to a "transparent" system of review with a right of appeal to an administrative court.

Factors limiting the complaint and denunciation mechanisms

There are three main reasons why the channeling of administrative grievances through the complaint and denunciation mechanisms has not contributed more to the juridification of state administration. The first involves technical deficiencies in the complaints procedures. Complainants are required to first petition the officials that made the offending decision before they can appeal the decision to the next highest level in the administrative hierarchy. Government reports have criticized this procedure for being "heavy handed," "closed," and lacking the distance required for impartiality.[42] Appeals are frequently referred back to the official who made the determination in the first place—making them judges in their own cause. Compounding the problem, few of the thousands of successful complaints made each year are enforced.[43]

The second problem with the complaints process is the limited scope for review. Complainants can only petition unlawful administrative actions. Questions of administrative bias, procedural unfairness and conflict of interest, which are particularly relevant to business licensing, are not reviewable. Take, for example, complaints about the registration of new companies under the Law on Enterprises.[44] Lawyers working in this area believe that most administrative abuses are not technically illegal, but rather arise from pedantic and "biased" interpretation of the incorporation rules. Abuses are intended to slow the approval process to extract facilitation payments from company promoters. Under the existing rules this type of misconduct is beyond review.

The Ministry of Planning and Investment, which oversees the incorporation process, is attempting to clarify the regulatory environment by issuing a series of official letters.[45] Incrementally the letters are developing a doctrinal base from which state officials and judges can uniformly regulate incorporation. The purpose of the guidelines is not to remove discretionary power, but rather to reduce the scope for rent-seeking by clearly defining discretionary powers. This experimentation with law-based administration is, however, confined to narrow, technical areas such as company incorporation and has not expanded into more complex areas of business licensing.

The third problem concerns the method of resolving complex disputes. The Government Inspectorate (*Thanh Tra Chinh Phu*), a state investigation agency, is called in by regulatory authorities to resolve "hard" cases that are not directly covered by statute.[46] Their method of resolving "hard" cases is well illustrated by cases concerning the compensation paid by the government for land compulsorily acquired for new infrastructure developments.[47] As Vietnam rapidly industrializes, state authorities are increasingly acquiring land for new factories, roads and government buildings. In some instances government inspectors have uncovered malfeasance by state land officials—clear legal violations. More typically, however, complaints relate to policy matters such as inadequate compensation values set by provincial authorities or other factors that do not directly violate the law.

The inspectorate soon exhaust legal reasoning as a means of resolving these complaints and turn to "reason and sentiment in carrying out the law" to broker compromises between complainants and state officials.[48] In land compensation cases, the inspectorate must balance at least three competing interests: claims for more compensation by citizens, the local government's desire to preserve the state budget and the national interest served by investment projects. They appeal to *hop ly* (reasonableness), backed by a mix of political, moral, legal and sentimental norms, to persuade local authorities and complainants to compromise. Outcomes aim for situational justice and little thought is given to crafting a universal set of principles that could apply to other cases. For example, the inspectorate search for opportunities to use *ho tro* (state compensation that does not involve the payment of money). Typically, local authorities are asked to find a land plot near the development site where the complainants can re-establish their business.

216 *John Gillespie*

It is possible to infer from this case study that the inspectorate will intervene in "hard" cases even when the complaint concerns policy matters that are technically beyond review under the Law on Complaints and Denunciations. This practice informally expands the scope of review well beyond the areas that the state is prepared to formally recognize. It is justified on the basis that some issues, such as land acquisition, housing disputes and business licensing, will generate social friction that needs an outlet. A problem with the informal system is that negotiated outcomes tend to favor those with political connections and ultimately undermine progress toward "rational" administration.

The inspectorate are reluctant to push the boundaries of review to consider questions of bias and breaches of procedural fairness. This type of behavior is considered a violation of civil service codes of conduct and is not a matter for public review. Evidently disciplinary action is only taken for the most flagrant administrative abuses that constitute dereliction of duty.[49]

A striking feature about the complaints and denunciation system is the ineffectiveness of law in resolving grievances. With the narrow exception of disputes concerning company incorporation, the legal system lacks clear doctrinal rules to assess whether legal violations have occurred. Law is only decisive where officials have clearly acted outside their authorized powers. In "hard" cases that are not directly addressed by law, remedies are only available when the inspectorate act like de facto ombudsmen and apply "reason and sentiment in carrying out the law" to resolve complaints. In an administrative system attuned to politics, morality and clientism, law lacks the authority to judge administrative action and is quickly displaced by other social norms and state policies.

Informal petitioning

The Vietnamese have been petitioning their leaders for centuries to protest administrative abuses. Their enthusiasm remains undiminished and approximately 20,000 petitions are sent annually to the People's Will Department, in the Office of National Assembly and even more are sent to National Assembly (NA) delegates and party leaders.[50] In contrast to complaints lodged under the Law on Complaints and Denunciations, petitioners can complain about any kind of administrative abuse.

Specialized committees within the NA deal with about 45 percent of petitions, and the Standing Committee deals with the remainder. Committees synthesize key issues into reports presented to the NA. Complaints are thus filtered many times before they are presented in summary form to delegates. The NA lacks the political resources to take action in all but the most egregious cases. With few exceptions, individual National Assembly delegates are not responsive to their constituents and rarely act on petitions.[51]

Petitions sent to provincial and central-level party leaders receive a more systematic response. In order to avoid *tu tap* (crowd gathering) and other spontaneous expressions of civil dissatisfaction, party leaders established a joint state and party facility to resolve otherwise intractable administrative complaints. The Office to

Receive Citizens' Complaints of the Central Committee of the Party and the State is composed of personnel co-opted from the Office of Government, Government Inspectorate and the Party Central Committee. In 2006 the facility received more than 50,000 letters of complaint and about 30,000 people presented their grievances in person.[52] Like the state inspectorate, officials in the facility employ "reason and sentiment in carrying out the law" to resolve complaints. As a central-level body located close to the main center of party power, the facility can muster considerable political resources to find pragmatic solutions to long-running grievances.

To recap, global forces promoting law-based complaints resolution systems are slowly influencing elite thinking. Party rhetoric supports processes that make state officials legally accountable to the public and the wave of amendments to the Law on Complaints and Denunciations aim to give citizens more effective mechanisms to check executive power.

What remains unclear is how far party leaders are prepared to allow reforms to progress. Will they give citizens broad powers to challenge executive action at all levels of government? The current system works well for the party, because it limits review to narrow questions of unlawful behavior while giving authorities broad discretionary controls over complex and sensitive complaints. Regulation through "reason and sentiment in carrying out the law" developed decades ago to deliver contextually relevant outcomes. Although it is nonsense to talk of total continuities, to some extent the administrative style and epistemological assumptions of the high-socialist period still inform the way the state resolves administrative complaints in contemporary Vietnam.

Administrative courts

Administrative courts with powers to review executive action were established in Vietnam in 1996.[53] Opponents of this reform used the Soviet "concentration-of-power" (*tap trung quyen luc*) doctrine to argue that the National Assembly, rather than the courts, should supervise executive action.[54] The prospect of judicial review also forced party cadres to contemplate whether they were equal to, and should submit to legal actions brought by ordinary people.

Social demand for administrative litigation

As it turned out, party cadres had little to worry about. During its first year of operation in 1996 administrative courts nationwide received 36 cases. By 1999 the caseload had grown to 409 and this figure increased to 1,172 in 2004.[55] When corrected for population differences this figure represents less than 15 percent of the new administrative law cases recorded in China each year.[56] Although the number of new cases is slowly increasing, they constitute only a minute proportion of the tens of thousands of unresolved administrative petitions.[57]

It is necessary to look beyond litigation rates to identify the factors constraining judicialization in administrative courts. There is a well-documented "shyness" (*tinh nhut nhat*) or reticence to litigate in Vietnam. Some respondents attribute this to pre-modern thinking that "only unlawful people are involved with courts."[58] Respondents in recent perceptional surveys expected courts to deliver "justice" but thought judges lacked the "impartiality and objectivity" (74 percent) to deliver these outcomes.[59]

There are more pragmatic reasons for not taking administrative action in the courts. The Ordinance on Administrative Court Procedures does not permit class actions or other forms of litigation that spread the risk of court action. More importantly, state licensing authorities use their close personal relationships to pressure businesses not to litigate. Officials have many opportunities to exact retribution against businesses foolish enough to ignore warnings. Unconstrained by close relational connections with state officials, foreign investment entities are more prepared to take regulators to court. Interviews with lawyers acting for foreign investors intimate that litigation is used as a tool, together with lobbying and newspaper articles, to publicly embarrass officials into correcting their malfeasance. State-owned enterprises litigate if they can mobilize political support for their action.

Judicial power

The discussion so far has considered social demand for litigation, but we need also to consider the internal (to the courts) structural and epistemological barriers to judicialization. One way to pursue this inquiry is to assess the potential for courts to acquire the powers to make binding decisions about important administrative issues. There are three generally accepted elements of judicial power: jurisdictional power, discretionary power and the authority to make binding decisions.[60] The following discussion uses the three powers to assess the scope for judicialization in administrative courts.

Jurisdictional powers

Powerful courts have jurisdiction over matters of controversy. Administrative courts in Vietnam are given wide powers to review the legality of administrative decisions regarding licensing, taxation, housing permits, compulsory acquisition of land and administrative penalties.[61] Any matters considered under the Law on Complaints and Denunciations 2004 can be appealed to administrative courts. Although jurisdictional power covers most administrative action that may infringe business interests, courts lack powers to review complaints about civil rights abuses such as curbing freedom of association and speech and arbitrary arrest and detention.

Another factor that limits jurisdictional power is the reluctance of some judges to accept responsibility for sensitive cases that may offend senior officials. Judges have a well-founded fear of retribution. To avoid hearing cases, some judges exploit procedural inconsistencies or simply delay proceedings.[62] For example, a private businessman seeking compensation from the Chairman of the Hanoi People's Committee, who had allegedly expropriated his business during the 1980s, eventually sought political intervention from the prime minister to convince the Hanoi Administrative Court to accept his case.[63]

Further limiting jurisdictional power, judges lack the power to order the discovery of documents and the attendance of state officials.[64] Judges currently rely on the goodwill of government agencies to produce documentary evidence and cannot compel the heads of government agencies to give evidence in court. Department heads are usually represented by junior officials who lack detailed information about the decision-making process. If the state honors its obligations under the BTA and WTO, courts may soon have powers to discover documents and subpoena witnesses.

Discretionary powers

Administrative courts have jurisdictional powers to review the legality of most commercial regulation, what they lack is discretionary power to make meaningful decisions. For decades provincial courts functioned as offshoots of provincial governments and saw their role as implementing rather than reviewing executive action. Court reforms in 2001 sought to distance courts from local government by placing them under the management of the Supreme Court.[65] But these reforms did not entirely sever the connections. Local government leaders still have a say over judicial promotions and as senior party officials they can exert considerable pressure on judicial decisions through court-based party cells.[66] Compounding this deferential relationship, the Supreme Court instructs judges to deal with administrative cases conservatively and avoid "interfering with the mechanisms of government."[67]

To provide some empirical understanding of the problem, during a five-year period from 2000 to 2005 administrative court judges in Ho Chi Minh City refused in 50 percent of cases to make administrative orders against government agencies found to have violated the law.[68] Instead they instructed the agencies to "re-handle the complaints." Some agencies acknowledged their wrongdoing and quietly withdrew their decisions, but others refused to make any concessions. During the same period the courts ordered government agencies to revoke their decisions in only 14 percent of cases.

Administrative courts tend to rely on government officials to gather evidence and in many cases determine liability.[69] For example, in resolving an administrative case the Hanoi City Court relied almost entirely on a report prepared by the government body accused of the wrongdoing.[70] The complainant asked the court to strike down an administrative decision by the Hanoi Housing Trust to purchase land from a state-owned company. He argued that the state-owned company had rights to manage the land, but had not acquired ownership rights. The judge requested the Hanoi Land Department, the authority supervising the Hanoi Housing Trust, to investigate the complainant's ownership rights over the land. The Trust's report concluded that as a matter of "policy" the state had acquired the land, even though there was no documentary evidence showing a transfer of ownership. Acting on the report, the court dismissed the complainant's petition.

In a more recent decision, the Ho Chi Minh City Administrative Court ruled in favor of a trader who challenged the legality of a state inspection.[71] In 2004 investigators from the Market Management Authority (MMA) (*ban quan ly thi truong*) searched premises leased by a private enterprise (Ky Quang Enterprise) and removed documents and 10,656 boxes of "Ballerine-Tea." The complainant petitioned the court to declare the search and seizure unlawful. He argued that the MMA violated procedural rules in the Ordinance on the Settlement of Administrative Violations 2002 by conducting a search without the written permission of the chairman of the local district people's committee. When the complainant lodged a petition under the Law on Complaints and Denunciations, the chairman of the district people's committee attempted to cure the mistake by retrospectively approving the inspection. When this did not satisfy the complainant, the chairman of the City People's Committee also retrospectively approved the inspection. The court ordered the MMA to return the documents and tea.

This case is unusual in a number of respects. Private entities rarely succeed in actions against state officials, much less high-ranking officials such as the chairman of the largest city government in Vietnam. Even more significantly, the judge agreed with the MMA that there were "sufficient signs of an administrative violation" made by Ky Quang Enterprise, yet decided that evidence of wrongdoing collected during an unlawful search could not support an administrative penalty.

It is possible to infer from these cases that in general administrative court judges passively and mechanically apply the law to resolve cases. The law is supposed to have already judged and judges must mechanically fit facts into the matrix of law. Naturally judges in civil law jurisdictions the world over arrogate some discretionary power to reconcile gaps between legislation and conditions on the ground. But Vietnamese judges are held accountable to an especially instrumental understanding of law. They are expected to assume that legislation is comprehensive, internally consistent and that for every social problem there is a governing rule. Without a doctrinal framework in which to place and resolve administrative complaints judges have little option but to rely on government reports and directives to determine the legality of administrative acts. Finally, although administrative courts rarely question the substance of government rulings, they are prepared to hold officials accountable to procedural requirements such as whether the correct steps were taken in making an administrative decision.[72]

Powers to enforce decisions

Administrative courts struggle to enforce their decisions, because government agencies frequently do not recognize the courts' authority.[73] For example, the business registration office in Ho Chi Minh City refused in 2005 to follow a ruling from the City Administrative Court to approve the incorporation of a company. This problem was sufficiently widespread for the central government to issue Decree No. 88 Implementing the Uniform Enterprise Law 2005, which directed business registration officials nation-wide to implement court rulings. Without the backing of government legislation state officials sometimes consider court rulings optional.

To a significant extent the reluctance of government agencies to follow court rulings is attributable to the low status of judges. Consider the statement made by Nguyen Van Thuan, Vice President of the Law Committee of the National Assembly, about judicial review over land administration. "It would be an honor" he declared "for the president of a provincial people's court to be invited to work with the chairman of a people's committee at the same level, so how dare an ordinary judge quash the chairman's decision in a land dispute case."[74] This criticism from one of Vietnam's most senior legal officials epitomizes the reluctance of government officials to accept the jurisdiction of administrative courts. Judicial authority is unlikely to increase until courts are seen as credible counterbalances to executive power. There is a compelling need to increase the discretionary powers of judges to make credible decisions. This will presumably send signals to officials that there are consequences for straying too far beyond the legal rules establishing their discretionary powers.

Summary

The discussion began with the proposition that low domestic demand for law-based administration is not inconsistent with a high demand for administrative complaint mechanisms. It was argued that domestic businesses are familiar with the contextual dispute resolution techniques used under the Law on Complaints and Denunciations 2004, but not with law-based and "arm's length" modes of state administration. In this view, administrative courts have failed to galvanize public support because they use law to resolve cases and cannot apply "reason and sentiment in carrying out the law" to reach compromises. Legal reasoning is not particularly attuned to resolving disputes to the satisfaction of all concerned—a key ingredient of Vietnamese notions of situational justice. This is because the role of law in judicial decisions is not to produce socially grounded decisions, but rather to make decisions based on legal rules, doctrines and fictions.[75]

It is unclear whether judicial power will automatically increase if Vietnam implements its obligations under the BTA and WTO and gives courts jurisdiction over procedural bias.[76] Questions of administrative bias are currently considered by the state inspectorate in context-based decisions and by internal review boards examining violations of the codes of conduct governing civil servants. These informal mechanisms have not developed the finely grained guidelines judges will need to evaluate highly subjective behavior of this kind.

So far the state has refused to yield to international pressure by giving administrative courts powers to review the constitutionality of administrative decisions, state laws and policies.[77] Only the Standing Committee of the National Assembly is entitled to interpret the constitution, a power it has rarely used. But as the next section suggests, further judicialization depends on whether the party is prepared to trust administrative courts with sufficient discretionary power to effectively review administrative action.

Political control over the courts

Party leadership over the state

There is one constant in the massive administrative and judicial reforms that have transformed Vietnam over the last two decades. The party is determined to remain the "force leading the state and society."[78] But this broad principle raises as many questions as it answers. For example, under what conditions will the party leave the formulation and implementation of law to constitutional institutions? In a Leninist administrative system do economic regulators owe their primary allegiance to the party or state-law? Can law-based administration and court-processes trump party policy?

Rolling back party control over the state

The party for decades has debated whether the Leninist concept of "party leadership" over the state weakens state authority and accountability.[79] PAR initiatives have unraveled some of the linkages between party and state, yet tensions remain about the role of the party as an economic regulator.[80] Riedel and Turley[81] summarized these concerns:

> Party and state functions need to be separated more clearly. The party must cease passing its directives through party committee secretaries and instead pass them through the government chain of command, allowing government officials to take full responsibility for implementation.

"Party leadership" has the potential to compromise state administration in three main ways. One, it creates polycentric power centers that blur responsibilities and lines of accountability between and within party and state organizations. Since state officials (including judges) are required to follow both state laws and the "party line" it is difficult sometimes to distinguish between "political" and "administrative" roles.[82] Attempts to bring decision-making within constitutional structures are resisted by the party and state because this reform unravels deeply entrenched collective decision-making and conflict management mechanisms.[83]

Two, the *nomenkultra* system (*to chuc can bo*), which places most senior officials and judges in their positions of power, confuses lines of authority and erodes the prestige of state-based recruitment and promotion mechanisms.[84] Yet without a constitutional system that gives rival political groups alternate turns in controlling the state, the *nomenkultra* system is needed to allow key party officials to place their followers in positions of status and authority within the state in ways that reflect the realities of political power.[85]

Three, the nuances of administrative law reside as much in party resolutions and pronouncements as they do in autonomous (from the party) legal rules and doctrines. This Leninist system undermines the development of coherent legal doctrines and jurisprudence that could increase the procedural transparency of administrative decisions and the discretionary power of administrative courts.

There is little question that the party has the capacity to influence court decisions. The pertinent question for this study is how (if at all) the party uses its powers to constrain judcialization in the administrative arena.

Privileging the "state benefit" in the courtroom

A central purpose of socialist legal systems is to promote the "state benefit" (*loi ich cua nha nuoc*). During the command economy, party resolutions and socio-economic plans described and announced the "state benefit." What constituted the "benefit" was never precisely defined to give planners flexibility to "fine tune" the economy. Following *doi moi* the party has moderated its hostility toward private commerce. As the pace of international integration gained momentum the former Prime Minister (Phan Van Khai) equated private business to revolutionary heroes by declaring that "entrepreneurial success in the marketplace is no less glorious than a victory on the battlefield."[86] The Politburo's Legal Sector Development Strategy issued in 2005 placed party rhetoric in a legal context by declaring that entrepreneurs can carry out any business that is not prohibited by law. This readjustment of the "state benefit" is reflected in the numerous laws that give private businesses legal rights to protect property, enforce contracts and incorporate companies.

Despite these changes, lawyers report that in administrative cases judges converse in twin narratives.[87] Judges are careful to portray their decisions as passively and mechanically applying the law—a textual narrative. But where textual narratives do not produce desired outcomes, judges quietly turn to party policy that permits extra-legal decision making to preserve the state benefit. For example, evidence produced in a case before the Thai Binh Provincial People's Court showed that businessmen had violated an administrative provision that prevented the commercial sale of VAT invoices.[88] The procuracy failed to prove the more serious criminal charge that the defendants had fraudulently dealt with negotiable instruments.[89] According to the defense counsel, when it became apparent to the trial judge (Nguyen Khac Son) that the businessmen might escape criminal prosecution, he used "legal analogy" (*ap dung phap luat tuong tu*) to expand criminal liability well beyond the textual authority of the Penal Code 1999. The use of "legal analogy" subordinates private legal rights to the "state benefit."

Lawyers claim that recent changes to the Civil Procedure Code 2005 have given them more opportunities to introduce evidence and raise legal arguments in the courtroom. To some extent just by being there lawyers are compelling judges to follow law-based rules. Pretending to be a judge while really pursuing politics is more difficult, when these purposes must be translated for the benefit of lawyers into an appropriate legal vocabulary.

The role of lawyers in promoting legal reasoning in the courtroom is constrained because there is little procedural compulsion for judges to listen to lawyers. Judges are supposed to recite legal arguments raised by lawyers in their judgments, but in practice jump from the facts of cases to the conclusion without providing much legal analysis. In addition, some lawyers rely more on bribery than legal arguments to secure favorable outcomes.

There is a growing awareness among a number of senior lawmakers that judges need secondary legal rules or doctrines to resolve the difficult commercial disputes generated by Vietnam's integration into world markets.[90] Party and state bodies cannot provide the detailed legal guidelines judges need to determine the "state benefit" in these cases. The Supreme Court is leading the way in synthesizing secondary rules from court decisions, academic commentary and other legal sources. It is transforming some "official guidance" instructions into generally applicable guidelines and it publishes similar fact case judgments (*nghi quyet hoi dong tham phan*) that show inferior court judges how laws should be applied in particular circumstances.[91] It also produces an annual report and guidance letters (*thong tu huong dan*) that give detailed legal solutions to commonly encountered substantive and procedural issues.

So far the development of internal (to courts) doctrines that give judges the means to interpret the "state benefit" are largely confined to commercial and civil cases and have not extended to administrative courts. Party resistance to strong administrative courts is not unexpected, because experience elsewhere shows that courts are usually the last state institution to gain power over political decision-making.

Conclusion

Global prescriptions for administrative law reform in Vietnam are preoccupied with mechanisms that make agencies accountable to executive supervision and judicial review. They presuppose transparent, stable and universal laws and clear administrative hierarchies. This chapter suggests a different understanding of administrative law in Vietnam, one best described as a series of negotiated relationships. Especially at the local level, public and private actors negotiate policy outcomes creating a type of participatory governance. Negotiations blur the law-based distinctions between public and private realms implicit in global notions of administrative law. They also challenge hierarchical concepts of administration. Government decision-making takes place more in an ongoing series of decentered negotiations than in constitutionally prescribed processes.

This description tells us little, however, about the forces that might propel the state toward law-based administration. As Vietnam integrates further into international trading networks, the central state is coming under more global pressure to "rationalize administration." So far the central leadership has lacked the capacity (and perhaps willingness) to bring local government inline with global expectations. Central legislation is too vague and opaque to circumscribe local decision-making. More importantly, central authorities tacitly allowed local officials to arrogate discretion to flexibly apply rigid central laws. Without domestic demand for "rational administration" there is little pressure on local officials to change.

Complicating reforms, the party still uses prerogative extra-legal powers to protect its interests. Although these powers are now confined to politically sensitive civil and economic cases, they are routinely used to resolve administrative complaints. The conundrum here is that the history of court reform suggests that independence from politics is not necessarily the most effective way to foster robust and effective courts.[92] Judgments create losers. Attacks on courts are inevitable, especially during their vulnerable inception period. Since judges lack the "purse and the sword" to defend themselves, to some extent courts must rely on politics to protect them from state and non-state interference. Politics thus threatens judicial power, but it is also vital for the protection of embryonic courts. The party is currently using its power to protect and expand the power of civil and economic courts. Perhaps in time, when the party is confident that administrative rules entrench its political position, it will also support administrative courts to review executive action.

Notes

1 See Tom Ginsburg's chapter, "Judicalization of administrative governance: Causes, consequences and limits," in this book.
2 Ta Van Tai, "Vietnam's Code of the Le Dynasty 1428–1788," *American Journal of Comparative Law*, vol.30, no.3, 1982, p.523.
3 G. Teubner, "Juridification: Concepts, Aspects, Limits, Solutions," in R. Baldwin, et al., eds., *Socio-Legal Reader on Regulation*, Oxford: Oxford University Press, 1998 (orig. pub 1987).
4 D. Nelken, "Law as Communication: Constituting the Field," in D. Nelken, ed., *Law as Communication*, Dartmouth: Aldershot, 1996, pp.3–30; J. Black, "Regulatory Conversations," *Journal of Law and Society*, vol.29, no.1, 2002, pp.163–74.
5 Dinh Gia Trinh, "May Y Kien Dong Gop Ve Van De Bao Ve Phap Che" (Some Opinions on the Protection of Legality), *Tap San Tu Phap*, no.3, 1961, pp.20–32.
6 Le Minh Tam, "Doi Tuong va Phuong Phap Nghien Cuu Cua Ly Luan Ve Nha Nuoc va Phap Luat" [Scope and Methodology for Studying the Themes of State and Law], in Hanoi Law University, ed., *Giao Trinh Ly Luan Nha Nuoc va Phap Luat* [Themes of State and Law], Hanoi: Nha Xuat Ban Cong An Nhan Dan, 1998.
7 Nguyen Nien, "Several Legal Matters Concerning Planning in Our Country," *Luat Hoc* [*Legal Science*], vol.22(2), April 1977, pp.22–8, translated by JPRS 70119, 24–26.
8 Nguyen Khac Vien, *Tradition and Revolution in Vietnam*, Berkeley: Indochina Resource Centre, 1974.
9 Hoang Quoc Viet, "Can Dam Bao Cho Phap Luat Duoc Ton Trong Trong Cong Tac Quan Ly Linh Te Cua Nha Nuoc" [We Must Ensure the Enforcement of Law in State Economic Management], in *Nghien Cuu Nha Nuoc va Phap Quyen* [Studies about State and Law], Hanoi: Truth Publishing, 1964, pp.35–6.
10 Pham Duy Nghia, "Noi Doanh Nhan Tim Den Cong Ly" [Where do Entrepreneurs Go for Justice?], *Tap Chi Nghien Cuu Lap Phap,* no.3, 2003, pp.45–54.
11 Hoang Quoc Viet, op. cit., pp.34–6.
12 J. Bentley, *Completion of Viet Nam's Legal Framework for Economic Development*, UNDP Discussion Paper 2, Hanoi: United Nations Development Programme, 1999.
13 Do Muoi, "Sua Doi Hien Phap, Xay Dung Nha Nuoc Phap Quyen Viet Nam, Day Manh Su Nghiep Doi Moi" [Revising the Constitution, Building a Law-Governed State and Promoting Renovation], *Tap Chi Cong San*, no.5, 1992, pp.6–7.

14 J. H. Berman, "Some Jurisprudential Implications of the Codification of Soviet Law," in R. M. Buxbaum, et al., eds., *The Soviet Sobranie of Laws: Problems of Codification and Non-Publication*, Berkeley: University of California Press, 1991, p.173.
15 Constitution 1992, article 4.
16 Vietnam is rated by Transparency International as one of the most corrupt regulatory systems in East Asia. See: Transparency International, Comparative Perception Index 2006; <http://www.transparency.org/news_room/in_focus/cpi_2006/cpi_table> accessed 26 January 2007.
17 VNA, "Concern Over Outdated Law on Petitions Proceedings," *IntellAsia News Services*, 20 May 2004.
18 Politburo Resolution No. 48 NQ/KW on the Strategy for the Development and Improvement of the Legal System of Vietnam to 2010 and the Direction for the Period up to 2020, 24 May 2005; Politburo Resolution No. 49-NQ/TW on Judicial Strategy until 2020, 24 May 2005.
19 A. Stone Sweet, *Governing with Judges: Constitutional Politics in Europe*, New York: Oxford University Press, 2000; R. Barro, *Determinants of Economic Growth*, Cambridge: MIT Press, 1997.
20 J. Gillespie, "Transplanted Company Law: An Ideological and Cultural Analysis of Market-Entry in Vietnam," *International Comparative Law Quarterly*, 51, 2002, pp.641–72.
21 CIEM, "Comparative Provincial Performance in Private Business Development," VIE01/025, Hanoi, November, 2003.
22 R. Mallon, "Managing Investment Climate Reforms: Viet Nam Case Study," unpublished paper, *World Bank Development Report*, Hanoi, 2005, pp.31–6.
23 CIEM, op. cit., p.23.
24 GTZ, "Business Licensing: Current Status and the Way Forward," unpublished paper, Business Issues Series, Hanoi: GTZ, 2006.
25 These comments are based on study conducted by the author of 70 firms operating in five industries in Northern Vietnam between 2004 and 2007.
26 Stone Sweet, op. cit.
27 M. Gainsborough, "Reforming State Owned Enterprises," unpublished paper, CERI, Science Po, Paris, December, 2006.
28 VNS, "Steel Producers Feeling Threatened by Chinese Imports," *Viet Nam News*, 12 March 2007, pp.15–16.
29 A. Santos, "The World Bank's Use of the 'Rule of Law' Promise," in D. Trubek and A. Santos, eds., *The New Law and Economic Development: A Critical Appraisal*, Cambridge: Cambridge University Press, 2006, pp.253–300.; World Bank, *World Bank Development Report 2002: Building Institutions for Markets*, Washington D.C.: The World Bank, 2002.
30 J. Meyer, "Globalization and the Expansion and Standardization of Management," in K. Sahlin-Andersson and L. Engwall, eds., *The Expansion of Management Knowledge: Carriers, Flows and Sources*, Stanford: Stanford University Press, 2002, pp.33–44.
31 Thang Van Phuc, "Public Administration Reform: Five Year Achievements (2001–2005) and Major Tasks to 2010," *Vietnam Law and Legal Forum*, no.138, 2006, pp.6–8.
32 Office of Government, *Public Administrative Reform Comprehensive Plan 2001–2010*, Hanoi, 2002; Doan Trong Truyen, "An Overview on Public Administrative Reform in the Socialist Republic of Vietnam," in UNDP, *International Colloquium on Public Administration Reform*, Hanoi: UNDP, 1996, pp.84–93.
33 M. Painter, "The Politics of Economic Restructuring in Vietnam: Contested Agendas and Uncertain Trajectories," *Journal of Development Studies*, vol.41, no.2, 2005, pp.261–83.

34 Hoang Hai Van, "Bo Tu Phap, UBND TPHCM de Nghi: Giu Nguyen Muc Thue Thu Nhap Doanh Nghiep 10% Cho Lien Doanh Phu My Hung" [Ministry of Justice and Ho Chi Minh City People's Committee Propose that Corporate Income Tax Rate Remain at 10% for Phu My Hung Joint Venture], *Thanh Nien-Online*, 17 February 2004, p.3.
35 See Official Letter No. 5, TP PL QT, 5 November 2003, Ministry of Justice.
36 Author Unknown, "Cloudy Reasoning in Phu My Hung Tax Row," *Sai Gon Giai Phong*, 21 August 2004, p.3, trans. *Development Vietnam*, Intellasia News Services, 25 August 2004, pp.14–15.
37 Ginsburg, op. cit.
38 Interviews with Nguyen Van Kim, Deputy Director, Legal Department, Thanh Tra Chinh Phu (Government Inspectorate), Hanoi October, 2006; interviews with Tran Van Son, Deputy Director, Claims Settlement Department, Office of Government, Hanoi, March 2007. Also see Nguyen Van Thanh and Dinh Van Minh, *Mot So Van De Ve Doi Moi Co Che Giai Quyet Khieu Kien Hanh Chinh O Viet Nam* [Some Issues about Renovating Mechanisms for Solving Administrative Complaints in Vietnam], Hanoi: Nha Xuat Ban Tu Phap, 2004, pp.76–147.
39 *Hoang Viet Luat Le* Nguyen Dynasty 1815, article 380.
40 For example, the Ordinance on the Settlement of Complaints and Denunciations 1981 directed officials to resolve grievances in accordance with law, the "state benefit" and the lastly, the citizens' "legitimate rights and interests." See Le Binh Vong, "Compliant and Denunciation Law-A Legal Guarantee for the Promotion of People's Democratic Rights," *Vietnam Law and Legal Forum*, vol.4, no.43, 1998, pp.17–19.
41 Laws regulating trade and services must by administered "in a uniform, impartial and reasonable manner," notably by independent administrative tribunals or procedures. General Agreement on Tariffs and Trade 1994, 15 April 1994; Marrakech Agreement Establishing the World Trade Organization, Annex 1A, art X, 1867 UNTS 187, 33 ILM 1153 (1994). See: Ngo Duc Manh, "Administrative and Legislative Issued Posed by WTO Accession," *Vietnam Law & Legal Forum*, vol.10, no.118, 2004, pp.2–8.
42 Tran Van Son, "Revising Complaints and Denunciation Law in Line with BTA and WTO Agreements," *Vietnam Law & Legal Forum,* vol.11, no.131, 2005, pp.16–18.
43 Ibid., p.20.
44 Interview with Nguyen Thi Huyen, Lawyer, NH Quang and Associates, Hanoi, October 2006.
45 Over 200 Official Letters were issued in 2006. Interview Do Tien Thinh, National Business Specialist, ASMED Hanoi, 22 October 2006.
46 Law on Complaints and Denunciation 2004. Editing Group 2007 *Project for Establishment of Administrative Tribunals in Vietnam*, unpublished paper, Hanoi, 13 March.
47 Nguyen Van Thanh and Dinh Van Minh, op. cit., pp.83–100.
48 Interviews Nguyen Van Kim, Deputy Director Legal Department, Thanh Tra Chinh Phu (Government Inspectorate), Hanoi, October 2006.
49 Interviews with Hanoi-based lawyers October 2006, March 2007.
50 Dao Xuan Tien, 'Responsibilities of Elected Deputies in Dealing with Citizen's Complaints and Denunciations', *Tap Chi Nghien Cuu Lap Phap,* no.2, 2005, pp.33–37. The National Assembly receives approximately 25,000 petitions each year, see: G. Andersson, et al., *Strengthening the Capacity of the Office of the Vietnam National Assembly*, SIDA Evaluation 12/12, Stockholm, 2002, p.28.
51 P. Solomon, "Courts in Russia: Independence, Power and Accountability," in A. Sajo, ed., *Judicial Integrity*, Kluwer: Dordrech, 2004, pp.205–6.
52 Petitions complaining about administrative abuses have also flooded the recently established Anti-Corruption Board (*Ban Chi Dao Phong Chong Tham Nhung*). See: Nhat Linh, 'Thu Tuong Nguyen Tan Dung Lam Truong Ban Chi Dao Phong Chong Tham Nhung' [Prime Minister is the Chief of the Guidance Committee For

Anti-Corruption] *Tuoi Tre* 29 July 2006, <www.tuoitre.com.vn> accessed 15 May 2007.
53 The Law on the Organization of People's Courts was amended 28 October 1995.
54 According to the "concentration of powers doctrine" the National Assembly is the paramount state agencies with powers to supervise other arms of the state. See: Bui Xuan Duc, "Van De Nhan Thuc va Van Dung Nguyen Tac Tap Quyen Xa Hoi Chu Nghia Trong Dieu Kien Hien Nay" [The Issue of Understanding and Implementing the Socialist Concentration of State Power Doctrine in the Current Situation], in Le Minh Trong ed., *Mot So Van De Ve Hoan Thien To Chuc va Hoat Dong Cua Bo May Nha Nuoc Cong Hoa Xa Hoi Chu Nghia Viet Nam* [Some Issues on Perfecting the Organisation and Operation of the State Apparatus of the Socialist Republic of Vietnam], Hanoi: Truth Publishers, 2001, pp.47–55.
55 These figures are taken from the "Bao Cao Cong Tac Nganh Toa An" (Supreme Court Annual Reports) from 1999–2004.
56 See: Peereenboom's chapter, "More law, less courts: Legalized governance, judicialization and *dejudicialization* in China," in this book.
57 A government report estimated that in a five-year period from 1999 until 2003 approximately 41 percent of administrative claims were legitimate, but only 800 cases from over 10,000 complaints were filed in administrative courts. See Author unknown, op. cit., 2004, pp.26–7.
58 UNDP, *Bao Cao Khao Sat Nhu Cau Cua Tao An Nhan Dan Cap Huyen Tren Toan Quoc* [Report on Survey of Needs of District People's Courts nationwide], Hanoi: Judicial Publishing House, 2007, p.208.
59 Ibid., pp.208–9; UNDP, "Access to Justice: Survey from the People's Perspective," unpublished paper, Hanoi 2004.
60 Solomon, op. cit., pp.226–30.
61 See Ordinance on Procedures for Handling Administrative Cases 1998 (amended 2005) article 11.
62 "Bao Cao Cua Chanh An Toa An Nhan Dan Toi Cao Tai Ky Hop Thu 6 Quoc Hoi Khoa 10 Ve Cong Tac Toa An" (Report of the Chief Judge of the Supreme People's Court at the Sixth Meeting of the Tenth Session of the National Assembly Regarding the Work of Court), No. 67 BC/VP, 22 October, 1999.
63 Author unknown, "Ca Mau Administrative Court Proves Toothless," *Thaoi Bao Te Sai Gon,* July 5 2001, p.4.
64 Nguyen Van Thanh and Dinh Van Min, op. cit., pp.140–7.
65 P. Nicholson and Nguyen Hung Quang, "The Vietnamese Judiciary: The Politics of Appointment and Promotion," *Pacific Rim Law and Policy Journal*, vol.14, no.1, 2005, pp.14–22; B. Quinn, "Legal Reform in the Context of Vietnam," *Columbia Journal of Asian Law*, vol.15, no.219, 2002. pp.245–6.
66 UNDP, op. cit., 2007, pp.298–9.
67 Toa An Nhan Dan Toi Cao [Supreme People's Court], "Giai Dap Mot So Van De Ve Hinh Su, Dan Su, Kinh Te, Lao Dong, Hanh Chinh va To Tung [Annual Report on Criminal, Civil, Economic, Labour, Administrative and Procedural Laws], Hanoi: Supreme People's Court, 1 February, 2000. pp.66–8.
68 Le Thi Hoang Thanh, "Buoc Thien Moi Trong Viec Thuc Thi Trach Nhiem Cua Nha Nuoc Truoc Cong Dan" [A Step Towards Development of the State Based on the Rule of Law], *Phap Luat va Phat Trien*, no.2, 2006, p.48; Nguyen Van Thanh and Dinh Van Minh, op. cit., pp.30–1.
69 Bui Ngoc Son, "Su Doc Lap Cua Toa an Trong Nha Nuoc Phap Quyen" [Judicial Independence in the Rule of Law], *Tap Chi Nghien Cuu Lap Phap*, vol.4, no.43, 2003, pp.43–50.
70 Judgment No. 1-HSST 21 December 1996, People's Court of Hanoi.
71 Judgment No. 21 HCST 11 May 2006, People's Court of Ho Chi Minh City.

72 Tran Xuan Thu, "Hoi Dap ve Phap Luat" [Legal Questions and Answers], *Nha Nuoc va Phap Luat,* no.9, 1996, pp.32–3.
73 Nguyen Van Thanh and Dinh Van Minh, op. cit., p.128–47.
74 Author unknown, "Nganh Toa An Kho Kham Noi Viec Xu Ly Tranh Cap Dat Dai" [Its is Very Tough for Courts to Resolve Land Disputes], Phap Luat <http://vnexpress.net/Vietnam/Phap-luat/2003/07/3B9C9DE9/> accessed 15 August 2003.
75 G. Teubner, "Alienating Justice: On the Surplus Value of the Twelfth Camel," in J. Priban and D. Nelken, eds., *Law's New Boundaries: The Consequences of Legal Autopoiesis*, Dartmouth: Ashgate, 2001, p.23.
76 See Article 7 BTA. Also see Politburo Resolution No 49-NG/TW on the Strategy for Judicial Reform to 2020.
77 Le Cam, "Cai Cach He Thong Toa An Trong Giai Doan Xay Dung Nha Nuoc Phap Quyen Viet Nam" [Reform the Court System to Build Up a Law Based State in Vietnam], *Tap Chi Nghien Cuu Lap Phap*, no.4, 2002, pp.21, 27.
78 Government of Vietnam, *National Programme on Public Administrative Reform*, 26 May 1994, pp.2–6; Doan Trong Truyen, op. cit., pp.84–93.
79 Le Duan, *Phat Huy Quyen Lam Chu Tap The Xay Dung Nha Nuoc Vung Manh* [Develop the Rights of Collective Mastery Build a Strong State], Hanoi: Nha Xuat Ban Su That, 1978, p.91.
80 Dang Phong and M. Beresford, *Authority Relations and Economic Decision-Making in Vietnam: An Historical Perspective*, Copenhagen: NIAS Publications, 1998, pp.92–4.
81 J. Riedel and S. Turley, *The Politics and Economics of Transition to a Market Economy in Vietnam*, Technical Paper No. 152, Paris: Organisation for Economic Cooperation and Development, 1999, p.37.
82 Ordinance on Public Servants (1998) (as amended) articles 4–6. See Government Steering Committee for Public Administration Reform, 2000 "Report of Group 3: Review of Public Administration Reform in the Field of Organizational Structure of Government Apparatus and State Management," Hanoi.
83 Painter, op. cit., pp.261–83.
84 Le Quang Thuong, "Mot So Van De Ve Cong Tac Dan Van Trong Tinh Hinh Hien Nay" [Several Problems Concerning Cadre Work Under the Current Situation], *Tap Chi Cong San*, 14 July 1996, pp.18–19.
85 T. Vasavakul, "Rebuilding Authority Relations: Public Administration Reform in the Era of Doi Moi," unpublished paper, Hanoi: Asian Development Bank, 2002.
86 Tu Giang, "The Nation's Corporate Spirit," *Vietnam Investment Review*, 12 September 2003, <www.vietnam.investmentreview.com.vn>.
87 Based on interviews with Hanoi based lawyers October 2006 and March 2007.
88 Case No. 57, First Instance Criminal Court, Thai Binh Provincial People's Court, 8 March 2004. Interview with the defense counsel, Hanoi, March 2005.
89 Criminal Code 1999, article 181.
90 Bui Ngoc Son, op. cit., pp.43–50.
91 Interviews Dang Quang Phuong, Director, Institute for Judicial Science, Supreme Court, Hanoi March 1999, September 1999, February 2000, March 2002.
92 B. Friedman, "The History of the Countermajoritarian Difficulty, Part One: The Road to Judicial Supremacy," *New York University Law Review*, 73, 1998, pp.333, 394–95.

11 The emergence of administrative justice in Thailand under the 1997 Constitution*

Peter Leyland

Introduction

This chapter seeks to provide a contextual overview of the current provision of administrative justice in Thailand. I will argue that a regime of administrative justice can be regarded as an important legacy of the 1997 Constitution. Thailand now has a developed system of administrative law and Administrative Courts closely modelled on the French system. However, it will also be apparent from this analysis that although the technical foundations have been firmly set in place, the constitutional malaise in Thailand has tended to undermine the effectiveness of the institutions set up to uphold the rule of law and promote good governance. Given the current political uncertainty the constitutional background is briefly outlined in the initial section of Part I of this chapter in order to frame the discussion that follows. We then proceed to situate the Administrative Courts as part of a multi-layered legal order in Thailand.[1] A comparative analysis of the Thai Administrative Courts is the focus of Part II of this chapter. After a detailed analysis of the jurisdiction, characteristics and powers of Thailand's Administrative Courts, Part III is mainly a case study. It begins by briefly mentioning the wider role of the administrative state in a nation which has been subject to economic liberalisation, and of particular relevance to this discussion, the privatisation and statutory regulation of significant industries. This is the prelude to an assessment of the role of administrative law and the involvement of the Administrative Courts in the field of the regulation of telecommunication, broadcasting and power generation under the 1997 Constitution.

Part I: The Thai constitutional and political context

There was a bloodless military coup in Thailand on 19 September 2006 which resulted in the suspension of the 1997 Constitution and the imposition of martial law. A temporary constitution was set in place, and a promise was made by the head of the military government, General Sonthi Boonyaratglin, that a new constitution would be drafted. There was a further commitment to hand back power to civilian rule with new elections within a year. This would be after a referendum approving the constitution had been held. A few weeks after the coup a former general, Surayud Chalanont, was appointed Prime Minister, and an appointed council was set up to rule alongside the military junta. A new constitution has since been approved by the Thai electorate following a national referendum held on 19 August 2007 and has now come into effect after a general election held in late 2007.[2] Given the fact that the 1997 Constitution was widely regarded as a major step towards democratic government, as it had many special provisions to root out corruption and establish good governance, this chapter seeks to set out the characteristics of the Thai system of administrative justice which was established as part of this new constitutional order.

Since the end of absolute monarchy in 1932 Thailand has lacked a stable system of constitutional rule.[3] In fact the nation had experienced a total of 17 new constitutions, including the 1997 Constitution. Periods of civilian government alternated with phases of military rule. The influence of the generals appeared to be in decline by the end of the 1980s. However, the military coup in 1991 failed to deliver an immediate transition to civilian rule. Street demonstrations for democracy were brutally suppressed, but the Bangkok business and urban class demanded a restoration of civilian rule and there were wider calls for political reform.[4] Influenced by the ideas of Thai liberal intellectuals, in 1995 a constitutional drafting assembly representing all regions of Thailand set about the task of reaching agreement on the essentials of a new constitution. The proposals which emerged were strongly resisted by certain entrenched elements such as generals, senators, judges and village heads.[5] In fact, it was the sudden economic crisis which prompted the introduction of this constitutional reform. A period of post-second world war expansion and then of economic boom during the 1980s and early 1990s ended with a spectacular financial slump in mid-1997.[6] A number of diverse groupings, ranging from monk intellectuals to the Democrat Party in Parliament, recognised that Thailand needed to strengthen its internal institutions if it was going to survive and prosper.[7] 'Bangkok's businessmen and middle class began to blame the crisis on mismanagement by politicians, and seized on the constitution as the way to bring politics into line with the needs of the globalised economy'.[8]

It certainly appeared at the time that a radically improved constitution offered a new way forward[9] since it contained measures designed to guarantee democracy and human rights, exclude military influence in the political process and eliminate corruption in public life. Indeed, this bold attempt at conferring greater power to the Thai people than had ever been granted before was regarded by some commentators as amounting to a revolution in Thai politics.[10] Although Thailand remained a constitutional monarchy, with the King as head of state at the apogee of power (mainly symbolically but also with limited capacity to intervene in certain circumstances),[11] the 1997 Constitution modified the electoral system, changed the composition of both Houses of Parliament, and reformed the structure of the courts.

A central problem is that:

> Those who would rule Thailand face the challenge of placating and managing innumerable vested interests, legal and illegal. Some political groups are

dominated by people who are deeply involved in activities that cover a broad range of illegality, from drugs and prostitution to gambling and smuggling.[12]

These observations alert us to that fact that as well as recasting the shape of the main institutions, a prime objective of the 1997 Constitution was to provide a basis for stable government, tackle corruption and protect basic human rights effectively. To achieve these goals a new set of watchdog organisations were set up under the constitution which have been the subject of much discussion. The Election Commission, the National Counter Corruption Commission, the Anti-Money Laundering Office and the State Audit Commission were each designed to tackle particular aspects of malfeasance and corruption associated with the political process.[13] Patrolling a different area, the Human Rights Commission was intended to deal with abuses of group rights and individual human rights. In the domain of law and administration a system of Administrative Courts and an ombudsman were introduced for the first time, to further protect citizen rights by extending the range of remedies available. Finally, the boundary of the entire constitutional scheme was patrolled by a new constitutional court. Despite some important flaws, the 1997 Constitution can be regarded as a remarkable achievement and, at one point, it looked like it might form the basis for a sustainable new chapter on the Thai political stage.

Thai legal process and administrative justice

In delineating the position of the Administrative Courts it is important to be aware of their jurisdictional scope in relation to other courts and the office of the ombudsman. With regard to constitutional issues, the 1997 Constitution established a Constitutional Court which consisted of a President and 14 judges.[14] Normally a quorum of nine judges presided over cases that came before it.[15] The Constitutional Court was responsible for hearing challenges to draft legislation, statutes and regulations on the grounds of unconstitutionality.[16] The court also determined matters of overlapping authority between official bodies under section 266 of the 1997 Constitution and it was designed to operate as a constitutional safeguard, particularly in relation to the protection of civil liberties and human rights.[17] As the judicial body with jurisdiction over many constitutional issues it was vested with formidable powers,[18] some of which are comparable to those exercised by the United States Supreme Court.[19] In such a capacity the Thai Constitutional Court was most exposed to political criticism and censure.[20]

An even more powerful Constitutional Court comprising a President and eight justices has been introduced under the 2007 Constitution. Apart from a familiar role of constitutional review and pronouncing on the validity of legislation its wide-ranging jurisdiction includes: determining the removal from office of members of Parliament; policing political parties, ratifying the appointment and dismissal of election commissioners; approving challenges to emergency decrees and so on.[21]

Also, it is worth noting that the 2007 Constitution allows any citizen to challenge the constitutionality of any legislation if he/she considers that his/her rights have been violated by any 'State organ or State agency' but in order to prevent this right of challenge before the highest court from being abused, the claimant must show that all other available remedies have first been exhausted.[24] In determining most constitutional issues the 2007 Constitution places the Constitutional Court above all other jurisdictions and thereby lowers the status of the Administrative Courts.[25]

Thailand has a system of criminal and civil courts with a jurisdiction operating in their respective fields. Further, the Administrative Courts have no jurisdiction over matters triable by other specialist courts,[26] matters of military discipline and matters falling under the remit of the Judicial Commission.[27] Where there is a dispute as to the jurisdictional limits of the Administrative Court the outcome is determined by a special committee comprising the President of the Supreme Court of Justice, the President of the Supreme Administrative Court and the President of the other court involved.[28]

As we will discover when discussing the iTV case later, in addition to the ordinary courts, Thailand has well developed systems of informal justice/alternative dispute resolution, and particularly of arbitration which is available through the Thai Arbitration Institute[29] (TAI), or under a scheme run by the Board of Trade. The recent Arbitration Act 2002 (BE 2545) in the main recognises UNCITRAL model law.[30] The arbitration approach offers the advantages of diverting cases from the ordinary courts, a less formal process,[31] with a model (usually binding) arbitration clause forming part of an agreement, and additionally, arbitration involves greatly reduced costs should there be a dispute. Normally, fees and expenses will be paid by the parties as specified in the award. Otherwise, the parties may request a court order to determine fees, expenses and remuneration of the arbitrator.[32] TAI and the Board of Trade have a specified rate for their schemes.[33]

Finally, the Office of the Ombudsman[34] (referred to hereinafter as the ombudsman although there are three Thai Ombudsmen in post) was conceived as *one* of several watchdog bodies that was custom designed under the 1997 Constitution to exercise a specialised oversight function.[35] In this regard the ombudsman was intended to work alongside the watchdog bodies listed earlier, but also, the ombudsman was granted a special role in relation to the referral of matters to the Constitutional Court and the Administrative Courts for formal legal resolution acting as a special guardian of the constitution itself.[36] In addition to dealing with routine administrative shortcomings the pressing reason for introducing an ombudsman in Thailand has been to combat the endemic corruption which has had the effect of undermining, not only the efficient running of government but also public confidence in the entire system of administration.[37] It was envisaged that the introduction of an independent ombudsman with formidable investigatory powers would extend beyond complaint handling and amount to another weapon in the armoury for tackling the particular forms of corruption associated with central and local government in Thailand.

The Thai ombudsman is empowered to consider and investigate complaints when an official at any level of government violates the law or exceeds the jurisdiction of his or her authority.[38] The ombudsman is also empowered to investigate when the action or inaction of a public body or official causes harm, damage or injustice to an individual or to the general public, whether or not this action or inaction by the public body or official is within his or her jurisdiction, and regardless of whether the action is in breach of the law. In addition, the ombudsman is competent to look into the 'performance of or omission to perform duties ... which unjustly causes injuries to the complainant or the public notwithstanding whether or not the action has been lawful'.[39] In other words, it is apparent that a wide jurisdiction was envisaged and has been granted to the Thai ombudsman. It encompasses routine complaints associated in other nations with the concept of maladministration,[40] it extends also to questions of legality[41] and goes beyond legal questions to allow investigation of injustice and unfairness. It will therefore be apparent that there is considerable potential for overlap with the role of the Administrative Courts. The essential difference lies in the type of role the respective bodies perform, with the ombudsman able to undertake investigations, recommend remedial action and granted the power to refer matters on to other bodies to pursue further, while the Administrative Courts lack an investigatory role but they have at their disposal a wide range of legal remedies. As with the Administrative Courts, following the military coup in 2006 the Office of the Ombudsman has continued to operate but the case load has declined from 4,343 in 2006 to only 1,051 in 2007. Out of a total of 16,528 cases that have been referred since the introduction of the office 2,149 claimants received compensation and a further 568 cases were referred for remedial action to be taken by the public body in question.[42] It is worth stressing, once again, that the constitutional apparatus was recognition of the need to introduce far-reaching controls over the exercise of public power, and that it appears that these institutions have been established as permanent fixtures under whatever constitution is in operation.

Thailand's Administrative Courts

The inspiration for the modern system of administrative law in Thailand is usually credited to Pridi Phanomyong who was a Thai politician, professor and judge of exceptional ability and energy.[43] Pridi trained in Paris and then returned to Bangkok where he was instrumental in introducing the teaching of administrative law as part of the curriculum for lawyers at the Ministry of Justice Law School in the years following his return from France. In fact the curriculum he introduced concentrated on constitutional matters such as the form of the state and the rights and liberties of individuals.[44] Pridi was a major player at the point when absolute monarchy was replaced by early forms of constitutionalism.[45] The Council of State was re-established by the Act on the Council of State B.E. 2476 (1933) and it was intended to perform the functions which had previously been exercised by the Advisory Agency of the State in the reign of King Rama V. The duties of the Law Drafting Department were transferred to the Council of State in 1933. The same body was also intended by Pridi to function as an Administrative Court to serve Thai citizens. Such a court could be petitioned to do justice against the government and state agencies.[46] However, the term 'Administrative Court' was not officially used.

At this point there were already certain options open to an aggrieved citizen. A case could be taken against an administrative official in the ordinary courts. A right of appeal to a court against the administrative act or order was sometimes available. A petition could be issued against the superior of an administrative official if wrongdoing was suspected. Finally, it was possible to petition the King directly.[47] The introduction of administrative law meant that if an administrative order was wrong, a process of petitioning to the Council of State would have become available. In order to perform a dual set of functions, the staff of the Council of State were divided into two categories: law councillors whose primary function was statutory drafting; and petition councillors who were entrusted to adjudicate administrative cases as prescribed by law.[48] From the 1930s when this upheaval was taking place, until recently, it would have been costly to introduce an Administrative Court, but, above all, there was well orchestrated opposition from prominent judges to the introduction of a new administrative law jurisdiction,[49] and therefore, the existing system of administrative appeals was expanded into the Petition Council of the Office of State to deal with the administrative cases that arose.

The 1997 Constitution provided for the introduction of the system of Administrative Courts in addition to the ordinary courts.[50] The Administrative Courts were designed to fill a particular gap in the grievance chain by offering full legal redress against official bodies. They were set up in 1999 by the The Act on the Establishment of Administrative Courts and Administrative Courts Procedure (hereinafter the 1999 Act) and began operating in 2001, replacing the Petition Council of the Council of State.[51] The new courts are based on a two-tier system: the Supreme Administrative Court and Administrative Courts of First Instance of which there are two: the Central Administrative Court (for Bangkok and provinces local to Bangkok) and the Regional Administrative Courts.[52] However, the characteristics of the courts and the limits of their jurisdiction can be distinguished from the ordinary courts and from other means of redress that are available under the constitution. The Supreme Administrative Court, apart from acting as an appellate court, hearing appeals from judgements of the Administrative Court of First Instance, exercises a jurisdiction which is directed at issues relating to the operation of central government. For example, it has competence to try cases concerning the legality of Royal Decrees or by-laws issued by the Council of Ministers. It also tries cases involving disputes in relation to decisions of a quasi-judicial council (as prescribed by the general assembly of judges of the Supreme Court).[53]

When it opened its doors in 2001 the newly formed Thai Administrative Court was staffed with a permanent cohort of professional judges. The appointing body, which also has responsibility for disciplinary matters is the Judicial Commission on the Administrative Courts (JCAC) composed of judges of the Supreme Court and the Administrative Court.[54] In order to be eligible for appointment as an Administrative Court judge any candidate must be a Thai national over 35 years of age with either a degree in law or the social sciences, but also with relevant experience. For example, at least three years as a petition commissioner, secretary to a Law Councillor, Administrative Court official, as a judge in a civil or criminal court or as a public prosecutor. In practice, all the judges appointed to date have been relatively senior legally qualified professionals.[55]

Part II: Characteristics of the Thai Administrative Courts

It is commonly assumed that Administrative Courts are fundamentally concerned with the accountability of public bodies and the containment of public power (as well as having other responsibilities, e.g. over administrative contracts and tort claims against public bodies) and, given this assumption, the reach of any public law jurisdiction becomes a question of crucial importance.[56] A separate public law jurisdiction has been justified on the basis that the state should have a monopoly over the exercise of certain types of coercive power, in particular the creation and enforcement of laws relating to the capacity of the state to act as an instrument of social regulation.[57] Thailand's French connection[58] has contributed to the local conceptualisation of a distinct public law which is associated with designing state organisations; ascribing varying degrees of importance to state agencies and state officials in regard to members of the public; formulating criteria and measures for controlling the discharge of state organs and officials.[59] In many European nations it has been increasingly recognised that any public/private distinction has been made more problematic by the emergence of a 'contracting state' in which there is expanding private sector involvement, for example, in the delivery of public services formerly provided by government and local government.[60] Other examples include the privatisation of formerly state run industries and the reliance of private companies to construct and manage many publicly financed enterprises.[61] Thailand is a nation which has also seen trends towards privatisation and a contracting state and the Thai Administrative Courts have been introduced as the most potent constitutional mechanism designed to regulate the exercise of these aspects of public power. In consequence, a restricted definition of what constitutes public law matters falling under the ambit of the Administrative Court would limit the application of public law remedies and exclude judicial supervision over functions formerly exercised by the state which now are manifested in private form.[62]

How then do the courts approach the task of determining their jurisdictional boundaries? In assessing a claim the court must decide whether the contested matter has a sufficient public law dimension to fall under its jurisdiction.[63] In cases where this issue is contestable the judge will consider: (1) whether the body/enterprise/individual is providing a public service; (2) whether a public power is being exercised. The test employed seeks to ascertain if a power has been granted that would not be granted or exercised in the private sector; (3) whether the body/enterprise or individual is exercising a public service function. From the reported case law it appears that the courts have defined public in a broad sense. For example, the court has heard cases involving privatised state enterprises which provide a universal service and has ruled that the Telephone Organisation of Thailand (TOT) remained an administrative agency subject to the jurisdiction of the Administrative Courts. The role of the *Tribunal des Conflits* in deciding contested matters of jurisdiction is closely replicated by the Thai Jurisdictional Conflict Tribunal which adjudicates when such disputes arise in the Thai legal context.[64] By way of comparison it is worth remembering that the major justification for the exclusivity principle as part of the modern law of judicial review in England and Wales was the introduction of both a special procedure and specially designed remedies.[65]

Turning next to remedies, the UK system of judicial review has been constructed around the remedies that were available. In particular, the courts were equipped with the ancient prerogative orders which allowed unlawful decisions of public bodies to be quashed; prevented bodies from taking decisions which were deemed unlawful; or commanded them to act where they were neglecting to perform a lawful duty.[66] The Thai Administrative Court is in possession of formidable powers when it comes to granting remedies[67] and many of the remedies it is able to award are tailored to suit an administrative law context. The court can issue a decree revoking a by-law or an order[68] and it can revoke an act in whole or part where it is alleged that an administrative agency or state official has done an unlawful act under section 9(1) of the 1999 Act. Furthermore, the court can direct whether any such decree is going to have retrospective or non-retrospective effect. In addition, the Administrative Courts have powers which roughly correspond to the mandatory orders and injunctive relief available to the English courts. They are granted powers to order the performance of a duty or order a person to act or to refrain from an act in compliance with the law. In addition the court has powers to order the payment of money or the delivery of property. The Thai system departs from the French most obviously in the way these far-reaching powers are set out. The decisions of the French Administrative Courts were normally obeyed without any need for enforcement but reforms were introduced to allow a follow-up to judgements where a decision has not been implemented, for example *astreinte*.[69] The lack of remedy has been regarded as a perceived weakness.[70]

In Thailand, as in France under *droit administratif*, there is an inquisitorial style of court procedure. It is specified that in the process of trial and adjudication the court has the power to inquire into the facts as is appropriate.[71] This procedure requires the judge to conduct investigations to ascertain the accuracy of the facts of the case (*inexactitude des fait*) and s/he is expected to draw the correct inferences from these facts.[72] At a preliminary stage a judge is put in charge of the case in order to consider any statements and documentary evidence submitted, the explanations of the parties and any other relevant facts. A memorandum is prepared with an opinion from the investigating judge which is submitted to the division to decide whether the matter can proceed further.[73] If the matter goes to trial another judge is made responsible for managing the case which will require an exchange of evidence so that both parties have full knowledge of the contested facts. At this stage the court is conferred formidable powers it can use against public bodies who fail to respond when the judge is conducting its fact-finding role.[74] When a case finally goes to trial the parties are allowed to make statements and call witnesses but without incorporating the adversarial style of routine examination and cross-examination.[75]

It has been emphasised that Thailand has a continental system based on legal codes which means that case law has a different status in comparison with a common law system where important decisions are reported in detail and the higher courts bind the lower courts on decided questions of law. In reaching a decision judges in the Administrative Courts are not bound by a doctrine of binding precedent. However, the judge is required to refer to any decided cases with similar facts. Any such authorities will be regarded as persuasive authority but they are not binding. Moreover, the Administrative Court of First Instance is not bound by the judgements of superior appellate courts (i.e. the Supreme Court which has a separate jurisdiction or the Supreme Administrative Court which shares the same jurisdiction and is the final Court of Appeal for administrative cases). A Supreme Court or Supreme Administrative Court judgement can be disregarded in the Administrative Courts if the judge has reasons to disagree with the judgement reached by the superior appellate court. However, the relevant precedent must be referred to in the course of arriving at the decision. Omission to make the appropriate reference would be a *prima facie* ground of appeal and would be regarded as a neglect of duty by the judge. Achieving consistency in decision-making may become an increasing problem in the absence of a settled doctrine of precedent. In France greater uniformity has been achieved since the reforms of 1953, which conferred an appellate jurisdiction on the *Conseil d'Etat* and required the decisions of the *Conseil d'Etat* to be circulated enabling them to be followed. In addition, the operation of local courts was overseen through a system of inspection by senior member of the *Conseil d'Etat*.[76]

Jurisdiction and grounds of intervention

As we have already seen, the Thai Administrative Court and the Supreme Administrative Court have a wide jurisdiction over administrative matters. The 1999 Act states that the Court can hear cases involving disputes in relation to the matters prescribed by the law to be under the jurisdiction of Administrative Courts[77] and it also gives the court jurisdiction over administrative contracts[78] (discussed later). A substantial caseload over the initial period indicates that there was a gap that needed to be filled by the new court.[79] However, the Thai Administrative Court has clearly circumscribed limits to its jurisdiction. But first we need to deal with the question of merits review. The connection with France is worth mentioning on this question before we proceed with more discussion of the grounds since the *droit administratif* has recognised that in the public domain decision makers are frequently vested with discretionary powers and if such powers are exercised lawfully there will be no opportunity for judicial intervention. In other words a principle has long been established that decisions cannot generally be challenged on merits grounds alone (*l'opportunité*). There is every indication that Thai Administrative Courts are very well aware of the dangers of stepping into the shoes of the executive and are unwilling to take decisions on a merits basis. Although the very general ground of 'bad faith' is mentioned, the act itself contains no reference to a threshold equivalent to

Wednesbury/Irrationality to be applied in order to determine when intervention is possible.

In regard to challenging administrative decisions, the Administrative Court may be regarded as a remedy of last resort which will only be available if other available avenues of redress have been exhausted.[80] Following an application to the court and before the matter proceeds to trial there is judicial discretion in deciding whether to proceed with a case.[81] In order to establish whether the court is in a position to intervene the concepts of objective legality and subjective legality are applied by the judge. Objective legality looks at whether the body concerned has a legal foundation for its actions. This approach has close parallels to the concept of illegality as part of the *ultra vires* principle where attention is directed to the type of power in the hands of the decision maker in order to see if the power has been exceeded. On the other hand, subjective illegality seeks to assess the situation by establishing whether the rights of the claimant/plaintiff have been directly impinged by the actions of an official or of a public authority.

It will be apparent from the discussion that follows that the Thai Administrative Courts are empowered to deal with comparable forms of illegality on the part of administrative bodies or state officials,[82] but the grounds for intervention in dealing with matters of illegality do not exactly mirror those under the *Droit Administratif* or those developed by the common law under the *ultra vires* principle. Turning to the grounds defined under the 1999 Act, we find that they have many elements in common. First, a challenge is possible against a public body for: 'acting without or beyond the scope of its powers and duties'. This is a ground which almost corresponds under *droit administratif* to *Incompetence* in the sense that the decision maker is acting without lawful authority.[83] It would seem to cover the ground of *L'inexistence* which is 'where a decision lacks an essential component'.[84] Exceeding the scope of powers and duties would constitute a form of 'illegality' under the categories identified by Lord Diplock under the common law[85] and it is broadly equivalent to what has been termed simple *ultra vires*. The basis for any such challenge is that a decision maker has acted in excess of their powers or has exercised a power that they do not possess.[86]

Second, the Act provides under the same sub-section that the courts may intervene if a public body behaves 'inconsistently with the law'. This might be understood in terms of acting at variance with a law or frustrating the legislative purpose. Although not expressed in quite the same terms, 'inconsistently with the law' could be equated under the common law with an implied duty recognised by the courts to promote the purpose under the act.[87] The purpose may be found to be improper because it fails to match the purpose set out under the law. Also, inconsistency with the law might be caused because of a failure by a decision maker in exercising a discretion to take into account relevant considerations, or alternatively, the fact that s/he has taken account of irrelevant considerations.

In a somewhat different sense, consistency as opposed to inconsistency is generally regarded as a principle of good administration[88] and it clearly overlaps with the related principle of legitimate expectation which is based on the idea of legal certainty. Among other things, legitimate expectation requires decision makers to act in conformity with the procedures they set in place. Consistency has been interpreted to suggest equal treatment to all comers. Expressed in the words of Lord Donaldson 'it is a cardinal principle of good administration that all persons who are in a similar position shall be treated similarly'.[89] However, given the provisions of the 1997 Constitution, it is not surprising that 'unfair discrimination' is explicitly recognised as a self-standing ground of review in its own right which will be construed in conjunction with Article 30.[90] We can see a parallel here as the constitution becomes a point of reference in rather the same way as the EC Treaty has become for member states. The principle of equality or non-discrimination is recognised as a principle of German administrative law[91] and it has been developed by the European Court of Justice to fill gaps and aid interpretation with reference to the EC Treaty Articles 12 (prohibiting discrimination on the grounds of nationality) and Article 13[92] (appropriate action to combat discrimination based on sex, racial or ethnic origin, religion or belief, disability, age or sexual orientation). The domestic courts of member states are required to adopt a stance which recognises the treaty obligations coupled with the jurisprudence of the ECJ when a discrimination issue comes before them. The capacity of the Thai Administrative Courts to intervene to correct unfair discrimination represents a significant mechanism for the enforcement of the equivalent constitutional principle.[93]

Third, the Thai Administrative Court is empowered to intervene where it is alleged there has been conduct 'amounting to undue exercise of discretion'. In regard to *droit administrif* it has been explained that the scope for intervention under this aspect of *violation de la loi*[94] will depend on whether the administrator under a statutory regime has no discretion, absolute discretion or limited discretion. This is where 'the administrative judge moves on to examine the actual contents of the administrative act itself in order to decide whether it conforms with the legal conditions set upon administrative action in a particular case'.[95] Under the common law there have been many judicial pronouncements asserting that discretion in an administrative law context is seldom, if ever, completely 'unfettered'[96] and that a discretion has to be construed within the statutory context. Moreover, it has been established under the common law that a decision maker conferred with a wide discretionary power must demonstrate that such power has been exercised even where the discretion is expressed in the broadest subjective language.[97]

Fourth, actions of public bodies can be challenged on procedural as well as substantive grounds. Section 9(1) provides that inconsistency can be not only with the law but also with 'the form, process or procedure which is a material requirement'. The 1999 Act thereby introduces a ground of review closely related under *droit adminstratif* to *vice de forme*. This ground of review includes any breach of fair procedure. Under this head can be included a general right to a fair hearing, proper notice, adequate consultation and the right to representation.[98] An inconsistency judged in respect of form, process or procedure is a ground that has been recognised by the common law. Procedural impropriety was set out as one of the three main grounds of judicial review by Lord Diplock in the GCHQ case.[99]

Administrative justice in Thailand 241

In the same case rather than the term 'natural justice' Lord Roskill preferred to define the requirement as 'the duty to act fairly'. It is worth noting that the common law rules of natural justice/fairness have developed to include legitimate expectation, both in terms of procedures and in certain limited circumstances, substantive outcomes. This is a concept borrowed from German administrative law which has an established place in EU law but the principle has not been recognised by the *Conseil D'Etat*.

The Thai Administrative Court has a jurisdiction which allows it to oversee the proper functioning of the administration.[100] An application can be made to the court over an alleged neglect of duty or unreasonable delay.[101] Equally, the court can be required to adjudicate over a 'wrongful act or other liability'[102] associated with the administration or state official in the discharge of legal duties.[103] In this sense the Administrative Court has a jurisdiction which potentially overlaps with that of the ombudsman. Indeed, the ombudsman is specifically empowered to refer matters to the court if, in the course of an investigation, he believes that any by-law or act of an administrative agency is unlawful.[104] Moreover, an official of the Office of the Ombudsman may take up a case on behalf of the Ombudsman in the Administrative Courts. In this sense the Administrative Court can be regarded as a body which lines up alongside the other organs of the state which have been designed to act as watchdog bodies at a number of different levels. Causing unnecessary process or excessive burden to the public is recognised as a ground of review in its own right. Additionally, a matter can be referred to the court by an administrative agency or state official to force a person or body to do a particular act prescribed by law or to prevent them from acting contrary to the law.[105]

Having looked briefly at the grounds of review we might end this section by noting that the English Administrative Court deals only with judicial review and as a result polices rather different territory. It has no competence concerning 'wrongful acts' in general. Perhaps the nearest equivalent is the tort of misfeasance in public office which comes under the jurisdiction of the ordinary courts, but cases in this area are extremely rare.[106]

Administrative contracts

The Thai Administrative Courts took over the jurisdiction previously exercised by the Court of Justice and the Petition Council for disputes relating to administrative contracts.[107] The introduction of the Administrative Court has established a system of parallel courts and this characteristic provides further evidence of French influence.[108] This jurisdiction incorporates a public/private law distinction that extends to contracting with the public sector. In essence, Thai law has moved towards a French definition of an administrative contract[109] as an agreement 'that relates to the public service and that reserves exceptional powers to the administration'.[110] The Supreme Administrative Court in Thailand has defined such a contract as where: '... an administrative agency or the person authorised by the state agrees with the other party undertaking or participating in the undertaking of public services, or it must be a contract containing peculiar provisions demonstrating the privilege of the state so that the exercise of administrative powers or the carrying out administrative activities – public services – can achieve their purposes'.[111]

In many cases contracts will be administrative in character, that is concerned with the management of public services, or to do with public construction projects.[112] However, another key characteristic is that such agreements are reached between 'unequal parties'. Often a special feature of administrative contracts is the power resting with public bodies to vary contractual terms unilaterally subject to certain conditions. The restricted right to enter into contracts afforded to administrative agencies is normally dictated by primary or secondary legislation, and this is a factor which has to be taken into account when looking at the formation of administrative contracts. For example, in Thailand many government procurement contracts require certain procedures to be followed which vary in accordance with the sums involved. The state, in the form of the administrative agency, is often granted special powers to supervise the performance of the contract.[113] The determination of whether a matter falls under the definition of an administrative contract is of considerable importance because the extent of the liabilities of the parties will often be greater under a private civil contract than under an administrative contract. A civil claim under private law would normally permit recovery in full where under an administrative contract adjustment may be made in accordance with the detailed circumstances of the case.[114]

An additional important point to note is that the jurisdiction over administrative contracts overlaps to some extent with other levels of dispute resolution.[115] In Thailand the civil procedure code[116] allows a dispute over an administrative contract to be settled by means of arbitration and this constitutes a significant divergence from the French position where recourse to arbitration is specifically prohibited under the French civil code. However, it has been held by the Administrative Court that in situations where an administrative contract provides for settlement by arbitration a case will not be heard until the arbitration process has been exhausted.[117]

Part III: Regulating government, decisions of the Administrative Courts and the wider role of administrative law in Thailand

In the final section of this chapter we will evaluate the role of administrative law and the performance of the Administrative Courts in providing judicial oversight in the regulation, ownership and control of bodies with a significant public function in telecommunication, the broadcasting media and power generation. It will be apparent from this discussion that the Administrative Courts, the Office of the Thai ombudsman and other watchdog bodies have been granted a crucial role in upholding the law, but obviously the ground rules for the formation of the administrative state in Thailand are set by legislators under whatever constitution prevails. Moreover, Thailand maintains a substantial civil service at central and local level, and although the public sector has been subject to a significant dose of privatisation, there has been a torrent of statutory regulation in many fields. Against this background the published throughput of cases provides a broad statistical indication of the prominence that these courts have assumed in the field of public law. Since they were introduced in 2001 until 31 May 2007 the Central Administrative Court has dealt with a total of 12,429 cases with an average referral rate of between 180 to 240 cases per month, while the Supreme Administrative Court has dealt with 5,876 cases with a current referral rate of between 110 and 160 cases a month. The referral rate of cases to these courts has not been affected by the recent political situation since the military coup in September 2006. Many of these cases concern routine matters such as administrative contracts, however in this section the focus will be on some of the courts' most important decisions in the domain of media and broadcasting.[118]

Recent experience confirms that a state broadcasting organisation protected under the constitution and at arms-length from interference, with a mandate to report news and current affairs from differing viewpoints needs to be established in Thailand as a matter of priority.[119] Any such constitutional provision supported by statutory rules will need to limit cross-media ownership and monopoly media domination through a revised regime of statutory regulation. Despite the absence of a codified constitution in the UK citizens are generally able to express themselves, and the freedom of the press and broadcasters to disseminate information is constrained by an intricate combination of formal regulation and informal safeguards. For example, the BBC and other broadcasters are expected to act as a conduit for political criticism. However, such criticism must not be part of an agenda set by the broadcaster. Likewise, Thailand needs to establish balanced news reporting, no matter what the ownership of the organisation which is broadcasting news, and this should be entrenched as a general constitutional requirement applying to all broadcasters and supported by a statutory licensing system. The state regulatory body should be placed under a statutory duty to revoke the licence of any broadcasting organisation which fails to adhere to the rules. In regard to these and other specified statutory duties the role of the Administrative Courts should be to ensure enforcement of the law following a referral of a contested matter to it.

The efficacy of aspects of such regimes have already been called into question before the Administrative Courts. To take one high profile example, the provision for and the regulation of telecommunications and broadcasting, securing accountability in this domain is clearly going to be of fundamental importance to the next stage in Thai constitution building.[120] Telecommunications and the print and broadcasting media were regarded as a business geared for profit under the Thaksin government (2001–2006), and there was widespread evidence of conflicts of interest and abuse of power for political advantage.[121] The intervention of the Administrative Court in upholding the rule of law in politically sensitive areas such as this often had limited effect under the 1997 Constitution. Turning to the much publicised example of public appointments in the field of telecommunications and media, following the liberalisation of the telecommunications industry, the National Telecommunication Commission (NTC) became the new telecommunications regulator[122] deciding on sensitive issues, such as the conversion of various state concessions granted to private operators into a licensing or tax system, and the privatisation of state agencies.[123] In March 2003 the Supreme Administrative Court upheld an earlier ruling by the Central Administrative Court in regard to the selection process for the National Telecommunication Commission.[124] It held that the selection committee, as it had been set up under the relevant legislation was a government agency and therefore conflicts of interest were expressly prohibited under the administrative code. The decision of the court resulted in a re-run of the selection process, but despite this earlier ruling many of the same names, with alleged conflicts of interest, appeared on the revised list.[125] There was an unsatisfactory outcome in this instance because the politicians and their associates[126] responsible for appointing the selection committee continued to ignore these procedural rules notwithstanding the aforementioned judicial intervention.[127] In a virtual repetition of this scenario the selection of candidates by the Senate for the National Broadcasting Commission in September 2005 was nullified by an order of the Administrative Court. This decision was on the identical grounds that the selection committee set up under the National Broadcasting Act had been partisan and not independent as required under the administrative code.[128] The decision by the Central Administrative Court was later confirmed by the Supreme Administrative Court.[129]

Equally, the Administrative Courts have been drawn into complex disputes involving other types of conflicts of interest that have arisen in relation to the ownership and control of the media. The most important examples have concerned iTV and the Shin Corporation.[130] We also observe in reviewing this litigation the engagement of the hierarchy of Thai justice, with the involvement of the Arbitration Court, the Administrative Courts and the Supreme Administrative Court. This TV channel (iTV) was created to provide an independent dimension to Thai broadcasting in 1995, with a concession granted until September 2025. Under a contract relating to this concession, that had been negotiated with the Prime Minister's Office, iTV were required to broadcast 70 percent news programmes and 30 percent entertainment programmes. Any failure to fulfil its obligations under this contract allowed the PM's office to exact fines and penalties of millions of Bts a day. A dispute arose when iTV sought compensation from the Prime Minister's office, arguing that it had been overcharged by the government (i.e. the PM's office) over the amount of the concession fee and that the programming stipulation, restricting the amount of entertainment broadcasting, was unreasonable. The matter was initially referred to the Arbitration Court for resolution which clearly found in favour of iTV in January 2004.[131] It was prepared to allow iTV to pay a lower fee and to continue with a programme ratio 50:50 which could be geared more towards entertainment. However, the Prime Minister's office lodged an appeal to the Central Administrative Court which, in turn, reversed the decision of the Arbitration Court. Not only did this ruling allow the PM's office to demand

Bt76 billion in penalties and fees (later increased because of the time that elapsed), but it also would require the programme ratio to revert to a preponderance of news scheduling.[132] Of course the effect of the ruling, if the financial penalties were paid was bound to have a drastic impact on the financial viability of iTV and if the company was forced into bankruptcy on all of its employees. The matter was referred to the Supreme Administrative Court for final determination which also found in favour of the PM's Office. As a result iTV has faced fines amounting to Bt94 billion.[133]

In addition, there has been a constitutional dimension to this matter further illustrating the degree of the conflicts of interest which underlie important governmental functions in Thailand. It was mentioned earlier that iTV was conceived as an independent broadcaster, but this role was compromised when in 2001 the Shin Corp Plc, a company owned by former Prime Minister Thaksin Shaniwatra and his family, became the major shareholder in iTV. During the time that he maintained his investment in Shin Corp plc, including most of his term as Prime Minister (2001–2006), apart from evidence of political interference in programme content[134] it suited Thaksin's personal commercial interest to push for lower charges from the government and to change the programme content to encourage increased audiences. In contrast, it was noted above that the original concession negotiated in the name of the PM's office was designed to serve a wider public interest. In consequence, the Arbitration Court and the Administrative Courts were called upon to determine a highly sensitive political issue. The imposition of these penalties by the Administrative Court in June 2006 was a judicially imposed setback for Thaksin which occurred after he had offloaded his financial investments in the TV company. However, his attempt as Prime Minister to ignore statutory rules was decisively rejected by the court.[135]

Although iTV's position had not at that point been resolved by the Administrative Courts the matter took a different turn in January 2006 when Thaksin and his family sold their majority investment in Shin Corp Group to Tamasek Holdings (a company which is Singapore's state investment arm). The sale was the subject of enormous controversy in Thailand. It resulted in popular protest, and it was one of the factors behind the military coup of the 19 September 2006, with Thaksin's opponents arguing that for example, the deal compromised Thailand's national security by giving another nation effective control of Thailand's communications (Shinsat), including defence communications. A challenge to the deal was mounted in the Central Administrative Court in March 2006 but the court held that the claimant lacked the necessary standing, as he had no contractual link to the takeover, a decision later overturned by the Supreme Administrative Court.[136] However, since the military coup a further challenge has been lodged with the Central Administrative Court in 2007 against the National Telecommunications Commission (NTC) and the Information and Communications Technology Ministry. It is alleged that the failure of these governmental bodies to safeguard the national interest by permitting the ownership of Shin Corporation to fall into foreign hands amounted to negligence.[137]

The *Egat Case* in November 2005 was another prominent decision in which the Administrative Courts ruled against the government.[138] The Thai government was proposing to privatise the Electricity Generating Authority of Thailand (Egat), Egat Plc.[139] However, a combination of 11 civic pressure groups, including the Campaign for Popular Democracy, the Consumer Protection Foundation, the Federation of Consumer Organisations, together with representatives from the Egat labour unions (and with the support of opposition parties) contested the government's privatisation plans. The objectors argued that the proposals were likely to result in greatly increased electricity prices for electricity consumers while giving disproportionate financial rewards for a small group of investors, including politicians with an interest in the scheme who stood to gain directly from the privatisation. The Prime Minister Thaksin Shinawatra and Energy Minister Viset Choopiban were among the five named defendants. It was alleged that there had been an abuse of power because the government was proceeding with the privatisation without any form of public consultation. although mandatory hearings were required for such a proposal. Further, it was argued that the sale of Egat shares violated the constitution[140] because the government had illegally used two royal decrees to appoint a panel to oversee electricity generation.[141] It was also argued that there were inadequate safeguards for consumers in regard to pricing levels and standards of service. The court found in favour of the objectors in November 2005, and it issued an injunction which prevented the privatisation from going ahead before hearings had taken place. The decision had far-reaching ramifications. The interruption of the schedule for flotation in a market sensitive area which is dependent on investor confidence called into question the economic viability of the entire scheme. At a political level the anti-privatisation campaign had developed into a personal campaign against the Prime Minister and the court's decision was a serious blow to a central plank of government policy. The fact that fundamental principles of legality were upheld by the court, especially given the extremely sensitive issues at stake in the case, suggests that, in this area at least, the 1997 Constitution had managed to establish a relatively independent oversight body.[142] The independence of the Administrative Courts in comparison to other watchdog bodies can, in part, be attributed to the court being perceived by politicians as having an oblique role in regard to deciding controversial political matters, certainly in comparison to the Constitutional Court, the Electoral Commission and the National Counter Corruption Commission. Although it attracted criticism from politicians from time to time, there was insufficient grounds to overtly politicise the court. An equally important reason for its relative independence is that the court was staffed from the outset with a permanent cohort of professional judges and lawyers appointed on merit. Thailand's higher judiciary has enjoyed a reputation for independence since the time of Rama V.[143]

Conclusion

This chapter has concentrated on providing a critical account of the introduction of a formalised system of administrative justice in Thailand. The Thai model has been strongly influenced by the French *droit administratif* and the *Conseil D'Etat*. At one level, it will be apparent that the Administrative Courts and the Office of the Ombudsman fill an important gap in the grievance chain by providing an impressive range of remedies for the aggrieved citizen against public bodies. Moreover, under the 1997 Constitution there was a genuine attempt to underline the separation of powers and functions between the executive and judicial branches in order to ensure the independence and the effectiveness of the Administrative Courts. For example, the funding for the court's administration was ring-fenced and a rigorous system of appointments limited the selection of judges to suitably qualified candidates. Once raised to the bench, these judges have been adequately remunerated.[144]

However, if the introduction of Administrative Courts (this point applies as much to the Constitutional Court) results in the strengthening of the judicial branch as part of any constitutional order embodying checks and balances, it also raises basic questions which will be familiar to constitutional commentators.[145] Should a group of non-politically accountable judges be empowered to frustrate the will of elected politicians? Thailand is a nation where the entire political process has frequently been subverted by systematic abuse of power, as was widely evident under Prime Minister, Thaksin Shaniwatra (2001–2006). Indeed, given the record of abuse in Thailand and the problems in embedding democratic government, it is difficult to place much credence on claims to political legitimacy that elected politicians might rely upon in resisting judicial intervention in defence of the rule of law. The case law in the field of regulation under the 1997 Constitution discussed in this paper might be cited as a useful test bed. It shows us that an appropriately balanced constitution should be designed to acknowledge a necessary tension between the desire of politicians to attain political objectives within the law, and judicial scrutiny of political decision-making and executive action to set the limits on the exercise of public power. The Administrative Courts made a repeated contribution by intervening in this controversial area with varying success due to government reluctance to comply with decisions of the court.[146] It should be noted however that the other watchdog bodies[147] under the 1997 Constitution had an even more indifferent record.

Professor Waldron has recently argued that the judicial resolution of disputes seldom provides a way for society to focus clearly on the real issues at stake when there are disagreements about rights.[148] This observation reminds us that in the modern part-privatised contracting state administrative law relies fundamentally on designing effective schemes of statutory regulation setting out the respective rights and duties of government, commercial interests and citizens. It also provides a system of oversight and enforcement, with the judges on the other hand, simply waiting in the wings to provide a remedy of last resort should cases be referred to the courts for resolution. Finally, the collapse of the constitutional foundations of the Administrative Court and its (temporary) replacement with an interim military regime introduced a different, but no less pressurised environment for Thailand's judges.[149] Nevertheless, it will be apparent that the Administrative Courts and the office of the Thai ombudsman have continued to function and remain in place to play an important part under the constitution.[150]

Notes

* I am very grateful to his honour Judge Dr Vishnu Varunyou of the Thai Administrative Court for supplying me with invaluable information and clarifying many matters during my work on this subject. I would also like to thank Professors Tom Ginsburg and Andrew Harding for their helpful comments on an earlier draft. In addition, thanks to Anna Razeen for her assistance with my research.
1. See also: P. Leyland 'Droit Administratif Thai Style: A Comparative Analysis of the Administrative Courts in Thailand' *The Australian Journal of Asian Law*, Vol.8, No.2, October 2006, pp.121–55.
2. The complex drafting process for the 2007 Constitution has been controversial as it was not regarded as inclusive (in contrast to the 1997 Constitution). Also, some of its provisions have also been criticised, particularly the fact that it will have a Senate which is appointed and, as a result, it has been regarded as less democratic than the 1997 Constitution.
3. Thailand has a population of 64 million, slightly larger than the United Kingdom, and covers a land area the size of France. For a historical introduction see C. Baker and P. Pongpaichit, *A History of Thailand*, Cambridge: Cambridge University Press, 2005.
4. Baker and Pongpaichit, op. cit., p.243.
5. M. Connors 'Framing the "People's Constitution"', in D. McCargo, ed., *Reforming Thai Politics*, NIAS, 2002, p.52.
6. For further economic and political analysis see P. Sulistiyanto *Thailand, Indonesia and Burma in Comparative Perspective*, Burlington, USA: Ashgate, 2003, Chapter Three 'Thailand's Boom' and Chapter Four 'Thailand's Crisis' particularly at p.103.
7. Ibid., p.256.
8. Baker and Pongpaichit, op. cit., p.255.
9. A. Harding, 'May There be Virtue: New Asian Constitutionalism in Thailand', *Australian Journal of Asian Law*, vol.3, 2001, pp.24–48.
10. P. Chambers, 'Good Governance, Political Stability and Constitutionalism in Thailand 2002', King Prajadhipok's Institute, 10 August 2002, p.16.
11. The Thai Constitution 1997 Chapter II recognised the King as head of state, as nominal head of the armed forces and confers on him powers to appoint Privy Councillors and officials of the Royal Household. He had the prerogative power under section 116 to dissolve the House of Representatives precipitating an election. Under Section 94 the King had the power to refuse the Royal Assent to legislation for up to a ninety day period. After which the matter would be referred back to the National Assembly. It would have required a two-thirds majority of the members present for the bill to be presented again for the Royal Assent.
12. D. K. Wyatt, *A Short History of Thailand*, 2nd ed., Newhaven: Yale University Press, 2003, p.307.
13. P. Leyland 'Thailand's Constitutional Watchdogs: Dobermans, Bloodhounds or Lapdogs?', *Journal of Comparative Law*, Vol. 2, Issue Two, 2007, 151–77.
14. This court was abolished at the time of the coup and replaced with a constitutional tribunal. The 2007 Constitution features a powerful Constitutional Court.
15. Thai Constitution 1997, Section 255. See 'A Basic Understanding on the Constitutional Court of the Kingdom of Thailand', *Office of the Constitutional Court*, 2003.
16. See ss.262 and 263 of the 1997 Thai Constitution.
17. The former Constitutional Court ruled on the constitutionality of organic laws, laws, regulations, draft laws and regulations, resolutions made by political parties, status of

the members of the House of Representatives and the Senate, actions of governmental organisations which may infringe upon basic rights and freedoms of the people, legal cases referred to by the courts of justice as provided under Section 264 of the constitution, status of Cabinet members and members of the Election Commission, conflicting jurisdiction of conflicting Constitutional bodies and questions referred to it by the National Counter Corruption Commission and the Ombudsman.
18 Under Section 268 of the 1997 Constitution: 'The decision of the Constitutional Court shall be deemed final and binding on the National Assembly, Council of Ministers, Courts and other State organs'.
19 Since the limits of its authority are not clearly defined in the constitution it was unclear whether the Constitutional Court was placed at the pinnacle of a hierarchy of jurisdictions or merely one jurisdiction amongst others. This became a matter of important debate in Thailand because it had a direct bearing on the limits of other jurisdictions. Although the majority of Thai jurists do not see the Constitutional Court as having higher authority, the Constitutional Court agreed to hear a case brought by the Electoral Commission contesting a decision by the Supreme Administrative Court.
20 For example, following a case brought against him alleging corruption which was decided on 3 August 2001, former Prime Minister, Thaksin Shinawatra, criticised the Constitutional Court and declared that the independent bodies should have their powers curtailed. Moreover, a petition was later filed demanding the removal of four Constitutional Court judges. See Chambers, 2002, p.28.
21 Constitution of the Kingdom of Thailand 2007, Articles 204–17.
22 Note removed.
23 Note removed.
24 Constitution of the Kingdom of Thailand 2007, Article 212.
25 Another reason for the criticism of the 2007 Constitution relates to the increased profile of the courts, particularly the constitutional and Administrative Courts, in resolving constitutional questions which some commentators believe could tend to politicise the judiciary.
26 Section 9(6) of the 1999 Act provided that the following matters are not within the jurisdiction of the Administrative Courts:

   (i) action concerning military discipline;
   (ii) action of the Judicial Commission under the law on judicial service;
   (iii) cases within the jurisdiction of the Juvenile and Family Courts, Labour Courts, Tax Courts, Intellectual Property and International Trade Courts, Bankruptcy Courts or other specialised courts.

27 The Judicial Commission is an organisation established by the Law of Judicial Organisation which deals with administration relating to the judges of the civil and criminal courts.
28 See Section 248 of the 1997 Constitution.
29 Thai Arbitration Institute: Administering Excellence and Due Process, Office of the Judiciary, 15th Anniversary, 2002: http://www.cdi.anu.edu.au/CDIwebsite_19982004/thailand/thailand_downloads/ThaiArbitrationReport.pdf
30 UNCITRAL Arbitration Rules (1976) (Adopted by the General Assembly on December 15, 1976): http://www.nortonrose.com/html_pubs/view.asp?id=2480, Accessed August 1, 2008.
31 Arbitration Act s.6: 'where the provisions of this Act empower the parties to determine any issue, the parties may authorize a third party or institution to make that determination on their behalves'.
32 Section 46.
33 Arbitration Act s.47 provides that bodies set up under the Act are empowered to prescribe 'fees, expenses and remunerations'.

34 See P. Leyland, 'The Ombudsman Principle in Thailand', *Journal of Comparative Law, Volume II, Issue One*, 2007 *137–51*. There had been much earlier proposals to introduce an ombudsman notably as part of the 1975 Constitution.
35 The first Thai ombudsman was appointed in 1999 and there are currently three in post. The Ombudsman Act 1999 s.18 provides 'each shall allocate duties among themselves in order that each may work independently, within agreed parameters'.
36 The Spanish Constitution provides an example of an ombudsman (Defensor del Pueblo) who is granted standing to bring actions of unconstitutionality. See Article 162 of the Spanish Constitution and Article 32 of the Organic Law No 2/1979 on the Constitutional Court.
37 See P. Pongpaichit and C. Baker, *Thaksin: The Business of Politics in Thailand*, Chiang Mai, Silkworm Books, 2004; 'Thailand's Rotten Politics' *New York Times*, April 14, 2006.
38 See Ombudsman Act 1999, section 16.
39 Ibid.
40 The term was explained in the UK Parliament during the debate on the 1967 bill as including: 'bias, neglect, inattention, delay, incompetence, ineptitude, perversity, turpitude, arbitrariness and so on' 734 HC Deb. (5th Series), col. 51. See also 1993 Annual Report, para 7.
41 Under section 197 of the Constitution the ombudsman is able to inquire into questions of legality coinciding with the review functions of Administrative Court, namely, a failure of public bodies to perform in compliance with the law or performance beyond their powers and duties as provided by the law.
42 A relatively low proportion of cases resulted in a remedial action: 6736 of the cases referred fell outside the jurisdiction under the act and a further 4,635 were investigated but declined. About 2,000 cases are still pending. See http://www.ombudsman.go.th/eng_version/statistics_stat.asp, Accessed August 1, 2008.
43 Chris Baker and Pasuk Pongpaichit (eds) *Pridi by Pridi: Selected Writings on Life, Politics and Economy*, Chiang Mai, Silkworm Books, 2000.
44 The use of the term 'administrative law' instead of 'constitutional law' was more acceptable during the period of absolute monarchy.
45 Baker and Pongpaichit, op. cit., p.121.
46 B. Bhalakula, *Pride and the Administrative Court*, Administrative Courts, 2001.
47 Ibid., p.9.
48 Ibid., p.13.
49 There were attempts by some judges to influence the drafting commission of the 1997 Constitution in order to prevent the creation of a separate Administrative Court.
50 It should be noted that Jean-Michel Galabert, former Président de la section du Rapport et des Études au Conseil d'Etat, played a part in the introduction of the Thai Administrative Courts. See Jean-Michel Galabert 'The influence of the Conseil d'Etat Outside France' *ICLQ*, Vol 49/3 2000 at p.700.
51 See 1997 Thai Constitution, Part 4, Section 276 which provided that: 'Administrative Courts have the powers to try and adjudicate cases of dispute between a State agency, State enterprise, local government organisation, or State official under the superintendence or supervision of the Government on one part and a private individual on the other part, or between State agency, State enterprise, local government organisation, or State official under the superintendence or supervision of the Government on one part and another agency, enterprise, organisation or official on the other part, which is the dispute as a consequence of the act or omission of the act that must be, according to the law, performed by such State agency, State enterprise, local government organisation, or State official, or as a consequence of the act or omission of the act under the responsibility of such State Agency, State Enterprise, local

government organisation or State official in the performance of duties under the law, as provided by law. There shall be the Supreme Administrative Court and Administrative Courts of First Instance, and there may also be the Appellate Administrative Court'.
52 See 1999 Act, Section 7.
53 See 1999 Act, Section 11.
54 See Chapter III of the 1999 Act. The potential.
55 Act on the Establishment of the Administrative Courts 1999, section 18. By way of contrast it is worth noting that the Constitutional Court under the 1997 Constitution was partly composed of non-lawyers (5 out of 15) and that the appointment process was more susceptible to political interference as candidates were voted on before the Senate which turned out not to be 'neutral' as was intended by the framers of the constitution.
56 See M. Hunt, 'Constitutionalism and the Contractualisation of Government' in M. Taggart, ed., *The Province of Administrative Law*, Oxford: Hart Publishing, 1997.
57 N. Bamforth, 'Public Law – Private Law Distinction: A Comparative and Philosophical Approach', in P. Leyland and T. Woods, eds, *Administrative Law Facing the Future: Old Constraints, New Horizons*, London: Blackstone Press, 1997, p.151.
58 The acceptance of a separate public jurisdiction based on the recognition of the distinct objectives of public law has been integral to the French system. See e.g. J. M. Auby and R. Ducos-Ader, 'Droit Public', in B. Rudden, *A Sourcebook on French Law*, 3rd ed., Oxford: Oxford University Press, 1991, p.14.
59 B. Bhalakula, 'Administrative Contract in the Thai Legal Context', Office of the Administrative Courts, Thailand, March 12, 2003, p.19.
60 P. Cane 'Accountability and the Public/Private Distinction', in N. Bamforth and P. Leyland, eds, *Public Law in a Multi-Layered Constitution*, Oxford: Hart Publishing, 2003, p.248.
61 I. Harden, *The Contracting State*, Buckingham: The Open University Press, 1992.
62 Hunt, op. cit., p.23.
63 It has been pointed out that in France, 'The key decision of the French Tribunal des Conflits in *Blanco* (1873) established the function criterion of service publique to define the boundary between the administrative jurisdiction and regular jurisdiction'. See Cane, op. cit., p.253.
64 Red Case Nos. 1733–1734/2002.
65 See Lord Diplock's discussion of these issues in *O'Reilly v Mackman* [1983] 2 AC 237.
66 In 2000 as part of the reforms to civil procedure the prerogative remedies were renamed to clarify their function. Certiorari is a quashing order, prohibition becomes a prohibiting order and mandamus is called a mandating order.
67 1999 Act, Section 72.
68 For example in March 2003, the Office of Consumer Protection Board issued regulations banning the sale of high pressure water guns which following commercial pressure were considered to be unlawful by the Administrative Court but remained in operation pending an appeal. See *The Nation*, April 13, 2004.
69 Enforcement through *astreinte* is a comparatively recent development, first introduced by the law of 16 July 1980 and it became available to the Cours Administratives d'Appel and the Tribunaux Administratifs from 1995.
70 N. Brown and J. Bell, *French Administrative Law*, 5th ed., Oxford: Oxford University Press, 1998, p.114.
71 Rule (2000), Clause 50.
72 The ground of 'Qualification juridique des faits' requires that proper inferences have been drawn from the facts.
73 This approximates to the permission stage in an application for judicial review, which is usually a form filling exercise to allow a judge to consider: first whether the procedural

requirements relating to time limits, locus standi and public as opposed to private issues are satisfied; second, to assess whether there is an arguable case based on the alleged grounds.

74 1999 Act, Section 57. 'In the case where an administrative agency or State official fails to take action within the time specified or shows such conduct as indicative of prolonging the case, the Administrative Court shall report to the superior, superintendent, supervisor or Prime Minister for proceeding with corrective action, giving directions or taking a disciplinary action, without prejudice to the power of the court to inflict a punishment by reason of a contempt of court'.

75 In France there is a heavy reliance on documents. Witnesses only given evidence in a separate procedure in advance of the final hearing.

76 Brown and Bell, op. cit., p.124.

77 Act on Establishment of Administrative Courts and Administrative Court Procedure 2542 (1999), Section 9(6).

78 See 1999 Act, Section 9(4).

79 In 2001 and 2002 the Central Administrative Court dealt with a total of 3,933 cases and the Supreme Administrative Court 642 cases. See table in T. Bureekul and S. Thananithichut, 'The Thai Constitution of 1997: Evidence of Democratization', *King Prajadhipok's Institute*, Bangkok, 8/9/2004 at p.14.

80 For example, it is provided in respect of administrative contracts that where arbitration is part of the contract this option has to be exhausted before recourse to the Administrative Court. Ombudsman also?

81 Rule of the General Assembly of Judges of the Supreme Administrative Court on Administrative Procedure BE 2543 (2000), Clause 37.

82 See Section 9(1) '...in relation to an unlawful act by an administrative agency or State official, whether in connection with the issuance of a by-law or order or in connection with other act, by reason of acting without or beyond the scope of the powers and duties or inconsistently with the law or the form, process or procedure which is the material requirement for such act or in bad faith or in a manner indicating unfair discrimination or causing unnecessary process or excessive burden to the public or amounting to under exercise of discretion'.

83 For example, in a ruling on 15 February 2005 the Administrative Court criticised the Anti-Money Laundering Office for launching an unlawful investigation into five political activists in 2001. 'This court finds that AMLO exercised its discretion to launch the investigation without allowing due process'. No financial penalty was granted against AMLO because the wrongdoing was detected and cancelled before any damage had been caused. See Keesinee Taengkhieo, Piyanuch Thamnukasetchai, *The Nation*, 19 February, 2005.

84 P. Birkinshaw, *European Public Law*, London: Butterworths, 2003, p.129.

85 See *Council of Civil Service Unions v. Minister for the Civil Service* [1985] AC 372, often referred to as the GCHQ case.

86 Classic examples include: *Attorney General v. Fulham Corporation* [1921] 1 Ch. 440; *Congreve v. Home Office* [1976] 1 All ER 697.

87 See *Padfield v. Minister of Agriculture Fisheries and Food* [1968] AC 997. Lord Reid '... the policy and objects of the Act must be determined by construing the Act as a whole and the construction is always a matter of law for the court'.

88 See e.g. K. Steyn, 'Consistency: A Principle of Public Law', *Judicial Review*, 22, 1997.

89 See *R. v. Hertfordshire CC, ex p Cheung, The Times*, 4 April 1986.

90 Article 30 of the Constitution provides: 'All persons are equal before the law and shall enjoy equal protection under the law. Men and women shall enjoy equal rights. Unjust discrimination against a person on the grounds of the difference in origin, race, language, sex, age, physical or health condition, personal status, economic or social

standing, religious belief, education or constitutionally political view, shall not be permitted'.
91 Article 3 of the German Constitution. See Nigel Foster *German Legal System and Laws*, 2nd ed. London, Cavendish, 1996, p.160. It is noted that: '... a number of general principles have been derived from the equality principle, such as equal access to public benefits, especially in the field of education, the principle of tax equity ..., and the equality of arms in legal procedure ...'. (p.161).
92 G. Anthony, *UK Public Law and European Law: The Dynamics of Legal Integration*, Oxford: Hart Publishing, 2002, p.106.
93 For example, Sirimit Boon-mul, a physically challenged lawyer, successfully appealed to the Supreme Administrative Court after the State Attorney Commission rejected a job application in 2001 on the grounds that he was incapable of performing the job due to a physical impairment. The decision of the court gave him the right to reapply for a job as a state attorney. See K. Taengkhiew, *The Nation*, 15 February 2005.
94 *Violation de la loi* as a ground also includes errors of law, using the wrong text, or misinterpretation of the law.
95 Brown & Bell, op. cit., pp.244 and 253. where the concept of *competence liée* is explained further.
96 Although it has also been acknowledged under the common law that there are occasions where a statutory discretion is so widely drawn that it might only be challenged if exercised irrationally or in bad faith. See *Padfield v. Minister of Agriculture Fisheries and Food* [1968] AC 997.
97 See W. Wade and C. Forsyth, *Administrative Law*, 9th ed., Oxford: Oxford University Press, 2004, p.356. In *Padfield v. Minister of Agriculture, Fisheries and Food* [1968] AC 997 Lord Reid rejected the all or nothing approach to the exercise of unfettered discretion and commented: 'Parliament must have conferred the discretion with the intention that it should be used to promote the policy and objects of the act ...'.
98 For example, it was reported in *The Nation*, June 1 2004 that the Khon Kaen Administrative Court heard the case of a Loei hospital director, Dr Kriengsak Vacharanu-kulkiete, who was removed for criticising his superiors at the Public Health Ministry. It was argued that an order for his removal to take effect within seven days was unfair.
99 See *Council of Civil Service Unions v. Minister for the Civil Service* [1985] AC 372.
100 Brown and Bell, op. cit., pp.56 and 82. The *Conseil d'Etat* exercises an advisory function for the administration as well as acting in a separate capacity in a role where it adjudicates over the administration. This aspect is referred to as the section contentieux. It is worth remembering the Diceyan critique of the *droit administratif* which concentrated on the fact that the Administrative Court was part of the administration.
101 Under 9(2) '... involving a dispute in relation to an administrative agency or State official neglecting official duties required by the law to be performed or performing such duties with unreasonable delay'.
102 For example, The Office of Atomic Energy for Peace (OAEP) OAEP was found negligent in the storage of spent isotopes around the country and was ordered by the Central Administrative Court in 2002 to pay Bt5.2 million to 12 survivors of the radiation leak. Original judgement referred to in *The Nation* 'COURT RULING: Long battle ends in Bt20 refund' 10 August 2004.
103 Under 9(3) '...involving a dispute in relation to a wrongful act or other liability of an administrative agency or State official arising from the exercise of power under the law or from a by-law, administrative order or other order, or from neglect of official duties required by the law to be performed or the performance of such duties with unreasonable delay'.

104 Rule of the General Assembly of Judges of the Supreme Administrative Court on Administrative Court Procedure BE 2543 (2000), Clause 28 'The referral by an Ombudsman of a matter, together with the opinions thereon, to the Court in the case where the Ombudsman is of the opinion that any by-law or act of an administrative agency or State official is unlawful ...'.
105 Section 9(5) provides: 'The case prescribed by law to be submitted to the Court by an administrative agency or State official for mandating a person to do a particular act or refraining there from'. Lord Roskill at 414.
106 Misfeasance in public office can be defined as 'even where there is no ministerial duty ... and even where no recognised tort such as trespass, nuisance or negligence is committed, public authorities may be liable in damages for malicious, deliberate or injurious wrong-doing' (Wade & Forsyth, 2004 p.781).
107 Section 9(4). It should also be noted that under 9(3) the Administrative Court is granted jurisdiction over 'wrongful acts' which can be understood in common law terms as for cases concerning public bodies which concern tort liability. See generally Administrative Contract in the Thai Legal Context.
108 See generally Bhalakula, op. cit., 2003.
109 The French jurisdiction has required a distinction to be made between *actes d'autorité* and *acte de gestion*. The jurisdiction of the Administrative Court only extends to actes de gestion. Contracts made by the state with private individuals were considered actes de gestion. A recent innovation in France has been to introduce a procurement code and to consider any contracts made in accordance with the code administrative contracts.
110 Brown & Bell, op. cit., p.202.
111 Resolution of the General Assembly of Judges of the Supreme Administrative Court, 6/2544, 10 October 2001. See p.32.
112 In Thailand there are five principal procedures of government procurement: price agreement; price inquiry; invitation for bidding; special procedure; and special case procedure. See Rule of the Office of the Prime Minister on Procurement 1992 and Act on Private Participation in State Undertakings 1992.
113 Bhalakula op. cit., 2003, p.12.
114 Petition Council No. 70/1992 is cited as an example by Bhalakula, 2003, p.24.
115 C. Okanurak and W. Yiamsamatha, 'New Arbitration Act and Administrative Contracts "Conflict is Inherent in Human Relations"'. Originally published in Public Law Net On Thursday November, 2004.
116 Chapter 3, sections 210–22. Further, see Thai Arbitration Act B.E. 2545 (2002). Section 15 specifically provides that in an agreement between a governmental agency and a private party, the parties may agree to resolve any disputes pertaining to the agreement by means of arbitration, and that such arbitration agreement shall be binding upon the parties.
117 Case No. Red 1454/2001 and Case No.1799/2001.
118 http://www.admincourt.go.th/amc_eng/02-KADEE/stat.htm, Accessed August 1, 2008.
119 iTV was intended to be an independent form of news based television, but it was taken over in 2000 by the Shin Corporation. See e.g. D. McCargo and U. Pathmanand, *The Thaksinization of Thailand*, NiAS, 2005 p.47.
120 Article 40 of the 1997 Constitution resulted in the introduction of the National Telecommunication Commission and the National Broadcasting Authority. See also V. Muntarborn, 'Mass Media Law and Regulations in Thailand', *Asia Media and Communications Centre*, Singapore, 1998.
121 In a different context, the civil courts were used by the former Prime Minister to suppress free speech and criticism in the media. For example, a defamation action was issued against Supinya Klangnarong for an article in the Thai Post in 2003, which drew attention to the profits being made as a result of improper political influence in

Administrative justice in Thailand 255

regard to media ownership. See P. Pongpaichit and C. Baker, *Thaksin: The Business of Politics in Thailand*, Chiang Mai, Silkworm Books, 2004, p.155.

122 See the Telecommunications Business Act 2001 (BE 2544).
123 'Thai Court Orders a New Candidate Selection Process for NTC', *Word Dialogue for Regulation for Network Economies*, 10 January 2003.
124 See 'NBC candidate choices nullified' *The Nation*, 5 March 2003.
125 See McCargo and Pathmanand, op. cit., p.46.
126 'PM blamed for telecom watchdog setback' *The Nation*, 11 January 2003 and for a report of the Supreme Administrative Court decision see 'NBC candidate choices nullified' *The Nation*, 5 March 2003.
127 See Pongpaichit and Baker, op. cit., pp.151 and 207.
128 'Broadcasting Panel: Additional doubt over NBC future', *The Nation* 29 September 2005.
129 'Rejection of NBC appeal upheld', *The Nation*, 7 June 2006.
130 For a discussion of the background to the case see McCargo and Pathmanand, 2005 pp.47–53.
131 Ibid p.61.
132 'iTV ordered to cough up Bt 77.7bn: OAG wants broadcaster to pay at once' *The Nation*, 20 June 2006. The judgements of the Administrative Courts are only enforced following the exhaustion of the legal process and thus depended on the decision of the Supreme Administrative Court.
133 'The Supreme Administrative Court ruled on Wednesday in favour of PM's Office over iTV saga', *The Nation*, 13 December 2006; 'Bankruptcy Looms for Reeling iTV', *The Nation*, 14 December 2006.
134 Pongpaichit and Baker, op. cit., p.149.
135 It is worth noting that under the draft Constitution of 2007 which was accepted in a referendum on 19 August 2007 such conflicts of interest are specifically prohibited.
136 'Shin Corp Deal in Jeopardy', *The Nation*, 6 October 2006.
137 'Shinsat Sale Row: Court accepts negligence case', *The Nation*, 1 May 2007.
138 See Editorial, *The Nation*, 16 November, 2005. 'Thai court delays sale of stake in utility' Wayne Arnold, *The New York Times*, 15 November 2005. Daniel Ten Kate 'Riding Thailand's Political Bandwagon', *Asia Times*, 12 January 2006.
139 http://pr.egat.co.th/prweb/new/EGATprofile.htm, Accessed August 1, 2008.
140 The Thai Ombudsman stated that he would forward the matter to the Constitution Court if he had grounds for believing the scheme was unconstitutional. See 'Opposition plans to test constitutionality of listing' *The Nation*, 16 November 2005.
141 These decrees were revoked by the Supreme Administrative Court in March 2006. See 'Egat listing shot down', *The Nation*, 23 March 2006.
142 'Ruling for Integrity', *The Nation*, 17 November 2005.
143 Of course, there is always the wider Thai context to consider. For example, we should also recognise the importance of other political influences and also of the direct intervention of the King. On 26 April 2006 following the disputed general election he addressed the judges (particularly of the Constitutional Court) and urged them to do their sworn duty under the 1997 Constitution and declare the election void.
144 See Leyland, op. cit., 2005, pp.129–32.
145 See J. Griffith, 'The Political Constitution', *MLR*, 1, 1979, p.14.
146 E.g., in regard to the selection process of the National Telecommunication Commission in 2003 see n.115 above.
147 These include the Constitutional Court, National Counter Corruption Commission, Election Commission, Anti-Money Laundering Office, Parliament Ombudsman and National Human Rights Commission.
148 J. Waldron, 'The Core of the Case Against Judicial Review', *Yale Law Review*, 115, 2006, p.1353.

149 See for example rulings by the Constitutional Tribunal under the interim constitution which disbanded Thai Rak Thai and banned 111 officials from politics for five years. 'Joy, relief, sadness and anger for most; for others it is poetic justice' *The Nation*, 2 June 2007.

150 Both bodies are recognised as part of the 2007 Constitution which was introduced in 2008 following elections in December 2007.

12 Administrative law and judicialized governance in Malaysia

The Indian connection

Gan Ching Chuan

Introduction

This chapter will focus its discussion on the actual judicialized administrative law or governance in Malaysia today and try to speculate on the roadmap for tomorrow. The central theme of this paper is two-fold. In the first part, an attempt will be made to examine how the Malaysian Judiciary has fared in its supervisory task of keeping the administration and its instrumentalities within the limits of their powers. Included therein is a brief survey on the judicialized governance of the modern day market-oriented regulatory regime where the courts particularly struggle to keep in check the privatized sector which has taken over and exercised many of the powers and tasks once assumed and discharged by the administrative bodies. Here the privatized bodies act as the agents or instrumentalities of the State and, therefore, the exercise of their powers may be subject to judicial review when challenged as being *ultra vires*. The second part will examine how the current administrative law regime is expected to respond to face the future challenges, particularly those problems posed by the implementation of the WTO economic and trading regime.

The chapter starts off by examining the administrative law regime in Malaysia via the perspective of judicial review of administrative action. This phenomenon contains two aspects. The first deals with what in administrative law parlance is referred to as *'common law review'*[1] by using the principles of judicial review as reformulated in the English case of *CCSU v. Minister for Civil Service*.[2] Owing to space constraints, this chapter will not deal with common law review, and any reference and discussion thereon has to be made elsewhere. The second aspect of Malaysian public law refers to what administrative lawyers would usually categorize as *'constitutional review'*.[3] The latter is associated with countries such as Malaysia, India, Fiji and South Africa, which possess a written Constitution and profess faith in the Rule of Law. In these countries, the Constitution contains a chapter guaranteeing fundamental rights to the individuals. The Constitution in these jurisdictions constitutes the supreme law of the land and no other law or administrative action may override or supersede it, or they will be struck down on the ground of unconstitutionality. At the outset, it must be pointed out and emphasized that constitutional review in Malaysia deals with the additional powers of the High Court over and above its inherent jurisdiction in the matter of judicial review of administrative action. It would constitute a crucial, fast developing and exciting area of the public law if the courts were to subscribe to the proposition that the Constitution is a living, organic and dynamic document primarily aimed at creating a dynamic society having faith in the Rule of Law and that the Government, particularly the Judiciary, is tasked with the constitutional duty of *'preserving, protecting and defending the Constitution'*.[4] This dynamic approach empowers the courts to construe fundamental rights enshrined in the Constitution broadly and liberally. Restrictions on rights are construed narrowly or restrictively against the administration. And, in the event of a conflict between two provisions in the Constitution or between the Constitution and a statutory provision, the doctrine of harmonious construction allows the more favourable construction to prevail.[5] Constitutional review offers greater prospects to applicants because the grounds of judicial review are wider and the potential remedies broader compared with the position at common law. Common law review under the *CCSU* principles is slower, and shackled with too many self-imposed restrictions. It is therefore crucial that the Malaysian system develops this constitutional aspect of judicial review quickly to secure the protection of fundamental rights. In this part of South-east Asia, the Malaysian system offers great prospects to perform and uphold the Rule of Law and constitutionalism.

To reiterate, constitutional review is important for the purposes of this chapter as it provides the basis for a liberal and broad interpretation of rights, broader grounds of judicial review and more powerful and effective remedies to address problems posed by the modern market-oriented regulatory regime associated with globalization. We also include a brief discussion of the need for a regional administrative law regime in Asia, consistent with the notion of global administrative law. Frequent references will be made to the more dynamic Indian public law jurisprudence, which is appropriate because the Indian Constitution had much influence on the Federal Constitution of Malaysia (the supreme law of the land), particularly the section on fundamental rights. Para 1, Schedule to the Courts of Judicature Act 1964 (Malaysia)[6] which confers additional powers of judicial review on the High Court[7] has its origin in Article 226 of the Indian Constitution.[8] It is important to note that the Indian jurisprudence on constitutional review is far more developed and rigorous than that of Malaysia. In India judicial creativity and activism in the field of public law emerged in the 1980s and has continued to develop over the years, showing no sign of abatement. The Malaysian position in this very crucial aspect of the public law unfortunately pales in comparison with that of India and is still in a stage of infancy.[9] Malaysians should therefore devote due attention to understanding how the Indian courts (the High and Supreme Courts) have imposed a rigorous discipline on the administrative powers of the State, particularly whenever human or fundamental rights are at stake in the exercise or, sometimes, non-exercise of discretionary powers of the State and its agencies.

Common law review

Malaysia is a common law country, so the English common law on judicial review is part and parcel of Malaysian public law, so long as it does not conflict with the supreme law of the land, namely, the Federal Constitution. In so far as common law review is concerned, the grounds of judicial review are those reformulated in the *CCSU* case.[10] These grounds are procedural impropriety, illegality and irrationality. Proportionality, discussed below, is not a ground of review under this formulation but is a possibility for the future.

Procedural impropriety refers to any failure to observe the basic rules of natural justice[11] or any failure to act with procedural fairness towards the person affected by the decision of a public authority. It covers also any failure by an administrative tribunal to observe any mandatory procedural rule expressly laid down in a legislative instrument conferring its jurisdiction.[12] Irrationality or super-*Wednesbury* unreasonableness refers to a decision which is so outrageous in its defiance of logic or of accepted moral standards that no reasonable person who has applied his mind to the question to be decided could have arrived at it. Illegality as a ground of judicial review refers to that part of the substantive *ultra vires* doctrine (excluding irrationality) incorporating simple *ultra vires*, 'sub-*Wednesbury* unreasonableness',[13] non-exercise of discretion,[14] misdirection of law and fact, legitimate expectations[15] and the equitable doctrine of estoppel in public law.[16] Owing to space constraints, these aspects of the *ultra vires* doctrine will not be discussed further, except to note that the law thereon corresponds fully with that of England.[17]

Constitutional review

What is it?

In a country with a written Constitution that guarantees fundamental rights to all persons living or operating within its territory, the question of constitutional review comes into play whenever the State or any of its instrumentalities or agencies takes an action which adversely affects a person's right or interest.[18] It may also arise whenever a State or its agency implements any rule or law that infringes or restricts or deprives a person of his or her right or interest. Whenever an action or a law is challenged in an application for judicial review[19] on the ground that the said action or law (either a statute or sub-statutory instrument) is unconstitutional, the question of proportionality may arise. In such an event,

> the court will see that the legislature and the administrative authority maintain a proper balance between the adverse effects which the legislation or the administrative order may have on the rights, liberties or interests of persons, keeping in mind the purpose which they were intended to serve. The legislature and the administrative authority are, however, given an area of discretion or a range of choices, but as to whether the choice made infringes the rights

excessively or not is for the court [to decide]. That is what is meant by proportionality.[20]

The reviewing court thus adopts a strict or heightened or most anxious scrutiny test and plays the role of a primary reviewer as to the validity or legality of the administrative action or law. Under this approach, the question of review on merits does not arise.[21] The intensity of review in such cases inevitably will be greater than in a case which does not involve constitutional review.[22]

In a recent Malaysian case involving an application for judicial review of the decision of the Registrar of Societies and the Minister rejecting the application of the appellant to register a political party at the national level, the Court of Appeal's pronouncement on the position relating to constitutional review is rather significant:

> The other aspect to interpreting our Constitution is this. When interpreting the other parts of the Constitution, the court must bear in mind the all pervading provision of Art. 8(1). That article guarantees fairness of all forms of State action (see *Tan Tek Seng v. Suruhanjaya Perkhidmatan Pendidikan & Anor*, [1996] 1 MLJ 261). It must also bear in mind the principle of substantive proportionality that art 8(1) imports (see *Om Kumar v. Union of India* AIR 2000 SC 3689). This doctrine was most recently applied by this court ... in *Menara PanGlobal Sdn Bhd v. Arokianathan a/l Sivapiragasam*, (2006) 3 MLJ 493. In other words, not only must the legislative or executive response to a state of affairs be objectively fair, it must also be proportionate to the object sought to be achieved. This is sometimes referred to as 'the doctrine of rational nexus' (see *Malaysian Bar & Anor v. Government of Malaysia*, (1987) 2 MLJ 165). A court is therefore entitled to strike down State action on the ground that it is disproportionate to the object sought to be achieved.

This *dictum*, declaring that Article 8(1) of the Federal Constitution in its constitutional dimension 'guarantees fairness of all forms of State action', is significant indeed in Malaysia. It means that in the matter of constitutional review, the reviewing court may look beyond proportionality. 'Fairness' includes both procedural and substantive fairness, and proportionality is merely a part of substantive fairness. Substantive fairness or unfairness is certainly a ground for judicial review,[23] and has several components.[24] More will be said of constitutional review in the next section.

Common law review contrasted

In cases not involving review of fundamental rights or where the attack is against the decision-making process of the administrator or decision-maker, then the role of the reviewing court is purely one of secondary review. In such cases, the *Wednesbury* or *CCSU* principles apply to test the validity of executive or administrative action taken or made in the exercise of a statutory power or discretion. The court can only go into the matter as a secondary reviewing body to find out if the executive or the administrator in its primary role has arrived at a reasonable decision on the materials before them. The choice of the options available is for the concerned authority to make. The reviewing court cannot substitute its discretion (namely, own view as to what is reasonable) for that of the authority concerned. Thus, the common law offers a more deferential test.

Right of access to court to enforce fundamental rights: Unique position in India and Malaysia

Position in Malaysia

Besides the inherent power of judicial review, the High Court in Malaysia also possesses some additional powers of judicial review.[25] The additional powers are enumerated in Paragraph 1, Schedule to the Courts of Judicature Act 1964 read together with section 25(2).[26] The provision of Paragraph 1 of the Schedule is reproduced below:

> Power to issue to any person or authority directions, orders or writs, including writs of the nature of *habeas corpus, mandamus, prohibition, quo warranto* and *certiorari*, or any others, for the enforcement of the rights conferred by Part II of the Constitution, or any of them, or for any purpose.

It must be pointed out and emphasized that the additional powers provided in Paragraph 1 are statutory powers.[27] They are traceable to the equivalent provision in the Indian Constitution, namely, Article 226. Before proceeding to dwell on the important provision in the Courts of Judicature Act 1964 (of Malaysia), a few words must be said about the Indian law and its jurisprudence in this area.

Position in India

As has already been mentioned, the Malaysian provision has its origin in the Indian Constitution and, hence, reference to the Indian law thereon is unavoidable. Another factor of equal importance is that the Indian jurisprudence on Article 226 is established and vast because the Indian High Court and Supreme Court have consistently developed a large corpus of case law thereon by way of judicial creativity and activism since the 1980s.[28] Conversely, the Malaysian jurisprudence in this area is limited and uncertain at the moment. There are two reasons for the disparity. First, the Malaysian courts only started invoking the Paragraph 1 powers in the mid-1990s. Second, the Malaysian Federal Court keeps on reversing the High Court and Court of Appeal cases,[29] turning the clock back to the antiquated pre-1996[30] position when common law review was all that was available. Despite this major setback, the prospects for change and advancement look promising if the Federal Court can be persuaded to discard its anti-fundamental rights mentality.

Reverting to the Indian position, a few statements should be made for the purpose of clarification:

- The Indian Constitution's Article 226 is primarily used for the enforcement of fundamental rights. Needless to say, the ambit of Article 226 is very broad indeed, and extends beyond fundamental rights enforcement. It could also include any legal right, human right as well as the ventilation of any issue of great public interest or importance in the field of public law. This is a very remarkable feature of the Indian public law jurisprudence which will be elaborated later.
- Moreover, the Indian system has an additional and narrower provision in its Constitution, namely, Article 32.[31] This provision empowers an individual to approach the Supreme Court directly for the purpose of enforcing fundamental rights only. Article 32 is in Part III of the Indian Constitution which confers and guarantees fundamental rights. Another difference between Article 226 and Article 32 is that the former is a constitutional right whereas the latter is a fundamental right guarantee. Article 32 is unique. It is confined to situations or cases which are urgent and where a prompt, decisive and authoritative stance needs to be taken for a particular public law dispute or issue and the decision of the Supreme Court thereon will bind all the parties to the dispute.
- Both Arts. 226 and 32 are very powerful provisions in the Indian Constitution and are considered a basic structure of the Indian Constitutional system, such that no law can dilute these rights without running the risk of being struck down as unconstitutional.[32]
- Arts. 226 and 32 have been construed and applied meaningfully, effectively and creatively in conjunction with the relevant fundamental right provisions of the Indian Constitution such as Arts. 14 and 21.[33] They have been used by public spirited citizens and public interest groups and the Indian courts themselves as the basis or habitat to espouse public interest litigation. More will be said later of the right of the individuals under the Indian system to approach or access the High Court and the Supreme Court for the purpose of enforcing fundamental and other rights.

Right to vindicate the rule of law

As pointed out earlier, the source of this right or power in Malaysia is in the Courts of Judicature Act 1964, namely, section 25(2) read with Paragraph 1 of the Schedule to the Act, quoted earlier. Paragraph 1 confers additional powers of judicial review on the High Court, conferring standing on individuals and provided the High Court is the power to grant any of the remedies specified therein including the power to fashion consequential relief in favour of an applicant. For purposes of discussion, we will refer to the Indian jurisprudence on the same level.[34] The salient and outstanding features of the provision of the Courts of Judicature Act 1964 may now be enumerated and highlighted as follows:

(1) 'For the enforcement of the rights conferred by Part II of the Constitution, or any of them'

This provision clearly indicates the primary purpose of Paragraph 1, namely, to secure the enforcement of fundamental rights or any of them as guaranteed under Part II of the Federal Constitution.[35] By using the doctrine of implied fundamental rights, other rights which are not expressly enumerated in Part II may also be incorporated therein. The approach taken by the Malaysian Court of Appeal in the landmark case of *Tan Tek Seng v. Suruhanjaya Perkhidmatan Pendidikan & Anor*[36] clearly illustrated the broad ambit of this provision. In that case, the word 'life' in Article 5(1) has been broadly and liberally construed, following the Indian authorities, to include other implied rights, particularly the important right to livelihood or employment.

(2) 'Or for any purpose'

Besides fundamental rights, the aforesaid phrase has been construed to include any legal or human or other rights. It has also been used to ventilate any issue of great public interest or importance.[37]

(3) Remedies obtainable under Paragraph 1

The remedies obtainable under Paragraph 1 are potentially broad, useful and powerful if Indian jurisprudence is a good guide. The following discussion supports this contention.

'Writs, including writs of the nature of'

This part of Paragraph 1 highlighted under this sub-heading refers not only to the traditional common writ remedies of *habeas corpus, mandamus, prohibition, quo warranto and certiorari*. The writ jurisdiction conferred thereunder is much broader. This can be inferred from the use of the phrase *'of the nature of'*. The most obvious consequence of this peculiar statutory formula is that the old and rigid English common law rules on the application of the writ jurisdiction, such as delay, *locus standi* and the notion that the reviewing court cannot substitute its own judgement for that of the administrator, and cannot come in the way of the application of the Paragraph 1 powers. The framers of the Indian Constitution had this feature clearly in mind when they drafted Arts. 226 and 32.

'Or any others'

The phrase *'or any others'* also empowers the High Court to issue the non-writ remedies of declaration and injunction. Again, the common law rules governing the grant of these remedies need not be rigidly followed by the High Court whenever these remedies are granted under the additional powers of the High Court. This part of Paragraph 1 clearly extends beyond the writ jurisdiction.

'Directions, orders'

The key words *'directions, orders'* empower the High Court to fashion the appropriate consequential relief in favour of the applicant 'to meet the ends of justice' in an application for judicial review under the Paragraph 1 powers. This may be considered the most outstanding feature of the Indian and Malaysian public law. This feature, together with that of granting the appropriate remedy[38] 'to fit the factual matrix of a particular case' as discussed earlier, were highlighted and emphasized by the Malaysian Court of Appeal in the case of *Hong Leong Equipment Sdn. Bhd. v. Liew Fook Chuan & anor appeal.*[39]

The power to fashion the appropriate consequential relief in each individual case includes:

1. The power to award interim payment to the victim of the tort or crime pending the hearing and conclusion of the case which may take time if the factual matrix of the case clearly shows that there is a clear *prima facie* case against the Government.[40]
2. The power to order *ex gratia* payment.[41]
3. The power to grant monetary compensation to the victim of a crime or tort or an unlawful State action.[42]
4. The power of the High Court to develop and formulate its own common law rules to govern the grant public law remedies under the Paragraph 1 powers.[43]
5. The power to formulate a temporary code of law to govern a particular public law dispute, in the absence of a law governing the same, pending appropriate law-making measures by the relevant authority or Legislature.[44] This power includes the discretion on the part of the reviewing court to move the law forward in an appropriate case if the law thereon is outdated and antiquated, so that it falls into accord with spirit and intent of the Federal Constitution.[45] It also necessarily means that administrators and lawyers representing the Government can no longer say that a particular public law grievance is not expressly protected under a particular piece of legislation because of a lacuna therein. This is because in such an eventuality, the Paragraph 1 powers could come to the rescue by construing a constitutional provision in the Federal Constitution, particularly any of those protecting fundamental rights, broadly and liberally so as to incorporate therein a common law right or human right or any other implied right or rights.[46]

To whom the writs may be issued?

The phrase *'any person or authority'* distinguishes Malaysian and Indian public law from that of England and the European Union. Under English and European

Union law, a writ may only be issued to 'a public authority' but under the Malaysian and Indian law, the same may be issued to a wider or broader group of respondents. The words *'any person'* is wide enough to include a legal entity such as a private commercial enterprise or corporation so long as its activity adversely affected the public interest or a fundamental right.[47] The word *'authority'*, too, is broader than the term 'public authority' at common law so long as the nature of the duty imposed is a public duty which is obligatory. In the era of privatization, many public law duties have been transferred to by private bodies which would not be regarded as 'public authorities' at common law, but today they are considered *'authorities'* under the Malaysian and Indian public law. This aspect of public law is also of particular relevance and significance in the era of globalization and the WTO regime because any over-zealous or exploitative implementation thereof is likely to adversely affect public interests or fundamental rights.[48]

Paragraph 1 powers: Basis to espouse public interest litigation

Public interest litigation (PIL)

The Indian courts have creatively used Arts. 226 and 32 of the Indian Constitution to cultivate public interest litigation. These provisions were used effectively in conjunction with Arts. 14 (equality before the law clause in particular) and 21 (life and personal liberty protection) and the Directive Principles of State Policy and Basic Duties resulting in the judicial policy that fundamental rights in the Constitution must be construed broadly in their cultural, social, economic and other contexts. In India, public interest litigation has developed and thrived since the 1980s and the *locus standi* rule has been liberalized to enable public interest groups to bring cases to court to vindicate the Rule of Law and to block unlawful action. The following discussion clearly illustrates the broad ambit of the PIL jurisprudence in India.

EXPLOITATION OF POOR LABOURERS

Public interest groups in India have utilized public interest litigation to champion the rights of poor labourers who had been exploited by the contractors or their employers.[49] For example, in *Bandhua Mukti Morcha v. India*,[50] an organization dedicated to the cause of release of bonded labour was allowed to vindicate the plight of bonded labourers before the Indian Supreme Court. The State Government was censured by the court for raising a preliminary objection to stall an inquiry into the complaint that a large number of peasants or workers were bonded serfs or subjected to exploitation by a few mine lessees, contractors or employers, or were being denied the benefits of social welfare laws.

PRISON LITIGATION

In *Hussainara (I)*,[51] a public interest suit was brought in the Indian Supreme Court seeking the immediate release of under-trials who languished in jails pending their trials. The Supreme Court held that a fair trial implied a speedy trial, and this right was an integral and essential part of the fundamental right of life and personal liberty enshrined in Article 21 of the Indian Constitution.

In another *Hussainara* case,[52] the Indian Supreme Court ruled that free legal aid should be provided to a prisoner who was unable to secure legal assistance by reason of poverty if justice required the State to provide such a service.

In *Sheela Barse*,[53] a woman journalist filed a writ petition in the Indian Supreme Court and raised questions about the welfare of children lodged in prisons while their mothers served jail sentences. The Supreme Court directed the Supreme Court Legal Aid Committee to take over and proceed with the case, upon application by the petitioner to withdraw the case when no progress was made. In another case, *Sheela Barse v. Maharashtra*,[54] the journalist went back to the Supreme Court and sought orders to prevent ill treatment of women in prison in Bombay. The Supreme Court gave orders to the relevant authority including the provision of legal assistance to the under-trial prisoners.

PROTECTION OF ENVIRONMENT

There have also been several high profile environmental protection cases. In *Vellore Citizens' Welfare Forum v. India*,[55] an NGO brought suit against tanneries causing serious pollution across several states, seeking orders of closure, orders to install pollution prevention devices in the tanneries and orders of compensation to the affected farmers and to rehabilitate the polluted rivers.[56] In the *Taj Mahal* case,[57] orders were sought to prevent damage caused to the ancient monument as well as the green belt surrounding the monument by visitors as a result of a musical concert organized and held in the vicinity of the monument. In *R L & E Kendra, Dehradum v. UP*,[58] also known the *limestone quarry*'s case, orders were sought against quarries operating at the foothills of the Himalayas as these quarries were causing ecological damage and imbalance in the affected area.

VENTILATION OF ISSUES OF GREAT PUBLIC INTEREST AND IMPORTANCE

In *George Mampilly v. State of Kerala*,[59] an order was sought to quash the decision of a state government to allow the sale of arrack (liquor) in polythene bags which was harmful to the health of people who consumed it. In *Janamohan Das v. State of Orissa*,[60] the High Court ordered the reopening of an inquiry into a liquor disaster that had killed many people. The state government initially closed the inquiry upon a newspaper report of involvement of government ministers. The state government was also ordered by the High Court to pay Rs 15,000 to each of the families affected by the disaster.

ABUSE OF DISCRETIONARY POWER BY THE EXECUTIVE

In *Chaitanya Kumar v. Karnataka*,[61] the Indian Supreme Court held that award of contracts by the Government to ineligible candidates over eligible applicants could be quashed on the ground of abuse of discretion even though no loss was caused to the State Exchequer. In the *Pergau Dam* case,[62] an oversea development grant to Malaysia made by the British Government under section 1 of the Overseas Development and Co-operation Act 1980 was blocked by an NGO because the said grant was *ultra vires* the statute under which it was made. The grant was meant for the promotion of economically sound development projects, but the project was shown to be so economically unsound that it fell outside the scope of the law even though it was permissible for the British Government to take into account wider political and economic considerations when deciding whether to make the grant.

No need for a writ petition to be moved

The Indian High Court or the Supreme Court itself may, of its own volition without a writ petition having been filed by any litigant before it, require a particular body or authority to appear before it to explain or show cause why action should not be taken against it for any alleged violation of any human or fundamental right protected under Part III of the Indian Constitution. The High Court or the Supreme Court may so act in pursuance of a letter written to it by a member of the public or as a result of newspaper report complaining of a breach of law by an authority provided there is a reasonable basis for so doing.[63]

Constitutional review: Recent Malaysian experience

Judicial creativity and activism: New frontiers in Malaysian public law

Until the mid-1990s, the Malaysian courts did not invoke constitutional review although they were empowered to do so by the Courts of Judicature Act since 1964.[64] The Court of Appeal began to invoke the Paragraph 1 powers in the *Tan Tek Seng* case[65] in 1996 and followed-up quickly in a number of other cases – *Hong Leong Equipment*;[66] *Sugumar Balakrishnan*;[67] *Utra Badi*.[68] The Federal Court did the same in *R. Rama Chandran*'s case.[69] The High Court also did so dramatically in *Abdul Ghani Haroon (No. 3)*[70] and *Abdul Ghani Haroon (No. 4)*.[71]

In *Tan Tek Seng*, the Court of Appeal started the liberal trend by construing the word 'life' in Article 5(1) of the Federal Constitution broadly to include employment. It then went on to say that once employment was adversely affected by way of disciplinary action initiated by the employer, procedural fairness would come into the picture to protect the affected employee as a result of the combined effect of Arts. 5(1) and 8(1) of the Federal Constitution. It further held that the doctrine of proportionality would also require that the punishment of the employee was not excessive or disproportionate to the wrong committed. In *Hong Leong Equipment*, the Court extended procedural fairness to include the right of the dismissed employee to know the reason for a particular decision, again on the bases of Arts. 5(1) and 8(1).[72] The right to procedural fairness was still linked to fundamental rights. Later in *Sugumar Balakrishnan*, the Court of

Appeal used the concept of substantive unfairness to strike down a substantively unfair administrative decision. It further extended procedural fairness to include the right to know the reason for an administrative decision whenever any right of a person has been adversely affected by an administrative decision. In this case, the Sabah State Government terminated the entry permit of the applicant (a lawyer) some six weeks before his permit expired on the ground of immorality. Again, Article 5(1) and Article 8(1) were relied upon to reach those liberal rulings. In *Utra Badi*, the High Court and the Court of Appeal extended procedural fairness further to include the right to a plea in mitigation after the finding of guilt by the disciplinary board in a proceeding against a civil servant alleged to have committed a disciplinary offence punishable with dismissal or reduction in rank. *Rama Chandran* and the *Abdul Ghani Haroon* cases were much awaited cases by the Malaysian legal fraternity, decided shortly after the landmark case of *Tan Tek Seng*. *Rama Chandran* was another employment case. The applicant was dismissed by his employer without just cause. When his case was heard at the Federal Court, he was already 51 years old, his chances of obtaining another job were not promising, and he had been out of work for quite some time. The Federal Court granted the appropriate consequential relief (including damages for loss of wages amounting to some 88 months)[73] in favour of the applicant and, in the interest of justice, did not resort to the usual practice of remitting the case back to the Industrial Court for reconsideration. The *Abdul Ghani* cases are classic *habeas corpus* cases. The High Court in *Abdul Ghani Haroon (No. 3)* found the preventive detention of the detainee unlawful on the ground of *mala fide* due to denial of the rights of the detainee to have access to his family members and counsel during his detention and right up to the time of the hearing of the writ. The court continued in *Abdul Ghani Haroon (No. 4)* to forbid the police to re-arrest the detainee in the 24 hours following his release on the same grounds of detention stated in the earlier detention order.[74] The court ruled the arrest and detention unlawful and *mala fide*.

On 12 July, 2007, in the case of *Kok Wah Kuan v. PP*,[75] the Court of Appeal struck down section 97(2)[76] of the Child Act of 2001 for unconstitutionality because it contravened the constitutional doctrine of separation of powers. The impugned provision of the Child Act purported to consign to the Executive[77] the judicial power[78] to determine the appropriate sentence that was to be served by a child (the appellant in that case) found guilty of murder by the High Court.[79] However, on appeal, the Federal Court unanimously overruled the Court of Appeal.[80]

Save for *Kok Wah Kuan*, these cases, together with the native customary rights cases,[81] constituted the high water marks of judicial creativity and activism in the protection of fundamental rights guaranteed under Part II of the Federal Constitution. The courts have assumed and displayed an activist stance, unlike the earlier cases[82] which were bent on 'killing' rights. For the first time, some four decades after the Federal Constitution came into force, they anchored Malaysian public law firmly on the constitutional review. By adopting this new approach, all disputes relating to public law, particularly those dealing with complaints of violation or deprivation of fundamental rights, were to be resolved by resorting to the supreme law of the land, namely, the Federal Constitution. The aspects of the English common law that interfere with the effective application of the supreme law must give way to the supreme law. In other words, the Federal Constitution will always pre-empt the common law where provisions differ.

Turning back the clock

The spate of judicial activism and creativity initiated by the Court of Appeal and the High Court was short-lived. The Federal Court did not endorse the broad and liberal construction approach adopted by the High Court and the Court of Appeal. The Federal Court struck down cases like *Sugumar Balakrihshnan*,[83] *Utra Badi*[84] and *Kekatong*.[85] Once again, Malaysian public law was thrown back to the pre-1996 restrictive phrase during which the general tendency of the courts was to interpret rights' issues narrowly and restrictively. The pre-1996 restrictive phrase can be summarized: the word 'law' in Article 5(1) that guarantees 'life and liberty of the person' did not include procedure;[86] the phrase 'liberty of the person' in Article 5(1) does not confer the right to travel abroad or obtain a passport;[87] and the court is not the avenue to determine whether the doctrinally implied limitation applied to the amending power of Parliament under Article 159 of the Federal Constitution and that the fine issue of constitutional law raised could only be resolved by addressing the matter 'to the legislature, and not the courts; they have their remedy at the ballot box'.[88]

The retrograde slide continued in subsequent Federal Court cases. Two such cases are discussed here. In *Beatrice Fernandez*,[89] the applicant unsuccessfully challenged her dismissal as a flight stewardess on the ground that she had breached a term in the collective agreement that she had to resign if she were to become pregnant. Once pregnant, she refused to resign and was dismissed by her employer, Sistem Penerbangan Malaysia (MAS or Malaysian Airlines). She challenged her dismissal chiefly on the ground of unconstitutionality for violating the 'equality before the law' protection clause of Article 8(1) of the Federal Constitution. The Malaysian courts (High Court, Court of Appeal and the Federal Court) found for her employer on grounds that the applicant had not proved that MAS was 'a public authority'; she was bound by the term of the collective agreement; there was not discrimination on the grounds of rational classification doctrine; and the collective agreement was not 'law' within the context of the phrase 'equality before the law' clause. Her case also fell outside the gender protection clause in Article 8(2) as the collective agreement was signed before the amendment incorporating gender equality in Article 8(2) came into effect. The Indian case law on the same was rejected.[90] The Indian Supreme Court struck down the dismissal of an Indian stewardess in similar circumstances on the ground of unconstitutionality, namely, arbitrariness and an insult to womanhood and hence violating the equality clause of Article 14 and the right to life clause of Article 21 of the Indian Constitution. It should also be pointed out that the Indian Supreme Court has taken the firm stance that fundamental rights cannot be waived by the weaker party on the grounds of public policy and unequal bargaining power.[91]

270 *Gan Ching Chuan*

In *Ketua Pengarah Immigresen Malaysia v. Heng Peo*,[92] a foreigner's complaint of threat to his personal safety or life, pleading for the protection of Malaysian law under Paragraph 1, Schedule to the Courts of Judicature Act 1964 was ignored. The Court of Appeal was more pre-occupied with procedural irregularities rather than realizing the importance of protecting the fundamental rights of the applicant.[93]

The refusal of the Federal Court[94] to endorse the broad and liberal interpretation of fundamental rights by relying on the enforcement provision of Paragraph 1 powers of the High Court is difficult to understand. It is sincerely hoped that the Federal Court will shed its 'more executive-minded than the Executive' mentality. In this context, it may be pointed out and emphasized that the Court of Appeal in *Tan Tek Seng*'s case took great pride in declaring that Malaysia has a dynamic, living and organic document in the form of the Federal Constitution. Public law operating under a written Constitution is constantly evolving in the effort to create a dynamic and progressive society, thereby maintaining relevance in response to changing times and circumstances. The American and Indian systems are classic examples of this constitutional model, featuring judicial creativity and activism and ensuring that the system operates as contemplated by their respective Constitutions. Reverting to the Malaysian position, it must be emphasized that members of the Judiciary are under a constitutional oath or duty 'to preserve, protect and defend the Constitution'.[95]

Weaknesses of the Malaysian constitutional system

Malaysian public law is not moving forward as it should in the post-*Tan Tek Seng* era. The backward slide as discussed earlier would not have occurred if the Federal Court had taken heed of the wake-up call sounded by the Court of Appeal in *Tan Tek Seng*'s case. The discretion to embark on constitutional review has been there since 1964 when the Courts of Judicature Act 1964 was enacted and came into force. However, for reasons best known only to the Federal Court itself, it continues to apply the rigid common law rules governing judicial review at the expense of the proper development of Malaysia's own common law based on its own legislation. Sometimes, important constitutional issues raised before the court are deliberately neutralized and converted into ordinary administrative law issues.[96] It is now time that the Federal Court abandons its anti-fundamental rights stance and takes the initiative to move Malaysian public law forward.[97]

The recent turn of events in Malaysia in the last quarter of 2007 provides some indication that the Rule of Law is under attack in the country. The attempts to ban or restrict activities organized by the Malaysian Bar (e.g. organizing Human Rights Walk and putting up banners at its premises to commemorate the International Human Rights Day), the prohibition of peaceful assemblies organized by NGOs and political parties, the demolition of Indian temples on the eve of Deepavali and the arrests, detentions and prosecutions of Hindraf (The Hindu Rights Action Force) members and supporters in the aftermath of their marches and protests are things which should not have happened in a country professing to be a democratic one based on and governed by the Rule of Law and a written Constitution guaranteeing fundamental and human rights.

Lessons from other jurisdictions

A common law jurisdiction based on the Rule of Law and whose written constitution contains a chapter guaranteeing fundamental rights may benefit greatly from the experiences of other jurisdictions which have displayed great courage and faith in the Rule of Law. This is especially so when its courts are construing the fundamental right provisions in the constitution. Outright rejection or refusal by the local courts to consider good case law precedents from other jurisdictions by offering lame excuses is difficult indeed to understand and justify.[98]

The rise of regulatory governance in Malaysia

Public undertakings or enterprises

Modern welfare states intervene actively in the national economy and undertake trade, commerce or business activities on an ever-increasing scale. They do so for various reasons: to gain proper control over the economic resources; to promote economic regeneration and development; to redistribute wealth; and to improve the socio-economic welfare of the people. Public enterprises or undertakings may be set up to provide essential services or utilities to the public or to engage in business. They may be operated to the exclusion of the private sector or in joint venture with the private sector or in competition with the private enterprises.

A few words may be said of this business phenomenon in Malaysia. The Malayan Railway was the first public enterprise to be set up by the Government in 1949, under the Malayan Railway Ordinance 1948. Other bodies came into being later, for example, the Federal Land Development Authority (FELDA) in 1959; the Malaysian Industrial Development Authority (MIDA)[99] in 1979; and the National Electricity Board (NEB)[100] in 1973. Some have been established to develop certain regions in the country, such as the Muda Agricultural Development Authority (MADA), established in 1972 to develop and commercialize rice cultivation in the State of Kedah.

Even State Governments are venturing into business and commercial activities. Each State has its own State Economic Development Corporation (SEDC) set up and corporatized as a statutory body. The primary objective of each SEDC is to promote and develop the economy of the State by venturing into activities such as building houses, shopping complexes and industrial projects, and undertaking logging, mining and transportation businesses.

Public enterprises may be categorized into several categories:

- socio-economic group;
- commercial and industrial group;

- public utilities; and
- financial institutions.

Control over such bodies is established in several ways. First these bodies are required to keep proper accounts for each financial year under the Statutory Bodies (Accounts and Annual Reports) Act 1980. The statement of accounts, within six months after the end of the financial year, is to be submitted to the Auditor-General for the audit to be carried out. The audited accounts are to be laid before each House of Parliament. The task of the auditor is to ensure that funds are used for the approved objectives and the objectives are implemented efficiently without wastage.

Parliament has a limited role in oversight. Although the audited accounts of statutory corporations are laid before Parliament, the usual practice is that no discussion is made on the accounts. Government companies, whose accounts are audited by private auditors, do not have to submit the reports on their audited accounts to Parliament.

Finally the relevant ministry exercises a good deal of control over public enterprises. The control may take various forms, including approval of the budget, borrowing and investment, making of regulations, appointment of members of the respective enterprises such the Chairman and other members of the board. Government companies are subject to control imposed under the Companies Act 1965.

Economic development planning and new economic policy

The Government formulates and implements economic development plans. Economic Development Planning in Malaysia began in 1950 with the publication of the Draft Development Plan of Malaya. Currently, the Ninth Malaysia Plan (2006–2010) is in its second year of implementation. An important and peculiar feature of this economic planning is the New Economic Policy (NEP). The NEP is primarily intended to assist financially and re-distribute wealth to the Bumiputras whose economic well-being and progress generally falls behind the other races. Under this policy, Bumiputra economic ownership was targeted at 30 per cent by the year 1990. The Government has announced[101] that this target is yet to be achieved. Under this policy, various bodies have been established and entrusted with a specific task or tasks to help to increase the Bumiputra economic participation and ownership.[102]

Privatization

The push towards turning Malaysia into a developed industrialized nation by the year 2020[103] began in the 1980s under the premiership of Dr Mahathir bin Mohamad (now Tun). Dr Mahathir had formulated several policies and implemented them towards this end. Under the Malaysia Incorporated Policy, the close partnership of the public and private sectors was necessary and important to promote growth. The public sector played the role of an active partner as facilitator and pacesetter, spurring on the private sector as the main engine of growth. As a result, the Privatization Policy has been actively implemented with several objectives in mind. Those objectives are:

- to reduce the financial and administrative burden of the public sector;
- to increase the efficiency and productivity in the public sector;
- to encourage economic growth. (If the private sectors are encouraged to utilize and develop the natural resources, then there will be a major boost to economic development);
- to increase efficiency in dividing our natural resources;
- hasten the objectives of the New Economic Policy;[104]
- by giving more opportunities to the private sector, the Government will be able to create more opportunities for the Bumiputras to establish and own more private enterprises.

The Economic Planning Unit (EPU) has been formed in the Prime Minister Department. It is composed of members from the Implementation Control Unit (ICU), Finance Ministry and Public Service Department (PSD) and headed by the EPU member itself. It is entrusted with the task of drafting a comprehensive guideline to implement the privatization plan. The government has since carried out privatization in various forms such as outright sale, leasing and management contracts. Of particular interest are the Build-Operate-Transfer (BOT) and the Build-Operate (BO) methods. The BOT method involves the construction of a public facility such as roads, ports or highways, by a private company at its own expense. The company then operates and manages it for a certain concessionary period. At the end of the period it transfers the facility to the government. Within the concessionary period, the company is allowed to collect a direct charge from users of the facility. In the BO method, the facility does not have to be handed back to the government.[105]

Economic roadmap for the future

With the recent re-adjustment to the target date to turn the country into a developed and industrialized country from 2020 to 2057, the ambitious plan towards fully developed nation status should be within the reach of the nation.[106] The 2020 target date was a good yet over-ambitious policy goal.

Government also participates actively in the field of business and commerce by setting up the so-called Government Linked Companies. These include some very large multinationals, with substantial government support, including such firms as PETRONAS, Permodalan Nasional Berhad (PNB), Khazanah Nasional Berhad, the Malaysian International Shipping Corporation (MISC); and CIMB Bank.

The public–private business and development partnership in developing the national economy and managing and regulating the country will eventually bear fruit. The system must be intermittently fine-tuned and constantly improved to continue moving forward.[107]

Regulatory mechanism

In order to ensure that the privatized commercial sector is not too profit-oriented and that quality and affordable services or utilities are provided to the public or consumers, it is advisable to set up a control mechanism that is fair and transparent to all parties – the Government, the privatized sector and consumers as well as other affected or interested parties. This body may also take on an additional role as a dispute resolution tribunal, but it may not supplant the role of the High Court as a supervisory body. Even the enactment of an ouster clause in the relevant statute may not have produced its purported intention of ousting judicial review if the *vires* or legality of an action or decision is questioned in the High Court.[108]

Judicial review

It has been accepted that both public and private enterprises are amenable to judicial review. Perhaps as a general rule, a governing power wherever located[109] and however the body under review is set up,[110] is subject to some constitutional limitations and thereby governed by the operation of the *ultra vires* doctrine. Even if incorporated as a private company, a body may still be regarded as an agency or instrumentality of the administration, and thus subject to judicial review under the statutory formula of *'any person or authority'*[111] when it conducts action that is understood as governmental in nature. Such a body may be regarded as 'an authority'[112] wielding a discretionary power when its exercise affects the rights or interests of a member of a particular group or profession or any member of the public. Sometimes, the dispute may be between the privatized body and the Government. For example, an Independent Power Producer (IPP) may question the decision of the Government seeking to alter the terms of the licence granted to the IPP to supply electricity to a particular area of a State citing non-compliance with procedural fairness[113] or any substantive or constitutional requirement.

Guidelines as to reviewability: Is a company subject to judicial review?

The Malaysian Court of Appeal has enumerated some useful guidelines for judicial review of actions by privatized companies:[114]

> At one end of the spectrum are limited companies (whether public or private it matters not) incorporated under the Companies Act 1965 whose shares are owned by two or more individuals or bodies. They perform no public function and are vested with no statutory powers. They are entirely private in character. The Federal or a State Government or both may own substantial shares in them. And as shareholders, they may dictate the constitution of the

board of directors. Malaysian Airlines is an example. Judicial Review cannot go to such a company.

Next in the spectrum are the hybrids. Some of these are former publicly owned service providers that have been corporatized under a privatization scheme. Tenaga Nasional and Telecom Malaysia are examples that spring to mind. Their shares are owned by many different persons, including Government, and they are just like any other limited company under the Companies Act 1965 except that they perform public functions which are regulated by statute. Parliament has also given them powers under particular statutes. That is why they are hybrids. And it is because they are hybrids, that their amenability to judicial review depends on the nature and character of the act or omission complained of. Where the company does something or omits to do something within the confines of its private character, then there can be no judicial review. But if it does something that is *ultra vires* the powers conferred on it by statute, then it becomes amenable to judicial review.

At the other end of the spectrum are companies of which the Government is the sole shareholder, are funded entirely with public money and have either statutory powers or duties conferred upon them. It is a misnomer to term such a company as purely private in character. It is axiomatic that the law looks at substance and not at mere form. In form these entities are companies. But in truth and substance they are each an instrument of Government. They are therefore a 'person or authority' referred to in Para. 1 of the Schedule to the Courts of Judicature Act 1964 and are amenable to judicial review.

A few comments may be made on the above-mentioned *dicta*. First, a fully commercial private enterprise in the first category may be open to judicial scrutiny if any of its operations falls within the purview of public law. For instance, its operation may have breached its corporate social responsibility, or adopted a collective agreement with its employees' union that breached the constitutional or fundamental rights of its employees.[115] Second, government companies in the third category may sometimes not be open to judicial review if the issue raised for judicial scrutiny is one that has strong governmental policy content or politically sensitive.[116] Third, the *locus standi* rule has to be construed liberally or broadly.[117]

Grounds of judicial review

An action or decision of a private company involved in providing services or utilities to the public may be called in question in a court of law. A few guidelines may be postulated for the conduct or operation of such a company:

1 The supply of utility or service has to be made to all without any favour or discrimination or ulterior motive.
2 A public utility provider must provide the utility to any consumer who applies for it subject to the conditions that it has enough supplies and is able to provide the utility.

3 The tariffs or prices charged for the utility supplied must be reasonable, fair and non-discriminatory.
4 The powers conferred on a public utility provider must not be exercised in a harsh, unreasonable, or cruel manner.[118]

Towards better administrative governance: A roadmap for the future

The forward march of public law: A phenomenon which can no longer be delayed!

This chapter has identified various weaknesses in the Malaysian constitutional framework and system hindering further judicialization. Rapid economic progress of the country in line with the Malaysia Incorporated Policy and in coping with the onslaught of the WTO regime necessitates the nation's legal and constitutional framework and practices to adapt. To achieve these lofty goals, the Government should consider the following steps:

1 The Federal Constitution needs to be amended to incorporate two new provisions along the lines of Arts. 226 and 32 of the Indian Constitution. Paragraph 1, Schedule to the Courts of Judicature Act 1964 needs to be upgraded into a constitutional right provision like Article 226 of the Indian Constitution. An additional constitutional provision similar to Article 32 of the Indian Constitution is needed to enable individuals to access the Federal Court directly to enforce fundamental rights in urgent cases. Once these provisions are in place, they will prevent any attempt, either administratively or by legislation, to dilute or deny any of the two constitutional rights of access to justice.[119]

2 The Malaysian Judiciary has to shed its anti-fundamental rights stance once and for all. The Malaysian legal and constitutional system must be liberated from the shackles of common law and other self-imposed restrictions and move forward quickly, in accordance with its constitutional duty. The Executive and the Legislature have somehow always failed to live up to their constitutional duty of preserving, protecting and defending the Constitution. In particular, a number of fundamental postulates need to be given priority:

 (a) The Federal Constitution is the supreme law[120] of the country by virtue of Article 4(1) of the Federal Constitution. Subject to contrary provisions in the Constitution, this constitutional command must be adhered to faithfully. Nothing (be it law, administrative decision or governmental policy or procedural or substantive rule) shall defy this important constitutional mandate.[121]

 (b) The Judiciary is under a constitutional duty 'to preserve, protect and defend the Constitution' under Article 124 of the Federal Constitution read with the Sixth Schedule of the Constitution. This duty has to be discharged faithfully bearing in mind that its power is conferred under Article 121.

(c) Fundamental rights must be broadly and liberally interpreted by the courts and any restrictions thereon must be narrowly and restrictively construed.[122]

(d) The courts have no constitutional mandate to re-write the Constitution by construing fundamental rights or the provisions of the Constitution narrowly.

(e) Save as otherwise clearly and expressly provided in the Federal Constitution, the finality of fundamental rights or any important question or issue of public law is to be decided by the superior courts with the High Court as the court of first instance.[123] The administration or any other body, partly also due to the *nemo judex in causa sua* objection, must not usurp this important judicial function.

(f) As a matter of public policy, fundamental rights cannot be waived.[124]

(g) In the field of public law if a judicial precedent on the interpretation of a fundamental right or on an issue of great public interest and importance is deliberately perverse, then there is no necessity to follow it as a precedent by virtue of constitutional command or mandate derived from Articles 121 and 124 of the Federal Constitution.[125] It must be emphasized that this is an exception to the general rule of *stare decisis*.

(h) The Constitution is dynamic and the primary duty of the courts is to resolve all issues of public law by resorting to its provisions.[126] The system must not leave citizens without any relief or remedy whenever their rights or interests have been adversely affected by the administration. The courts must not shirk or abdicate their important constitutional duty whenever they are called upon to resolve important constitutional issues or disputes howsoever sensitive they are. The superior courts are also under a constitutional duty and mandate to develop their own common law that is to govern the grant of public law remedies based on the legislation of the country.[127] The rigid common law rules on judicial review may have to be modified or even discarded if they obstruct the application or development of the local public law, and applications for judicial review should not be dismissed on technical or procedural grounds in fundamental rights cases.[128]

3 For the Rule of Law to prevail, there must exist a strong and independent Bar and an informed public, with a vigorous civil society. Together these forces serve as an effective and powerful mechanism to check any abuse of government discretion.

4 A separate Administrative Court Office (ACO) should be established at all levels of the superior courts, staffed by judges with the necessary expertise who can create a corpus of administrative or public law in accordance with the spirit of the Federal Constitution. The current system is not conducive towards this end. At the moment, everything depends on the orientation of the judge

or judges assigned to a case. The current judicial trend and climate is towards construing the Federal Constitution narrowly.[129] This trend should not go on forever.[130] The Federal Constitution turned 50 years old on 31 August 2007. A positive change is urgently needed in anticipation of the full implementation of the WTO economic regime.

5   So far as the operation of *ultra vires* doctrine is concerned, we are governed by the Rule of Law, not the whims and fancies of the administrators. Discretionary powers are to be exercised for the public good and not detrimental to public interest.

6   It is vital to reiterate that public law is ever evolving and constantly adapting to meet the needs of our contemporary society, and all other laws including personal laws should move forward responsively in the era of globalization.

Regulatory regime or governance in the field of public law: Need for judicial review

As the policy of privatization is becoming the norm, and the Government plays the role of an active regulator, judicial review as to the legality or *vires* of the decisions or actions of privatized bodies remains necessary whenever members of the public or consumers are adversely affected or complain of their unlawfulness or unreasonableness. Sometimes, the dispute over the legality or constitutionality of an action or a law arises between Government and a particular privatized body. A vibrant review mechanism provides an adequate remedial system to the complainants. Such a framework should be composed of a combined system of common law and constitutional review. Some elements of the French system of *droit administratif* may also be incorporated therein.

Public law response to the WTO regime

In the WTO era, an MNC that invests in a country will demand that its investment as well as its professional expatriate staff be protected by local law. In India, Article 19(1)(g) of the Constitution expressly provides protection for the right 'to practise any profession, or to carry on any occupation, trade or business' in the territory of India. Article 19(6) empowers the Indian Government to impose reasonable restrictions on those rights in the general interest of the public. The Indian constitutional framework is touted as WTO compliant and ready. It may be recalled that the Indian Constitution contains two other provisions, Arts. 226 and 32, that guarantee an individual the right of access to the High Court and the Supreme Court respectively to enforce fundamental rights. The long arms of these two provisions may even reach commercial enterprises or companies that violate fundamental rights or commit a serious breach of the law. These bodies clearly fall within the crucial phrase 'person or authority'. A company incorporated and registered as a private company under the Companies Act is a legal entity for the purpose of the word 'person'. Such 'a person' may be the subject of a writ petition or action provided that any of its activities adversely affects any of the fundamental rights guaranteed under the Constitution. And for the purposes of Article 226 and Article 32, public interest litigation is permitted as the actual aggrieved person or persons is or are usually not in a position to come forward before the court to ventilate and vindicate his/her or their constitutional rights by reason of poverty or ignorance or any other impediment. Reverting to Part II of the Malaysian Federal Constitution, that part contains no equivalent provisions of the Indian Article 19(1)(g) and Article 19(6) and this being the case, an amendment to achieve a similar effect in the Malaysian Constitution is certainly called for in order to render the Malaysian constitutional framework WTO ready and compliant.[131] Commencing a public law action under either Article 32 or Article 226 is to be preferred rather than commencing a tort action because the public law remedies are far superior to those of private law actions owing to the breadth of those provisions and the vast power of the reviewing court to grant the appropriate remedy in favour of the applicant in order to suit the factual matrix of each individual case. The relevant enforcement agency or agencies could also be directed by the reviewing court to act accordingly in order to ensure that all parties comply with the court's orders. An administrative agency could even be held jointly liable if its failure to enforce the law led to an industrial accident or disaster. A good example is an escape of poisonous gas from a factory at night that killed many people living in the vicinity of the factory.[132] If the company is not financially able to pay the victims, then the State may be held jointly liable for its failure to regulate the factory.

Global or regional administrative law in the making?

From time to time, we come across news reports that an MNC unjustifiably resorted to unlawful practices to reap huge profits at the expense of human rights or the environment.[133] In some cases, seeking legal redress in the host countries will be meaningless because of the poor quality of the justice system. This may lead to the need for some kind of international administrative law, in which all the delinquent parties, including the governments involved, may be sued.[134] Some countries, such as India, would treat these actions as public interest litigation, in which costs may be waived and the court may waive technical common law rules that might block the application. Corporate social responsibility of the delinquent corporation and the duty of the delinquent governments to preserve, protect and defend human and fundamental rights may additionally provide a strong basis to commence such public law actions against the perpetrators.

On a smaller scale, a regional convention on human rights for Asia or within the Association of South-east Asian Nations may be helpful. Human rights activists also campaign seriously for an Asian Convention on Human Rights and Asian Court Human of Rights on the European model. Human and fundamental rights should not be left to be decided with finality by the domestic courts. A higher level or tier of law and tribunal is needed to ensure that the Rule of Law is upheld by the countries in this part of the world.

Notes

1 Emphasis added.
2 [1985] AC 374. These principles have been adopted *in toto* in Malaysia in the case of *Rama Chandran, R.v. The Industrial Court of Malaysia & Anor*, [1997] 1 AMR 6:433; [1997] 1 MLJ 145, (FC).
3 Emphasis added for reasons to be explained. In brief, the additional powers are statutory in nature but the fundamental rights are to be found in the Federal Constitution. When read together, the two components empower the High Court to engage in constitutional review.
4 Emphasis added. This is a peculiar and outstanding feature of the Indian public law upon which the Malaysian system is modelled. The supremacy of the Constitution has already been emphasized.
5 The Court of Appeal in particular adopted this approach after the landmark case of *Tan Tek Seng v. Suruhanjaya Perkhidmatan Pendidikan & Anor* [1996] 1 MLJ 261. See in particular *Sugumar Balakhrishnan v. Pengarah Immigresen Negeri Sabah & Anor* [1998] 3 MLJ 289 at 308, (CA).
6 Read with §25(2) of the Courts of Judicature Act 1964.
7 For the Court of Appeal and the Federal Court, a similar power is also exercisable when each respective court hears an appeal coming from the lower court. See the discussion thereon in the case of *Rama Chandran* [1997] 1 MLJ 145, (FC).
8 The Indian Constitution contains an additional provision not found in the Malaysian Constitution. Article 32 of the Indian Constitution confers similar powers (original jurisdiction, not appellate, and confined only to the enforcement of fundamental rights) on the Indian Supreme Court.
9 Constitutional review will be discussed in Part 3. Part 3 of this paper is built around or on the proposition that there is much justification and prospects for constitutional review in Malaysia if one is anxious and optimistic about the forward march of Malaysian public law in the not too distant future. Malaysian public law has no choice but to move forward in the face of the onslaught of the WTO regime. It would be a terrible mistake and disastrous to restrict the courts to common law review. Of course, we should not terminate common law review. Malaysia is after all a common law country and common law will stay so long as it does not come in the way of blocking the operation of the Federal Constitution. In fact the two systems can operate and co-exist harmoniously.
10 *CCSU v. Minister for Civil Service* [1985] AC 374. Prior to this, the principles applicable were those of the *Wednesbury* unreasonableness (of the super-*Wednesbury* and sub-*Wednesbury* categories) and the rules of natural justice. They are still in vogue today. *Associated Provincial Picture Houses Ltd v. Wednesbury Corp*, [1948] 1 KB 223.
11 For a classic re-statement of the rules of natural justice, see the case of *Ketua Pengarah Kastam v. Ho Kwan Seng,* [1977] 2 MLJ 152. For procedural legitimate expectation, see the case of *JP Berthelsen v. DG of Immigration*, [1987] 1 MLJ 134. For a case on the test of personal bias, see the case of *Majlis Perbandaran Pulau Pinang v. Syarikat Bekerjasama-sama Serbaguna Sungai Gelugor dengan Tanggungan*, [1999] 3 MLJ 1, (FC).
12 *Narinder Singh Jaswant Singh v. Ketua Polis Daerah Georgetown & Ors*, [1997] 1 CLJ Supp 592.
13 Sometimes also known as 'general unreasonableness'. For a broad and liberal interpretation of what amounted to *mala fides*, see the case of *Mohd Ezam v. KPN & Or Appeals*, [2002] 4 CLJ 309, (FC).
14 See the recent case of *Lam Eng Rubber Factory (M) Sdn Bhd v. Pengarah Alam Sekitar, Negeri Kedah dan Perlis & Anor*, [2005] 2 MLJ 493, (CA), on a specific aspect of non-exercise of discretion.

15 For substantive legitimate expectation, see the case of *Dr Chandra Muzaffar v. Universiti Malaya*, [2002] 5 MLJ 369.
16 For errors of law committed in the face of an ouster clause, see *Syarikat Kenderaan Melayu Kelantan Bhd v. Transport Workers' Union* [1995], 2 MLJ 317. For the application of the *ultra vires* doctrine in respect of subsidiary legislation, see MP Jain, *Administrative Law*, Kuala Lumpur: *Malayan Law Journal*, 1997, V–VII.
17 See also the relevant parts of the paper in this volume by Prof. Johannes Chan, Dean, Faculty of Law, HKU.
18 Rights means any fundamental right or human right or any right recognizable by law.
19 Sometimes, it may also arise in an appeal. For example, in the recent case of *Kok Wah Kuan v. PP*, [2007] 5 MLJ 174, (CA).
20 *Om Kumar & Others v. Union of India*, [2001] 2 SCC 386, Paragraph 28.
21 See *dicta* in the case of *R. (on the application of Begum (by her litigation friend, Rahman) (Respondent) v. Headteacher and Governors of Denbigh High School (Appellant)*, [2006] UKHL 15, Paragraph 51.
22 See the principles enunciated in *Om Kumar v. India*, AIR 2000 SC 3689 or *Union of India v. G. Ganayutham*, AIR 1997 SC 3387.
23 *Preston v. IRC*, [1985] 2 ALL ER 326, (HL). See also, *Sugumar Balakhrishnan v. Pengarah Immigresen Negeri Sabah & Anor*, [1998] 3 MLJ 289, (CA); [2002] 3 MLJ 72, (FC). It may be pointed out that the ruling of the Court of Appeal (Malaysia) on substantive unfairness as a ground of judicial review constituted a better view in the field of public law because the doctrine of fairness or unfairness in its constitutional dimension (as contrasted with *CCSU* or *Wednesbury* review) is a broad one based on the authorities cited and relied upon by the Court of Appeal.
24 Including substantive legitimate expectation and estoppel. From the perspective of common law review, it includes abuse of discretion and non-exercise of discretion. Applied extensively, it is hoped that the common law review may eventually be subsumed under the sub-head of constitutional review based on the proposition that Article 8(1) of the Federal Constitution is the basis or source of the *ultra vires* doctrine in Malaysia.
25 See also the South African Constitution (Section 34 and Section 38) and Fijian Constitution (Section 41). South Africa has probably the best of the modern day constitutions. The Fijian Constitution was drafted after the Indian, Malaysian and South African constitutions. A Malaysian Judge was appointed to advise the drafting of Fijian Constitution. On the whole, the Fijian model is better than that of Malaysia. In particular, the right to access the High Court (under Section 41) for the enforcement of fundamental rights in Fiji is itself a fundamental right.
26 Section 25(2) of the Courts of Judicature Act 1964. That provision confers additional powers on the High Court which are enumerated in Paragraph 1 of the Schedule to the Act. The position of Singapore is similar to that of Malaysia. However, the High Court in Singapore is yet to invoke its additional powers of judicial review.
27 Note the difference with that of the position in India, Fiji and S. Africa. This may possibly constitute the weakness of the Malaysian law, depending on how one views the matter in question, namely, positively or negatively.
28 See a recent case of the Indian Supreme Court. *I.R. Coelho v. State of Tamil Nadu & Ors* [2007] INSC 31.
29 *Sugumar Balakhrishnan v. Pengarah Immigresen Negeri Sabah & Anor*, [1998] 3 MLJ 289, (CA); [2002] 3 MLJ 72, (FC). *Utra Badi a/l K. Perumal & Anor v. Lembaga Tatatertib Perkhidmatan Awam*, [1998] 3 MLJ 676, (HC); [2000] 3 MLJ 281, (CA); [2001] 2 MLJ 417, (FC) is another example.
30 *Tan Tek Seng v. Suruhanjaya Perkhidmatan Pendidikan & Anor*, [1996] 1 MLJ 261 constituted the starting point for constitutional review in Malaysia. This case ushered in a new era or a new constitutional dimension in judicial review in the field of public law in Malaysia.

31 Malaysia does not have a similar provision in its Courts of Judicature Act nor in the Federal Constitution.
32 MP Jain, *Indian Constitutional Law*, (Nagpur: Wadhwa, 2003), Vol. 1 & 2 , pp 460, 461, 462 & 1926.
33 For a good discussion of the Indian jurisprudence on Arts. 226 and 32, read MP Jain, *Indian Constitutional Law*, (Nagpur: Wadhwa, 2003), Vol. 1, pp.461–508. Article 14 (India) is *in pari materia* with Article 8(1) of the Malaysian Constitution. Article 21 (India) is *in pari materia* with Article 5(1) of the Malaysian Constitution. This is the life and personal liberty provision.
34 Including that on Article 32. It must be noted that Malaysia does not have a provision similar to that of Indian Article 32 in its law.
35 From Arts. 5 to 13: Article 5 (life and personal liberty); Article 6 (prohibition of slavery and forced labour); Article 7 (prohibition of retrospective criminal laws and repeated trials); Article 8 (equality); Article 9 (freedom of movement and prohibition of banishment); Article 10 (Freedom of speech, assembly and association); Article 11 (freedom of religion); Article 12 (rights in respect of education); and Article 13 (rights to property).
36 [1996] 1 MLJ 261.
37 *Janamohan Das v. State of Orissa*, AIR 1993 Orissa 157 – the liquor disaster case. *George Mampilly v. State of Kerala*, AIR 1985 Kerala 24 – the case of the sale of liquor in polythene bags. See also, n. 40.
38 Remedy here includes the grant of an injunctive or a declaratory relief.
39 [1996] 1 MLJ 481, at 543–44.
40 *DK Basu v. W. Bengal*, AIR 1997 SC 610.
41 For an order of interim and *ex gratia* monetary payment in favour of the victim of a public tort, see the Indian case of *Naresh Dutt Tyagi v. UP*, (1995) Supp(3) SCC 144.
42 *Rama Chandran, R.v. The Industrial Court of Malaysia & Anor*, [1997] 1 MLJ 145, (FC).
43 See *dictum* of the Malaysian Court of Appeal in *Hong Leong Equipment Sdn. Bhd. v. Liew Fook Chuan & anor appeal*, [1996] 1 MLJ 481, pp.543–44.
44 *Vishaka v. State of Rajasthan*, AIR 1997 SC; *DK Basu v. State of West Bengal*, AIR 1997 SC 416. Perhaps in the field of commercial law, a law-making power of this sort is needed in order to prevent the courts from alleging that it is powerless to deal with a particular complaint because there is a lacuna in the law.
45 *Sagong bin Tasi & Ors v. Kerajaan Negeri Selangor & Ors*, [2002] 2 MLJ 591, (HC); [2005] 6 MLJ 289, (CA).
46 *Vishaka v. State of Rajasthan*, AIR 1997 SC 3011; 6 SCC 241.
47 *T. Gattaiah v. Commissioner of Labour*, (1981) Lab IC 942; *Union Carbide Corp v. India*, (1991) 4 SCC 584. In the former, a private company retrenching its workers was held to be bound by the law protecting the retrenchment of its workers. In the latter, a settlement fund by the factory was insufficient to compensate the victims of a gas leak, the Indian Supreme Court ordered the Indian Government to make good the deficiency because it had allowed the factory to operate without complying with the law.
48 See in particular, MP Jain, *Indian Constitutional Law*, (Nagpur: Wadhwa, 2003), vol.1, pp.476–81.
49 *People's Union for Democratic Rights v. India*, AIR 1982 SC 1473 (*Asiad Games Village* Case); *Labourers Working on the Salal Hydro-Project v. Jammu & Kashmir*, AIR 1984 SC 177 (*Salal Hydro Electric Dam* case).
50 *The Bonded Labour*'s case, AIR 1984 SC 802.
51 *Hussainara Khatoon v. HS, State of Bihar*, AIR 1979 SC 1360.
52 AIR 1979 SC 1360 at 1369; (1980) 1 SCC 81.
53 (1988) 4 SCC 226.
54 AIR 1983 SC 378.

55 AIR 1996 SC 2715.
56 See also *MC Metha* – (also known as the *Ganga Water Pollution*'s case, (1987) 4 SCC 463.
57 *MC Metha v. India*, (1998) 9 SCC 93.
58 AIR 1985 SC 652.
59 AIR 1985 Kerala 24.
60 AIR 1993 Orissa 157.
61 AIR 1986 SC 825.
62 *R.v. SS for Foreign and Commonwealth Affairs, ex p. World Development Ltd*, [1995] 1 All ER 611. It is to be noted that this is not an Indian case.
63 See MP Jain, *Indian Constitutional Law*, Nagpur: Wadhwa, 2003, Vol. 2, pp.1551 & 1554.
64 Namely, the additional powers of judicial review of the High Court as provided for in Paragraph 1, Schedule to the Act. There were earlier sporadic attempts to the same effect but not on the bedrock of the Paragraph 1 powers.
65 *Tan Tek Seng v. Suruhanjaya Perkhidmatan Pendidikan & Anor*, [1996] 1 MLJ 261, (CA).
66 *Hong Leong Equipment Sdn. Bhd. v. Liew Fook Chuan & anor appeal*, [1995] 3 MLJ 742, (HC); [1996] 1 MLJ 481, (CA).
67 *Sugumar Balakhrishnan v. Pengarah Immigresen Negeri Sabah & Anor*, [1998] 3 MLJ 289.
68 *Utra Badi a/l K. Perumal & Anor v. Lembaga Tatatertib Perkhidmatan Awam*, [1998] 3 MLJ 676, (HC); [2000] 3 MLJ 281, (CA).
69 *Rama Chandran, R.v. The Industrial Court of Malaysia & Anor*, [1997] 1 AMR 6:433; [1997] 1 MLJ 145, (FC).
70 *Abdul Ghani Haroon v. KPN & Anor Application (No. 3)*, [2001] 2 CLJ 709, (HC).
71 *Abdul Ghani Haroon v. KPN & Anor Application (No. 4)*, [2001] 3 CLJ 606, (HC).
72 The fairness limb is composed of equality before the law clause and the equal protection clause.
73 Departing from the usual rule of practice of the Industrial Court. The usual practice is to award damages for loss of wages up to the maximum limit of 24 months for dismissal without just cause and excuse.
74 See also, *Mohd Ezam v. KPN & Or Appeals*, [2002] 4 CLJ 309, FC. In this case, *mala fide* was construed broadly to include a situation if the arrest and detention was made for a 'collateral' or 'ulterior' purpose other than what the legislature intended in passing the law of preventive detention.
75 [2007] 5 MLJ 174, (CA).
76 This sub-section provided that 'in lieu of a sentence of death, the Court shall order a person convicted of an offence to be detained in a prison during the pleasure of ... the Yang di-Pertuan Agong if the offence was committed in the Federal Territory of Kuala Lumpur'. This section applied to a child who had been found guilty of the criminal offence of murder under section 302 of the Penal Code.
77 The Yang di-Pertuan Agong.
78 Being nevertheless still housed in Article 121 of the Federal Constitution despite the fact the expression 'judicial power' was removed therefrom by Act A704.
79 Although this case was not a case on judicial review, it is contended that the same issues raised before the Court of Appeal could nevertheless be raised in an application for judicial review. See the earlier case of *Sivarasa Rasiah v. Badan Peguam Malaysia & Anor*, [2002] 2 MLJ 413, (CA).
80 23rd October 2007. Of particular interest is the judgement of His Lordship Richard Malanjum, CJ (S & S) citing and relying on the basic feature doctrine for the first time.
81 *Adong bin Kuwau & Ors v. Kerajaan Negeri Johor & Anor*, [1997] 1 MLJ 418, (HC); [1998] 2 MLJ 158, (CA). See also, *Sagong bin Tasi & Ors v. Kerajaan Negeri*

Selangor & Ors, [2002] 2 MLJ 591, (HC); [2005] 6 MLJ 289, (CA). These cases used Arts. 5(1), 8(1) and 13 of the Federal Constitution for the purpose of protecting the proprietary rights and interests of the natives under their respective customs particularly those over the land which they settled, cultivated and forayed, the loss or deprivation of which would adversely affect their livelihood.

82 A couple of cases could be given here. *Loh Kooi Choon v. Government of Malaysia*, [1977] 2 MLJ 187; *Loh Wai Kong v. Government of Malaysia & Ors*, [1978] 2 MLJ 175.
83 [2002] 3 MLJ 72.
84 [2001] 2 MLJ 417.
85 *Kekatong Sdn Bhd v. Danaharta Urus Sdn Bhd* [2003] 3 MLJ 1, (CA); [2004] 2 MLJ 257, (FC). In this case, the Court of Appeal used Article 8(1) as the source of the right of equal access to justice to strike down an anti-injunction provision (s. 72) in Pengurusan Danaharta Nasional Berhad Act 1998 as unconstitutional.
86 *Karam Singh* [1969] 2 MLJ 129.
87 *Loh Wai Kong* [1978] 2 MLJ 175.
88 *Loh Kooi Choon* [1977] 2 MLJ 187.
89 *Beatrice a/p AT Fernandez v. Sistem Penerbangan Malaysia & Ors* [2004] 4 MLJ 466, (CA); [2005] 3 MLJ 681, (FC).
90 *Air India v. Nergesh Meerza*, AIR 1981 SC 1829.
91 *Nar Singh Pal v. India*, AIR 2000 SC 1401.
92 [2007] 2 AMR 395, (CA).
93 The retreat from the Rule of Law could also be deduced from the use of defamation suit to suppress free speech and the prosecution of a social activist who spoke up on some alleged human right violations by a certain detaining authority.
94 In the case of the Court of Appeal, see, for example, the case of *Heng Peo*. See n. 104.
95 In Malaysia, see the oath of office prescribed in the Sixth Schedule of the Federal Constitution.
96 For example, *Chai Choon Hon v. Ketua Polis Daerah Kampar* [1986] 2 MLJ 203.
97 But this was the rare view taken by the Federal Court in *Rama Chandran* [1997] 1 MLJ 145, 198. In the words of the court 'In doing so, I trust that we have pointed the way to new horizons in the forward march of judicial review.' (Per Edgar Joseph Jr, FCJ, as his Lordship then was.) There are other weaknesses present in the Malaysian constitutional system that will be discussed later under the sub-heading of 'The Way Forward'.
98 See the approach of Malaysian courts in the recent case of *Beatrice Fernandez* [2004] 4 MLJ 466, (CA); [2005] 3 MLJ 681, (FC). See also, *Karam Singh v. Menteri Hal Ehwal Dalam Negeri Malaysia* [1969] 2 MLJ 129. On the other hand, it must be reiterated that the Indian case law in particular cited and discussed in this part of the paper are most enlightening. See also, *Vishaka v. State of Rajasthan*, AIR 1997 SC; *Derbyshire CC v. Times Newspapers Ltd.* [1993] AC 534; *Case of Steel and Morris v. UK* (2005) EctHR 68416/10; (2005) TLR 93. For an idea of the rapid advancement of the public law jurisprudence in South Africa in the post-Apartheid era, visit the website of its Constitutional Court at http://www.constitutionalcourt.org.za/site/home.htm, Accessed August 1, 2008. Common law countries operating under written constitutions could take a leaf from the rapid progress made by the South African Constitutional Court ever since February 1995. In particular, see sections 2, 7, 22, 23, 24, 28, 32, 33, 34, 36, 38, 39 and 167 of the South African Constitution. In respect of South African statutes, see Promotion of Administrative Justice Act 2000 (PAJA), Promotion of Access to Information Act 2000 (PAIA), Promotion of Equality and Prevention of Unfair Discrimination Act 2000 (PEPUDA).
99 Its predecessor was FIDA, 1967.
100 Now known as Tenaga National Berhad.

101 Sept. 2006.
102 It is argued that affirmative action to assist the poorer sections of the non-Bumiputras to progress socially and economically could be based on the combined reading of Arts. 5(1) and 8(1) of the Federal Constitution in particular.
103 The target date has now been shifted to 2057. From newspaper reports of the Prime Minister's press statement on 15 June 2007. The front page of *The Star* newspaper reported under the heading of 'Beyond 2020'.
104 This policy has since been extended and renamed as the National Development Policy.
105 For more information on privatization, See the following site: http://www.epu.jpm. my/New%20Folder/application%20and%20approval/priva.htm, Accessed August 1, 2008.
106 See *The Star*, front page news entitled 'Beyond 2020'. 15 June 2007.
107 Three recent development plans are worth mention here. The masterplan for the Northern Corridor Economic Region (NCER), a development initiative expected to draw investments worth RM177 billion from 2007 to 2025, was launched in July this year. The Iskandar Development Region (IDR) was launched in November 2006 and designated as a special economic zone in the South. It is expected to draw investment up to 10 billion ringgits over a period of 15 years. The East Coast Economic Region (ECER) was launched in October 2007. This development plan is expected to attract RM112 billion of investment projects over the next 15 years.
108 *Syarikat Kenderaan Melayu Kelantan Bhd v. Transport Workers' Union* [1995] 2 MLJ 317.
109 *RD Shetty v. The International Airport Authority*, AIR 1979 SC 1628; *Sukhdev Singh v. Bhagatram*, AIR 1975 SC 1331.
110 *OSK & Partners v. Tengku Noone Aziz* [1983] 1 MLJ 179. Kuala Lumpur Stock Exchange (KLSE), a non-statutory body, registered under the Companies Act 1965 and subject to the control and direction of the Minister was subject to judicial review when it exercised its power to discipline a member of the KLSE. See also the English case of *R. v. Panel Take-Overs & Mergers, ex p. Datafin & Prudential Bache Securities Inc.* [1987] 1 All ER 564.
111 Emphasis added.
112 Meaning an instrumentality of the State. Within the scope of Paragraph 1, Schedule to the Courts of Judicature Act 1964.
113 *Wong Ah Suan v. Sarawak Electricity Supply Corp.* [1982] 2 MLJ 89.
114 *Tang Kwor Ham & Ors v. Pengurusan Danaharta Nasional Bhd. & Ors* [2006] 5 MLJ 60, 79–80.
115 *Air India v. Nergesh Meerza*, AIR 1981 SC 1829. The Malaysian case of *Beatrice a/p AT Fernandez v. Sistem Penerbangan Malaysia & Ors* [2004] 4 MLJ 466, (CA); [2005] 3 MLJ 681, (FC) is simply a perverse decision.
116 For example, if the issue raised touches on the implementation of the New Economic Policy. In such a case, the court is likely to show judicial self-restraint by declining to intervene.
117 See rule 2(4), of the Rules of the High Court 1980. *QSR Brands Bhd v. Suruhanjaya Sekuriti & Anor* [2006] 3 MLJ 164, (CA).
118 It must be pointed out that the list is not exhaustive. *Dai-Ichi Electronics (M) Sdn Bhd v. Tenaga Nasional Bhd.* [1996] 4 MLJ 506. *Claybricks & Tiles Sdn Bhd v. Tenaga Nasional Berhad* [2007] 1 MLJ 217. Of the two cases cited, the former represented a better view of the issue raised. See also, *Public Textiles v. LLN* [1976] 2 MLJ 58 on the possible operation of the doctrine of estoppel against LLN. See also, *TNB v. Perwaja Steel*, 15 Aug 1995, High Court, unreported. See also the case of *TNB v. Tekali Prospecting Sdn. Bhd.* [2002] 2 MLJ 707, (CA), on the need to exhaust the statutory appellate procedure before moving the High Court for judicial review.

119 See one additional amendment needed to render the Federal Constitution relevant in tandem with the move towards globalization. Other necessary amendments needed include a Preamble to the Federal Constitution and an additional part similar to Part IV of the Indian Constitution on Directive Principles of State Policy and Basic Duties.
120 As opposed to parliamentary supremacy which does not exist under the Malaysian system. It is thus a fallacy to argue that Malaysia is an Islamic state by virtue of the combined effect of Arts. 3(1), 4(1) and 121(1A) of the Federal Constitution.
121 As to the position of any pre-Merdeka law that violates the Constitution, see Article 162(6). See also the case of *Kerajaan Negri Selangor & Ors v. Sagong Tasi & Ors* [2005] 4 CLJ 169, (CA).
122 *Datuk James Wong Kin Min* [1976] 2 MLJ 245 at p.251. Reverting to the constitutional power and duty of the reviewing courts (under Arts. 121 and 124 of the Federal Constitution respectively read with the additional powers of judicial review under Paragraph 1 of the Schedule to the Courts of Judicature Act 1964) to administer, for example, social-economic justice on behalf of the poor, weaker and marginalized groups (including protecting the rights of women, children and foreign labourers) in our society, the Court of Appeal cases of *Sagong Tasi* and *Adong bin Kuwau* clearly indicate that the Malaysian Judiciary is mindful of its constitutional power and duty to protect the customary rights of the natives. However, the same was not exercised in *Beatrice Fernandez* and *Sugumar Balakrishnan*. In *Sugumar Balakrishnan* [2002] 3 MLJ 72, (FC), for example, an individual lawyer fought against the powerful State government which had abused its power under the Immigration Act, but the Federal Court threw its weight behind the State Government.
123 Reading Arts. 4(1), 121, 124 and Part II of the Federal Constitution together.
124 *David Tan Boon Chee* [1980] 2 MLJ 116. *Nar Singh Pal*, AIR 2000 SC 1401.
125 For example, see the case of *SKMK* where the Court of Appeal declined to follow the earlier authority of *SEA Firebricks*. See also the case of *Tan Tek Seng* where the Court of Appeal refused to follow *Karam Singh* on the question of whether the word 'law' in Article 5(1) of the Federal Constitution included procedural law. A further proposition must also be added. That the word 'law' in the phrase 'save in accordance with law' in Part II of the Federal Constitution denotes not any law *simpliciter* but a law that complies with the requirement of fairness and reasonableness (both substantive and procedural) in Article 8(1) of the Federal Constitution.
126 See *dictum* to this effect in *Tan Tek Seng* at [1996] 1 MLJ 261 at p.281, (CA).
127 See *dictum* to this effect in *Hong Leong Equipment* at [1996] 1 MLJ 481 at p.543, (CA).
128 See *dictum* of the Court of Appeal in *Sivarasa Rasiah* [2002] 2 MLJ 413, 422.
129 *Beatrice Fernandez* (CA & FC); *Ooi Kean Thong & Or* (FC); *Heng Peo* (CA); *Sugumar Balakrishnan* (FC); *Utra Badi* (FC).
130 Recent calls for the establishment of a Judicial Commission in Malaysia to appoint the judges of the superior courts may be viewed as timely and appropriate.
131 Another amendment is needed for Directive Principles of State Policy and Basic Duties. See Part IV of the Indian Constitution.
132 *Union Carbide Corp v. India* (1991) 4 SCC 584.
133 For example, engaging bonded labour, practising slavery or paying the workers below minimal wages; or causing water and air pollution.
134 For information on Global Administrative Law, please visit the webpage of NYU Law School on the GAL Project.

13 The judicialization of governance
The case of Singapore

Jolene Lin

Introduction

Singapore is often viewed as that tiny island in Southeast Asia that has worked a miracle of transformation from a poor ex-colony into an economically powerful nation within a relatively short span of time. A significant, if not dominant, feature of Singapore's post-independence economic success is the role the government has played. It is widely acknowledged that Singapore's economic rise has been largely orchestrated and driven by the ruling government's singular pursuit of economic growth as a key platform of the country's strategy for survival as a viable nation state.[1] Like the other countries of the "East Asian miracle," a term coined by the World Bank in its famous 1993 study, the Singapore government has not followed the model of a passive or minimalist state but has intervened extensively in the nation's economy and played a highly active role in promoting exports and supporting specific industries.[2] The concept of the developmental state was formulated to explain the exceptional growth performance of some Asian economies, primarily Japan, South Korea, Taiwan, Hong Kong, and Singapore.

> ... The core features of the developmental state may ... be described as the intervention of the state in the economy but under the form of policies that are credible and oriented towards growth, not of the ownership and direct control by the state of large pieces of the economy.

Thus, for example, active development strategies are pursued, especially industrial policies such as targeted taxation, incentives for the banking sector and training in technology.[3] By this description, Singapore is a developmental state because of the dominant role played by its government in coordinating all aspects of economic and social activity in pursuance of developmental goals.

What is interesting about the developmental state of Singapore, however, is the degree of resemblance it bears to an administrative state.[4] Singapore is the quintessential administrative state: government ministries, agencies, and statutory boards form a regulatory labyrinth covering healthcare, environmental planning and conservation, public housing, trade development, financial markets, and almost every other conceivable aspect of caring for the citizen from cradle to grave.[5] The reaction to the rise of the administrative state in the UK has been the development of administrative law as the courts seek to protect the rights and liberties of the individual against the omnipresent and omnipotent state.[6] In the United States, there has been a similar judicial reaction but prompted more by concerns to prevent the unconstitutional concentration of power in the executive branch of government.[7] The judicial check becomes all the more important when the legislature effectively grants significant law-making powers to the executive because, among other reasons, it lacks the time, resources, and expertise to pass the minutiae of laws, rules and regulations required for the proper functioning of the state's various regulatory regimes.

This is where the experience of Singapore as an administrative state departs from the historical trajectory seen elsewhere. Despite the presence of a large regulatory machinery that affects all citizens in one way or another, administrative law is a relatively undeveloped area of Singapore law. The judiciary is not often asked to pronounce on the legality of administrative action which leads to the judiciary playing a relatively small role in regulatory governance and its limited influence on executive decision-making. Further, the judiciary exercises significant self-restraint and has demonstrated great reluctance to interfere with executive decisions. With the judicial branch playing a limited role in regulatory governance, Parliament granting extensive law-making powers to the executive branch (as evidenced by the wealth of delegated legislation that is promulgated by the executive branch, including informal rules and codes of practice by statutory boards), regulatory governance in Singapore may be described as executive-dominated. One of the purposes of this chapter is to analyze whether Singapore has "departed" from the historical trajectory of the typical administrative state whereby increasing regulation has led to a more active role for the judiciary, or whether the "judicialization of governance" in Singapore is yet to come. For the purposes of this chapter, "judicialization" refers to the expansion of the role of the courts and the use of court-like processes in regulatory regimes which may eventually lead to the displacement of technical, bureaucratic, or political decision-making about regulation with judicial decision-making through courts and tribunals.[8] A regulatory regime, in turn, can be taken to possess three basic components. First, the setting of standards; second, processes for monitoring compliance with the standards; and finally, enforcement mechanisms to ensure compliance.

It will be suggested that extensive governmental regulation or the existence of an executive-dominated regulatory framework in Singapore has not prompted the same reactions to the rise of the administrative state seen elsewhere because the administrative apparatus in Singapore was created from the outset intentionally to pursue the national goal of economic survival. While the rise of the regulatory state in the UK, for example, has been described as a "Trojan horse"[9] of increasing governmental intervention in an unsuspecting society, suggesting a certain disdain or skepticism of it (and therefore the need to keep it in check), regulation in Singapore is not seen in quite the same fashion. Because economic and social regulation in Singapore is almost entirely oriented toward the developmental agenda, which has been successfully promoted as a shared national aspiration for all sectors of Singaporean society, there has not been that demand for external checks on the regulatory machinery. Instead, it appears to be conceded that the executive branch needs all the powers, discretion, and flexibility it can have to pursue economic development for Singapore. Within this paradigm, the overarching goal of regulation is economic survival and progress. Law may be said to be an instrument of regulation, its role being facilitative of economic development and the role of the courts is to maintain the rule of law that is necessary for creating and maintaining an attractive business environment. In this regard, the judiciary may be described as "... well attuned to the national policy goals of [its government] and [does] not wish to undermine them."[10] Thus, in the area of regulatory governance, the courts are not often asked to scrutinize executive action and when they are, tend to restrict themselves to "narrow" judicial review, that is, ensuring that powers devolved from Parliament onto the executive are exercised in accordance with the law, primarily through applying the low-threshold test of *Wednesbury* unreasonableness in the scrutiny of administrative decision-making processes.[11] Finally, various methods of oversight and control over interest groups also prevent the emergence of public interest litigation in areas of social regulation, such as consumer protection, land use planning, and environmental conservation.

As regulation in various economic and social spheres becomes more complex, it is unlikely that the judiciary will perceive a more active role for itself. The courts have consistently maintained that their role in governance is a limited one of ensuring that a regulatory agency (usually the statutory board, in Singapore's case) operates within its statutory mandate and adheres to certain well-established principles of good governance in administrative law. As regulatory regimes and policy-making becomes more complex, the judiciary is likely to continue to defer to the "experts" of the regulatory authority, a la *Chevron* style.[12] International factors such as WTO requirements for administrative proceedings will not have a significant impact on Singapore's regulatory governance as the rule of law in the commercial and related fields is already well-established and will continue to be upheld with the highest rigor as the maintenance of a sound business environment is seen as critical to Singapore's survival.

Part I of this chapter describes the rise of the administrative state in Singapore as the creation of a comprehensive regulatory framework was essential to carrying out the country's development plans and socio-economic programs. Part II provides an overview of the administrative law framework in Singapore. An attempt will be made to situate the analysis of the role and performance of the judiciary within that of the wider socio-economic context described in Part I. Part III will explore the various reasons for the present state of judicial review in Singapore. These reasons include the prevailing regulatory culture that discourages confrontation between the regulator and the regulated, and the absence of other elements of good governance such as rights of public participation in administrative rule-making and freedom of information within the overall architecture of regulation and governance in Singapore. Part IV concludes that the "judicalization of governance" has not happened because of the unique social, economic, and political conditions in Singapore. Gazing into the crystal ball, one might fathom some seeds of change but only time will tell what the future holds.

Part I: The origins of the Singapore administrative state

The industrialization program

On the eve of independence in 1965, high unemployment, squalid living conditions, and social discontent was rife in Singapore.[13] How the government was going to ensure this young nation's survival was a troubling question. Having lost a large domestic market with the separation from Malaysia, import-oriented industrialization was no longer an option. Export-oriented industrialization was therefore the only choice Singapore had if it wanted to lift itself out of poverty. Singapore therefore embarked on a national industrialization strategy based on the recommendations of the *United Nations Proposed Industrialization Programme for the State of Singapore* which emphasized three approaches: (1) the disciplining of a politically activated and strike-prone labor force; (2) the development of industries which were natural for Singapore in light of its port and geographical location; and (3) the attraction of foreign and multinational investment.[14]

Such an industrialization program required state activism of an extensive nature. Hence began the process of active state intervention in areas as diverse as labor, social and physical infrastructure, investment in human resources, industry and services, to create and maintain favorable economic conditions in Singapore in order to attract the multinational corporations (MNCs).[15] For example, extensive investment incentives were offered to foreign investors to entice them to set up operations in Singapore as well as to later persuade them to transform the nature of their investments from lower to higher-technology industries. No other country in the world at that time was willing to offer such attractive tax incentives.[16] In the area of education, the government had two main objectives. The first was to mass produce the sort of trained manpower required by the government-targeted clusters of industries.[17] The other objective was to respond to the specific manpower needs of certain MNCs or clusters of MNCs, usually by promoting several joint training programs.

As part of the industrialization program, the creation of an extensive regulatory apparatus was intended to regulate all aspects of social and economic life in Singapore to create conditions attractive to foreign investors. It should be noted that this would not have been possible without the aid of an efficient and incorrupt bureaucracy.[18] From the outset, the civil service was enlisted in the ruling government's national developmental agenda.[19] It is widely perceived to be competent, honest, and efficient in formulating and implementing national policies. In fact, the role of the elite of Singapore's civil service is often analogized to the system of mandarins that served in the Chinese empire. They are selected after the most demanding examinations, induced into a life-long service and are entrusted by the leaders with considerable powers and discretion.[20] Arguably, among the reasons for the few legal challenges of administrative action in Singapore is the relatively high regard that the civil service enjoys and the almost indistinguishable fusion of the civil service and the ruling government in the eyes of the public. In the words of S. Rajaratnam, Singapore's first Foreign Minister, "... we involved [the civil servants] in something far more challenging and satisfying than just being civil servants – building houses, roads, keeping the city clean. They were being stretched. It did not take long before we established a close link between us and the civil service. In fact, after the first two elections, the PAP became really an administration. It was no longer a party. And the civil service became a part of that." [21]

Statutory boards

Apart from the civil service (that is, the ministries), many government activities and powers are performed by statutory boards in Singapore.[22] Statutory boards are autonomous corporate bodies established by Acts of Parliament. The statutory board has been defined as "... a legal entity which is separate from the civil service and does not enjoy the legal privileges and immunities of government departments. However, the latter disadvantage is offset by the greater autonomy and flexibility enjoyed by statutory boards in the performance of their functions as they are responsible for their law suits, agreements and contracts, as well as the acquisition and disposal of property in their own names."[23] Statutory boards also tend to enjoy a greater degree of autonomy and flexibility in their day-to-day operations and financial matters than the civil service proper. However, they are theoretically under the supervision of the Minister of the statutory board's parent ministry and therefore answerable to Parliament.[24]

From the outset, the statutory board was the choice vehicle for implementing Singapore's economic development plans and socio-economic programs because it was seen as being more flexible and able to perform efficiently the tasks of national development without encountering the constraints faced by the civil service.[25] Today, the ministries are seen as the entities responsible for the formulation of policies, which are then executed by the statutory boards under their purview. The first statutory board established in Singapore is the Housing and Development Board (HDB) which is responsible for public housing in Singapore.[26] The success of the HDB and the Economic Development Board led to the establishment of several other statutory boards, such that there is one in almost every important socio-economic field. To sum it up, "[the state] played the all-embracing roles of entrepreneur, regulator, venture capitalist and facilitator. Through the visible hands of nearly 100 statutory boards and several hundred government-linked companies the state itself practiced economic development."[27] From an administrative law perspective, that these statutory boards also carry out the type of regulatory functions that are typically the responsibility of government agencies is problematic if these statutory boards are not subject to some sort of oversight akin to that of government departments. In 1997, the Singapore High Court, in the case of *Lines International Holdings Pte Ltd v. Singapore Tourist Promotion Board and Port of Singapore Authority*,[28] recognized the need for statutory boards to formulate policies, guidelines, or such other "quasi-laws" which are essential for the operation of the modern state, particularly the conducting of governmental policy through quasi-autonomous bodies operating at arm's length from the government. Importantly, the courts also ruled on the need to hold these rule-makers accountable. In this regard, the court's articulation of conditions that validated the adoption of a general policy by a statutory board indicates that the courts regard such guidelines as somewhat akin to delegated legislation.[29]

It will be useful at this juncture to gain a sense of the "players" in Singapore's regulatory landscape and the predominance of statutory boards. The list of ministries and statutory boards below does not include government-linked companies (GLCs) which have played a critical role in Singapore's economical development but do not perform regulatory functions per se.[30]

Government ministries[31]

- Ministry of Defence (MINDEF)
- Ministry of Education (MOE)
- Ministry of Finance (MOF)
- Ministry of Foreign Affairs (MFA)
- Ministry of Health (MOH)
- Ministry of Home Affairs (MHA)
- Ministry of Information, Communications and the Arts (MICA)
- Ministry of Law (MINLAW)
- Ministry of Manpower (MOM)
- Ministry of National Development (MND)
- Ministry of the Environment and Water Resources (MEWR)
- Ministry of Trade and Industry (MTI)
- Ministry of Transport (MOT)
- Prime Minister's Office (PMO)[32]

Statutory boards

- Accounting and Corporate Regulatory Authority (ACRA)
- Agency for Science, Technology and Research (A*STAR)
- Agri-Food & Veterinary Authority of Singapore (AVA)
- Board of Architects (BOA)
- Building and Construction Authority (BCA)
- Central Provident Fund Board (CPFB)
- Civil Aviation Authority of Singapore (CAAS)
- Civil Service College (CSC)
- Competition Commission of Singapore (CCS)
- Defence Science & Technology Agency (DSTA)
- Economic Development Board (EDB)
- Energy Market Authority (EMA)
- Health Promotion Board (HPB)
- Health Sciences Authority (HSA)
- Hindu Advisory Board (HAB)

- Hindu Endowments Board (HEB)
- Hotels Licensing Board (HLB)
- Housing and Development Board (HDB)
- Infocomm Development Authority of Singapore (IDA)
- Inland Revenue Authority of Singapore (IRAS)
- Institute of Southeast Asian Studies (ISEAS)
- Institute of Technical Education (ITE)
- Intellectual Property Office of Singapore (IPOS)
- International Enterprise Singapore (IESINGAPORE)
- JTC Corporation (JTC)
- Land Transport Authority (LTA)
- Majlis Ugama Islam Singapura (MUIS)
- Maritime and Port Authority of Singapore (MPA)
- Media Development Authority (MDA)
- Monetary Authority of Singapore (MAS)
- Nanyang Polytechnic (NYP)
- National Arts Council (NAC)
- National Council of Social Service (NCSS)
- National Environment Agency (NEA)
- National Heritage Board (NHB)
- National Library Board (NLB)
- National Parks Board (NPARKS)
- Ngee Ann Polytechnic (NP)
- People's Association (PA)
- Preservation of Monuments Board (PMB)
- Professional Engineers Board, Singapore (PEB)
- Public Transport Council (PTC)
- Public Utilities Board (PUB)
- Republic Polytechnic (RP)
- Science Centre Board (SCB)
- Sentosa Development Corporation (SDC)
- Sikh Advisory Board (SAB)
- Singapore Corporation of Rehabilitative Enterprises (SCORE)
- Singapore Dental Council (SDC)
- Singapore Examinations and Assessment Board (SEAB)
- Singapore Labour Foundation (SLF)
- Singapore Land Authority (SLA)
- Singapore Medical Council (SMC)
- Singapore Nursing Board (SNB)
- Singapore Polytechnic (SP)
- Singapore Sports Council (SSC)
- Singapore Totalisator Board (SINGTOTE)
- Singapore Tourism Board (STB)
- Singapore Workforce Development Agency (SWDA)
- Standards, Productivity and Innovation Board Spring Singapore (SPRING)

- TCM Practitioners Board (TCMB)
- Temasek Polytechnic (TP)
- Urban Redevelopment Authority (URA)

The role of law

In addition to creating a regulatory regime to facilitate economic development, the law itself was also a facilitative tool for growth in Singapore. In her study, *Eyes on the Prize*, Connie Carter has described Singapore's economic development laws as "mature policies" as government policies were essentially a few steps from becoming law.[33] She observes that each People's Action Party (PAP) government has consistently stated that its objective is to achieve economic development and nationhood for Singapore and the nature of Singapore's laws is derived from these objectives.[34] She further suggests that the PAP and its governments embraced the mid-1990s neo-liberal parlance of "good governance" but

> ... whereas neo-liberals translate this to mean keeping the government from interfering with the market, in Singapore, the concept supplies the justification for state intervention. In this sense the rule of law in Singapore has become rule *by* law – a trusted pragmatic tool. It is a tool wielded by the government to effect policies and guide actions and behavior. Its value is measured by its success in achieving the pragmatic goals of the enterprise, Singapore Inc. Thus the *nature* of law in Singapore exhibits more holistic or integrated, communitarian, duty-based and regulatory tendencies than rights-based, individualistic western law.[35]

In other words, the rule of law is appreciated in utilitarian and functional terms, for its value in creating a pro-business environment which was deemed instrumental to Singapore's industrialization and economic development.[36]

It is arguable that the judiciary is sympathetic toward this pro-development philosophy. This is reflected rather obliquely in the field of administrative law whereby the judiciary's self-restraint is arguably an implicit nod to the extensive role of government in pushing forward the development strategy. Some of the case law (see discussion later) further illustrates how the judiciary itself plays its role by its acceptance of expressed national development policies as provided for in schemes such as the Land Acquisition Act and the implications of such policies, including the weakening of protection of individual rights for the greater benefit to the community. Let us now turn to the administrative law framework in Singapore and then try to situate it within the wider socio-economic background described earlier.

Part II: The administrative law framework in Singapore

Like most former colonies, the law of Singapore has its foundation in the body of English law that was transplanted onto local soil.[37] In the area of administrative law, the law in England had developed in the absence of a written constitution and where Parliament reigns supreme. Singapore, on the other hand, has a written constitution. This means that there are constitutional limits on legislative power, and the judiciary is the final arbiter of these limits in accordance with Article 43 of the Constitution. It also means that Singapore courts have greater powers of review than the English courts since Parliamentary supremacy necessarily means that there can be no legal limits on Parliament's legislative competence. However, the approach of the Singapore courts to administrative law has been generally conservative, drawing heavily on English case law but not engaging in creative elaboration of existing principles or issues in judicial review.[38]

In fact, the Singapore judiciary has not articulated any express policies or conceptualized theory of judicial review to this day. In a seminal 1985 essay on administrative law in Singapore and Malaysia, Professor Chinkin concluded that

> [t]he cases reveal that frequently the principles enunciated by the British judiciary have in fact been followed with little or no attempt to analyse their effect, impact or suitability for adoption. With few notable exceptions amongst the Malaysian judiciary [footnote removed], these appears to be an unwillingness to set forth explicitly the judicial attitude towards review. Thus prevailing policies have to be deduced from the judgments [footnote removed] ... The prevailing judicial attitude appears to be one of formal lip service to the common law principles without any expansion or modification of them, rather than any creation of a distinctive administrative law.[39]

While this conclusion generally still holds true today, it must be noted that in recent times, the Singapore judiciary has reiterated on a number of occasions the need to be discerning while applying UK administrative law principles because of its increasing "Europeanization" as a result of the Human Rights Act 1998.[40] The concern that UK law may no longer be as relevant for Singapore in light of the influence of European Community law on English jurisprudence was raised in the Singapore Parliament as early as 1989. The Minister of Home Affairs, in the course of parliamentary debates prior to the legislative overruling of the seminal case *Chng Suan Tze v. Minister of Home Affairs*,[41] expressed his concern that the judgment in this case was heavily influenced by foreign cases, particularly from the UK, where the influence of "the European court has no concern whatsoever to Singapore."[42] It may also be argued that the judicial articulation of a locally oriented conception of administrative review is not too far off in the horizon in light of the bench's sharp awareness of the importance to develop an indigenous legal system. In a recent High Court case, the esteemed Judge of Appeal Andrew Phang took the opportunity to articulate his views on this matter:

> ... English law, having been "exported" to so very many colonies in the past, has now to be cultivated with an acute awareness of the soil in which it has been transplanted. It must also be closely scrutinized for appropriateness on a more general level – that of general persuasiveness in so far as logic and

reasoning are concerned. This is the essence of the ideal of developing an autochthonous or indigenous legal system sensitive to the needs and mores of the society of which it is a part. Only thus can the society concerned develop and even flourish .... It is therefore to be welcomed that the English law is no longer accepted blindly. This is not to state that it has not served jurisdictions such as Singapore, even outstandingly well. But there ought to be departures where either local conditions and/or reason and logic dictate otherwise.[43]

Institutionally, there isn't a separate system of specialized administrative courts in Singapore, unlike most civil law jurisdictions. The constitution and the powers of the Supreme Court of Singapore are set out in the Supreme Court of Judicature Act.[44] Judicial review, an aspect of the courts' supervisory jurisdiction, is exercisable only by the High Court. It is also a remedy of last resort. Where there are available statutory procedures for redressing a grievance with an administrative order, these should generally first be pursued. It is only after exhausting available appeal procedures that an aggrieved person may then apply for judicial review.[45] There is no legislation equivalent to an Administrative Procedure Act.

Delegated legislation

Delegated legislation (also known as secondary, administrative or subsidiary legislation) is a familiar feature of Singapore's legal landscape. Subsidiary legislation abounds in almost every area of the law, and is widely recognized to be where the "law" lies (i.e., that primary legislation merely contains the broad legal framework which is fleshed out by the intricate details of subsidiary legislation).

Section 2 of the Interpretation Act defines "subsidiary legislation" as "any order in council, proclamation, rule, regulation, order, notification, by-law or other instrument made under any Act, Ordinance or other lawful authority and having legislative effect."[46] In determining whether an instrument constitutes delegated legislation, a substantive rather than formal test is applied. There are substantive and procedural requirements that a purported piece of subsidiary legislation must satisfy in order to be valid (and hence be of legal effect).[47]

For purposes of judicial review, "enabling provisions" in primary legislation confer the power to enact secondary or delegated legislation and it is often to such enabling provisions that we turn to understand the permitted content and nature of the delegated legislation. Any secondary legislation that is enacted outside the terms of the enabling provisions will be *ultra vires* and susceptible to judicial review. Many enabling provisions simply confer the power upon the administration authority to enact secondary legislation for specific purposes laid down in the statute.

For example, Section 77 of the Environmental Pollution Control Act[48] states:

(1) The Agency may, with the approval of the Minister, make regulations —

   (a) for or in respect of every purpose which is necessary for carrying out the provisions of this Act;

(b) for prescribing any matter which is authorised or required under this Act to be prescribed; and

(c) without prejudice to the generality of paragraphs (*a*) and (*b*) for or in respect of the matters specified in the Third Schedule.

(2) All such regulations shall be presented to Parliament as soon as possible after publication in the *Gazette*.[49]

As this example shows, these enabling clauses are usually drafted broadly so as to grant the administrative branch a high degree of flexibility to promulgate the type and quantity of regulation it deems fit. This is a pragmatic measure that recognizes the reality that Parliament does not have the time, resources, and technical expertise that is required to create comprehensive regulatory regimes. However, such broadly defined powers make it more difficult to control delegated legislation through the *ultra vires* doctrine if the administrative agency can claim in its defense that such broad powers were indeed granted to it by Parliament.

The "modest undertaker"

At the heart of much of administrative law – and certainly of the practice of judicial review of administrative action – stand fundamental and seemingly intractable theoretical questions about the role of courts in government. What, if anything, gives judges the general authority to review governmental action? What is sought from such review and what can it achieve?[50]

Cotterell identified three basic positions in response to the above questions. The first, which he named "the modest undertaker," sees the judicial role as simply policing the rule of law by interpretation. The second bestows the judiciary with greater flexibility, allowing them to "tap into values inherent in [a] fuller sense of democracy."[51] The third proposition is that of the courts enabling popular participation in two ways. The first is through the enforcement of procedures in governmental decision-making that allow popular input into decision-makers' deliberations. The second is for judges to enable popular participation by allowing their own procedures to be used for this purpose, i.e., by providing opportunities for influence on administrative matters by citizens as litigants.[52] It is safe to suggest that judges in Singapore see themselves as "the modest undertaker." The following passage from the High Court judgment in *Wong Keng Leong Rayney v. Law Society of Singapore* nicely encapsulates the approach of the Singapore courts to judicial review:

> ... there is a clear distinction between the powers that a superior court exercises in judicial reviews and appeals ... Judicial review is almost invariably limited to examining, *inter alia*, whether the tribunal has exceeded its jurisdiction, whether there has been an abuse of discretion or a failure of natural justice, and whether the tribunal has acted irrationally, unreasonably or in bad faith. In other words, it hinges on the legality of the decision. An appeal, on the other

hand, has a wider scope: an appellate court may in limited circumstances evaluate the substantial merits of the decision arrived at by the tribunal ... the basic distinction between an appeal and a review operates at two levels: one is formal and the other is substantive. At the formal level, the reviewing court cannot substitute its decision for that of the administrative body under review. This is because the task of determining the rights of the parties has been statutorily conferred on the administrative body, not the court. The reviewing court may declare that the task has been performed badly in law but it cannot take the further step of actually performing the task itself.[53]

The strict adherence to the "legality/merits" dichotomy is an indication of the courts' reluctance to venture beyond the role of "the modest undertaker."[54] The words of a former Attorney-General of Singapore, Mr. Tan Boon Teik, in a lecture delivered in 1987 still ring true today: "The avoidance of examining the merits or substance of a decision represents a self-conscious deference by judges toward the decisions of persons who have relatively greater technical and substantive expertise and are consequently better equipped to decide."[55] Such judicial deference, it may be argued, helps to maintain the status quo that implicitly gives the executive extensive control, through the regulatory regimes, to direct all aspects of economic and social life in Singapore toward the national developmental agenda.

There are occasions on which the judiciary comes out quite plainly in favor of deferring to the executive because of the perceived need to empower the executive, as far as possible, to carry out the task of governing Singapore and pursuing the country's best interests. There also appears to be a judicial assumption that the executive (and its agencies) always works in the best interests of society, which means that allegations of abuse of power or bad faith are taken very seriously. Below are selected cases that, in their legal reasoning, appear to support the hypothesis I venture to make above. It is necessary to make the following caveats at this stage. The following judgments have been selected to show that the argument can be made that the Singapore judiciary is willing to defer to the executive because of the perceived need for the executive to be as well equipped as possible to pursue Singapore's best interests, whether in the social, economic, and political context as they are all intrinsically linked to the nation's survival. There are, of course, many cases in which government agencies such as the police force have been taken to task by the courts within the ambit of "narrow" judicial review. Cases involving national security and international relations have also not been chosen for consideration here because it is reasonable for courts to defer to the executive's judgment in these political issues.

Galstaun and Another v. Attorney General[56]

This case was a classic challenge mounted by a private land owner against the public authorities for acquiring land under the Land Acquisition Act in an allegedly *ultra vires* and illegal manner.

Section 5(1) of the Land Acquisition Act provides that "Whenever any particular land is needed (a) for any public purpose; ... the President may, by notification published in the Gazette, declare the land to be required for the purpose specified in the notification." Section 5(3) states "the declaration shall be conclusive evidence that the land is needed for the purpose specified therein as provided in sub-s (1) of this section."

Counsel for the plaintiff submitted that the government cannot take more land than is needed for the specified public purpose and that, in the present case, some part of the plaintiffs' land has been acquired not for the specified public purpose.[57]

Dismissing the claim, the court held that "The Government is the proper authority for deciding what a public purpose is. When the Government declares that a certain purpose is a public purpose it must be presumed that the Government is in possession of facts which induce the Government to declare that the purpose is a public purpose."[58]

Teng Fuh Holdings Pte Ltd v. Collector of Land Revenue[59]

This is another case involving land acquisition. It is interesting that some 26 years have lapsed since *Galstaun and Another v. Attorney General* but the legal reasoning in this High Court case is an echo from the past.

The plaintiff owned some lands and properties which were eventually acquired under Section 5 of the Land Acquisition Act.[60] A declaration that the land acquired was "needed for a public purpose, viz.: General Redevelopment" was published in the Government *Gazette* of 26 February 1983. The plaintiff received compensation on the basis of the market value of the land as at 30 November 1973 and continued to occupy the land as a licensee from 1983 to 2005. In 2005, the plaintiff sought leave to apply for an order quashing the declaration, as well as an order that the acquisition was void. The plaintiff argued that it had suffered a terrible injustice because nothing had ostensibly been done with the property for 22 years. It also alleged that the acquisition had been made in bad faith by the defendant who had acquired the land for public purposes although the land was subsequently zoned for residential purposes.

Section 5(1) of the Land Acquisition Act states:

> Whenever any particular land is needed (*a*) for any public purpose; (*b*) by any person, corporation or statutory board, for any work or an undertaking which, in the opinion of the Minister, is of public benefit or of public utility or in the public interest; or (*c*) for any residential, commercial or industrial purposes, the President may, by notification published in the *Gazette*, declare the land to be required for the purpose specified in the notification.

Section 5(3) states that "The notification shall be conclusive evidence that the land is needed for the purpose specified therein as provided in subsection (1)."

The interesting part of the judgment, for present purposes, is as follows:

> Section 5(3) is in fact consistent with the underlying rationale and purpose of the Act itself and, in particular, with the idea that the relevant government fund authority is in the best position to determine whether or not the land concerned is required for one or more of the purposes set out in s 5(1) ... However, does that mean that s 5(3) of the Act cannot be questioned in any court? *This is not an implausible proposition, having regard to the nature and policy of the Act itself.* However, bad faith, particularly in the governmental context, does not sit easily in any (and, especially, the modern-day) context ... it is important to note that the Act was promulgated not only for the public benefit but also because land is an extremely scarce and therefore valuable resource in the Singapore context. These are in fact inextricably related reasons. This being the case, *it is clear why much more latitude and flexibility is given to governmental authorities.* As a corollary, it is not the task of the courts to sit as makers of policy. This would in fact be the very antithesis of what the courts ought to do. But latitude and flexibility stops where abuse of power begins. Such abuse of power is most commonly equated with the concept of bad faith. At this point, the courts must – and will – step in. But, in the nature of both the concept itself, such abuse of power will not be assumed (let alone be found) at the slightest drop of a hat. It is a serious allegation. There must be proof. (emphasis is mine)

The Court of Appeal, however, came to a slightly different conclusion. It held that when the allegation of bad faith is founded on a very substantial period of inaction, an explanation should be given. Prolonged inaction, if not explained, could constitute a *prima facie* case of reasonable suspicion that the land was not needed for general redevelopment when it was acquired in 1983. Unfortunately, the application was made out of time and therefore had to be dismissed. The court noted that "... if the application had been made in time, a reasonable argument could have been made for leave to be granted for the appellant to proceed with the action, *which in turn would have merited serious consideration*" (emphasis is mine).

Chee Siok Chin and others v. Minister for Home Affairs and another[61]

The facts of this case are as follows: The three applicants and another person ("the protestors") held a "peaceful protest" outside the Central Provident Fund (CPF) Building.[62] Two of the protestors wore T-shirts with the words "National Reserves" and "HDB GIC" inscribed on them. The other two protestors wore T-shirts with the words "Be Transparent Now" and "NKF CPF" inscribed on either side. One of them also held up a placard which read "Singaporeans spend on HDB; whole earnings on CPF; life savings – but cannot withdraw when they need" while another of the protestors held up a placard with the word "Accountability" written in Chinese.

The police arrived at the scene and a senior police officer (DSP Baptist) told the protestors to disperse, whereupon the protestors sought the legal basis for the dispersal order. DSP Baptist stated that the offence was one of public nuisance under the Miscellaneous Offences (Public Order and Nuisance) Act. The protestors alleged that DSP Baptist also asserted that the gathering constituted a seizable offence and that they could be arrested. Shortly thereafter, the protestors walked to the back of the CPF Building where they removed their T-shirts. They handed over their T-shirts and placards to the police upon the latter's request.

The applicants then commenced proceedings, seeking declarations that the Minister for Home Affairs and the Commissioner of Police had acted in an unlawful and/or unconstitutional manner in ordering them to disperse during their protest and in seizing the items. The applicants contended, *inter alia*, that they were exercising their rights to freedom of speech and expression, and freedom of peaceful assembly under Article 14(1) of the Constitution.

As noted in the judgment, there was "no hint or suggestion of violence and/or any threatened breach of peace."[63] The most striking feature of the protest would have been the words associating the CPF with the NKF (the National Kidney Foundation). Coupled with this were references to the HDB (Housing and Development Board), GIC (the Government of Singapore Investment Corporation Pte Ltd), the "National Reserves," and a clarion call for "Transparency" and "Accountability" as well as a suggestion that "Singaporeans were for some inexplicable reason unable to withdraw their CPF 'life savings' when they needed it."[64]

The judge took judicial notice of the fact that, at the time of the protest, the NKF was mired in adverse publicity whereby information that entered the public domain as a consequence of litigation involving its former chief executive officer, suggested that there were inexplicable accounting practices, corporate unaccountability, lack of financial disclosure and questionable management practices in the NKF. The learned judge was of the view that "An objective view of the printed words on the T-shirts and the placards would leave no doubt that the protestors ... were patently attempting to undermine the integrity of not just the CPF Board but also the GIC and the HDB by alleging impropriety against the persons responsible for the finances of these bodies ... in addition, they were calling into question the dealings of the institutions with the 'National Reserves.' This was a conscious and calculated effort to disparage and cast aspersions on these institutions and more crucially on how they are being managed." This, in his view, was unacceptable:

> The integrity of public institutions and *more specifically of the persons entrusted with these institutions*, forms an integral part of the foundation that grounds Singapore. *It accounts in no small measure for the singularly stable and upright stature Singapore has managed to uphold. Undermining confidence in these institutions and/or the persons responsible for them*

> *without any justification, apparent or otherwise, can hardly be described as a "peaceful protest."* Domestically as well as internationally, public governance in Singapore has been equated with integrity. To spuriously cast doubt on that would be to improperly undermine both a hard-won national dignity and a reputable international identity.[65]

What is also worth noting is the judge's unequivocal rejection of the principle of proportionality and the reasoning behind this position:

> Proportionality is a more exacting requirement than reasonableness and *requires, in some cases, the court to substitute its own judgment for that of the proper authority*. Needless to say, the notion of proportionality has never been part of the common law in relation to the judicial review of the exercise of a legislative and/or an administrative power or discretion. Nor has it ever been part of Singapore law. (emphasis mine)[66]

It is arguable that the Singapore court's lukewarm attitude toward the principle of proportionality has more to do with its unwillingness to go beyond its "modest undertaker" role than with the fact that the principle has never been part of the common law and "… has infiltrated British law, since British law must conform to European Union law."[67]

Part III: Reasons for the state of judicial review in Singapore

It is not often that the Singapore courts are asked to review executive action. One reason for this may be that the judicial self-restraint as described above discourages litigation by citizens who are well aware of the potential outcome. What other reasons may explain the relative dearth of administrative law cases, specifically judicial review of alleged administrative malpractice? At this juncture, it is worth noting that the Singapore courts do hear many administrative law-type cases each year but these cases tend to involve the review of decisions by disciplinary bodies constituted by a statutory source (for example, the Singapore Law Society and the Singapore Medical Council), and not malpractice by the executive branch of government. This distinction is important to note because when an appeal is made to the High Court to review such decisions of disciplinary bodies, its role is not confined to ascertaining whether natural justice rules have been breached or whether the decision of the disciplinary body has been honestly reached (i.e. the traditional scope of "narrow" judicial review which the Singapore courts tend to adhere to). The scope of review is enlarged by the right of appeal pursuant to which the High Court is empowered on appeal to hold a rehearing according to Order 55 Rules 1 and 2 of the Rules of Court.[68] This indicates that one of the ways in which the judiciary is involved in regulatory governance in Singapore is through oversight of the various "self-regulating" professions. Nonetheless, there are relatively few administrative law cases involving judicial scrutiny of alleged executive malpractice.

Prevailing regulatory culture

A reason for the relative dearth of judicial review cases in Singapore is arguably that the regulatory culture in a broad sense discourages the use of judicial review by regulated persons to alter agency decisions or to influence a policy-making process. Take the following, for example: Under the Securities and Futures Act[69] and the Financial Advisors Act,[70] a financial intermediary that wishes to provide services regulated by the above-mentioned Acts has to be licensed or come under the relevant exemptions. The application for a license or for an exemption is usually made to the relevant department in the Monetary Authority of Singapore (MAS) which will assign an officer to the case. The applicant is usually represented by a law firm, and as there are relatively few law firms practicing securities law in Singapore, the lawyer/law firm will usually be known to the officer-in-charge or they may even have worked on other such applications before. The application process usually requires detailed financial and other confidential information to be provided to the MAS and there is frequent correspondence between the applicant (and his lawyer) and the MAS. There tends to develop a relationship of trust and confidence.[71] This should not suggest the risk of regulatory capture. Instead, it suggests that the regulatory culture is one that is more cooperative, less confrontational, and antagonistic. It is arguable that such a regulatory culture deters regulated entities from using legal means to circumvent regulation or to alter agency decisions. This is not a phenomenon unique to Singapore. In the United Kingdom, the more cooperative and non-confrontational style of regulation that is characteristic of the environmental agency makes businesses in the UK less likely to engage in litigation to challenge environmental regulations, which is in contrast to the situation in the US.[72]

A rather different illustrative example is that of the relationship between non-governmental organizations (NGOs) and the statutory boards responsible for land use planning and nature conservation in Singapore. NGOs in Singapore operate within an organized system of oversight and control.[73] In the case of environmental NGOs, a government-initiated and sponsored institution of public character called the Singapore Environment Council (SEC) acts as an "umbrella organization."[74] It sits above the various NGOs and allocates funds to them through the government's Central Environmental Fund Scheme. There are other formal and informal means by which NGOs in Singapore are controlled, including legal registration under the Societies Act[75] and government-articulated "out of bounds markers" which dictate the boundaries of politically acceptable involvement in public debate and contribution to policy implementation. Because of the constraints within which these NGOs have to operate, the way in which they usually contribute to policy planning is by informal interaction or consultation with the relevant statutory boards. Over time, the development of good relations marked by mutual trust and shared concerns means that both NGOs and statutory boards find such informal consultation beneficial. In such a context, NGOs may find it more strategic to maintain good ties with the relevant statutory boards than to pursue policy change through contentious methods such as legal challenges.[76] It is not surprising that there has not been any public interest litigation in the context of land use planning and environmental protection in Singapore thus far.

Relationship between the citizen and the state

The relationship between the citizen and the state in Singapore is arguably a contributing factor. According to a certain line of argument, the government's legitimacy lies in its successful achievement of its political mandate of delivering housing, jobs, and meeting other "bread and butter" needs since independence. As the government has been able to deliver its side of the bargain, there has been a sustained if implicit compact between the people and the government, under which the latter is given an almost complete monopoly of power to pursue economic performance. This creates a "virtuous dynamic between polity and economy that has helped to propel the whole development process."[77] Thus, it may be argued that the courts are not often asked to review administrative or governmental action because the citizen is not willing to challenge governmental action which has been beneficial to him thus far and which would otherwise disturb the social equilibrium achieved by this political compact. This portrayal of the meek citizen suffering in indignant silence despite his grievances may be a tad simplistic. The average citizen with grievances does not appear to hesitate lodging complaints with his electoral constituency's Member of Parliament (who is expected to take up the issue with the relevant statutory board, whether it has to do with public housing, public transportation, workplace health, and safety, etc.) or to flood the statutory board or parent ministry with demands for redress of his grievances.[78] Instead, it is arguable that the average citizen is not likely to pursue legal remedies because of the length of time required, the costs involved as well as a certain pragmatic streak that values positive outcomes over the preservation of rights so to speak. To the extent that the positive outcome may be gained through non-legal methods, the aggrieved citizen is unlikely to insist on the legal vindication of his rights.

Absence of other elements of 'good governance'

Finally, it is arguable that judicial review is a useful form of oversight of executive action only when the other elements of 'good governance,' such as rights of public participation in administrative rulemaking and freedom of information, are present within the overall architecture of regulation and governance. It is a truism to note that, quite apart from the more "legal concerns" such as *locus standi* and ripeness, the lack of information and participatory rights in rule making on the part of the citizenry hinder their ability to hold regulators accountable through the courts. For example, Singapore does not have any laws mandating environmental impact assessments (EIAs).[79] Briefly, EIAs require a comprehensive, integrated, and detailed study of all potential impacts on the environment, including ecological and sociological impacts that may result from an activity. It is also a hallmark of EIAs that they allow some degree of public participation. Without the performance of an EIA, many development projects come to the public's attention only after the decision to go ahead has *already* been taken. As no proper study of the impact of the project in question would have been conducted, there will be little if any information available to the public should it wish to question certain aspects of the decision-making process (unless it chooses to or has the resources to conduct its own EIA). Thus, the lack of rights of public consultation or involvement in administrative policy-making in Singapore reduces the efficacy of judicial review as a check on governmental action in the area of land use planning and environmental conservation.[80] Considering that this is a contentious area that requires the delicate balancing of economic, environmental, and social interests, it is not surprising that the government would wish to limit public participation, especially if such participation should equip the public to bring the courts into the decision-making arena. To the extent that the limitation of such rights has prevented the emergence of judicial review of planning and environmental regulation in Singapore, the Singapore courts have been prevented from playing a significant role in environmental governance.[81]

Part IV: Judicialization of governance?

Recently, the courts in Singapore have begun to hear more cases involving administrative law principles. The bench has demonstrated a willingness to engage in rigorous analysis of administrative law issues, and judges with differing views have not been reluctant to engage one another in their judgments over administrative law concepts.[82] While this is a positive sign of the potential development of administrative law in Singapore, a careful reading of these cases does not indicate that the courts are going to start taking a "hard look" at executive action. As regulation in various economic and social spheres becomes more complex and technical, it is unlikely that judges will feel more comfortable playing a more interventionist role in regulatory decision-making.

However, the impetus for greater judicial involvement may come from other forces. In January 2004, prior to his appointment as Singapore's third Prime Minister, Mr. Lee Hsien Loong gave a landmark speech to the Harvard Club of Singapore in which he outlined a new style of state–society relations. Acknowledging that he had "… no doubt that our society must open up further …," Prime Minister Lee went on to develop his vision of how Singapore could "… promote a political culture which responds to people's desire for greater participation …," the creation of more space for citizens to "look after their own affairs" and the encouragement of civic participation and public debate. Prime Minister Lee's claim was, at least implicitly, that there would be more "openness" during his leadership. It would be a long shot to claim that greater civic participation, public consultation (note that in this speech, Mr. Lee also carefully set out the "rules of engagement" for such public consultations which were developed by a team of civil servants) and feedback in Singapore would lead immediately to greater public scrutiny of governmental action and legal challenges. However, it is arguable that the gradual development of a more engaged citizenry, rising education levels and growing rights awareness, and the development of procedures in governmental decision-making that allow a degree of popular input into decision-makers' deliberations, will create an environment that is more conducive of public scrutiny of policy-making. To the extent that litigation is one of the tools within the public scrutiny toolkit, the judiciary may inevitably be led to play a greater role in Singapore's regulatory governance.

Providing a brief overview of administrative law in Singapore, this chapter has sought to show that the ultimate goal of regulation in Singapore is to harness all aspects of life toward achieving economic progress, while administrative law may be said to be an instrument of regulation. As demonstrated in this chapter, the instrumental value of administrative law or even law in general lies in its enforcement of legal norms so as to maintain investor confidence in Singapore Inc. In this scheme of things, it is not surprising to find that the courts play a limited role in governance given that it is not obvious that the courts should be a primary actor in policy making in pursuit of economic progress. To the extent that the legality of governmental action provides the necessary comfort to foreign investors and is an essential element of a conducive business environment, the courts have a role to play. It should, however, be noted that litigation is no virtue in itself. The lack of litigation in the field of administrative law in Singapore should not be taken as a sign of the lack of social progress. However, given the high degree of regulatory activity by the numerous agencies that comprise the executive branch, the dearth of administrative law litigation is somewhat surprising. As this chapter sought to demonstrate, the factors behind this phenomenon lie outside the law itself. It is therefore sound to suggest that, as long as the socio-economic conditions that maintain the status quo in Singapore persist, changes within the legal sphere per se, for example, judicial attitudes toward certain administrative law principles, will be of limited impact. Yet, such changes may gain momentum and set in motion a process toward greater involvement of the courts in regulatory governance, which may in turn elicit responses from the executive such as "litigation-proofing" their decisions by the adoption of law-like procedures and decision-making tools, e.g., cost–benefit analysis. However, at this point in time, these are speculative thoughts about the future. Presently, governance in Singapore is primarily dominated by the executive, which is the ruling government virtually unopposed in Parliament and supported by a battalion of statutory boards to carry out the work of the regulatory state. The judiciary has always played a limited role in this scheme of governance, and as the discussion in this chapter suggests, it is unlikely that, barring fundamental change in the way Singapore is currently governed, the "judicialization" of governance will happen in Singapore anytime soon.

Notes

1 The People's Action Party (PAP) has been the ruling government since Singapore's independence in 1965. For an interesting account of the early history of modern

Singapore, see H. C. Chan, *Singapore: The Politics of Survival 1965–1967*, Oxford University Press, 1971.
2 The World Bank, *The East Asian Miracle: Economic Growth and Public Policy*, Washington D.C.: The World Bank, 1993.
3 A. Sindzingre, *Financing the Development State: Tax and Revenue Issues*, presentation at the Overseas Development Institute (ODI), London, 5 April 2006, pp.4–5.
4 The work of the administrative state apparatus is, to put it succinctly, regulation. There are various definitions of the term "regulation." For the purposes of this chapter, I adopt the following definition: a "sustained and focused control exercised by a public agency over activities that are valued by a community." This definition excludes from the concept of regulation the traditional areas of criminal law and the concerns of the criminal justice system by emphasizing "valued activities." See A. Ogus, *Regulation: Legal Form and Economic Theory*, Oxford: Clarendon Law Series, 1994, p.1.
5 This is not unique to Singapore. As explained in H. W. R. Wade and C. F. Forsyth, *Administrative Law*, "If the state is to care for its citizens from the cradle to the grave, to protect their environment, to educate them at all stages, to provide them with employment, training, houses, medical services, pensions, and, in the last resort, food, clothing and shelter, it needs a huge administrative apparatus. Relatively little can be done merely by passing Acts of Parliament and leaving it to the courts to enforce them" at p.4.
6 The phenomenon of the rise of the administrative state is well-documented. See, for example, the opening chapter of H. W. R. Wade and C. F. Forsyth, *Administrative Law*, 9th edition, Oxford University Press, and that of Carol Harlow and Richard Rawlings, *Law and Administration*, 2nd edition, Butterworths, for excellent introductory reading.
7 As encapsulated in the Federalist Papers, No. 47, "The accumulation of all powers, legislative, executive and judiciary, in the same hands ... may justly be pronounced the very definition of tyranny."
8 See Colin Scott's discussion of judicialization within regulatory regimes in his chapter, "Agencification, regulation and judicialization: American exceptionalism and other ways of life" in this book.
9 M. Hill, *The State, Administration and the Individual*, London: Fontana, 1976, p.27 *cited in* Carol Harlow and Richard Rawlings, *Law and Administration*, 2nd edition, Butterworths, p.11.
10 C.M. Chinkin, "Abuse of Discretion in Malaysia and Singapore" in A.J. Harding (ed.), *The Common Law in Singapore and Malaysia*, Butterworths Singapore, 1985 at pp.267–8.
11 The term "*Wednesbury* unreasonableness" is a shorthand legal reference to the classical judicial approach expounded in *Associated Provincial Picture Houses, Limited v. Wednesbury Corporation* [1948] 1 KB 223 *per* Lord Greene MR, at 229: "In short, the basis of the quashing of a decision is that it is so outrageously defiant of 'logic' and 'propriety' that it can be plainly seen that no reasonable person would or could come to that decision."
12 *Chevron USA v. NRDC*, 467 U.S. 837 (1984). See the discussion of this case in Tom Ginsburg's chapter "Judicialization of administrative governance: Causes, consequences and limits" in this book.
13 For a succinct account of how Singapore became independent, see D. K. Mauzy and R. S. Milne, *Singapore Politics Under the People's Action Party*, Routledge, *Politics in Asia* series, 2002, Ch. 2.
14 P. N. Pillai, *State Enterprise in Singapore: Legal Importation and Development*, Singapore: Singapore University Press, 1983, p.30. For a historical overview of Singapore's industrialization program, see Teck-Wong Soon and C. Suan Tan, *The Lessons of East Asia: Singapore – Public Policy and Economic Development*, Washington D.C.: The World Bank, 1993.

15 W. G. Huff, "Turning the Corner in Singapore's Developmental State?," *Asian Survey*, vol.39, no.2, 1999, p.228.
16 Ibid., p.227.
17 The selection of industries by the government to incubate and promote is a practice that is very much alive today. For example, the Research, Innovation, and Enterprise Council announced last year their approval of three strategic research sectors: Biomedical Sciences Phase II; Environmental and Water Technologies; and Interactive and Digital Media. Prime Minister Lee Hsien Loong, Chairman of the RIEC, said, "Singapore is committed to invest in R&D as a driver for economic growth and as a foundation for our long-term competitiveness. Our priorities are firstly, to build up core R&D capabilities in selected strategic areas, and secondly, to attract and develop a significant concentration of talent to sustain a critical mass of advanced research activity into the long term. The abundance of career opportunities in R&D will encourage more to pursue advanced higher education." See Press Release, 7 July 2006, "Research, Innovation and Enterprise Council Approved Plans for Three Strategic Research Sectors and a Campus for Top R&D Talent," Research Innovation Enterprise Council, Prime Minister's Office.
18 It has been argued that Singapore has succeeded in reducing corruption because of the commitment of Singapore's political leaders, the promulgation of comprehensive anti-corruption legislation, and the establishment of a powerful anti-corruption agency that investigates and enforces the Prevention of Corruption Act: J. Quah, "Singapore's Experience in Curbing Corruption" in Heidenheimer, et al., eds., *Political Corruption: A Handbook, 4th ed.*, New Brunswick, NJ: Transaction Publishers, 1997. For an interesting account of Singapore's fight against corruption, see Lee K.Y., *From Third World to First: The Singapore Story: 1965–2000*, Singapore: Straits Times Press, 2000, Ch. 12.
19 S. Tay, ed., *A Mandarin and the Making of Public Policy: Reflections by Ngiam Tong Dow*. Singapore: National University of Singapore Press, 2006, pp.229–33. The heading of this sub-chapter is instructive – "Mandarins and Masters: The Political and Constitutional Context."
20 Ibid. at p.6.
21 Cited in Teck-Wong Soon and C. Suan Tan, *The Lessons of East Asia: Singapore – Public Policy and Economic Development*, Washington D.C.: The World Bank, 1993, p.19.
22 For example, the Monetary Authority of Singapore (MAS), established by the Monetary Authority of Singapore Act (Cap. 186), acts as the banker to and financial agent of the Singapore government. Under Section 21, responsibility for regulating the securities market, insurance industry, and banking industry, *inter alia*, was transferred to the MAS.
23 J. S. T. Quah, "Statutory Boards" in J. S. T. Quah, et. al, eds., *Government and Politics of Singapore*, Oxford: Oxford University Press, 1985, p.121.
24 Supervision of the statutory board by the parent ministry and the government is also ensured by the composition of the board of directors of such statutory boards. Under Section 7 of the MAS Act, for example, the chairman "shall be appointed by the President on the recommendation of the Cabinet" and the managing director is appointed by the President on the advice or recommendation of the Public Service Commission (Section 9 of the MAS Act). It is interesting to note that "The directors, including the managing director, and the officers and employees of the [MAS] of every description shall be deemed to be public servants within the meaning of the Penal Code (Cap. 224)" (Section 16 of the MAS Act).
25 J. S. T. Quah, op. cit., p.125.
26 The government has been very successful in making good and affordable public housing available to the majority of Singaporeans. In 1973, T. J. S. George had this to say, "Spectacular as Singapore's business and industrial growth was, the greatest

achievement of them all was its many-splendoured low-cost housing scheme ... It was what made Singapore a topic of discussion round the world"; quoted in Mauzy and Milne, op. cit., p.90.
27 C. Carter, *Eyes on the Prize: Law and Economic Development in Singapore*, The Hague, Netherlands: Kluwer Law International, 2002, p.126. See also Huff, op. cit., pp.214–42; L. Low, "The Singapore developmental state in the new economy and polity," *The Pacific Review*, vol.14, no.3, 2001, pp.411–41.
28 [1997] 2 SLR 584. The Court of Appeal dismissed an appeal from the plaintiffs on 9 July 1997. Endorsing Judith Prakash J's judgment, the Court of Appeal decided not to write separate grounds of judgment. (See Editorial Note in the High Court judgment).
29 Ibid. at para. 78.
30 GLCs (and statutory boards) were created in the late 1960s to jumpstart economic development. GLCs are incorporated under the Companies Act (Cap. 50, Sing. Rev. Ed.) and do not come under the direct purview of Parliament. Pioneer GLCs include the Keppel, Sembawang, and Jurong Shipyards, which spearheaded Singapore's development as a major shipbuilding and ship repair centre, and the Development Bank of Singapore (DBS) which provided development financing. Temasek Holdings was set up in 1974 as a limited holding company to manage the government's investments in the GLCs. According to information on the Temasek Holdings website, seven of the first-tier GLCs are listed on the Singapore Exchange and contribute to approximately 21 per cent of the market capitalization of all companies listed on the Exchange. The total market value of these companies is about S$91 billion; http://www.temasekholdings.com.sg/news_room/mediakit_faqs.htm (accessed on 10 June 2007). See C. Ramirez and Ling Hui Tan, "Singapore, Inc. versus the Private Sector: Are Government-linked companies different?," in *IMF Working Paper WP/03/156*, Washington D.C.: IMF Working Institute. Some statutory boards have been corporatized into GLCs, for example, the Port of Authority of Singapore (PSA) was converted into PSA Corporation in 1997.
31 The list of government ministries and statutory boards is compiled from information available on the Singapore Government Directory Interactive (SGDI) website www.sgdi.gov.sg (accessed on 1 July 2007).
32 The Prime Minister's Office co-ordinates the activities of Ministries, the general policies of the Government, and overall policy direction.
33 Carter, op. cit., p.259.
34 Ibid., p.261.
35 Ibid., p.262. See also, S. Sudo, "Regional Governance and East and Southeast Asia: Towards the Regulatory State?," *Japanese Journal of Political Science*, vol.4, no.2, p.341, where the author describes one component of good governance in Singapore to mean "not only that 'leaders are elected by the people and are accountable to them', but also that 'once elected, the task of governing should be left to the governing elite who will exercise independent judgment on what is in the long-term interest of the people and act on that basis'."
36 For an interesting discussion of how the concept of rule of law is understood and utilized in Singapore, see L. Thio, "Rule of Law within a Non-liberal 'Communitarian' Democracy: the Singapore Experience", in R. Peerenboom, ed., *Asian Discourses of Rule of Law*, London, New York: Routledge Curzon, 2004 p.183.
37 See the writings of Judge of Appeal Andrew Phang on the importance of developing an indigenous legal system in Singapore, e.g., A. Phang Boon Leong, *The Development of Singapore Law: Historical and Socio-Legal Perspectives*, Singapore: Butterworths, 1990.
38 Thio Li-Ann, "Law and the Administrative State," in K. Y. L. Tan, ed., *The Singapore Legal System*, 2nd ed., Singapore: Singapore University Press, p.167.

39 C. M. Chinkin, "Abuse of Discretion in Malaysia and Singapore" in A. J. Harding, ed., *The Common Law in Singapore and Malaysia*, Singapore: Butterworths, 1985, pp.268–9.
40 See discussion of *Chee Siok Chin and Others v. Minister for Home Affairs and Another* below and footnote 62.
41 [1989] 1 MLJ 69.
42 *Singapore Parliamentary Debates*, 25 January 1989, col. 468.
43 Paras. 27–28, *Tang Kin Hwa v. Traditional Chinese Medicine Practitioners Board* [2005] SGHC 153.
44 Cap. 322, Sing. Rev. Ed.
45 *PP v. Chiam Heng Hsien* [2004] SGDC 125 at [55], following *Tan Gek Neo Jessie v. Minister for Finance* [1991] SLR 325. The process of application for judicial review is set out in Order 53 of the Rules of Court (Cap. 322, Section 80).
46 Cap. 1, Sing. Rev. Ed.
47 For example, a legislative instrument (as opposed to an administrative one) must be published in accordance with Section 23(1) of the Interpretation Act. In *Cheong Seok Leng v. PP* [1988] 2 MLJ 481, Chan J. affirmed the mandatory nature of this publication requirement.
48 Cap. 94A, Sing. Rev. Ed.
49 The Third Schedule, *Subject Matters of Regulations*, sets out the subject matters in which the National Environment Agency may promulgate regulation. These matters include, *inter alia*, the prescribing of the types of tests to be carried out and the records to be maintained by occupiers of industrial or trade premises with respect to emission of air impurities, the types of air pollution control equipment that may be used by industrial facilities, noise standards, control of discharge of trade effluent into drains and the sea.
50 R. Cotterell, "Judicial Review and Legal Theory" in G. Richardson and H. Genn, eds., *Administrative Law and Government Action*, Oxford: Clarendon Press, 1994, p.13.
51 Ibid. at 18.
52 A leading American administrative law scholar, Professor Richard Stewart, famously argued that the function of administrative law is the facilitation of interest group participation in administrative decision-making; R. B. Stewart, "The Reformation of American Administrative Law," *Harvard Law Review*, 88, 1975, p.1699.
53 [2006] SGHC 179.
54 The great American administrative law scholar, Lon Fuller, famously argued that certain problems, described as "polycentric" because they involve a complex network of interests and considerations, are unsuitable for resolution by adjudication: see L. Fuller, "The Forms and Limits of Adjudication", *Harvard Law Review*, 92, 1978 92, p.353. The Singapore judiciary is likely to share this view and that the courts are not the only mechanism for ensuring accountability of government.
55 "The Singapore Law Review Lecture," *Singapore Law Review*, 9, 1988, pp.74–5.
56 [1980–1981] SLR 345; [1980] SGHC 17.
57 Ibid., at para. 8.
58 Ibid., at para. 9.
59 [2006] 3 SLR 507; [2006] SGHC 93.
60 Cap 152, 1985 Rev Ed.
61 [2006] 1 SLR 582; [2005] SGHC 216.
62 The Central Provident Fund (CPF) is Singapore's national compulsory savings scheme that was put in place to ensure that citizens would have sufficient savings for their retirement years. Over time, the functions of the CPF have greatly expanded and diversified to include provision for partial payment of the cost of some social services (for example, loans for tertiary education and Medisave (healthcare)), government facilitation of investment by CPF members, and "topping up" of members' accounts by the government; see discussion of the CPF at Mauzy and Milne, op. cit., pp.86–90.

63 At para. 120.
64 Ibid.
65 At para. 133.
66 At para. 87.
67 The learned judge added emphasis to these words in citing an account of the principle of proportionality by Wade and Forsyth in para. 87 of the judgment: "In the law of a number of European countries there is a 'principle of proportionality' which ordains that administrative measures must not be more drastic than is necessary for attaining the desired result. This doctrine has been adopted by the European Court of Justice in Luxembourg and so it *has infiltrated British law, since British law must conform to European Union law.* More significantly, it is freely applied by the European Court of Human Rights in Strasbourg, and so is taken into account in Britain under the Human Rights Act 1998. [emphasis added]."
68 *Ling Uk Choon v. Public Accountants Board* [2004] 3 SLR 517.
69 Cap. 289, Sing. Rev. Ed.
70 Cap. 110, Sing. Rev. Ed.
71 These observations of the license application process are the author's own based on her experience as a legal associate practicing securities regulation. The observations are corroborated by her conversations with other lawyers and acquaintances working in the MAS.
72 See D. Vogel, *National Styles of Regulation: Environmental Policy in Great Britain and the United States*, Ithaca : Cornell University Press, 1986.
73 Y. Tanaka, "Singapore: Subtle NGO control by a developmentalist welfare state" in S. Shigetomi, ed., *The State and NGOs: Perspective from Asia*, Singapore: Institute of South East Asian Studies, 2002.
74 The SEC describes itself as "... nationally oriented, independently managed body, to nurture, facilitate and co-ordinate environmental causes and groups in Singapore" as well as a "... tree offering shelter and roots to green groups, in aid of a better world and a better Singapore." See the "About Us" page of the SEC website: http://www.sec.org.sg/abtus_htm/abt_us_framset.htm.
75 Cap. 311, Sing. Rev. Ed.
76 Using the campaign against the de-gazetting of the Lower Pierce Reservoir Catchment Area as a case study, Maria Francesch-Huidobro looks at the tensions in the relationships between the ministries and the statutory boards, on one hand, and the statutory boards and NGOs, on the other, in light of the fact that the common ground that the statutory boards shared with the environmental NGOs was often at variance with the policy positions of the ministries. See M. Francesch-Huidobro, Statutory Bodies, "Land Use Planning and Conservation in Singapore: Issues and Challenges for Governability," *Public Organization Review*, Vol.6, no.3, 2006. pp.277–88.
77 Sudo, op. cit., p.333.
78 According to anecdotal evidence gathered by the author, these complaints are not infrequent and junior officers are told to address these complaints. Also, complaints that are transmitted via Members of Parliament are dealt with swiftly, especially if the Member of Parliament is a cabinet minister or high-ranking civil servant.
79 See Lye Lin Heng's chapter on Singapore in T. Mottershead, *Environmental Law and Enforcement in the Asia-Pacific Rim*, Sweet & Maxwell Asia, 2002, p.426.
80 In response to calls for greater public accountability and transparency, various statutory boards including the National Environment Agency do invite public comments on environmental policies (for example, the recently concluded public consultation of the national climate change strategy) but usually only *after* the policy has been drafted. The public consultation exercise then becomes akin to a public justification of the favored policy.

81 It is interesting to note that in the field of economic regulation, there appears to be less aversion to public consultation, perhaps because the regulatory agency sees a real need to respond to the needs of the regulated entities which are doing business and therefore contributing to economic development in Singapore. For example, the MAS and the Accounting and Corporate Regulatory Authority (ACRA) regularly circulate their policy papers for public consultation and input.

82 For example, two recent High Court cases, *Tang Kin Hwa v. Traditional Chinese Medicine Practitioners Board* [2005] SGHC 153 and *Re Shankar Alan s/o Anant Kulkarni* [2006] SGHC 194, have given the Singapore courts an opportunity to develop the local jurisprudence relating to the rule against apparent bias.

14 "Government by judiciary" in the Philippines

Ideological and doctrinal framework

Raul C. Pangalangan

> [The Court] has unwittingly transformed itself into ... a *"government by the Judiciary,"* something never intended by the framers of the Constitution when they provided for separation of powers ... and excluded the Judiciary from policy-making.[1]

> [A] society so riven that the spirit of moderation is gone, no Court can save; [] a society where that spirit flourishes no Court need save; [] a society which evades its responsibility by thrusting upon the Courts the nurture of that spirit, that spirit will in the end perish.[2]

> In the complex life of to-day, the business of government could not go on without the delegation, in greater or less degree, of the power to adapt the rule to the swiftly moving facts.[3]

Introduction and summary

Governing the Philippines did not become judicialized overnight. Judicialization is deeply rooted, an instinctive preference for law-like techniques that Justice Oliver Wendell Holmes Jr., no less, chastised when the Philippines was still a U.S. colony. He lamented the Philippine Supreme Court's excessive reliance on legalistic interpretations that ignored either the equities or practicalities of cases, such legal formalism that saw the great powers of government in "fields of black and white [divided] with mathematical precision ... into watertight compartments."[4]

What Holmes lamented persists until today – the idealization of seemingly objective standards embodied in law hand-in-hand with the aversion to any form of discretion and open-ended decision making – and has been exalted as the quintessence of the Rule of Law, indeed one of the proudest achievements of its post-Marcos democracy.

The fetish for rules and rule-bound decision can be understood at various levels. The simplest, most obvious explanation is historical, but though valid and compelling, it is by no means complete. It merely provides the formal and institutional expression of deeper cultural predilections that have been codified into its constitution, laws, even more workaday matters like school admissions and judges' appointments.

I propose that the explanation lies in the Filipinos' lack of a communal ideology by which to legitimize decision and the lack of any institution that can be trusted to make those decisions. Who is right and who is wrong can be answered only in relation to a genuine community that shares a common moral universe. Absent that nomos, the next best option is to devolve that decision to trusted persons and institutions.

But that trust has often been betrayed, either by failed institutions or flawed leaders. And, here the historical explanation reappears. In the stalemate wherein no single leader or social group commands enough respect to lead the way, the last recourse is to insulate all decision-makers from illegitimate subjectivities (e.g., ideological bias, personal debts of gratitude, familial loyalties) by shackling decision-making with rules. And voila, a new secular religion is found in law-based decision, de-personalized, de-politicized, and de-ideologized.

Doctrinal evolution of judicialization

The cornerstone of "judicial sovereignty" in Philippine law today is the 1987 Constitution, the charter that was adopted under President Corazon Aquino after the peaceful uprising against Ferdinand Marcos. The drafting commission consisted of 48 men and women handpicked by President Aquino from the coalition that topped Marcos. The resulting charter thus reflects the internal contradictions of that coalition.

Codification of policy objectives and substantive norms

Directive principles: Preempting the democratic process by constitutionalizing norms

The first step was to codify welfare state obligations and directive principles into law. The 1987 Constitution contains a *Declaration of Principles and State Policies*[5] described as "a constitutional inventory of fundamental community values and interests."[6] In addition, it positivized a protectionist and statist economic theory in a separate article on the *National Economy and Patrimony*[7] and institutionalized affirmative action in the article entitled *Social Justice and Human Rights*.[8]

The drafters' goal was to freeze into the Constitution the socio-economic agenda of the democratic coalition that ousted Marcos in February 1986.

> We have been called to this Commission by a revolutionary government to the extent that it is a government that is a product of the February revolution.... Therefore, what we are trying to formulate here is a constitution that will set up structures capable of continuing the goals of the revolution. It is said that the revolution of February was primarily a *political revolution*. It was a revolution that released from the political oppressions that were institutionalized under the old regime ....

But it also said that we still have to complete a social revolution. And if we look at the Bill of Rights ..., we find guarantees which by themselves are *self-executory. But when it comes to guarantees of social and economic rights, the farthest we can go is to set goals for future legislatures to attain* ... because we, as a Constitutional Commission, cannot legislate fully effective means for attaining these social and economic goals.

What we need today is the *completion of a peaceful social and economic revolution.*[9]

Thus the charter recognized substantive claims to a "right to health,"[10] to a "balanced and healthful ecology,"[11] and to "education"[12] and to a "self-reliant and independent national economy effectively controlled by Filipinos."[13]

That the drafters of the Constitution were appointed, and not elected, is most significant in this regard. They had a clear distrust of the subsequent legislators who would be elected, and preferred to bind the hands of future congresses to their welfare state program. In the classic concept of pre-commitment, the drafters aimed to preempt what they conceded to be the political compromises intrinsic to the give-and-take of democratic politics.

Economic protectionism: Advancing a "nationalist" ideology through law

The president of the commission that drafted the 1987 Constitution referred triumphantly to the article on National Economy and Patrimony as "pro-poor, pro-people and pro-Filipino," because it insulated the economy from foreign control, and openly advanced a "Filipino First" policy.[14] By way of example, the following clause codified into the charter a policy of preferential treatment for nationals.

> The State shall promote the preferential use of Filipino labor, domestic materials and locally produced goods, and adopt measures that help make them competitive.[15]

The goal, it was said, was

> to constitutionalize the Filipino-First policy, first expressed in Commonwealth Act No. 138,[16] giving native products and domestic entities preference in government purchases, Republic Act No. 912[17] requiring use under certain conditions of Philippine-made materials or products in government projects, including public works, whether done directly by the government or through contractors; and Republic Act No. 5183, reserving to Filipino citizens or to corporations owned 60% by Filipinos the award of contracts to supply government agencies, government-owned or controlled corporations, and municipal corporations.

This was extended to the practice of the professions, which was related to the principle that national patrimony and economy be under the control of Filipinos, which includes professions.

> ... The practice of all professions in the Philippines shall be limited to Filipino citizens, save in cases prescribed by law.[18]

These protectionist clauses ensure "a self-reliant and independent national economy effectively controlled by Filipinos"[19] and reflect the anti-foreign, "nationalist" ideology that animated the democratic movement against Marcos. It drew its power from the anti-colonial revolution against Spain that erupted in 1896, which was channeled into parliamentary lobbying during the period of American colonialism until 1946, and which was sustained in the left-inspired anti-imperialist rhetoric of the student protests right before the declaration of martial law by Marcos in 1972. It was this orthodoxy that prevailed in economic policy, and which was calcified into constitutional norms in the 1987 Constitution.

Social justice clauses: Statist consequence of redistributive claims

Redistributive claims historically were recognized in Philippine constitutional law under the rubric of "social justice." First constitutionalized in the 1935 Constitution that was written while the country was still a U.S. colony and under which it became independent, the Philippines disavowed *laissez-faire* in favor of the welfare state.[20]

In the 1987 Constitution, the social justice clause[21] is considered the "centerpiece" because it provided the "material and social infrastructure for the realization of basic human rights, the enhancement of human dignity and effective participation in democratic processes."

> The State shall promote a just and dynamic social order that will ensure the prosperity and independence of the nation and free the people from poverty through policies that provide adequate social services, promote full employment, a rising standard of living, and an improved quality of life for all.[22]
>
> The Congress shall give highest priority to the enactment of measures that protect and enhance the right of all the people to human dignity, reduce social, economic, and political inequalities, and remove cultural inequities by equitably diffusing wealth and political power for the common good.[23]

Next, the drafters of the Constitution laid down the legal doctrines needed to reconcile affirmative action and preferential treatment, on the one hand, with the equal protection clause on the other. They expressly recognized the social function of private property and the principle of stewardship.

> To this end, the State shall *regulate* the acquisition, ownership, use, and disposition of *property* and its increments.[24]

"Government by judiciary" in the Philippines 317

> The State shall apply the principles of agrarian reform or *stewardship*, whenever applicable in accordance with law, in the disposition or utilization of other natural resources, including lands of the public domain under lease or concession suitable to agriculture, subject to prior rights, homestead rights of small settlers, and the rights of indigenous communities to their ancestral lands.[25]

Note that each time the Constitution identifies a vulnerable group or affirms the principle of social justice, it at the same time pays due homage to free market principles.

> The use of property bears a social function, and all economic agents shall contribute to the common good. *Individuals and private groups, including corporations, cooperatives, and similar collective organizations, shall have the right to own, establish, and operate economic enterprises*, subject to the duty of the State to promote distributive justice and to intervene when the common good so demands.[26]
>
> The State shall afford full protection to labor, local and overseas, organized and unorganized, and promote full employment and equality of employment opportunities for all.
>
> The State shall promote the principle of shared responsibility between workers and employers and the preferential use of voluntary modes in settling disputes, including conciliation, and shall enforce their mutual compliance therewith to foster industrial peace.
>
> The State shall regulate the relations between workers and employers, *recognizing the right of labor to its just share in the fruits of production* and *the right of enterprises to reasonable returns on investments, and to expansion and growth.*[27]

The Supreme Court has affirmed the exceptional character of redistributive justice in takings cases arising from agrarian reform. The Constitution codifies the claim to a "just distribution of all agricultural lands."

> The State shall, by law, undertake an agrarian reform program founded on the right of farmers and regular farm-workers, who are landless, to own directly or collectively the lands they till or, in the case of other farm-workers, to receive a just share of the fruits thereof. To this end, the State shall encourage and undertake the just distribution of all agricultural lands, subject to such priorities and reasonable retention limits as the Congress may prescribe, taking into account ecological, developmental, or equity considerations, and *subject to the payment of just compensation*. In determining retention limits, the State shall respect the *rights of small landowners*. The State shall further provide *incentives for voluntary land-sharing.*[28]

Pursuant to this clause, the Philippine Congress adopted the Comprehensive Agrarian Reform Law.[29] The Supreme Court upheld the law in *Luz Farms v. Secretary of Agrarian Reform*,³⁰ and characterized redistributive takings the "*mingling* of the police power and the power of eminent domain."

> However, we do not deal here with the *traditional* exercise of the power of eminent domain. This is not an ordinary expropriation where only a specific property of relatively limited area is sought to be taken by the State from its owner for a specific and perhaps local purpose. What we deal with here is a *revolutionary* kind of expropriation.³¹

Yet what began as a substantive program to minister to the disadvantaged and the vulnerable has resulted, ironically, in a long series of constitutional clauses that begins with the words "The State shall ...." In other words, social justice, thus conceived, is statist at its core, because the state is seen as the only viable agent for communal action, and all other collectivities are seen, potentially, as mobs. Stated otherwise, the Philippine concept of social justice bespeaks both an excessive trust in the formal mechanisms of the State, and a fear of the raw power of collectivities unrestrained by law.

Expansion of judicial power

Second, the 1987 Constitution expanded the power of the courts to encompass hitherto non-justiciable political questions. The most pronounced legacy of the anti-Marcos struggle is the deliberate downgrading of the "political question" doctrine. The drafters of the Constitution felt that, during the Marcos regime, judges unduly deployed the political question doctrine to avoid confronting the dictatorship. Thus the new definition of judicial power:

> Judicial power includes the duty of the courts of justice to settle actual controversies involving rights which are legally demandable and enforceable, and to determine whether or not there has been a grave abuse of discretion amounting to lack or excess of jurisdiction on the part of any branch or instrumentality of the Government.³²

This definition expands judicial power in two ways. *One,* the courts have the "duty" to settle disputes before it and may not wash their hands in the face of highly contested issues, derided during the Marcos years through the euphemism "judicial statesmanship." *Two,* the "grave abuse of discretion" standard, hitherto applied solely to the review of judicial decisions,³³ now encompasses non-judicial decisions by "any branch or instrumentality of the Government." The irony therefore is that these branches (executive or legislative) or instrumentality (administrative) typically exercise open-ended discretion with minimal objective safeguards. When a judge wields this broad review power, he or she inevitably is called upon to exercise his or her own discretion and to second-guess the discretion of the original decision maker.

[T]he political question doctrine is no longer the insurmountable obstacle to the exercise of judicial power or the impenetrable shield that protects executive and legislative actions from judicial inquiry or review.

The second part of the authority represents a broadening of judicial power to enable the courts of justice to review what was before forbidden territory, to wit, the discretion of the political departments of the government. As worded, the new provision vests in the judiciary, and particularly the Supreme Court, the power to rule upon even the wisdom of the decisions of the executive and the legislature and to declare their acts invalid for lack or excess of jurisdiction because tainted with grave abuse of discretion. The catch, of course, is the meaning of "grave abuse of discretion," which is a very elastic phrase that can expand or contract according to the disposition of the judiciary.[34]

The expanded scope of judicial power thus alters the balance in the separation of powers scheme in the Constitution. It shifts to unelected judges the power to apply their own discretion in reviewing decisions by the politically accountable branches of government and, worse, to dress up the review in the language of the law.

Direct judicial enforceability of directive principles

Third, the *coup de grâce* for judicialized governance was dealt by the Supreme Court when it subsequently made the grand normative statements directly enforceable by the courts, without need of legislative implementation. At the outset, it was recognized that this has thus "propel[led] the courts into the uncharted ocean of social and economic policy making."

The Supreme Court held that the "right to a balanced and healthful ecology in accord with the rhythm and harmony of nature"[35] – though merely a directive principle – actually gave rise to an actionable claim to stop the issuance of timber-cutting licenses.

> While the right to this balanced and healthful ecology is to be found under the Declaration of Principles and State Policies and not under the Bill of Rights, it does not follow that it is less important than any of the civil and political rights enumerated in the latter. Such a right belongs to a different category of rights altogether for it concerns nothing less than self-preservation and self-perpetuation – aptly and fittingly stressed by the petitioners – the advancement of which may even be said to predate all governments and constitutions.[36]
> *Minors Oposa v. Factoran*, G.R. No. 101083, Feliciano, J., Separate Opinion (1993).

Significantly, a separate opinion surfaced the key underlying dilemma. The juridical difficulty derives from the broad and general language of the Declaration and related clauses, despite the fact that they lack "language of a lower level of generality."

It is in fact very difficult to fashion language more comprehensive in scope and generalized in character than a right to "a balanced and healthful ecology." The list of particular claims which can be subsumed under this rubric appears to be entirely open-ended: toxic fumes in the air, sewage in the rivers, garbage collection, nefarious mining practices, dynamite and cyanide fishing, ground water contamination, etc.[37]

He concluded that the Court had thereby declared the directive principles "self-executing and judicially enforceable even in their present form," notwithstanding that it fails to state "a more specific legal right – a right cast in language of a significantly lower order of generality." In conclusion, he zeroed-in on the lethal combination of constitutionalized norms and expanded judicial power.

> *When substantive standards as general as "the right to a balanced and healthy ecology" and "the right to health" are combined with remedial standards as broad ranging as "a grave abuse of discretion amounting to lack or excess of jurisdiction," the result will be, it is respectfully submitted, to propel courts into the uncharted ocean of social and economic policy making ....* Where no specific, operable norms and standards are shown to exist, then the policy making departments – the legislative and executive departments – must be given a real and effective opportunity to fashion and promulgate those norms and standards, and to implement them before the courts should intervene.[38]

The Court has also stopped the relocation of a petrochemical plant, citing the protectionist clause securing a "self-reliant and independent national economy effectively controlled by Filipinos." In *Garcia v. Board of Investments*,[39] the Court reversed a petrochemical plant investor's decision to relocate a proposed plant, citing the duty of the state to "develop a self-reliant and independent national economy effectively controlled by Filipinos," and using policy arguments to explain why the investor's decision was bad for the nation. Strong dissenting opinions argued for judicial restraint, citing the dangers of "government by the judiciary."

> [C]hoosing an appropriate site for the investor's project is *a political and economic decision* which, under our system of separation of powers, only the executive branch, as implementor of policy formulated by the legislature ..., is empowered to make.[40]

> [The majority has] decided upon the *wisdom* of the transfer of the site ...; the *reasonableness* of the feedstock to be used; ... the *undesirability* of the capitalization aspect ...; and *injected its own concept of the national interest* ...

> ... By no means [does the Constitution] vest in the Courts the power to enter the realm of policy considerations under the guise of the commission of grave abuse of discretion.[41]

The Court has allowed a losing Filipino bidder to match post hoc the bid of the winning foreign bidder for the historic Manila Hotel, citing the clause granting preferential rights to nationals. In *Manila Prince Hotel*,[42] the Court went out of its way to apply the clause in a highly controversial decision about the sale of the historic Manila Hotel (which the Court, absent an executive determination, had first to declare as "historic"), the Court holding that the losing bidder, a Filipino company, had the right to match post hoc the winning bid of a Malaysian company.

> The Filipino First policy is a product of Filipino nationalism. It is embodied in the 1987 not merely to be used as a guideline for future legislation but primarily to be enforced; so it must be enforced. ... [I]t is not the intention of this Court to impede and diminish, much less undermine, the influx of foreign investments. Far from it, the Court encourages and welcomes more business opportunities but avowedly sanctions the preference for Filipinos whenever such preference is ordained by the Constitution.
>
> Privatization ... should not take precedence over non-material values. A commercial, nay even budgetary, objective should not be pursued at the expense of national pride and dignity. For the Constitution enshrines higher and nobler non-material values .... *[T]here is nothing so sacrosanct in any economic policy as to draw itself beyond judicial review when the Constitution is involved.*
>
> Protection of foreign investments, while laudable, is merely a policy. It cannot override the demands of nationalism.[43]

Finally, in *Tatad v. Secretary of Energy*,[44] the Court struck down the Oil Industry Deregulation Law for failing to carry out the constitutional mandate against monopolies. The Court was painfully aware that it has been accused of judicial overreach, as expressed in *Oposa*.[45] The Court confronts that criticism, and essentially explains the basis for judicialized governance in Philippine constitutional law.

> With this Decision, some circles will chide the Court for interfering with an economic decision of Congress. Such criticism is charmless for the Court is annulling [the Oil Deregulation Law] *not because it disagrees with deregulation as an economic policy but because as cobbled by Congress in its present form, the law violates the Constitution.* The right call therefore should be for Congress to write a new oil deregulation law that conforms with the Constitution and *not for this Court to shirk its duty of striking down a law that offends the Constitution....* Lest it is missed, the Constitution is a covenant that ... guarantees both the political and economic rights of the people. The Constitution mandates this Court to be the guardian not only of the people's political rights but their economic rights as well.[46]

This is in stark contrast to the settled constraints on judicial oversight of regulatory discretion, and the longstanding recognition of the need for managerial leeway.

> Discretion is not unconfined and vagrant. It is canalized within banks that keep it from overflowing. [T]he separation of powers between the Executive and Congress is not a doctrinaire concept to be made use of with pedantic rigor. There must be sensible approximation, there must be elasticity of adjustment, in response to the practical necessities of government, which cannot foresee to-day the developments of tomorrow in their nearly infinite variety.[47]

In contrast, in the *WTO Ratification* case,[48] the Court saw its way to reconcile economic protectionism with globalization. "Economic nationalism should be read with other constitutional mandates to attain balanced development of the economy."

> All told, while the Constitution indeed mandates a bias in favor of Filipino goods, services, labor and enterprises, at the same time, it recognizes the need for business exchange with the rest of the world on the bases of equality and reciprocity and limits protection of Filipino enterprises only against foreign competition and trade practices that are unfair. In other words, the Constitution did not intend to pursue an isolationist policy. It did not shut out foreign investments … in the development of the Philippine economy. While the Constitution does not encourage the unlimited entry of foreign investments, it does not prohibit them either.[49]

Strengthening of private right of action

Fourth, as a final shot, having enabled the Courts to apply constitutional norms without legislative intervention, the Supreme Court has relaxed the traditional requirements for standing, thus enabling citizens more latitude to file taxpayers' suits, and then consummate the judicialization of governance by ensuring the citizens' access to information.

The Philippines has long followed American doctrine on standing, and as a rule required "injury-in-fact" and the presence of Hohfeldian plaintiffs.[50] Further along this line of doctrine, it has also allowed public interest cases through taxpayer standing.

Under the 1987 Constitution, however, the Court loosened the requirements by allowing standing in cases of "transcendental significance," itself a standard that is malleable and elastic. The classic example is *Chavez v. Presidential Commission on Good Government*[51] where the Court upheld the right of a citizen to bring a taxpayer's suit on the recovery of Marcos's ill-gotten wealth.

> [T]he matter of recovering the ill-gotten wealth of the Marcoses is an issue of "transcendental importance to the public." [O]rdinary taxpayers have a

right to initiate and prosecute actions questioning the validity of acts or orders of government agencies or instrumentalities, if the issues raised are of "paramount public interest," and if they "immediately affect the social, economic and moral well being of the people."

Moreover, the mere fact that he is a citizen satisfies the requirement of personal interest, when the proceeding involves the assertion of a public right, such as in this case. He invokes several decisions of this Court which have set aside the procedural matter of *locus standi*, when the subject of the case involved public interest.[52]

Other decisions would trace this to the Court's expanded powers under the 1987 Constitution.

Considering the importance to the public of the cases at bar, and in keeping with the Court's duty, under the 1987 Constitution, to determine whether or not the other branches of government have kept themselves within the limits of the Constitution and the laws and that they have not abused the discretion given to them, the Court has *brushed aside technicalities of procedure* and has taken cognizance of these petitions.[53]

[I]n line with the liberal policy of this Court on *locus standi*, ordinary taxpayers, members of Congress, and even association of planters, and non-profit civic organizations were allowed to initiate and prosecute actions before this Court to question the constitutionality or validity of laws, acts, decisions, rulings, or orders of various government agencies or instrumentalities.[54]

* * *

[I]nsofar as taxpayers' suits are concerned [the Court] is not devoid of discretion as to whether or not it should be entertained. .... As such ... even if, strictly speaking, they [the petitioners] are not covered by the definition, it is still within the wide discretion of the Court to waive the requirement and so remove the impediment to its addressing and resolving the serious constitutional questions raised.[55]

Kilosbayan v. Guingona[56] was eventually reversed in *Kilosbayan v. Morato*,[57] the Court saying that standing doctrine applies only when constitutional issues are at stake. In these two cases, Kilosbayan, an NGO, challenged the legality of a lottery franchise. In *Morato*, the Court applied the "personal stake in the outcome of the controversy as to assure that concrete adverseness which sharpens the presentation of issues upon which the court so largely depends for illumination of difficult constitutional questions," the Court citing the U.S. case *Baker v. Carr*.[58] The Court held that standing doctrine applied only in constitutional cases, and that – significantly for our study – no such issue was at stake because the good morals clauses from the Constitution which were invoked in the case were not self-executing. "They do not embody judicially enforceable constitutional rights but guidelines for legislation."

The Declaration of Principles and State Policies enhances the citizens' direct right of action by ensuring greater access to information.

> Subject to reasonable conditions prescribed by law, the State adopts and implements a policy of full public disclosure of all its transactions involving public interest.[59]

And then in the next article, the Bill of Rights, access to information is transformed into a right.

> The right of the people to information on matters of public concern shall be recognized. Access to official records, and to documents, and papers pertaining to official acts, transactions, or decisions, as well as to government research data used as basis for policy development, shall be afforded the citizen, subject to such limitations as may be provided by law.[60]

These "twin provisions" mutually reinforce each other, as explained in *Chavez v. Public Estates Authority*,[61] wherein the Court allowed a private citizen access to public records and eventually nullifed a Manila Bay reclamation project.

> These twin provisions of the Constitution seek to promote transparency in policy-making and in the operations of the government, as well as provide the people sufficient information to exercise effectively other constitutional rights. These twin provisions are essential to the exercise of freedom of expression. If the government does not disclose its official acts, transactions and decisions to citizens, whatever citizens say, even if expressed without any restraint, will be speculative and amount to nothing. These twin provisions are also essential to hold public officials "at all times ... accountable to the people," for unless citizens have the proper information, they cannot hold public officials accountable for anything. Armed with the right information, citizens can participate in public discussions leading to the formulation of government policies and their effective implementation. An informed citizenry is essential to the existence and proper functioning of any democracy.[62]

Judicialization as default mechanism: Institutional correction of democracy's flaws

I propose that the Philippines has judicialized its governance as a mode of correcting the deficiencies of democratic processes. Lofty norms are proclaimed officially but betrayed in day-to-day transactions. If the majoritarian process is unable to vindicate public norms, the only other mechanism *compatible with liberalism* is "decision according to law" rendered by neutral institutions.

The Brazilian legal philosopher Roberto Mangabeira Unger describes the typical circumstance of Third World democracies, a description most apt for the Philippines. There is a confusion, he says, in the people's "social imagination," a "particular incongruity between the *spiritual ideals* they had accepted as properly governing the life of the society and the vision of *social life they in fact live out.*"

> In their *professed beliefs* ... they had embraced a *liberal view* of social relations as well as of governmental organization. ... The official political dogmas of this ruling and possessing class enshrined the equality of *right*, the cult of *consent*, and the idea that power had to be ennobled by sentiment in the family, controlled by ... *legal rule in the state*, and justified by *voluntary agreement* [*in economics*].
>
> But their *actual social life* was another story.... There they treated each other as *patrons and clients* and traded in favors and dependencies. There they showed their almost complete disbelief in all institutions not founded on *blood, property, or power*. There they acted *as if a moment of personal presence was worth a thousand promises* and as if any exercise of *power could be tolerated so long as the veil of sentiment covered it.*[63]

Given this gap, the drafters of the 1987 Constitution deliberately codified their moral and policy preferences into the constitution because they did not trust the subsequent legislatures. In other words, they felt that the democratic process, left to itself, would betray those values. It was, at its heart, a distrust not just of the institutions of popular democracy; it was "disdain for the popular power." Thus the "chronic fetishism of the Constitution," the "extravagant if not obsessive reverence for the icons, liturgies and orthodoxies of Our Constitutionalism," that "dwarfs the political capacity of the people, and deadens its sense of moral responsibility."[64]

The counter-majoritarian thesis of judicial review posits that certain rights and claims must be insulated from shifting political majorities, and that correction of legislative and administrative mistakes must come from outside, through unelected judges. The function then of judicial review is "to contain or to retard, to tame or to manipulate" the raw power of the people.[65] It privileges a "higher" politics (because constitutional) that "transcend ordinary politics" (because it is subject to electoral and legislative give-and-take). It is this traditional and essentially anti-populist notion of judicial power that is idealized in the Philippines.

The best examples of Filipino formalism are two cases decided when the Philippine was still a U.S. colony, and the U.S. Supreme Court had the power to review decisions by the Philippine Supreme Court.

Cariño v. Insular Government,[66] arose from a land claim by the leader of an indigenous people. Mateo Cariño was a tribal chief of the Ibaloi tribe, one of the peoples in the Cordillera mountain range in northern Luzon. When the Philippines became an American colony, the U.S. authorities took over tribal lands for a military base and sanitarium in the mountains. Cariño sued for payment, but the Philippine Supreme Court upheld the government's claim. The Spanish colonial government had earlier required all inhabitants to register their lands, but Cariño failed to do so.

What is interesting is that the Philippine Supreme Court used the most mechanistic application of the rules, and effectively divested Cariño of all claims of title. In contrast, it took the U.S. Supreme Court, through Justice Oliver Wendell Holmes, to read Philippine land laws more justly and, indeed, more creatively. Holmes declared that it was not as if the Spanish colonial authority could overnight transform Cariño into a trespasser in his own home by token of its land registration law.

Springer v. Philippine Islands,[67] likewise began in the Philippines and ended at the U.S. Supreme Court. The Philippine Court had held that the power to appoint the board directors of a state corporation belonged to the executive (namely, the Governor-General), and not to the legislature. Again, it took Holmes, joined by Brandeis, to admonish the Philippine justices against mechanistic thinking.

> The great ordinances of the Constitution do not establish and divide fields of black and white. Even the more specific of them are found to terminate in a penumbra shading gradually from one extreme to the other.[68]

* * *

> [H]owever we may disguise it by veiling words we do not and cannot carry out the distinction between legislative and executive action with mathematical precision and divide the branches into watertight compartments, were it ever so desirable to do so, which I am far from believing that it is, or that the Constitution requires.[69]

Notice then the Philippine Supreme Court's almost fetishistic adherence to legal formalism in these landmark cases. It was not until the progressive ferment in the late 1960s and early 1970s that the fictions of liberal legality were exposed by a Maoist counter-culture, essentially an extraneous assault on legal formalism, the closest Philippine equivalent of the legal realist critique of formalism that transpired in American law.

The democratic resistance against Marcos, however, during the decade and a half of military dictatorship from 1972 to 1986, largely adopted the language of liberal democracy, and aimed, in its formal rhetoric, to restore a liberal constitution and all its trappings: elected representatives, a bill of rights, separated powers of government, and independent courts.

However, instead of merely reinstating liberal institutions, the newly restored democracy of Corazon Aquino likewise codified welfare state objectives into the 1987 Constitution. Thus the unique jurisprudential challenge, namely, legal realist objectives sought to be attained by courts that aspire, nay, pretend, to be legal formalists – and *able to do so* because the welfare state agenda has been formalized into law.

Stated otherwise, neither the Court nor the Filipino public outgrew its legal formalism. Rather, a transformed milieu rewrote what they were formalist about. The Philippines' post-Marcos Constitution is an attempt to reconcile the popular cause of social transformation with the distrust of power. Judicialized governance is at best a temporary corrective mechanism for democracy's failings, or at worst the abdication of a people's raw power to make hard choices and make them stick.

Notes

1 Garcia v. Board of Investments, G.R. No. 92024, 191 SCRA 288, 302, Nov. 9, 1990 (Melencio-Herrera, J., *dissenting*).
2 Pratap Bhanu Mehta, "The Rise of Judicial Sovereignty," *Journal of Democracy*, 18, 70, 2007, *citing* Learned Hand, *The Contribution of an Independent Judiciary to Civilization*.
3 Panama Refining Co. v. Ryan, 293 U.S. 388, 442 (1935) (Cardozo, J., *dissenting*).
4 Springer v. Philippine Islands, 277 U.S. 189, 210 (1928) (Holmes, J.).
5 Const. art. II.
6 F. Feliciano, "The Application of Law: Some Recurring Aspects of the Process of Judicial Review and Decision-Making," *American Journal of Jurisprudence*, 37, 1992, p.17.
7 Const. art. XII.
8 Const. art. XIII.
9 RECORD OF THE CONSTITUTIONAL COMMISSION [hereinafter, CON-COM RECORD], Vol. 2, Record No. 35 (21 July 1986).
10 Const. art. II, §15.
11 Const. art. II, §16.
12 Const. art. II, §17.
13 Const. art. II, §19.
14 Con-Com Journal, Vol. 2, Journal No. 63, Aug. 23, 1986.
15 Const. art. XII §12.
16 (1936).
17 (1953).
18 Const. art. XII §14.
19 Const. art. II §19.
20 ACCFA v. CUGCO, G.R. No. 221484, 30 SCRA 649, Nov. 29, 1969.
21 Const. art. II §10.
22 Const. art. II §9.
23 Const. art. XIII §1 ¶1.
24 Const. art. XIII §1 ¶2.
25 Const. art. XIII §6.
26 Const. art. XII §6.
27 Const. art. XIII §3 (emphasis supplied).
28 Const. art. XIII §4 (emphasis supplied).
29 Rep. Act No. 6657 (1988).
30 G.R. No. 86889, 192 SCRA 51, Dec. 4, 1990.
31 Association of Small Landowners v. Secretary of Agrarian Reform, G.R. No. 78742, 175 SCRA 343, 385, July 14, 1989 (emphasis in original).
32 Const. art. VIII §1.
33 Rules of Court, Rule 65.
34 Oposa v. Factoran, G.R. No. 101083, 224 SCRA 792, 810, July 30, 1992 citing Isagani Cruz, Philippine Political Law, 226–27 (1991 ed.).
35 Const. art. II §16.
36 Oposa v. Factoran, G.R. No. 101083, 224 SCRA 792, 804–5, July 30, 1992.
37 Ibid., at 815, (Feliciano, J., *concurring*).
38 Ibid., at 818, (Feliciano, J., *concurring*) (emphasis supplied).
39 G.R. No. 92024, 191 SCRA 288, Nov. 9, 1990.

40 Ibid., at 299, (Griño-Aquino, J., *dissenting*).
41 Ibid., p.302, (Melencio-Herrera, J., *dissenting*).
42 G.R. No. 122156, 267 SCRA 408, Feb. 3, 1997.
43 Ibid., p.447.
44 G.R. No. 124360, 281 SCRA 330, Nov. 5, 1997.
45 Oposa v. Factoran, G.R. No. 101083, 224 SCRA 792, Jul. 30, 1992.
46 Tatad v. Sec. of Energy, G.R. No. 124360, 281 SCRA 330, 370, Nov. 5, 1997.
47 Panama Refining Co. v. Ryan, 293 U.S. 388, 441 (1935), (Cardozo, J., *dissenting*).
48 Tañada v. Angara, G.R. No. 118295, 272 SCRA 18, May 2, 1997.
49 Ibid., pp.58–9.
50 *See e.g.,* Valmonte v. Philippine Charity Sweepstakes, G.R. No. 78716, Sep. 22, 1987 *and* Tan v. Macapagal, G.R. No. 34161, Feb. 29, 1972.
51 G.R. No. 130716, 299 SCRA 744, Dec. 9, 1998.
52 Ibid., pp.758–9.
53 Kapatiran ng mga Naglilingkod sa Pamahalaan ng Pilipinas, Inc. v. Tan, G.R. No. 81311, 163 SCRA 371, 378, June 30, 1988.
54 Kilosbayan v. Guingona, 232 SCRA 110, 137, Aug. 25,1994.
55 Ibid., p.137.
56 Ibid.
57 Kilosbayan v. Morato, G.R. No. 119326, 246 SCRA 540, July 17, 1995.
58 369 US 186, 7 L.Ed. 2d 633 (1962).
59 Const. art. II §28.
60 Const. art. III §7.
61 G.R. No. 133250, 384 SCRA 152, July 9, 2002.
62 Ibid., p.184.
63 R. Mangabeira Unger, "Social Theory: Its Situation and Its Task. A Critical Introduction to Politics," *Constructive Social Theory,* 73, 68, 1987 (emphases supplied).
64 Richard Parker, *Here the People Rule: A Constitutional Populist Manifesto*, Cambridge, Harvard University Press, 1994.
65 Ibid.
66 41 Phil. 935 (1909), *and* 212 U.S. 449, 457 (1909).
67 50 Phil. 259, 276 (1927), *and* 277 U.S. 189 (1928).
68 Springer v. Philippine Islands, 277 U.S. 189, 210 (1928) (Holmes, J., *dissenting*).
69 Ibid., p.212.

15 Administrative law and judicial review in Indonesia

The search for accountability

Stewart Fenwick

Introduction

Administrative review has operated in Indonesia for just over 15 years. The Administrative Courts were seen as offering a vehicle for challenges to state authority in the latter years of the Soeharto regime. However, the promise of a significant contribution to accountability was not sustained. The Court has steadily declined in prominence, and has not found a voice in post-reform Indonesia. In many respects the jurisdiction is largely invisible, and is notable for its comparatively light caseload, poor enforcement powers, and an apparent inability to generate significant jurisprudence. A new draft law seeks to re-vitalize administrative review procedures in the pursuit of civil service reform, President Yudhoyono's anti-corruption agenda, and the establishment of principles of good administrative governance as the foundation for executive action. While the draft Law on Government Administration sets out new standards for administrative decision-making, it does not alter the framework for review mechanisms in any fundamental way.

The Administrative Courts therefore must be seen in the context of political and legal transition in Indonesia more generally. The lack of impact of the Courts only reflects the marginal role of the Court system, until recently, to act as a check upon state authority. The truncated authority and degraded capacity of the Court system has begun to be systematically addressed, and recent experience with judicial review is contributing to a new mindset. Judicial review, in the sense of reviewing laws for consistency with the constitution, is now taking hold as the most important avenue for legal review in Indonesia, and eclipses in significance the reforms that led to the establishment of Administrative Courts. However, the overall framework of accountability through judicial oversight – across all levels of government and legislative authority – is fractured, lacking in procedural consistency, and conceals significant scope for the abrogation of constitutional protections.

Almost ten years after Soeharto's departure, the whole conception of the Indonesian state – its nature, purpose, and administration – continues to evolve. The judiciary is beginning to play a part in this process of re-definition, but a new and coherent theory of public law is yet to crystallize, and the anatomy of the state itself remains novel and, at times, puzzling. Accountability may be partial precisely because the state itself is a hybrid creature; partly de-regulated, partly de-centralized, and partly judicialized. Under the circumstances, the search for accountability is perhaps rather more an aspiration than an expectation. Questions that flow from this predicament include whether, or for how long, Indonesia will remain suspended in what might be described as its "pre-regulatory" condition? What are the limitations of this situation? Specifically, will the administrative law field remain a jurisdiction in search of a cause? More fundamentally, what further changes – if any – are required in the structures, procedures, or mentalities of government?

Indonesian transitions: Regulation and reform

Law and development has recently been re-conceived by David Trubek and Alvaro Santos[1] as being situated at the point of convergence of three disciplines – law, economics, and institutional practice. Therefore some preliminary observations will clarify the way in which the concepts of governance, administration, and modes of regulation being addressed in this volume apply to the case of Indonesia. As prefaced by Kanishka Jayasuriya in this volume, the emergence of the regulatory state carries different implications for developing nations in comparison to developed democracies. For Indonesia in particular, the story is more about efforts to constitute the public domain, not reconstituting it in line with new conceptions of governance. Similarly Dan Lev, in one of his last commentaries, asserted that one should start from the assumption that Indonesia has no functioning state at all.[2] More specifically, with regard to Indonesia's law and legal institutions, Lev proposed that we seek to understand "how a reasonably useful legal system was destroyed and what forces counted most in reducing it to rubble."[3]

This does not mean that elements of what has been called "new governance"[4] are irrelevant to this case study, or that Indonesia is not influenced in a variety of ways by transnational regimes and economic forces. Indonesia has instituted a number of legal and institutional reforms in its process of transition, many in direct response to international pressure.[5] Some of these developments reflect a broader pattern of reform, in which the notion of the state in East Asia is moving away from a model of state as provider, and in which new regulatory frameworks are emerging.[6] Indonesia has, for example, several regulatory institutions that would be familiar to foreign observers: the Business Competition Supervisory Commission (KPPU); the Capital Market and Financial Institutions Supervisory Agency (Bapepam-LK); and a National Consumer Protection Board (BPKN). The experience of the KPPU, though, provides some indication of the difficulty of changing the practice of governance in Indonesia. The emergence of the KPPU in 2000 reflected long-standing local demands for reform of business monopolies, but the institution has been subject to criticism since its inception for a lack of commitment, and incapacity to exercise its core competencies.[7] During 2007 the KPPU evaluated the investments of Singapore's Temasek Holdings in two Indonesian communications companies, a challenge described as likely to determine if the agency would "retain what little trust the public still has in its integrity and technical competence."[8]

The Commission held against Temasek, and its decision has indeed been criticized as revealing significant technical weaknesses.[9]

The accountability referred to in this chapter therefore is primarily that of public legal institutions, and their contribution to the rule of law in the conventional sense.[10] The relatively confined terms of this case study reflect the low base from which the *reformasi* process commenced. The pace of this process was, and remains, determined by the complexity of unraveling the extreme anti-governance that characterized the New Order regime of President Soeharto. The hallmarks of this regime were heavily centralized authority, a comprehensive and highly effective system of corruption, and a degraded and compromised legal system. Despite these factors, and contrary to theory, investor confidence remained stable and economic growth high for a sustained period of time due to Soeharto's capacity to manage the system of bribery, and preserve property rights for investors.[11] The management of corruption was particularly sophisticated, resembling a complex franchise arrangement spanning all institutions – administrative, judicial, legislative, military, and commercial – and all levels of administration – national, regional, and down to village level.[12]

Given the pre-reform pathology of governance,[13] judicial reform and the emergence of judicial review is one of the most important stories to emerge from contemporary governance reform in Indonesia. Ultimately, this is a story about the rehabilitation of the judiciary, and while there is still a significant amount of institutional reform left to do, the importance of developments to date should not be underestimated. By far the most interesting dimension is the contribution made by the new Constitutional Court in Indonesia which is beginning to play a significant role in re-conceiving the rule of law. This reform offers considerable scope for reflection on the process of judicialization both in terms of its impact on the state in Indonesia, and on theories of constitutional and political reform in Asia.

A note on judicial authority in Indonesia

The failure of law and legal institutions under the New Order regime was the perfection of a process of de-legitimization that commenced with Sukarno's Guided Democracy, and both were in turn built on a constitutional framework hostile to liberal legal order. The intellectual foundations of Indonesian constitutional order following independence drew upon European organicist thought, leading to the development of a theory of the integralist state, a model in which the state and individual were understood to be more or less united (a "village republic").[14] Despite the Indonesian state having a structure and legal logic derived from European sources, the *Pancasila* philosophy of state was at odds with the legality inherent in the broader structure.[15] Sukarno's 1961 declaration that "you cannot make a revolution with lawyers" succinctly describes the climate his revolutionary politics generated for the law state (or *negara hukum*), but constitutional democracy had already been discarded, and this was a critical turning point for the rule of law in Indonesia.[16] Following the arrival of Soeharto in

1965 (using means that were definitively extra-constitutional) lawyers and legal officials quickly realized they need not adjust the (bad) "habits" initiated under his predecessor Sukarno.[17]

There should be no misunderstanding about the fact that the power of judicial review, and the independence of the judiciary more broadly, were eliminated through deliberately targeted legal and administrative measures. During the 1950s the judiciary struggled, and failed, to achieve reforms to their salary (which was similar to that of prosecutors) and independence from the civil service (they remained covered by civil service regulations), with the consequence that legal skills shrank in importance with the rise of bureaucratic politics among legal agencies.[18] The judiciary lobbied Parliament for independence from the Ministry of Justice, and for the establishment of a power of constitutional review, but these proposals were lost with declaration of martial law in 1957.[19] In 1960 the Supreme Court Chairman (Chief Justice) was appointed to Sukarno's 100-member Cabinet, and there followed a "barrage of substantive and political steps" to subject judges to Sukarno's increasingly "grandiose" ideology.[20] These measures included replacing the traditional scales of justice as the symbol of the courts with a banyan tree (a traditional symbol of protection), but the keystone of the new legal architecture was Law No. 19/1964 on the judiciary which empowered the Executive to interfere at any stage of the judicial process "in the interests of the revolution."[21] The Elucidation to a subsequent law, No. 13/1965 (also dealing with judicial power) put the matter beyond any doubt, proclaiming that "the idea of the separation of powers doctrine (*Trias Politika*) no longer applies in Indonesian society."[22]

Following the establishment of Soeharto's New Order a "definitive symbolic reform battle" took place between 1968 and 1970 over amendments to the law on the judiciary.[23] Two key claims promoted once again by the judiciary (with support from the private profession) were administrative independence and powers of judicial review, but a third measure was also pursued – the upgrading of the constitutional framework to a balance of powers (as opposed to a mere separation of powers) system.[24] The new law, No. 14/1970, however, did not provide the sought-after reforms. In contrast to the 1964–65 legislation, it reinstated a measure of separation of powers by affirming that the judiciary was "free from any interference from any other power of government," but the judiciary remained under departmental control.[25] The law's Elucidation also spelt out the administration's conclusive view on the nature of judicial review in Indonesia: the 1945 Constitution did not provide for constitutional review; legislation could not provide the Supreme Court with this power; only specific constitutional amendment could grant this power to the Court.[26] The 1970 legislation did introduce a limited form of review, with article 26 of Law No. 14 providing the Supreme Court with the authority to invalidate instruments below the level of statute on grounds that they were in conflict with statute.[27] This restricted power of judicial review (or *hak uji materiil* in Indonesian) was further truncated in its implementation because it was ultimately the prerogative of the relevant agency to rescind any invalid law, and – in practice – the court focused only on older colonial-era statutes and was extremely reticent to read down post-Independence legislation.[28]

Perhaps the major contribution of the New Order regime was to achieve total political domination of the judiciary through consistent interference in the management of both the Supreme Court and lower courts. This co-option of the judiciary "cut deeper and would last longer" than any of the previous conflicts or challenges, and was distinguished by further encroachments into judicial administration and independence.[29] Sebastiaan Pompe catalogues the strangulation of the judiciary between 1970 and 1998.[30] It was achieved through complete control of administration by the Department of Justice, and the appointment as Chairman of the Supreme Court of a series of political appointees from outside the judicial career corps. There were also other critical compromises made to the institution of the judiciary. For example, the courts at all levels of administration, national down to regional, from the early 1980s were included in informal councils of justice sector officials, other government agencies, and the military, which were a peculiar tool of coordination and control instituted by the regime, and which effectively bound the justice sector to the authority of the military.[31]

The courts also became increasingly notorious as a player in corruption, and the "judicial mafia" (*mafia peradilan* as it is still known in Indonesia) was publicly exposed through the revelations of a member of the Supreme Court, who detailed the collusion rampant in the highest levels of the judiciary, and corruption was by no means confined to the superior court.[32] One of the final, and perhaps the most unusual, indicators of the decline of judicial standards was the revelation during the 1990s that there was an entrenched practice of the use of so-called *surat sakti* or "magic memos" by the Chairman of the Supreme Court. This was a method by which the Chairman issued instructions countermanding verdicts in particular cases on the instruction of the executive when – according to a former Chairman – it was in the interests of national development.[33] This reflected a pattern of direct intervention in cases by both Ministers of Justice and Chairman of the Court that had become commonplace many years earlier.[34] It is against this summary of the central issues affecting judicial authority in Indonesia that I will turn to the development of the system of administrative justice.

The emergence of administrative justice

Between Independence and the New Order of Soeharto, administrative law in Indonesia was experienced through Dutch-influenced actions in government tort.[35] This is evidenced particularly by a body of jurisprudence from the period of parliamentary democracy of 1950–1959. The groundwork for a separate administrative jurisdiction was established through the adoption by the Provisional People's Congress in 1960 of an eight-year plan that included the establishment of a system of administrative justice. Subsequently, the otherwise retrograde 1964 law on the judiciary included a reference to an Administrative Court as a branch of the judicial arm. The most likely explanation for the rather sudden, and somewhat contradictory, emergence of the concept of administrative justice in the 1964 law appears to be the personal commitment of the then recently appointed Minister for Justice. The reason for its appearance earlier in the state development plan is not apparent.

Eighteen years were to pass before a government-sponsored Bill was submitted to Parliament. During this time there was what one observer called a "summer of liberal influence" in the early New Order (which took place in the years 1966–67).[36] A parliamentary committee considered the proposed Administrative Courts, and a draft Bill was prepared by reform minded parliamentarians, but the overwhelming focus of attention was the debate on rehabilitation of the status of the judiciary.[37] Research and studies took place throughout the late 1960s and early 1970s, both by professional and government-affiliated bodies, including a visit to France in 1976 by a number of judges that allowed them to learn first-hand about administrative justice. Then, for reasons that are not entirely clear, Soeharto announced in his annual speech to parliament in 1978 that Administrative Courts would be established. A government team went on to prepare a draft law, but it failed to gain political support upon introduction to Parliament in 1982, and it was not adopted. The 1982 Bill was revised, although it remained in most respects substantially the same, and was adopted as Law No. 5/1986 – the Law on Administrative Justice.[38]

The closing provision of the Law, article 145, allowed a period of up to five years for the commencement of the Law, in order to ensure that the appropriate physical and personal infrastructure was in place. The new jurisdiction would be developed "in stages," and only following enactment of the Law would the government consider what preparations were necessary.[39] A little over four years following the passage of the legislation, the Law on Administrative Justice came into effect, on 14 January 1991.[40] Thereafter Administrative Courts were established across Indonesia in batches, with judges also recruited in groups, largely due to resource constraints at the Ministry of Justice, which was responsible for court administration (for reasons outlined in the previous section).[41]

The framework for Administrative Justice

The Law on Administrative Justice introduced the principle of judicial review of administrative action, and it established the Administrative Courts and their rules of procedure. The Law is not, however, a comprehensive statement of administrative law or procedure, it did not set standards for administrative decision-making, nor address the process of seeking administrative remedies from state agencies. Therefore a significant number of the Law's provisions deal exclusively with matters concerning the establishment, staffing, and administration of the two levels of Administrative Court. As with the General Courts in Indonesia, the jurisdiction consists of a first instance court (State Administrative Court) at the District level, and an appeal court (High Administrative Court) at the Province level. The Court's jurisdiction extends to administrative action taken at both the central and district government level (article 1(1)).

The Administrative Courts can only receive a challenge to an administrative decision after any relevant administrative appeals have been exhausted (article 48). An administrative "appeal" can be made when the relevant legislation requires a separate or higher institution to handle complaints, such as in the case of disciplinary matters relating to civil servants. The administrative decision itself informs the party concerned whether or not administrative review is available to them. Following this initial administrative review procedure, the challenge may be taken to the High Administrative Court (article 51), and by inference, judicial review of all other administrative decisions may be filed at the State Administrative Court.

Administrative decisions are defined (article 1(3)) as a written decision given by a body or administrative official, consisting of acts under administrative law based on legislation, that are "concrete, individual, and final, and that give arise to legal consequences for a person or legal entity." Under article 3, administrative decisions include those that officials fail to make when so authorized, as well as decisions not taken within a specified time. Persons or legal entities affected by the decision may seek judicial review under article 53(1), and may seek to have the decision declared "void or illegal," with or without an accompanying claim for compensation or "rehabilitation." The grounds for judicial review originally included (article 53(2)) were:

- the decision contravenes the relevant legislation;
- at the time of making the decision, the body or administrative officer used their authority for a purpose other than that for which it was granted;
- at the time of making, or not making the decision, in question, after properly weighing all the relevant considerations, the body or administrative official should not have arrived at the decision (or the failure to make the decision).

In 2004 the second and third grounds cited in the 1986 legislation were removed, and decisions were made subject to challenge if in contravention of "general principles of proper administration."[42] The Elucidation to the 2004 law describes these principles as including, along with "legal certainty," the following:

- rules of state management/organization;
- transparency;
- proportionality;
- professionalism;
- accountability.

Including these principles is the Elucidation cross-references Law No. 28/1999 on Clean State Management Free of Corruption, Collusion, and Nepotism.[43] This post-New Order act sought to reverse the slide in standards of public administration, particularly rampant corruption, known to Indonesians as *KKN* (an acronym for corruption, collusion, and nepotism). The intention of the amendment therefore appears to tie the work of the Administrative Courts to the broader reform agenda of better public administration, and also thereby to provide standards against which administrative decisions might be measured. However, in neither law does there appear to be a provision – for example – obliging all decision-makers to apply these principles of good government in fulfilling their legislative responsibilities, so the overall outcome appears more aspirational than substantive.

The stipulations for enforcement of the Court's judgment include provisions (article 116) nullifying a decision that has not been rescinded within four months of the judgment, or within three months when the Court requires the issuing of a revised decision, or the issuing of a decision when none had previously been made. The 1986 law then provided that in cases of continuing interference by the relevant official or body, the Chairman of the Court could require compliance. Following any further delays in execution, the Chairman of the Court could then bring the matter to the attention of the President. The provisions concerning execution were tightened in 2004 (article 116(4)) to allow the imposition of a fine or administrative sanction against the official in question in cases of non-compliance. Should this measure still fail to result in compliance, the Registrar of the Court may publicize the matter in local print media (article 116(5)).

A further amendment was introduced through Law No. 5/2004 which revised rights of appeal to the Supreme Court. Litigants in Indonesia have largely unrestricted rights of appeal to the Supreme Court, which is at the apex of the system of General Courts. Under the 1986 Law on Administrative Justice, cases from the Administrative Courts could, as with other jurisdictions, be taken on cassation to the Supreme Court, and further to an appeal procedure within the Supreme Court known as *peninjauan kembali* (and usually translated as "judicial review") (articles 131–132). In 2004, the right of appeal on cassation to the Supreme Court in administrative cases arising from decisions of district officials was removed (article 45A of Law No. 5/2004).[44] Thus, administrative decisions in regional Indonesia may not proceed beyond the level of the High Administrative Court, located at provincial level. This amendment appears to have potentially far-reaching consequences given that a significant amount of government services in Indonesia have been decentralized.[45] At the time of writing, however, this restriction to the appeal processes applying to local level decision-making had become the subject of a challenge in the Constitutional Court, and its status is therefore uncertain.[46]

Current administrative law reforms

A draft Law on Administrative Governance was released in February 2007 which aimed to introduce a number of significant reforms for administrative law in general, and for the Administrative Courts.[47] Two key reasons advanced for the latest reforms are poor standards in public administration, and the fact that after almost 20 years of a system of administrative justice decisions of the Administrative Courts frequently fail to be effectively executed. Notes accompanying the draft law therefore propose that the law will provide a new basis for relations between the state and its citizens, as well as providing a basis for examining administrative decisions in the Administrative Courts.

The draft law seeks to apply an exhaustive list of principles of proper administration to the acts of all officials and agencies (article 2). This list consists of no fewer than 20 principles, including those introduced to the Law on Administrative Justice in 2004 (such as transparency and accountability) but also including accuracy, justice, appropriateness, protection of philosophy of life and/or private life, the public good, as well as efficiency and effectiveness. The draft law also provides that this list of principles can continue to develop according to development in knowledge, social needs, and jurisprudence (article 2(4)). Further, the law establishes procedures for making administrative decisions, requiring, for example, that officials exclude themselves when they have an interest in the decision in question, allowing interested parties to be heard before making a decision, and providing access to relevant documents during the process (articles 10–20).

The draft law then sets out the requirements for administrative decisions (article 21), which include 11 "material" conditions. These include the requirement that the decision fulfills 20 principles of good government stipulated in article 2, as well as others such as taking into account the balance of interests expressed by concerned parties, consistency with previous decisions, and not being in contravention of responsibilities arising in the community concerned, and numerous others. The reasons forming the basis of the decision must also be provided (article 24). The reasons for which a decision may be nullified include (article 30) a mistake in one of the material conditions, a party that should be excluded from having input in the decision is proven to have been involved, or the decision involved bribery or corruption. The draft also proposes a system of administrative objection for all administrative decisions not already the subject of their own review procedures (article 36) and provides for recourse to the national or regional Ombudsman Commissions in situations where an official or agency has failed to respond adequately, or at all, to a request for review of a decision (article 38).[48]

The draft Law on Government Administration provides that parties may challenge an administrative decision in the Administrative Courts (article 39). It is clear from the above brief analysis that the draft law potentially expands the range of considerations for a judge of the Administrative Courts far beyond any of the considerations included in Law No. 5/1986, as amended. Should the proposals be enacted as drafted, judges will face a difficult and complex challenge to identify and weigh the very large number of principles, conditions, and procedures that will be associated with administrative decisions. However, the draft law also offers significant potential to expand the range of matters coming before the courts. The draft does this in two ways. First, it proposes expanding the range of actors capable of making an administrative decision beyond merely government officials, to include decisions made by "other legal entities that conduct government functions based on laws and regulations" (article 1(1)). The draft defines other legal entities as "organizations or officials that conduct government functions on assignment, delegation or transfer of authority based on law or regulation."

Second, it proposes expanding the definition of "decision" to include oral decisions (article 1(4)). Finally, in an effort to increase the level of enforcement of decisions of the Administrative Courts, the draft law proposes that any fine imposed by the Court for non-compliance with its decision may be administered by the Court Bailiff (article 7).

In the opinion of a senior judge who participated in drafting the proposed Law on Government Administration, the law would expand the jurisdiction of the Administrative Courts, and potentially clarify the distinction between the roles of these courts and the General Courts.[49] Thus, all decisions or legal acts taken under public law – whether by a government official or any other legal entity – could be challenged in the Administrative Courts, and all private acts would be funneled to the civil jurisdiction.[50] In the view of the senior judge in question, the new framework for administrative law would embrace the work of commercial entities delivering government services. The Elucidation prepared for the draft law does not address this important development at all.

The Administrative Courts at work

Adriaan Bedner's study of the Administrative Courts[51] is the most comprehensive analysis of the jurisdiction in its early years of operation. While the Court was still relatively new at the time of his research, his conclusions remain of value despite the adjustments made in 2004. On the question of the Court's understanding of its jurisdiction, he found that there were many inconsistencies in approach, resulting in dubious decisions. The distinction between what was an administrative and a civil case was not always clear, and the Court was quite flexible in allowing a wide range of defendants to be named. Perhaps more worrisome was inconsistency in approaches taken to the principal question of whether or not a particular act met the requirements of the definition in the legislation (concrete, individual, final). Moreover, the application of the provisions establishing grounds for review showed considerable variety of opinion. In particular there was a strong body of opinion that general principles of proper administration were accepted by judges as being a ground for administrative review, even though this did not appear in the legislation until the 2004 amendments. This principle was simply appropriated by the judges from Dutch law, and implied among the grounds of review.[52] Selection of exactly what principle the Court thought applied in a particular situation appeared, in some cases, to be almost random.

Despite these technical limitations, the early work of the Court has been celebrated, most notably its decision in the case challenging the Government's 1994 banning of the independent weekly magazine *Tempo*. While the claimant in the case ultimately failed, the case offered a taste of what might be achieved through the process of administrative review. In that case the Administrative Courts overturned the government ban, basing its decision on a failure to follow principles of good administration, and applying an assumed power to set aside a regulation for inconsistency with a higher law – that is, employing a further form of judicial review, as yet unavailable in the courts.[53] The Supreme Court duly accepted the Government's appeal against the decisions of the lower courts, and – for good measure – transferred the presiding judge from the first instance court to a distant post.[54] The lower court judgments attracted attention precisely because the concept of challenging the system was novel. There are other examples of decisions of the new court attracting publicity in its early years, which are all the more notable because the gradual roll-out of the court meant that there were very few Administrative Courts in place at the time.[55]

Contemporary decisions of the Administrative Courts are difficult to locate, owing to the current poor state of documentation of the work of the court system generally. The Supreme Court has no uniform system in place for publishing its own judgments, let alone those of lower courts.[56] One case study recently published in a weekly current affairs journal offers a snapshot of a fairly typical case in the Administrative Courts, as well as some insight into decision-making in the Supreme Court. Under the heading "One Object Two Decisions,"[57] the piece relates the story of a land dispute and a series of associated administrative decisions dating back to 1961. Land in the suburb of Pondok Indah, South Jakarta, was acquired from parties claiming it as part of an inheritance. The other party, a land developer, had since constructed a golf course and housing complex on the land. In 1961 the inheritors were awarded compensation by the Government in the form of a piece of land approximately one-fifth the size of their original plot. A subsequent determination in 1984 offered them a smaller plot, and a further decision in 1987 determined that they should receive a sum of Rp 146,000,000.[58] In 1999 the Head of the National Land Agency issued a determination withdrawing both the 1987 and 1984 decisions, therefore in effect reinstating the earliest, and in the opinion of the inheritors most generous, compensation offer. The land developer challenged the 1999 decision in the Administrative Courts, ultimately coming to the Supreme Court on cassation, at which point the developer lost.

In 2003, two separate claims for judicial review (*peninjauan kembali*) were filed, one each by a company director and deputy company director of the land developer. In September 2004, the same panel of Justices at the Supreme Court, with the same Justice chairing the panels on both occasions, upheld the appeal in the case of one of the representatives of the property developer, and refused the appeal in the case of the other representative. The confusion that this result caused the original land owners, and the lack of a response from the Supreme Court when approached to explain the differing results, led the landowners to send the case files to the journal in an effort to gain some support for their case.

Recent data published by the Supreme Court may help in reviewing contemporary practice in the Administrative Courts, and at least allows for a comparison to be made of the workload of the Administrative Courts with that of other courts (see Table 15.1).

The Administrative Courts clearly handle a tiny fraction of the total caseload of the Indonesian court system at first instance. The 2006 caseload of 840 compares with 627 cases in 1995, and 330 cases filed in 1991.[60] Despite this increase in filings over time, the judges at first instance are vastly under-worked in comparison with their colleagues in other jurisdictions: on average, Administrative Courts judges

Table 15.1 Workload in Indonesian courts, 2006[59]

Jurisdiction level	No. Cases	% (by level of court)	No. Judges	Output (case/judge)
General				
First Instance	2,636,689	92.53	2,787	946
Appeal	8,202	73.23	334	25.5
Religious				
First Instance	206,780	7.25	2,203	93.8
Appeal	1,952	17.42	239	8.1
Administrative				
First Instance	1,203	0.04	180	6.7
Appeal	621	5.54	30	10.7
Military				
First Instance	4,628	0.16	73	63.4
Appeal	425	3.79	9	47.2
Total First Instance	**2,849,300**		**5,243**	**543.44**
Total Appeal	**11,200**		**612**	**18.30**

decide just under seven cases each per year. There are Administrative Courts in some districts in Indonesia handling as few as eight cases per annum, and even the busiest court handled a total of only 175 cases at first instance in 2006.[61] The relatively high volume of cases at the appeal level derives from the allocation of jurisdiction (discussed earlier) in which the High Administrative Court accepts not only cases on appeal from the State Administrative Courts, but also cases previously the subject of other administrative review procedures. I will return later to the issue of the volume of cases handled by the Indonesian court system, as the workload of the General Courts in particular requires further interpretation.

A recent study of the caseload at the Supreme Court offers better insight into the docket of the Administrative Courts.[62] Figures from the Supreme Court docket may not reflect accurately the composition of the caseload of the Administrative Court at lower levels, but the Administrative Court does not compile data about its caseload, so an accurate assessment cannot be made of the breakdown of cases in this jurisdiction.[63] Further, the figures that appear in Table 15.2 are estimates only, based on a review of almost 19,000 cases in circulation at the Supreme Court in 2006, and there is some inaccuracy in the data recording processes (which primarily reflect variations in administrative procedures within the Supreme Court). However, the table presents a breakdown of the nearly 2,500 cases managed by the Administrative Law Division of the Supreme Court, by subject matter.

The predominance of land disputes is striking, as is the high profile of labor, tax, and civil service cases.[64] It is worth looking in a little detail at the issue of land. A breakdown of causes of action in civil cases on appeal at the Supreme Court shows that at least 30–40 percent of all civil cases relate in some way to land disputes. This does not take into account inheritance cases, which in many instances would also include land issues, so the overall percentage of civil disputes

Table 15.2 Cases in Administrative Division of Supreme Court by subject matter, 2006

Subject matter	%
Land	30.0
Labor	21.5
Tax	12.5
Civil Service	9.0
Permits and approvals	5.0
Challenge to regulations	4.5
Decision at district level	4.0
Other	13.5
Total	**100.0**

at cassation level involving land could reach as high as around 50 percent. In total, therefore, land disputes in both the administrative and civil jurisdictions may account for around 25 percent of all cases at the Supreme Court.[65]

Fewer than 5 percent of cases in Table 15.2 involve a challenge to a regulation – the total number of cases of this type in the Supreme Court in 2006 was approximately 110. This group of cases is the sum of the Supreme Court's workload in conducting judicial review of regulations. They form part of the Administrative Law caseload because a Supreme Court regulation requires that judicial review be managed by the Administrative Law Division of the Court.[66] This number of cases seems incredibly low, despite the fact that figures recently compiled by the Cabinet Secretariat show that since 1945 over 3,400 Government regulations have been passed, with a total of 686 passed since 1998.[67] Since Independence a further 10,468 Presidential instruments of various types have been signed into law, and during the same time a total of 1,343 pieces of legislation have become law.[68] Overall, the volume of regulatory instruments below the level of legislation (and which potentially fall within the Supreme Court's power of judicial review) outnumber the volume of Acts of Parliament by a ratio of 10:1. While the small volume of work handled by the Administrative Courts is itself interesting, the low volume of judicial review work is perhaps even more telling. This component of judicial authority, which forms a critical counterpart to the role filled by the Administrative Courts, might rank as the least used element of judicial authority in Indonesia.

The judiciary post-1998

Following the end of the Soeharto era in 1998 there has been a renewed focus on the judiciary. Critically, there has been a reversal of previous policy in relation to the two key issues – management and administrative responsibility for the judiciary, and constitutional review – and these reforms have been accompanied by an expansion in the jurisdiction of the courts, with a number of specialist courts having been added to the ranks of the judiciary. The early years of *reformasi*, though, saw no action from the judiciary itself. According to Pompe, the courts failed to react to the opportunity presented by the widespread political reform going on around them, thus the major developments affecting the Supreme Court during the early years of reform were externally driven.[69]

The short but significant Law 35/1999 – the so-called *Satu Atap* (literally "one roof") law – dismantled control of the judiciary by the bureaucracy.[70] It provided for the transfer of administrative control over all four branches of the judiciary – general, religious, military, and administrative – from the Ministry of Justice and other Departments to the control of a single body, the Supreme Court. This change was cemented after a five-year transition period. A second significant change was the filling, in 2000, of 20 vacancies at the Supreme Court – around half the total positions – through a transparent process in which Parliament publicly scrutinized candidates for the bench.[71] In this way a large number of non-career candidates were appointed, changing the gene pool at the top of the judiciary, and leading to the selection of one of the new appointees as Chief Justice – Bagir Manan. Under his leadership the Supreme Court has pursued a reform agenda based on several "blueprints" for reform of the judiciary, developed in close consultation with civil society representatives.[72] This program has allowed the judiciary to present a fairly respectable profile in what continues to be a very dynamic time in Indonesian legal and judicial reform.

A further reform era development was the refinement made to the Supreme Court's power of judicial review. In 2004 amendments were introduced to the legislation for the Supreme Court to strengthen the Court's power of judicial review.[73] Now a successful challenge to regulation, or other subordinate instrument such as a Presidential or Ministerial decree, has immediate legal effect rather than requiring remedial action on the part of the relevant agency, as had been the case since the introduction of judicial review in 1970.[74]

One of the most striking developments in the reform era, however, has been the proliferation of new courts, evidenced by the establishment of a total of eight new jurisdictions between 1998 and 2006 – an average of one new court per year.[75] Table 15.3 summarizes this expansion of courts, with the year referring to the time the new jurisdiction became operational.

All of the courts listed in Table 15.3, except for the Constitutional and *Syariah* Courts, form part of the General Courts system in Indonesia. They are not separate court systems in their own right and so, for example, the Commercial, Human Rights, Corruption and Industrial Relations Courts are physically located in, and administered by, existing District Courts. According to the Chief Justice of the Supreme Court, the development of new specialist courts is a phenomena of the reform era, but he has cautioned against courts being established merely as a response to the wishes of particular interest groups.[76] In part these concerns reflect experience with the Anti-Corruption Court, which was the subject of a successful constitutional review in the new Constitutional Court (see next section), and a concern among the judiciary that special courts weaken the existing judicial infrastructure. In reality the development of specialist courts has, to an important degree, been motivated by the obvious weaknesses of the judiciary and

Table 15.3 New courts established post-Soeharto

Year	Court	Law
1998	Commercial	Law 4/1998 enacting Government Regulation in Lieu of Law 1/1998 Concerning Amendments to the Bankruptcy Law
2000	Human Rights	Law 29/1999 on Human Rights; Law 26/2000 on Human Rights Courts
2002	Tax	Law 14/2002 on Tax Courts
2003	Constitutional	Third Amendment to 1945 Constitution, 2001; Law 24/2003 on the Constitutional Court
2004	Corruption	Law 30/2002 on the Anti-Corruption Commission
2004	*Syariah*	Law 4/2004 on the Judiciary; Law 18/2001 on Special Autonomy for Aceh
2006	Industrial Relations	Law 2/2004 on the Resolution of Industrial Relations Disputes
2007	Fisheries	Law 31/2004 on Fisheries

its reluctance to embrace reform. Thus the Chief Justice has also acknowledged that in the longer term, the judicial system may "re-absorb" the specialist courts once the weaknesses of the judiciary have been done away with.[77]

In most instances, these new courts are found in very few locations. As we saw in relation to the establishment of the Administrative Courts, the practice is, and continues to be, that new courts are established gradually in a few locations at a time. Thus the Human Rights Court operates in Jakarta, Makassar, Medan, and Surabaya – although these last two locations have not to date received a single case.[78] The Commercial Court, similarly, is physically present only in Jakarta, Medan, Makassar, Surabaya, and also Semarang. The Corruption Court exists only in Jakarta. The case of the Tax Court is different again, with the previous taxation dispute body being re-badged as a Court under the 2002 legislation, and the Court itself sitting as a special chamber of the Administrative Court.[79] In the case of the *Syariah* Courts, these are the existing Religious Courts in Aceh with a new name, and with an expanded jurisdiction. In addition to the existing jurisdiction of the Religious Courts (in which over 90 percent of all cases are divorce cases for Indonesian Muslims),[80] the Courts in Aceh have been granted special jurisdiction as part of the autonomy package granted to Aceh. This includes Islamic moral offences such as gambling, for which criminal penalties (including caning) apply.[81]

The reason that most of the new specialist courts fall under the General Courts lies in the structure of the judiciary mandated by the Constitution. Article 24 of the Constitution specifies that judicial authority is vested in the following judicial bodies: public courts (what I have been referring to as the General Courts); religious courts; military courts; the state administrative courts; and the Constitutional Court. Therefore, the establishment of a free-standing jurisdiction would require a constitutional amendment, which significantly raises the stakes for legal policy makers, and results in something of a strain on – or at the very least a complication to – judicial administration in the General Courts. The earlier analysis is only a brief review, and not sufficient to explain the particular histories of, and motivations for, each court. The Commercial Court, for example, has its genesis in the dialogue between Indonesia and the international community post-economic crisis.[82] The Anti-Corruption Court was instituted as a special forum for the prosecution of cases handled by the new Anti-Corruption Commission,[83] and the special case of the *Syariah* Court has been outlined.

There are no comprehensive published figures available to indicate the volume of work flowing to, or generated by, the different jurisdictions created between 1998 and 2006. Some national statistics are available, however, and Pompe records a large increase in the volume of cases handled by the General Courts at first instance over recent decades – 95,000 cases filed in 1969 rising to nearly 2,000,000 cases in 1994.[84] A comparison of case statistics with population figures demonstrates that the rise in filings is not just an increase in absolute terms, but that filings have risen more rapidly than the corresponding increase in population over the same time. Thus between 1971 and 2006 the caseload at first instance per capita has risen from one action for every 735 citizens (1:735), to an average of one action for every 85 citizens (1:85). Table 15.4 sets out the data on national case filing statistics and population growth between 1971 and 2006.[85]

The fact that new specialist courts are very recent arrivals means that the creation of jurisdictions by itself is not responsible for this dramatic effect in overall caseload. Increasingly litigious behavior is a possible factor,[86] but one problem in determining the cause with accuracy is the lack of complete data. The caseload at first instance in the General Courts covers all forms of criminal and civil cases. Litigious behavior is associated with the employment of civil actions by private parties, but without a breakdown of causes over time it is not clear what the source of the expansion in cases might be, and whether it is consistent across both civil and criminal matters. It seems, in fact, that the volume of civil litigation in Indonesia may be quite low. Of all cases filed in the first instance of the General Courts in 2006, approximately 32,000 were civil cases.[87] This means that over 98 percent of the 2.6m cases in the Indonesian court system in 2006 (see Table 15.4) were criminal matters. Further, of these criminal cases the vast majority are minor traffic matters – perhaps around 93 percent, or approximately 2.4m cases.[88] The 32,000 civil actions in the courts amount to an average of around 100 civil cases per annum in each first instance court (there are a total of 323 District Courts in Indonesia).[89] Although the number of civil cases dwarfs the 840 filings in the Administrative Courts, for a nation of over 220 million people there is clearly little demand for

Table 15.4 Caseload in Indonesia at first instance, per capita

Year	Cases	Population	Ratio
1971	162,323	119.2m	1:735
1980	322,429	147.3m	1:457
1990	1,245,365	179.2m	1:144
2006	2,636,689	222m	1:85

formal legal process to settle civil disputes. Further research is needed, therefore, to determine what the causes may be for this per capita increase in court usage, and what it indicates about court administration and the resort to law by both state and citizen.

The Constitutional Court

The second key reversal of judicial policy in the reform era was the institution of a system of constitutional review. Four amendments to the Constitution were passed between 1999 and 2002, with the power of judicial review of legislation being granted to a new Constitutional Court in the Third amendment, adopted in November 2001. Under transitional provisions adopted in the Fourth amendment (in 2002) the Constitutional Court was to be established no later than Independence Day, 17 August, 2003. The legislation establishing the Court was signed into law four days prior to the expiration of the deadline, on 13 August, 2003.[90]

A program of substantive institutional change was developed to reflect the aspirations of the reform movement, and the Third amendment to the 1945 Constitution was the most significant in terms of institutional reforms. This amendment package recognized the sovereignty of the people, introduced Presidential impeachment procedures, and provided for substantial reforms to the judiciary through the new Constitutional Court and a Judicial Commission.[91] However, Andrew Ellis concludes that despite the fundamental nature of the changes brought down in late 2001 "almost nobody noticed it happen," and the full implications of the changes did not begin to sink in until some time in 2002. The Chair of the parliamentary team responsible for oversight of the constitutional reform process also holds to the view that most observers missed the major changes that were being introduced. In fact, it is possible that if more politicians had been aware of the substance of the reforms being tabled, they may not have agreed to them as passed.[92]

In addition to review of laws against the Constitution, the Constitutional Court's jurisdiction (article 10, Law 24/2003) includes settlement of disputes between state institutions identified in the Constitution, the dissolution of political parties, electoral disputes, and parliamentary petitions for impeachment of the President or Vice President. The Court's bench of nine Justices is composed of appointees nominated by each of the three branches of government; that is, three nominations each from the Supreme Court, Parliament, and President (article 18). Justices are appointed for terms of five years, and may be selected for a second term (article 22). The nomination of Justices must be conducted in a transparent and accountable manner (article 19), although each of the agencies with authority to nominate candidates has responsibility for regulating this process in respect of their nominees (article 20). As we have seen, the legislation for the Constitutional Court was passed only days before the expiry of the deadline for the Court's establishment. What is more, and despite the provisions requiring transparent selection of Justices, the tight deadline meant that the first bench was appointed a mere two days after the passage of the legislation, with Justices sworn-in the following day.[93]

With regard to its power of judicial review, the Court may only examine challenges to legislation arising after the First Amendments passed to the Constitution in November 1999 (article 50). The Court has held on several occasions, however, that this provision is itself in breach of the Constitution, and so it has reviewed laws passed prior to this date.[94] The Constitutional Court must inform the Supreme Court within seven days of the filing of a judicial review application (article 53), and the Supreme Court is required to suspend any review of regulations under the legislation in question until a decision is rendered by the Constitutional Court (article 54). Other than these provisions, no formal relationship is established between constitutional challenges and judicial work in the ordinary courts.

This lack of mutual recognition among these two parts of the Indonesian judicial system is a matter of significant interest, and has become sharply defined by criminal cases involving the death penalty. The Constitutional Court held in 2004 that the prosecutions of those responsible for the 2002 Bali night club bombings breached the constitutional protection against the retrospective use of law (article 28I of the Constitution), as the legislation applied (originally framed as an emergency regulation) was passed after the bombing.[95] The convictions have been challenged in the Supreme Court, with the applicants relying upon the Constitutional Court's 2004 decision as the basis for this review. The challenge of at least one of the bombers was recently rejected by the Supreme Court and – through a spokesperson – the Court explained that it did not regard the successful constitutional challenge as new evidence, which is what is usually required to mount a *peninjauan kembali* review.[96] The Constitutional Court itself maintains that its decisions operate purely prospectively.[97] This could be seen as a classic civil law position, and appears to reinforce the disconnect between the work of the two superior courts, if only because any successful constitutional challenge cannot influence the outcome of a case previously concluded in the General Court system. I will return to consider further the split of responsibilities between the review powers of the two courts later.

The Constitutional Court at work

The Court rendered a total of 145 decisions in its first four years of operation (2003–2006), with a peak of 82 decisions handed down in 2004, many relating to elections disputes from that year's general election.[98] Several decisions are worth considering here for their relevance to the development of the judiciary, and one other decision has particular significance for the issue of regulatory activity in the broader sense.

The Judicial Commission began operations in 2005, and it originally possessed two functions: to select candidates for appointment to the Supreme Court, and to monitor judicial conduct. The implementation of this second part of its mandate caused significant concern at the Supreme Court, to the extent that in 2006 31 Justices of the Supreme Court challenged the Commission's supervisory powers in the Constitutional Court.[99] The filing of the case was preceded by a series of public maneuvers including the refusal by the Chief Justice to submit to questioning by the Commission in relation to a corruption allegation, a call by the Commission for the sacking of the entire Supreme Court bench, and the leaking of the names to the press of Justices who had been the subject of complaints by the public. The Constitutional Court found in favor of the applicants, holding that the constitution protected the exercise of judicial power, and that the Commission could not investigate judicial decision making (as opposed to judicial conduct). The decision, while fundamentally seeking to protect judicial independence, paralyzed the Commission and arguably set back the process of developing a more publicly accountable judiciary.[100]

In another 2006 decision the Constitutional Court once again delivered a verdict with significant implications for judicial administration. A number of individuals charged with corruption offences arising from the execution of their duties as members of the General Election Commission, had been prosecuted by the Anti-Corruption Commission in the special Anti-Corruption Court.[101] The Constitutional Court held that the establishment of the Anti-Corruption Court (under article 53, Law 30/2002) was in contravention of several provision of the constitution. One reason provided by the Constitutional Court was that article 24A of the Constitution requires that judicial bodies be established "by" law, when in this case the Anti-Corruption Court was set up via a provision within the law establishing the Anti-Corruption Commission (suggesting that the Court needed its own statute).

A more convincing argument advanced by the Constitutional Court in support of its decision was that the special Corruption Court operates in tandem with prosecutions in the General Courts, leading to a "dualism" in corruption enforcement. The Court found that establishment of the new court therefore breached human rights protections in the Constitution, specifically article 28D which allows for "protection and certainty before a just law, and of equal treatment before the law."[102] In short, the treatment or outcome received by corruption suspects could differ depending upon whether the prosecution was conducted in the single Jakarta-based Anti-Corruption Court, or in one of the hundreds of District Courts, under normal criminal procedure. Acknowledging that this outcome would hinder law enforcement, the Court set a three-year sunset period for the Anti-Corruption Court, to allow time for the preparation of new legislation clarifying the status of specialist corruption courts.

These decisions show the Court deciding matters of direct relevance to the structure and functionality of the public law accountability system, which is the focus of this chapter. The Court has, however, also delivered several decisions in an area of relevance to the state's role in market regulation. The decisions highlight an unusual feature of the Indonesian constitution which is of critical importance to the future of regulatory mechanisms in Indonesia, and also graphically demonstrates the impracticality of Indonesia's approach to judicial review. In a series of cases all arising from privatization or forms of private sector engagement in production or resource exploitation, the Court has been required to rule on article 33 of the Constitution.[103] This provision defines an approach to national economic management that has been described as "the people's economy": the article holds that the economy shall be founded on what is known as "the family principle"; prescribes state control for important branches of production; and further provides for state control of natural resources, which are to be used for the greatest possible prosperity of the people.

In its decision on the validity of Law 20/2002 on electricity, which sought to institute unbundling of electricity generation, transmission, distribution, and sale, the Court declared the legislation to be in breach of article 33.[104] The Court argued that regulation of an industry was insufficient to meet the requirement of control specified in the Constitution, and that as the Government already possessed inherent power to regulate, state control must be read more broadly. The Court did not prohibit privatization as such, indicating that control did not require 100 percent state ownership. The decision therefore leaves the door open for private sector involvement in utilities, so long as the state retains sufficient interest to control decision and policy making. Two months after the decision the Government issued a Regulation which was very similar to the earlier unconstitutional legislation, to provide certainty to investors in the aftermath of the Court's decision, and to facilitate a tender process by the state electricity company. The Regulation cannot be challenged in the Constitutional Court because judicial review of other statutory instruments lies with the Supreme Court, and so the Executive was able to circumvent the successful constitutional challenge to the electricity law.

Courts and accountability in Indonesia

Indonesia now possesses a recognizable public law accountability framework. It has the necessary judicial institutions, empowered with adequate authority, to conduct review of executive and legislative action. The most recent addition to the public law armory is the Constitutional Court, but the other elements have been in place for a much longer time in the form of powers to review regulations, and – subsequently – the Administrative Courts. It was noted at the outset that notwithstanding the existence of several regulatory agencies, there are few signs that Indonesia embraces newer approaches to accountability and regulation. The primary method of regulation in the public sphere therefore remains centered on judicial institutions, and judicial institutions themselves are in the process of rehabilitation. This process is taking the courts from a position of subservience to the executive to one of independence, and is measured through observing changes to administrative control of the court system, and the granting of expanded judicial review powers. For these reasons I have described Indonesia as situated in a "pre-regulatory" condition.

The development of independent judicial authority, together with the expansion of jurisdictions discussed above, may also be taken as signs of judicialization. However, these developments must be seen as part of the process of dismantling decades of authoritarian rule, in which successive regimes have systematically degraded the judicial function. They also reflect Indonesia's particular experience of judicial power as a European colony, and the excruciatingly slow process of re-establishing the judiciary post-Independence. It took many years for the Administrative Courts to be fully established across Indonesia, and even today the executive lacks the funds to establish new jurisdictions on a national basis. For these reasons, judicialization in Indonesia is also only a partial condition.

The Court statistics examined earlier also tell us something about the role and capacity of the courts in Indonesia, and in particular they seem to demonstrate serious limitations in the function of review of administrative and of regulatory action. The weakness of these review functions – maintained by the Administrative Courts, and in the Supreme Court's original jurisdiction to review subordinate legislative instruments – are evidenced by extremely small case filings both for the Administrative Courts and in the judicial review function (*hak uji materiil*). Case volumes might not, of course, be entirely representative of the health of judicial functions. However, Indonesia has traditionally been governed through executive action – this is demonstrated by the very high proportion of subordinate instruments below the level of statute (and executive control is the mark of authoritarian rule). In this case, why is it that the administrative law field still appears to be a jurisdiction in search of causes of action?

Pompe points out that it is ironic for the Indonesian judiciary to routinely lobby for the power of constitutional review during the decades prior to democratization.[105] The judiciary has had the power to "strike at the heart" of the regime by reading down regulations and Presidential instruments for some time, but has consistently refused to employ its power of judicial review. What would the Indonesian judiciary have done with full powers of judicial review if granted any earlier? He suggests that it was the indivisibility and – therefore – unaccountability of state power that caused this situation, and that the arrival of the Constitutional Court theoretically provides the opportunity to change decades of old practices. Certainly the Constitutional amendments transformed the whole framework of state governance. But, as Lindsey points out, institutional transformation itself is not sufficient to transform systems of administration and governance, particularly when the rule of law had been replaced by "ideology and violence," resulting in the complete marginalization of law under Soeharto.[106]

The work of the Constitutional Court to date suggests that it is in fact making a positive contribution to the framework of accountability. Initially there appears to have been some confusion as to what an appropriate response was to its decisions, but now the legislative program in Indonesia clearly prioritizes legislative amendments required as a result of Constitutional Court decisions.[107] The Government's handling of the decision in the electricity privatization case indicates a degree of hostility to the outcome in that case, and also a conscious exploitation of the distinction between the two forms of judicial review available in the Supreme and Constitutional Courts. This type of reaction is to be expected when politics is judicialized via constitutional review.[108] Indeed it is arguable that in the case of Asian Constitutional Courts there is a very high likelihood of this form of conflict between the executive and judiciary. This is because superior courts of this type are destined to play a highly political role, positioned as they are to deliberate upon core issues of state, and therefore dealing with potent issues of the day as a matter of course.[109]

The mentality of government is therefore clearly beginning to shift. The acceptance of judicial review as part of the broader process of democratic transition in Indonesia is a major success, all the more so when contrasted with the ongoing limitations of, and slower pace of change seen in, the General Court system. The low court usage rates, though, are perhaps an indication that a more profound shift is yet to take place. Weak court infrastructure has meant that there has (up until surprisingly recently) been a lack of physical capacity to dispense justice. This resulted in a physical separation between the people and the courts.[110] Bridging this gap has been a deliberate policy for a long time, but the motivation for this has been primarily to extend state authority through expanding the footprint of the courts. This in fact may be one of the factors contributing to the rise in per capita filings over time. The statistics on the number of civil and administrative actions might be interpreted, on the other hand, as indicating that the national court infrastructure remains either out of reach for many people, or the judiciary remains out of favor. It is important to recognize that with a large population living in regional and remote areas, many in poverty, large parts of Indonesia may be indifferent to the state courts.[111] Therefore, even should the Supreme Court continue to lead the way in rehabilitating the judiciary, both through implementing reformist policies and strengthening judicial administration, it may take more significant changes in local economy and culture across Indonesia for access to the judiciary to be valued as an accountability mechanism by the average citizen.

An equally difficult question is whether the distinct roles of the Supreme and Constitutional Courts in judicial review requires reform. While this distribution of powers has the potential to abrogate constitutional protections, it is a model that exists elsewhere. The Chief Justice of the Constitutional Court himself has highlighted the similarity between the Indonesian and South Korean models, in which the Constitutional Court reviews legislation and the Supreme Court reviews lower level instruments.[112] The similarity is not exact, though, as the Supreme Court in South Korea has the authority to review regulations against the Constitution.[113] On the other hand, the Indonesian Constitution does not explicitly preclude reference to the Constitution in the Supreme Court's judicial review function – it merely states that the Court has the authority to review regulations (article 24A(1)). The Indonesian Court has in the past read its authority broadly and annulled colonial era legislation,[114] so a precedent exists for this interpretation of its role.

The South Korean model also provides an example for the Indonesian Constitutional Court, should this court choose to consider expanding its role. The South Korean Court unilaterally decided that it had implied jurisdiction over administrative regulations, in a 1990 case.[115] The trend of decision-making in the Constitutional Court suggests that it may be capable of expanding its authority. It has already amended its own legislation (widening its jurisdiction temporally, to include pre-reform legislation) and has also experimented with implied rights, and may in the future mine the unexplored ground of the Constitution's Preamble.[116] It has already applied the human rights provisions of the Constitution, including the requirement for certainty and equal treatment before the law, which could also be a source of an expanded authority. For the moment, however, the presumption remains that there is a distinction between the two powers, and that neither Court might consider entering the others' domain.[117]

Conclusion

There are significant differences between the conditions that brought about Indonesia's system of administrative justice in the 1980s, and the newer judicial review process 20 years later. However, the precise motivations for the creation of both courts seem to remain somewhat obscure, especially the critical political forces at play, despite the information that is available about their origins. The key question about the Administrative Courts is how they could come into being in a climate so hostile to judicial oversight? This was, after all, the New Order at its peak, and it must be assumed that the Soeharto regime calculated that it could manage the associated risk.[118] Several theories have been advanced as to particular factors that may have motivated the regime to institute the new Court including the need to reassure foreign critics and investors about the regime's reform credentials; to provide a tool to assist in rationalizing the bureaucracy, and to provide the Indonesian public with some measure of redress in the face of an incompetent and corrupt public sector.[119]

What is probably more significant is the choice of model and the powers granted to the Administrative Court. Ultimately, the limitations of the Court's powers of review have been sufficient to ensure a marginal role for the Administrative Court, despite similar weaknesses being remedied long ago in the Netherlands.[120] The failure of the Supreme Court's judicial review function is perhaps more a reflection of the Court's subjugation to the executive, which has resulted in the complete sublimation of its inherent power to check authority. Ambiguity and lack of transparency in its decision-making remain a key limitation on its capacity to command respect as the head of the General Court system. Consistent efforts at reform will be needed to raise the profile of the courts as an avenue of redress against the administration.

The Constitutional Court, on the other hand, owes its existence to the sweeping constitutional reforms introduced during Indonesia's first years of post-authoritarian government. The absence of legislative review had preoccupied jurists for decades, but beyond this there remains limited evidence of what drove the political players responsible for introducing this important reform. For this reason it may be difficult to apply current theories for the development of judicial review to the case of Indonesia, at least with any conviction.[121] Beyond the fact that the Constitutional Court fills an important gap in the framework for public accountability, what its early work highlights is that only now can the task of re-defining the values that are to be applied within this framework properly begin. As the business of administration is increasingly subject to legal challenge, questions as to the nature and purpose of the Indonesian state are exposed. The lack of consensus at the level of "state purpose" in Indonesia is borne out by decisions of a Court that must face up to the inherent contradictions of the reform-era

Constitution.[122] The combination of continuity and change in the Constitution has resulted in liberal individual rights co-existing with the Socialist-inspired "people's economy" of article 33, under the overarching *Pancasila* principles, which in the past have been employed as a tool of state ideology. The judiciary in Indonesia is now beginning to play a positive role in determining what these values mean, and how they will be applied, as Indonesia continues its transition to a model of the regulatory state.

Notes

1 D. Trubek and A. Santos, *The New Law and Economic Development: A Critical Appraisal*, Cambridge: Cambridge University Press, 2006, pp.3–5.
2 D. Lev, "The state and law reform in Indonesia," in T. Lindsey, ed., *Law Reform in Developing and Transitional States*, New York: Routledge, 2007, p.236.
3 Lev, op. cit., p.237.
4 See for example D. Trubek and L. Trubek, "New Governance & Legal Regulation: Complementarity, Rivalry, and Transformation," *Columbia Journal of European Law*, vol.13, 2006, p.4.
5 T. Lindsey, "Legal Infrastructure and Governance Reform in Post-Crisis Asia: The case of Indonesia," *Asian-Pacific Economic Literature,* vol.18, no.1, May 2004, p.13.
6 K. Jayasuriya, "Beyond Institutional Fetishism: From the Developmental to the Regulatory State," *New Political Economy*, vol.10, no.3, September 2005, p.384.
7 Lindsey, op. cit., p.29.
8 V. Lingga, "KPPU Integrity on the Line with Indosat Case," *Jakarta Post*, 15 August, 2007.
9 Editorial, "Barking up the Wrong Tree," *Jakarta Post*, 19 November 2007.
10 J. L. Mashaw, "Accountability and Institutional Design: Some Thoughts on the Grammar of Governance," in M. Dowdle, ed., *Public Accountability: Designs, Dilemmas and Experiences*, Cambridge: Cambridge University Press, 2006. Mashaw discusses different forms of accountability regime, and provides a critique of the traditional public governance processes.
11 A. Macintyre, "Investment, Property Rights, and Corruption in Indonesia," in J. Campos, ed., *Corruption: The Boom and Bust of East Asia*, Manila: Ateneo University Press, 2001, p.38.
12 R. H. McLeod, "The Struggle to Regain Effective Government Under Democracy in Indonesia," *Bulletin of Indonesian Economic Studies*, vol.41, no.3, 2005, pp.369–71.
13 As to the "pathologies of legal process" in Indonesia, see Lev, op. cit 2007, pp.241–6.
14 D. Bourchier, "Magic Memos, Collusion and Judges with Attitude: Notes on the politics of law in contemporary Indonesia," in K. Jayasuriya, ed., *Law, Capitalism and Power in Asia*, New York: Routledge, 1999, and "Positivism and Romanticism in Indonesian Legal Thought," in T. Lindsey, ed., *Law and Society in Indonesia*, Sydney: The Federation Press, 1999; B. Quinn, "Indonesia: Patrimonial or Legal State? The Law on Administrative Justice of 1986 in Socio-Political Context," in T. Lindsey, ed., *Law and Society in Indonesia*, Sydney: The Federation Press, 1999, p.259.
15 Bourchier, op. cit., p.235. This term refers to the five core principles underpinning the theory of state in Indonesia: belief in Almighty God; humanity or humanitarianism; nationalism, or state unity; democracy through deliberation; and achievement of social justice. The *Pancasila* are found in the closing words of the preamble to the Constitution and continue to drive public debate about the nature of the Indonesian state, see A. Salim, "Muslim Politics in Indonesia's Democratisation: The Religious Majority and

The Rights of Minorities in The Post-New Order Era," in R. McLeod and A. MacIntyre, eds., *Indonesia: Democracy and the Promise of Good Governance*, Singapore: Institute of South East Asian Studies, 2007, pp.133–4.
16 D. Lev, "Judicial Institutions and Legal Culture," in *Legal Evolution and Political Authority in Indonesia: Selected Essays*, The Hague: Kluwer International, 2000, p.172; and Lev, op. cit., 2007, pp.239–40.
17 Lev, op. cit., 2007, p.243.
18 D. Lev, "The Politics of Judicial Development in Indonesia," in Lev, *Selected Essays*, pp.74–88.
19 S. Pompe, *The Indonesian Supreme Court: A Study of Institutional Collapse*, New York: Cornell University, 2005, pp.51–2.
20 Ibid., p.58.
21 Bourchier, op. cit., p.237; Pompe, op. cit., pp.52–3; Lev, "The Lady and the Banyan Tree: Civil Law Change in Indonesia," in *Selected Essays*, pp.119–42, at 119.
22 Pompe, op. cit., p.52.
23 Lev, op. cit., 2007, p.243.
24 Pompe, op. cit., p.79.
25 Ibid., p.109.
26 Ibid., p.110.
27 Bourchier, op. cit., p.237; Pompe, op. cit., p.110.
28 Pompe, op. cit., pp.136–7; Quinn, op. cit., p.260. While this review power remains the same today, post-Soeharto reforms have theoretically made its implementation less dependent on the bureaucracy, see text accompanying note 73.
29 Pompe, op. cit., pp.111–74.
30 Pompe, op. cit., Chapter 4.
31 Bourchier, op. cit., p.238.
32 Bourchier, op. cit., p.239, and pp.246–7; Lev, op. cit., 2007, pp.243–4.
33 Bourchier, op. cit., p.246; S. Butt, "The *Eksekusi* of the *Negara Hukum*: Implementing Judicial Decisions in Indonesia, in Tim Lindsey, *Law and Society in Indonesia*, Sydney: The Federation Press, 1999, pp.253–4. For an analysis of a number of high profile cases attracting the attention of the Executive see Pompe, op. cit., pp.149–70.
34 Pompe, op. cit., pp.127–8.
35 A. Bedner, *Administrative Courts in Indonesia: A Socio-Legal Study*, The Hague: Kluwer Law International, 2001, p.7. The following discussion draws on Bedner, *Administrative Courts*, Chapter 2. D. Linnan, "Decentralisation Versus Administrative Courts: Which Path Holds Greater Promise?," in T. Lindsey, *Law and Society in Indonesia*, Sydney: The Federation Press, 1999, pp.223–4, outlines the protection of private rights offered by the Dutch Indies Civil Code, involving both private and state actors.
36 Lev, "Judicial Authority and the Quest for an Indonesian Rechstaat," in *Selected Essays*, pp.215–43, at 234.
37 See Lev, op. cit. 2007, pp.234–8; and Pompe, op. cit., pp.88–110.
38 *Peradilan Tata Usaha Negara*, or alternately State Administrative Justice.
39 Article 145, Law 5/1986 and accompanying Elucidation.
40 Government Regulation No. 7/1991.
41 See Bedner, *Administrative Courts*, Chapter 8 on the establishment and staffing of the courts. The situation of recruitment was at one point so dire it was decided to allow Registrars to take up positions as judges in the new courts. The problem of resources for courts is an old one, reflecting in part a history of constrained national budgets and pressures within the court system following changes to the judicial structure following independence, see Lev, "Judicial Unification in Post Colonial Indonesia," in *Selected Essays*, pp.33–70; Pompe, op. cit., pp.186–9.
42 Law No. 9/2004 on Amendments to Law No. 5/1986 on Administrative Justice.

43 Article 3 of Law 28/1999.
44 Article 45A(2)(c) provides that cases excepted from cassation include "administrative law cases in which the object of the challenge is in the form of a decision of a regional official the validity of which has effect in the area of the region concerned."
45 Decentralization of authority in Indonesia has taken place through two rounds of legislation, in 1999 and 2004. Legislation passed in 1999 (Law No. 22/1999 on Regional Government) was revised and re-enacted in Law No. 32/2004 on Regional Government because the earlier legislation was not felt to be consistent with "developments in conditions" in Indonesia, state administration, and the requirements of decentralization. The distribution of powers, though, is broadly the same in both laws. That is, the national government retains powers in regard to foreign affairs, defense, security, justice, national monetary and fiscal policy, and religion (article 10, Law No. 32/2004). The Provinces and Districts across Indonesia are allocated the balance of authority for a wide range of areas of government administration and services including health, education, investment, land, small and medium enterprise etc. (articles 13–14). In order to administer their responsibilities, Districts have received a transfer of staff from the national government, although they remain members of a single national civil service (articles 12, 129), and local parliaments in each District have the power to pass regulations to implement of their administrative responsibilities (articles 40–42, and 136–149). The distribution of powers between the levels of government cannot be read literally. In April 2007, for example, a new Investment law was signed into law at the national level – Law 25/2007 – which aims to improve conditions for economic development, notwithstanding that investment is allocated to the regions under decentralization legislation.
46 Case 23/PUU-V/2007, applicant Hendriansyah.
47 As at the time of publication, the draft law was still listed as a priority bill for consideration by parliament during 2008. Developed with the help of the German technical assistance organization GTZ, the draft is described in their literature as the Administrative Procedure Act. (See http://www.gtzsfgg.or.id/ Accessed June 1, 2008 under Administrative Reform).
48 The jurisdictions of Ombudsmen at national and local level in Indonesia remain confused and require clarification. For a discussion of this see M. Crouch, "Indonesia's National and Local Ombudsman Reforms: Salvaging a Failed Experiment?," in T. Lindsey, ed., *Law and Society in Indonesia 2ed.*, Sydney: Federation Press, 2008.
49 Private communication, 28 March 2007.
50 Bedner proposed this as a solution to broadening the court's jurisdiction, *Administrative Courts*, p.263.
51 Bedner, *Administrative Courts*. This section draws on Chapter 3.
52 Quinn, "Patrimonial or Legal State," p.261.
53 J. Millie, "The Tempo Case: Indonesia's Press Laws, the *Pengadilan Tata Usaha Negara* and the *Negara Hukum*," in T. Lindsey, ed., *Law and Society in Indonesia*, Sydney: The Federation Press, 1999.
54 Pompe, op. cit., pp.165–6.
55 Quinn, op. cit., p.262.
56 Indonesian court decisions are traditionally available in various journals, but publication has been inconsistent over recent years. Measures were under way at the time of writing to rejuvenate the Supreme Court's publication of decisions, including the publication of a Supreme Court regulation on access to information, and the uploading of judgments to the Court's website. On the history and current practices in the field of judicial publications and jurisprudence see Pompe, op. cit., pp.448–56, and also Bedner, op. cit., p.215.
57 T. Alwie, et al., "Satu Obyek Dua Putusan" [One Object Two Decisions], *Gatra*, vol.XIII, no.30, 7–13 June 2007.

Law and judicial review in Indonesia   355

58 Approximately US$15,000, but a considerably more valuable sum prior to the devaluation of Indonesia's currency by the regional economic crisis.
59 See *2006 Annual Report, Supreme Court Republic of Indonesia*, Jakarta: Supreme Court, April 2007.
60 The comparative figures are found in Bedner, *Administrative Courts*, p.198.
61 Figures obtained from the Report of the Junior Chief Justice for Administrative Law, National Meeting of the Supreme Court, September 2007, copy on file with author.
62 Internal review of case statistics at Supreme Court, copy on file with author. This work was carried out as part of a case management project supported by Australian government funds.
63 On seeking data about caseload and case type at first instance in the Administrative Courts, I was advised by a senior administrator that this information was not collected. Private communication, 17 July 2007.
64 Previous analyses of the Administrative Court docket have shown that land and civil service disputes predominate, see Bedner, *Administrative Courts*, p.8; Quinn, "Patrimonial or Legal State," p.262.
65 Daniel Fitzpatrick proposed that the best solution to land law in Indonesia was the establishment of a dedicated land court, "Disputes and Pluralism in Modern Indonesian Land Law," *Yale Journal of International Law*, vol.22, pp.171–212, 1997.
66 Supreme Court Regulation No. 1/1993 on Judicial Review (*hak uji materiil*).
67 Figures are drawn from an unpublished analysis of legislative instruments conducted by the Cabinet Secretariat in early 2007. Copy on file with author.
68 Source as for n66. Evidence for the continuing appeal of executive regulations as a tool of governance is Presidential Decision 13/2006 on the National Team for the Alleviation of the Sidoarjo Mud Flow. This order establishes a team of state officials and industry representatives to resolve the "mud volcano" that erupted at a drilling site in East Java in 2006, causing a national and international sensation. This Presidential instrument requires that the costs of the team's work be borne by a private company, PT Lapindo Brantas, operator of the drilling site. The drilling operator's parent company is owned by Aburizal Bakrie, a Cabinet member and prominent businessman.
69 Pompe, op. cit., pp.472–3.
70 Lindsey, op. cit., 2004, pp.20–2.
71 Pompe, op. cit., pp.474–5.
72 Pompe, op. cit., pp.59–77, and "Understanding the Indonesian Blueprints for Court Reform," *Jentera: Jurnal Hukum*, Edisi 15, Tahun IV, January–March 2007, pp.59–77. This policy package covers the reform of personnel management and finances, judicial education, judicial supervision, and the development of a judicial commission, and includes policy papers on specialist courts for commercial law and corruption cases. It represents a far-reaching and highly strategic set of objectives; Lev, op. cit., 2007, p.260, and p.265, n50.
73 Law No. 5/2004 on Amendments to Law No. 14/1985 on the Supreme Court.
74 See text accompanying notes 26 and 27.
75 If we expand our frame of reference by one year, to the final year of Soeharto's rule, we find the establishment of yet another court, a Children's Court (Law 3/1997).
76 Comments of the Chief Justice of the Supreme Court at the Inauguration of the Fisheries Court of Medan, 4 October, 2007. Copy on file with author and available at the time of writing at www.mahkamahagung.go.id, Accessed June 1, 2008.
77 The Chief Justice highlights the system of "ad hoc" judges as one of the key developments arriving with the specialist courts. In fact the Administrative Courts were the first court to introduce the concept of using "ad hoc" or non-career judges (article 135 Law 5/1986). While the Administrative Courts did not go on to engage ad hoc judges (private communication, 28 March 2007) they have been an important feature of the

work of the Anti-Corruption Court, where a majority of judges on its judicial panels are composed of non-career judges. On this issue and the operations of the Anti-Corruption Court see S. Fenwick, "Measuring Up? Indonesia's Anti-Corruption Commission and the New Corruption Agenda," in T. Lindsey, ed., *Law and Society in Indonesia 2ed.*, Sydney: Federation Press, 2008.

78 "Revisi UU Pengadilan HAM Disiapkan" [Revised Law on Human Rights Courts Has Been Prepared], *hukumonline*, 18 September, 2007. The issue of accountability for human rights violations in Indonesia is an important story in its own right, and reference to human rights courts should also include the ad hoc human rights courts established to try individuals for rights violations during Indonesia's withdrawal from East Timor. See S. Linton, "Accounting for Atrocities in Indonesia," *Singapore Yearbook of International Law*, vol.10, pp.1–33, 2006, for an examination of these issues.

79 Mahkamah Agung [Supreme Court], *Indonesian Legal System*, Jakarta: Mahkamah Agung and Faculty of Law, University of Indonesia, 2005, p.65.

80 On the Religious Courts see B. Hooker and T. Lindsey, "Public Faces of *Syariah* in Contemporary Indonesia: Towards a National *Madhhab*?," *Studia Islamika*, vol.10, no.1, 2003, pp.23–64. The authority of the Religious Courts was expanded in 2006 with the addition of responsibility for oversight of aspects of the Indonesian *syariah* economy, article 49, Law 3/2006 on Amendments to Law 7/1989 on the Religious Courts.

81 Article 25(2) Law 18/2001 provides that the authority of the *Mahkamah Syariah* is based on regional regulations, known as *Qanun*. See for example article 23(1) *Qanun* 13/2003 on Gambling which imposes caning as the penalty for the act of gambling. See Salim, "Muslim Politics in Indonesia's Democratisation," for a discussion of the human rights implications of *Syariah*-inspired regulations in Indonesia.

82 For a detailed discussion of this see T. Lindsey, ed., *Indonesia: Bankruptcy, Law Reform and the Commercial Court*, Sydney: Desert Pea Press, 2000.

83 See Fenwick, op. cit.

84 Pompe, op. cit., p.283.

85 Figures for caseloads are taken from Pompe, op. cit., Appendix 2, Court Dockets in Indonesia, 1969–1993, and statistics from the Supreme Court's 2006 annual report (Supreme Court, 2007). Population data is sourced from M. Ricklefs, *A History of Modern Indonesia Since c.1200*, Stanford: Stanford University Press, 2001, and National Statistics Agency, National Development Planning Agency, and UNFPA *Indonesian Population Projections 2000–2025*, Jakarta, 2005.

86 Pompe, op. cit., p.283.

87 Unpublished research conducted at the Supreme Court during 2007, copy on file with author.

88 Source, unpublished research referred to in n87.

89 There are a little over 700 first instance courts in Indonesia: 323 General Courts; 346 Religious Courts; 26 Administrative Courts; and 19 Military Courts. (Source: unpublished annual budget documents for the Supreme Court. Copy on file with author).

90 Law 24/2003 on the Constitutional Court.

91 There were a number of political imperatives on the agenda immediately following the end of the New Order including a special emphasis on increased political freedoms, the formation of new parties, and decentralization via a regional autonomy package. See A. Ellis, "Indonesia's Constitutional Change Reviewed," in McLeod and MacIntyre, *Indonesia: Democracy and the Promise of Good Governance*, Singapore: Institute of South East Asian Studies, 2007, pp.24–33, on the political turmoil prevailing at the time, and on the question of the level of awareness of decision-makers as to the nature of the constitutional amendments.

92 Senior political figures who played a key role in the establishment of the Court gathered at a function in Jakarta in 2007 to celebrate the Constitutional Court's fourth

anniversary (attended by the author). Neither the significance of the development for the rule of law in Indonesia, nor any of the political metrics applying at the time of the reforms were touched on by those in attendance at the function. Akbar Tanjung, who was the speaker of People's Consultative Assembly at the time of the constitutional amendments, and a representative of the Golkar party (the powerful central party that effectively dominated politics during Soeharto's rule), mentioned simply that the need for a Constitutional Court was in his party's policy platform at the time the amendments were passed. Former President Megawati Soekarnoputri was in power when the legislation for the establishment of the Court was enacted, as well as leader of a major party during the amendment process. In her remarks at the event the former President recalled discussions regarding selecting a plot of land for the Court, but offered no recollections as to her hopes or expectations for the new Court, although her signature appears at the bottom of the Constitutional Court's legislation.

93 See History of the Constitutional Court at www.mahkamahkonstitusi.go.id. Anecdotal information also holds that at least one of the nominees (a judge proposed by the Supreme Court) was unaware of his nomination until advised that he had been selected to join the Court.
94 S. Butt, "Judicial Review in Indonesia: Between Civil Law and Accountability? A Study of Constitutional Court Decisions 2003–2005," unpublished PhD thesis, University of Melbourne, December 2006, p.182.
95 See S. Butt and D. Hansell, "The Masykur Abdul Kadir Case: Indonesian Constitutional Court Decision No. 013/PUU-I/2003," *Asian Law*, vol.6, no.3, 2004, pp.176–96.
96 "Supreme Court rejects final Amrozi Appeal," *The Jakarta Post*, 8 September, 2007.
97 Butt, op. cit., p.69.
98 2006 Annual Report of the Constitutional Court, Jakarta: The Constitutional Court, January 2007, p.84.
99 Case No 5/PUU-IV/2006, and see Simon Butt, "The Constitutional Court's Decision in the Dispute Between the Supreme Court and the Judicial Commission: Banishing Judicial Accountability?," in McLeod and MacIntyre, *Indonesia: Democracy and the Promise of Good Governance*, Singapore: Institute of South East Asian Studies, 2007, pp.178–99. It has been said that the applicants did not include the Chief Justice of the Supreme Court, or either of the Vice-Chief Justices, in order to avoid the case being characterized as a dispute between state institutions, and thus falling under another of the Constitutional Court's powers of review.
100 Draft amendments to the Judicial Commission's legislation were with the parliament at the time of writing; Ramidi, "Fangs for the Commission," *Tempo*, 10 September, 2007.
101 Cases 012–016 and 019/PUU-IV/2006, applicants Drs Mulyana and others. See also the discussion in the context of corruption reforms in Indonesia in Fenwick, op. cit.
102 The second set of constitutional amendments introduced in August 2000 inserted a large number of well-established international human rights standards into the foundation document in an expanded article 28.
103 This discussion draws on S. Butt and T. Lindsey, "Defending the 'People's Economy'? The Constitutional Court, Article 33 and Privatisation in Indonesia," *Bulletin of Indonesian Economic Studies*, 2008, forthcoming.
104 Cases 001–021–022/PUU-I/2003.
105 Pompe, op. cit., p.147.
106 Lindsey, "Indonesia: Devaluing Asian Values – Rewriting the Rule of Law," in R. Peerenboom, ed., *Asian Discourses of Rule of Law*, London; New York: Routledge Curzon, 2003, p.296.
107 "*Prolegnas 2008 Prioritaskan UU yang Dibatalkan MK*" [2008 Legislative Program Prioritizes Laws Annulled by Constitutional Court], *Kompas*, 2 October, 2007.
108 See T. Ginsburg, *Judicial Review in New Democracies: Constitutional Courts in Asian Cases*, Cambridge: Cambridge University Press, 2003, p.255.

109 In contrast to superior courts in the Anglo-Saxon tradition where there is unease about the interaction of the fields of politics and law. See Stewart Fenwick, "Realpolitik and Renewal in Asian Governance: The Role of Constitutional Courts," book review of Ginsburg, *Judicial Review in New Democracies*, in *Asian Law*, vol.6, no.2, 2004, p.210.
110 See Pompe, op. cit., pp.197–204.
111 The issue of the relationship between state, society, and law in Indonesia has been examined in great detail by Lev (for example see "Judicial Institutions") and cannot be adequately summarized here. Pompe (referenced at n109) besides addressing the physical separation of the people and the court system, also discusses the interaction between bodies of traditional and state law. This issue does not feature in contemporary debates about judicial reform in Indonesia. For an introduction to the issue see, for example, Hedar Laudjeng, *"Mempertimbangkan Peradilan Adat"* [Considering *Adat* [Traditional] Justice], *Seri Pengembangan Wacana*, no.4, 2003, a study conducted by the non-government organisation HuMa (The Collective for Law Reform Based on Society and the Ecology), funded by the Ford Foundation.
112 Prof. Dr. Jimly Asshiddiqie, *Konstitusi dan Konstitusialsime Indonesia* [The Constitution and Constitutionalism in Indonesia], Jakarta: Constitutional Court, 2006, p.245.
113 Ginsburg, op. cit., p.239.
114 Pompe, op. cit., pp.136–7.
115 Ginsburg, op. cit. p.240.
116 Butt, op, cit., Chapter 7.
117 Prof. Dr. Jimly Asshiddiqie, *"Judicial Review: Kajian atas Putusan Permohonan Hak Uji Materiil terhadap PP. No.19 Tahun 2000 tentang TGPTPK"* [Judicial Review: A Reading of the Decision in the Request for Judicial Review of Regulation No.19, Year 2000 regarding the TGPTPK (an acronym for a corruption fighting body)], *dictum*, edisi 1, 2002, pp.41–2.
118 See, for example, Ricklefs, *A History of Modern Indonesia*, Chapter 22, "The New Order at its Peak, 1976–88." The years during which the administration was preparing for the arrival of new Administrative Courts were the same years in which it introduced compulsory national training in the state *Pancasila* ideology, the state-sanctioned murders known as the Petrus killings took place, as well as the killing of civilians by the military at Tanjung Priok. See also Bedner, *Administrative Courts in Indonesia*, p.49.
119 Lev, op. cit, p.245.
120 The limitations of the model were appreciated by the Dutch, and in 1994 – only a few years after the establishment of the Indonesian courts – a new and more extensive system of judicial review was launched in the Netherlands. Bedner, op. cit., p.7.
121 Butt, op. cit., pp.38–50, finds that Ginsburg's "insurance" model has some traction in the Indonesian setting, but concludes that "problems of proof" make it difficult to determine whether a particular theory can be applied – that is, convincing evidence cannot be found to support adoption of a model. At the very least, he suggests, the absence of the "ideological competitors" to judicial review that had existed during the New Order facilitated the process of adopting a process of constitutional review.
122 D. Linnan, "Like a Fish Needs a Bicycle: Public law theory, civil society and governance reform in Indonesia," in T. Lindsey, ed., *Law Reform in Developing and Transitional States*, New York: Routledge, 2007, p.274.

16 Conclusion

Reflections on administrative law and judicialized governance in East and Southeast Asia

Albert H.Y. Chen

This volume is the fourth in a series of books on law in Asia; three of the four volumes represent the outcomes of three conferences held at the University of Hong Kong which this author has participated in organizing during the last few years. The first volume, *Asian Discourses of Rule of Law*,[1] provides an overview of the conceptions of and discourses relating to the Rule of Law in Asia, as well as the basic institutional framework of Asian legal systems. It was intended to provide the foundation of and pave the way for more specialized studies in subsequent volumes of the series. The second volume, *Human Rights in Asia*,[2] explores the theory and practice of human rights in various Asian jurisdictions. Given the importance of human rights and the close connection between the Rule of Law and the protection of human rights, the second volume naturally and logically proceeds on the basis of the first. This present volume is more specialized than the three previous volumes and investigates into a specific domain of substantive and procedural law – administrative law, and a specific dimension of the legal system – the judiciary. It is intended to add to the growing body of scholarship on how law and the Rule of Law operates in Asia – particularly East and Southeast Asia, and how legal theories and practices transplanted to Asia in the course of colonization and modernization have been adapted to local circumstances and culture and to meet the challenges faced by Asian societies in this era of democratization, globalization and other great political, economic and social changes.

This concluding chapter is divided into three parts. Part I constructs a theoretical framework for the purpose of understanding the development of administrative law and the phenomena of juridification and judicialization, drawing mainly from the experience of the West. Part II summarizes the main findings in this volume as regards administrative law, juridification and judicialization in various Asian jurisdictions. Part III attempts to interpret these findings in the light of the theoretical framework developed in Part I.

I A theoretical framework

Administrative law may be understood both from the perspective of legal science and that of social science. From the point of view of legal science or legal doctrines, administrative law, together with constitutional law, forms the core of public law – that part of the law that concerns the exercise of state power and the relationship between the government and the people. While constitutional law deals with the basic structure of the governmental system and the fundamental rights and freedoms of citizens as enshrined in a written constitution, administrative law concerns the exercise of power in the day-to-day operations of governmental agencies on which ordinary legislation has conferred power which the legislation also limits and subjects to procedural, judicial and other constraints and checks. Thus administrative law simultaneously empowers and restrains governmental agencies.

From the inter-disciplinary perspective of the social sciences, there is a close relationship between administrative law, governance and regulation, and administrative law may be regarded as one of the many tools of regulation or one mode of governance. 'Mode of governance' may be broadly defined as 'the social mechanism by which the rules in place in any given community are adapted to the experiences and exigencies of those who live under them'.[3] 'Regulation' may be broadly defined as 'sustained and focused control exercised by a public agency over activities that are valued by a community'.[4] Regulation therefore consists of governmental actions designed to influence people's behaviour, primarily for the purpose of promoting the public interest. Apart from using the law to 'command and control'[5] or to create 'rights and liabilities'[6] (e.g. criminal law, administrative law), there are many other means of regulation, such as administrative means (e.g. using codes of practice, or encouraging self-regulation), or 'to deploy wealth', 'to harness markets', 'to inform', or 'to act directly'.[7] Regulatory actions may be taken by departments of the national government, local governments, independent regulatory agencies, courts or tribunals.[8] As Ginsburg points out in this volume,[9] administrative law may be conceived of as being concerned with the 'regulation of regulation', which may take place at the 'retail' level (e.g. ex post facto review of administrative actions by courts in litigated cases) or at the 'wholesale' level (e.g. ex ante controls at the point of the making of rules, such as allowing affected persons to comment on proposed rules).

From a historical perspective, the classic examples of regulation that began in the nineteenth century were in the domains of public health and employment conditions.[10] Furthermore, '[d]evelopments in the supply of railway, water, gas, and electricity services led to the introduction of controls over prices, safety, and quality of service'.[11] The concept of 'juridification' should also be understood in a historical context. As Scott points out in this volume, juridification refers to 'the governance of social and economic spheres' being increasingly 'shaped by juridical norms and processes'.[12] Similarly, Ginsburg defines juridification as 'the spread of legal discourse and procedures into social and political spheres where it was previously excluded or minimal'.[13] The word 'juridification' comes from the German term *Verrechtlichung*, which was originally used to describe the legal formalization of labour relations in the labour law of the Weimar Republic, and to criticize this development for depoliticizing class conflicts and dampening social movements.[14] Teubner highlights the significance of Habermas' analysis of the 'four epoch-making thrusts of juridification' in modern Western history:[15] (1) juridification at the moment of transition from absolutism to the bourgeois state at which the economic and political systems were differentiated, their 'new autonomy' was safeguarded in legal form, and the 'classical system of civil law' emerged; (2) legal constitutionalization, in which administrative power was subordinated to the principle of legality or the Rule of Law; (3) democratic constitutionalization, or the democratization of state power, with 'universal and equal franchise and freedom of organization for political associations and parties' being enshrined in law; (4) social constitutionalization, with the emergence of the 'social state' or the welfare state, 'the juridification of the modern world of industry and labor', and the law being used 'as a means of control to constitutionalize the economy'.[16]

Taking into account this history of juridification, Teubner points out that juridification is not just a matter of 'legal explosion' in terms of the quantitative growth of legal norms and standards,[17] but involves 'qualitative aspects' that are even more important.[18] '[J]uridification does not merely mean proliferation of law; it signifies a process in which the interventionist social state produces a new type of law, regulatory law'.[19] Juridification in the age of social constitutionalization is characterized by the use of law to fulfil the 'societal need for social protection' against the 'phenomena of economic power',[20] and is exemplified by developments in modern labour law, company law, antitrust law and social security law.[21] Such juridification involves a process of the politicization and socialization of the law, or what Weber calls the materialization of formal law, thus giving rise to the phenomenon of 'regulatory law'.[22] In this process, the functions, structure or 'inner order' as well as the mode of legitimation of law has undergone significant changes.[23] Teubner also discusses the 'ambivalence of juridification',[24] in the sense that its effects may not be entirely positive. 'Dysfunctional consequences' or 'regulatory failures' may result from the 'inadequate structural coupling of politics, law and the area of social life'[25] or the 'limits of this structural coupling' being 'overstepped'.[26] An example of such dysfunctional consequences is what Habermas calls the 'colonization of the life-world': juridification may endanger 'the self-reproductive spheres of the life-world'.[27]

Juridification is therefore a concept which tackles the relationship between the legal system and the political and economic systems of the society in which it exists, as well as the relationship between the legal system and what Habermas calls the 'life-world'. As a component of the legal system, administrative law in the West has followed a trajectory of development that has been largely determined by the progression of the stages of juridification as described above. Contemporary administrative law is characterized by a set of core principles or public law values of legal certainty and predictability, fair procedure, giving reasons for decisions, rights of review and appeal, judicial review, transparency, public participation in the making of rules and decisions, accountability of decision makers, etc.

For the purpose of the comparative study in the present volume, it may be useful to develop a notion of the degree of juridification in administrative law. It is proposed that the following factors are relevant in evaluating the degree of juridification in administrative law in a particular legal system: (1) To what extent are the law and judicial processes used in regulation and governance? (2) To what extent does reference to and adherence to legal norms govern the interactions between citizens and business enterprises on the one hand and governmental organs on the other hand, or are such interactions governed instead by personal and social relationships and networks (i.e. the question of the Rule of Law *versus* the 'rule of *guanxi* (personal and social relationships'),[28] negotiation and consensus, informal understandings, customary practices or administrative policies? (3) To what extent is the exercise of executive power subject to effective legal restraint, procedural controls and judicial checks, or can executive power and discretion be exercised in an absolute, unfettered or arbitrary manner without being subject to any such restraint, control and check? (4) To what extent are the principles of modern administrative law or public law values recognized and institutionalized in the legal system?

We now turn from the concept of juridification to that of judicialization. While the former focuses on the amount, nature and role of legal norms in a society, the latter can best be understood as being concerned with the phenomenon of litigation or 'adversarial legalism'[29] and the role of courts in society. Thus Ginsburg in this volume defines judicialization primarily as 'the expansion of the range of activities over which judges exercise significant authority'.[30] Dowdle (Chapter 2 in this volume) usefully adds that whereas it is natural to expect that 'the more government regulation, the more areas of social and political life the courts help regulate' because 'courts are a foundational part of government regulation', the concept of judicialization should be understood to refer to 'an expansion in judicial role *relative to* other governmental actors'.[31] By analyzing carefully the motives of litigants and the social and political meanings of court trials and judgements, Dowdle is able to identify four kinds of judicialization: 'centralizing judicialization' (implementing centrally enacted laws and policies in different localities), 'experimental judicialization' (courts using 'local knowledge' to adapt national policies to local conditions), 'expressive judicialization' (litigants articulating their grievances and the state being required to respond to complaints and to justify its acts publicly), and 'resistive judicialization' (litigants using the courts to promote policies – such as those relating to minority rights – that cannot be successfully advanced through the political domain).[32]

For the purpose of the comparative study in this volume, a notion of the degree of judicialization of administrative law in a particular society may be employed. The factors affecting such degree may include the following: (1) To what extent is litigation used by citizens and businesses to challenge administrative actions affecting their rights or interests? (2) To what extent are the courts active in reviewing and striking down administrative actions, or to what extent are they deferential to the administration? (3) To what extent do the courts engage in judicial activism in determining controversial political issues or intervening in matters of social, economic and other policies and shaping such policies, or to what extent do they practise judicial restraint?

The basic conceptual framework for studying the findings in this volume has been developed above. It remains to investigate the relationship between administrative law and the great changes in the world since the late twentieth century that are captured by the concepts or terms of privatization, deregulation, liberalization and globalization.

The late twentieth century world – particularly the Western world – has undergone a 'market revolution' in the sense that the large public sector of the welfare state has been criticized for its inefficiency and has been in retreat, and there has been a growing recognition that market forces should be given more free space to operate. The resultant policies include privatization (with industries, utilities or services previously under public ownership being privatized, statutory monopolies being removed, and contracting-out of public services being introduced), deregulation (reducing state control over economic activities so that competition and market forces can play a greater role), and liberalization (also a reduction of state control over economic activities but to a lesser extent than deregulation).[33] These developments seem to have entailed the following consequences for administrative law and judicialization. First, new modes of regulation and new regulatory agencies have come into being that were not necessary at a time when the relevant industries or services were run by the state.[34] Privatization and deregulation have thus ushered in a new type of 'regulatory state',[35] a state that does not control or intervene in the economy as extensively or intensively as before, but seeks to regulate market-based economic activities in the public interest. Thus a new body of administrative law has arisen to deal with this new mode of regulation.[36] The activities of the new regulatory agencies are subject to judicial review.[37] Second, the fact that formerly state-operated services and activities have been privatized should not mean that they can escape supervision and accountability as far as matters of public interest are at stake. Thus some of the principles of administrative law and public law values have been extended to apply to this new part of the private sector.[38] Third, privatization and deregulation, which have multiplied the number of firms in liberalized sectors of the economy, have also meant that some of the original practices between business and government that were based on close relationships, negotiation and consensus can no longer survive, and are being replaced by more law-governed interactions and increasing incidence of litigation.[39] In other words, privatization and deregulation can serve to promote juridification and judicialization.

We finally turn to the issue of globalization. Globalization as a term is now commonly used, but its precise meaning is not easy to define. Roughly speaking, it refers to various economic, social, political and cultural phenomena, forces and movements that transcend national boundaries and influence the world as a whole. Holm and Sorensen defines globalization as the 'intensification of economic, political, social and cultural relations across borders'.[40] Braithwaite and Drahos distinguish between three types of globalization with the relationship between them being only contingent – the globalization of firms (firms spreading their operations throughout the world), of markets (business transactions being conducted in a global market) and of regulation.[41] 'The globalization of regulation involves the spread of some set of regulatory norms'.[42] In so far as some of these regulatory norms find expression in administrative law, one can speak of the globalization of administrative law. For example, for some countries, becoming members of the World Trade Organization (WTO) means that they need to reform their systems of administrative law so as to conform to WTO requirements regarding publicity of norms, transparency, notice and comment procedures and independent review of administrative actions.[43] Globalization of firms and markets may also promote the development of administrative law and juridification in countries where administrative law and juridification have been relatively under-developed, if these countries come to recognize that such development will better enable them to increase their competitiveness internationally and to attract capital and investment.[44]

Another aspect of globalization is the emergence of what Teubner calls 'global law without a state'.[45] This refers to 'a new body of law that emerges from various globalization processes in multiple sectors of civil society independently of the laws of the nation-states',[46] particularly in the discourses of specialized and technical global communicative 'networks of an economic, cultural, academic or technological nature'.[47]

What Teubner calls global law seems to be closely related to the new administrative law developing outside the state system that Jayasuriya discusses in Chapter 4 of this volume. Whereas Teuber cites the *lex mercatoria* as 'the most successful example of global law without a state',[48] Jayasuriya's examples of the new 'global administrative law' include labour standards, accounting standards, and regulatory norms relating to trade, the environment and public health. While Teubner refers to specialized and technical communicative networks, Jayasuriya refers to the public domain constituted by 'various specialized functional policy and private orders'[49] as sites for the emergence of the new administrative law. He highlights the importance of 'transnational non-government standard setting organizations'[50] in this process. He points out that 'new methods and forms of public monitoring, review, and even grievance mechanisms that lie outside the formal governmental process'[51] have been established; new 'accountability communities' composed of 'private actors, transnational organizations, and national governments'[52] and 'embody[ing] public law principles, participation, review, and reasoned decision making'[53] have come into being. In this sense he speaks of 'new modes of governance'.[54]

II Findings regarding Asian jurisdictions

The chapters in this volume on individual countries or jurisdictions provide a significant body of information regarding developments in administrative law in East and Southeast Asia and the political, social and economic contexts in which such developments have taken place. The main findings will now be summarized, with particular reference to the issues of the degrees of juridification and judicialization in administrative law which have been conceptualized and explained in the preceding part of this chapter. We shall start with countries in

Northeast Asia – Japan and South Korea, then move to Taiwan, Hong Kong, then to countries in Southeast Asia – the Philippines, Thailand, Indonesia, Malaysia and Singapore, then finally to the communist states of the People's Republic of China and Vietnam.

Japan

Japan's Administrative Litigation Law was enacted in 1962. Since the 1990s, major reforms in administrative law have been introduced. Important developments include the enactment of the Administrative Procedure Law in 1993 and the Information Disclosure Law in 1999, and the revisions of the Local Government Law, the Privacy Law, the Administrative Litigation Law and the Administrative Procedure Law in 1999, 2003, 2004 and 2005 respectively. The reforms were designed to promote fair procedure, transparency, accountability and open government. The Administrative Procedure Law introduced procedures of public participation and transparency, including notice and hearing, notice and comment during the rule-making process, and subjected the existing and important practice of administrative guidance to statutory boundaries and judicial control. At the same time, reforms of the judicial system and of legal education have been introduced. Civil society groups have been active in litigation against the government, as evidenced by suits regarding disclosure of government information and local government spending. However, the plaintiff prevailing rate in administrative litigation is still low (at 10 per cent). Self-restraint is apparently still practised by the judiciary. In Chapter 5 in this volume, Ushijima points out that these developments may be better understood against the background of the collapse of the 'bubble economy' in the early 1990s, regulatory reform and deregulation, the changing relationship between citizens and business on the one hand and government on the other, international pressures for legal harmonization associated with the WTO and the OECD, and the desire of the ruling Liberal Democratic Party to secure public support. In this author's opinion, the case of Japan is one of a significant movement towards juridification in administrative law, accompanied by an increasing but still very limited degree of judicialization in administrative law.

South Korea

As one of the 'Four Little Dragons' of Asia, South Korea was once an authoritarian 'developmental state'. Its current era of democratization dated back to the introduction of a new Constitution in 1987 following the People's Uprising at the time. Since the 1990s, major developments in administrative law include the enactment of the Administrative Procedure Law 1996 (revised twice subsequently), the Official Information Disclosure Act 1996, the Local Government Act 1999, the Anti-Corruption Act 2001, and the Ombudsman of Korea Establishment and Operation Act 2005.[55] The Administrative Litigation Act, first introduced in 1951 and revised in 1984, was revised again in 1994. The Local Government Act and its revisions provided for citizens' initiative, referendum and citizens' lawsuits (taxpayers' lawsuits). The Local Government Finance Act 2005 introduced citizens' participation in the budget-making process. Significant government reforms were introduced by the Kim Dae Jung administration (1997–2002), which implemented a new 'Public Management Model' involving privatization, and by the Roh Moo Hyun administration (2002–2007), which introduced more decentralization and participation and adopted the slogans of 'participation government' and 'transparent and effective government'. The number of cases of administrative litigation increased four times between 1998 and 2005. In Chapter 6 of this volume, Jongcheol Kim cites several cases to illustrate the increasing activism of both the ordinary courts and the Constitutional Court in political and administrative matters. Kim points to the rising rights consciousness of the Korean people, their confidence in the courts being higher than that in other branches of government, and the growing demand for judicial checks on the administration as a means of democratization. In this author's opinion, the case of South Korea is one of increasing degrees of both juridification and judicialization in administrative law.

Taiwan

Taiwan, another of the 'Four Little Dragons' of Asia, had also been an authoritarian 'developmental state'. Its era of democratization began in 1987 with the end of the long martial law period and the liberalization of restrictions on civil and political rights. Previously, in the era of the developmental state, '[d]evelopment policies were mainly incarnated in policy statements and administrative regulations without any need for prior legislative authorization'.[56] Since the 1990s, strides in administrative law have been made. Major enactments include the Fair Trade Act 1991, the Act on Property Declaration by Public Servants 1993, the Consumer Protection Act 1994, the Environmental Impact Assessment Act 1994, the Data Protection Act 1995, the revisions in 1998 of the Administrative Appeals Act, the Administrative Litigation Act and the Administrative Enforcement Act, the Administrative Procedure Act 2000, and the Government Information Disclosure Act 2005. Since the 1990s, the courts, particularly the Constitutional Court (the Council of Grand Justices) and the administrative courts, have engaged in considerable judicial activism. In Chapter 7 of this volume, Jiunn-rong Yeh provides evidence of such activism, and seeks to explain it with reference to the forces of democratization (including demands for transparency, participation and accountability), legislative empowerment of the courts, the activism of the 'media-court link' in supervising the state, the spillover of controversial issues in a contested political environment to the courts (which illustrates the theory that fragmentation of political power in a democratizing polity can contribute to judicialization),[57] and a vibrant civil society. Yeh also points out that the courts' approach, though activist, is 'process-centric',[58] encouraging political dialogue rather than imposing their own policy preferences. In this author's opinion, the case of Taiwan is a clear case of increasing degrees of both juridification and judicialization in administrative law.

Hong Kong

Hong Kong, the third of the 'Four Little Dragons' discussed here, was a British colony until its incorporation into the People's Republic of China as a Special Administrative Region (SAR) in 1997. Democratization began in the mid-1980s but has yet to been completed, in the sense that the Chief Executive of the SAR and half of the members of the legislature are not yet elected by universal suffrage. As Johannes Chan demonstrates in Chapter 8 of this volume, the enactment by the colonial government of the Hong Kong Bill of Rights in 1991 and the coming into effect of the Basic Law of the Hong Kong SAR in 1997 have both enhanced the role of the Hong Kong courts in the adjudication of major issues of politics and policy. Since the 1990s, there has been a significant rise in the number of applications for judicial review of governmental actions, which covered a broad range of social and political issues. Simultaneously, there has been a rising rights consciousness among the populace; civil society and the Bar have been politically active; the new Court of Final Appeal has been eager to assert its authority. The availability of legal aid, liberalized *locus standi* requirements and the innovative use of pre-emptive costs order have contributed to the growth of public interest litigation. Litigants have attempted to use the courts as a forum to ventilate their grievances against the government, to hold the government accountable and to pursue social reform agendas which they failed to advance in the political domain (which is reminiscent of Dowdle's theories of 'expressive' and 'resistive' judicialization mentioned above), while the courts have practised some degree of judicial restraint and exercised their power cautiously. Chan considers the rise of and increasing prominence of administrative law litigation in Hong Kong a sign of the 'democracy deficit'[59] of the SAR and the ineffectiveness of its political system. '[T]he court was dragged to the forefront of governance.... Reluctant as it may be, the court was driven to become the "involuntary hero"'.[60] In this author's opinion, the case of Hong Kong is another case of increasing degrees of juridification and judicialization in administrative law.

The Philippines

Like South Korea and Taiwan, the Philippines also experienced authoritarian rule. However, Western liberal values had been transplanted to the Philippines long before Marco's declaration of martial law in 1972. Pangalangan points out in Chapter 14 of this volume that '[t]he democratic resistance against Marcos ... during the decade and a half of military dictatorship from 1972 to 1986 largely adopted the language of liberal democracy'.[61] The Rule of Law has become 'one of the proudest achievements of [the Philippines'] post-Marcos democracy'.[62] The 1987 Constitution codifies not only civil and political rights but also economic and social rights, welfare state obligations and principles of social justice. It provides for the right to health, ecology and education. It provides for a self-reliant and independent national economy and preferential treatment for nationals in this context. It provides for the social function of private property

368 *Albert H.Y. Chen*

and the principle of stewardship. It also expands judicial power to encompass political questions. Pangalangan points out that the intention of the draftsmen of the Constitution was to codify their own moral and policy preferences so as to bind future legislatures and to pre-empt democratic politics, because they were motivated by a distrust of subsequent legislators (which is reminiscent of Ginsburg's theory of 'political insurance'[63] and Hirschl's theory of 'hegemonic preservation').[64] And they were apparently successful. The courts have made the directive principles in the Constitution directly enforceable in judicial proceedings, and have actively intervened on major issues of policy. Private rights of action have been strengthened; standing requirements have been relaxed; taxpayers' suits have been facilitated; and the right of access to governmental information has been affirmed by the courts. In this author's opinion, the case of the Philippines is another clear case of increasing degrees of juridification and judicialization. Pangalangan believes that judicialization in the Philippines is actually 'deeply rooted',[65] and is explicable by a 'fetish for rules and rule-bound decision',[66] the lack of a communal ideology by which government decisions can be legitimated, and the lack of trust in other institutions, so that the law as administered by courts has become 'a new secular religion'.[67]

Thailand

Although not one of the original 'Four Little Dragons', Thailand was recognized by the World Bank in 1996 as the top growth country in the world for the decade of 1985–94.[68] Since 1932, when absolute monarchy was replaced by constitutional monarchy, a total of 18 constitutions have been successively enacted, that last two being the 1997 and 2007 Constitutions. There had been rule by military governments and 'strongmen', as well as attempts at 'managed democracy'.[69] But '[e]lectoral democracy had prevailed in Thailand throughout the 1980s and 1990s, except for one year in 1991–92'[70] when the military was again in power. Since 1992, Thailand appeared to be consolidating its democracy, until the military coup in 2006 toppled Thaksin Shinawatra who was popularly elected in 2001. It appears from Peter Leyland's Chapter 11 in this volume that as far as Thailand's regime of administrative justice is concerned, the 1997 Constitution made a significant contribution. It amounted to 'a revolution in Thai politics' and represented a 'bold attempt at conferring greater power to the Thai people than had ever been granted before'.[71] It established a new Constitutional Court, a new system of administrative courts modelled on the French system, an ombudsman, and other 'watchdog organizations'.[72] The administrative courts have had a considerable caseload, and have ruled against the government in a number of politically controversial cases. Leyland points out that economic liberalization and privatization has meant more statutory regulation of business and industry and in turn a greater role for the administrative courts. Leyland also notes the remarkable fact that 'Thailand's higher judiciary has enjoyed a reputation for independence since the time of Rama V'.[73] In this author's opinion, the case of Thailand since the adoption of the 1997 Constitution is also one of considerable increase in degrees of juridification and judicialization in administrative law.

Indonesia

Indonesia, the most populous nation in Southeast Asia, had experienced a period of parliamentary democracy in the 1950s.[74] Authoritarian trends began in the late 1950s during the later years of the presidency of Sukarno, and intensified during the long strongman rule of Soeharto and his 'New Order' regime (1965–1998). A body of jurisprudence based on Dutch-influenced administrative law had developed in the period of parliamentary democracy. However, under Soeharto's rule, the legal system was 'degraded'[75] and the judiciary 'strangulated'.[76] The courts were not only subordinated to the executive, but were also corrupt and suffered from a decline of judicial standards. A positive development in administrative law nevertheless occurred in 1991 when a system of administrative courts, the planning for which was first announced by Soeharto in 1978, was finally established in accordance with the Law on Administrative Justice 1986. Various significant developments have taken place in the post-1998 era of democratization. The grounds for judicial review of administrative action were broadened by the 2004 amendment of the 1986 Law. In 2007, the draft Law on Administrative Governance was introduced which exhaustively sets out the principles of proper administration. Whereas a 1964 law empowered the executive to interfere in the judicial process, a 1999 law now 'dismantled control of the judiciary by the bureaucracy'.[77] Judicial reforms were introduced which have 'allowed the judiciary to present a fairly respectable profile'.[78] Various new courts have been established, including Human Rights Courts in 2000 and the Constitutional Court in 2003. The Constitutional Court has power to review and strike down legislation, while the Supreme Court may review instruments below the level of statutes – a power it had been given as early as 1970 and strengthened by legislative amendment in 2004. The new Constitutional Court has decided a number of high profile cases and asserted its authority. However, the volume of civil litigation has been very low, and still lower in the administrative courts. And the judiciary has 'consistently refused to employ its power of judicial review' of regulations and Presidential instruments.[79] In this author's opinion, Indonesia has experienced a small increase in the degree of juridification in administrative law in the post-1998 era, and a still smaller increase in the degree of judicialization; its existing levels of juridification and judicialization are low even by the standards of East and Southeast Asia.

Malaysia

Unlike most of the countries of East and Southeast Asia, Malaysia has been under the rule of the same governing party since its independence in 1957. There had been a period of full and open democracy in the 1960s, but the level of political freedoms was lowered after the racial riots of 1969.[80] The New Economic Policy was introduced which discriminated in favour of the Malays.[81] Malaysia seemed to move further away from Western-style liberal democracy during the prime ministership of Dr Mahathir Mohamad (1981–2003).[82] A severe blow to the independence of the judiciary occurred in 1988 when the government removed from office the top judge of the country and two senior judges.[83] There was afterwards 'a growing public unease concerning the true independence of certain judges'[84] and 'a diminution in public confidence in the judicial institution'.[85] In Chapter 12 of this volume, Gan Ching Chuan points out that the Malaysian Constitution was largely modelled on the Indian Constitution. Whereas the Indian courts have been activist and creative since the 1980s, particularly with regard to public law and public interest litigation, and Indian constitutional jurisprudence is now highly developed, the Malaysian position 'pales in comparison with that of India':[86] Malaysian public law is 'still in a stage of infancy'.[87] Gan points out that there were a number of cases beginning with *Tan Tek Seng*[88] in 1996 in which the Court of Appeal started to become more activist and creative, but the development was soon reversed by the Federal Court. It appears from Gan's chapter that there seems to be no significant movement towards juridification and judicialization in administrative law in Malaysia in recent decades.

Singapore

Like its neighbour Malaysia, of which it was once a part, Singapore has also been ruled by the same governing party since its independence, and Lee Kuan Yew's personal visions have significantly shaped the development of this city-state. As a developmental state, the Singaporean government has intervened extensively in the economy. As Jolene Lin's Chapter 13 in this volume demonstrates, there exist in Singapore a large regulatory machinery, a wealth of delegated legislation (made under broadly drafted enabling statutes), informal rules and codes of practice, and many statutory boards. Singapore has practised a kind of 'rule by law', with the law being used as a pragmatic tool for development. Its conception of law is communitarian and duty-based. Its regulatory governance is executive-dominated. Few cases of judicial review of administrative actions have been litigated in the courts. The courts in such cases have been conservative and deferential to government. The judiciary shares the government's 'pro-development philosophy';[89] there 'appears to be a judicial assumption that the executive (and its agencies) always works in the best interests of society'.[90] Lin points out that there has been no public interest litigation in Singapore. The regulatory culture 'discourages confrontation between the regulator and the regulated'.[91] Interest groups in civil society and NGOs are subject to governmental oversight and control, and they prefer to maintain good relations with the government and practise informal consultation rather than litigation. There is no right of public participation in administrative rule-making or right to access governmental information, and, in the domain of the environment, no law mandating environmental impact assessments. 'As the government has been able to deliver its side of the bargain, there has been a sustained if implicit compact between the people and the government, under which the latter is given an almost complete monopoly of power to pursue economic performance'.[92] Thus there seems to be a relatively low degree of juridification of administrative law and a still lower degree of judicialization in Singapore.

People's Republic of China (PRC)

China is the most populous nation on earth and one of the largest and fastest growing economies in the world. Developmental trends in China are of great international interest. China's legal system had been devastated during the Maoist era,[93] and its reconstruction did not begin until 1978 with the introduction of Deng Xiaoping's 'reform and opening' policy. Considerable progress has been made: Peerenboom points out in Chapter 9 to this volume that when China is judged relative to other countries in the same lower middle income class, China's performance in terms of the Rule of Law is actually 'better than average'.[94]

Significant developments in administrative law have taken place in China in recent years, including the introduction of the Administrative Licensing Law 2003, the State Council's Implementation Outline for Promoting Administration by Law 2004, the Administrative Compulsory Enforcement Law 2005, the Law on Civil Servants 2005, and the Regulations on Open Government Information 2007 (but China is yet to enact its Administrative Procedure Law). The level of transparency and public participation in rule-making and in the supervision of the implementation of laws has been raised. Over the years the number of cases of administrative litigation has risen, the range of disputes litigated in such cases has broadened, and a 'support structure' for 'impact litigation' consisting of social activists, interest groups and lawyers has emerged in civil society.[95] 'Plaintiffs prevail in whole or in part in approximately 30–40 per cent of administrative litigation cases in China, in comparison to 12 per cent in the U.S. and just 8–12 per cent in Japan and Taiwan'.[96] On the other hand, Peerenboom notes that in recent years, the total number of disputes submitted to the courts as well as the number of administrative law suits have levelled off. There have even been 'signs of retrenchment' or 'dejudicialization'.[97] Attempts have been made to limit access to the courts in controversial or politically sensitive cases; there has been a renewed emphasis on mediation; official efforts were made to rein-in activist litigation support groups. Peerenboom points out that courts in China are still 'relatively weak',[98] dependent on the local government and generally deferential to party and government authorities, and are 'not the best forum for resolving' certain types of issues,[99] particularly what he calls 'politically sensitive' cases and 'cases that reflect the growing pains of developing countries',[100] such as those involving the taking of land for development or environmental issues, because courts are often incapable of providing effective remedies in such cases. He concludes that 'China demonstrates that increasingly assertive and independent courts are possible within an authoritarian regime, albeit within certain limits'.[101] In this author's opinion, the case of China is one of increasing degrees of juridification and judicialization in administrative law in recent decades, although the existing levels of juridification and judicialization are apparently lower than in some of the countries and jurisdictions discussed above.

Vietnam

Like China, Vietnam is also within the 'Confucian cultural sphere' and has been a communist state undergoing economic reform. As in China (particularly China in the 1950s), the development of Vietnamese law had also been influenced by the Soviet Union. As John Gillespie points out in Chapter 10 to this volume,[102] the Soviet concept of 'socialist legality' and Soviet administrative law were imported into Vietnam from the 1960s. 'Following reunification in 1975, the 1980 Constitution borrowed deeply from the 1977 Soviet Constitution'.[103] The 1992 Constitution, enacted pursuant to the decision of the Vietnamese Communist Party at its seventh Party Congress in 1991 to pursue political reform concurrently with economic reform, puts greater emphasis on the Rule of Law and human rights.[104] Administrative courts with power to review the legality of administrative actions were established in 1996. Significant judicial reforms were introduced in 2001, placing the courts under the management of the Supreme Court and thus distancing them from local governments. In 2005, a series of strategies for legal and judicial reforms were promulgated, emphasizing the accountability of government bodies and access to justice. Gillespie points out, however, that although foreign investors and international agencies desire and encourage the rationalization and improvement of administrative law and procedures in Vietnam, there is as yet little domestic demand for the use of law and the courts to check state power. Neither is the Communist Party keen to cede more power to the courts or to grant them greater independence. Although the caseload of the administrative courts has increased over the years, '[w]hen corrected for population differences this figure represents less than 15 per cent of the new administrative law cases recorded in China each year'.[105] Many disputes are resolved through other channels, such as 'administrative complaints'[106] or 'informal petitioning'.[107] Interaction between business firms and local government is largely based on the personal relationships generated by 'business networks'[108] rather than 'arms-length, law-based relationship with state regulators'.[109] In this author's opinion, the case of Vietnam seems to be one of an increase in the degrees of juridification and judicialization in administrative law in recent decades, but the existing levels of juridification and judicialization are still quite low, and probably lower than that in China.

III Interpretations

On the basis of the findings summarized in Part II above, it may be concluded that most of the countries and jurisdictions in East and Southeast Asia covered by the studies in this volume have in recent decades experienced an increase in the degrees of juridification and judicialization in administrative law, with Malaysia and Singapore being possible exceptions. Apart from *changes* in the degrees of juridification and judicialization, the *existing* degrees or levels of juridification and judicialization are also important factors. For example, Japan's existing level of judicialization is probably quite low by Western standards; the existing levels of juridification and judicialization in Indonesia and Vietnam are probably quite low even by the standards of East and Southeast Asia.

The findings in the present volume may be usefully compared with those in the report of a study commissioned by the Asian Development Bank on *The Role of Law and Legal Institutions in Asian Economic Development 1960–1995* (hereafter called 'the Report'),[110] which covers six Asian economies – the PRC, India, Japan, South Korea, Taiwan and Malaysia. The main findings of the Report were presented by employing a typology developed in the Report of four kinds of legal systems based on two dimensions of a legal system – the resource allocative dimension and the procedural dimension, which can be further explained as follows.[111]

As regards the resource allocative dimension, the Report points out that a legal system can provide for allocation of economic resources by the state or by the market. Thus laws can be state-allocative or market-allocative. Market-allocative laws are basically Western laws of contract, property, tort, corporations, etc. that have been transplanted to Asian jurisdictions. On the other hand, state-allocative laws confer on the state significant powers in regulating the economy.

As regards the procedural dimension of a legal system, the Report points out that the procedures adopted by a legal system can be either ruled-based or discretionary. The distinction between these two kinds of procedure lies mainly in the extent to which the executive is, in the exercise of its powers, subject to effective legal constraints enforced by an independent judiciary. Rule-based procedures correspond to the notions of due process of law and effective legal limitations on state power. By contrast, discretionary procedures refer to the unfettered discretion which the executive may exercise, or discretion that is not effectively controlled by judicial review. In the Report, the concept of discretionary procedures is also extended to the law-making process where the executive engages in norm-making by way of administrative rules, interpretation and guidance.

The two dimensions mentioned above thus generate the following four-fold typology of legal systems:

(1) a market/rule-based legal system;
(2) a market/discretionary legal system;
(3) a state/rule-based legal system;
(4) a state/discretionary legal system.

The Report postulates that legal systems of Western industrialized nations belong to category (1). Its main findings as regards the Asian jurisdictions studied are that (a) each jurisdiction experienced in some earlier stages of the period 1960–1995 a category (4) legal system; (b) since the 1980s all the jurisdictions studied (with the possible exception of Malaysia) have moved towards category (1), particularly in the resource allocative dimension of their legal systems, and also, albeit to a comparatively smaller extent, in the procedural dimension.[112]

It seems that the concept of 'rule-based procedures' (as contrasted with 'discretionary procedures') as used in the Report overlaps significantly with the concepts of juridification and judicialization as used in this volume and particularly this chapter. Thus the findings in the present volume converge with and reinforce the findings in the Report as far as the trend in Asia towards rule-based procedures, juridification and judicialization is concerned. As the Report only covers developments up to 1995 whereas the study in this volume is more up-to-date, the findings in this volume suggest that the trend towards 'rule-based procedure' that was identified in the Report has continued since 1995.

As to the possible explanation for the move towards category (1) legal systems, the Report focuses on changes in economic policy. The Report points out that there was a congruence between the type of legal system that existed in a particular period and the prevailing economic policy adopted by the state in that period.[113] Thus in periods of active government direction and regulation of and intervention in the economy, the legal system exhibited the features of category (4). On the other hand, when governments introduced privatization, deregulation, greater openness in trade and foreign investment, and liberalization of the financial market and relied more on the private sector and market forces for economic development, the legal system moved towards category (1).

In a previous comment on the Report,[114] this author has pointed that while this economic explanation is certainly plausible in dealing with the move in the resource allocative dimension of the legal system (from state-allocative law to market-allocative law), it fails to address adequately changes in the procedural dimension and the move towards 'rule-based procedures'. It was further suggested that to explain the latter, political developments in the society concerned may have to be taken into account:

> A hypothesis ... is that it may well be the case that the evolution of the 'procedural dimension' of law is more governed by the dynamics of the political system of the country concerned than by economic factors. If whether a legal system is dominated by 'market-allocative laws' or 'state-allocative laws' is largely determined by economic policy factors, whereas whether 'rule-based procedures' and 'discretionary procedures', prevail in its procedural dimension is dependent on the political, constitutional and democratic evolution of the country concerned, then there may not be a necessary connection between the allocative and procedural dimensions of law.[115]

In this regard, it seems that the present volume provides a missing link regarding the explanation for the evolution of the procedural dimension of many Asian legal systems towards 'rule-based procedures', juridification and judicialization, and confirms that, as this author hypothesized previously, such explanation indeed lies mainly or at least partly in the political dimension.

Most of the chapters in this volume attest to the important role of political factors, particularly democratization, in influencing developments towards juridification and judicialization in administrative law in various jurisdictions in East and Southeast Asia. They also provide some evidence that the economic and international factors identified in Ginsburg's Chapter 1 in this volume have also been relevant.[116] For example, most of the chapters on country studies in this volume make some reference to the WTO and its possible relevance to administrative law developments in the countries concerned.

We now turn to reflect on the possible similarities and differences between the Western world and East and Southeast Asia as far as juridification and judicialization in administrative law is concerned. Some of the authors in this volume put forward the idea of a transition in some Asian jurisdictions from the 'developmental state' to the 'regulatory state',[117] with increasing degrees of juridification and judicialization in the course of such transition. In so far as the 'developmental state' is largely an East Asian phenomenon[118] and is not a concept applicable to the West, the idea of such a transition seems to suggest that the trajectory of juridification and judicialization of Asia is one quite different from that in the West, even though both have been affected by the forces of privatization, deregulation, liberalization and globalization in recent decades.[119] But what exactly is the nature of the difference in the trajectories?

In Part I of this chapter, Habermas' model of the four stages of juridification in modern Western history has been alluded to. If this model represents the trajectory of legal modernization in the West, then it is obvious that not many Asian countries have followed the same trajectory. For example, where (as in the Philippines or Indonesia) the state is weak and does not enjoy much autonomy from powerful interest groups or economic interests in society, the conditions of even stage (1) of the Western model may not have been fully satisfied. Where (as in South Korea, Taiwan, the Philippines and Indonesia before their democratization) the Rule of Law is not well developed and the executive enjoys absolute powers and unfettered discretions, the requirements for stage (2) may not have been fulfilled. Where (as in present-day PRC and Vietnam or Hong Kong before the 1990s) the political system has not been democratized, the features of stage (3) do not exist. In the West, stage (4) – social constitutionalization in the welfare state – built on the achievements of the preceding stages, whereas in a communist state (such as the PRC and Vietnam at certain moments), the state may seek to provide comprehensively for people's welfare without practising either the Rule of Law (stage (2) of the Western model) or democracy (stage (3) of the Western model). Thus the evidence in this volume demonstrates that there is no universally applicable trajectory of legal modernization, juridification and judicialization. There is no 'natural law' that governs the legal evolution of societies from one stage to another according to the sequence of the specific stages of legal modernization in the West. Instead, there are many possible permutations and combinations of circumstances that can give rise to juridification and judicialization and different degrees thereof at various moments of the history of the evolution of a particular society.

Although the *histories* have been different, there are similarities between the *phenomena* of juridification and judicialization in the West and in Asia.

The concepts of juridification and judicialization as defined in Part I of this chapter are universally applicable for the purpose of studying relevant legal developments in different countries and jurisdictions. Thus one can observe that in those Asian societies that have been experiencing increasing degrees of juridification and judicialization, their legal systems and cultures are coming closer to those in the West. In this sense one can speak of a 'convergence' in legal developments.[120]

A final point to ponder is whether the trajectory of juridification and judicialization, once started when a legal system reaches a particular point in its development, is not only determined by exogenous political, economic and international circumstances, but also governed by an internal logic or dynamics of its own. According to Teubner's theory of *Law as an Autopoietic System*[121] and of the 'self-referential nature of law',[122] law should 'be understood as a self-producing and self-reproducing process'; 'the operations of the law are dependent on its inner states'.[123] Sweet points out that third-party or 'triadic dispute resolution' (TDR), of which litigation in the courts is one mode, is associated with a 'normative structure' whose 'dynamics of change ... are endogenous to the logic of dyads, triads, and rules'.[124] 'Once individuals have moved to the triadic level, the internal dynamics of TDR will drive processes of judicialization'.[125] For example, TDR has the capacity to generate a '*social* process of reasoning about rules';[126] it 'perpetuates a discourse about the pertinence of rules to behaviour'.[127] '[T]hose who initiate TDR cannot meaningfully control the outcomes produced by triadic rule-making.... [T]he world of triadic governance evolves according to the logic of path dependence'.[128] Or as Ginsburg and Kagan put it: 'if political authorities want credit for establishing *credible and reliable* courts and legal institutions, they must grant those institutions a visible measure of independence. Once so empowered, however, judges tend to adopt minds of their own'.[129]

Although judicialization may have an inner logic of its own and may evolve 'according to the logic of path dependence',[130] its precise dynamics remain to be more fully explored, in the West as in Asia or elsewhere. The complexity of the interplay between juridification and judicialization, their inner logic of development and external political, economic, social, cultural and global circumstances is such that the future trajectories of juridification and judicialization remain unpredictable, both in Asia and elsewhere. And this is as things should be, if, as Teubner speculates, 'law is essentially self-referential and unpredictable'; 'it is dependent on the past, but cannot be predicted'.[131] If this volume is able to contribute a little in elucidating a segment of this past in East and Southeast Asia, then its objective would have been achieved. The future is uncertain, as the 'end of history'[132] has not yet arrived, nor has the end of the legal history of juridification and judicialization in administrative law.

Notes

1 R. Peerenboom, ed., *Asian Discourses of Rule of Law: Theories and Implementation of Rule of Law in Twelve Asian Countries, France and the U.S.*, London: Routledge, 2004.

2 R. Peerenboom, et al., eds, *Human Rights in Asia: A Comparative Legal Study of Twelve Asian Jurisdictions, France and the U.S.A.*, London: Routledge, 2006.
3 M. Shapiro and A. Stone Sweet, *On Law, Politics, and Judicalization*, Oxford: Oxford University Press, 2002, p.55. It is also pointed out that '*government* – the activities of hierarchically ordered, organizationally differentiated structures one finds in the modern state – constitutes one form of governance, but not the only one' (ibid., p.14; emphasis in original). Another type of governance is 'third-party dispute resolution' (including dispute resolution by a court of law) (p.15).
4 R. Baldwin and M. Cave, *Understanding Regulation: Theory, Strategy, and Practice*, Oxford: Oxford University Press, 1999, p.2.
5 Ibid., p.35.
6 Ibid., p.51.
7 Ibid., p.34. Some of these means may also involve the use of the law.
8 R. Baldwin and C. McCrudden, *Regulation and Public Law*, London: Weidenfeld and Nicolson, 1987, p.4.
9 See Tom Ginsburg's chapter, 'Judicialization of administrative governance: Causes, consequences and limits', in this book, at p.1. See also T. B. Ginsburg, 'The Regulation of Regulation: Judicialization, Convergence, and Divergence in Administrative Law', in K. J. Hopt et al., eds, *Corporate Governance in Context: Corporations, States, and Markets in Europe, Japan, and the US*, Oxford: Oxford University Press, 2005, p.321 at 326.
10 Baldwin and Cave, op. cit., p.3.
11 Ibid.
12 See Colin Scott's chapter, 'Agencification, regulation and judicialization: American exceptionalism and other ways of life', in this volume, at p.47.
13 See Ginsburg, op. cit., this volume, at p.3.
14 See G. Teubner, 'Juridification: Concepts, Aspects, Limits, Solutions', in R. Baldwin, C. Scott and C. Hood eds, *A Reader on Regulation*, Oxford: Oxford University Press, 1998, p.389 at 395.
15 Ibid., p.397.
16 Ibid., pp.397–8.
17 Ibid., p.392.
18 Ibid., p.393.
19 Ibid., p.405.
20 Ibid., p.401.
21 Ibid., pp.392, 401.
22 Ibid., p.390.
23 Ibid., pp.401–5.
24 Ibid., p.389.
25 Ibid., p.408.
26 Ibid., p.391.
27 Ibid., pp.410–11. See also Ginsburg's discussion of the costs and benefits of judicialization and of 'American adversarial legalism' in his chapter in this volume, at p.14.
28 See e.g. C. A. G. Jones, 'Capitalism, Globalization and Rule of Law: An Alternative Trajectory of Legal Change in China', *Social and Legal Studies*, vol.3, no.195, 1994; A. H. Y. Chen, 'Rational Law, Economic Development and the Case of China' *Social and Legal Studies*, vol.8, no.97, 1998.
29 Ginsburg, op. cit., in this volume, at p.14.
30 Ibid., at p.1.
31 See Michael Dowdle's chapter, 'On the regulatory dynamics of judicialization: The promise and perils of exploring "judicialization" in East and Southeast Asia', in this volume, at p.28. Emphasis supplied.
32 Ibid., at p.31.

33 See Baldwin and McCrudden, op. cit., pp.22–4.
34 See, e.g., D. J. Galligan, ed., *A Reader on Administrative Law*, Oxford: Oxford University Press, 1996, pp.8–13.
35 See generally Scott's chapter in this volume.
36 See Baldwin and Cave, op. cit., pp.3–4.
37 See generally J. Black et al., eds, *Commercial Regulation and Judicial Review*, Oxford: Hart Publishing, 1998.
38 See generally M. Taggart, ed., *The Province of Administrative Law*, Oxford: Hart Publishing, 1997, Chs.1 and 7.
39 See Scott's chapter in this volume, at p.47; C. Scott, 'The Juridification of Relations in the UK Utilities Sector', in Black et al., op. cit., p.19 at 19–21, 55–57; T. Ginsburg and R. A. Kagan, 'Introduction: Institutional Approaches to Courts as Political Actors', in T. Ginsburg and R. A. Kagan, eds, *Institutions and Public Law: Comparative Approaches*, New York: Peter Lang, 2005, p.1 at 8–9.
40 H. Holm and G. Sorensen, 'Introduction: What Has Changed?' in H. Holm and G. Sorensen, eds, *Whose World Order: Uneven Globalization and the End of the Cold War*, Boulder, Colorado: Westview, 1995, p.1 (quoted in J. Braithwaite and P. Drahos, *Global Business Regulation*, Cambridge: Cambridge University Press, 2000, p.8).
41 Braithwaite and Drahos, op. cit., p.8.
42 Ibid.
43 See, e.g., Ginsburg's chapter in this volume, at p.9.
44 See Ginsburg, 'The Regulation of Regulation', op. cit., pp.323, 333.
45 G. Teubner, ed., *Global Law Without a State*, Aldershot: Dartmouth, 1997.
46 G. Teubner, '"Global Bukowina": Legal Pluralism in the World Society', in Teubner, *Global Law*, op. cit., p.3 at 4.
47 Ibid., p.7.
48 Ibid., p.3.
49 See Kanishka Jayasuriya's chapter, 'Riding the Accountability Wave? Accountability Communities and New Modes of Governance', in this book, p.60.
50 Ibid., p.59.
51 Ibid., p.69.
52 Ibid., p.65.
53 Ibid., p.72–3.
54 Ibid. See the title of his chapter.
55 The predecessor of this Ombudsman was first instituted in 1994: see p.111 of this volume.
56 See Jiunn-rong Yeh's chapter, 'Democracy-driven transformation to regulatory state: The case of Taiwan', in this volume, at p.128.
57 See Ginsburg's chapter in this volume, at p.7; Ginsburg and Kagan, op. cit., pp.6–7.
58 At p.137 of this volume.
59 Chan's chapter in this volume, at p.165.
60 Ibid., p.164.
61 See Raul C. Pangalangan's chapter 'Government by judiciary in the Philippines: Ideological and doctrinal framework', in this volume, at p.324.
62 Ibid., p.311.
63 See T. Ginsburg, *Judicial Review in New Democracies: Constitutional Courts in Asian Cases*, Cambridge: Cambridge University Press, 2003; Ginsburg and Kagan, op. cit., p.6.
64 See R. Hirschl, *Towards Juristocracy: The Origins and Consequences of the New Constitutionalism*, Cambridge, MA: Harvard University Press, 2004.
65 Pangalangan's chapter in this volume, at p.311.
66 Ibid., p.311.

Conclusion 379

67 Ibid, p.312.
68 D. King, 'Thailand', in I. Marsh et al., eds, *Democracy, Governance, and Economic Performance: East and Southeast Asia*, Tokyo: United Nations University Press, 1999, Ch. 8, at p.203.
69 See, e.g., P. Church ed., *A Short History of South-east Asia*, Singapore: John Wiley & Sons, 4th edn. 2006, pp.167–74.
70 King, op. cit., p.206.
71 See Peter Leyland's chapter, 'The emergence of administrative justice in Thailand under the 1997 Constitution', in this volume, p.229.
72 Ibid., p.230.
73 Ibid., p.245. Rama V reigned in 1868–1910.
74 See, e.g., Church, op. cit., pp.51–3.
75 See, e.g., C. Mason, *A Short History of Asia*, New York: Palgrave Macmillan, 2nd edn. 2005, pp.217–27.
76 See Stewart Fenwick's chapter, 'Administrative law and judicial review in Indonesia: The search for accountability', in this volume, p.331.
77 Ibid., p.340.
78 Ibid.
79 Ibid., p.347.
80 See, e.g., Church, op. cit., p.96; Mason, op. cit., p.241; H. P. Lee, 'Human Rights in Malaysia', in Peerenboom, Petersen and Chen, op. cit., p.191 at 233.
81 Lee, op. cit., p.243.
82 Church, op. cit., pp.99–105; Mason, op. cit., p.241.
83 H. P. Lee, 'Competing Conceptions of Rule of Law in Malaysia', in Peerenboom, *Asian Discourses*, op. cit., p.225 at 243.
84 Ibid.
85 Ibid., p.246.
86 See Gan Ching Chuan's chapter, 'Law and judicialized governance in Malaysia: The Indian connection', in this volume, p.256.
87 Ibid.
88 [1996] 1 MLJ 261.
89 See Joline Lin's chapter, 'The judicalization of governance? The case of Singapore', in this volume, p.292.
90 Ibid., p.296.
91 Ibid., p.287.
92 Ibid., p.302.
93 See, e.g., A. H. Y. Chen, *An Introduction to the Legal System of the People's Republic of China*, Hong Kong: LexisNexis Butterworths, 3rd edn. 2004, Ch. 3.
94 See Randall Peerenboom's chapter, 'More law, less courts: Legalized governance, judicialization and dejudicialization in China', in this volume, at p.175.
95 Ibid., p.182.
96 Ibid.
97 Ibid., p.174.
98 Ibid., p.189.
99 Ibid.
100 Ibid., p.190.
101 Ibid., p.195.
102 See John Gillespie's chapter, 'The juridification of administrative comlpaints and review in Vietnam', in this volume, p.204.
103 J. Gillespie, 'Evolving Concepts of Human Rights in Vietnam', in Peerenboom, Petersen and Chen, op. cit., p.452 at 455. See also Truong Trong Nghia, 'The Rule of Law in Vietnam: Theory and Practice', in *The Rule of Law: Perspectives from the Pacific Rim*, Mansfield Center for Pacific Affairs, p.123 at 129–30.

104 Gillespie's chapter in this volume, at p.205; Nghia, op. cit., pp.132–6.
105 Gillespie's chapter in this volume, at p.215.
106 Ibid., p.211.
107 Ibid., p.214.
108 Ibid., p.206.
109 Ibid., p.207.
110 New York: Oxford University Press, 1999. The Report was prepared for the Asian Development Bank by Katharina Pistor and Philip A. Wellons. The discussion of the Report here draws on my previous article, 'Law, Development and the Typology of Legal Systems' (1999–2000) 4 *Journal of Chinese and Comparative Law* 30.
111 See the Report, pp.3–7, 27–8, 53–5.
112 See the Report, pp.13–15, 18–19.
113 Ibid., pp.63–64, 109.
114 Chen, 'Law, Development and the Typology of Legal Systems', op. cit., pp.43–5.
115 Ibid., p.46.
116 See Ginsburg's chapter in this volume, at pp.5–6, 9–11.
117 See Scott's Chapter 3 in this volume, at p.44; Yeh's Chapter 7, at p.127; Kim's Chapter 6, at p.113.
118 See A. MacIntyre, 'Business, Government and Development: Northeast and Southeast Asian Comparisons', in A. MacIntyre ed., *Business and Government in Industrialising Asia* (St Leonards: Allen & Unwin, 1994), Ch. 1: MacIntyre points out that whereas South Korea and Taiwan were 'developmental states' (strong states that were relatively insulated from business interests and 'distributional societal pressures' (p.4), able to implement their policies effectively and intervening extensively in the economy to promote development), the four Southeast Asian states of Thailand, Malaysia, Indonesia and the Philippines – 'lacking the strength of the Northeast Asian NICs, but equally not being hopelessly corrupt or captured' – were 'intermediate cases' lying in 'a continuum of state structures ranging at one end from the developmental states of Northeast Asia, through to predatory and "klepto-patrimonial" states such as that of Mobutu's Zaire' (p.10).
119 Indeed, in the case of Britain, the term or notion of the 'regulatory state' only came to be used widely *after* the introduction of such privatization, deregulation and liberalization: see Scott's chapter in this volume, at pp.40–1.
120 For the 'convergence' thesis, see, e.g., Ginsburg, 'The Regulation of Regulation', op. cit.; and the Report, op. cit., Ch. 8.
121 G. Teubner, *Law as an Autopoietic System*, Oxford: Blackwell, 1993.
122 Ibid., p.2.
123 Ibid.
124 A. Stone Sweet, 'Judicialization and the Construction of Governance', in Shapiro and Sweet, op. cit., p.55 at 59.
125 Ibid., p.72.
126 Ibid., p.85. Emphasis in original.
127 Ibid.
128 Ibid., p.86.
129 Ginsburg and Kagan, op. cit., p.11. Emphasis in original.
130 Sweet, op. cit., p.86.
131 Teubner, *Law as an Autopoietic System*, op. cit., p.2.
132 Francis Fukuyama, *The End of History and the Last Man*, New York: The Free Press, 1992.

Index

accountability communities 59–78; codes of conduct 66–7; global administrative law, and 64–9; governance and state transformation, and 72–3; private rule making, and 66–9; 'public' conception 68; reconstitution of public domain, and 64–9; technocratic politics 65, 71–2
accountability wave 59–78
administrative law: operation of 1–2
agency-related firm: agencification, and 48–50
American exceptionalism: agencification, and 38–58
Asia: findings regarding 364–72
Australia: agencification 43

Cambodia-US bilateral textile trade agreement 67–8
Canada: agencification 43
China 28, 30–1, 33–4, 36–7, 175–201, 371–2; constitutional review of laws and regulations 185–6; constructing regulatory framework for administrative law regime 177; dejudicialization 175–201; dejudicializing disputes 191–4; explaining limited judicialization 186–9; improvement of mechanisms to check administrative power 181; improving civil service 178; judicial review of laws and regulations 185–6; judicialization 175–201; legalization of administrative law and governance 176–82; legalized governance 175–201; limited deregulation 178–9; limited government 177; limits on judicial review of specific acts 184–5; local explanations for limited judicialization 188–91; more law, less courts 175–201; new conception of governance 177; privatization 178–9; public participation 179–81; retrenchment 191–4; transparency 179–81; yifa xingxheng 177
Consumers 50

Delegation 54

Europe: agencification 43–4
European Commission 52
Expertise argument 42

Financial services regulation 41, 39–40

global administrative law 61–4; accountable governance, and 62–3; exercise of public power, and 61–4; forms of rule making 61; participation 63–4
global law: administrative law, and 364
globalization: meaning 363–4

Hong Kong 143–74, 367; Administrative Appeals Board 154; administrative law 143–74; administrative system 149–55; Commission of Inquiry 155; de-judicialization of governance 155–65; Director of Audit 155; engine for social reform 161; from Wednesbury to proportionality 158–61; governance 143–74; harbour reclamation 161–2; historical perspective 143–7; interception of telecommunications 163–5; judicial review 150–4; judicialization of governance 155–65; legitimate expectation 157–8; Municipal Service Appeals Board 154; Ombudsman 154; politics 143–74; proportionality 157–65; public housing 162–3;

substantive legitimate expectation 157–65; trend of judicialization 148–9

Independent Regulatory Agencies 39–41, 45
Indonesia 329–58, 369; administrative law 329–58; administrative courts at work 338–41; caseload at first instance per capita 344; cases in Administrative Division of Supreme Court 2006 341; Constitutional Court 345–6; courts and accountability 348–51; current administrative law reforms 336–8; emergence of administrative justice 333–4; framework for administrative justice 334–6; judicial authority 331–3; judicial review 329–58; judiciary post-1998 341–5; new courts established post-Soeharto 343; reform 330–1; regulation 330–1; search for accountability 329–58; traditions 330–1; workload in courts 2006 340
Interstate Commerce Commission 39–40

Japan 81–100, 365; ACLL 92–5 administrative law 81–100; administrative process 83; administrative remedies 86–7; administrative state 82–3; APL 88–92; Constitution 1946 82; future developments 95; judicial review of administrative action 92–5; judicial system reform 87–8; judicialized governance 81–100; legislative process 83; principles and procedural control of administrative guidance 90–1; reform of administrative law 85–7; regulatory reform 84
Judicialization: agencification, and 38–58; centralizing form 28–9; changing constitutional role of courts,and 26; character of courts, and 34–5; China, and 28, 33–4; civil disobedience, and 30; common law courts 24; convening power 29; decentralization, and 30; definition 27–32; development of administrative bureaucracy, and 25; developmental implications 32–5; diversity of trajectories 32; early history 24; effects 55; "experimentation" 29; history 23–7; industrialization, and 26–7; judicial surrogates 35; kinds of 27–32; litigation strategies, and 32; modernism, and 25–7; original function

of courts, and 23–5; policymaking, and 28; "regulation, and" 36; regulatory dynamics 23–37; regulatory mapping 34; resistance, as 30–1; retreat of courts' policymaking capacities 25–6; "rule of law", and 27; standard model 33; triadic dispute resolution, and 31
Judicialization of administrative governance 1–117; "adversarial legalism" 14; American experience 12–14; Asian Financial Crisis 1997 7; benefits 14–15; causes 1–17; concept 3–5; consequences 1–17; costs 14–15; democratic consolidation, and 7; developmental state model 2; East and Southeast Asia 1–2; economic complexity, and 6; economic factors 5–6; globalization 5–6; international factors 9–11; judges 8; judicial "solution" 10; juridification 3; "legal complex" 9; liberalization, and 6; limits 1–17; local interest-group structures 8–9; normative debate 11; normative question 17; one-way process, whether 4; political coalitions, and 8; political factors 6–9; supranational regulatory regime, and 9–10; timing 4; triadic structure of dispute resolution 3–4; WTO, AND 9–19
Juridification: history of 361

Korea 101–125, 365–6; accountability and judicialization 115; administrative adjudication in ACC Korea 120; administrative litigation law reform 121–2; administrative litigations 1998–2005 118; administrative procedure law reform 108; citizens' initiative 110–11; citizens' lawsuits 109–10; citizens' participation in budget-making process 110; citizens' request for audit and inspection 109; democratization 101–2; development of public law 101–25; e-government 113–14; efficiency 104–6; evaluation system reform 104–5; globalization 102; government reform 101–25; increasing quasi-judicial committee 119; information disclosure system reform 107–8; informization 102; institutions 118; judicialization 101–25; mediation institution 120; Ombudsman 112–13; participation 109–14; policy coordination reform 105; public participation in administration 109; recall 111–12; referendum 111; reform for decentralized organizational design 105–6; Saemangeum Reclamation Project case 117; Salamander case 117–18; statistics 118; transparency 107–9; transparency of discretion 108–9

legal instrumentalism: technocratic politics, and 69–72
legal system: life-world, and 361
Licensing 49
life-world: legal system, and 361

Malaysia 257–86, 369–70; access to courts to enforce fundamental rights 261–2; administrative law 257–86; better administrative governance 276–9; common law review 259; constitutional review 258, 267–70; economic roadmap for future 273–4; Indian connection 257–86; judicial review 274–6; judicialized governance 257–86; lessons from other jurisdictions 271; no need for writ petition to be moved 267; Paragraph 1 powers 265–7; privatization 272–3 public interest litigation 265–7; regulatory regime in public law; right to vindicate rule of law 262–5; rise of regulatory governance 271–3; roadmap for future 276–9; weaknesses of constitutional system 270–1; WTO regime
Market revolution 363

Natural law 375
New Zealand: agencification 43

Philippines 313–28, 367–8; advancing nationalist ideology through law 315–16; codification of policy objectives 314–15; codification of substantive norms 314–15; direct judicial enforceability of directive principles 319–22; Directive principles 314–15; doctrinal evolution of judicialization 314–16; doctrinal framework 313–28; economic protectionism 315–16; expansion of judicial power 318–19; governance by judiciary 313–28; ideological framework 313–28; institutional correction of democracy's flaws 324–7; judicialization as default mechanism 324–7; social justice closures 316–18; statist consequence of redistributive claims 316–18; strengthening of private right of action 322–4;
Political factors: judicialized governance, and 374–5
Privatisation 363; agencification, and 40–1

Regulatory regimes 45–8; judicial element 48; judicialization within 46–8; litigation, and 47; pre-history in European countries 47; understanding 45
Resource allocation 373

Self-regulatory bodies: agencification, and
Singapore 287–312, 370–1; administrative law framework 294–302; administrative state 287–8; Chee Siok Chin and others v Minister for Home Affairs and another 300–2; delegated legislation 296–7; economic success 287; Europeanization 295; Galstaun and Another v Attorney general 298–9; government ministries 292; industrialization program 290–1; judicial review 294–302; judicialization 287–312; judicialization of governance 305–6; modest undertaker 297–8; origins of administrative state 290–4; regulatory framework 288–9; role of judiciary 289; role of law 294; statutory boards 291–4; Teng Fish Holdings Pte Ltd v Collector of Land Revenue 299–300
Social sciences: inter-disciplinary approach 360

Taiwan 127–42, 366; analyzing transition from development to regulatory state 134–8; civil society 130; democracy-driven transformation to regulatory state 127–42; development state before 1987 128; Electronic Toll Collection case 138–9; executive control 130; from developmental to regulatory state 128–34; impact of transition 140; judicial adjudication 129–30; legislation 129; National Health Insurance divide 139–40; Nuclear Installation controversy 139; process-centric transformation in legislative dimension 138; process-centric transformation of judicial adjudication 138–40; regulatory state after 1987 131–4

Thailand 230–56, 368–9; administrative courts 234–6; administrative justice 232–4; administrative law 242–6; Constitution of 1997 230–56; emergence of administrative justice 230–56; legal process 232–4; regulating government 242–6

United Kingdom 40–3, 47–8, 51
United States: activist approach of courts 13; administrative bureaucracy 25; administrative history 24; Administrative Procedures Act 15, 25; administrative state 12–14; Cambodia-US textile trade agreement 67; constitutional role of courts 26; constitutional traditions 2; drug courts 29; FIRA model 39–40; Interstate Commerce Commission 39–40; judicial review 12–13; judicial system 24; judicialization 1; legal instrumentalism 70

Vietnam 205–29, 372; administrative complaints mechanisms 213–17; administrative courts 217–18; changing role of legality in state administration 206–8; complaints and denunciations 213–17; constructing law-based state 206–8; demand for law-based interactions with state officials 208–13; judicial power 218–21; juridification of administrative complaints and review 205–29; political control over courts 272–4; rolling back control over state 222–4

eBooks – at www.eBookstore.tandf.co.uk

A library at your fingertips!

eBooks are electronic versions of printed books. You can store them on your PC/laptop or browse them online.

They have advantages for anyone needing rapid access to a wide variety of published, copyright information.

eBooks can help your research by enabling you to bookmark chapters, annotate text and use instant searches to find specific words or phrases. Several eBook files would fit on even a small laptop or PDA.

NEW: Save money by eSubscribing: cheap, online access to any eBook for as long as you need it.

Annual subscription packages

We now offer special low-cost bulk subscriptions to packages of eBooks in certain subject areas. These are available to libraries or to individuals.

For more information please contact webmaster.ebooks@tandf.co.uk

We're continually developing the eBook concept, so keep up to date by visiting the website.

www.eBookstore.tandf.co.uk

Routledge Paperbacks Direct

Exclusive offers for eUpdate subscribers!

This exciting new initiative makes the best of our hardback publishing available in paperback format for authors and individual customers only.

Routledge Paperbacks Direct is an ever-evolving programme with new titles being added regularly. To find out how to become an eUpdate subscriber or to take a look at the titles available visit....

www.routledge.com/paperbacksdirect

Routledge Paperbacks Direct

Routledge Paperbacks Direct is an exciting initiative that makes the best of our hardback research publishing available in paperback format for authors and individual customers to purchase directly from the dedicated Routledge Paperbacks Direct Website

Paperbacks direct includes titles from our publishing programmes in Philosophy, Politics and International Relations, Military and Strategic Studies, Asian Studies, Economics, Business and Management.

www.routledgepaperbacksdirect.com